VIETNAM MAILBAG

VOICES FROM THE WAR: 1968-1972

NANCY E. LYNCH

ISBN 978-0-615-24454-9 · ©2008 · ALL RIGHTS RESERVED

★ TABLE OF CONTENTS ★

TO THE VIETNAM VETERANS
WHO FOUGHT THE LONG FIGHT
THANK YOU FOR YOUR SERVICE
AND YOUR SACRIFICES

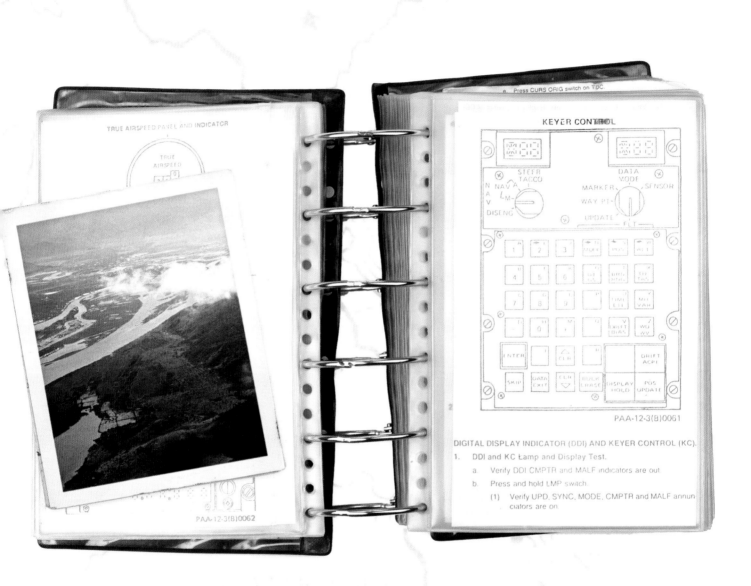

★ FOREWORD ★
U.S. SENATOR THOMAS R. CARPER

While Nancy Lynch was writing her Vietnam Mailbag column from 1968 to 1972, I was serving three tours in Southeast Asia as a naval flight officer aboard Navy P-3 patrol aircraft. The P-3 is still flying today, retrofitted for new missions in Iraq and Afghanistan, but in the Vietnam War, we flew low-level missions off the coasts of Vietnam and Cambodia searching for infiltrator trawlers disguised as fishing boats whose real mission was to resupply the Vietcong.

When we weren't doing that, we frequently flew surface surveillance missions monitoring shipping traffic entering or leaving Vietnam's Haiphong harbor, as well as shipping traffic in the South China Sea and throughout parts of the western Pacific and the Indian Ocean. As Cold War warriors, we also tracked Soviet submarines in that part of the world and – when we weren't deployed overseas – in the eastern Pacific, too.

Like today's servicemen and women in Iraq, and like the many soldiers, sailors, airmen and marines who wrote to Nancy four decades ago, the 300 or so men in my squadron held a wide range of views about the war in which we served. Many of our enlisted men had joined the Navy as an alternative to the draft. While a number of our officers were U.S. Naval Academy graduates or – like me – former Navy ROTC midshipmen, others had signed up for duty in the Navy in lieu of being drafted.

Some of my squadron mates felt that America's presence in Southeast Asia kept a tide of communism from sweeping throughout that part of the world. Others viewed our involvement as meddling in a civil war aimed primarily at uniting Vietnam into one country again. And some shared neither opinion.

U.S. Sen. Tom Carper is the highest-ranking Delaware public official to have served in the military in Southeast Asia during the Vietnam era.

He settled in Delaware in 1973 after five years of active duty as a naval flight officer. His career in public service began in 1976 when he was elected to the first of three terms as Delaware's state treasurer. In 1982, he was elected to represent Delaware in the U.S. House of Representatives. After serving five terms in the House, he was elected governor in 1992 and won a second term in 1996. He was elected to the U.S. Senate in 2000 and is now serving his second term.

After completing his military active duty, he continued to serve in the Naval Reserve until retiring in 1991 with the rank of captain.

"Looking back now, I've concluded that I was mistaken in my earlier views that we had won the battle in Vietnam only to lose the war. Instead, I believe we lost the battle, but in a very real sense, we've won the war for the hearts of the Vietnamese people."

They were just glad to be flying or maintaining our 13-man, four-engine aircraft whose missions did not include making bombing runs over Hanoi. They were also grateful that our jobs did not entail slogging through the jungles of Vietnam fighting an elusive foe on behalf of a South Vietnamese government that did not enjoy the broad support of its people.

As protests against the war rose in the United States during the late '60s and early '70s, I remember reading the words of George Aiken, a crusty old Republican senator from Vermont. His advice on the war was to declare victory and bring the troops home. In the end, that's pretty much what we did, although after we pulled out, the North overran the South in 1975 and united the country under a Communist regime.

For many years, I reflected on that series of events and concluded that – for the U.S. – it was a little like winning the battle and losing the war. I wasn't the only one who saw it that way either.

Sixteen years after the fall of Saigon, though, I led a congressional delegation of five other U.S. representatives who had served in the Vietnam War. One of them – Pete Peterson, a Democrat from Florida – had been held as a POW in the Hanoi Hilton for six years.

The six of us returned to Southeast Asia at a time when many Americans were convinced that the Vietnamese, the Laotians and/or the Cambodians were holding hundreds of American MIAs in secret POW camps or prisons. We went there in an effort to learn the truth, and we also witnessed the ineffectiveness of American efforts to recover the remains of our missing in action or determine their fates. We subsequently recommended and successfully pushed for a major overhaul. The cooperation that the United States was receiving from the governments of Vietnam, Cambodia and Laos didn't measure up either, and we let the leaders of those countries know it at every opportunity.

We also shared with the leaders of Vietnam a roadmap to normalized relations that the Bush administration had briefed us on prior to our departure for Southeast Asia, and we strongly encouraged those leaders to pursue that roadmap with our government, prom-

ising that our country would reciprocate for every positive step Vietnam took. Within a year, the first tentative steps were taken by the Vietnamese and by the United States. In time, many other steps would follow.

Seven years later, in 1998, I returned to Vietnam as governor of Delaware, leading a trade delegation from our state. We were welcomed at the Hanoi airport by the new U.S. ambassador to Vietnam, my friend and former House colleague Pete Peterson.

By then, the United States and Vietnam had normalized relations, exchanged ambassadors and opened embassies. They were beginning trade and other exchange activities. Vietnam had begun to change.

I've not been back since 1998, but I've welcomed a number of Vietnamese delegations and leaders to Delaware and to Washington, D.C., over the intervening years. The longstanding animosity between our countries has been replaced by a surprising and growing trust. Trade continues to flourish. U.S. naval vessels occasionally call today on Vietnamese ports. A free market economic model has largely replaced communism. And while there is still work to be done in that regard and Vietnam has not yet become a democracy, advances are being made, with dissent and freedom of religion more widely tolerated.

Looking back now, I've concluded that I was mistaken in my earlier views that we had won the battle in Vietnam only to lose the war. Instead, I believe we lost the battle, but in a very real sense, we've won the war for the hearts of the Vietnamese people. Oftentimes when I'm with other veterans of the Vietnam War, I urge them to travel back to that part of the world if they ever have a chance. If they did, their reflections on modern-day Vietnam might make for an interesting postscript to Nancy's Vietnam Mailbag which you'll read about in the pages that follow.

Thomas R. Carper

Thomas R. Carper, U.S. Senator

IN THE BEGINNING

WOULD I CONSIDER, MY EDITORS ASKED IN THE SPRING OF 1968, CORRESPONDING THROUGH A WEEKLY COLUMN WITH SEVERAL HUNDRED DELAWARE SERVICEMEN IN VIETNAM? As a young, single, newly-employed general assignment reporter at the News-Journal Company in Wilmington, Delaware, I embraced the opportunity.

Gathering my thoughts for Nancy's Vietnam Mailbag, I first drafted a blanket letter in April to my new pen pals, explaining that the column was really theirs, a forum for them to express their opinions on everything from the war to the weather. The Mailbag was also a vehicle for them to exchange ideas, to vent, to gripe, and to meet other Delawareans serving in Vietnam. Whatever they wished to correspond, I encouraged them "to tell it like it is."

We dispatched more than 800 letters to Vietnam. Military addresses were supplied by the News-Journal's circulation department. As a public service, the then-privately held media company, which published morning and evening newspapers Monday through Saturday, provided free subscriptions to *The Morning News* to Delaware servicemen in the combat zone.

Days later, letters from Vietnam, marked "Free" and in frayed envelopes striped in red, white and blue, started trickling in to the Mailbag. Then they poured in. We were in business. The first column was published on May 20, 1968, with an upbeat story and picture from Army Spc. John W. Morgan who had befriended a tiny Vietnamese tot in Chu Lai. That Monday, we also welcomed more than a dozen other Delawareans who eagerly told us where they were stationed and shared their stories.

The volume of mail grew so rapidly that, in less than a month, the Mailbag expanded to two columns a week. On June 15, 1970, the Mailbag began appearing three times a week, a frequency that was sustained for more than a year before cutting back to twice a week, then to once a week. The last Mailbag was published on December 18, 1972, after receiving a total of nearly 900 letters. Our troops, finally, were coming home.

Throughout our time together, we celebrated promotions, birthdays, anniversaries and arrivals of children yet unseen. The Mailbag even engineered an engagement or two. In addition to printing letters from the war zone, we provided servicemen with information on absentee ballots, benefits and a bonus from the state Veterans Military Pay Commission.

We requested free flags from the Delaware State Development Office, kept ever-changing military addresses current and personally answered nearly every letter the Mailbag received. The war was close to us too – with my brother, a neighbor, friends, and high school and college classmates on the front lines.

As we got to know many of these brave men and women over those five years, we marveled at their buoyancy, self-sufficiency and confidence at danger's door. Unselfishly, they airmailed their unvarnished, war-torn, homesick selves to us week after week. Between the lines, we read their apprehension and fear and, yes, optimism and hope. Despite the grimness of battle, they found time to express wit and humor and gladly shared with us their zest for life in the face of death.

NANCY LYNCH
VIETNAM MAILBAG – REPORTER

They made us proud to know them.

Though their letters were directed to Delaware, we soon realized their words clearly resonated far beyond the boundaries of the nation's second-smallest state. Delawareans indeed spoke for all Americans through their letters, and, in the process, gave those of us at home an unprecedented window on the war.

In *Vietnam Mailbag, Voices of the War: 1968-1972*, we celebrate these exemplary war letters and safeguard them today as touchstones of time.

In Part I, a chapter is devoted to each of the five years of the column. Most letters have been excerpted; a few are printed in their entirety. All have been edited for ease of reading. A Delawarean's name, branch of service and rank, location in Vietnam and date of correspondence, if known, are printed following each letter or excerpt. In the back of the book, a glossary translates most frequently used military jargon.

Part II takes us to the present, through a series of contemporary interviews of Vietnam veterans. From their experiences and perspective, they tell us how the undeclared and unpopular war affected them, both in Vietnam and back at home. They also share their thoughts on today's undeclared and unpopular war in Iraq, decades after Vietnam.

Join me now as we salute the authors of these war letters that transcend generations with their timeless relevancy and enduring spirit. And, to all Delawareans who braved so much to bear America's freedoms to a foreign land, know how very privileged I felt, through the Vietnam Mailbag, to be in your service.

Nancy

EDITOR'S NOTE

In *Vietnam Mailbag, Voices From the War: 1968-1972*, we have attempted to fashion a social history of the Vietnam War, as seen through the eyes of hundreds of servicemen, most of them from Delaware, who served their country during those five years. While the chapters of the book are arranged chronologically, the letters within each chapter are not. We have organized the chapter around the primary themes the servicemen covered in their letters each year. So, different portions of a single letter may appear on several pages within a chapter.

We have introduced each letter with the first sentence in bold type. At the end of each letter, we have identified its author and when it was written (if the letter was dated) or the date it was published in Nancy's Vietnam Mailbag. Mailbag correspondents didn't always include their branch of service in their letters. In most of these cases, we have been able to identify their branch through references to military units in the correspondent's return address. When verification was not possible, an individual's branch is not listed.

In preparing the book, we have occasionally made minor edits to the letters – correcting misspellings or grammar when necessary to ensure that they read clearly.

The book also includes numerous excerpts from Nancy's Vietnam Mailbag and from several other publications. Excerpts of one paragraph or more appear in italic type.

PART I

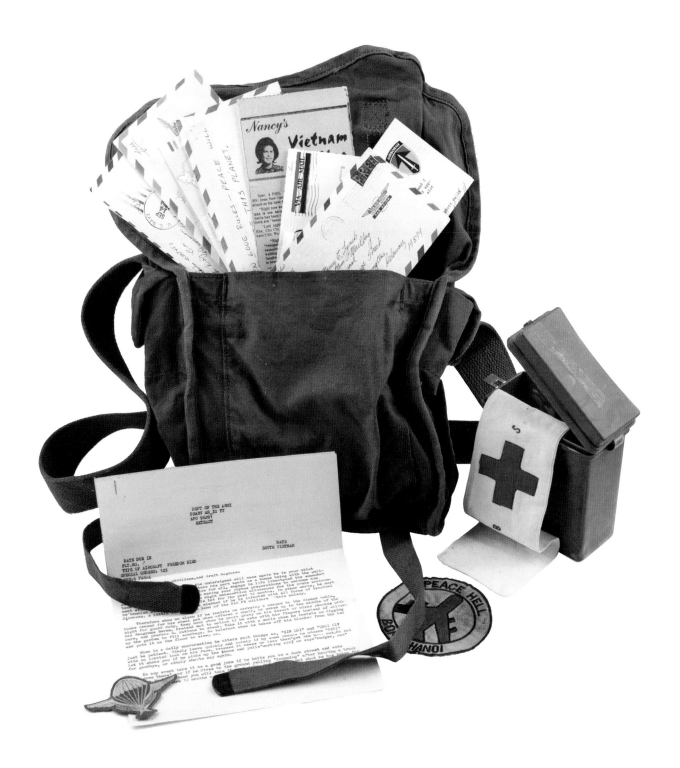

★ LETTERS FROM VIETNAM ★
THE WAR IN THE SERVICEMEN'S OWN WORDS

An icon of the Vietnam War, the Army's Cobra helicopter ushered in a new era of aerial warfare with its multiple machine guns and rockets and logged more than a million operational hours in the combat zone. A sweep team (opposite) from the 2nd Battalion, 34th Armor of the 25th Infantry Division checks the road ahead of a convoy out of Cu Chi. Detecting underground explosives mitigated one of the greatest dangers to American troops.

1968

A PERFECT STORM OF TUMULTUOUS EVENTS THUNDERED THROUGH THE UNITED STATES IN 1968, PRECIPITATING REBELLION, RACE RIOTS AND RANCOR. THE POST-WORLD WAR II BABY BOOMERS, VANGUARD OF THE NATION'S LARGEST GENERATION, PREPARED TO VOTE IN THEIR FIRST PRESIDENTIAL ELECTION.

Americans protested the undeclared war in Vietnam, raged at the assassinations of the Rev. Dr. Martin Luther King Jr. and U.S. Sen. Robert F. Kennedy and thumbed the establishment with draft-card burnings. The national mood soured on the endless – and seemingly unwinnable – war in Vietnam, 12,000 miles distant yet telecast into millions of homes each evening. In 1968, its deadliest year, the unde-clared war claimed the lives of 16,592 American forces. Delaware, the country's second-smallest state, mourned the loss of 55 men.

Civil rights leader King was slain in Memphis on April 4 while supporting a sanitation workers' strike. His death triggered racial tension and urban chaos throughout the country. Two months later, Kennedy, challenging Vice President Hubert H. Humphrey for the Democratic presidential nomination, was also felled by an assassin's bullets, shot in a pantry at the Ambassador Hotel in Los Angeles as he left a victory celebration following the California primary.

Coming into its own, a defiant, long-locked generation found favor with iconic liberals Dr. Benjamin Spock, Yale University's William Sloane Coffin and others convicted June 14 for aiding draft evasion. In separate cases, the Rev. Daniel J. Berrigan was twice convicted for tampering with and burning draft files.

Wilmington, Delaware's largest city, mirrored the nation's festering malaise. In the summer of 1967, Democratic Gov. Charles L. Terry Jr., armed with groundbreaking, bipartisan-backed emergency powers legislation, quashed racial violence on the city's West Side. He placed Wilmington under a state of emergency and ordered the National Guard on standby. He also predicted more civil unrest for the summer of 1968.

The tempest struck sooner.

Five days after King was killed, rioters in Wilmington's West Center City burned buildings, looted businesses and lobbed firebombs at city police. Mayor John E. Babiarz Sr. called for the National Guard. Terry didn't hesitate, activating 3,500 guardsmen. Although order was restored in a few days, the city was placed under curfew until April 14.

Babiarz canceled the state of emergency on May 2, but Terry refused to halt the Guard's jeep patrols. Wilmington was the only municipality in the country with militia on active duty, prompting 30 leaders of the city's African-American community to circulate a statement labeling him a "racist governor." Undeterred, Terry hunkered down. Not until political newcomer Russell W. Peterson, a Republican and former DuPont Co. chemist, narrowly defeated Terry and was inaugurated governor on January 21, 1969, was the Guard removed from Wilmington. Peterson's first official act ended the longest military occupation of a U.S. city since the Civil War.

But the growing cancer at home and throughout the country was Vietnam. Army Spc. Walter L. Rainard of Wilmington, writing from Saigon in 1968, described the conflict as "a confusing and complicated commitment."

A commitment President Harry S. Truman made in 1950 when he sent a military assistance advisory group to train the South Vietnamese in the use of U.S. weapons. In October 1954, President Dwight D. Eisenhower offered direct economic aid to South Vietnam, now partitioned from North Vietnam along the 17th parallel. Four months later, in 1955, Eisenhower dispatched military advisors to train South Vietnamese forces.

The first U.S. troops arrived in Vietnam in December 1961, when President John F. Kennedy ordered 400 uniformed Army personnel to Saigon to man two helicopter companies to support South Vietnam's effort to maintain its independence. Within a year, the United States had flexed its military muscle by deploying 11,200 troops to Vietnam. And five years later, in 1967, President Lyndon Baines Johnson pronounced U.S. troop strength would stand at 525,000 by 1968. Weary of the interminable war, Americans at home worried and waited. And demonstrated.

In this climate, Delawareans serving in Vietnam found a voice. As a public service, the News-Journal Co. offered a free subscription to *The Morning News* to every First Stater in Vietnam. Editors in 1968 created Nancy's Vietnam Mailbag as a column of correspondence between those in uniform and me. Writing from the combat zone to the Vietnam Mailbag, Army, Navy, Air Force, Marine Corps, Red Cross and USO personnel aired their perspectives, opinions, concerns and gripes, giving Delaware an unprecedented window on the war, a vantage far more personal than newscasts viewed on television.

Starting with the first column on May 20, our servicemen expressed their views eloquently or simply but always passionately on the war, protesters, race riots, the King and Kennedy assassinations, politics, the bombing halt and the Paris peace talks. They penned battlefield narratives, described their jobs and explained their civic action projects. And they gifted us with their good humor.

First, though, they overwhelmingly endorsed the Vietnam Mailbag.

"**I received your letter today concerning your new assignment on Delaware GIs in Vietnam.** It sounds like a great idea and I certainly wish you well. I've got a subscription for both the *Evening Journal* and *The Morning News* and I'm constantly looking for articles on other 'Diamond Staters' in Vietnam. It's really encouraging to see that there are people concerned with what we are doing here. Thank you and I hope to hear from you soon."
Army Staff Sgt. Ronald Bailey, April 26

The first Vietnam Mailbag appeared May 20 in *The Morning News* with this introduction: "Nancy's Vietnam Mailbag starts today as a regular Monday column in *The Morning News*. Reporter Nancy E. Lynch has written to more than 800 Delaware servicemen in Vietnam explaining that the new column will be devoted exclusively to them: Their achievements, opinions, experiences, humor and gripes." These letters (opposite), written in late April and May, were among the first the column received. Servicemen's enthusiastic response to the Mailbag boosted the column from once to twice weekly less than a month after its debut.

4   Morning News, Wilmington, Del. * * * Monday, May 20, 1968

Nancy's Vietnam Mailbag

By NANCY E. LYNCH

"**I hope that this column helps ...** both in Delaware and Vietnam, to clear up the minds of people who don't know what is going on here, as well as we who don't have the true picture of home."
Army Spc. James Fitzgerald, April 28

"**I received your letter about the new column you are starting in the Wilmington newspaper and was pleased to hear that the newspaper is doing it.** It gives the serviceman from Delaware [a chance] to express his opinions about the war in Vietnam and to add humor to keep his spirits high. It also gives the Delaware serviceman a chance to find who actually are the servicemen from Delaware fighting over here."
Marine Lance Cpl. Richard M. Magner, April 28

"**I'll be staying over here for another four months unless something drastic happens and I can do without that.** In the meantime, I'll be watching for your bit in *The Morning News* that comes all the way over here to Camp Eagle."
Army Chaplain (Maj.) Jim Peterman with the 101st Airborne Division near Hue, April 28

"**I was quite amazed at the information people want to know about this beautiful country which they haven't been able to receive from the usual writings of Vietnam and the war.** It seemed to me that the people know we're at war in some far-off land but know nothing of that land where their own sons are dying."
Army Spc. Frank C. Woerner Jr., April 28

"**I think that the idea of a column voicing our gripes, humor and opinions is a good one.** It will give the people an idea of what it's like over here and what some of the men go through.

Regardless of whether we belong here or not is (pardon the cliché) a world of experience. I have only been over here a short time but I have learned a lot and I have also grown to appreciate the small things that I had back home.

Back home the people don't have the real picture of what it is like over here. The column might give them a better idea of what it is like over here. Overall, most of the people over here have a wealth of information that we can share with everybody instead of just our parents. How many people have been more than say 500 miles from home? Well, we can give them an idea of what another country is

like and even an idea of a different cultural, social, political and religious system than what we are used to. I think it is a great idea. Help us to help enlighten the people back home."
Army Spc. Hugh R. Dougherty, April 30

"**I received your letter and I think it is a great idea.** I know Delaware is a small place but we must have more than 3 men over here. Thank you much for thinking of us over here. You don't know how much it helps. I get *The Morning News* everytime the mail comes through and all the men in my squad, even though they are from other states, think you and the rest of the staff have excellent coverage of the war. Keep up the good work."
Marine Cpl. William Tilley, April 30

"**I am sure [by] merely printing some of the comments made by Delawareans, many people will obtain a view of the war uncovered by the wire services.** So much is involved here. We so often tend to resort to a black or white analysis of the situation."
Army 2nd Lt. John C. Henry in Nha Trang, May 4

"**I was really glad to hear of your editors' new idea for the guys here.** I think it is great. I'm glad you said you'd like to keep the column informal. I always like to speak in plain words. Just thinking about your paper itself, I'd like to congratulate the [paper] on a great job of coverage of this situation and of course [columnist] Bill Frank does a great job."
Marine Pfc. Alan Greenwell, May 17

"**I think this is a really good idea having this column in the paper.** I really enjoy it and I show the column to all my buddies because they say Delaware's so small I'm the only one over here."
Army Spc. Bruce Hunter in An Khe, June 29

"**First, I would like to say that looking forward to reading your column has certainly helped to pass the time over here.**

Being a career man, with just over two years before I retire, I look at this tour as a very necessary job in which we all have to do our part. It is most gratifying to know there are people back home that appreciate our efforts."
Navy Chief Petty Officer E.H. "Manny" Caralivanos in Nha Be, Aug. 5

For more than a decade, American troops waged an undeclared and unpopular war in South Vietnam, a politically unstable agrarian nation about the size of the state of Washington. The country's challenging terrain of mountains, plateaus, plains and deltas, combined with oppressive tropical weather, tested traditional methods of warfare.

SERVICEMEN SOUNDED OFF ON PROTESTERS OF ANY PERSUASION. Throughout 1968, soldiers wrote in, blasting everyone from university students holding campus buildings hostage to those demonstrating against the war. First, they wondered aloud about the unimaginable events unraveling in their small state of Delaware.

"I'm almost sorry that *The Morning News* is being sent to me while here in Vietnam. Life here is depressing enough at times and one can only think of getting 'Home' – I read the paper and I think to myself, 'Come home to what,' curfews, looting and rioting? I'm beginning to think I'm safer over here with the Vietcong. Day after day I care for sick and wounded GIs, not to mention all the innocent wounded Vietnamese children. The 'war' at home in my town of Wilmington is far greater than this one over here. Many of us here live in fear of being wounded, mortared and rocketed – do I have the same thing to live in fear of at 'Home' too? There are a few of us Delawareans here that are frankly disgusted with Wilmington – Negro and white alike!! You can't imagine what it's like to be confined for a year – and then to face the confinement at home too. I feel pity for all of you at home and in the same breath hope that the situation 'at home' improves. Please make America the best place to live."
Army Nurse Corps Lt. Diane King with the 17th Field Hospital in An Khe, April 30

"Please encourage [the people back home] to call a halt to the civil disturbances for the thirty-day period beginning 28 September 1968. That's when I get home and I really don't know if I could stand the excitement."
Army Capt. Jon M. Peterson near Phu Bai, May 3

"Now my gripe is I receive *The Morning News* from you and on the front page was a picture of police pushing back rioters and a story of snipers and riots all over Delaware. Could anyone in the states realize how depressing that is?

To think I'm in Vietnam fighting and my National Guard friend who joined to get out of fighting is fighting! That's quite a joke to me. Up until now I used to think it would really be great [to] return to a world of peace and nonviolence. But now it seems when I finish my tour over here I will return to almost the same thing as what I'm doing here.

I wish people would realize there's enough trouble and turmoil in the world without causing more!

In closing I would also like to say may I never meet or hear of anyone burning their draft card or defecting to another country. Though my views on Vietnam are not 100% pro, I am an American and I am fighting for my country."
Army Sgt. Gerald W. "Jerry" Thompson, May 7

A downtown theater locked its doors (opposite) while national guardsmen patrolled city streets and strategized in Wilmington, Del., following the April 4,1968 assassination of civil rights leader Rev. Dr. Martin Luther King Jr.

"Up until now I used to think it would really be great to return to a world of peace and nonviolence. But now it seems when I finish my tour over here I will return to almost the same thing as what I'm doing here."

Army Sgt. Gerald W. "Jerry" Thompson

"I just received *The Morning News* dated 10 +12 April. Boy, they really upset me. I can't imagine anything like that happening in Wilmington. That one article about the Hungarian immigrant whose little boy was hit with a brick really upset me. People must be crazy doing things like that, burning, throwing bricks, etc. Don't enough people get hurt and killed over here? If they want violence, why don't they come over here?

When guys ask me where I'm from in the states, anymore I try to change the subject. I'm becoming more and more ashamed to say that I'm from Wilmington, Delaware.

I recently returned from R&R to Japan and enjoyed it very much. I'm seriously thinking about going there to live after I get out of the Army. At least there you don't have to worry about what part of town you walk down, or having your son hit by a brick or your store being burnt to the ground by some group of young people who don't have anything better to do than cause trouble for other people.

I probably shouldn't have written this letter but I'm still upset. I'd hate to come home after a year of dodging enemy mortars and rockets and get hit by a wild bullet or a flying brick. You can't imagine how most of the guys feel when we hear about riots back in our hometowns.

Oh well, I'll probably regret shooting off my 'pen' but what the heck, 'War's Hell.'"
Army Spc. Paul M. Grifantini, May 7

"I am glad that I'm going home in nine days. For a while there I was not sure I want[ed] to come home or not because of the trouble you had back home. I thought it was safer over here. I still have my thoughts about coming home or not."
Army Spc. George S. Walker in Vinh Long, Sept. 19

After learning of the violence not only in their home state but throughout the United States, others expressed their indignation.

"I'll feel very good when the day comes that I can tell my son of my year in Vietnam, while the frightened, immature, drug addict, mamma's boys hide behind [their] protest signs safely in a country where freedom is taken for granted. A freedom which men are giving up their lives for every day and will be as long as their country needs them. Truly, this is the main 'gripe' of every man away from home. I ask myself why should I have to serve in one war zone and then come home to another? One which is much worse than Vietnam because of its nature."
Air Force Airman 1st Class Robert D. Mayfield, April 26

On April 9, 1968, Gov. Charles L. Terry Jr. deployed the National Guard to Wilmington at the request of Mayor John E. Babiarz Sr. A week later, Babiarz requested the troops be withdrawn but Terry refused and kept them in the city until his term ended in January 1969.

During the 1960s, riots caused mass destruction in many U.S. cities, including Wilmington, Del. Firefighters and National Guard members patrolled Jefferson Street after it was stormed by protesters reacting to the April 1968 assassination of Rev. Dr. Martin Luther King Jr.

"All the other marines whom I work with wonder if it's safer here or in the states. These riots are so ridiculous. Here we're fighting a war so people can keep what they have, freedom. And now almost everyone home is shooting one another, robbing and burning....

Since I've been in Vietnam, I find that I've picked up a very warped sense of humor. Things that are not really amusing, I laugh at, but I guess it could be the harassment around the place I work. At times I find myself in a very fatuous way. Majority-wise, everyone around here is like that, to keep from going insane."
Marine Lance Cpl. Tim J. Rineer, April 28

"And about the draft dodgers, all I can say is more power to them. They don't want to go into the Army and risk their [lives] for nothing when us boys over here are fighting and risking our lives for everything and for them to enjoy life and peace. Maybe when they get older, they will realize this."
Army Pfc. Bruce W. Biscoe, May 1

"The things that really gripe the guys over here are when you see your buddies killed in action fighting for freedom and you come back to your area and hear the news of riots in the states. The main thing is that the people complaining and rioting don't know anything about Vietnam or the Vietnamese people because they have never been here and experienced war.

If they knew what Communist aggression can do to a country and how the people live in fear all the time, they'd more than likely change their story. I'd like to know how they would like to work 10 hours a day, six days a week for about 26 American dollars a month. After they have been paid this they have to forfeit almost half of it for self-protection. I also would like to know how American women would like to go to work with a pick and shovel. It will some day come to that unless we can stop Communist aggression here in Vietnam."
Navy Petty Officer 3rd Class Joseph Forrest Jr. in Da Nang, May 13

"We'd like to see the hard-core rebels of places like Columbia University over here on our side. Anyone who can capture and hold an administration building against such overwhelming opposing forces would definitely be a tactical asset."
Army Pfc. Tim Smith with the 101st Airborne Division, May 14

"I am prepared to give my life in defense of my country; but now there is a question mark! To what do I surrender my life if the time should come? To rioters, racists, murderers, or corrupt politicians? No, only to these strong-hearted people of South Vietnam, for I am ashamed, ashamed of my own people. I hope the people could only realize how they tear down the morale of the fighting man in Vietnam at a [time] when he must be fully in control of his wits. Do you know how scared I am to return home? I'd rather take my chances with Charlie. I pray for peace once more in the United States of America.

The wishes of my comrades are the same as mine. May the Good Lord guide you, my fellow Americans!"
Army Spc. Robert V. Hudson in Vung Lau, June 10

"[One gripe I have is] the war protesters. If they don't like war and want to protest it and don't like the U.S. being in it, tell them there are ships and planes leaving the U.S. every day and I wish they'd be on them. Of course, they are only a minority, so no big thing. If anyone protests us fighting the Communists, then they must be Communists. What more can I say?"
Marine Sgt. Earl A. Heston near Da Nang, June 17 Mailbag

"Those damn hippies and protesters don't realize it but we are fighting so that they can go on and be free and have public [gatherings] and marches. The only people that can do this are free. And that's what we are fighting for – to keep people free."
Army Sgt. Pete Rago in Quang Tri, Aug. 1

A Delaware National Guard soldier in full riot gear (opposite) patrols in riot-torn Wilmington, Delaware's largest city.

"I'm serving here in Vietnam with 'L' Co. 3rd BN 27th Marines. Last night while receiving a few rounds, I started thinking about things going on back home. So I started writing and ended up with the following. I sure hope you consider printing it.

My God, how can it be that one boy lies rotting from malnutrition and torture in a jungle prison camp in North Vietnam and another boy spits and TRAMPLES ON THE FLAG OF HIS COUNTRY ON THE STEPS OF THE UNIVERSITY OF CALIFORNIA.

That one boy lies sightless in a U.S. naval hospital from communist-inflicted face wounds and another boy uses a Communist flag to drape himself in defiance of the laws of his country.

That one man of medicine begins his thirteenth straight hour standing over an operating table in pursuit of life for men serving his country. And another man of medicine implores groups of young men to refuse to serve their country.

That one soul brother holds the face of his dead chuck comrade in his arms and cries pitifully in a dirty foxhole in Vietnam. And another soul brother screams with hate against his chuck brothers on the streets of countless American cities.

That one boy lies in a coffin beneath the ground because he believed in duties to his country, and another boy lies on a dirty cot giving blood to the enemies of his country.

That one man of God shields a wonderful boy from an enemy bayonet with his body and dies, and another man of God uses his cloth as a shield to preach hate, dissension and lawlessness."
Marine Pfc. Joe B. Henderson, July 20

"I don't want to argue the politics of this war because we are here. But I do have one big gripe. And that is when the war protesters talk about how immoral we are. Yet I never hear immorality laid at the feet of the VC or NVA. I would like to cite several examples of VC-NVA immorality:
1. Shooting at medical evacuation helicopters
2. Mass murder in Hue during Tet
3. Assassination of civilians
4. Enslavement of Montagnards
The first and third items I speak of from first-hand experience. I think these protesters should be as honest in their thought as they are free in their speech."
Army Spc. Larry R. Kipp in Lui Khe, Aug. 5 Mailbag

"America is a great place and it's a privilege to live there. But you must earn this privilege. Just because a person is born there doesn't mean that they have a right to make a fool of their country. This is what they're doing with their demonstrations and such but, like I say, these people are in the minority so they don't really count.

I know that once I'm home, I'll feel I've done my part. It will give me peace of mind."
Marine Cpl. Charles R. Straughn at Marble Mountain near Da Nang, Aug. 24

"One thing does get to me and that is the way that some of the people are acting back in the STATES. I tell you if any person spent one year in Vietnam that they would be glad to get back in any part of AMERICA. I know that I sure do want back in good old DELAWARE. As you say, it is the first and the best."
Army Pfc. Winfield Scott Walls near Saigon, Aug. 29

"This war has been going on too long. There is one thing all of us feel hurt that we are over here fighting to keep freedom, sacrificing our girls, our wives, our children, our parents and the wonderful things we all did before coming over here. But yet in the states, there are people that do not have the backbone to fight for something that is right. But we are all proud to be fighting for the freedom of our country. And we all will give our lives for freedom."
Cpl. Ken Machamer in Phu Bai, Sept. 13

"Ask the war protesters and draft dodgers to think about what the late President Kennedy said. 'Ask not what your country can do for you, ask what you can do for your country.' I'm more than willing to die for the country I love."
Marine Cpl. H.B. "Burty" Todd in Chu Lai, Sept. 13

"As for my gripes, well, I don't have the paper to list them all but here are a few: sand, rain, no girls, the food, the working hours, no girls, the pay, no girls, and, above all, the demonstrations and rioting that are going on back in the United States. I realize that it is a minority but that is all I ever read in the *Stars and Stripes* and also *The Morning News*. I just wish all those hippies and yippies knew just how good they have it in the good ole USA. If they could spend a couple of months over here, I'm sure they would change their outlook 180°."
Marine Cpl. Scott Price in Chu Lai, Sept. 27

"As far as Da Nang goes, I think it's a real safe place, especially when I read about what's going on in the states! I can't complain about the way Uncle Sam's treating me here, but I could name a few other places in the world I'd much rather be!"
Navy Seaman Joe Gaynor in Da Nang, Oct. 14 Mailbag

As a sober reminder of the price of freedom, one serviceman gathered his thoughts for students at Rehoboth High School, his alma mater.

"I'd like to talk about a war, a person, a people and a decision. It's Nov. 26 and I'm writing to you, the students of Rehoboth. Some of you may remember me. If you don't, I don't really blame you because I wasn't the local celebrity.

I'd like to talk about a war, a person, a people and a decision.

A war – one nobody wants, everybody talks about, few people seem to care or know about, and some people are dying in. Dying – how do you define an 18-year old guy dying for his country? It's not easy. He could be here reading this article and saying, 'What a nut this guy must be to write this.'

A person – You, for example. What do you think of this war? Hope we win, newspapers flash out. 'GIs kill 300 NVA. Marines take Hill 810.' But there are other sides to it. After reading the newspaper and seeing the newsreel, you say, 'Our guys got the situation well in hand.'

But our guys have many other things to cope with besides the enemy himself: loneliness, missing a family, a country, a freedom, fighting in a war they don't really understand. Listening to a radio announcer say, 'Students march on Capitol, protest war and killing in Vietnam.' What then? A young man's mind turns over and wonders: Doesn't anyone care? Tell me, are your fellow Americans expendable? NO!! It's my buddy, your brother and friend, most of all, your fellow American. He's all alone and wants to come home!

A people – yes, youth, all young Americans. Yea! You can't vote or drink. Neither can they (the soldiers), most of them. But you can speak up for the men in Vietnam. All they want is to know you care, that you're backing them, not with words alone, but with 100 percent participation in a thing that concerns the cause they fight and die for.

A decision – it's yours. You can turn the page and forget this little note, but can you forget them? Remember while you read my little note, a guy is sitting in a cozy, muddy bunker, his thoughts traveling back to the days when he was in school. He would have cared! But his thoughts are interrupted by a small incident, a war, lonely, silent and most deadly. Sleep well tonight, my friends, because he's watching over you."
Marine Cpl. Gerard C. Flaherty, Nov. 26

Throughout 1968, antiwar protesters gathered to demonstrate their opposition to the war in Vietnam. Marches were common, although many demonstrators, like these in New York City's Union Square, assembled to vocalize their displeasure.

IMMEDIATE UNCONDITIONAL *HALT* TO ALL U.S. BOMBING

STOP THE WAR MADNESS NOW!

FIFTH AVE. VIETNAM PEACE PARADE COMMITTEE 17 E. 17ST N.Y.C. 10003

R NOT VER!

MADNESS NOW!

COMMITTEE 17 E. 17ST. N.Y.C. 10003

"Our guys have many other things to cope with besides the enemy himself: loneliness, missing a family, a country, a freedom, fighting in a war they don't really understand. Listening to a radio announcer say, 'Students march on Capitol, protest war and killing in Vietnam.' What then? A young man's mind turns over and wonders: Doesn't anyone care?"

Marine Cpl. Gerard C. Flaherty

Artillery assignments necessitated heavy lifting. The gun crew of the 1st Battalion, 8th Artillery, load a 155-mm howitzer during a firing mission.

DESPITE THE NATION'S CIVIL UNREST, SERVICEMEN HONORED THEIR COMMITMENT TO THEIR COUNTRY. Most were proud to serve their nation and accepting of the dangerous duty overseas.

"Married March 11, 1967, my wife and I had five months together before I was sent to Vietnam. Hate it!! No one could have hated the idea of a year in Vietnam any more than I did. Now I'm counting the days, 114 more of them in fact, till I'll be returning to the wonderful, wonderful states. Although I dreaded my being sent to Vietnam, I can truly say I'm very proud to be serving my country in this period of crisis."
Air Force Airman 1st Class Robert D. Mayfield, April 26

"I can say the Vietnam War and the fighting the American soldier does is for a cause. I just wish we had the backing of all the people in the USA."
Army Staff Sgt. Ernie Miller in Da Nang, April 27

"As much as I would love to go home and along with all of the bad things of a war, I am proud to be an American. I am proud to serve my country, defend it, and fight for the cause of peace. I think that has been my greatest achievement, to find out just how wonderful it is to be an American."
Army Pfc. Bruce W. Biscoe, May 1

"There are quite a few people who frown upon this war. As for myself, all I can say is that this is where my country sent me, this is where she wanted me to serve her. So here I am."
Army Sgt. Edmund S. "Ted" Cox, May 19

"I don't think anyone is in favor of war in general, but if it takes this to stop the communists from taking over the world, I'm in favor of it one hundred percent.... If the president didn't think the war in Vietnam was necessary to the security of our nation, he wouldn't have sent us here. Sure, we're helping the Vietnamese people now, but we're helping ourselves in the long run in the years to follow."
Marine Sgt. Earl A. Heston near Da Nang, June 17 Mailbag

"I hope that everyone who serves in Vietnam gains as much from their tours as I have from mine. It gives you an understanding of how awful an effect communism can have on a country and its people. It really makes you appreciate how fortunate we are to live in a free and progressive land. Let's hope it will always be that way!"
Army Spc. Don White in Chu Lai, June 18

Army Sgt. Charles E. Cole, a tank commander for the 2nd Battalion, 34th Armor, rests after the second day of fighting NVA forces near the Ho Bo Woods.

"I feel that a lot of us are here not because we want to be but because it's our job and we know it. I don't exactly love it here in Vietnam, and, to be honest with you, I can't wait to leave.

We are definitely accomplishing our mission over here and I'm glad I'll be able to say I did my part while being here. I'm due home on 31 Aug. 68."
Army Sgt. Ralph Walsh, July 2

"Ah, yes, I am the sometimes infamous 'Scrounge Hound' [at the University of Delaware].... I look upon those days with great longing, for today in my new job I am a horse of a different color.

Two things tend to alter my personality: a) I'm a convert from the Reserves and everyone knows a convert to a cause is generally very rabid and b) I'm a volunteer for this Vietnamese vacation, which means my personal convictions in this cause are rather strong."
Army Capt. Jon M. Peterson, July 17

"I feel that the war in Vietnam [has] got a purpose.... The people here are living a two-way war to survive. When we are here, we are number 1. They respect and fear us, knowing if they got caught dealing with the VC they are in grave trouble. And when we leave and the VC move in, the VC are number one so that they can survive peacefully."
Marine Pfc. Bill "Rock" Watkins on Hill 29 near Chu Lai, Sept. 13

"The war, in my opinion, is for a cause, that is to free countries of communist control and let them have a safe and democratic life. I was born in the USA, so I will fight and die for my country. It's as simple as that."
Navy Seaman Al Temple at the DMZ, Sept. 17

"Being in the service, and now especially in 'Nam, has made me take life a lot more seriously than I did a few years back. I guess matured would be the best word. The war – well, I'll simply say I think it's necessary! For the fact that I actually wouldn't want my children's children living under communism. I'm pretty sure every American feels the same way. Although I wonder sometimes after being home [on a 30-day leave]. One incident that sort of sticks in my mind happened while I was at a drag strip in New Jersey. At the beginning of every meet, the national anthem is played, during which everybody is supposed to stand. I noticed a couple of 'fellow Americans' sitting down while it was played. Acted like it was a joke. I wonder if they would think the 'Killed in Action' list that is put out every day over here is a joke too!"
Navy Petty Officer 3rd Class Jim Belay in Da Nang, Sept. 26

Army Capt. Herbert C. Pratt (wearing hat) of the 2nd Battalion, 34th Armor MEDCAP team listens as ARVN soldiers describe their symptoms. Fire brigade medics, Army Sgt. Robert J. Dinardo of Fremont, Calif., and Army Spc. Jose R. Soto of Milwaukee, Wis., accompany Pratt.

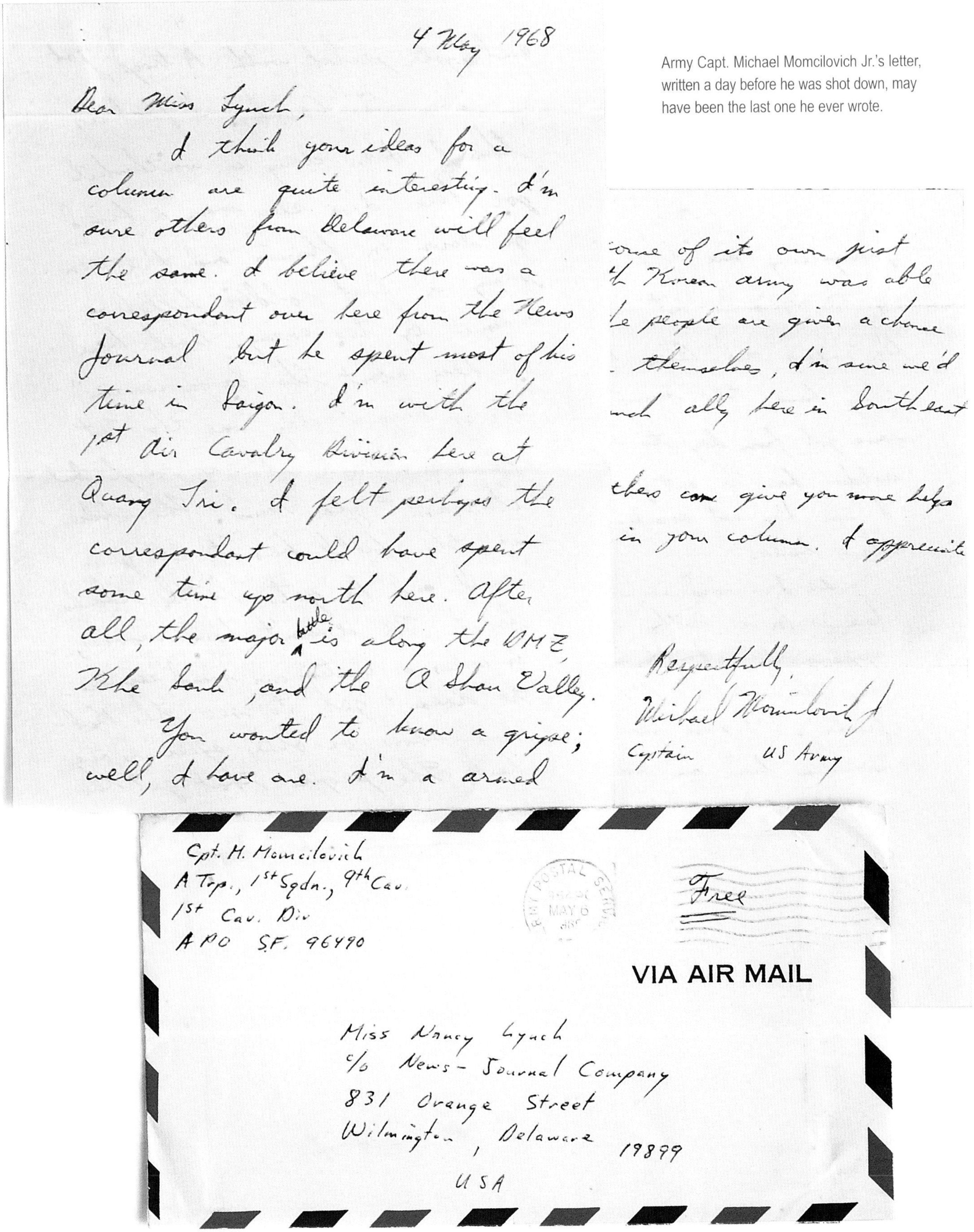

4 May 1968

Dear Miss Lynch,

I think your ideas for a column are quite interesting. I'm sure others from Delaware will feel the same. I believe there was a correspondent over here from the News Journal but he spent most of his time in Saigon. I'm with the 1st Air Cavalry Division here at Quang Tri. I felt perhaps the correspondent could have spent some time up north here. After all, the major *battle* is along the DMZ, Khe Sanh, and the A Shau Valley.

You wanted to know a gripe; well, I have one. I'm a armed

Army Capt. Michael Momcilovich Jr.'s letter, written a day before he was shot down, may have been the last one he ever wrote.

...ome of its own just ...h Korean army was able ...he people are given a chance ...themselves, I'm sure we'd ...nd ally here in Southeast ...

...thers can give you more helps in your column. I appreciate

Respectfully,
Michael Momcilovich J.
Captain   US Army

Cpt. M. Momcilovich
A Trp., 1st Sqdn., 9th Cav.
1st Cav. Div
APO SF. 96490

Free

VIA AIR MAIL

Miss Nancy Lynch
c/o News-Journal Company
831 Orange Street
Wilmington, Delaware 19899
USA

> "I feel the work here is for a worthy cause. At times it appears the South Vietnamese aren't too sure they want to pay the price for freedom. I have seen some ARVN units withdraw from an enemy force much smaller than their own and other times I have seen ARVN units hold their own when confronted with quite formidable odds."
>
> Army Capt. Michael Momcilovich Jr.

An Army officer offered additional insight. He had been wounded about a month before writing this letter.

"I'm an armed helicopter pilot with a troop, 1st Squadron, 9th Cavalry. I feel as though I'm doing a worthwhile job here. I've seen many a friend go down in flames and I've seen many a foot soldier killed or maimed by the enemy. Back home we hear about the 'Saigon warrior' whose biggest day was the Tet Offensive. True it was rough but it wasn't year round. The soldier in the field has it all year round and he gets little thanks for it. He doesn't have movies, or Cokes, or continuous mail service. He doesn't get to see the Bob Hope show or other specials over here. The people that get the pampering are the stock clerks and gate guards at places like Qui Nhon, Da Nang and Bien Hoa. Of course they have the monotony of doing the same job from day to day while the field soldier has to outguess a very sly enemy. I hope I'm not sounding too pointed along these lines....

I feel the work here is for a worthy cause. At times it appears the South Vietnamese aren't too sure they want to pay the price for freedom. I have seen some ARVN units withdraw from an enemy force much smaller than their own and other times I have seen ARVN units hold their own when confronted with quite formidable odds. With better guidance and some patience I'm sure the Vietnamese Army will come of its own just as the South Korean Army was able to do. If the people are given a chance to decide for themselves, I'm sure we'd have a staunch ally here in Southeast Asia."
Army Capt. Michael Momcilovich Jr. at Quang Tri, May 4

Capt. Momcilovich, 24, who graduated from Brandywine High School in 1961 and the U.S. Military Academy at West Point in 1965, was killed a day after writing to the Mailbag, when the Cobra helicopter he was flying was shot down by hostile ground fire. The 77th Delawarean to die in Vietnam, Capt. Momcilovich was one of 187 U.S. troops killed on May 5, the date America sustained the most casualties in a single day during the entire war. His decorations included the Air Medal and the Purple Heart.

An excerpt from Capt. Momcilovich Jr.'s obituary as it appeared in the News-Journal on May 13, 1968 read:

After spending two years in West Germany with an armored unit, he was sent to Vietnam last November.
He returned to the United States briefly for helicopter training at Ft. Wolters, Tex., and then returned to Vietnam. He was wounded in April and then learned to fly the Cobra and returned to duty.
Capt. Momcilovich is survived by his widow, Mrs. Lynne Momcilovich; a daughter, Kristin; his parents, and two brothers, Peter and Mark, both at home.

When a high explosive round's primer detonated but the main charge failed to fire, quick reaction by a soldier prevented an untimely explosion. He yanked the round out of its barrel and ran it back into a clearing.

"My feeling about this war is that the United States should support an all-out effort over here to destroy the Communist insurgent forces. As it stands now, they are doing a pretty good job at it, but many of our fellow servicemen are losing their lives still. We should submit all our manpower to destroy the Communist aggressors."
Marine Lance Cpl. Richard M. Magner

Another marine had reason to be bitter. The closing of his letter was ominous.

"**Hi! I guess that's a good way to start this letter.**
I really don't know what to say. My name is Cpl. Ron Bleacher.
I lived in Wilmington and Elsmere all my life.
I won't say how long I've been in Vietnam, I'll just tell you I have 44 days left.
I am with Hotel Co 2nd Bn 5th Marines at An Hoa. I saw your article with Cpl. John Carrow.
About 10 minutes ago I was just talking to him. We've been out in the field now for 27 days and his company was just choppered into our area.
We both talked for about 20 minutes before he left.
He told me to write.
Myself, I really don't think we should be over here. Two of my best friends were killed over here for what? These ungrateful people? This country?
If this is what they died for, it isn't a hell of a lot.
He told me to say what I thought, so I am.
All I want to know is for what, or why?
I'm just glad I'm getting out of here.
Bye, Ron"
Marine Cpl. Ronald T. Bleacher at An Hoa, Sept. 8

Three weeks later, on September 29, Cpl. Bleacher was shot and killed by enemy gunfire during a military operation. His obituary was published October 2 in the News-Journal with those of two other Delawareans, Marine Pfc. Aaron Zane H. Glazar, a former Wilmington resident, killed September 23, and Army 1st Lt. Werner Curt Brown II of Greenville, who died September 29 and was the son of Werner C. Brown, a vice president of Hercules Inc. These three losses brought the Delaware death toll in Vietnam to 105.

For some, frustration with the war was inevitable, in spite of their commitment to their country.

"**My impression about this war isn't very good.** I think it is a dirty, rotten, demoralizing war. The people over here are wondering why the U.S. isn't doing more to step up this war or to escalate it to the point that everyone goes home. It is just a politicians' war and no one else's.... Just don't get me wrong, I am all for this war. We have lost too many men over here to pull out."
Marine Cpl. Mike Fleetwood with the 3rd Tank Battalion
near Dong Ha and Quang Tri, July 11 Mailbag

"**I feel I'm right in being here, but I'm afraid our government doesn't know they play for keeps over here.** I've had my share of perimeter guard and seen my share of action. I've seen young men die needlessly because of some officer or staff NCO.... In many ways this war is very disgusting and heartbreaking and only by being over here, a part of it, will then you understand what I mean. It's too hard to explain with words. I just hope and pray that this will end soon as I hope my 17-year-old brother never has to come here."
Marine Lance Cpl. Larry Depew in Da Nang, Oct. 20

Marine Cpl. Ronald T. Bleacher, 19, wrote on Sept. 8, just three weeks before he was killed. The letter appeared in the Sept. 30 Mailbag, a day after his death. Cpl. Bleacher had joined the Marines in July 1966 and was sent to Vietnam in October 1967. He was survived by his parents, an older brother, Robert, and his paternal grandparents.

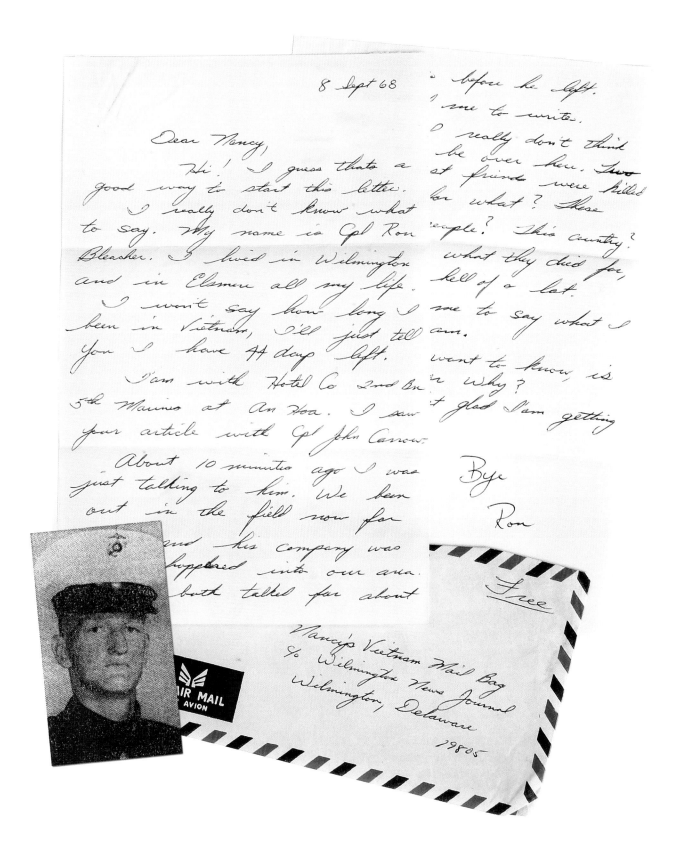

8 Sept 68

Dear Nancy,

Hi! I guess that's a good way to start this letter. I really don't know what to say. My name is Cpl Ron Bleacher. I lived in Wilmington and in Elsmere all my life. I won't say how long I been in Vietnam, I'll just tell you I have 44 days left.

I'am with Hotel Co 2nd Bn 5th Marines at An Hoa. I saw your article with Cpl John Carrow. About 10 minutes ago I was just talking to him. We been out in the field now for ___ and his company was ___ happened into our area. ___ both talked for about

before he left. ___ me to write. ___ really don't think ___ be over here. Two ___ st friends were killed ___ or what? These ___ ple? This country? ___ what they died for, ___ hell of a lot. ___ me to say what I ___ am.

___ want to know, is ___ Why? ___ glad I'am getting

Bye

Ron

Free

Nancy's Vietnam Mail Bag
% Wilmington News Journal
Wilmington, Delaware
19805

AIR MAIL
AVION

"Because of the inaccessibility of the hill, everything is rationed. You can't shave or wash. The water you get is for drinking. You can imagine we are a pretty scroddy bunch of characters up here. As for my gripes, I could give you a list a mile long. The living conditions are terrible, the working hours are too long, the food terrible."

Marine Cpl. E.R. "Rich" Moore

Canned rations or C-rations date back to World War II and have sustained American troops in the field for more than a half-century. In Vietnam, servicemen often sparred over favorites like peanut butter and crackers, spaghetti and fruit. An anxious sergeant (opposite) radios his tank driver during a sweep in the Filhol Plantation south of Cu Chi.

DESPITE THEIR DOUBTS, SOME SERVICEMEN CHOSE TO EXTEND THEIR TOURS OF DUTY. One correspondent extended his tour for six months but asked that information not be printed in the Mailbag as he hadn't yet told his parents. He joined the Marine Corps in July 1966 and arrived in Vietnam in October 1967. He wrote from Hill 304.

"**I'm with the 3rd Marine Division, Headquarters Company, Radio Relay Platoon.** Our job is to supply communications for the division. It is pretty complicated to explain in writing. The best definition I can give you is we supply multi-channel communications from outlying 3rd Division units to 3rd Division forward, which is Dong Ha. That's the best I can give for a definition, just please don't get us confused with a radio operator – we aren't.... There are three of us on a team. We are attached out from our home unit, which is Dong Ha, to outlying units.

I've been just about everywhere there is to go in the I Corps area, from Da Nang (a very short time) to Khe Sanh on the west, to the east and Con Thien north. At the present time, I'm on Signal Hill, more commonly known as Hill 304. I've been here for a month and will probably remain here until I go home.

Because of the inaccessibility of the hill, everything is rationed. You can't shave or wash. The water you get is for drinking. You can imagine we are a pretty scroddy bunch of characters up here.

As for my gripes, I could give you a list a mile long. The living conditions are terrible, the working hours are too long, the food terrible, etc. These gripes are in comparison to the states but we aren't in the states over here. In the situation we are in and under the circumstances, we are getting the best there is.

As for my opinion on the war, I have neither the paper nor the ink to express the way I feel, and I'm not a writer. I've been over here, I feel I know what's going on. I feel there have been a lot of statements made and a lot of things written by people who only have half an idea about what is happening. I'm not against protesting and demonstrations against the war. That's why I'm here, so people of America have the right to say what they think. We may be going about this war wrong and we have made mistakes. Until someone comes up with a better solution, and we are trying to do so, all we can do is try and an attempt is better than doing nothing at all.

I may be wrong in saying it, but I don't think we can win a military victory over here. We have to show the common Vietnamese people that we are interested in them and by doing this they will take an interest, not just in their small farms but in their country and their place in the world. Everyone has heard of our war with the VC and NVA but we are also waging a war with the Vietnamese people. When we win their confidence and interest, then and only then will this war end. After reading over this, it is kind of confusing but this is my opinion. I hope I haven't bored you with it.

I have met two other First Staters over here, Mike Fleetwood from Seaford, whom I enlisted with, and a guy from Wilmington. I can't remember his name. He should be home by now."
Marine Cpl. E.R. "Rich" Moore near Dong Ha, Sept. 16

Others extended their tours of duty as well. A few shared their thoughts with the Mailbag.

"**This is my second tour in Vietnam.** I keep trying to tell myself the reason I am here is to keep those children of mine from having to go through what I am now."
Capt. Anthony P. DiBendetto, April 29

"**This is my third tour in Vietnam and I am sorry to say there isn't much humor over here.** As for gripes, I don't have any of them either, mainly because I am the one who wanted to come over again and if I have any complaints, I have to blame myself and no one else. But I am happy to say I have a good bunch of people I work for.

We are right at the mouth of the Mekong Delta where we try and keep the waterways open going into Saigon for the shipping. We also control how much traffic goes to and from Saigon."
Navy Petty Officer 3rd Class Joseph Kopec Jr. in Cat Lo, July 7

"**Well hello and how is everyone back in Wilmington?** First of all I would like to say thanks for taking your time to do something for us guys over here. So many times we wonder if the people back home really care by the way they act sometime. I have learned you cannot judge by a few.

I'm now in Vietnam for my third time. I was in Germany for eight months and requested duty in Vietnam. After my first twelve months I requested a six-month extension. I served that and took six more. Some people say I'm a fool, but all us fools are born everyday. I'm now a squad leader. My job consists not only in leading twelve men, but at any time I'm ready to explore Vietcong bunkers and tunnels. All of this comes under a Combat Engineer. We are attached to the 11th Armed Calvary Regt. under the command of Col. George S. Patton III. In my time here I have seen a good part of the Nam. If they were not at war and with a little help this could and will be a great country. I only hope and pray that I see that day come soon."
Army Sgt. William H. Chance at Xuan Loc, Nov. 28

Jungle sweeps were one of the prime missions of the 34th Armor during the dry season. This tank crew, alert for any enemy movement in the fender-high growth, included driver James C. Riley of Sturgis, Mich., Clifford McDonald of Dunellon, Fla., William R. Mosier of Bells, Tenn., and Kevin M. Hatley of Erie, Pa. Ground forces (above) also were vigilant as they pounded the bush.

SERVICEMEN IN THE WAR ZONE HAD STRONG OPIN-IONS ON NATIONAL EVENTS AS WELL. Mail filtered in with their feelings about the Rev. Dr. Martin Luther King Jr. and Robert F. Kennedy assassinations, the bombing halts in North Vietnam and the 1968 presidential election.

"I am writing this letter in hopes you will publish it so the USA will see what one GI out of so many feels about Senator Kennedy's death.

I write in hope that the USA will try and see what it is slowly but surely turning into. After we heard Senator Kennedy was dead, we just don't understand anymore. 99% of the servicemen in Vietnam just don't understand what is going on in USA today. I sincerely believe that it is a rotten shame for GIs to come over here, die for this country, to try and explain to the Vietnamese that freedom is great, to tell them to live the USA way, when our own country cannot live in peace.

I also believe that if they took all those "Hippies," demonstrators, draft-card burners, rioters, and all those (PEO-PLE) ????? who want to fight so much, and send them to Vietnam – They would soon find out that they have something to live for. THEIR LIFE!!!!!!!

It is disgusting to know that after days, weeks, months of running for bunkers, hoping that the next round doesn't have your name on it, and to dream of my rotation date when I will be going home – when you stop and wonder – HOME – fights, riots, assassinations, hippies, draft-card burners????? Is this really home????? Can I really say to myself I will be so happy to go home? Sometimes we think that it is actually safer over here. So a GI says to the people back home – Stay with us, support us, and believe in us – for without you – what can we live for?? A letter from a GI in Vietnam – 'You HAVE TO BE THERE BEFORE YOU CAN CRITICIZE.'

P.S. I enjoy your column very much and it is a pleasure to know someone cares."
Army Staff Sgt. Ernie Miller in Da Nang, April 27

"There is a popular song over here called 'I Wanna Go Home.' Whenever an entertainment group starts singing it, all of us usually join in. I sing it too but do I want to come home? John F. Kennedy, the Rev. Dr. Martin Luther King and now Sen. Robert Kennedy. When somebody ran in the dispensary and shouted, 'Kennedy has been shot,' it was like being back on that day in November '63.

U.S. Sen. Robert F. Kennedy's bid for the White House ended when he was slain shortly after midnight as he left a victory celebration following the June 4 California primary.

"It is disgusting to know that after days, weeks, months of running for bunkers, hoping that the next round doesn't have your name on it, and to dream of my rotation date when I will be going home – when you stop and wonder – HOME – fights, riots, assassinations, hippies, draft-card burners????? Is this really home?????"
Army Staff Sgt. Ernie Miller

Why? America seems to be changing. I don't think I am going to know America when I get home. Over here during the elections, there are guards on the proposed candidates. Sure, this is a country at war with the enemy trying to do anything that will disrupt the government. The assassination of candidates is considered part of the fight. But in America – my America?"
Army Spc. Philip D. Johnson in Phu Loi, June 9

Concerning the assassinations of John F. Kennedy, the Rev. Dr. Martin Luther King Jr. and Robert F. Kennedy, a 1965 John Dickinson High School graduate, Army Spc. William F. Andress, sent the Mailbag this poem in November. "Memories of the Three Ks" was written by his friend and platoon sergeant, Hubert R. Ralmer. Williams had returned home in the fall of 1968 after 20 months in Vietnam.

There were two Kennedys and Mister King
All three stood for wonderful things
They worked hard and searched diligently
So that all men can have equality
They preached, practiced and lived by love
The same as we were taught from above
Let not their ideas fall or die
We will complete them as the days go by
The world has mourned their passing away
But their memories are here to stay
They worked hard and with lots of grace
To bring perpetual love and peace to the human race
These three men had no fear
Of the danger waiting out there
For this trio was of men brave and bold
Doing all that was right to reach their goal
So let's complete the work left undone
Because of some idiots that possessed a gun.

30

As a peace gesture, President Lyndon B. Johnson on March 31 stopped U.S. bombing over most of North Vietnam. Hanoi applauded the move, which opened the door to peace talks between the United States and North Vietnam in May in Paris. Many servicemen disagreed with their commander-in-chief's decision to halt the bombing.

"**Why did Johnson stop the bombing?** I tell you it will not work, I know for sure too, Nancy. Just tonight I have to sleep with all my clothes on because of strong reports of the VC and North Vietnamese regulars in the area. It's really even worse than strong reports but I cannot and I will not say the approximate number around us tonight.

I have never been through a ground attack. The last one at this base was just last Jan. 31st but I was in Hawaii at the time on my way over. It all breaks down to this: when the bombing was stopped, the North Vietnamese armies (hereafter referred to as NVAs) were building up more so than you can imagine. One of my buddies was talking to a pilot that flew [reconnaissance] recently over North Vietnam. The pilot stated that the NVA's supply line looked like the New Jersey Turnpike. Of course, that was hearsay on my part but who am I to doubt the word of someone who was there?

Anyway, I personally think the war is far from over. I think that there will definitely be another attack on my base within the next few days. I bet by the time you get this letter you will read of it. It scares me to think who will get it, will it be my buddy or the guy who's always making everyone laugh. You don't want anything to happen to anyone but it's inevitable at this stage. The last attack we lost only 4 guys to God but I just know that we will lose so many in the next episode that 4 guys will seem nothing.

Tonight, I'm on 10-minute alert status in my sleep. What it amounts to [is] when they attack, my outfit (Quick Response Team) will be one of the very first to meet 'Charlie' coming across the fence. I'm scared to do it but I also want to do it. It's really quite a funny feeling."
Air Force Airman 1st Class Sandy Shaner at Tan Son Nhut Air Base, April 26

"**I, for one, and most of the guys here think that the bombing halt is a bad move.** I don't think we should let up on them at all. Hit them hard and keep hitting them from the air and ground and we'll make these rotten Communists come to their knees."
Army Spc. Denny Skirvin near Tam Ky, April 29

"**There are so many opinions about us being over here.** As for mine, I wish we would bomb all the important targets in the north and if they don't surrender, then invade. These peace talks won't amount to anything."
Marine Lance Cpl. John P. Carrow, May 10

"**I understand peace talks are getting underway in Paris.** They will never settle anything in talks. Hanoi will never meet our terms and vice-versa."
Army Spc. Richard Glazier in Phan Thiet, May 10

"**I'm proud to have served aboard the Lowry.** Not to mention being over here. The war as a whole would go a lot better for us if they would lift the restrictions and go all out to win which I think would happen if they did."
Navy Seaman Wayne R. Zimmerman aboard the USS Lowry, Sept. 14

"**You mentioned the presidential campaign and what my feelings are towards it.** Well, I'm gonna tell you how myself and many other Marines over here feel. The three persons up for president [Richard M. Nixon, Hubert H. Humphrey, Eugene McCarthy] are all good men and all three know what they're doing except for one thing, 'Stop the Bombing!'

A lot of us feel if this is done the enemy will start walking all over South Vietnam. That means all the men who have died, been wounded, or driven crazy by this country have served no purpose. The ones that will still be here, well, I don't know about them.

I know about the [Paris] peace talks and all that but so far nothing has come of them yet except for more killing and fighting. I think if the B-52s opened up one good, hard time on Hanoi, the peace talks would all of a sudden bust wide open."
Marine Lance Cpl. Walt Maier near the DMZ, Sept. 15

"**As far as the 'bombing halt' goes, I have to disagree with President Johnson's decision.** I think it is going to make things worse instead of better. If you knew exactly how the North Vietnamese and Vietcong work, you would understand why."
Army Sgt. Robert A. Elliott in Pleiku, Nov. 10

"**As for the [South] Vietnamese government's present indifferent attitude toward the Paris talks is concerned, I agree with Clark Clifford, the secretary of defense.** He said in his recent press conference that if Saigon doesn't want to talk in Paris, then the U.S. has the right to go ahead without them. I go further and say that the U.S. should go ahead without them. If Saigon was really that interested in peace and freedom for all the Vietnamese, then they would see the Paris talks as a means toward hastening peace and then they would discuss political considerations. You can't resolve anything political while you are still shooting at each other. It seems to me all too symptomatic of our foreign policy to back the first person who has the word 'democracy' spewing from his mouth, no matter what sort of petty dictatorship he is running. That's how we got stuck with such staunch 'democratic' allies as Battista, Diem, Trujillo and Franco."
Army Spc. Robert W. Ketchum Jr., Nov. 14

"The bombing halt was a very stupid mistake. It just gives the commies another edge in the propaganda war. I'm glad Nixon won. I think he will stand up to the commies. LBJ was too much of a dove."

Marine Lance Cpl. John P. Carrow, Dec. 29

More than a quarter of all American fatalities in Southeast Asia occurred in 1968, the deadliest year of the war. Of the 58,193 troops lost during the undeclared war, 16,592 were killed that year.

"As you know by now, they stopped the bombing and as far as I can see it has done no good at all. They say all the time if we make the first move they'll talk peace but they back out [of] it. I don't think this war will end by the time I leave here but [it] would be real great if it would!"
Army Pfc. Edsel Ford Norris Jr., Nov. 22

"I am against stopping the bombing over North Vietnam because it is they who are the aggressors, not us. Therefore, it should be them the ones to give us a break and not for us to give it to them, knowing that they are going to take advantage of the situation to make things worse for us. Also, they are attacking South Vietnamese cities such as Saigon, My Tho and Tan An, killing civilians who have nothing to do with the war. I feel that if they can do this to the South Vietnamese people, there is no reason why we shouldn't go over to North Vietnam and do the same thing to them."
Army Sgt. Emilio Santos in Tan An, Nov. 24

"About the bombing halt: I'm in a Marine gunship squadron and since I fly so much I see quite a bit of this area. Since the halt, it seems like everything is stepped up. The goonies (bad guys) seem braver in the way they're hitting us and everything is just a little 'hotter' than before.

Nobody here at Marble Mountain likes the idea at all. In fact, before the halt we hadn't been hit in over 2 months but right after the halt we were hit twice in a week, once with mortars and the second time with rockets and mortars both. Nobody likes mortars but the rockets are worse. Very bluntly, they scare the hell out of you. I honestly think this can be attributed to the bombing halt.

What really burns me is here we take the brunt of the halt but in Paris they're arguing about what type of table they're going to sit at."
Marine Cpl. Charles R. Straughn at Marble Mountain, Nov. 30

"If you care what I feel towards the bombing halt, I'll say I wish they would start it up once again. In that way it would keep the VC up north where they belong."
Air Force Sgt. James F. Wachter Jr., Dec. 23

Comments on the 1968 presidential election ran the gamut. "My feelings about the presidential elections [are] whoever the Democrats select I'll back him 100%," wrote Marine Lance Cpl. Richard M. Magner in his September letter. With President Lyndon B. Johnson's March decision not to run for re-election and the assassination of Robert F. Kennedy in June, the field winnowed to Democrats Hubert H. Humphrey and peace candidate Eugene McCarthy, Republican Richard M. Nixon and the American Independent Party candidate George C. Wallace, former governor of Alabama.

"My opinion of the presidential campaign, Nixon would be my choice. Because I disagree with the HHH [Hubert H. Humphrey] points of view."
Army Spc. Olindo Damiani in Vung Tau, Sept. 12

"As for the presidential campaign, I'm for Richard M. Nixon all the way. He has the experience that we need. He's the answer to the Vietnam War. Eight years of the Democratic Party is enough for me. The eight years prior with the Republican Party were a lot better, I believe."
Marine Cpl. H.B. "Burty" Todd in Chu Lai, Sept. 13

"As I'm not quite 21 and won't be until after the election, I'm not really too hot on the presidential campaign. I was hoping Senator Gene McCarthy would be nominated and elected. Since he wasn't, I lost even more interest as neither of the two candidates [Hubert H. Humphrey and Richard M. Nixon] are men that I'd want to vote for."
Navy Seaman Wayne R. Zimmerman aboard the USS Lowry, Sept. 14

"About the presidential campaign, I've been hearing quite a bit about [it] over the radio. My feeling about [it] is that no matter who is elected, I do not think he will do any better than President Johnson. You see, this is like when we were fighting for our independence, we are here for a cause…. How do you think we feel at times when we hear of our generation burning their draft cards? To me, I thank God that I was born an American, and this one year away from home, it's hard, but I know that I am here for a very good reason and also that I'm protecting my family and friends and my First State."
Army Spc. Joseph Baray in Da Nang, Sept. 17

"As for the elections, I really haven't formed any opinions. However, it seems like all of the candidates want to pull out of Vietnam, which I completely disagree with. If only they could see these people after Charlie hits them with rockets or mortars. They really need and want our help. Of course, I don't agree completely with the way some things are done here either."
Marine Cpl. William Tilley in Dong Ha, Sept. 19

"Concerning the election, the *Saigon Daily News* ran a daily poll of the servicemen's choice for two months prior to Nov. 5. The results were something like this: Wallace-398 votes; Nixon-216, Humphrey-98, McCarthy-24, Reagan-16, Dick Gregory-3 and Rockefeller-3. Fortunately, George Gallup was more accurate.

The Vietnamese citizens were largely in favor of Nixon's election. Even here in Saigon, 12,000 miles from the normal campaign grounds, there were numerous Nixon/Agnew signs decorating telephone poles and billboards ... a nostalgic reminder to us servicemen."
Army Spc. Jim Cresson in Saigon, Dec. 4 Mailbag

"I can't say too much about the election. I'm just glad Wallace didn't get it. I think Nixon will do a good job as our commander-in-chief. He's had a lot of experience. About the bombing halt, well, President Johnson did what he thought was best. At least, he's trying to end this war."
Marine Sgt. Earl A. Heston near Da Nang, Dec. 16 Mailbag

OF THE MANY BATTLE NARRATIVES WE RECEIVED IN 1968, THESE WERE PARTICULARLY POIGNANT. First, two servicemen wrote of imminent assaults on their bases while others described events after the fact.

"**Right now we are as close to an attack as possible.** All it will take is one second of that siren to have us all in the bunker. A battle has been raging outside our perimeter all day. As we put it, there are 'beaucoup VC' out there, all trying to get in. Last night they hit Phouc Vinh, Tan Son Nhut Air Base, Loi Khe, Cu Chi, and Saigon. There was little damage done. Phu Loi wasn't hit but we all said we were next. I guess we are.

Right now some of us (medics) are out on the 'resupply line' and in various areas to check for casualties The rest of us are sitting in the dispensary – waiting. There is a card game in progress, and nervous laughter. Somebody has their tape recorder on, low enough to hear the siren over it. The outside noises are intense. We hear the 'thrump' of mortars and the firing of rockets and heavy artillery. The most reassuring sound is the beat of a copter's blades and the staccato of a gunship. More so is the deafening sound of a jet making a low pass outside the perimeter.

Tonight my hopes are for the 'grunts' (the infantry). They have formed their own wall, a human perimeter, that separates our bunker line and the VC. All of this is about a mile from us. We have our secondary bunker line manned too – in case.

All we can do now is sit here and wait. It is up to Charlie now. We are ready. The card game pauses each time there is a series of loud explosions. Are they ours – or theirs? Coming in or going out? The guy with the tape recorder pauses, then returns to his music. The game progresses. We have some new guys here. To us they are 'green.' They are the ones already in the bunker, sitting extremely quiet. We laugh to ourselves for we know we did the same thing once. We know too that after a while they will change. They will learn the difference between an outgoing and an incoming round. There is a definite sound difference. They are probably thinking we are out of our minds for acting so calm. But they will learn. Nobody is calm now. However, it is reassuring to each other to look this way. We do things like write letters. (If you get this letter, we are all right.) We do things that really are silly. Some of us who have tape recorders, especially now, put them under desks, for protection.

It is about 8:30 now. I am going to try to get a few winks of sleep. Tonight will be a long, long one."
Army Spc. Philip D. Johnson in Phu Loi, April 5

"Right now we are as close to an attack as possible," wrote Army Spc. Philip D. Johnson about an April 5 scare at Phu Loi. Home to several units, Phu Loi Army Airfield was located west of Bien Hoa about 25 miles north of Saigon. Tanks from the 1st Battalion, 5th Mechanical Infantry sweep the area after contact with the Vietcong.

"**At the present time I'm sitting in a bunker being mortared, and rockets coming in.** This has been going on for the past three days and nights, plus we've already had one ground attack and expect another tonight! [Despite] the lack of sleep, incoming rounds, and constant weapons fire, morale is surprisingly not that bad."
Army Sgt. Gerald W. "Jerry" Thompson, May 7

"**It has been a little while since I've worked on this letter, but I've been awful busy lately.**
Miss Lynch, I want to tell you a little story, part of which you probably know about.

You no doubt remember the Tet Offensive, when our base was overrun by VC. Well, there were VC all over our base, around our barracks, and small arms fire was intense. You didn't dare leave your barracks for fear of getting shot by a sniper, you stayed out of the bunkers because no one wanted to get trapped in such a place.

Well, we had no weapons. We only got a weapon when we pulled guard detail or shotgun for a convoy. I volunteered for these extra duties all the time, just to have a weapon so I could protect myself.

At work, we had five weapons, and we pulled guard detail around our complex, which is a trailer unit.

We did come under sniper fire one night, but luckily no one was hurt, except Charlie.

Then the rockets came. Scared; boy, what a noise, it's a lot different than the sound of artillery or mortars, and a lot more deadly.

All our bunkers are above ground, and not very safe. So everyone started digging bunkers underground. A stop was soon put to this and we were made to fill them back up.

Then came the big plan. A plan was drawn up to arm everyone on base if we should get overrun again. As soon as Charlie breaks through our perimeter, we will be issued one M-16 and two clips of ammo, or possibly 60 rounds.

Well, I sat down one night with a couple of guys, and we started doing some figuring. There were eight of us in our group, supposed to defend our position for fifteen hours. So we figured the amount of ammo we had and the time we were to defend our position, with eight men.

We came up with this. Each man, only one at a time now, could stand up every four minutes and fire one round. Thus at one shot every four minutes, we could hold our position for the required fifteen hours. Good Luck, GI."
Air Force Airman 1st Class Robert D. Mayfield, April 27

"**It's hard to believe they have relegated so many of us over here.** So many innocent people are dying.

Here at F.L.C. (Force Logistic Command), which is the biggest supply base in Vietnam, we receive sniper rounds from the perimeter. And rockets from the mountains that surround the base. Rocket attacks are our main problem. We have no defense whatsoever. All we can do is sit in our bunkers and pray as they come in on us."
Marine Lance Cpl. Tim J. Rineer, April 28

"**Our battery hasn't received much trouble from the enemy, only once about 3 months ago when we were south of our present position did we receive heavy mortar fire from the enemy in which the battery sustained heavy casualties (wounded).** I was wounded in the right leg and arm by mortar shrapnel during a night attack. It was at this position that our battery acquired the name of 'DINGING DELTA,' which was given to us after knocking out enemy mortar positions with our artillery."
Marine Lance Cpl. Richard M. Magner, April 28

"**I just returned from Vung Chua Mt. near Qui Nhon where I had to make a report on an attack by the VC.** I stayed there overnight and helped inspect the guard periodically. Needless to say, it was scary business. No one takes any chances as far as defense goes. I had a machine gun and a pistol with me and wore a flak jacket. Since the attack a couple of nights ago, they have been on red alert all the time with 50% of the personnel manning the firing positions. The mountain is one of those places you might think is impregnable when you first see it. It's about a mile high, almost straight up from sea level, and has very steep slopes leading to its perimeter. But the VC are the most unconventional savages I've ever heard of. They're not dumb either. Their attacks are very well planned and coordinated. The preparation for a single raid may begin several months before the planned attack. Luckily in this instance they didn't attack in a large enough force, so not too much damage was done.

I was really amazed when I first saw the view from up there. It was what you might expect a South American resort city to look like. The scene was equally impressive at night with several ships sitting in the bay, all the lights of the town, and hundreds of native houseboats with their lighting reflecting off the water."
Army 1st Lt. James L. Deese, Aug.17

Several servicemen attested to the perilous conditions along Vietnam's waterways.

"**Down here in the [Mekong] Delta is the worst part of the war now.** It started during Tet. I was not here for all of Tet because I was wounded the morning of Jan. 31…. From Jan 31 to Feb. 7, the guys said it was 8 days of Hell and I can believe it. Since I got back, this compound has been getting hit about every week. Before, they only hit once a month and sometimes 2 or 3 months would go by without being hit. When I got back from the hospital, I had to drink so I could go to sleep at nights. That is how bad it is in Vietnam in the Mekong Delta."
Army Spc. George S. Walker in Vinh Long, Sept. 19

"**Another day's sunset turns the beautiful Vietnamese landscape into a nightmare.** [And] we, the men of RivDiv 521, stand ever ready to carry the fight to 'Charlie' on his terms to ensure safe passage for civilian and supply craft on waterways of Vietnam's I Corps."
Navy Petty Officer 3rd Class Ralph W. "River Rat" Kessler, Dec. 24

Soldiers of the 2nd Battalion, 34th Armor tank crew clean a .50-caliber machine gun before remounting it on top of the turret in front of the tank commander's position.

Marine Lance Cpl. Henry L. Smith Jr. wrote to us from his location near the Ben Hai River. Like most servicemen, he expressed his wish for the war to end.

"Right now, we're on an operation inside the DMZ about 400 meters from the Ben Hai River. I hope it's over soon.... Now I am not only section leader for 60 mortars, I handle all supply in the field for my company. I find that this job takes up most of my time. Also, I find the busier you are, the faster days pass."

Marine Lance Cpl. Henry L. Smith Jr.

Death was the omnipresent foot soldier of war, crouched at everyone's back. Letters nine days apart concerning a near-miss experience riveted Mailbag readers.

"We're sitting here on our hill. At least it's ours today but nightfall might bring something else. It's overlooking Khe Sanh. We watch as Charles throws rounds in on the unfortunate marines as we watch the black smoke from them and wonder when he will turn the guns our way. It's hot and windy and gets worse everyday. All the men are lonely and wish mail would come but it won't. We even wonder when we'll get our next 'C' ration meal and water. We hear about the things back in the states and wonder if the war will ever end. Sure there [are] peace talks but what will they do? While the talks are going on so are the NVA southward and making our job even harder. Some don't even want to come home for sometimes we think the real war is at home. Why don't we go north to the home of the fire and put it out? I would like for you to use this in your column and send me an issue of the paper. Please, we want all the people of the United States to know what it's like here in Nam.

P.S. War is our business and business is damn good."
Marine Pfc. Terry Ivie near Khe Sanh, May 8

"Hope things are fine with you. They [are] pretty bad for now here. I had a few more things to tell you is why I'm writing. When as you can see the peace talks aren't doing any good and the bombing is still stopped, my unit was almost wiped out the 12th of the month. I'm on a hospital ship now. Out of 1,133 good marines, 312 are left. So you can see as well as I can what's happening here.
P.S. Just you and me, right, God?"
Marine Pfc. Terry Ivie near Khe Sanh, May 17

Others landed in hospitals, narrowly escaping death.

"Sorry to say that I am no longer in Vietnam. 'Well,' not really but I am sorry that I won't be able to help you. Last January Mr. [News-Journal reporter Bill] Frank was coming over there and I wrote to him inviting him to visit my unit and told him I would give him a ride in my chopper. I am sad to say I was shot down before I got a chance to mail it. If I were Mr. Frank, I would not feel too bad about not being there to share in this unique experience. A thing like that can ruin your whole day, in fact, it ruined several of mine because I am still in the hospital. Anyway, I will be out soon so maybe I just got to get home early."
Chief Warrant Officer George N. Porter, May 13

"I was in Vietnam and I was medevaced from Vietnam. I spent time in Hawaii and then I was sent to Valley Forge General Hospital. From Valley Forge I was sent to Ft. Bragg in North Carolina, where I am presently serving out the rest of my 81 days in the Army.

I appreciate, I'm sure, along with the rest of Delaware's soldiers in Vietnam, the concern that someone cares about us. Thank you.

I feel now that I have served my time for this country and now I will fade into the crowd and take my place with the rest of my fellow Americans. I appreciate all those who have cared for me and the rest of America's fighting men."
Army Spc. Donald L. Herman, July 10

**COMMENDATION FOR THE SOLDIER IN THE FIELD WAS
FREQUENT.** One writer provided a thoughtful commentary
from his base as well as the Mailbag's 200th letter from Vietnam.

"**I was happy to receive your invitation to write since I've always
had it at the back of my head to send my observations on
Vietnam, solicited or otherwise, to my favorite paper.** I guess
everyone feels like an instant correspondent after arriving in
Vietnam. Opinions and impressions are easy to come by. If you'd
like to read them, I'd like to pass on my observations as another
instant expert.

I've been here for a little over four months, serving as 1st Platoon
Leader, D Co., 2nd/12th Cav, 1st Air Cavalry. Right now, I'm attend-
ing USARV Advisory School. Next week, I'll begin duty as an advisor,
part of a 5-man American team assisting the Vietnamese Regional
Forces/Popular Forces in a district of Quang Nam Province (in the
Da Nang area).

The questions asked most frequently about Vietnam are those
concerning policy and morality. Why are Americans fighting here?
Are we justified in being here? There are no simple, quick, pat
answers. This is a political war, a war of propaganda and guerrilla
action, terrorism and confusion. The man in the field pounding the
boonies finds it rather futile to pursue answers to these questions.
Whatever the reason, he is here.

Ideology means little to the grunt. In some cases, he does not
understand the Johnson administration's views on the war. Others
understand the administration policy and vigorously agree with it.
Still others find it asinine. It doesn't really make any difference, hard

as that may be to believe, in his competence as a soldier. The grunt
does not see his mission here as a matter of burning down villages
and creating refugees. Nor does he picture himself as the courageous
friend of the struggling Saigon government. Politics are anathema to
GIs and GIs avoid letting politics interfere with soldiering. Soldiering
is a simple matter of doing your job while trying to cover your bottom as thoroughly as possible – and your buddy's too, if you can.

The whys and wherefores of our involvement in Vietnam are rather
immaterial to a guy ducking a satchel charge in a bunker or hiding
from AK-47 rounds behind a foot-high paddy dike. A soldier is by
necessity a pragmatist.

The morale of the GI in Vietnam is very high, as you have undoubtedly heard over and over again. It is not, however, the high morale of
the basic trainee going on his first overnight pass. It is not exactly
elation. No GI is deliriously excited about being in scenic Vietnam.
Ask a soldier if he'd rather be here or in the states and expect a reply
that begins with a blank-faced stare of sheer disbelief followed by a
burst of articulate profanity. The term 'high morale' is relative to the
situation. What it means is that the men bear up as well as can be
expected or even better than can be expected, considering the circumstances – the place, the discomfort, separation from home, etc.

The GI has three enemies, not one: boredom, discomfort, and, of
course, Charley. He confronts these enemies every day for a long,
long year. A year, in case you didn't know, is 365 days, 8,760 hours,
525,600 minutes, 31,536,000 seconds, and 10, 712,000 breaths. An
hour can pass very, very slowly when you spend it caught in the
middle of a firefight. A day of rest, on the other hand, can seem like
a week when it means lying around all day cleaning your M-16 over

and over and rereading the same old magazines and letters. A night on ambush can seem like an eternity when you're lying shivering in the mud and muck caused by the ever-present rain.

Days pass, though, and some of them go by surprisingly quickly. The amazing logistical support we have is the source not only of instant resupply, but in many cases, instant happiness. After tromping through the mountains and jungles of the Central Highlands all day, it's funny how excited you can get when a chopper comes to your little LZ and drops off mail, hot chow, and – wonder of wonders – cold beer and Cokes! Only in America.

No other Army in the world takes such pains to pamper its individual soldiers. No soldiers appreciate the pampering more.

Another morale builder is the Army's policy of substituting supporting fires whenever possible for infantry charges. Our artillery and air support are unparalleled. Without parallel also is the value we place on the life of each grunt. This all makes life a little more bearable.

You know, the camouflage cover on a shell pot makes an excellent canvas for self-expression. A quick glance at the helmet of any grunt can tell you more than you want to know about the owner's life, loves, and artistic ability. Typical GI graffitti: always a calendar of the bearer's time remaining in Vietnam, hometowns, home states, names of girlfriends, names of children, and sundry Cav cliches – 'God is Airmobile,' 'Black Power,' 'War is Hell,' 'Flower Power,' 'God is My Point Man,' and various and assorted profanities. But by far the most popular message is 'Make Love – Not War.'

Hope you've been able to make this out – my penmanship isn't always decipherable."

Army Lt. Bob Nylen near Da Nang, Sept. 29

> **"A year, in case you didn't know, is 365 days, 8,760 hours, 525,600 minutes, 31,536,000 seconds, and 10,712,000 breaths. An hour can pass very, very slowly when you spend it caught in the middle of a firefight."**
>
> **Army Lt. Bob Nylen**

South Vietnamese forces (opposite) fought during the Tet Offensive. A mobile unit of the Army's 1st Battalion, 8th Artillery prepares for a firing mission. A must-have item from the combat zone was a South Vietnamese-made leather watchband, shown with a spent 20-mm projectile or small cannon shell.

SHOCKING STORIES CONTINUED TO POUR IN FROM NAM.
During the war, South Vietnam's black market was booming. Two servicemen provided disturbing accounts of the scope of the thriving underground economy.

"**I came to Nam in August, after a tour in Bremerhaven, Germany.** I'm now stationed with the 300th Military Police Company, 92nd Battalion.

Our job here is to provide security for the Saigon port, and to escort the convoys that leave here.

We don't see much action here, as a matter of fact the only fighting you'll see us doing is in a bar in Saigon with one of the girls that work there; and 9/10 of the time we wind up losing that and half our pay too.

When I first got here I was told how illiterate and stupid these people were. Well, they may not all have a high school education but, believe me, they're not stupid.

They all know where the money is and how to make it.

They know more ways of making money than the Mets know how to blow a ball game. The black market proves that. It keeps getting bigger than the DuPont Company every day.

Here at the port, we have guards at every ship, walking the area, and at exits-entrances, and we still lose about $1,000 a day in materials.

But as long as they don't start stealing the MPs that work here, and selling them on the black market, until after next August, I could really care less, because then, I'll be one happy civilian again."
Army Spc. James Casula, Dec. 12 Mailbag

South Vietnamese peasants, downtrodden from years of war in their country, eked out a meager agrarian existence. Army Spc. Hugh R. Dougherty (opposite) with confiscated black-market items in An Khe. Contraband Coca-Cola and Pepsi cost $2.40 a case at the PX but sold for $12 on the black market.

An estimated 50 to 90 percent of the Vietnamese economy in 1968 was supported by the black market, Hugh R. Dougherty of Elsmere told me when he stopped by my office after his tour ended. On the edge of my seat, I took copious notes as he talked. His comments and pictures later filled an entire Mailbag.

The black market, he said, infiltrated the entire country and involved as many, if not more, Americans than South Vietnamese. Prime contraband items were canned beer and sodas, medicine, gasoline, drugs, alcohol, cigarettes, building supplies, money, falsified orders, documents, visas, passports and tickets.

Drugs and medicines cornered the market. Morphine, opium, heroin and marijuana filtered down from the north. Medicines, such as antibiotics like penicillin, were gathered and French labels applied when their potency had expired. Then they were resold.

In April 1968, when he was based at An Khe, Hugh said he, two other American MPs and a Korean MP would apprehend 30 to 40 soldiers a day for possession of marijuana. An AWOL GI was caught with $250,000 of heroin on his person.

In the United States, Hugh said the cache would have been worth perhaps four times that much. In Vietnam, it is illegal to possess, sell or smoke drugs.

Gasoline and JP-4, a fuel for helicopters, were also popular contraband as was hard liquor, a cheap commodity at the post exchanges. Hugh said 30 to 40 percent of American liquor at the PX ended up on the black market. A carton of cigarettes sold for an average of $1.45 at the PX, $5 on the black market; Coca-Cola was $2.40 a case at the PX, $12 on the black market, a bottle of liquor $3.20 at the PX and $10 on the black market.

Falsification of documents was a common occurrence, Hugh said. He could have bought tickets and a passport to Sweden for $1,100. All he had to do was sign out for an R&R in Tokyo and he would have been finished with the service – had he wanted to.

Hugh recalled meeting a soldier at the military hospital in Phu Bai who had been trying to get on a plane with some black-market orders. After a thorough check, the soldier was found to be carrying 20 sets of orders from 20 different outfits. In addition, he had countless identification cards and driver's licenses, all with the same picture, but each with a different name. The soldier, it turned out, was mentally ill, completely disoriented and suffering from combat fatigue.

Hugh said he could substantiate all the information he gave me with records and statistics culled during his tour. What he told me, he added, barely scratched the surface of the black market. In fact, he said he was expecting a footlocker from Vietnam, one made by the Vietnamese from black market building materials. Village chiefs, he explained, were given lumber and other building supplies free. Within five days, those materials would be on the black market.

Practicing the world's oldest profession, a young woman (opposite) solicits her next customer. Shown here is the quarter-mile strip of Plantation Road in Saigon which was a GI hotspot during off-hours. Prostitution was commonplace, as was the GI "hustle," according to Army Spc. Walter L. Rainard.

The Mailbag received some interesting correspondence from a Salesianum School graduate from Wilmington who had been attending Columbia University. Halfway through his initial one-year tour, he planned to extend for another nine months. Based in Saigon, he worked 12- to 15-hour days with the Regional Communications Group. He offered his perspective on leisure time and the world's oldest profession.

"**Perhaps the most insightful diversion in Saigon during the off-hours is to hit the bars.** [They] account for every other building on the quarter-mile strip of Plantation Road between Cholon and [Tan Son Nhut] which runs perpendicular to the Regional Communications Group Compound (which is quite small) main road, and which is about two blocks from my billet.

I don't know whether this is common knowledge but the rate of prostitution in Saigon is perhaps the highest in the world, and I personally know several girls who make over a thousand dollars a month and yet in general physical appearance would not pass for more than a 'plain Jane' at home.

The amazing thing about these girls is that they can make off with half a GI's money without ever fulfilling the implied contract of prostitution. They play on the frustration of GIs on a 3-day pass to Saigon from the tough field assignments in the 'boonies.' By the time the GI figures out what has happened, his pass is over and he's due back at his unit. For those of us stationed in Saigon, the advantage of foreknowledge prevents the 'hustle' from ever progressing past the preliminary stages.

Mud-caked, war-weary GIs enter a bar, sit down and one dainty Vietnamese dish quickly moves in ... opens with, 'Hello, honey' in sing-a-ling English. 'What's your name?' 'You buy me tea?' The famous Saigon tea is a third of a shot glass filled with regular tea, which costs about two dollars, of which the girl gets half. One 'dainty' Vietnamese girl can drink about ten an hour without ill effect. The mistake is to buy the first one because the rest appear almost as if by magic. A mixed drink of basic proportions goes for anywhere between $2.50 and $4.00.

Most of the girls who work in these bars are educated to at least the high school level and can't afford not to work in a bar as it pays too well. It is a highly accepted if not respected role to play in Saigon and every night around eight o'clock, when the bars close, the girls who have been teasing and hustling GIs all day hop on the back of their Vietnamese boyfriend's Honda, or maybe their father is driving, and head for home. This is the general rule, but of course there are exceptions.

The bar girls of Saigon are of course economically cutting the throats of their fellow countrymen by promoting inflation, and the GIs do their part by paying exorbitant prices – and perhaps this will be one of the tragic remnants of a confusing and complicated commitment, if and when it is ever fulfilled."

Army Spc. Walter L. Rainard, Sept. 16

On the first day of his special leave home in December, Army Spc. Robert W. Ketchum Jr. of Wilmington stopped by my office for a nearly two-hour chat about all things Vietnam. Bob mentioned a peculiar habit cultivated by generations of Vietnamese.

They chewed the betel nut, fruit of the betel palm tree, with leaves of the betel pepper, a tropical climbing plant of the pepper family, as a mild stimulant. However, after years of this practice, their lips turned crimson red and their teeth black.

The 212th Military Police Sentry Dog Company was reactivated in 1966 for duty in Vietnam. By 1968, about 240 soldiers and dogs in six detachments pulled security detail in the combat zone. The breed of choice was the German shepherd. Shown here is dog handler Army Pfc. Robert S. Biss with his beloved King.

JOBS IN THE COMBAT ZONE WERE AS VARIED AS THE TROOPS SERVING THERE. One of the Mailbag's earliest contributors, who became one of the column's most prolific penmen during three tours from 1968 through 1970, generously supplied us with lots of commentary on and photographs of his intriguing job in Vietnam. And he always added his pal's name when he signed off.

"I am a dog handler with the first of two sentry dog companies here in Vietnam. I became a dog handler because of my tremendous love for dogs. However, now that I am part of the program, I find that it is little known to the people back home. My mother tells me that people are always asking her (she's a nurse) exactly what I do and what the dogs are used for. Well, I'm very proud of what I'm doing, and the purpose of the dogs.
Sincerely,
Bob and King (my dog)"
Army Pfc. Robert S. Biss in Long Binh, April 27

"As you can see I'm no longer in Long Binh. You see, the 212th has six detachments throughout Vietnam (well, below Cam Ranh Bay, that is) and I have been sent to our detachment in Vinh Long.
I'm right in the middle of the [Mekong] Delta. As a matter of fact, our motto for this detachment is 'the Nose of the Delta.' Our mission here is to protect the airfield [from] infiltrating VC and guarding the choppers. It seems that we are doing a more important job here than we were at the ammo dump in Long Binh and the conditions for working our dogs are much better. King seems to like it better too.

I must admit that the change from Long Binh to here was quite drastic. However, just because this place resembles a WWII POW camp doesn't mean that it doesn't have its advantages. One of the biggest is the fact that we have running water in our hooch, which means flushing toilets. The compound has a central water system. There is also an on-limits town which gives one a place to go to get away from the compound.... This place has Long Binh beat in more ways than one. The main reason – and anyone who has spent time in L.B. will know this – is the lack of harassment. You see, in L.B. the United States Army Vietnam (USARV) has its headquarters and that makes the post as harassment-filled as a post back in the world.
Sincerely,
Bob and King"
Army Pfc. Robert S. Biss in Vinh Long, July 16

While Air Force Sgt. Robert Wiesner wasted few words on his work, saying, "I regret to inform you that I am under secret orders and cannot participate in your program," many servicemen embellished descriptions of their daily work with anecdotal information.

"I'm an intelligence specialist, so I work in an air-conditioned office, 12 hours a day, seven days a week, but I don't worry much about fighting. It's the guys in the field who have it rough. You might say we're 'sitting on easy street here,' if you could call it that. Oh, it's not always easy street. We've had our share of hell, and we live every day praying to see the next."
Air Force Airman 1st Class Robert D. Mayfield, April 26

Army Spc. Richard Glazier (second from left) with intelligence specialists from the Vietnamese Army.

"I've been in Vietnam 5 1/2 months now as a field corpsman with the 2nd Battalion 4th Marines. [I] have been fortunate enough to have traveled from the DMZ to Cam Ranh Bay. We have encountered everything from booby-trapped 105 [mm] rounds to NVA in their full glory."
Navy Hospital Corpsman Donald L. Godwin, April 27

"Right now, I'm located in a regiment on Hill 55 about 12 miles south of Da Nang. I'm in 81's mortar platoon attached to India Co., which is the same company Capt. [Charles L.] Robb [President Lyndon B. Johnson's son-in-law] is with and he is our commanding officer. I've seen him a couple times, but never had the opportunity to talk to him yet."
Army Pfc. Larry Hughes on Hill 55, April 29

A 22-year-old sailor who was interviewed by News-Journal columnist Bill Frank in February 1968 during Bill's second visit to Vietnam was qualifying for his rank as a Navy diver at a Navy Mobile Construction Base (Seabees) at Da Nang. Assigned to the 128th Battalion, he joined the Navy in April 1966 and had been in Vietnam since October 1967.

"As you probably know, [News-Journal columnist] Bill Frank saw me while I was diving in Da Nang. I finished up that job in a few weeks. We repaired a few underwater fuel lines to ships in the harbor working for 3 days. Upon return to my outfit, MCB128, I started pole climbing once again. We are presently working on lighting an ammunition supply area. We set 146 poles, ran over 49 miles of wire and placed 2 lights on every pole. The only bad part about it was that some poles were in old rice paddies while others were on a mountain slope of Hill 327. This job will probably last until my outfit returns home in early July. My first job climbing was a hot one because I became a subject of interest for a VC sniper. You know there's no place to hide up a pole? Thank goodness he was a poor shot! Thanks for your letter and I hope this one will help you. P.S. Tell Mr. Frank I receive the paper regularly and enjoy reading it in my 'spare time.' I also forgot to mention our supply resources are rough so here's our motto in the Bees: We've done so much with so little for so long, we can do anything with nothing FOREVER!"
Navy Petty Officer 3rd Class Louis C. Remmers Jr., May 1

"For the past 11 months, I have flown an armed helicopter over here. The first unit I was in was the 335th Assault Helicopter Company, 'the Cowboys,' when we worked in the Dak To area with the 173rd Airborne. The end of November, I was transferred to the 135th Assault Helicopter company in the Bien Hoa area, and we now live at a place called 'Black Horse.'
Our unit is the only joint Australian-American Aviation Company in Vietnam at this time. We have several Australian navy pilots in our company and two of them fly armed helicopters, 'gunships,' with me. Our company has been lucky since it came to Vietnam. We were supporting all of III Corps during Tet and we suffered only light losses.

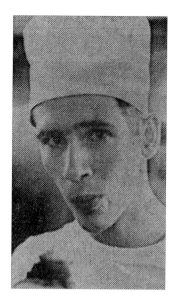

Navy Seaman Steven Cool was assigned to KP aboard the destroyer USS *Collett* with the Seventh Fleet off the coast of Vietnam. The sailor gained notoriety but no weight as he daily chowed down seven meals. "He's always nibbling at something," a shipmate was quoted as saying in the August 1 Mailbag. "I don't know where he puts it all. And the beauty is, he doesn't even gain an ounce." As a cook, Steven was privy to the pantry yet philosophical about his appetite. "The Navy has good chow and I enjoy eating," he commented, "So why not cook the food and eat all I want?

Our main job is to support the Royal Australian Task Force, but we have been called upon for missions in support of the entire III Corps area. Flying over here is always a challenge to us, and it is very unforgiving of any mistakes.
When I return to the states in July, I will be assigned to Fort Rucker, Alabama, as a flight instructor for new helicopter pilots. The men I will train have all volunteered to serve as pilots over here when they finish their flight training.
I can only say that I am proud to have been part of what is probably one of the most demanding professions of our time, that of the combat aviator."
Army Warrant Officer David Saxton near Bien Hoa, May 29

"My job over here is an intelligence advisor for the ARVN (Army of the Republic of Vietnam) intelligence section. Quite often, I accompany the ARVN intelligence platoon on search-and-destroy operations. They are a real good unit and I always feel pretty safe when I'm out in the field with them. Most of my days here are spent trying to find out what the enemy is up to and it is very interesting work."
Army Spc. Richard Glazier in Phan Thiet, June 2

"I'm a helicopter mechanic with the 48th Assault Helicopter Company. Hope to one day soon be a crew chief. My wife and parents live in Seaford and in 286 days I shall be back."
Army Spc. James M. Rowe at Ninh Hoa, June 3

"I have been sitting here for more than an hour trying to come up with something to write about. My job is not as interesting to hear about as some of the ones I have read in your column.... I am a weapons specialist on the A1E Skyraiders."
Air Force Airman 1st Class Edward C. "Red" Redmond Jr. at Pleiku Air Base, July 2

Navy Lt.j.g. John D. Jackson finished his second six-month deployment to Vietnam at the end of October 1968, and was transferred to Newport, R.I. Before stateside reassignment, he sent photos of the USS *Edson* and its crew to the Mailbag, along with a letter describing different operations the ship's sailors had participated in. "The USS *Edson* has been used primarily to provide gunfire support for allied forces ashore in South Vietnam. We have worked with the 1st Division of the Army of the Republic of South Vietnam, South Korean Marines, U.S. 101st Airborne Division, U.S. 1st Air Cavalry, and the I and III U.S. Marine Divisions. We have also operated off the coast of North Vietnam participating in Operation Sea Dragon ... the Navy's effort to stop the flow of men and supplies into South Vietnam from North Vietnam."

"**Hi, I had a few spare minutes so I used them to drop you a line.** I am stationed at the Force Logistic Command (a few miles from Da Nang) where I work in the disbursing office. My job is to get the troops over here paid every month."
Marine Sgt. William J. Gibson near Da Nang, Sept. 12

"**My job here is a weapons mechanic.** At Da Nang, I load the fastest gun, the M-61 built by General Electric. I'll sure be glad to get home after a year here."
Air Force Sgt. Kevin Kirkpatrick in Da Nang, Sept. 15

"**I'm in the 7BN and 11ARTY, 'B' battery and I'm a 'gun-bunny.'** That's what they call us, cause we have to 'hop' to get the job done. One thing for sure, the hours are bad! You're on 24 hours a day!"
Army Pfc. Edsel Ford Norris Jr., Sept. 16

"**I am an interrogation officer with the Division Interrogation Section.** I have been here for nearly six months now."
Army Lt. Ron Love in Chu Lai, Sept. 24

"**I am a door gunner on a UH-1B helicopter and work as a part-time company clerk.** I come home in May, approximately the second day. And my birthday was 24 September and I turned 19 that date."
Army Spc. Art Irelan near Quang Tri, Sept. 30

"**My helo [helicopter] is always ready, able and willing.** It's the best, cleanest, not quite the fastest, but it always flies. It's the only one that does. What are a few hydraulic leaks here and there? We can always auto-rotate down. Boy! You should see it! It's a real veteran, full of all sorts of holes and patches. It only went in the water twice and a rice paddy once. We can hack it!"
Navy Airman Jon C. Bonnett, Sept. 30

"**My job is squad leader.** Proud to be an infantryman. (We do the fighting in the [Mekong] Delta). Our job is to look for Charlie and get him before he gets us. So far we have been very successful, thanks to God."
Army Sgt. Emilio Santos near Tan Tru, Oct. 24

"**The [USS] Intrepid is a support aircraft carrier (CVS) operating as an attack carrier (CVA).** It was 25 years old this August 9, 1968, and it has an impressive battle record. We have just won our 4th battle efficiency 'E,' which is commendable for this old ship.

I am an Aviation Support Equipment Technician, Mechanical, 3rd Class. My job is to keep the necessary gear ready to support a launch and recovery, plus many types of aircraft maintenance gear, such as hydraulic test stands, etc.

I help maintain a pool of 'up' or ready-to-use tractors, jet starters (gas turbines), and mobile electric power plants. It is a never-ending job because the gear takes quite a beating on the flight deck.

The 'Fighting I' pulled out of her home port of Norfolk [Va.] on June 4, 1968, and will return early in 1969. The date is not certain yet."
Navy Petty Officer 3rd Class Rick Nock aboard the USS Intrepid, Nov. 14 Mailbag

"The 3rd MP BN is part of FLC (Force Logistics Command). The battalion is located a little ways from Da Nang Air Base. I'm a squad leader in a security platoon. All we do is run patrols, go on sweeps every now and again and we have an OP (outpost) about 12 miles from our battalion area. We stay out on the OP usually two weeks at a time. I like it out there because there are no 'lifers' to play silly games with you."
Marine Sgt. Earl A. Heston near Da Nang, Dec. 16 Mailbag

"I guess I have it easy on board ship. I am a baker and work nights on the bread watch. It wasn't until some marines came aboard for Thanksgiving and Christmas dinners that I got to talk to someone who really has it tough. But like one marine said, 'You have your job. We have ours.'"
Navy Petty Officer 3rd Class Edward F. Blest aboard the USS New Jersey, Dec. 30

Others provided details beyond the standard job description.

"I am a lance corporal recently promoted this month and have been in Vietnam 7 months. I am with an artillery battery (Delta) 2nd Battalion, 11th Marines, 1st Marine Division (Rein), FMF, located a few miles south of Phu Bai. Our battery is small in comparison to other units but we are a close unit. All our men have a wonderful disposition. I am now presently the battery administration chief, but I have been school trained as a field radio operator so I guess I am stuck with my present position as an office worker. My job is keeping the paperwork involved in running a small unit up to date.
I just got back from 5 days R&R in Bangkok, Thailand, which was wonderful. The people there are very nice and are glad to show their appreciation to American servicemen. I was very sad upon leaving Bangkok, 'cause it was just like leaving home, but it will be better to leave Vietnam for my own home in Newark."
Marine Lance Cpl. Richard M. Magner, April 28

"I myself fly helicopters over here. It's one of the most rewarding jobs in Vietnam. You really get a chance to help out others. I think people back home really care about what we are doing over here. The Vietnamese people want us here [and] need our help. When you see all the suffering these people go through, you can understand our purpose in Southeast Asia. My seven months over here have been filled with many types of experiences. The first time I took bullet holes through the fuel cells of my chopper, I guess I was scared to death. After seeing the crew were all OK, it didn't seem so important. I like my job and wouldn't want to be anywhere else right now besides home. I guess we think about home most of our leisure time. Mail call is our favorite time of each day. The food isn't bad, but I sure miss fresh milk."
Army Chief Warrant Officer Paul P. Stoddard, May 9

"The 45th Medical Company is commonly known as Dust Off. The Army refers to us as [their] Air Ambulance. It's our job to get casualties to a hospital as quickly as possible, which is not more than 15-30 minutes after they have been hit. But we do more than that. Anybody that needs to be taken to a hospital, we'll take. I've flown with NVA, VC, Viet [civilian] war casualties, ARVNs, Mike Forces (Cambodian Freedom Fighters, fighting in and for South Vietnam). I would also like to point out that we pick up Viet civilians who were in accidents not involving the U.S. or free world forces of the war. We pick up pregnant women and men run over by their own cattle."
Army Spc. Larry R. Kipp at Lui Khe, Aug. 5 Mailbag

"My real job is antisubmarine warfare. While here in Vietnam, we usually operate close to shore and the water is shallow, so there's no need to worry about subs. My job here is manning either the machine guns or one of the [USS] Lowry's gun mounts. My ship has been involved in three types of duty: gunfire support for our troops ashore, escorting carriers on Yankee Station, and Sea Dragon operations off the coast of North Vietnam.

> "In a place where you're warned not to become too close to a buddy because he, or you, can be killed at any time, it's impossible not to develop friendships that go beyond just being 'friends.' When you eat, sleep, fight, etc. alongside a guy, the word 'friend' seems a bit insufficient."

Marine Lance Cpl. Gary D. Chastain

A VC anti-tank mine, planted near Trung Lap, is destroyed by the 65th Engineers. The mines had been set to blast a task force returning from the Boi Loi Woods. Soldiers (opposite) keep tanks in top fighting form.

We've given support to the 101st Airborne at Phan Thiet and other units in the II Corps area. We've escorted the USS *America* on Yankee Station twice.

While we were on [Operation] Sea Dragon, our job was to suppress shore batteries while the cruiser's bigger guns fired on inland targets. We also sunk some VC barges and small craft there. Our ship has acquired a lot of praise from the various commands we've operated with."

Navy Seaman Wayne R. Zimmerman aboard the USS Lowry, Sept. 14

"My MOS is 0311 which is infantry, whose job is to walk your legs off and hunt out the NVA. After about two months, I picked up a weapon called the M-79 Grenade Launcher, which is a weapon that shoots a 40- by 46-millimeter grenade and explodes. After picking up the rank of lance corporal in June, I decided it was time to move up some more. So in July, I dropped the launcher and became a team leader in charge of three or four other people. Since then, I've kept that position."

Marine Lance Cpl. Walt Maier near the DMZ, Sept. 15

"My job with Charlie Co. is platoon radioman but that is apt to change as there is a constant reshuffling of men and changing of jobs. We are currently situated at the L.Z. Stud, just between the Rockpile and Ca Lu. This is our jumping-off point for our seemingly endless operations. We are completing an operation now which took us across the Ben Hai River and into the N. Viet side of the DMZ. Ours was the first outfit to penetrate this far north, so we have something on the rest of the 9th Marines.

The men of Charlie Co. are really an outstanding group of guys. I guess the average age is about nineteen (I'm 20), but yet our work is definitely man-sized. Despite the fact that we get very little rest and go on op after op, the morale is still high. It's rather a difficult thing to explain but I suppose we of Charlie 1/9 have what they call plenty of esprit de corps. In a place where you're warned not to become too close to a buddy because he, or you, can be killed at any time, it's impossible not to develop friendships that go beyond just being 'friends.' When you eat, sleep, fight, etc. alongside a guy, the word 'friend' seems a bit insufficient. I think perhaps that instead of being buddies, we are more like brothers."

Marine Lance Cpl. Gary D. Chastain at Landing Zone Stud, Sept. 21

"I am an S-1 clerk (here in division artillery). We handle just about every kind of personnel action, including R&R allocations, extensions, adjusted DEROS (Date Estimated Return From Overseas), and any other correspondence necessary in support of the many, many troops assigned to Division Artillery. I do like my job, however, it is a long day from 0730 hours to about 2100 hours (better known as 9 p.m.). We do get to see an occasional show (LIVE) once in a while and usually have scheduled movies in our outdoor theater (benches under the stars)."

Army Spc. Donald L. Shepherd in Pleiku, Oct. 9

"I am stationed at Camp Haines, Vietnam. It's about 80 miles north of Da Nang and just a few miles from the ocean. This is my first trip over here. I'll be here for 9 months, stay in Port Hueneme, California, for 5 months and come back here for 9 more months. We are right next to the big Army base at Camp Evans.

I've been on KP for the first month and, believe me, it's no 'skate' job. From 4:30 a.m. until 8 p.m., we work hard all day long. We have more than 900 Seabees to feed three times a day. Little thanks do we get. I joined the Navy because I was classified 1A and about to be drafted. I guess I joined to get out of going to Vietnam. Now look where I am. In the Seabees, in the middle of Vietnam, and I've never set foot on a ship. I'm not complaining, though. We have it pretty good over here. We get great food for the place we are in. There's a small village a few miles away, about 900 people. The village chief comes 3 times a day and takes our garbage back to the village to feed to the people. Believe it or not, it's a lot better than what they've been getting.

We haven't seen too much fighting as yet. Everyday, though, we hear the war going on around us only a few miles away. I think we're right helping these people, but I sure would like to be home for Christmas. I don't think the 100° temperatures are going to be too fun in the summer either."

Navy Seaman Apprentice Ron Weatherlow at Camp Haines, Nov. 16

Servicemen from the 2nd Battalion, 34th Armor on a Combined
Reconnaissance Intelligence Patrol (CRIP) encounter some
friendly followers along the way.

CIVIL ACTION OR PACIFICATION PROGRAMS ATTEMPTED TO IMPROVE THE QUALITY OF LIFE OF THE OPPRESSED SOUTH VIETNAMESE. But building or rebuilding infrastructure and providing services could be difficult. Navy Petty Officer 3rd Class Stephen A. Nash, with Mobile Construction Battalion Five, referred to these efforts as Vietnam's "second war."

Battalion Five, headquartered at Camp Barnes near Dong Ha, was the northernmost Seabee battalion in Vietnam and operated in support of U.S. forces in the northern I Corps area. In April, he wrote that his job involved handing out food, clothing, toys and building materials to villagers and Montagnard refugees in the Cam Lo area. The food and clothing came from various U.S. organizations while the building materials were scraps left over from battalion construction projects.

The program was often hampered by enemy harassment but the battalion persevered and planned to build a school in Cam Lo to replace one destroyed during the Tet Offensive. Steve wrote:

"**The feeling I get [as] to the authenticity and value of this program doesn't seem to register quite as well with the folks back home as it should.** Because I work through our Battalion Chaplain's Office directly in civic action work, I feel I am qualified to give a pretty accurate, knowledgeable, first-hand report.

If some people are skeptical enough to feel that we are losing this war and should leave, I think they are most definitely wrong. In 80-90% of the cases I've been connected with, the people are very appreciative of our presence here and consider it as almost a gift from heaven. Even in these rural districts of the northern I Corps area, one can plainly see how we have helped their standard of living. It's true, their dwellings might make Harlem look like Park Avenue to them, but still things are improving.

If you could let the people know that their undying support of our effort would be of a greater help, I'm sure the good American citizens of Delaware would rally to our cause. It doesn't matter if they feel our being here is just, right or wrong, or what have you, the fact remains, WE ARE HERE, and the support should be given."
Navy Petty Officer 3rd Class Stephen A. Nash, April 30

Tragic victims of the war, these children lost their parents and lived in orphanages near Chu Lai. Servicemen asked Mailbag readers to send toiletries and school supplies for the children.

Children amuse themselves at an orphanage in Phan Thiet. Vietnamese villagers (opposite) during a MEDCAP visit by a pacification team on a routine mission to dispense supplies and medical attention.

One writer appealed directly to Mailbag readers, requesting specific items for Vietnamese children.

"These children do without a lot of the basic necessities that even our poorest children grow up with. Some of these children don't even have parents and live in an orphanage in Bong Song. It is called the Bong Song-Tenlon Evangelical Church and Orphanage. These children are fairly well taken care of in the Vietnamese standard, but it still leaves a lot to be desired. Also, this orphanage depends upon the donation of the Vietnamese people and the American GI.

There is also a Catholic church down near Phu My that has a school. The children that attend this school come from the farms in the surrounding area. Most of these children are extremely poor. In fact, this whole area is composed of poor farmers.

Besides these two places, there are quite a few schools in the area. The children, as I have said before, are poor. To them we are like millionaires. We come from a land where there are more advantages and chances to get ahead. You might say that we are the du Ponts, Rockefellers, Raskobs and Vanderbilts over here.

As a result, our Battalion chaplain has organized a program.... Below is a list of what he would like those who want to support our program to send. A cloth bag containing:

1. Crayons
2. Soap
3. Ballpoint pen
4. Toothbrush and toothpaste
5. Hard candy
6. Coloring book
7. Notebook

In regards to this matter, I'd like to leave one last thought. Besides helping somebody less fortunate than us, you might save some GI's life. By helping them they may help us by telling us where the VC are. It will help them realize also, that we are sincerely interested in their welfare. I'd like to leave one last thought and that is, 'War is Hell' (pardon the cliché) and it is the kids over here that suffer."
Army Spc. Hugh R. Dougherty at Landing Zone Uplift, June 14

Two months after publication of Hugh's plea, we received another note from him. He was on the move in Vietnam but wrote asking that we again print the address to which packages could be sent.

Other servicemen, including a Navy hospital corpsman, also commented on civil action projects, both large and small.

"A letter to you and even more important, to those who read your column. I am finishing up my tour here in Vietnam at Dong Ha, seven miles from the DMZ. A big change for me since leaving Charlie Med at Khe Sanh. But here we are doing something possibly even more important toward winning the war!

Here at Delta Med we have opened a 60-bed children's hospital to serve the people of the northern I Corps Area. A population of over six million. The hospital opened last week and already we have had over 500 children patients – luckily for us most could be treated as outpatients. We have two children's wards and a nursery, which I run, a modern two-room operating room, laboratory and X-ray unit. All the conveniences offered to the fighting men of America over here. But there are many things we are lacking – supplies for a war just do not include the things for a child's happiness and care. We are in desperate need of baby bottles, blankets, toys and games, bibs, pacifiers, all the little things to make life a little easier for these youngsters.

Over here TB, malnutrition, meningitis and malaria are all prevalent. And of course, explosive wounds, some grossly infected. We see them all. And thus far, most have been cured. And this is our reward – the happy faces of the mothers who know that without us, their child would have died.

Though I leave soon, the hospital will continue to function. It will continue to help those little tykes and give them a chance to live. Can you, the people back home, help us? Help us win these people to our side. For by showing them our good help and care, we will end this war sooner."
Navy Petty Officer 3rd Class David Rusher, Sept. 12

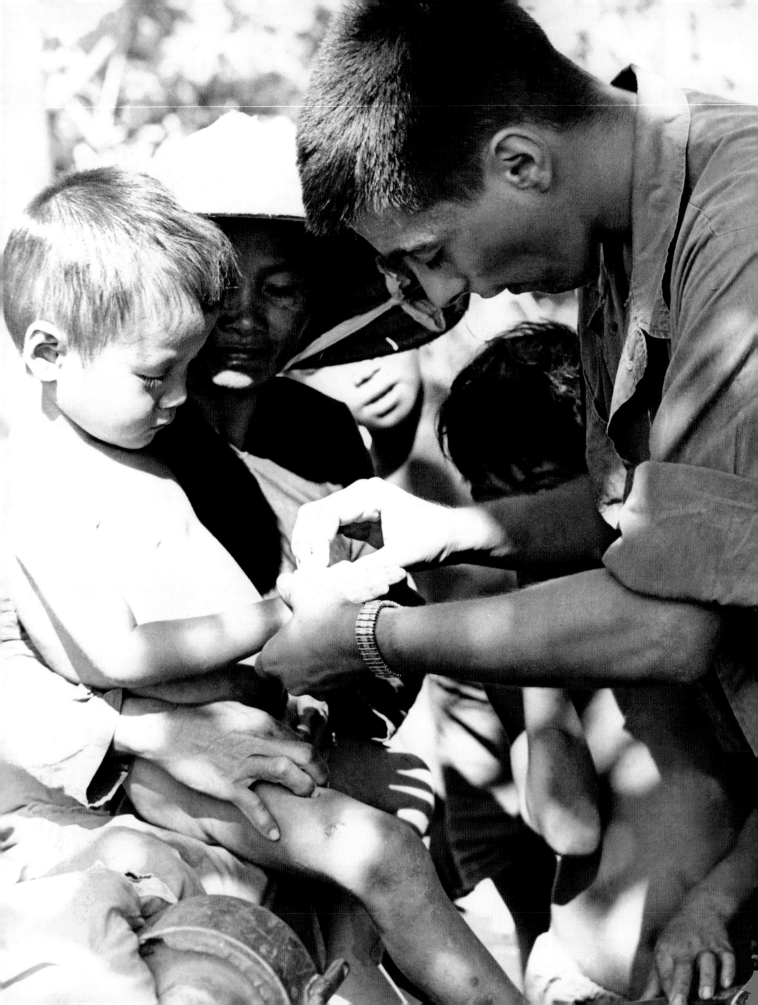

A soldier couldn't wait to tell us about his personal pacification project. His letter was published in the inaugural Mailbag on May 20.

"**I go down [to the village] once a week to see a little 2-year-old baby that runs up to me when she sees me coming down the road.** She knows which pocket I keep my gum or candy in. All she gets out of my pocket at once is one piece of gum or candy. I wrote and asked my mother to send me a little sunsuit for her. When I got the package, I found two suits for her. My mother and sister both got her one, along with shoes and socks. I'm enclosing a picture of her with one of the sunsuits on."
Army Spc. John W. Morgan in Chu Lai, April 26

And there were other examples of goodwill.

"**My company has been taking up a collection to send some Vietnamese children to school.** It doesn't take a whole lot to send a child to school for one month over here. So far, we have enough to send about 16 kids. I really believe that this is a worthwhile project."
Army Spc. Robert A. Elliott at Camp Holloway, July 12

Army Spc. John W. Morgan's April 26 letter included this photograph of a 2-year-old Vietnamese toddler wearing a sunsuit given to her by his family. An Army medic (opposite) tends to an injured South Vietnamese child.

"**One of the girls that works on the post broke her ankle.** We had it X-rayed and then applied a cast. Teaching her to walk with the cast was a lot of fun. The cast seemed to weigh as much as she did. I think the greatest enjoyment here is the look on these peoples' faces when we help them, treat their illnesses and injuries. It makes [us] feel great and that being here isn't bad after all."
Army Spc. Philip D. Johnson with the 11th Civic Action Battalion in Phu Loi, June 9

"**Vietnam is a very beautiful country.** It was certainly different than what I had expected. It's too bad that the country has to be at war and the countryside destroyed by artillery craters and bomb craters. But we are needed over here and these things sometimes have to be done.

It took a little while to get used to some of the customs, but after a while picking up a few words and using sign language you get to know the people. They are really great people, a little confused, but who wouldn't be if one day you go into their villages and explain the reason you're here and the next day come and destroy half of their village and tear up their crops with tanks because of the Vietcong activity.

Myself, I've fallen in love with the little kids over here. They are really great [and] they're the ones that get the raw deal over here."
Marine Lance Cpl. Philip S. Young, May 5

LETTERS ABOUT CHANCE MEETINGS IN VIETNAM ALWAYS MADE GOOD READING. The hard-to-miss calling card in the combat zone was the Delaware state flag, a silk-screened, full-color flag that measured three feet by five feet. The Delaware State Development Office offered free flags to all First Staters serving in Vietnam. Once they learned of this "freebie," everyone wanted one. And the Mailbag itself soon became a vehicle for scouting others.

One of the more unusual random encounters occurred early on and involved neither the flag nor the column.

"**I have a interesting story for you about a meeting between three hometowners – Galicia Navigator, a ship registered in Wilmington, William McLaughlin and myself.**

Bill and myself are military policemen but we're not the usual MP. Our job is to ride 'shotgun' on the merchant ships on their way up the river to the Saigon ports and the tugs to the towns on the Mekong Delta waterways.

It was early in the morning when we met. We were on a tug working our way out to the different ships when a voice called out, 'McLaughlin, Miller, get your gear together.' As we approached the fantail of the ship I read the name Galicia Navigator Wilmington Del. I thought to myself, 'Gee, a ship from my hometown.' Before the thought was out of my head a voice next to me said 'Hey, that ship is from Wilmington, my home.' That's when Bill McLaughlin and I met. And on to the Galicia Navigator (formerly Our Lady of Peace) we climbed.

Well, that's the end of the story. It just goes to show you. You never can tell when you're going to run into a hometowner. It happens every day. And 12,000 miles away from home off the coast of Vietnam in the South China Sea is a strange place for it to happen."
Army Pfc. Andrew D. Miller, May 24

Some meetings were better late than never. And some, unfortunately, never occurred.

"**I have been here seven months and until three days ago, I had not met or heard of anyone from Wilmington.** I lost one of my personnel due to rotation and, believe it or not, his replacement was from good old Wilmington. His name is Richard Windon and he lives on Marsh Road. We both went to Mount Pleasant High School, even though it was four years apart."
Marine Sgt. George E. Hijar in Cua-Viet, May 18

"**I'm the only one from the 'First State' onboard the USS *New Jersey* so I pass my paper on to some guy from Maryland.** I miss someone from Delaware to talk to though. Every time – which is often – I talk about Wilmington or Delaware, I get the same pat question, 'Where's that?' Then I launch into my speech about the First State, du Ponts, and how progressive we are, etc.! It doesn't sink in, but they do know Delaware exists. I won't let them forget it!"
Navy Petty Officer 3rd Class Edward Blest aboard the USS New Jersey, Dec. 30

Army Pfc. Andrew D. Miller (left) met fellow Delawarean Army Pvt. William P. McLaughlin 12,000 miles from home on duty aboard the *Galicia Navigator.*

"**I'm stationed here at Tan Son Nhut, outside of Saigon.** We live at Pershing Field, a military police compound housing about 700 men. There are now four of us from Delaware with the 92nd MP Battalion. I am a courier with the headquarters detachment. Sgt. Elijah Weathersby is with the C/87 Infantry, pulling security guard duties. He's from Lewes. Pvt. William P. McLaughlin from Wilmington is with the 560th M.P. Battalion, pulling vessel security between Saigon and the Mekong Delta. Army Spc. Clifford O. Joseph, from Millsboro, is with the 188th M. P. Co. and works road patrols between Long Binh, Saigon and points in the Delta."
Army Spc. Kenneth Gerard at Tan Son Nhut, April 27

At first, this soldier hadn't met anyone from Delaware. Then he did. He wrote before and after letters to the Mailbag. His correspondence was only a few weeks apart.

"**I only hope you can help me.** My problem is that I've been stationed in Vietnam for seven months and haven't found one person from Delaware. I've been reading your column quite frequently and have never found any addresses close by. I am stationed at a small receiver site about two miles from Long Binh Post. There are only 24 of us here. So I would really like to meet someone from my home state."
Army Spc. Robert H. Johnson near Long Binh, Sept. 12 Mailbag

"**I just wanted to inform you that I have finally met a fellow GI Delawarean from around this area.** He is stationed approximately two miles from our location at IIFFV. His name is Winfield Scott Walls. He is from Millsboro and knows quite a few people from the First State. He drops over a few times a week and we reminisce. He's due to stay the night about Thursday. It's going to be a reunion for old Delaware. I wish to thank everyone in Delaware for all the support they are giving us here. It helps a lot. Oh, before I forget, would you please send Scott and me a First State flag so we can brag how better our state is than theirs, which it is anyway, but I want to be the first on my block to have one. We have an extra flag mast here and I will place it there. I'll probably get strung up with it, but that's war."
Army Spc. Robert H. Johnson near Long Binh, Sept. 25

Others also swapped news of friendly encounters.

"**There is another guy from my shop who is from Delaware.** He is from north Wilmington on River Road. He is Gary Olmstead. A mutual friend of ours, Gordon DeNight, also a Delawarean, was aboard last week with HE-7, a Search and Rescue (SAR) Helo Squadron.

My brother Johnny [Nock] is also over here. He is a marine with the 3rd Marine Division, H&S Co. I hear from him every now and then. His morale is surprisingly high. He has to spend almost six months longer than me in Vietnam.

Well, tomorrow is another busy day so I'd best close for now. I've accounted for four Delawareans!"
Navy Petty Officer Third Class Rick Nock aboard the USS Intrepid, Nov. 14 Mailbag

"Yesterday, I met Ronnie Annone from Claymont. He's at Red Beach. He came out here to Liberty Bridge. The bridge is about five miles from An Hoa. So far, there has been no enemy buildup in this area. The weather is still real nice. I get home the first week of February."
Marine Cpl. John P. Carrow near An Hoa, Nov. 21

However they said it, most agreed Delawareans were a rare breed in Vietnam.

"I am not a great writer but I will try to tell you a little something about myself. I did not go to school in Delaware. I came from Virginia in 1950 and prior to going into the Army in 1952, I worked at a few places [in Wilmington]: Keil Motor Company, Berger Brothers, and what used to be Service Block Inc. Since that time, I have been in the Army. I have three tours in Germany, one in Korea, and now Vietnam.

I have been here since September 1967, and I do hope to be leaving here next month. My unit here is Co. E, 2nd Battalion, 60th Infantry and is located at Tan Tri, which is south of Saigon. Right now, I am the platoon sergeant of a 4.2-inch mortar platoon. I have met a few First Staters in my battalion but we are few. I am glad to see each one of them and will be glad to get back [home]."
Army Staff Sgt. James L. Mayfield at Tan Tri, Sept. 21

Early on, one sailor offered a plan for meeting others.

"The main thing I would like to suggest would be add a few addresses with the column. Because our state is so small and it has a relatively small number of representatives over here, it is hard to find someone from home to talk to. And, believe me, one of the greatest morale boosters is to be able to sit and shoot the breeze with someone from close to your home."
Navy Petty Officer 3rd Class Stephen A. Nash at Dong Ha, April 30

Steve wrote again nine weeks later.

"One other reason I especially enjoyed that particular column was that also mentioned was a marine, Cpl. William Tilley (9th Mt. Bn.) [who] was stationed at Dong Ha, the same as I am. If time permits, this will lead to a meeting of two men from the same area, something that is always welcome. The reason I said if time permits is because in just 16 days, I will be headed back to the 'world.'"
Navy Petty Officer 3rd Class Stephen A. Nash at Dong Ha, July 5

Like most servicemen, Army Staff Sgt. James L. Mayfield was eager to come home. When he wrote, Mayfield had less than a month of duty left on his tour. Members of the 2nd Battalion, 34th Armor (opposite) ready a 4.1-foot mortar for firing.

Two soldiers sent a tag-team letter from Camp Wilson near Pleiku with a special plea to the distaff side.

"**This letter is from two of us, both from Wilmington, Delaware.** We are graduates of P.S. du Pont High School, Class of '67. We were in the same classes together all four years of high school. And have known one another even longer.

I, SP/4 Warren W. Evers Jr. (nickname 'Sonny'), am 21 years old and will be 22 on the 23rd of November 1968. I live at 523 Springer St. in Wilmington. At present I'm attached to HHD 124th Transportation Battalion as a chaplain's driver, and I enjoy my job immensely. I believe my mission over here is 'just,' and most essential. I hope this war will soon come to an end. I will be coming home on the 27th of June 1969.

I, SP/4 Robert G. Lynch (nickname 'Bubbles'), am 20 years old and will be 21 on the 6th of January 1969. I live at 2411 West St. Wilmington. I'm assigned to Goer Trans Co., 'the only one of its kind in the world.' As a clerk, I enjoy my job very much. And believe in fighting for my country. I also hope the war will soon be over. On the 8th of July 1969 I will be on my way home.

Sonny and I met in Qui Nhon on July 14, just six days after I arrived in country. It sure was a surprise to see someone from your hometown."
Army Spc. Warren W. "Sonny" Evers Jr. and Army Spc. Robert G. "Bubbles" Lynch near Pleiku, Nov. 8

Tales of Delawareans meeting others from their home state reached the Mailbag, like the letter we received from Army Spc. Warren W. "Sonny" Evers Jr. (left), who wrote of his chance reunion with his high school classmate, Army Spc. Robert G. "Bubbles" Lynch (opposite).

"Sonny and I met in Qui Nhon on July 14, just six days after I arrived in country. It sure was a surprise to see someone from your hometown."
Army Spc. Robert G. "Bubbles" Lynch

News of other meetings unquestionably boosted morale.

"**I'm stationed in Pleiku right now and I've met some fine people but no 'First Staters!'** Could you put something in your column that might help me find them? I would really appreciate it."
Army Spc. Evan L. Jones in Pleiku, June 20 Mailbag

"**Just thought I would let you know that I have met two more Delawareans and they are in the same company as I am in.** Their names are Chief Warrant Officer Paul Stoddard and Capt. Howard A. Murray. CWO2 Stoddard is from Christiana and Capt. Murray is originally from Selbyville but now makes his home in El Paso, Texas. There are a couple of more Delawareans who are stationed here at Camp Holloway, but I haven't gotten around to meeting them. I saw in one of your columns where a guy named Evan L. Jones hasn't met any First Staters. He is stationed just a couple of miles away from me. If I ever get the chance, I will try to find him."
Army Spc. Robert A. Elliott at Camp Holloway, July 12

"**As I mentioned earlier, I have been here almost a week and I have seen about four Maryland flags flying from both inside and on tops of the huts we sleep in around here.** [Getting a Delaware flag] may also help locate any Delaware marines that may be stationed here also."
Marine Lance Cpl. Andrew J. Manning at Camp Red Beach, Da Nang, Aug. 19 Mailbag

"**Finally, I settled into a personnel management job at Fort Sill, Oklahoma.** It was there that I met Anthony Undorf (of Lea Boulevard in Wilmington) and pulled a few strings to get him assigned as a personnel specialist with me. (We First Staters are a fraternal lot, aren't we?) Anyway, that involved changing his Army branch from artillery to adjutant general, but we did it.

And luckily, too. Less than six months later he was sent here and landed a job with the US Army Vietnam (USARV). He was to determine assignments for new Vietnam arrivals. And when I received orders for the 'Pearl of the Orient' this August, it was old pal Tony whom I wrote.

When I finally arrived at Bien Hoa Air Base [on] September 10, Tony was waiting with my new assignment: news reporter for the Information Office, Headquarters, Vietnam Regional Exchange (PX). He had pulled a few strings too."
Army Spc. Jim Cresson, Dec. 4 Mailbag

> ## "The owner of the third chute is perched on my shoulder. Actually it seems that his craft, a flaming doghouse, went down unnoticed."
>
> Navy Petty Officer 3rd Class Terry Reiswig

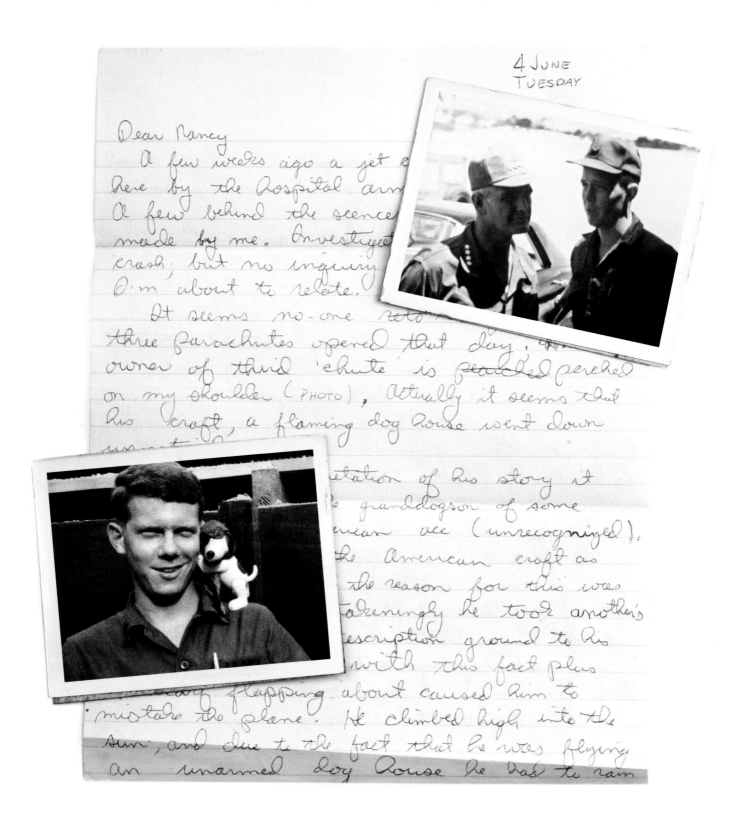

4 JUNE
TUESDAY

Dear Nancy

A few weeks ago a jet ~
here by the hospital arm~
A few behind the scenes ~
made by me. Investigat~
crash; but no inquiry ~
I'm about to relate.

It seems no-one ~
three parachutes opened that day. ~
owner of third 'chute' is perched
on my shoulder (PHOTO). Actually it seems that
his 'kraft,' a flaming dog house went down
~

~tation of his story it
~ granddogson of some
~ ace (unrecognized).
~ the American craft as
~ the reason for this was
~keningly he took another's
~escription ground to his
~ with this fact plus
~ flapping about caused him to
mistake the plane. He climbed high into the
sun, and due to the fact that he was flying
an unarmed dog house he had to ram

DESPITE THE DAILY PRESSURES OF A COMBAT ZONE, HUMOR SERVED AN IMPORTANT ROLE. Our servicemen in Vietnam mostly were an optimistic and fun-loving lot. Despite daily dangers, they enjoyed sharing their stories, real and fabricated, news of their jobs and projects, anecdotes about meeting one another – or not meeting one another – and, of course, their unflagging humor.

"**Charlie tries to get us one or two times a week with rockets, mortars, and recoilless rifles.** We are afraid he may get us, so we fire back like a nut at times."
Army Cpl. Joseph W. Dawson Jr., April 28

"**It is, as people say over and over, 'hell' over here.** But within a squad, the men get to be brothers over here regardless of race or religion and learn to live this life and take it in stride, smile, and keep on pushing."
Army Sgt. Jim Dawson near Khe Sanh, May 3

"**This base is not too well known and till the other day it was unhit.** But that's past history now. Like last night, I was shaving and here comes the mail in, crump, womp and away we go again. Well, what was I wearing – shower shoes, big beach towel, flak vest and hard hat. Talk about humor. Man, it's funny what we have on when we hit the bunkers."
Air Force Tech. Sgt. Frank Lloyd Wright in Phu Cat, May 11

Some expressed their creative talents as well. Even their carping made us smile. To all of them, though, mail, family, and coming home mattered most.

Soon after the Mailbag was underway, one sailor wrote of an unforgettable chance meeting.

"**Recently while stationed in Cam Ranh Bay, South Vietnam, I had a pleasant experience.** While serving in ground support of Market Line Air patrols, I was personally confronted by General William C. Westmoreland. Since I was not part of an escort, I felt proud that he took time before he left for his helicopter.

When he approached me all I saw were 16 stars from his hat and four on each collar. When he put his arm around me I was absolutely speechless. I thought he was going to ask me (a sailor) what I was doing in an Air Force uniform. Instead he asked me how I was doing, what I did and when I was going home.

Presently we of Patrol Squadron Six are preparing to return to our home base in Barbers Point, Hawaii. But I will surely remember distinctly my short tour of duty in Cam Ranh Bay. The general's stars will remain quite bright in my mind."
Navy Petty Officer 2nd Class Ralph J. Boyer, June 18

Random encounters, both real and imaginary, filled many letters to the Mailbag. Navy Petty Officer 2nd Class Ralph J. Boyer met Gen. William C. Westmoreland (top) while stationed in Cam Ranh Bay. Navy Petty Officer 3rd Class Terry Reiswig wrote a humorous account of reconnoitering with a fictional war hero.

Another sailor rewarded us with a battle "tale" and the sighting of another highly visible hero.

"**A few weeks ago a jet crashed on Route One here by the hospital armory where I work.** A few behind-the-scenes inquiries were made by me. Investigation will verify the crash; but no inquiry will reveal the story I'm about to relate.

It seems no one realized that three parachutes opened that day. The owner of the third chute is perched on my shoulder. Actually it seems that his craft, a flaming doghouse, went down unnoticed.

From my interpretation of his story it seems that he is the grand-dogson of some famous WWI American ace (unrecognized). It seems he took the American craft as one of the enemy's; the reason for this was that mistakenly he took another's goggles (his were prescription ground to his specifications) and with this fact, plus the scarf flapping about, caused him to mistake the plane. He climbed high into the sun, and due to the fact that he was flying an unarmed doghouse, he had to ram the other craft. This maneuver caused his craft to catch fire like any wooden doghouse would. Putting his craft into a steep dive toward a sandy area, he then 'hit the silk' and landed safely.

Due to the fact that this dog has been such a great morale factor to our troops, I don't think any disciplinary action should be taken against him. Truly he is an unsung hero of Vietnam; he rides with many pilots, co-pilots, navigators and crews on their missions. Snoopy power is a good power to have on your side!"
Navy Petty Officer 3rd Class Terry Reiswig, June 4

A rather humorous article involving Lt. John C. Hill of Dover and some fancy math appeared in the August 1968 edition of *Swift & Company* magazine. It read, "Lt. John C. Hill, a helicopter pilot, sent a photo to his father, J.H. Hill, manager of the Felton [Del.] plant, who in turn sent the photo to a local newspaper. They printed it with the following caption: 'Lt. John Hill of Dover poses by a mileage sign in Long Binh. He writes that Pittsburgh is spelled wrong on the signs, and that he can't vouch for the accuracy of the mileage.'"

A staff writer for the magazine saw the photo and wrote the following letter to John: "Having seen your picture with various mileage markers and showing a question mark for Dover, the Delaware State Development Department decided to check the mileage between Long Binh and Dover.

"After trying several sources, I finally called the computer center at the University of Delaware. They took the coordinates of Dover (39 degrees, 10 minutes north latitude and 75 degrees, 35 minutes west longitude and of Long Binh (10 degrees 10 minutes north latitude and 105 degrees 50 minutes east longitude) and by applying the Pythagorean triangle theory came up with a distance between the two cities of 10,543 miles.

"In case you are a horse racing fan, it may interest you to know that this is 84,344 furlongs. And flying the northern route from Dover Air Force Base via Elmendorf Air Force Base and Yokota Air Force Base, the air mileage is approximately 9,000 miles.

Good luck during the rest of your tour, and may you return safely to Dover."

29 November 68

Dear Nancy,
Yep, it's me again. Ole "Mop." Sorry I haven't written for awhile but I've been stuck with several new duties since I received my promotion. Oh, didn't I tell you? They promoted me to Sergeant. They didn't want to at first, but then I threatened to re-enlist for 10 years. My new duties are real cool. They include: supervising the bathing of all dogs and cats in the base camp; capturing flies and tying tags on their legs for study in the new Vietnam wildlife control program; and, of course, making up the battalion commander's bed in the morning. Oh well, that's the only way to make Major.
Oh yes, did I tell you that we've recently changed base camps? We're not in Quan Loi anymore, we're in Lai Khe. The _____ral didn't want to move, but with the dry season coming on all that red d___ _____thering my asthma. They've got a swimming pool here in the camp. It t___ _____ but then so is Delaware, so what the heck. I immediately orga_____ _____ball team". After awhile no other teams wo___ _____ly us. _____ an unfair advantage due to ___ _____t. So

As Always,
Tom
Mop McBride
TOM "MOP" McBRIDE

Headquarters
1st Battalion, 28th Infantry
Lions of Cantigny
(1)

AFTER 5 DAYS RETURN TO

SP4 Tom McBride
Co B, 1st Bn, 28th Infantry
1st Inf Div, APO SF 96345

ZIP CODE

PAR AVION
VIA AIR MAIL
MIT LUFTPOST
CORREO AEREO

Wilmington Morning News ATTN: Nancy
Wilmington, Delware
19899

Humor also helped morale in Vietnam. In his April 28 letter to the Mailbag, Sgt. Jimmie F. Wardell shared an article by *Pacific Stars and Stripes* correspondent Bob Cutts who reported the men at Binh Thuy Air Base, a small Mekong Delta airfield, regarded the Vietcong as their best alarm clock. For nearly three months, the enemy had shelled the air base every other night, always between midnight and 3 a.m., just like clockwork. Every building on base had a few shrapnel holes. Cutts wrote:

The VC, who approach the base at night, fire a few rounds and sneak off before they can be pinpointed, added insult to injury one evening at the Officers' Club. Without warning, a mortar shell hit the roof of the men's room, perforating everything inside except one extremely startled captain who happened to be using the facilities.

Muttering something about violations of his right to privacy, the lucky officer ran to a nearby bunker and waited out the raid.

Throughout his tour, one soldier regaled readers with his zany and mostly-fabricated adventures. He never sent us a picture of himself so we could only imagine our roly-poly reporter, nicknamed "Mop" by the Vietnamese, which he told us, meant plump. His letters always made us laugh. In his first letter, he introduced himself.

"**My name is SP4 Tom McBride.** I'm from Wilmington. I'm stationed here with Company B, 1st Battalion, 28th Infantry, 1st Infantry Division 30 miles north of Saigon, near the Iron Triangle, in War Zone C, in Quan Loi Base Camp. I'm currently a morning report clerk, but previously served in the field. I simply must tell you about Ho Bo Woods, it was H_____!!! We were on a Recon in Force operation in the Ho Bo Woods in the Iron Triangle, 5 kilometers from Lai Khe Base Camp. The lead elements had made contact with a large Vietcong force. Being a red-blooded Delawarean, I immediately moved forward where I could better assess the situation. It was then, with complete disregard for my personal safety, I scampered across the area to our battalion commander to advise him. Anyway, we gained a decisive victory that day. Funny, though, not many days later I was given a clerical job, and soon to follow was a letter from the division psychiatrist to my unit. Guess he also wanted to commend me on a job well done. I've got to go take my medicine now so I'll close. I hope to see mention of me in your column before I receive my Bugs Bunny mugs and Smiling Pitcher I ordered."
Army Spc. Thomas F. McBride in Quan Loi, July 11 Mailbag

More letters arrived from Mop throughout the year:

"**Just a few lines to let you know I'm fine and still hold memories of our fair state.**

Oh, yes, I have received my Smiling Pitchers but, unfortunately, lack the Bugs Bunny mugs. Oh well, I can rough it. I was really touched by all the copies of my last letter that appeared in your column that were sent to me by my numerous fans. I hope my letter served as an inspiration to all other citizens of our state serving in this war-torn country.

I'm really doing a great job in my company clerk position and have really acquired many friends, one of them being the division psychiatrist, a regular old pen pal. I really hate to complain, but I haven't been regularly receiving *The Morning News*. If at all possible, please help me in this respect.

Though I've not been in any recent battles, I must share with you my nickname bestowed upon me by the Vietnamese people that work for our unit. They call me 'Mop,' meaning plump, which is quite strange considering my exquisite physique. I'm actually quite robust at my height of 5 feet 6 inches and a healthy 230 pounds.

If it would not be asking too much of you, Nancy, please publish a personal request for me to our fellow citizens. To maintain my vitality, I am in dire need of such items as Carnation Slim, banana and strawberry Metrecal beverages, diet wafers and non-fat dry milk. Your aid would really be appreciated.

Well, Nancy, it'll soon be midnight snack time and soon after I'll need my medicine again. I won't be able to write for quite some time as I'm currently in the midst of organizing a health club but I promise to jot down a few more lines when the time permits."
Army Spc. Thomas F. McBride in Quan Loi, Aug. 16

"**Hi, I'm really sorry I've taken so long to write but our cooks have been outdoing themselves lately, you know how it is.** The health club has been a complete success. We've got some really outstanding physical specimens here (next to me, of course). I've added 20 more pounds of muscular strength. This will be a great aid to the career I plan as a Sumo wrestler when I depart from the Army. By the way, I don't think I ever mentioned my latest attribute (besides, of course, my obvious physical supremacy). I've become a really accomplished Montagnard flute player. Just recently I've won a great many prizes in local talent contests that I'll forever treasure. My tribal warrior loincloth I'll never part with as well as my hard-earned Vietnamese festival kettle capable of holding a half of a cooked pig (MMMMMMMM).

I'm glad to say that my old buddy the division psychiatrist has written again. He must be a great guy 'cause my commanding officer and all the NCOs in my battalion write him all the time. Though I'm very humble, I'm proud to say that I'm really in great demand within our division. I've actually heard senior officers argue as to which unit I should go.

Oh yes, this should be of great interest to our younger generation. I'm on the verge of becoming the leader of a 'Vietnamese Love Colony.' I've also successfully organized and proudly lead and play kazoo for an excellent musical group, 'Mop's Multiple-Vitamin Enriched Malnourished Slenderized Gourmet-Appealing Appetizing Pasteurized Dehydrated Vaccinated Pulverized Devoured Ragtime Skiffle Band Balladeers.'

Well, my practice session is right after I take my medicine so it's so long for now. We'll send you a few more lines real soon."
Army Spc. Thomas F. McBride in Quan Loi, Sept. 19

"**This is your old roly-poly buddy 'Mop' speaking again.** Say, I got a letter from my sweet old mother today. She said that you'd called and inquired about the possibilities of obtaining a picture of me in all my masculine splendor for possible use in a TV show. Boy, that'd be fantabulous. You could even throw in a plug for my health club and band. My band has been having some difficulty getting jobs lately. There isn't too much demand for a sextet composed of a bass washboard, kazoo, crushed-toenail maracas, 'Dick Tracy' police whistle, hambones, and beer can vibes. Even our relatively conservative costumes of blonde wigs, purple tights and thongs don't seem to attract much of a crowd. My mother also mentioned that you were doubtful about using me on your show because some doubt had arisen as to whether I had actually written all those letters. Well, put your mind at ease, Nancy old girl. I just told my mother I didn't do it to save her unnecessary embarrassment and personal anguish. I'd be honored to be part of your show. I'll even see if I can round up a picture of myself for the occasion. Well, 'til next time, this is 'Mop' signing off."
Army Spc. Thomas F. McBride in Quan Loi, Oct. 28

Tom's last letter of the year arrived a month later.

"**Yep, it's me again.** Ole 'Mop.' Sorry I haven't written for awhile but I've been stuck with several new duties since I received my promotion. Oh, didn't I tell you? They promoted me to sergeant. They didn't want to at first, but then I threatened to re-enlist for 10 years.

My new duties are real cool. They include: supervising the bathing of all dogs and cats in the base camp; capturing flies and tying tags on their legs for study in the new Vietnam wildlife control program; and, of course, making up the battalion commander's bed in the morning. Oh well, that's the only way to make major.

Oh yes, did I tell you that we've recently changed base camps? We're not in Quan Loi anymore, we're in Lai Khe. The general didn't want to move, but with the dry season coming on, all that red dust was bothering my asthma. They've got a swimming pool here in the camp. It's sort of stagnant. But then so is Delaware, so what the heck. I immediately organized a 'water volleyball team.' After awhile no other teams would play us. They complained that I had an unfair advantage due to my webbed feet. Sore losers.

With the presidential race so close this year, I decided that I may as well get in the running. I did some fast campaigning around the base camp, running on the Obesity Party ticket. I adopted the motto, 'Fatness is Fun.'

I took a solid stand on all the major issues:

a) Crime – There's too much of it and it should be made illegal.

b) Poverty – I propose to start a new Poverty Prevention Commission headed by Mr. Robin Hood. He and his merry band will swipe from the rich and give to the poor.

c) The War in Vietnam – If elected, I would declare a 20-year truce. By the time it's up everybody will have forgotten what they were fighting over.

I amassed a grand total of 3 write-in votes. The only people that voted for me were myself, my mother, and Captain Newman, our battalion adjutant. I bribed him with a personally autographed photo of the commanding general and a bite of a 3 Musketeers candy bar.

My band has really been hanging in there. We just cut a smash record called, 'If You Can Guess How Many Rolls I Have On My Belly, I'll Let You Punch Me In My Double-Chin.' We did it to the tune of Buffy St. Marie's big hit, 'Ground-Hog, What Makes You Smell So Bad?' I'll send you a courtesy copy for $10 postage and handling. Well, that's about it for now, Nan. There's dogs to be washed.'

'Til next time, this is SGT 'Mop' signing off."
Army Sgt. Thomas F. McBride in Lai Khe, Nov. 29

TUNNEL RAT

NON GRATUM ANUS RODENTUM

In Army Pfc. Fred "Fritz" Hensing's April 28 letter, he shared his musical endeavors with Mailbag readers. "You said you'd like to be informal in your new column. I think it's a great idea. Here is a start. I've written a song on Vietnam and I usually sing for my platoon every night." He continued, "I have another friend in Vietnam from Camden, Del. His name is Bruce King and he is a member of the 'Dirty Half Dozen,' a group formed during our A.I.T. training back in the states (the 'world'). I carry an M-79 grenade launcher and I've [earned] one Purple Heart. I'm 21 years old and dying to get back to Delaware. If you would like some photos, contact my father. He has plenty from me here in Vietnam."

28, April 68

Dear Nancy,

You said you would like to be informal on your new column. I think it's a great idea. Here is a start. I've written a song on Viet Nam & I usually sing for my platoon every night. I have another friend in Viet Nam from Camden, Del. His name is Bruce King & he is a member of the "Dirty Half Dozen", a group formed during our A.I.T. Training back in the states ("The World"). I carry an M-79 Grenade Launcher & I've won one Purple Heart. I'm 21 years old & dying to get back to Delaware. If you would like some photos contact my father at 108-4 Simca ln. He has plenty from me here in Viet Nam. Good luck!

Sincerely Yours

Fred.

P.S. My nick name is Fritz!

CREATIVITY RANKED HIGH IN THE WAR ZONE. Songwriters and poets came forward to entertain those of us at home. Army Pfc. Fred "Fritz" Hensing shared that he had written a song and a few weeks later, Fritz's father, John Hensing, sent the song to the column on his behalf.

VIETNAM
A war is raging across the sea,
Bringing man tragedy.
Ain't no sense feeling blue,
It's a job that we must do.
It's something people will never see
This crazy war and its tragedy.
Home is where I'd like to be,
But there's one hundred more just like me.
Vietnam is an ugly place,
Bringing man so much disgrace;
But this world and its human race
Will take its course in time and space.
But I guess we'll never learn
That Communism must always burn;
But soon you will learn to see
Vietnam's not the place to be.
Maybe in the years to come
If I have a little son,
He will learn to have his fun
Playing under the warm yellow sun.
Who can tell what's going to be?
Maybe we'll have time to see.
Hope he will always be free

Instead of ending in tragedy .

Another soldier sent his song from Vietnam. He explained:

"I'm sorry it's taken me so long to write but we've been on the move a lot.

I'm also inclined to agree that this [column] could be fun. As for our humor, gripes, achievements and our opinions, well (1) our humor is always high, (2) our gripes, I must say, are really few, (3) our achievements we hope are many, and (4) our opinion on this war is to never withdraw without victory on our side. These views are not only mine but most of the men of Bravo 1/9. All I can send you is a little song we made up at Khe Sanh (Jan. 21-April 25). It isn't much but it's the way we all feel."
Marine Cpl. Walt Meekins, June 5

The song, Walt told us, was sung to the tune of *On Broadway*, a popular 1960s hit by the Drifters.

AT KHE SANH
They say the air-strikes
Are out of sight at Khe Sanh
They say the goonies move
at night around there
There they are I know
They are 'cause I can hear
Them they're not too far
We'll have to stay here
And fight it out for Khe Sanh
We've paid the price
We've lost some men at Khe Sanh
They say we've been here
60 days or more – at Khe Sanh
For what we've got, we know
Not what
We plan to move 'cause the
Weather's hot
And we will find another
Spot around Khe Sanh
From Alpha outpost the
NVA plague Khe Sanh
From Bravo outpost they
Try to get to us
At our lines the men fought
Back – and cease the enemy attack,
But in the end we'll stop the
Rush for Khe Sanh
We hope and pray that some day
We will leave Khe Sanh
We'll shed a tear for those
We left behind
When we get home the joy will
Last, 'cause Khe Sanh now is
A thing of the past
And we'll remember the
Time we had at Khe Sanh

This poem, published in the second Mailbag on May 27, was written by Navy Petty Officer 3rd Class Earl T. Evon Jr. of Waterbury, Conn. He wrote: "I am a corpsman in the U.S. Navy attached to Gulf Company, 2nd Platoon 2/9 with [Delawarean] Pvt. Steve F. Eastridge. Steve asked me to write to you because he will be coming home soon and he doesn't feel he would be able to add much to your column. I have a poem that I composed which sums up most of the feeling of the men in 'Nam."

"The 'war' at home in Wilmington is far greater than this one over here. Many of us live in fear of being wounded, mortared and rocketed — do I have the same thing to live in fear of at home too?

"You can't imagine what it's like to be confined for a year and then to face the confinement at home too. I feel pity for all of you at home and in the same breath hope that the situation improves. Please make America the best place to live."

The poem was written by HM3 EARL T. EVON JR. (3d MAR DIV REIN FMF) from Waterbury, Conn. His buddy, Pvt. STEVE F. EASTRIDGE (G CO 2/9 2d PLT) from Delaware, was on his way home when he got our letter about the column.

Earl sent the poem which he calls "A Serviceman's Poem." He says it sums up the way the majority of men feel.

Take a man, then put him alone,
Put him 12,000 miles from home.
Empty his heart of all but blood,
Make him live in sweat and mud.

This is the life I have to live,
And why my Soul to God I give.
You have a ball without even trying,
While we're over here dying.

You burn your draft cards, march at dawn,
Plant your signs on the White House lawn.
You all want to ban the bomb.
"There is no real war in Vietnam."

Use your drugs and have your fun,
And then refuse to use a gun.
Is there nothing else for you to do?
Am I supposed to die for you?

There is one thing you don't know:
And that is where I think you should go.
I'm here and it's too late,
I've already traded my love for hate.

I'll remember this till the day I die
For I have heard my buddies cry,
I saw one's arm a bloody shred,
I heard them say, "This one is dead."

It's a large price to pay,
To see your buddy blown away.
He had the guts to fight and die,
He paid the price, but do you know why?

By his death, your life he buys.
But who gives a damn when one Marine dies?
His wife, his sweetheart, his parents or his son,
But they are about the only ones.

★ ★ ★

. . . Pfc. LARRY HUGHES (H&S CO 81 MM MORTAR PLT), the fella who raised Delaware's blue and gold flag atop Hill 55, about 12 miles south of Da Nang, writes that his commanding officer is Capt. Charles L. Robb, the President's son-in-law. Larry says he's seen Robb a few times but hasn't spoken with him. Let us know if you ever corner him, Larry. Larry's been in Vietnam since December. He's from Ashley Heights . . .

. . . Chaplain (Maj.) JAMES A. PETERMAN (OFFICE OF THE DIVISION CHAPLAIN 101st AIRBORNE DIVISION), from Milford, is based at Camp Eagle, just outside Hue. He was a parish priest at St. Patrick's Catholic Church in Wilmington six years. He says he enjoys The Morning News—it is delivered to his tent daily . . .

. . . Spec. 4 FRANK C. WOERNER JR. (870th TRANS CO TS) from Newark spent almost 15 months at Cam Ranh Bay. He's put in for six months' extra duty. Frank, you mentioned you felt Americans didn't know much about the Vietnamese. Why not write to us about them from your experiences? . . .

LETTERS WE RECEIVED WERE NOT ALL FULL OF "WAR TALK." What happened outside the battle zone was always of interest to our readers. Servicemen didn't disappoint in providing commentary and insight with their slice-of-life musings.

"**Oh, yes, heard the Dover [Delaware] radio station noon news the other day.** The AFN [Armed Forces Network] has a different one on every day."
Army Pfc. Curt Calloway at Dong Tom Base, April 27

"**In the past six years, almost two years have been spent in Nam.** Right now, I'm on a Seabee team stationed in Can Tho in the Delta region. Can Tho is the headquarters for the IV Corps region. Mostly we refer to it as the 'hub of the mud.' In the rainy season, you can't tell where the ocean begins or ends. It's all water!"
Navy Petty Officer 2nd Class Chuck Riley, April 27

"**Phu Loi isn't big, the town is about the size of New Castle [Delaware], with a population of about 3,000.** Phu Loi isn't usually shown on maps of Vietnam. If you find the provincial capital of Phu Cuong, that is close enough. Phu Loi is to Phu Cuong, in distance, as New Castle is to Wilmington."
Army Spc. Philip D. Johnson in Phu Loi, April 28

"**To tell a tale on myself, I guess it would be my many tries to bring a little home comfort to Vietnam.** At 1223 [Evergreen Road, Carrcroft Crest in Wilmington], we used to have a little home garden in which grew tomatoes, beans, lettuce, etc. Well, I have tried three times to grow some over here and failed all times. My first attempt the seeds were carried away by ants, the second attempt was eaten up by these lizards we have over here, and my last attempt failed due to a strong sand storm."
Army Cpl. John W. Ferguson at Chu Lai Airfield, May 30

"**How is everything back in good ole Wilmington?** Yesterday we flew from Phu Bai in C-146 cargo planes here to An Hoa. All of 5th Marines is moving here. It's a heck of a lot hotter down here on the flat lands than it was up north in the mountains."
Marine Lance Cpl. John P. Carrow in An Hoa, July 30

"**Next week, I'll be comin' back to good ole Wilmington [Delaware].** However, I voluntarily extended my tour over here for eight months, so I'll only be home for 30 days. It sure will be good to get home and see all of my friends and relatives.
Last month, I went on my R&R to Bangkok, Thailand. That place is something else! I really had a wild five days."
Army Spc. Richard Glazier in Phan Thiet, Sept. 1

Despite the unrelenting demands of a war zone, American troops savored the sense of normalcy provided by such mundane tasks as getting a haircut or writing a letter.

"**I've been receiving *The Morning News* for several months now and find it interesting to follow such things as the progress of Interstate 95, the battle of the the DNG [Delaware National Guard] between Gov. Terry and Mayor Babiarz, and the rise of the American Independent Party.** So far I've spent three months in such places as the Iron Triangle, Ho Bo Woods, and Boi Loi.
I've spent another three months at Tan Son Nhut Air Base, where my Delaware state flag was torn by shrapnel from a 122-mm rocket back on 3 June."
Army Lt. Bruce C. Ward in Cu Chi, Sept. 17

"**I am writing with a flashlight inside my bunker.** It's awful hot in here so I plan to get out soon! Am still in the field and have heard we may stay here for a couple more months. Will be home for the 1969 4th of July but I think I've had enough of all fireworks and guns! Isn't any way in H___ anyone will ever get me to go hunting!"
Army Cpl. Edsel Ford Norris Jr. to his mother, Dec. 18

COMPLAINTS WERE COMMONPLACE IN LETTERS. While inevitable gripes painted Vietnam unfavorably, Army Spc. Richard Glazier offered a mostly optimistic spin on his experience in Phan Thiet. He wrote in May, "The city has almost everything a guy could want; a beach, a main street, an airfield and even some VCs running around. The only gripes I have about Vietnam is that it's too hot and there's no racetracks."

Others, like Army Spc. Paul M. Grifantini, weren't so positive. "I really haven't anything good to say about this place," he wrote in his April letter. Paul continued, "There's a saying over here that 'when God finished making the world he took what was left over and put it all in one place – Vietnam.'"

Gripes from the war zone poured in throughout the year.

"**The traffic situation here in the Saigon-Cholon area has to be the worst I have ever seen.** The Kirkwood Highway would be nothing to drive down compared with some of the traffic jams you get stuck in over here. At least on the Kirkwood Highway you don't have bikes and motorcycles collecting around you like flies."
Army Spc. Bob Weatherby, May 5

"**About the only gripe I have about this place is all this sand.** Another thing that all of us have to gripe about is our mail. Some days we get mail and then again we go maybe two weeks without getting a thing. Sometimes we have to gripe about our chow. The steak is either raw or burned. And the potatoes are instant. Really though, we shouldn't gripe about our chow because just think of the fellows out in the field that have to eat C-rations from a can."
Army Spc. John W. Morgan in Chu Lai, April 26

"**One thing people should try to do more of here in Vietnam is clean it up.** These people are, in my opinion, dirty."
Army Spc. Skip Fleischut, April 26

"**My biggest complaint is being sent overseas with only nine months left in the Army.** This happens all the time to guys with even less time than I had. I am glad, though, because I can always say I have done my part."
Army Spc. Robert A. Elliott near Pleiku, May 1

"**About the biggest problem here with me and the food is that we seem to have an excess of chicken and roast beef.** Sometimes, I think that's all they know how to fix. Seven more months and I'll be back and I can forget about their chows."
Army Pfc. Edsel Ford Norris Jr. at Tay Ninh, Sept. 16

"**I would like to tell you about the Army.** But my father always told me if you don't have anything good to say, don't say it."
Army Spc. William R. Lilley, June 17 Mailbag

"**The only thing wrong with this unit is too much guard, KP and other details.** The war is something you can't stop by talk, you have to fight for what you have. I guess we are lucky to have what we have back in the states. The food is awful but the cooks do the best they can."
Army Pfc. Bob "Weasel" Arnold in Chu Lai, Oct. 24

A street scene near Chu Lai shows rampant poverty. A light anti-tank weapon carried by infantrymen in the field (opposite) replaced the World War II-era bazooka. Made of fiberglass and aluminum, it held a single 4-foot mortar and was used to destroy enemy tanks or bunkers.

Age-old sniping between those drafted and those serving a career in the military also reached the Mailbag. We presented both sides.

"**I think I'll start off with my gripes.** Ordinarily, I would have to write a book to tell you all of them. But to be kind, I'll just mention a few. I think about my worst gripe is the NCOs over here. They think you're still in the states. They stay on you about having your haircut and your fatigues pressed every day. You see, I'm in the Security Police and you just can't do it, being in that dust all day. But the NCOs stay on your back. I think I would rather be a cook or something other than a policeman."
Air Force Airman First Class Sandy Shaner in Saigon, April 26

"**We also have those lifers over here.** They are the ones that don't think it is bad enough just being here so they try to make it worse by using what little free time you have to do some silly detail or something. [As] soon as you finish all necessary work, there they are looking for something [for us] to do instead of relaxing for a while and writing letters. I sometimes [think they think] you're not even human."
Army Pfc. Edsel Ford Norris Jr., Nov. 22

"**Most of the lifers are afraid to leave the battalion area anyway (please don't print that last sentence).** It's getting so bad that the trenches for mortar and rocket attacks have reserved signs on them (that's just a joke)."

Marine Sgt. Earl A. Heston, Dec. 16 Mailbag

A career soldier offered a rebuttal.

"**I have no intention of attempting to use your column as a 'battleground'; however, I am a 'First Stater' and feel I must speak out on a word that keeps appearing in your column....**
The word is 'lifer.' To see it used as it has been lately, it points to us career men as something like a machine; no brains, no feelings, just robots taking orders and enforcing unnecessary and foolish orders.
I have been in the Army for over 11 years.... I am presently in the Data Service Center located at Long Binh. I have a section of 19 men at work and am also a barracks sergeant in charge of 68 men.
I have been taught to judge each man as an individual, not to classify as a group. Just as in civilian life, there are good and bad. This term 'lifer' refers to men, of whom I am a proud one, that have made serving their country a career.
I am proud of the uniform and of the country I serve. Granted, lack of common sense is predominant in many barracks and individuals, however, I don't believe any more so than in civilian life.
We are also men with families, feelings and compassion. One man had said, as a joke, about the bunkers being reserved. Well, I am in a safe area compared with many in Vietnam. However, I have, in the course of my duties here, been from Long Binh to Dong Ha, six miles from the DMZ, and many areas in between....
I speak for all of us over here when I say thanks to all at home who, regardless of their faith, creed or beliefs in this war, do try to back the men here and judge them as individuals, not the system or reasons they are here."
Army Sgt. 1st Class Eugene F. Nittinger in Long Binh, Dec. 22

Throughout the war, SOS Vietnam sent homemade cookies, canned goods, personal items and news to our soldiers serving in Vietnam. Notes like this one accompanied every package. Troops always appreciated the bennie boxes and mail from home, even my second "form" letter (opposite) encouraging troops to write to the Mailbag.

September 26, 1968

Dear Servicemen:

GOD BLESS AMERICA

No-It's Not "Passe" to LOVE OUR GOD
Nor to be PROUD of OUR GREAT COUNTRY!
Let's hold on to this heritage
For our future generations to see!

Sometimes it may be a little heavy
To carry the load we find
But with a WONDERFUL COUNTRY like OURS
I'm SURE that none of us mind!

For AMERICA is the LAND OF THE FREE
And it's the VERY BEST PLACE to live
Her faults are in the MINORITY
Compared to the PRIVILEGES she gives!

Yes! We still get sentimental when
The STARS and STRIPES we see
And we stop to think just a little bit
HOW GRATEFUL WE ALL SHOULD BE!

"FROM FOLKS THAT CARE IN DELAWARE"

(PEOPLE WHO DON'T TAKE HER FOR GRANTED)

SOS-VIETNAM
"INTERDENOMINATIONAL CENTER"
Red Lion Methodist Church
Red Lion, Bear, Del. 19710

MAIL FROM HOME WAS MANNA. Servicemen in Vietnam treasured letters and packages from loved ones and even strangers. In addition to receiving correspondence from family and friends, they looked forward to their free subscriptions to *The Morning News* and monthly 5-pound bennie boxes from SOS Vietnam, the Interdenominational Center at Red Lion United Methodist Church in Bear.

Founded to Serve Our Servicemen, the all-volunteer, non-profit organization packed boxes the last Thursday of every month and vowed to continue until the last Delawarean was home from the combat zone. From February through August 1968, SOS mailed 1,677 packages at a cost of nearly $2,500. Homemade cookies, canned goods, toiletries, toys and sundry other donations delighted those serving. The monthly SOS newsletter accompanied each box. The first page featured an original drawing and verse and always ended with "From Folks That Care in Delaware!"

Holiday packages, however, were distributed to Delaware servicemen through the "Shop Early" program. In addition, the Delaware Chapter of the American Red Cross delivered packages filled with books, games, and recreation articles, all contributed by business firms, organizations and citizens throughout the state.

Delawareans appreciated all bennie boxes from SOS, letters, newspapers and packages – and wanted everyone to know.

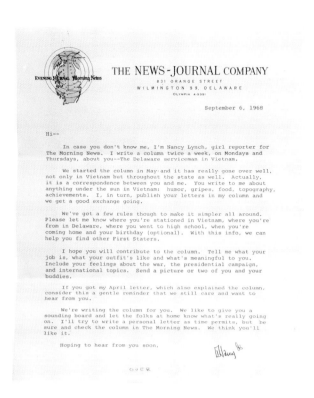

"My reasons for writing were to thank all the people back home who have helped so much to keep our spirits up over here. Their letters and packages have been truly enjoyed and are always welcome. I realize there aren't many people from Delaware over here, however, the support we receive from home could fill the state of Texas."
Army Cpl. John W. Ferguson at Chu Lai Airfield, May 30

"You have no idea how it is to receive news (local) from back home. Again, I thank you very much."
Army Spc. Robert W. Curro in Da Nang, June 10

"You can't imagine how much current, local news from home on a daily basis means to us who spend a year of our life to protect our country's freedom. The support we receive is fantastic and a credit to everyone back in the states. It makes all the political unrest and racial trouble insignificant by comparison."
Army Pfc. Charles M. Danner in Plei Markang, July 19

"I have only 95 days left so I figured it's about time I wrote and told you how much I have enjoyed your column. It usually never fails that whenever I read over your column, I'll run across a name of someone I knew or went to school with…. It is very seldom you run across a fellow Delawarean here, but I guess I was lucky in having a First Stater, Spc. 4 [Robert] Scott from Seaford, here in my own company. When I first found out Scotty was from Delaware, we had plenty to talk about even though he is from Seaford and I from Bear….

We have a group of people from Delaware who are doing a great job and service for Delawareans in Vietnam. These people use their own free time to help ship packages to us over here. Believe me when I say that it's not only the packages that are appreciated, but also the thought that our people back home care. This is the Interdenominational (whew) Center, located at Red Lion Church.

I believe that they can be proud in knowing that of all the people I talk to from different states, that Delaware is the only one that has such a program."
Army Spc. Pete Romano, July 29

"The division asked for pictures of people reading hometown papers and it turns out that I am the only one on the entire landing zone who gets a hometown paper. So you may have the very great pleasure of seeing me in print."
Army Spc. Gerald R. "Jerry" Smith at Landing Zone Betty near Hue, Aug. 26 Mailbag

"[Receiving *The Morning News*] is like a big, long letter from the city of Wilmington and I appreciate your sending it to me as a gift. I read it so thoroughly that I probably know more about what happened in Wilmington … than I do about what's happening in Saigon."
Army Pfc. Robert A. Hoey in Dong Ha, Sept. 21

"I'd like to use your column to express a personal thanks to SOS Vietnam…. They sent me a package – with everything in it! Packages create a special interest for just about everyone here and we all share whatever is inside."
Army Spc. Donald L. Shepherd in Pleiku, Sept. 30 Mailbag

"Yes, it's beginning to look a lot like Christmas. This becomes more and more apparent as my stacks of fruit cake tins, cookie tins, and other wrapped packages of canned goods, that have been sent from the greater Wilmington area, continue to grow daily, Thus, the reason for the present writing. I wish to thank the participants in SOS Vietnam, my friends, and neighbors for their recent benevolence."
Army Pfc. Michael E. Brelick, Dec. 9

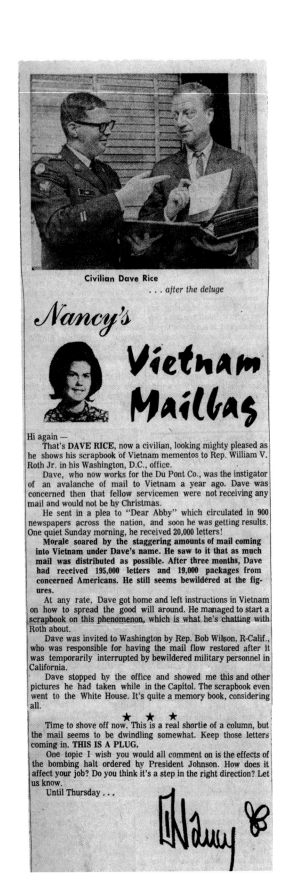

Civilian Dave Rice
. . . after the deluge

Nancy's
Vietnam
Mailbag

Hi again —

That's **DAVE RICE**, now a civilian, looking mighty pleased as he shows his scrapbook of Vietnam mementos to Rep. William V. Roth Jr. in his Washington, D.C., office.

Dave, who now works for the Du Pont Co., was the instigator of an avalanche of mail to Vietnam a year ago. Dave was concerned then that fellow servicemen were not receiving any mail and would not be by Christmas.

He sent in a plea to "Dear Abby" which circulated in 900 newspapers across the nation, and soon he was getting results. One quiet Sunday morning, he received 20,000 letters!

Morale soared by the staggering amounts of mail coming into Vietnam under Dave's name. He saw to it that as much mail was distributed as possible. After three months, Dave had received 195,000 letters and 19,000 packages from concerned Americans. He still seems bewildered at the figures.

At any rate, Dave got home and left instructions in Vietnam on how to spread the good will around. He managed to start a scrapbook on this phenomenon, which is what he's chatting with Roth about.

Dave was invited to Washington by Rep. Bob Wilson, R-Calif., who was responsible for having the mail flow restored after it was temporarily interrupted by bewildered military personnel in California.

Dave stopped by the office and showed me this and other pictures he had taken while in the Capitol. The scrapbook even went to the White House. It's quite a memory book, considering all.

★ ★ ★

Time to shove off now. This is a real shortie of a column, but the mail seems to be dwindling somewhat. Keep those letters coming in. THIS IS A PLUG.

One topic I wish you would all comment on is the effects of the bombing halt ordered by President Johnson. How does it affect your job? Do you think it's a step in the right direction? Let us know.

Until Thursday . . .

Nancy

Army Spc. William D. "Dave" Rice received coverage in the Mailbag when he generated tons of mail for lonely servicemen in Vietnam with a single letter to syndicated columnist "Dear Abby."

Mail was so important to soldiers that one serviceman decided to take the initiative on behalf of those who received little or no mail. But mild-mannered Army Spc. William D. "Dave" Rice's good intentions led to unintended consequences.

Dave gained international attention during his first tour in Vietnam by jolting lonely servicemen out of their doldrums with mail from home.

Tons of it.

Concerned because so many of his fellow soldiers were not receiving mail regularly, if at all, and had little to look forward to during the holidays in late 1967, Dave expressed his dismay in an August 1967 letter to Dear Abby, whose advice column was syndicated in 900 newspapers across the country.

"Dear Abby," he wrote, "For Christmas, I'd like to see some smiles on the faces of lots of my buddies over here. They don't get any mail. If any of your readers (from 15 to 80) have a 5-cent stamp and time on their hands, please have them write to 'Any Lonely Soldier' in care of me, and I'll see that he gets it."

Dave told me later he also was practicing his typing when he composed his letter to Abby. "I was a clerk with the 29th General Support Group's OMSI [Operation Maintenance Supply Inspection] and was going out in the field on a new job that required preparing reports and had to qualify for typing. I was using a manual typewriter in my tent, typing from the *Pacific Stars and Stripes* when I came to 'Dear Abby.' So I decided to write her."

Abby published his letter. Dave waited patiently for a response from the home front. Nothing happened for several weeks. Then, without warning on a quiet Sunday in Vietnam, he received 20,000 letters from the states, all addressed to him in Bien Hoa for distribution to lonely servicemen.

On that day, Dave's headaches began. He was overwhelmed – and so were postal authorities at Army post offices in San Francisco and Seattle. The mail backed up stateside. Dave sought and received assistance from U.S. Rep. Bob Wilson, a California Republican from San Diego, to sort out the postal overload.

"He made one phone call to the Pentagon, which released all of it after an investigation by the FBI and other agencies to rule out a scam," Dave recalled. "We turned a bunk house for 18 people into our mail room. We got mail twice a day, seven days a week. I went through every mailbag separating out letters addressed 'To Any Lonely Soldier.' I was worn down to practically nothing."

By December 1, Dave had accumulated 125 mailbags to take north to Da Nang, the DMZ and surrounding areas. In just three months, he received a total of nearly 200,000 letters and 19,000 packages. Dave's lone letter precipitated an avalanche of mail for servicemen who longed for it and paved the way for mail to lonely soldiers serving in future conflicts like Desert Storm, and in Afghanistan and Iraq today. Dave left Vietnam in May 1968, but left instructions for distributing the deluge of goodwill throughout the combat zone.

On Dave's return to the states, Wilson invited him to Washington to talk about his famously good deed. There, he shared a scrapbook of his postal phenomenon, which also made rounds at the White House. Dave also showed the memory book to U.S. Rep. William V. Roth, also a Republican and Delaware's only representative in Congress, and stopped by the News-Journal office to share it with me.

The irony of this story is that Dave volunteered for a second tour in Vietnam in 1972. His assignment: mail clerk.

THOUGHTS OF COMING HOME AND REUNITING WITH FAMILY CONSUMED MANY SERVING IN VIETNAM. Often, letters mentioned a countdown in days, and some in hours and minutes. One put a face to his DEROS (Date of Estimated Return Overseas).

"Well, the magic number today is 120. This is till I become a full-fledged citizen....Well, everything comes to an end. I wish it was the war but it's my letter."
Army Spc. Robert H. Johnson, Sept. 24

"As of this writing I have exactly 30 days, 11 hours and 23 minutes left to go over here. The only bad thing about coming home now will be that it will be so cold. I remember when I came home on thirty-day leave back in March of this year it took me about two weeks to get used to the change in climate."
Army Spc. Robert W. Ketchum Jr., Nov. 14

"In the year I've spent over here, I've logged over a thousand hours of flying time in an Assault Helicopter Company, the 189th Ghostriders. I'm looking forward to coming home soon and getting back to the world."
Army Chief Warrant Officer Paul P. Stoddard, Sept. 23

"We (MCB 10-Seabees) are so short in country (Vietnam) that we sleep under M-16 bore patches. It will be good to get back to the good old U.S.A. and Delaware."
Navy Seabee George F. Stalnaker in Quang Tri, April 30

"We're doing a job that must be done. It's an experience I can talk about the rest of my life. After seeing the way many of the Vietnamese people must live and try to exist, I'm proud that I can help improve their future in my small way. It also makes me so thankful for all I have back in the good old U.S.A. There is no country better in the world.

I'm about halfway through my tour and I don't regret being here, but I sure am looking forward to coming home."
Army Spc. William Mahan near Da Nang, July 24

"I miss being at home but with the hometown newspaper I'm not too homesick. I read the newspaper every day when I was home so I'm asking if you could send [it to] me every day. Although it won't be up to date, I would like to read one every day. I used to be a paperboy."
Marine Pfc. Stanford Avant in Dong Ha, July 15

Leaving Vietnam couldn't happen fast enough for most servicemen (opposite). Army Spc. Robert H. Johnson's countdown appeared in the Oct. 3 column. His exuberance about the number of days until his DEROS was obvious.

"As you noticed in my other letter, I haven't used my name or any inkling of identification of who I am. Reason being my mother worries a lot and as far as she knows I'm in the securest area in Vietnam. I believe you'll understand my situation."
Army Sgt. Gerald W. "Jerry" Thompson in I Corps area, May 7

A marine wrote about a family situation that ended well, based on his two letters, sent a few weeks apart.

"I receive *The Morning News* here and I saw my brother's name in it in your column.
I arrived here in April and I went to Saigon to visit my brother (a place called Plantation about 15 miles outside of Saigon). I'm happy to say that I talked him into leaving this place (only one brother is supposed to be in country at one time). I thought this might be interesting to you since not too many brothers are here."
Marine Cpl. Charles R. Straughn near Da Nang, July 6

"My brother who was in Saigon has about 12 days left. I envy him but it's good to know that finally one of us is going home. Don and I are the only ones in the family and it's real hard on Mom but this will make it somewhat easier on her."
Marine Cpl. Charles R. Straughn near Da Nang, Aug. 28

Soon after the Mailbag received Chuck's letters, Mrs. Straughn explained to me her sons had enlisted at different times, Chuck with the Marines and Don with the Army. When they found they were both going to Vietnam, they tried to get each other shipped out. After about a month of red tape, Don won. With nine and a half months' service in Vietnam, he left Saigon for South Korea, followed by a 30-day home leave in September 1968. He was reassigned to Fort Bliss, Texas. Chuck got home safely in April 1969.

Homecoming was an exhilarating experience for this sailor.

"Received your letter a couple of days ago and was very pleased to hear from you. As I'm sure you know by now, we [the USS *Enterprise*] are now back in the states. Your letter was held up for about three weeks while we were en route home.
It was really great going under the Golden Gate Bridge of San Francisco and our return to the states with a warm reception from those of the San Francisco Bay area. After visiting other countries, it sure makes me realize what a great country it is that we live in. For those who find it easy to knock our country all the time, they should take a good look at the many things we have that other countries don't."
Navy Petty Officer 3rd Class William E. Ayers aboard the USS Enterprise, July 27

In the combat zone, contact with loved ones was as essential as breathing. And many in uniform wanted those at home to know exactly how they felt.

"Nancy, got a small favor to ask you, if I'm lucky enough to have my letter answered again in your column. I was wondering if you could tell a certain young lady I miss her very much and I'm sending my love!
Her name is Brenda! She lives in Michigan but she'll see the column. Went up to Michigan twice to see her while I was home, and I'm counting the days till I see her again. How would you like to be invited to a wedding?"
Navy Petty Officer 3rd Class Jim Belay in Da Nang, Sept. 26

"I guess that I will start out by telling you something about myself and my family for they are the most important to me as you can guess.... I am married to Linda Jo Walls and we have a son by the name of Winfield Scott Walls Jr.... He is 8 1/2 weeks old. He was born on the 21st of June and at the present he is unemployed.
Linda just had our first anniversary on the 12th of August. It is just too bad that we had to spend it 12,000 miles apart. I am not griping for I know that I only have eight months left until we are together again, along with our son whom I have not seen yet except through the many pictures that his mother has sent to me. We have a lot to look forward to when we are together again."
Army Pfc. Winfield Scott Walls near Saigon, Aug. 29

"I'm married and have one child and one is due this month. I have four more months to do in Vietnam, so if you could I'd also like for you to put this little poem in the Mailbag. I call it 'Keep Faith in Me.'
If now the letters you receive are few, and so very far apart,
Please do not worry, darling, and please do not blame my heart.
I love you just as much or more than ever before.
I long to gaze into your eyes and listen to your voice,
To be with you each day and every night.
But mine is not the choice.
I have my duty to perform until that certain day.
When we embrace again and all our fears will fade away.
So, darling, keep your courage up, the same as I must do
And trust me with your heart and soul, as I have faith in you."
Marine Lance Cpl. Keith W. Allen near Da Nang, Aug. 21

In a country of contrasts, South Vietnam's lush mountain ranges near Da Nang segue to fertile rice paddies only a few miles from its sandy coastline on the South China Sea.

SEASON'S GREETINGS

Dear Nancy

I enjoy reading your column, as well as a number of non-Delawareans do, here very much. It's a wonderful thing The Morning News is doing for the Delaware Serviceman. Few other states will send the home town paper. I'm located at an Air force installation near the coastal city of Qui Nhon. April is my "magic month" @ back to The "world". Thanks for your column, keep up The good work.

Frank Green

AS 1968 WOUND DOWN, THE FRACTIOUS YEAR'S PASSING WOULD BE CELEBRATED BY FEW. U.S. troops in Vietnam stood at nearly their peak strength of more than 550,000 while total American deaths in the war topped 30,000 by the end of December. Delaware still had several hundred men serving in Vietnam and counted 108 casualties since the state's first loss, Army Capt. James Harold Johnson Jr. of Milford on October 3, 1963.

Delawareans at home and in uniform continued their outpouring of mail. One serviceman shared a humorous plea to Santa in his letter. The piece was written by fellow serviceman H. Behrent whom he'd never met but added he and his colleagues shared the author's sentiment.

"**Dear Santa: I have decided to ask for only one present this year.** Since there is no snow here in Vietnam, you can't land your sleigh so just wrap the present and I'm sure the postal department will take care of your delivery. Santa, can you imagine the joy on my face when I open your gift and find the one thing that I want for Christmas – an Anti-Vietnam War Demonstrator?

First thing, I'll give him a haircut – if I have to do it with a bayonet. But I can't promise to keep him clean the way I'd like to because baths are pretty scarce over here. I'll share my cold food with him, and even give him my miserable bunk. I'll share the impossible steaming heat with him.

I'll share the heartbreak of seeing my buddies fall beside me. I'll share the misery of trying to identify the bodies that the [Vietcong] have left behind. I'll share my hours with him sitting beside me, waist deep in mud and water-filled foxholes.

Army Staff Sgt. Frank Green expressed his thanks for the newspaper in his Christmas card to the Mailbag. Army Pfc. Wayne Baldwin (opposite), a machine gunner with the 9th Infantry Division, finds a moment to read greetings from home at Bear Cat, about 16 miles northeast of Saigon.

But, Santa, I'll be warm with joy of giving a deserving welcome to this Christmas present you were thoughtful enough to send me. I will be so careful of him and will watch out for the things he deserves. The next time one of our patrols is attacked by the Cong, I will be the first one to let him run to the front to tell them that he loves them and wants to give them a flower.

Santa, I don't want to ask for a present just for me, so do you think that maybe you could send my buddies a demonstrator of their very own?

…Just thought you might like to know first-hand how the boys over here feel about our brave young men at home.

In essence, what we are trying to say is, Will the realists please stand up? The idealists are 'out of order.' Indeed, they are."
Army Pfc. Michael E. Brelick, Nov. 7

During the holidays in Vietnam, goodwill was evident, behind the lines and even on the battlefield.

"**Christmas day is over now or just about.** It was a real nice day except that we were not in the states. We had steaks that we cooked on a grill, cold beer and we played Christmas carols on a tape recorder. Yesterday I went to the Bob Hope show, I was pretty far away from stage but I used a pair of binoculars."
Marine Lance Cpl. Carl H. McNeely, Dec. 25

The family of Army Pfc. Jim Stewart shared his December letter about being so far from the hearth during the holidays.

"Dear Mom and Dad,
Now I know what it's like to be away from home at a very special holiday. I can say that it is very lonely, even though we still have Christmas trees, and music, and most of the boys even have gifts!

But on Christmas Eve, I wonder what the boss will be thinking about that special night, while they're pulling guard or something that's entirely different from what they remember as their Christmases at home?

I know what they think about and you can bet that if you give them a small chance they would be home for the holidays! For on the eve of the birth of Christ, these boys should be home with their loved ones, but they are not. Instead they are here to ensure that there may be many more Christmases for the people, their families, to have.

And some may never see their families again or another Christmas at home. They pay a great price to see that America goes on being! I don't know about most boys, or the people of America, but on Christmas Eve, I will be thinking not only of my family, but also of the thousands of boys who never will see a 'White Christmas' at home."

As the countdown to 1969 began, Americans at home and in Vietnam wondered what the new year would bring.

1968 – YEAR IN REVIEW

JANUARY 30
Communist NLF (Vietcong) and NVA launch pre-dawn Tet Offensive attacks in major South Vietnamese cities and at the U.S. Embassy in Saigon. U.S. troops repel the enemy but hope dims for a military victory.

FEBRUARY 23
Heaviest shelling by North Vietnamese during the siege of the remote Marine base at Khe Sanh.

MARCH 16
My Lai massacre of hundreds of unarmed men, women and children by troops from the Army's Americal Division. The atrocity was hushed until November 1969.

MARCH 31
President Lyndon Baines Johnson announces partial halt of U.S. bombing of North Vietnam as a peace gesture. He sends additional 13,500 troops to Vietnam, far short of Gen. William C. Westmoreland's request.

MAY 13
Peace talks open in Paris between the U.S. and North Vietnam and falter within two weeks.

JUNE 27
Marines start dismantling the firebase at Khe Sanh and later abandon it.

JUNE 29
U.S. death toll for first half of 1968 nearly surpasses total KIAs for all of 1967.

SEPTEMBER 29
Navy's battleship USS *New Jersey* anchors off the coast of Da Nang. Its 16-inch guns boost naval presence and provide massive firepower near the DMZ.

OCTOBER 31
Johnson announces the complete halt of bombing of North Vietnam.

NOVEMBER 1
Paris peace talks are expanded to include South Vietnam and the NLF.

NOVEMBER 26
President Nguyen Van Thieu's South Vietnamese government finally joins peace talks but disagreement over the conference table's shape delays a four-way dialog until 1969.

DECEMBER 14
U.S. fatalities in Vietnam since early 1960s total more than 30,000. Number of U.S. troops in Vietnam nears peak of about 550,000.

Marine Pfc. Lawrence R. Spry wrote his family he had seen plenty of action during Tet. The 19-year-old was in country until March 1970. Army Cpl. Bohdan R. "Bo" Tanchuk (opposite) was a frequent contributor to the Mailbag from Saigon.

1969

WITH THE EBB OF THE SELF-ABSORBED SIXTIES, A NEW TIDE OF POLITICS WASHED OVER THE COUNTRY IN THE LAST YEAR OF THE DECADE. RICHARD M. NIXON, THE CALIFORNIA REPUBLICAN WHO WAS VICE PRESIDENT WHEN PRESIDENT DWIGHT D. EISENHOWER SENT U.S. MILITARY ADVISERS TO VIETNAM, WAS INAUGURATED ON JANUARY 20, 1969 AS THE NATION'S 37TH PRESIDENT.

His triumph over Democrat Hubert H. Humphrey, the vice president under Lyndon Baines Johnson, repudiated the former president's massive troop buildup in Vietnam. The war-weary Johnson, who had declined to run for re-election, retired to his Texas ranch.

Nixon's inauguration would prove perhaps the most predictable of the headlines that would be bannered across the nation's newspapers in 1969. In July, U.S. Sen. Edward M. Kennedy, younger brother of slain President John F. Kennedy and presidential candidate Robert F. Kennedy, drove his car off a bridge on Chappaquiddick Island off Massachusetts, causing the death of one of Robert Kennedy's former secretaries.

Just two days later, astronaut Neil Armstrong took a giant leap for mankind, becoming the first human to walk on the moon. In August, Woodstock rocked the Catskills, as more than 400,000 people converged on a farm near the small upstate New York town for a four-day music festival. Earth Day debuted in April, the New York Mets improbably won the World Series, and the first reports of the My Lai massacre in Vietnam surfaced.

In Delaware, Gov. Charles L. Terry Jr. left office after his defeat in November by Republican Russell W. Peterson, a DuPont Co. chemist who capitalized on public opposition to Terry's insistence on maintaining a long-term National Guard presence in Wilmington.

Following civil unrest in the city after the April 1968 assassination of the Rev. Dr. Martin Luther King Jr., Terry had ordered the Guard into the city and refused to withdraw the troops, convinced rioting would resume if he did. The Guard left Wilmington when Terry left Woodburn, the governor's mansion. On January 21, 1969, immediately after taking his oath of office, ironically in the National Guard Armory in Dover, Peterson halted the Guard's jeep patrols and ended a national embarrassment.

The war droned on for everyone. Within months of being sworn in, Nixon announced the first troop withdrawals in Vietnam: 25,000 by August 1969, and another 65,000 by year's end, scarcely a dent in the muster of more than 550,000 troops. "Vietnamization" became the new administration's buzzword for the increased shouldering of responsibility by the South Vietnamese for the war in their country.

Regardless, Americans were becoming increasingly restless. On October 15, Vietnam Moratorium Day, millions collectively rallied against the conflict in their hometowns, a stunning display of curbside democracy that demonstrated back-burner sentiment against the war had reached the boiling point. A month later, more than 500,000 marched in Washington, D.C., to protest a war that now was claiming an average of 40 American lives a day, a war that robbed them of their husbands, sons, brothers and boyfriends.

Now in its eighth year, the war wrought a significant attitudinal shift among some servicemen. Doubt, pessimism and frustration eroded the once gung-ho certainty about America's ability to achieve victory in Vietnam.

Stationed near Saigon, my good friend and former University of Delaware classmate, Army Cpl. Bohdan R. "Bo" Tanchuk expressed his futility in the June 30 Vietnam Mailbag. "Over here," Bo wrote, "one lives from day to day, never quite sure of tomorrow and, for that matter, today."

He added a troubling observation, "As you drive through Tan Son Nhut Air Base, one sees a country club with golf course, tennis courts, bar, etc. Many Americans patronize this club, mostly officers and businessmen, maybe even civilian government workers. To them, the war seems far away by the expressions on their smiling faces.

"But fifteen miles away, young Americans are making their greatest sacrifice for the people of Vietnam by dying and suffering so that they may someday have what we have had for so long – freedom. When one thinks of the club people and the miserable infantrymen in the sweltering heat of the jungle, somehow one realizes something is amiss and one asks the ultimate question: is there any justice and purpose for this war?

"So the search ... continues in the event that we may someday find the answer."

"We were sucked into this tragic carnage because of military pride and a grotesque high-level ignorance of the situation. For this we have 37,000 dead Americans."

Army Spc. John Tolbert

Grenades, small metal bombs detonated by a fuse and thrown by hand or fired from a gun, were deadly instruments of combat. The World War II-era pineapple grenade (center), initially used by American troops in Vietnam, was replaced by the round or baseball grenade. The Vietcong and NVA used a Chinese communist grenade, shown with a wooden plug instead of a fuse at its base. More Americans died in the conflict from grenades and satchel charges than bullets. Another deadly weapon was the fragmentation rocket, whose nose cone (left) is shown.

Several others volunteered their perspectives to the Mailbag. One offered his take from the vantage of nearly four years in Vietnam. He was with the 82nd Airborne Division at Firebase Hardcore when he wrote.

"**After fighting with two combat units (attached to 1st Cavalry and 82nd Airborne Division, 3rd base) and having been with an evacuation hospital (67th Evac) for a total of four years (Aug. '65-Aug. '69) and having operated in I, II, III and IV Corps of South Vietnam, I can personally state that I have not seen any real improvement (for our side) for the past four years.**

While I feel we (U.S. government) made a terrible mistake in committing our ground troops in Vietnam, I know we cannot just walk out at this moment.

Also, I'd like to state the following: while many Americans do not support this war and for good reason (In fact, I am getting out of the Army ASAP, I've only been in the Army for 4 years, 3 months), let's not forget we are Americans over here. If you do not want to support your government, support your fellow Americans. Well, enough of a sad situation.

Give my best regards to everyone in Delaware and let the family of 1st Lt. Roger A. Akin know he just left today heading for Wilmington."
Army Staff Sgt. Richard Williams Jr., June 13

Some servicemen reversed their opinions about the war, as was the case when an old friend of mine wrote the Mailbag. At first against the war, he wrote his feelings started to change after landing in Vietnam.

"**I never thought I would be doing something like this – fighting for my country – but here I am.** I had no idea what Vietnam was really like but I thought it was wrong, regardless, for the United States to be involved in any type of aggression. I'm a new guy over here but I can feel the patriotism in these other guys over here and, believe me, it tends to reel off. Recently, my picture was in your paper, connected with the Valley Garden Park ordeal. At the time, I was proud to stand up and speak out against the war. Now, I am not so sure of myself."
Army Spc. George L. Allen, May 18

Once enthusiastic about the war, an interrogator with the 199th Light Infantry Brigade wrote to us detailing his about-face in July.

"**I joined the Army 2 years ago, immediately after high school, a gung-ho, nearly chauvinistic youth with but one thing in mind: the fight against the specter of international communism.** My opinions began to change while I studied Vietnamese for 47 weeks in Ft. Bliss, Texas. Since arriving in Vietnam, my opposition to the war has been unshakeable, and my compassion for the Vietnamese peasant complete.

I love my freedom and hence my country. But I cannot believe that U.S. forces were sent to Vietnam to stop communist aggression. If there was aggression, the origin is debatable. We were sucked into this tragic carnage because of military pride and a grotesque high-level ignorance of the situation. For this we have 37,000 dead Americans.

Following any battle, large or small, an after-action report was complied and a sweep of the area made. American forces tally a body count of Vietcong after a skirmish.

But the blame must be shared by the calloused men in Hanoi and Saigon who willingly send hundreds of thousands of young men and women to their deaths.... But this is their country, and I for one do not pretend to understand the Asian mind.

I am an American and am entitled to my opinion on our actions. I've seen a woman from Cholon (sister city of Saigon) visiting a village for the day get killed in a U.S. helicopter attack. A swarm of flies where her skull should have been.

In this same attack, 4 little girls were shot up. The American pilots said they drew fire from the hut, yet no weapons were found. I heard an American boast that he ran over three Vietnamese with his APC ('gooks,' as he called them).

Every day we alienate enough Vietnamese simply by our behavior to make a VC battalion. This is probably why the VC are always able to replace their losses. We GIs have a popular saying over here: 'Let me win your heart and mind or I'll burn your hooch down.'

And then there's the old reliable, 'The only good gook is a dead gook.' Perhaps this kind of an attitude was acceptable in World War II, but when you're trying to win the people's loyalty, it'll never work.

To all the idiots who believe in the communist cause, and American righteousness: Come to Vietnam and see your beliefs shattered. In 268 days, I will be discharged from the Army. Perhaps then I'll resign from the human race too!"
Army Spc. John Tolbert, July 8

In June, after just four months in Vietnam, a marine wrote about how the war had discouraged him.

"I'm in 60 Mortar Team over here with the grunts. They call us 'Death from Above.' Most of our operations now are in the Arizona Territory, which isn't a pleasant word to anybody in the 5th Marines. We stay out there for two weeks up to 52 days, which we have done once and hope we never have to do it again.

I'm just waiting and doing my job until the day comes when I can come back home. This will be one year and 20 days I will never forget as long as I live.

This is for your information, Nancy, and please don't print it. The guys over here hate this war and you can't blame them. We fight to protect our country from such things that could happen back in the world. The way they treat us, the Marines who are fighting this war, we come to the rear to rest and what do they do: [The top brass] put us on working parties all day and [had us] stand lines at night. We'd be better off staying in the bush.

By writing these letters, we don't mean any disrespect toward the men fighting this war because they are America's finest men. We take great pride in serving our country but we wonder what our country is coming to.

Just something to think about, Nancy. They say all American troops will be pulled out by the end of 1970; how many more men will die before then?"
Marine Lance Cpl. Norman Townsend, June 25

During the Vietnam War, ground troops were usually attacked by enemies from all sides, so artillery and bombers earned the nickname "Death from Above." Army Spc. Richard Glazier (opposite) poses with a member of his intelligence platoon, months before the man was killed.

Drawing on family history, a soldier was equally negative about the war in his letter published in the column.

"I've been over here 6 1/2 months now and I've seen more than I ever wanted to see. I'm the third son of three to be over here. One of my brothers was here when I got in the country. I was with 3/21 196th until I got a transfer to the 71st Assault Helicopter Company as a door gunner.

As I see it, this isn't our war. Most of the South Vietnamese people are either farmers or fishermen. The political leaders of the country are distant and unimportant to these people. I can't understand why Americans are fighting and dying for a people who don't care who wins.

We have CAs (combat assaults) every week. Some are hot, some are cold. When one is expected to be hot, GIs are sent in, not ARVNs. My ship was flying for a lieutenant colonel who was an ARVN advisor. When a battalion of ARVNs ran into a platoon of Vietcong, the ARVNs ran.

The Americans are the ones who are putting their lives on the line. Why should we take more chances than the ARVNs when it isn't even our war?

To see one's closest friends killed is a nightmare I'll never forget. And back in the world, people just push this war out of their minds. Most of the South Vietnamese people want us to stay only because of the 'extras' we bring in.

The Vietnamese never had it so good after spending a day at the trash dump. As for the GIs, most of the Vietnamese people hate us. We don't like these people and hate being here. Since when are American lives worth a boost to industries? What a sorry time we live in."
Army Spc. S. Garry Miller, Aug. 18 Mailbag

"Anything Nixon says about the war he has said before. When he stops talking and starts acting, I'll have something to say. We could have been out of here if Washington would stop kissing _____!"

Air Force Airman 1st Class R. Lance Hall, Nov. 9

"Fighting to make it better," wrote Army Sgt. Emilio Santos (third from left) on the back of this picture. Soldiers flanking him, from left, were Capt. Hixon, Lt. Adams, and Spc. Rores.

understand this situation, the American public should get a hold of a damn good book, *Our Own Worst Enemy*, by the co-author of *The Ugly American*, Mr. William J. Lederer. It's a great book filled with truthful facts."
Air Force Airman 1st Class R. Lance Hall, Aug. 8

"**This war is entirely too political.** Everybody has their fingers in it.... I like the Marine Corps for what it is: the best fighting outfit ever put together. But politicians trying to run the services is the biggest reason why I could never make a career out of it."
Marine Sgt. Jim Harris, Oct. 15

Throughout 1969, the Mailbag continued to receive a range of commentary, often insightful and just as often sarcastic. One serviceman expressed his disdain in two letters.

"**I read your column whenever I get the paper.** Mainly to see who else is spending a lovely tour in this beautiful country trying to help these brave little people fight communist oppression and establish a democracy for the populace. Who are we trying to kid?"
Army Sgt. James M. Carney, May 5

"**It's been a long 13 months but with a 5-month early out I shouldn't complain.** I'll leave the bad times in Vietnam and only retain the 'high points' of my tour.... I was one of the more fortunate people.... I'm coming home. Many aren't. Too many aren't. The games people play with others' lives."
Army Sgt. James M. Carney, Sept. 28

Others, too, were upset.

"**I don't want to be hanged for bad-mouthing the government.** I would like to mention one thing though. We have been losing this war, we are losing this war, and we will lose this war as long as we are involved. To fully

"**I don't really care how people are reacting to this futile conflict in this vast wasteland known as the Republic of Vietnam.** I do know one thing: this entire operation is as far-fetched as can be imaginable.

I feel that I have a duty to perform for my country and I really shouldn't consider whether this war (hassle) is right or wrong. Personally, I feel it is wrong, but I feel that those who protest the war and avoid the draft are in greater error than any policies our country upholds. I really can't see where we are accomplishing anything worth speaking of over here. To me, the government is just wasting its time, money and efforts."
Army Spc. Mark D. Castelow, Nov. 12

"**Personally, I see the U.S. involvement in Vietnam as a political farce and a complete waste of manpower and money.** I feel that my time spent in Vietnam is nothing but a waste of a year. I know that I'm not alone in my feelings."
Army Pfc. Mike Moore, Dec. 28

Americal Division troops fortify Fire Support Base San Juan Hill. Soldiers posted there were nicknamed "gimlets."

"I'M NOW ON MY FOURTH TOUR OF DUTY IN 'CHARLIE' COUNTRY," WROTE NAVY PETTY OFFICER 2ND CLASS ROBERT "CHUCK" RILEY. "I have spent a total of 40 months over here." Despite those who questioned America's continued presence in Vietnam, many servicemen remained unfazed by the long and arduous undeclared war. And they wrote to let those at home know the extent of their commitments.

One soldier provided a reasoned pro-war argument in his letter, signed by 10 of his buddies.

"I'm into my eighth month now, on line, not in the rear, so I consider myself qualified to write about this war….

I attended Conrad High School and graduated in 1968. I'm from Elsmere. I like long hair and good times as anyone will tell you that has ever been associated with me. I'm a 2-year man in the service, and will get out with only 19 active months.

So, by no means can anyone call me a 'lifer,' or in your words, a 'career soldier.' My views aren't bent towards the service. My views are coming from a 20-year-old man who won't be able to vote or drink a beer legally when I get home. I don't know if you people back there realize it or not, but every time we receive a newspaper or magazines we see headlines 'Demonstrations!!!' and second news fronts about counter-demonstrations!!! Most of us realize these headlines are for selling purposes, but it is depressing!!! We'd like counter-demonstration headlines always….

You know a simple letter of appreciation means more to the guys than 500 demonstrations! Especially from people they don't normally hear from.

Yesterday, I received a package from a Methodist Church in Bear, Delaware!!! I'm from Elsmere and I'm a Catholic!!! It was the first time in eight months anything like that ever happened to me….

My feelings on the war are as follows: the United States has the 'freedom to vote.' Consequently, the people vote for our president. Our president and his staff have us over here for reasons we have no right to question. To stop communist aggression should be enough! It's enough for me and my friends over here.

My company has seen the death of fellow GIs, VC, NVA, pacification, the heat and the rain. And we still feel it's worth it. Uncle Sam asked us for two years of our lives and that's all. A man will give him this, a boy wants anybody else but him to do this!!!

We're proud to do our part for freedom and we're proud of the men who have laid down their lives for it. To pull out of Nam now would be a loss and I hope our government won't let these men die in vain!!!

Progress is slow and hard, it costs blood, sweat and guts. But we are making progress. We can and we will win this war if we stay!!! And stay we must!!!

My feelings towards the people back home: a total lack of support!!!

I don't know how many people back home have seen war but I'll bet one thing, if war ever came to the United States, the soldiers fighting it would get 100% backing!!!

My feelings towards hippies and alike: the U.S. is a free land. Freedom of speech, press, etc. and the only reason why is because men fought and died for these freedoms. Hippies and alike have the right to do their own thing as far as I can see if they've served their time protecting these rights. When I come home, if I grow my hair long and buy a motorcycle, I think I deserve the right. But people who haven't done a thing for the government but scorn and deface it have no rights!!! Draft dodgers: any man of able body and mind who hides or lies to get out of the service isn't much of a man and I hope his family and friends are very proud of him!!! And I hope he enjoys the freedoms other men have died for!!!….

My feelings toward the government: you people voted for it. Like I said before, I can't vote for three months after I come home. I think it needs some changes but these things take time. I don't blame the government for sending me here because they didn't, you did!!! But I don't blame you either. So, back your government and us!!! If enough good people got together, you could stop all the things that need to be stopped and start the needed things. Get together!!! To all the wives and families of fallen servicemen: your loved ones never died in vain; they died for what they believed in and for you and me…. These views I expressed in this letter aren't mine alone, they are shared by the men I'm with 24 hours a day. Sure, we complain: no bed to sleep in, C-rations, dirt, no cold drinks, rain, mountains, and, most of all, away from our loved ones, but we are here and we are proud!!! Proud of what we stand for and proud of what we're doing…. We would like to thank all our supporters and tell everyone that deserves it to enjoy our free world and don't let a few people ruin it for everyone!! As long as there are men left and not boys, we will have a 'free world!!!'"
Army Spc. Michael J. Freebery, Dec. 4 Mailbag

Uniform insignias worn in the war zone were olive drab to avoid enemy attention. With its looser weave, this patch (opposite) was likely made in Vietnam. The men in Army Spc. Miichael J. Freebery's unit endorsed his opinion on the war. His letter closed with a postscript: "Dear Nancy, These are only 10 names. The first 10 guys that I let read this. My whole company backs this, but I realize you can't print 150-plus names."

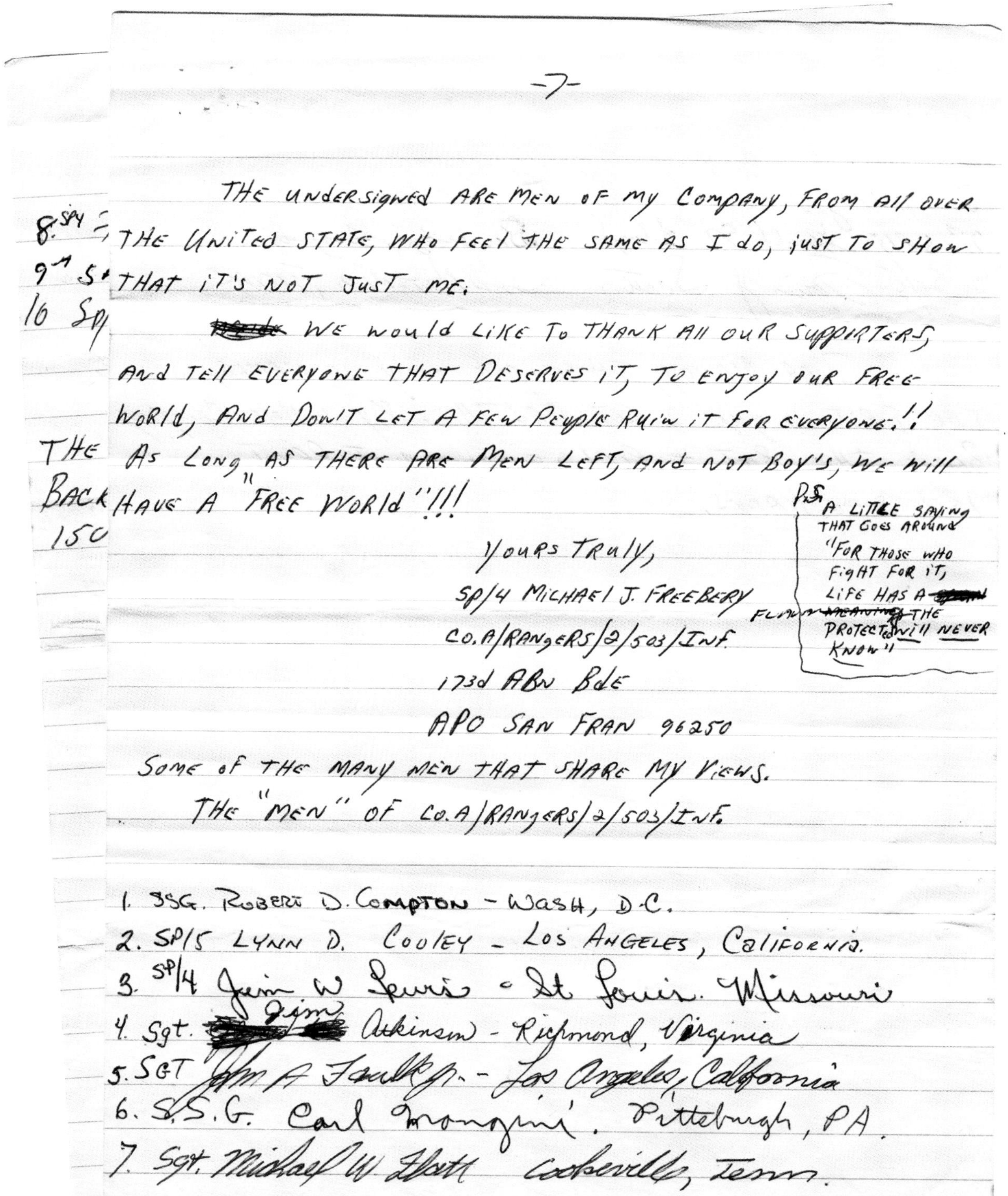

-7-

THE UNDERSIGNED ARE MEN OF MY COMPANY, FROM ALL OVER THE UNITED STATE, WHO FEEL THE SAME AS I do, just TO SHOW THAT iT'S NOT JUST ME.

~~~~ WE would LIKE TO THANK All OUR SUPPORTERS, And TELL EVERYONE THAT DESERVES iT, TO ENJOY OUR FREE WORld, And DON'T LET A FEW PEOPLE RUiN iT FOR EVERYONE!!
As LONG AS THERE ARE MEN LEFT, And NOT BOY'S, WE Will HAVE A "FREE WORld"!!!

P.S. A LITTLE SAYING THAT GOES AROUND "FOR THOSE WHO FiGHT FOR iT, LiFE HAS A ~~~~ FLAVOR ~~~~ THE PROTECTED will NEVER KNOW"

Yours TRULY,

SP/4 MICHAEL J. FREEBERY

CO.A/RANGERS/2/503/INF.

173d ABN Bde

APO SAN FRAN 96250

SOME OF THE MANY MEN THAT SHARE MY ViEWS.

THE "MEN" OF CO.A/RANGERS/2/503/INF.

1. SSG. ROBERT D. COMPTON - WASH, D.C.
2. SP/5 LYNN D. COOLEY - LOS ANGELES, California.
3. SP/4 Jim W Lewis - St Louis. Missouri
4. Sgt. ~~Jim~~ Atkinson - Richmond, Virginia
5. SGT John A Faulk Jr. - Los Angeles, California
6. S.S.G. Carl Mongini. Pittsburgh, PA.
7. Sgt. Michael W Flatt Cookeville, Tenn.

101

"Believe me, I wish I were getting hit with that East Coast snowstorm rather than these east coast [of Vietnam] rockets. Charlie sure has been putting in overtime on the night shift."

Army 1st Lt. Robert G. Ralston, Feb. 28

CAUGHT IN THE LINE OF FIRE OR FACING AN IMPENDING BATTLE TESTED THE BEST METTLE. Wistful thoughts often permeated servicemen's correspondence about their frontline situations. "We are right outside Da Nang at Marble Mountain," Army Spc. Alfred C. Smith wrote on March 14. "I work on trucks at the 245th motor pool. We get hit with rockets {B-122s] a lot. Right now we are expecting a ground attack." He added, "I won't be home until next August and I'm going to be an uncle this month. I just wish I could be home." Others expressed apprehension.

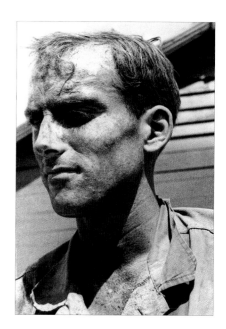

"**If anyone in the 'land of the big PX' cared about what was happening over here, they would have done something when Saigon was rocketed last week.** Nixon is supposed to give a speech tomorrow, so I hope he shows some sign of guts or he will lose about a half-million votes from Viet vets in '72. When senators say that we provoked the attacks, it disgusts me. It seems OK to them if we recon and survey the enemy situation, but don't dare shoot anyone or we are asking for trouble.

I hope I don't sound militaristic because I'm not. I just believe, like many others, that we are here, so let's do the job while we are in a position to help someone."
Army Sgt. James M. Carney, March 4

"**In January of '68, I arrived here in Da Nang.** I was assigned to the Armory.... I traveled on inventories to Chu Lai (south), Hue, Dong Ha, Tan My and Cua Viet (north). I saw a lot of this Vietnam. Months later, I worked at the station hospital.... That assignment helped me find myself. I saw men die before my eyes. How do you tell someone this? I saw pieces of people. I sorted weapons and gear from people. Some of the things that happened, you'll never know or read about in a paper. You can't give too much credit to the corpsmen there. Among blood, sweat, excrement and plain stinking messes, they were there along with the doctors trying to save lives....

Those poor 'grunts' that came in, not all were battle casualties. Some came in due to poor judgment (leadership, whatever).... An officer would push a squad too far and they'd want to just lie down and sleep. To hell with death, that could come too, but they needed sleep and rest. The rains were the worst part. Continually it would rain. One Negro came in with exposure. Two days and nights of solid rain...."
Navy Petty Officer 2nd Class Terry Reiswig, April 9

"**Thank you for the write-up in the paper about me.** May I add that, although the medals were for me, if not for my buddies who died on the fatal day of the 22nd of December [1968] I would not have them. So it is with great honor to them that I wear [the medals] and walk proudly. No man wants to die and I am sure that no one wants someone else to die for them so I can only say may God give us peace and understanding with hope for our future."
Emanuel Marino, April 15

A gunner from the 2nd Battalion, 34th Armor, picks out his target. Army Spc. Douglas R. Elliott (above) after his last mission before returning stateside, a five-day firefight in August near Nui Ba Den.

A CALL TO ALL

It is night in Viet Nam, very lonely
dark, and hollow.
I stare at the darkness - but it is not
the darkness staring back at me, it is
my life.
The enemy lies very close to my front,
and death may easily wait for me, as
I wait in fear of it.
I find myself looking back at my life in
flashes. I am beginning to discover many mistakes
I have made.
I see my biggest mistake was that I did
not see. I never saw what a wonderful
loving family I have, and how much I really
love my family. I see my girl as she really
is, kind, sweet, gentle, generous and full of love.
How I wish I had been able to see all of
these and (nay) many other things which I
see so clearly now. I pray that it
is not to late for me to make
amends.
It is not to late for the rest of
the world, I call to all of you
to stop, face death in your imagination
and see what beautiful things you
have and are taking for granted.

A Delaware Soldier

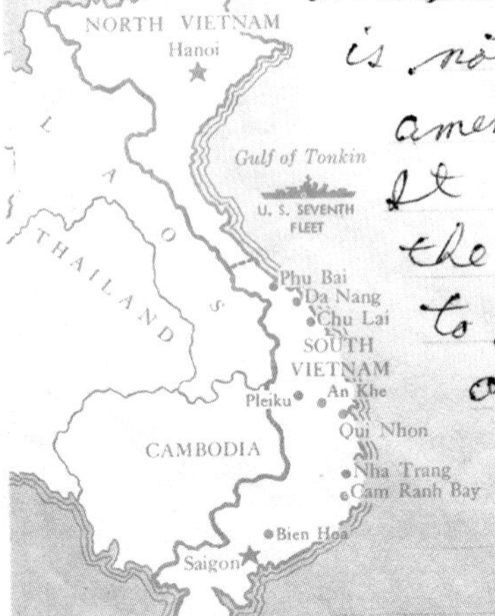

"I'm in the 2nd Battalion, 320th Artillery of the 101st Airborne Division and we are air mobile and thus move frequently depending on where needed. We have moved our firebase twice in ten days between May 7 and 16. We are now located in Tien Phoc, where the action is fairly hot. We have been averaging about 800 rounds per day firing…. We artillery support the infantry and the grunts have it bad in most places.

Myself and Lee Sylvester from New Castle are in A Battery here at Tien Phoc. The NVA has been giving us a real workout lately and we have hit them hard in the short time we have been at this location."
Army Pfc. Peter J. McCorkle in Tien Phuc, May 24

One soldier wrote two months apart:

"**In the last few days, we've had two early-morning rocket attacks (Charlie was kind enough to wait until it was just about time to get up anyway), a bomb going off downtown and an airplane crashing on the beach and the heavily traveled adjacent road.**

I became involved with the airplane crash, which presented the most gruesome scene I've ever seen. None of the bodies or vehicles involved were in less than several pieces and they were strewn all around.

The rocket attacks caused no American casualties and almost no damage. They did, however, kill a few Vietnamese.

It is now monsoon season here and it rains heavily quite a bit of the time, especially late in the afternoon and early in the evening. Apparently, Charlie likes this sort of thing."
Army Capt. William J. Taylor III, Oct. 12

A flamethrower attached to a tank from the 1st Battalion, 5th Mechanized Infantry aims a stream of ignited flammable liquid at hardcore NVA resistance. A rare anonymous letter (opposite), haunting for its content, was published on Memorial Day in the May 30 Mailbag. The author titled it, "A Call To All."

"**You probably heard about the Air Vietnam DC-6 crash here.** I did the investigating and it was quite a scene. All kinds of wild body counts have gotten out over the air and through the press. So far, the actual confirmed body count is 35, not 125 or 135 or anything like that. Of course, 35 is 35 too many! The stench at the [scene] was fantastic. We managed to get quite a bit of info quickly and I believe much of the data for the early reports came from our efforts."
Army Capt. William J. Taylor III, Dec. 28

These soldiers were more pragmatic about their sorties.

"**We haven't had it too bad since I've been here, except for booby traps.** I've been down to the Saigon River several times but the worst place I've ever been is the Ho Bo Woods. Our company is now building a fire support base (to be called Patton) right on the outskirts of the Ho Bo Woods."
Army Pfc. Larry Smith, May 30

"**God only knows what I'm doing in an infantry unit but at least I'm in the best.** Tomorrow I fly into the A Shau Valley and begin my apprentice OJT as an infantry platoon leader. Today a cot, tomorrow a rucksack."
Army 2nd Lt. Henry A. "Alex" Wise, July 23

About three weeks later, Alex wrote:

"**Well, I am back in the rear for a few days and glad to be back from five days in the A Shau Valley.** I can safely and proudly say that I am one [of] very few armor officers to wear the Air Medal for a combat assault by helicopter under hostile enemy fire and the CIB (Combat Infantry Badge) for serving in an infantry combat slot for a certain length of time. Putting it plainly, I'm not a 'cherry' any more."

At "the sands" near Hue, the 101st Airborne Division infantry joins 2nd Battalion, 34th Armor tank crews on an operation with South Vietnamese Popular Forces, local militias that protected their villages from Vietcong attacks.

Col. George S. Patton's letter, sent to the Mailbag by Army Sgt. William H. Chance, praised members of the 11th Calvalry Regiment, who wore the Blackhorse patch, for their reputation as "the best and fiercest unit in the United States Army." A yellow NVA flyer offers a reward of 10,000 piastres (about $300) "for any capture made with or without injury. Imperialist America is our despicable enemy." Hue (pictured), Vietnam's ancient imperial capital on the Huong River, sustained massive damage during the Tet Offensive.

THERE WAS NO DOUBT, EVER, THAT COMBAT VICTORIES BOOSTED MORALE. One serviceman wrote of the pros and cons of serving in an elite unit.

"**Well, here I am once again.** May I say in a very happy mood after a very successful five-day operation in which the 11th Cavalry Regiment scored a great victory. Without a doubt in my mind, a terrible blow was dealt to the Vietcong. In five days, members of the M Co., H Co., L Troop and two squads from the 919th Engineering Co. inflicted well over two hundred losses to the Vietcong. All this was done under the command of Col. George S. Patton III (now General Patton). We have been on the go for some two weeks and have really confused the Vietcong. We should be out in the field at least two more months."
Army Sgt. William H. Chance, April 10 Mailbag

One letter described several successful skirmishes with the enemy over many months and the devastation in Hue. The letter mentions Larry Maroney and Bob Brown, both serving in the Navy's River Division 521, and Jim Sharpe, assigned to the division's Mobile Support Base 1.

"**Last May [1968], Larry and I were the only Delawareans in the Riv Div.** On May 7, we found out what the war was all about. Our boats came under B-40 rocket and heavy automatic weapons fire, resulting in three guys seriously wounded and four with minor wounds. Then things quieted down.

During the Tet Offensive, RivDiv 521 was instrumental in providing safe passage for supply craft carrying vital supplies to the besieged city of Hue.

During the past months, RivDiv 521 has participated in numerous successful operations with the 2nd Brigade of the 101st Army Airborne Division.

On Aug. 9, two sailors of RivDiv 521, led by a patrol officer, and two PacVs (Navy air cushion boats) of Coastal Group 17 swept the Dam Sam, a shallow lagoon five miles northeast of Hue, while the airborne units swept the adjoining shores, thereby catching the Vietcong and the NVA in a trap. This highly successful one-day operation resulted in 42 VC killed in action and one NVA and 393 VC prisoners captured with no friendly casualties.

On Sept. 9, our sailors again provided a blocking force for Army Airborne on the Dam Thuy Tu, a long lagoon 10 miles east of Hue, to prevent hostiles from escaping by water. This operation lasted over two weeks, resulting in over 700 VC-NVA killed or captured. Unfortunately, a Vietnamese National policeman assigned to our RivDiv was killed when two sailors came under heavy automatic weapons fire while attempting to stop a VC crossing.

Then, men of RivDiv 521 created a scholarship fund for the policeman's children living in Hue. He was truly a man who made us realize what we were fighting for….

That pretty much sums it up for now. Will write you of Larry, Bob and my individual jobs at a future date…. Oh yes, I have extended my tour in Vietnam."
Navy Petty Officer 3rd Class Ralph W. "River Rat" Kessler, Jan. 13 Mailbag

The battle on Hill 937, more commonly known as "Hamburger Hill," represented a major U.S. effort to clear the A Shau Valley of infiltrators from the north. The 10-day encounter in May cost 70 U.S. soldiers their lives. Another 372 were injured. The need for the battle was questioned in the U.S. Senate and in the news media, especially after the new commander of the 101st Airborne abandoned the position on June 5. The battle also prompted a reappraisal of U.S. strategy, from "maximum pressure" against the North Vietnamese to "protective reaction" for U.S. and South Vietnamese troops threatened with attack. It also brought some letters to the Mailbag.

"**I read in the paper where Ted Kennedy said that the battle for 'Hamburger Hill' was unnecessary.** Well, myself and all the other GIs here feel that Sen. Kennedy is very wrong. How can anyone say that it was unnecessary? When we can start defeating the enemy in what are his safe areas, then we are making progress. I think Sen. Kennedy was very much in the wrong and only made those statements for political reasons."
Army Spc. Richard Glazier, June 8

"Enclosed is a paper sent down through our sergeant and a prisoner of war. The 11th ACR is becoming one of the most hated units in Vietnam. A price tag has been put on the head of any GI with a Blackhorse patch on his shoulder. Would you believe I'm worth a whole three hundred dollars?"

Army Sgt. William H. Chance at Firebase Gem, May 15 Mailbag

"Me and my buddies feel the same about 'Hamburger Hill.' It was necessary. I was on LZ Carolyn where we were hit by a regiment of North Vietnamese. If you could get a May 6 paper, you would read about it. We killed an estimated 450 North Vietnamese. I'm glad."

Army Cpl. Thomas Hobson near Tay Ninh, July 4

Army Sgt. Charles E. Cole lets a link fly from his crackling .50-caliber machine gun. Humorous commentary (below) often adorned the covers of xenon searchlights on M-48A3 medium battle tanks. Army Spc. Courtney Cosgrove (opposite), a mortarman from Van Wert, Ohio, takes a break in a bunker at Fire Support Base Emory, two miles east of Cu Chi.

Smoke grenades were used as a ground-to-ground or ground-to-air signaling device, a target or landing zone marking device, or a screening device for unit movements. They came in a wide spectrum of colors.

While many provided details about their illnesses, one serviceman contacted the Mailbag in July complaining of a lack of adequate medical treatment for a sickness he did not define. He wrote of his condition and requested a call to action from those at home.

"**This letter is in reference to my status as an infantry soldier.** I entered the Republic of Vietnam on April 6. Since then, I've been extremely sick and it seems the doctors won't help me anymore. They say it's just a GI disease and are willing to let it go at that.

My attempts to obtain medical help over here have not been completely futile but I know that something more can be done for me than they have done in the past or intend to do in the future. So I'm writing to the commonwealth of Delaware.

The state is responsible for my being drafted and my being here in Vietnam. The state is responsible to help me in returning to the United States so I can obtain better medical attention.

I feel that a petition signed by the people and presented to our congressman or a senator would definitely help my situation. I will be forever grateful to whoever starts and signs such a petition."
Pfc. George J. Turak, July 12

HEALTH CONDITIONS WERE OF UTMOST IMPORTANCE TO THOSE SERVING IN A DISEASE-RIDDEN, WAR-TORN LAND. Servicemen didn't hesitate to update readers on their well-being, share stories of injury or express concerns. One marine first wrote of hardships in the field in March.

"**We have been on Operation Taylor Common since Dec. 8 [1968].** We've been up here in the mountains since Jan. 2. We have gone up until now without a shower or bath. Who knows how much longer we will have to wait until we get to clean up? We've gone without water, chow, and sleep quite a bit."
Marine Lance Cpl. R. W. "Bobby" Green, March 4

Two days later, Bobby wrote home with news of a health scare. His family shared the letter with the Mailbag. "Well, I'm in the rear because I have blood poisoning of the left hand. I got stuck with a rusty nail. It's pretty sore but I really needed to get in the rear for a rest, plus I haven't had a shower in about 49 days now."

He added, "I'm going out to the bush after I see the doctor. I'm not supposed to, but I am going to help carry out mail, beer and sodas to the guys. I bought $35 worth of all kinds of goodies for 2nd platoon. I'll do everything I can for these guys. They're the greatest."

Bobby then wrote the Mailbag again, updating readers on his condition six days after his letter to his family.

"**I am in the hospital (1st Med) at this time.** They aren't sure what is wrong yet. I have all the signs of malaria but they don't think that's what I have. They're still taking tests."
Marine Lance Cpl. R. W. "Bobby" Green, March 12

Another shared his concerns.

"**The month of April has been a pretty busy one for us.** [In addition to] the work of holding sick call, doing all administrative work, sanitation and patrols, we have had accidental shootings and jeep accidents. It's bad enough losing our men in battle, but by our own bullets and auto accidents is really too much. Being with a unit that has no doctor really puts a lot of pressure on us but I don't think I would have it any other way."
Navy Hospital Corpsman Larry D. Gum, May 8 Mailbag

My friend was diverted to Japan during his tour in Vietnam but remained philosophical in his letter to the Mailbag.

"**I am in the 24th Medical Evacuation Unit waiting to disembark for Japan.** After a slight mishap, the doctors have ordered me to go to Tokyo for a spinal operation. I should be gone for approximately six to eight weeks. It seems as though my luck is running high, I hope it continues."
Army Spc. George L. Allen, June 3

Less common was praise for medical service, although one soldier wrote about his good care in May.

"**I had the misfortune of being medevaced back in September.** The whole thing wasn't too bad. I had a hot shower and a bed to sleep in, not to mention the chow. The few days I spent on the USS *Sanctuary* were the best days I've had since I've been in country."
Marine Lance Cpl. John M. Nock, May 26 Mailbag

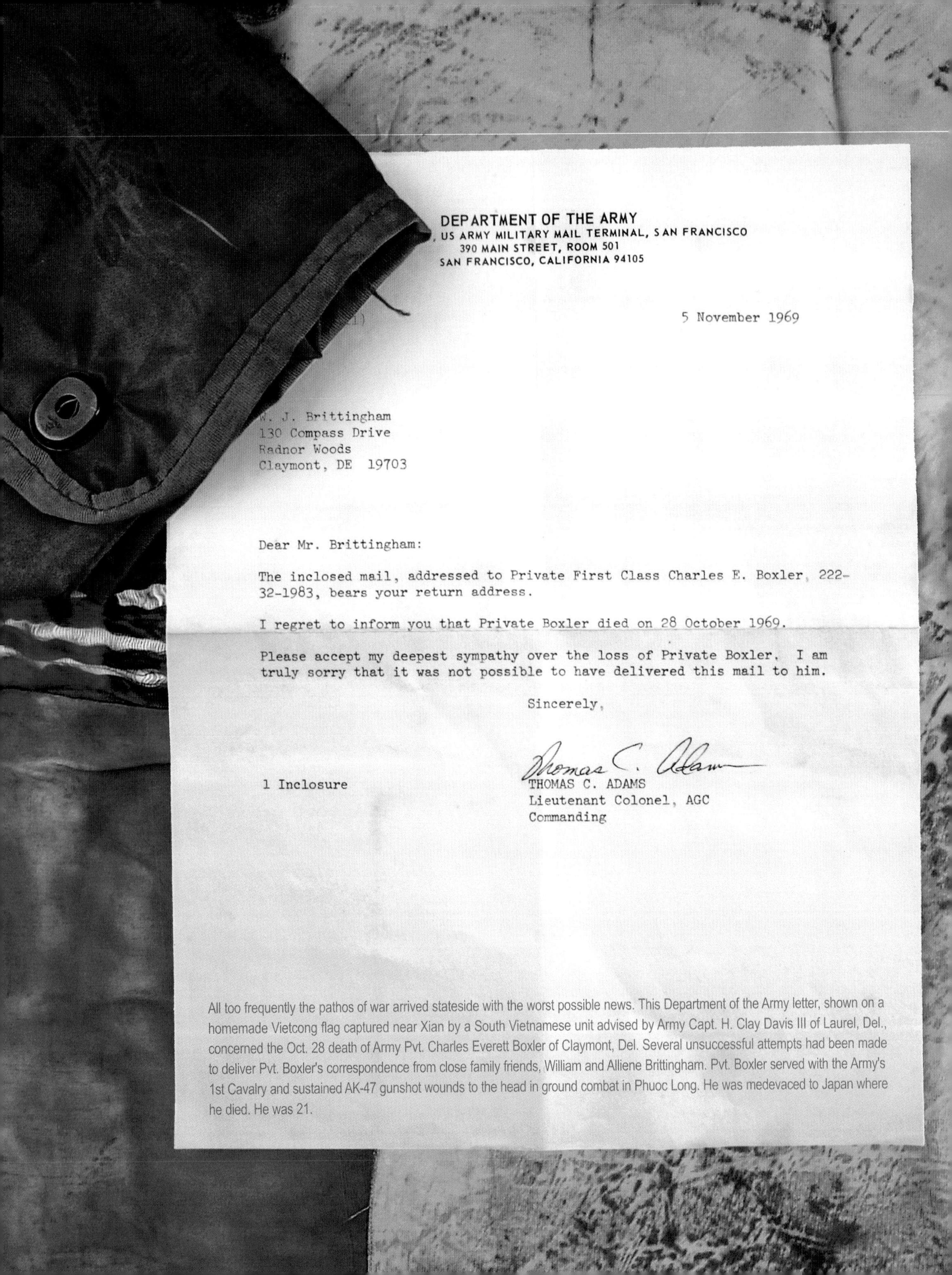

DEPARTMENT OF THE ARMY
US ARMY MILITARY MAIL TERMINAL, SAN FRANCISCO
390 MAIN STREET, ROOM 501
SAN FRANCISCO, CALIFORNIA 94105

5 November 1969

W. J. Brittingham
130 Compass Drive
Radnor Woods
Claymont, DE 19703

Dear Mr. Brittingham:

The inclosed mail, addressed to Private First Class Charles E. Boxler, 222-32-1983, bears your return address.

I regret to inform you that Private Boxler died on 28 October 1969.

Please accept my deepest sympathy over the loss of Private Boxler. I am truly sorry that it was not possible to have delivered this mail to him.

Sincerely,

THOMAS C. ADAMS
Lieutenant Colonel, AGC
Commanding

1 Inclosure

All too frequently the pathos of war arrived stateside with the worst possible news. This Department of the Army letter, shown on a homemade Vietcong flag captured near Xian by a South Vietnamese unit advised by Army Capt. H. Clay Davis III of Laurel, Del., concerned the Oct. 28 death of Army Pvt. Charles Everett Boxler of Claymont, Del. Several unsuccessful attempts had been made to deliver Pvt. Boxler's correspondence from close family friends, William and Alliene Brittingham. Pvt. Boxler served with the Army's 1st Cavalry and sustained AK-47 gunshot wounds to the head in ground combat in Phuoc Long. He was medevaced to Japan where he died. He was 21.

Claymont
Mt. Pleasant
heartsick...
the gam...
his fue...
grandm...
Kim je...
what...
she so...
tell you...
us...
work...
day...
I fe...
hea...
afra...
sh...
fu...
th...

And doing quite well. He works fast
... you see they are

4.

you come home to see. This was
the most beautiful wedding I have
ever seen. Thelma Lou, Holly, Valerie.
And Bill's two sisters and Leslie ine
Kim looked just beautiful. It was
out of this world... I wish you had been
home you would ... invited.
because of Les...
were there
enjoyed them...
and I mus...
I'm still so...
If you ...
Army, ...
laugh I know...
you and maybe I can...
kids around here to write
So long for now
Hope everything is well with you.
Mrs. Buttingham
and the kids

6.

PFC Charles E. Butler
249 GH 96267

WILMINGTON DEL
PM
27 SEP 1969

An unidentified soldier has the "thousand-yard stare," a term given to the unfocused gaze characteristic of combat stress reaction known as shell shock (opposite). This clipping from the March 8 edition of *Pacific Stars and Stripes*, sent by Army Spc. Larry R. Kipp, shows Henry Cabot Lodge, chief U.S. negotiator at the Paris peace talks, and a young victim of a communist rocket.

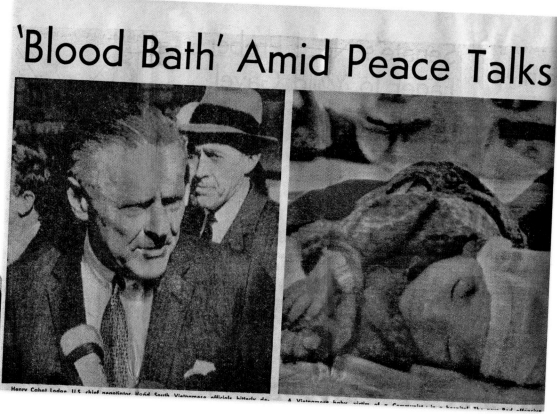

'Blood Bath' Amid Peace Talks

Henry Cabot Lodge, U.S. chief negotiator World South Vietnamese officials bitterly de-

A Vietnamese baby victim of a Communist in a hospital. The new Red offensive

THE PARIS PEACE TALKS WERE ANOTHER HOT TOPIC FOR THE MAILBAG. Begun in May 1968 between the United States and North Vietnam, they were expanded later that year to include South Vietnam and the Vietcong National Liberation Front. The talks sputtered and stalled. Many servicemen viewed the initiative as a hollow attempt to restore peace to a ravaged South Vietnam.

"**Paris peace talks – Well, the talks have been going on for almost a year now.** So far, they've decided on what shape table they want. I realize that you don't just walk in, sit down and sign a treaty, but THIS IS RIDICULOUS!"
Army Spc. Paul J. Walker III in Saigon, Feb. 24

"**Well, it's about time that I got around to answering your question about how I feel about the Paris peace talks.** Well here goes. Hope you print this because I'm not the only one in my company that feels the way I do. About 55% of the people I asked agreed with me.

In my total career of 15 months in the United States Army, I have read and heard quite a bit about the 'Paris peace talks.' I feel that I can give you and the readers a good opinion from what I've learned.

These talks are utterly disgusting and completely ridiculous. While men are dying on the battlefield, the 'fat cats' are quibbling about troop withdrawal.

Once again, the Land of the Free and Home of the Brave has come to the rescue. Protection for these people, yes, all the material and equipment they need. As far as American blood is concerned, NEVER!!! There is no alternative now but to play the game. We put our foot into it in the beginning and immediately went up to our eyeballs. If we pull out now, we would lose more face than we have already.

I'm not saying that the United States should get out of Vietnam. Let's face it, we have already committed ourselves. I'm saying that Mom, home and apple pie should be more cautious before jumping into the fire.

You think I am being ridiculous? See what parents say whose sons are over here. Also, what happened to the talks over the Pueblo [the Navy intelligence vessel captured by North Korea in early 1968]? A year later then something was done. It took a bunch of women to demonstrate, 'Remember the Pueblo,' to get some action.

Well, as big as this country is economically, defense-wise, you mean we couldn't buy the ship back? The U.S. has bought everything else it needed."
Army Spc. Bob Marciniszyn, May 1 Mailbag

"**I have been reading your column for about two months now.** Before, I didn't really have much to write about but one letter I read boiled me up and got this letter going. Paris peace talks – I agree with the newsman. Take them out of their plush hotel in Paris and put them in a foxhole somewhere in Vietnam and see how long it takes to come to some sort of agreement."
Air Force Staff Sgt. Robert E. May, May 8

PRESIDENT NIXON'S PROPOSAL TO CONDUCT A DRAFT LOTTERY IN MAY 1969 DREW COMMENTS FROM SERVICEMEN. Touted as a step toward fulfilling his campaign promise to replace the draft with an all-volunteer armed forces, the plan called for 19-year-olds being most vulnerable for one year only. The proposal, had it passed, would have eliminated the uncertainty eligible men faced for eight years, from ages 19 to 26. Our men weighed in on the subject:

"**I think that a draft by lottery would represent little, if any, improvement over the present system.** People drafted would still have the same ill feelings about the fact that they were drafted while others were not. Personally, I look forward to the day when all people around the globe get straightened out to the point where both the draft and the ABM (Anti-Ballistic Missile) system are superfluous."
Army Capt. William J. Taylor III at Cam Ranh Bay, June 3

"**The draft seems to be an ever-present subject and maybe I could throw in my comment.** As I see it, if enough people were interested in their country, as far as its being their country, a draft wouldn't be necessary. Uncle Sam doesn't grab people for no reason or just to have larger armed forces. We do have commitments that must be met in order that just maybe my son or yours won't have to fill if we fill them. I'm not interested in a career in the Marine Corps or any other branch of the service, but I do feel it's my obligation to do at least 'my part.' I joined and I'm fighting for what I believe in, in my own way."
Marine Lance Cpl. Vern H. Ranney Jr., June 4

"**As for the new system of draft that Nixon is thinking of, I feel that it is wrong.** I feel that it is the duty of every able young American to do his part for his country. After all, if it were not for the young men like my father who fought for freedom during WWII, this country might not be free now. And if I didn't fight now like I am and the others over here with me refused to fight, where would my young brothers be in a few years? I want my son to live a life of freedom like I have. That is why I think that every young man [should] be drafted into the armed forces at 19; also, because a 19-year-old can adjust to the new way of life faster than a 23- or 24-year-old. Not to knock the old, but it's the young 18-year-old PFCs and the 19-year-old Sp4s that are winning freedom for both Vietnam and the world."
Army Spc. John E. Rubincan, Nov. 6

Known as a "bunker-buster," this practice rocket-propelled grenade (RPG) was about three feet long. RPGs were used to destroy enemy defensive positions. Fighting was fierce as a tank from the 2nd Battalion, 34th Armor engaged the NVA near Nui Ba Den, the Black Virgin Mountain.

Nixon's November 3, 1969 address to the nation coined a new word: Vietnamization. The cornerstone of the Nixon Doctrine, the plan allowed for American troop withdrawal when the South Vietnamese became strong enough to defend their own freedom. "I recognize that some of my fellow citizens disagree with the plan for peace I have chosen," President Nixon said. "Honest and patriotic Americans have reached different conclusions as to how peace should be achieved." Although many wanted immediate withdrawal from Vietnam, the president did have some support.

"I heard President Nixon's Vietnam speech and had chills running up and down my spine.... Vietnamization can work if given the time. Too many people are guided by their emotions and shortcomings. They want out but they do not realize that it is not that simple. Nixon has some excellent ideas which will eventually get us out of Vietnam and possibly prevent another from happening. Furthermore, a lot of people protest and open their mouths with little knowledge of what it is all about.

When you know what is happening, you realize how ignorant people are, especially when it comes to believing what one reads and sees in print.

We get most of the magazines from the states, and we just laugh at some of the simple and ignorant conclusions which are drawn. Things that happen every day over here are blown out of proportion to defend certain statements or positions.

One example is a recent picture in *Life* magazine showing Vietnamese soldiers hiding in a ditch while they were under attack. These pictures were so-called proof that the process of Vietnamization was not working and the soldiers were not capable of fighting.

Your natural instinct when under fire is to hide, even though this is wrong. You have to be trained to counter this instinct and then learn how to exercise the correct technique in an actual situation. The next time these soldiers come under attack, they will know better.

Furthermore, from talking to many veterans, they all agree that the Koreans were in worse shape during the Korean War than the Vietnamese are now. They are feared over here more so than the Americans.

It all boils down to the fact that you have to be here and know what is going on before you can make a statement. The papers tell you very little, and much of it is slanted to express or stress a specific view."
Lt. Thomas W. Van Grofski, Nov. 17 Mailbag

REPORTS OF THE MY LAI MASSACRE IN VIETNAM FUELED ANTIWAR SENTIMENT IN THE UNITED STATES. First accounts of the March 1968 atrocity did not appear until November 1969. Army Lt. William L. Calley Jr. was charged with having responsibility for the murders of scores of unarmed civilians in the village as well as with killing a civilian about six weeks before My Lai.

Calley, who faced trial by court martial, was found guilty by a military jury in 1971.

Soon after the accounts appeared, one soldier sent his thoughts on the massacre and enclosed an article published in the *Pacific Stars and Stripes* headlined "How Could A Massacre Happen?" by Associated Press writer John T. Wheeler. The article, prompted by the My Lai murders, analyzed the emotional transformation a GI undergoes in Vietnam.

"**I look forward to reading your articles with messages from those of us here in the war zone.**

Lately, I've noticed a few about the GIs' feelings towards the war. I think the enclosed newspaper article consolidates the feelings of most of us here in Vietnam."
Army Spc. Robert C. Booth, Dec. 18 Mailbag

Here is some of what Wheeler wrote:

No spark sets off a fire unless it falls into combustible material. The sparks that ignite American GIs are snipers, mines and booby traps. The major cause of casualties in Vietnam are mines and booby traps. Snipers are also a major factor. The three are all the more hated because each is hidden and after the damage is done, there is usually no chance for the American infantryman to even the score because no enemy can be found.

Often intelligence will pinpoint a village as the source of the mine and booby trap makers and snipers. Repeated sweeps through the hamlet turn up little or nothing except more casualties. And hatred builds up for the villagers who know the snipers and know where the hidden traps are but don't tell. Then one day something snaps in one or more men. The frustration and fear drives them across that line of civilized conduct that in combat zones is a hazy mark at best.

There are indications that these things might have been at work on the men who are accused of massacre in My Lai last year....

In war, everything is realer than real. 'The capacity for great violence rises to the surface, but so does a capacity for great compassion,' an Army doctor said. Remember, part of the brutalizing men undergo is necessary to their survival. You can't look war in the face with the kind of emotional responses we use in the states. You would go mad.

Another Army specialist made some interesting points when he commented on My Lai in his letter.

"**The recent publicity for supposed massacres in Vietnam points out one of the great truths about the type of war being fought over here and the true number of casualties.** The figure quoted by Sen. [Edward M.] Kennedy (D) from Massachusetts of 800,000 wounded and 200,000 killed in the past four to five years is much closer to the truth than the figures quoted by the general press.

Killing civilians over here is a sport for certain units – however, it remains a closely guarded secret and to the Vietnamese it is a sure death to publicize objections. The attitude is most aptly expressed by the huge white lettering on the bottom of the gunships of a certain platoon in the Nam – 'birth control.' The publicity this war receives is a pressure valve for population-conscious people all over the world. North Vietnam has 200,000 men reaching draft age each year – fodder for the cannon. The recent Vietnamization of the war is proving highly successful – the ARVN troops are starting to jell – showing a lot of pride and desire to pursue 'Charles.'

One point that is of great interest and curiosity to many GIs over here is whether the published casualty figures (American) are anywhere near correct. Most combat vets feel they are grossly understated as there have been many massacres of companies of GIs over here which never received any publicity.

In Vietnam, you never can be sure who Charlie is – you don't have many Vietnamese friends over here, even among the military. War is a destructive experience for the most part and whether it is necessary and/or moral, I don't believe anyone can judge until they've been through one under combat conditions."
Army Spc. Walter L. Rainard, Dec. 13

"Killing civilians over here is a sport for certain units – however, it remains a closely guarded secret and to the Vietnamese it is a sure death to publicize objections."

Army Spc. Walter L. Rainard

How Could a Massacre Happen?

Allegations that American GIs massacred South Vietnamese civilians during a raid on a village complex last year have stunned the United States. How could it happen? is the most frequently asked question. In the following analysis, John T. Wheeler, who reported the war in Vietnam for the Associated Press for several years, gives an insight into the conditions of a strange war in which anything can happen.

By JOHN T. WHEELER
Associated Press Writer

To try to understand the alleged massacre by American GIs of civilians at My Lai it is necessary also to understand the atmosphere of a war which has led many U.S. fighting men to feel they are as much at war against Vietnam as for it.

While the communiques speak of battles involving companies and battalions—the clash of professional soldiers doing their grim job—each GI carries with him the certain knowledge that in any village there may be men, women, and even children who are also the enemy, waiting for the time and place to attack him.

Brutality, and indifference to human life, are commonplace in Vietnam. Even the disfigurement of dead GIs is common.

In Vietnam the killing of civilians was a practice established by the Viet Cong as a major part of the war long before the first U.S. ground troops were committed in March 1965.

By official count ―
mund ―

thoroughly terrorizing the countryside that resist. The total now is more than 3,00‒ enemy in Hue when they held ― weeks. At Hue, the victims wer‒ of all ages. Many were killed sin‒ behind their backs, shoving them ― ing them alive.

It was into this conflict that t‒ were plunged. They had been told t‒ who were bad and woo the peas‒ enemy because he had no ch‒ official line went, Vietnam wante‒ ‒ree cratic just like America.

But the GIs found a war o‒ ‒undered‒ divided allegiances to any regi‒ ‒ Saigon.

In a Strange War—Anything C‒

(Continued From Page 1)
the enemy's professional troops living in the jungle.

In short, the GIs felt—and still do—there were few they could trust.

There is no front in Vietnam, no rear, no safety. To the GI of a rifle company everyone outside the perimeter can be suspected of plotting to kill him.

In Vietnam the word civilian does not describe noncombatants. It describes dress more certainly than occupation.

In Vietnam the GI has plenty of reason for his distrust and fear:

Item: An elderly woman notebook for her ready smile and broken betel nut-stained teeth, was caught smuggling out a detailed map of the defenses of an American base where she worked as a laundrywoman.

Item: U.S. Marines found begging children to whom they had been giving food were stealing

Item: After one night attack by a large enemy force, Americans sweeping the perimeter of the camp's found the body of a rifle. He barber, still clutching the assault to had been leading the way through the show the way at its weakest barbed wire point.

Item: A U.S. truck was blown up, killing all aboard, on highway 13, called "bloody Route 13" because of the frequency of minings. GIs from another truck quickly traced out the electrical wires to the detonator and found a young girl still holding the handle. They shot her.

The Pentagon say that today's soldiers are the most sophisticated in history. But more than being able to operate intricate electronic equipment and the like, the GIs in Vietnam also could see at first hand the corruption, the indifference of Vietnamese soldiers to winning the war, the contrast between the

poverty in the countryside and the comparative wealth of the cities and the way Vietnamese merchants, bar girls and even children selling black market American soft drinks gouged them. Added to this were the deaths and maimings of friends. Cynicism mixed with anger rapidly replaced the early idealism among combat troops.

No spark sets off a fire unless it falls into combustible material. The sparks that ignite American GIs are snipers, mines and booby traps. The major cause of casualties in Vietnam are mines and booby traps. Snipers also are a major factor. The three are all the more hated because each is hidden and after the damage is done, there usually is no chance for the American infantrymen to even the score because no enemy can be found.

Often intelligence will pinpoint a village as the source of

the mine and booby trap makers and snipers. Repeated sweeps through the hamlet turn up little or nothing except more casualties. And hatred builds up for the villagers who know the snipers and know where the hidden traps are but don't tell. Then one day something snaps in one or more men. The frustration and fear drives them across that line of civilized conduct that in combat zones is a hazy mark at best.

There are indications that these things might have been at work on the men who are accused of massacre in My Lai last year.

They certainly were on a group of American Marines I accompanied into a village south of Da Nang in 1965. A half squad, out of a regimental size force, went on a brief rampage killing a group hiding in a civilian air raid shelter.

The battalion was due to rotate home in four weeks. In the previous month, 15 per cent of the battalion had been killed or wounded by snipers and booby traps. None of the Marines had seen a Viet Cong soldier during the time.

After the reports of the incident were published in the United States, Maj. Gen. Lewis Walt, then U.S. Marine commander in Vietnam, issued a public statement saying the killings "grieve me deeply. And I express my deep sympathy to the loved ones of such innocent victims as I do the loved ones of the Marines who have given their lives."

The U.S. Command's position has been from the beginning that civilians are not to be harmed. But the case for the sanctity of civilian life is weakened by the knowledge that there are South Vietnamese assassination teams—sometimes led by Americans— operating in

Army Spc. Walter L. Rainard (opposite, right) enclosed a picture with his letter. Army Spc. Robert C. Booth sent a *Pacific Stars and Stripes* article headlined "How Could A Massacre Happen?" about the My Lai civilian murders. A chilling excerpt from the second page of the article read, "U.S. Marines found begging children to whom they had been giving food were stealing grenades that were tossed back at the Leathernecks during the night."

War scenes captured by combat photographer Army Spc. Douglas R. Elliott include (clockwise) a tank on the move, soldiers digging in for a night position, a 2nd Battalion, 34th Armor soldier relaxing on a cot on an armored bridge tank and an ARVN soldier reaching for blocks of C-4 explosive to destroy an enemy bunker.

PACIFICATION OR CIVIL ACTION PROGRAMS IN THE WAR ZONE WERE DESIGNED TO BUILD OR REBUILD INFRA-STRUCTURE AND PROVIDE SERVICES FOR THE DOWN-TRODDEN SOUTH VIETNAMESE. These positive steps were often hamstrung by enemy harassment but U.S. perseverance generally prevailed. The Mailbag published many letters from servicemen involved in these efforts.

Navy Petty Officer 3rd Class Stephen A. Nash, assigned to Mobile Construction Battalion Five, was a frequent correspondent in 1968. By extending his tour a second year, his reaffirmed his commitment.

"**It's a little hard to continue something started almost a year ago but a promise I made must be kept….**

I have spent 3 months in Monterey, California, at a Vietnamese Language School. Now, I am set to go back and continue with the work I was doing last year, working in the Pacification Program.

Our battalion is leaving next week for the Seabee Camp, Camp Hoover, in Da Nang…. I'll be writing to you periodically letting you know how we are making out."
Navy Petty Officer 3rd Class Stephen A. Nash, Jan. 27 Mailbag

Steve wrote again, after he arrived in Vietnam.

"**I have come to learn that in the past six months all military units have stepped up their civic action programs in an effort to win more people over to the side of the Vietnamese government.**

I haven't been here long enough to make an analysis but, from what I've seen of the Da Nang area thus far, it appears to be working.

In the short time we've been here, my counterpart, a native Californian, and I have completed several civic action projects. We are also teaching English in a Buddhist school on a regular basis. It's amazing how quickly these youngsters pick things up.

I have found that by learning their language, the people are much more sociable than I had realized. They seem to appreciate it when they don't have to learn our language to be able to communicate."
Navy Petty Officer 3rd Class Stephen A. Nash, Feb. 18

Army Spc. Joseph Uniatowski (above) relaxes with a young audience near Long Binh. South Vietnamese children benefitted from civil action efforts.

Rudimentary housing near Chu Lai defined the standard of living for most South Vietnamese.

A letter of appreciation commended the civic action work Steve and his outfit performed at Bo De School in the village of Hoa Phat. Written by an unidentified South Vietnamese youth, the tribute was titled "A Subtle Battlefield." After Steve's parents, Mr. and Mrs. Wadsworth H. Nash, delivered the letter to me, it was published in the Mailbag.

Naturally these following lines have been written by a Vietnamese young citizen who is responsible for a Vietnamese school existence.

At the first beginning of these lines, I should like to concern the oldest word, LOVE, but Love is a most powerful combatant who can subdue all.

The first time they came here at our school to visit us. I am very sincere to say that we were very happy to receive them. Soon I knew that they are American officials working for MCB5 civic action program. And they did come here with their love to carry on their mission of mercy.

They are Steve Nash, Bruce West and Chaplain Kirstein. We have been receiving school supplies, clothing and scholarships also from their love since January. Because of their goodwill reserved for our high school students, they have been coming to our school to teach English four times a week regularly. I know that they want to assist us to beat down the dangerous ignorance because they are combatants. Our students like to learn English taught them, especially their good, clear pronunciation.

As I write these lines, I also remember the last Tet. We had a Tet to remember. Why? At 9:30 o'clock on Thursday, Feb. 13, 1969, a big truck full of wooden boxes stopped outside our village school. Then toys, candies, clothes, tea were given out to over 1,200 children. The children were very happy and merry with fresh flowers smiling naturally on their innocent lips. How can we forget that moment on which a source of pleasure overflowed in our hearts?

One day, West asked me about the pupils who are so poor that they can't keep on their study at our school. The following day Phung Dinh Sinh, Do Thi Thuong and her young sister came back to school to continue their study, thanks to the donation of money and clothing from MCB5's civic action program. I was much surprised at the matter and I was oscillated by my own emotion.

Bruce has also let me know that MCB5 has been progressing a special plan to present some more scholarships to Bo De Hoa Phat students. Besides, our school has recently accepted a lot of books of different subjects, donated by this program.

Furthermore, Steve and Bruce are very fond of finding to understand about our Vietnamese special characters and traditional customs too. They also showed us how to play checkers and chess in time of our entertainment. Reciprocally, they were shown how to play Co Tuong, a noble game from long-ago China.

Summarily, I think that they are gentle, latent and brave combatants who are serving our mankind as a bridge between people and people and their only equipment is: Sincere communion in love.

Using common chopsticks, South Vietnamese children demonstrated their ingenuity as well as their dexterity during a curbside game of pick-up-sticks. Orphans of the war (opposite) often owned little more than donated clothing.

Sgt. Luu Huu Cuong (above), an interpreter for Company D, 2nd Battalion, 34th Armor, annouces the arrival of a MEDCAP (Medical Civil Action Program) team in a Vietnamese village, while Army medic Jerry Cedillo of Bettendorf, Iowa, drives. Eileen May, wife of Air Force Staff Sgt. Robert E. May, sent the Mailbag pictures that show his barracks, complete with boardwalk, and an orphanage under construction. MEDCAP (opposite) dispensed vital health care throughout South Vietnam.

Another old-timer in terms of correspondence to the Mailbag was Army Spc. Hugh R. Dougherty. Hugh stopped by the office to chat in March 1969. He was a civilian then but had been involved in what we called "Operation Children" during his 1968 tour in Vietnam. Through the Mailbag, we successfully lobbied support in Delaware for the project started by his battalion chaplain at an orphanage in An Khe. Hugh told us the story behind the orphanage.

GIs treasured bennie boxes, boxes of goodies from home. Hugh and his outfit made it a practice to share cookies and candy from the boxes with the children in various hamlets and villages. One day they went on patrol to a small village with a normally bustling marketplace. The village was deserted and there was an uneasiness in the air.

Without warning, a couple of children jumped out from the bushes and made wild pointing gestures. Their parents appeared from nowhere and hauled them to safety. The GIs were already trapped. The children had tried to warn them the VC were present. For the next two hours, they were held at bay. Hugh emphasized the situation could have been a lot worse without the children's actions. From that day on, Hugh said, bennie boxes accompanied every patrol and the children received treats.

Eventually, treats turned to assistance for youngsters in various communities and led Hugh and his battalion chaplain to aid the orphanage in An Khe. At the time of Hugh's visit, the chaplain remained in An Khe working with the orphans.

A Navy hospital corpsman wrote in February about a U.S. civilian medical aid program and its positive effect on the Vietnamese people and sent a follow-up letter.

"I would like to say I'm proud to be over here helping these people in any way possible. Since being here, I've become more appreciative of what I have at home. From our MEDCAP program our doctor (D.D. Henning) managed to send a little Vietnamese girl and her mother to the United States for heart surgery in California. We spent Christmas Eve at the home of the father and were treated like royalty. It was one of the best Christmases a guy could possibly spend away from home. These people do appreciate what we are doing for them even if the people in the United States don't get to see it."

Navy Hospital Corpsman Larry D. Gum in Da Nang, Feb. 3

"Just yesterday I had the opportunity to enjoy myself. I attended a homecoming party for a little Vietnamese girl who has just returned home after having heart surgery in California. The party was given by her parents to show how grateful they were for her recovery. It was a most enjoyable and unforgettable time."
Navy Hospital Corpsman Larry D. Gum in Da Nang, May 8 Mailbag

In late spring, a sailor wrote about another dimension of civic action for the South Vietnamese.

"I am stationed at NSA Da Nang and I work for civic action. If you're not familiar with my department, I will give you the rundown on it. First off, we are one of the very few departments that are self-supporting, though we do get some money but not very much.

Our program is a self-help program for the Vietnamese people. It is on the same basis as VISTA and CARE, etc. We have 18 VATs (Village Assistance Teams) who live in the many villages that make up Da Nang.

We live with the people and help them build schools, houses and do medical and dental assistance. The people do most of the work but we do some. The reason behind this I will not go into. We are mainly advisors and what we do here reflects the image of the Americans. Living in a VAT sometimes can be very dangerous because some of the VATs are very close to populous Vietcong villages. It's not like being out in the bush, but sometimes it gets dangerous.

We also teach English in our off hours. We also have a price of about $400 that the Vietcong placed on us. We are mainly advisors to the Vietnamese people. We offer scholarships to the very poor children so they can go to school. This money is all voluntary contributions from people back in the states.

My job here is getting supplies for the VAT teams and I go on to the open market a lot and see many of the sights and sounds that many people do not see.
Navy Seaman Michael S. Solomon in Da Nang, May 24

133

Army 1st Lt. Robert G. Ralston, an officer for the 39th Signal Battalion, provided background and detailed a plan of action for the battalion in his letter. He told readers about programs he was initiating "in an attempt to help these war-ravaged people." He sent a picture taken during a presentation of gifts to injured South Vietnamese soldiers. Despite the invasion of their country by Americans, South Vietnamese children (opposite) developed an affinity for U.S. Servicemen.

28 Feb 69

DEPARTMENT OF THE ARMY
HEADQUARTERS DETACHMENT, 39TH SIGNAL BATTALION (SUPPORT)
APO San Francisco 96291

SCCPVSGSBG

27 February 1969

SUBJECT: Civic Action

ALL PERSONNEL
39th Signal Battalion
APO 96291

Since the French military disaster at Dien Bien Phu in May 1954 approximately seven million South Vietnamese people have been orphaned or left homeless. This staggering number of refugees represents more than one third of the total population of South Vietnam.

Today the ARVN (Army of the Republic of Vietnam) soldier is being trained and motivated to repel the Communist aggression which has terrorized his family and ravaged his homeland for so many years.

When we take a closer look at the ARVN soldier, we learn that the rigors of his military life require this family-oriented man to spend about 95% of his time away from home. Consequently, his family is unintentionally neglected. If the family is fortunate enough to have a makeshift shower, who is available to repair it when it breaks down? If paint is procured, who can paint the "house"? The South Vietnamese "house" often consists of a flimsy, wooden framework with roof, walls and floor made of plywood, cardboard or sheets of tin. Under these conditions, poverty and disease are most prevalent.

In an effort to improve the living condition [...] people, the United States Military Advisors [...] chiefs to determine project priorities with [...] "pacification plan". Unfortunately, the fu[...] another question. Often funds are diverted [...] governmental levels.

Fortunately, by the establishment of "self[...] do our part to help. By providing the nee[...] do the construction themselves. As an ex[...] and a simple pump are being used in one [...] community well to the houses themselves. [...] insecticides and rat poison are desperat[...] disease. These families also need item[...] soap and simple toys for the children.

The ultimate cessation of open hostili[...] will probably not be effected by the u[...] order to fulfill our mission, we must [...] and minds of the South Vietnamese. Let us unite [...] of stone.

ROBERT G. RALSTON
1LT, SigC
Civic Action Officer

Others wrote less frequently about pacification programs but their voices were equally important.

"**The reputation and 'can do' spirit of the Seabees has been demonstrated over and over again in the Republic of Vietnam as well as other parts of the world.** Their constant devotion to and participation in civic action programs is to be esteemed and admired. I mention the latter because I fear that many of the good deeds that are performed in the midst of this great tragedy are overlooked and ignored, and only sensationalism becomes news."
Navy Petty Officer 3rd Class Richard Panadero, Feb. 3

"**I'm an interpreter-translator for a civic action team.** I'm completely involved with the pacification program. You know, winning the hearts and minds of the people. I suppose I could write a documentation of my experiences working and trying to help these wartorn people. I thank the 'powers that be' because I'm one of the lucky guys who hasn't had to become a paid killer. Kind of bitter, eh? I don't want my political ideas to stain this note.... I'll be home, playing civilian, March 18!"
Army Spc. Terry W. Arnold, Feb. 21

In their makeshift blacksmith shop in a remote South Vietnamese village, men repair cooking utensils and wheels. Seeing adult males in villages was a rare sight; most were conscripted. Children cared for children (opposite) at an orphanage near Chu Lai.

Some shared firsthand information about living conditions under the Vietcong.

"**Presently, I'm located about 5 miles north of Saigon in Gia Dinh Province in the suburbs.** Basically, Saigon and the suburbs are one huge slum, not unlike the ones back in the 'World.'

Poverty is a way of life here and if one compared this life to the so-called poverty at home, I'd say that person was insane. The living conditions of these miserable wretches are unthinkable and despicable – can't understand how the poor devils survive.

But this is a very different culture from ours and the people seem to do their best with what they have. Saigon has more motorcycles and three-wheeled cabs than I've ever seen in my life and if you think New York has traffic problems, you should see this place. Wow!"
Army Cpl. Bohdan R. "Bo" Tanchuk near Saigon, June 17

"**I'll tell you that at first I didn't think much about coming over here, but now that I'm here I'm glad.** Just to look at the people and the way they live, and we're helping them too. There are lots of Vietnamese people that work in the shops and are learning a trade and a better way of life. And it makes me realize that we are over here for a reason. Don't get me wrong, because I wish it were all over and all of us GIs were home again."
Army Spc. Steve McElwee in Nha Trang, June 18

"**I'm stationed at Phuc Vinh with the 1st Cavalry Division (Air Mobile).** My job is assistant psyop [psychological operations] for the division. It is quite interesting and informative. I was involved in the defection of the VC-controlled village of Duc Bon around Song Be. Talking to these people, I have received a first-hand report of life under VC control. Forced labor, excessive taxation, starvation and disease were their daily plight. This microscopic version of life under the VC was reconfirmed by the defection of two more VC-controlled villages around Song Be. Duc Bon was not the exception, but the rule. Quite different from the ideal socialistic state we studied at the U of D.

I wrote this letter to acquaint the people back home with certain facts. For the people of Vietnam, the issue is basic, life and all the necessities that are required to sustain it. Protest marches, moral righteousness and complete freedom in all pursuits are the luxury of the well-fed, healthy members of an advanced democracy where they are guaranteed these privileges. Vietnam (South) hasn't achieved that status yet. Nor will it ever under communist domination."
Army Cpl. Mike Falkowski in Phuc Vinh, Nov. 17

One soldier offered a U.S.-guided, agrarian-based solution to better South Vietnam's economy. The letter was addressed to: "Those Interested in Helping the People of South Vietnam."

"**I am a GI in South Vietnam and a friend of one of you asked me recently what the people in my area needed and whether I could distribute charitable items such as clothes or shoes.**

First, let me say that South Vietnam does not need charity. What it does need is a secure, stable base upon which to build its own nation. It doesn't need communism and it doesn't need capitalism.

South Vietnam needs security. It needs an honest economy based initially on agriculture. It needs technological advice. And it needs foreign investments.

The U.S., after a bitter struggle with the communists, has begun to win security for the established pro-Western government. We are training the South Vietnamese to defend themselves from foreign attack and to maintain internal peace and order.

But let us look at the situation a little closer. We have told the people here that to grow and prosper they have to start making money. But in order to make money, one must have something to sell.

Residents of Hoi Than near Cu Chi string barbed wire to prevent the Vietcong from infiltrating their village at night. Materials were provided by the Army's 2nd Battalion, 34th Armor. The Vietnamese made do with materials at their disposal for their housing (opposite) and even fashioned sandals from discarded tires.

The South Vietnamese have large quantities of rice which many people want. That in fact is one of the things this war is about. But there is a great demand here for things other than rice. Wherever the U.S. Army goes, large amounts of money are spent.

So the people are madly selling all types of new goods and services to get some of the money that is to be had. Most of the profits unfortunately are controlled by the black market and other illegal concerns.

A look at Saigon will show that graft, quick business and prostitution are its livelihood and easy wealth and pleasure its lure. Will this country's largest city ever become more wholesome and worthwhile than Hong Kong or Las Vegas?

I see an impending economic disaster and subsequent loss of governmental stability that we all have fought so hard to win. That is, unless we realize the falseness of this frantic economy and plant its roots where they belong – in the soil.

South Vietnam's chief resource is agriculture and unless its economy is based initially on that, its foundation will crumble and its new house will fall.

What can we do to help the people of South Vietnam? We can see to it that the United States plays the part of an honest, conscientious, yet detached guardian of its adopted foster child rather than just one more smug, egotistic adult botching its job of parenthood."
Army Spc. Richard B. "Blake" Ohsol, Jan. 20 Mailbag

Throughout the year, servicemen wrote more about Vietnam's black market. Two servicemen shed light on the subject.

"You can't believe the waste and black-marketing that goes on here! Some men (last year) were running a black-market syndicate on tape recorders, radios, TVs, record players and stuff of that nature.

The bar girls are another unbelievable item. Would you believe up to $200 in tips alone a week is what they make sometimes! They get GI boyfriends to buy them cigarettes, soap, cookies, perfume, watches, candy and on and on. All this goes on to the black market and bolsters the girls' economy. But no amount of preaching will stop these 'fishes' from being hooked into compromising situations."
Navy Petty Officer 2nd Class Terry Reiswig, April 9

"I would like to talk about a small group of people who, through black-market activities, are helping to ruin the economy of this war-torn country. They are the Koreans. In Saigon, the Koreans are now the largest organization making money off the black market. I have observed them for the last nine months of my Vietnam tour, and have seen just how they operate! The Korean officers, who make up the largest number of the countrymen in Vietnam, go to the many PX facilities here in Saigon and buy up everything that can be bought and then take it out on the streets of Saigon and sell it on the black market, making extremely high profits.... Early in the morning when the PX opens, they are always the first in line. They number as many as 100 sometimes.

While in the PX, they proceed to buy merchandise such as suitcases, irons, foods and anything else that can be hand-carried from the PX to that little Vietnamese who will buy it from them for an arm and a leg.... Anyone who has been in Saigon for any length of time can tell you the story of the Koreans and the PX. It is my opinion that the only way to cut down on this black marketing is to deny the Koreans the right to buy in American Armed Forces PX facilities."
Army Spc. John E. Rubincan, Dec. 27

With a maximum load perfectly balanced, a South Vietnamese woman trots down a street between Chu Lai and Da Nang. Streetside shops in Phu Bai sold all manner of food and goods, even black-market items.

LETTERS FROM SOLDIERS OCCASIONALLY MENTIONED ANIMALS, AS THEY WERE OFTEN ADOPTED OR USED AS WAR MASCOTS. One letter, perhaps the most unusual request the Mailbag received in five years of publication, requested pet food for a rescued dog. Retired Maj. Jim Richardson of Rehoboth Beach wrote concerning a young Navy Seabee in Vietnam who had saved a dog's life there and decided to adopt it but had a tough time providing food for the animal.

Richardson suggested an appeal in the column for canned dog food or small boxes of dog kibble or biscuits on behalf of Navy Seaman Gilbert Gray, his nephew.

We agreed and made the unprecedented pitch in the January 23 Mailbag and included the sailor's address in Vietnam. In a May note, Gilbert wrote, "I'm not too much at writing but I would like to take the time to thank you for your help on my dog food problem. I received enough food to start my own store. Your readers were very generous."

Another serviceman, Army Spc. Jerry Smith, sent readers his animal story in January. A reporter for *The Cavalier*, the newspaper of the 1st Air Cavalry, he wrote, "Eighteen mascots and pets were shot on Landing Zone Sharon today. A veterinary team from the 175th Veterinary Detachment visited the LZ. Its mission: to vaccinate all mascots and pets of the canine family against rabies." He continued, "The team, from Da Nang, is carrying on a program which they hope will protect the men and animals of the 1st Air Cavalry. All 18 animals are now immunized against rabies."

A friendly four-footed mascot peeks out of the ammo box of a .50-caliber machine gun mounted on a tank. Embracing the softer side of the war, Army Spc. Joseph Uniatowski of Wilmington, Del., is at ease with White Rabbit (opposite). Sent to the Mailbag by the Army Home Town News Center in Kansas City, the photo appeared in the June 2 column. According to the press release, both man and furry friend were familiar faces in Long Binh where White Rabbit apparently took up residence in the back of one of the 313th Signal Battalion's three-quarter-ton trucks.

SERVICEMEN CONTINUED TO REGALE READERS WITH "ON THE JOB" STORIES. Often letters incuded job descriptions and miscellaneous personal information.

"My tour here in Vietnam has been varied; for 5 months I was Battalion Adjutant before going to the Comm. Center. Here at Long Binh, we're known as the 'chair-borne GIs' and I must admit that there isn't much action in our area. However, it does have its disadvantages. The Comm. Center is one of the busiest in Vietnam, handling about 40,000 messages per month. Much of it is sensitive in nature. We have the rather unpleasant task of sending all the casualty messages back to the states.

Vietnam is full of challenges, no matter where you happen to be. The GIs in the field get all the glory, and they deserve much of it, but if it wasn't for those back at the base camps and in the supply points, the field-borne GI would be in a sad fix. And then again, we are occasionally called upon to drop our pencils to defend our perimeter.

I suppose my job is much better than many. I work in air-conditioned facilities. However, in my job, mistakes, even little ones, can bring all sorts of trouble. The pressure here is on the mind and there are those who are unable to take it.

I am also involved in civic action. The battalion supports an orphanage and I am custodian of the funds. We visit every week. I am also the editor of my own paper for the battalion. We publish the *Signal Sounds* every month. The paper contains articles from the chaplain, commanding officer, myself, as well as news of, by and for outstanding soldiers – our byline."
Army 1st Lt. C.K. "Ken" Savage, March 17

"I work in a Supply Unit, which is called DSU (Direct Support Unit). I work for a section called S-4 TROOP COMMAND. We clothe, feed and shelter all personnel who work in the Army Depot Long Binh, which is on Long Binh Post.

At night, I show a movie to the Officers Club and have a whale of fun watching movies such as 'The Dirty Dozen' and 'Princess and the Pill,' etc. So when Charlie Cong isn't around, things aren't too bad, but here lately, he won't or hasn't let us sleep too much. But things are a lot better than in February!"
Army Spc. Donald B. Patton, April 12

"Sitting here writing by candlelight. Thought I would drop a few lines to you. It's about 10:30 now and I'm in my bunker, staying alert for any 'fire mission' that might come down from our Fire Directory Center.

I'm in an artillery unit working with a 105-mm howitzer gun. I have been in Vietnam for 3 months now and I'm stationed in Tay Ninh at Fire Support Base Buell.

We have been fortunate so far because we've been at this location for about 5 months and this is the longest any battery has been in one position for this length of time. I must say also that we haven't had contact with Charlie since I've been here. (Thank God)."
Army Pfc. Thomas E. Hudson at Fire Support Base Buell, April 14 Mailbag

Away from the rigors of the bush, soldiers on stand-down spent three to four days relaxing in the rear at this divisional base near Chu Lai and were exempt from guard duty. Servicemen uniformly were good-natured and appreciated time away from the war.

sent me to Vietnam and planted me behind a desk.

Here I am, the R&R clerk, awards clerk, correspondence clerk and general gofer, and as you can see, I can't type. But I pull no duty, have a real bed and try to ignore all the general harassment that is so typically army. Nonetheless, it is Vietnam, it is the army, and I have 242 days left.

You ask for comments on controversial issues.... As far as the draft goes, I had some strong opinions on that last June, but I can't say that it worries me at the moment. Without the draft, how many young men would get to see the Orient with its culture, flies, malaria, etc.

Well, that's enough drivel for now. Somewhere out there in Delaware land are the former company clerks of this war and others who can appreciate the special plight of working with antique typewriters, etc."
Army Spc. Warren E. Taylor, May 29

"**I'm a radio technician and work as a radio operator too.** Our job is to supply communication for convoys we run up north and south to Da Nang .... As for being over here, I believe we're doing a good job, everybody gets their share of combat and everything."
Marine Lance Cpl. Robert C. Just at Quang Tri, June 21

"**I'm located over here in a place called Duc Pho.** It's a small base camp about 50 miles south of Chu Lai. I work in food supplies over here so I'm pretty busy most of the time. As long as you stay busy over here, the days really fly by. Since I've been over here, our base camp has had about 53 attacks but, like I say, 'It's all in the mix.'"
Army Spc. Marty Basara, June 22

"**Well I never thought I'd get here but I did.** I went through staging in Oct. with Bill Moffa, whom I came in with. Upon arriving I saw Bill who was just returning from R&R. I'm stationed with the 'grunts.' I'm a radio 'humper.' I'm in tactical air control. I go out and call in air strikes, gun strikes and medical evacuations for the grunts. Out in the field we are forward air controllers. The job used to be left up to an officer but through the years it's changed until all FACs are all enlisted men.

I stayed in the rear for 7 days learning procedures and the board. Now I'm going out on a 45-day operation with B Company.

You have to be very careful. It's very easy to get your own men. That's why I have to be with one of the guys that are experienced for a week to learn."
Marine Lance Cpl. Stuart D. Swalheim, April 17 Mailbag

"**I'm afraid that this letter won't be very interesting because it is sorely lacking in tales of woe, hardship and excitement....** I am at the LZ that the Vietcong don't even want, so take heart, mothers of Delaware, there are some soft, safe jobs in Vietnam. Uncle Sam spent $14,000 and 12 weeks teaching me to repair Huey helicopters, then

"**The [USS] *Garrett County* has one of the least likely jobs of the war.** Its mission is to support PBRs [Patrol Boats River] in the Mekong Delta. We are part of Operation Game Warden along with three other LSTs. The ship is now located in Vinh Long on the Co Chien River about 65 miles south of Saigon.

River Division 535 is now embarked onboard and carries out all its operations from the ship. The ship has just been awarded the Navy Unit Commendation. It also has just earned the Battle Efficiency Award."
Navy Petty Officer 2nd Class Robert J. Manelski, July 7

"**I am stationed at Lai Khe, with the 314th Aviation Support Detachment.** I am an air traffic controller and work in the airfield control tower giving landing instructions to aircraft."
Army Spc. Ganett Legates Jr., July 8

Even in the combat zone, downtime was necessary. A soldier (above) refuels an unarmed LOH before a scouting mission. Despite numerous attacks on their base camp in Duc Pho, Army Spc. Marty Basara (on right) and his Mississippi pal take a minute to mug for the camera.

June 22, 1969

Hi Nan[cy]
What
is the
can sa
But
over
alread[y]
I a[m]
Base
to
that
P.
s
o
t
o

you "for [   ] my birthday in your column.
My buddi[es]   wished that [I] had
something   "L.T. said, "Delaware ma[de]
Nancy,
my bud[dy]
the rig[ht]
My
any
pictu
my
Well
now. I have to ge[t]
night. Be looking forwar[d] [to]
again.

A shortimer Delawarean,
Marty

P.S - In the picture, both of us are giving the
peace sign. That's what all of us over
here want, peace. Do you think, that we will
ever get it? I hope so.

So long for now.

"**I am an F-100 Super Sabre pilot flying combat missions out of Tuy Hoa.** The F-100 is a single-seat, single-engine jet fighter bomber that carries a variety of bombs and has four 20-mm guns.

We support Army troops on the ground, including U.S. troops, Australian, Korean and Vietnamese troops, and we interdict enemy supply routes in enermy territory.

I have flown 175 combat sorties and I am now leading flights of two F-100s on combat missions. We always fly in a formation of at least two aircraft so that in case someone gets shot down, the other pilot can protect the downed pilot.

I have enjoyed my tour here, but I am anxious to come home. The war has steadily deteriorated since I got here and it will be interesting to see if it picks up when the monsoon season ends.

It is much more exciting to fly missions when the war is really hot because we always support the ground troops, which gives us the most satisfaction. But on the other hand, the ground fire becomes more intense and I can get along without that."
Air Force 1st Lt. Sam Jorgensen at Tuy Hoa Air Base, Aug. 28

"**I feel rather bad about not writing you for over 6 1/2 months, so after much thought (222 days worth), I finally made up my mind to give it a try….** My first 6 1/2 months in country were spent out in the boonies as a grunt. The 1st Air Cavalry is airmobile, so I've been moving here and there. My battalion worked off LZ Cindy (Bien Hoa area) for about 2 months; from there we went to LZ Jake (by the Cambodian border) for a month, Phuoc Vinh for a month and right now I'm at LZ Grant, up around Tay Ninh and the Black Virgin Mountain.

We have been working off Grant for just over 2 months so far. The enemy situation up here is ever-changing, but one thing remains unchanged: there are always plenty of gooks around!

Army Sgt. Tom Harden of Whitefish, Mont., drove over a rice paddy dike while sweeping an area near Cu Chi during the dry season. Air Force 1st Lt. Sam Jorgensen of Bellefonte, Del.,(opposite) boards a F-100 Super Sabre.

I have been working for about the last month in the Battalion Tactical Operations Center located on LZ Grant. It is our job to coordinate and control everything of a tactical nature in the battalion. I personally work with air traffic in our area of operation. I expect to work in this capacity until I come home in early January.

I won't discuss lifers, ABM or the morality issues of this war as others before me have. These subjects and others are for each man to decide himself. But I will say this: you can't really understand Vietnam unless you have been here and even then you're not sure.

Here's a little saying I've heard since I've been here that sort of sums it up:
You have never lived
Until you have almost died.
For those who fight for it
Life has a flavor
The protected will never know."
Army Spc. Thomas D. Skelly near Tay Ninh, Sept. 1 Mailbag

"**I went through school in San Diego to be a radio technician.** I graduated and went to Camp Pendleton where my wife is stationed. My wife is a woman marine and the best-looking woman marine the corps has, to my way of thinking. We were stationed together for about 9 months then I came over here.… I should be getting out when I get back. My wife gets out November 26 this year. We hope to live an even happier life as civilians."
Marine Sgt. Jim Harris, Oct. 9 Mailbag

After a seige on the Ho Chi Minh Trail along the Cambodian border, members of the 8th Field Artillery, 25th Infantry Division found themselves fighting the 88th NVA Regiment forces at the base of Nui Ba Den, the Black Virgin Mountain, near Tay Ninh Province. The firefight ended after several days, when the surviving NVA forces retreated at night and escaped into Cambodia.

A member of the 101st Airborne Division's Command Parachute Demonstration Team, nicknamed the "Screaming Eagles," during inspection before a mission. The An Khe Air Base (opposite) was located in the Gia Lai Province in Vietnam's Central Highlands.

One serviceman literally put his job to song in his letter.

"I am a platoon leader in a truck company stationed at Pleiku and a convoy commander running to places with names like Qui Nhon, An Khe, Ben Hit, Kontum, Polei D'Jereng. My drivers have a hard lot. It occurred to me while running a convoy one day that a paraphrase of a modern-day folk song by Gordon Lightfoot called 'Where I'm Bound' might be very apropos. If it's possible, considering copyright laws, I should like for you to print it:

It's a long and dusty road
It's hot and I've a heavy load
And the places I go aren't always kind
Some are bad and some are good
And I've done the best I could
But all have a long, long road behind
And I can't help wondering where next I'm bound
Where I'm bound
But when 12 months have gone by
And I'm on a freedom bird on high
And San Francisco has come in sight
I won't know what I've won
All I know is it's over and done

And home to my loved ones I shall write
And now I know, I know
Where I'm bound
Where I'm bound

These fellas really do a grand job under very difficult conditions. Driving a 5-ton tractor is a job that's pretty tough pulling a 12-ton trailer, especially if you've only been doing it for a couple months. But then when a man does for as long as seven or eight hours a day, seven days [a week], often along rough roads under dangerous conditions, it becomes quite a chore.

These men deserve a big hand, no praise is too great."
1st Lt. Robert H. Hallsted, Oct. 28

In describing his duties, an airman added praise for soldiers.

"I am now stationed at Tuy Hoa Air Base, which is probably the best base in Vietnam. Our mission is one of close air support. I am in the Munitions Maintenance Squadron and once in a while I am a gunner on an AC119 gunship. This way I see a little action, but nothing like the men on the ground. They are the ones that really have it bad and my hat is off to them."
Air Force Airman 1st Class Edward VanSant at Tuy Hoa Air Base, Dec. 15

Dear Nancy,

I am now working in the main communications center of Vietnam, located
at Long Binh. I am working in the top secret crypto section, so I cannot
tell you exactly what I do. However, I do get a complete and first hand look
at all the aspects of the war from the messages received, and I am more
convinced than ever that this war is not only killing people here, but also
back in the states.

Although I cannot quote you verbatim, the messages that come through
here, I can paraphrase, in my own words, what we receive. What I am concerned
with is the casualty report sent through the Red Cross, which comes in daily.
One tells of a soldier who has serious wounds in both legs, both arms, and both
eyes. Another tells of another soldier who was seriously wounded, and his
mother, hearing the news, is on the verge of a nervous breakdown. It seems
she has lost two sons already. I could go on, but the stories are only more
gruesome, and would only make your skin crawl. The point is, look at the
tremendous hardship and suffering this war is causing the American people,
as well as the Vietnamese. It is senseless and wrong to feel that we are
accomplishing anything constructive over here.

I leave Vietnam in May, and although I will have another year to serve
in the Army, most likely in the states, I will participate in everything possible
to make it known that being in Vietnam is wrong, and that we should withdraw
immediately. No one can say that I do not have a clear perspective as to what
is going on, because   here, I can see it, and I do not like it.

                    Agnew and all the rest of the pro-war people
                    firsthand, have them talk to the soldiers to find
                    we are doing over here, and then see if he and
                    ss generalities they have stated recently.

                    his war stinks, and should be ended immediately.

                                        Sincerely,

                                        Mark

                                        Mark L. Goodman

                    I made for you at work.

Army Spc. Mark Goodman encoded top-secret military communications in Long Binh.

One puzzled serviceman wrote the column about a job snafu. Upon arriving in Saigon, Army Pfc. Mark L. Goodman received an assignment that wasn't at all related to the training the Army had given him. After writing to his congressmen, Mark explained his situation to Mailbag readers in the Oct. 13 column. His dilemma got me invited to Washington, D.C., to spend a day with Delaware's U.S. Rep. William V. Roth.

The day after the column appeared, Roth's office called me to say the congressman had not received Mark's letter. An aide said Roth was most concerned that Mark felt the lack of a reply indicated that the congressman didn't care about his situation. I spent most of Oct. 29 with Roth and was impressed with his handling of inquiries and problems from Delawareans in Vietnam. Roth had been in contact with Delaware's U.S. senators, John J. Williams and J. Caleb Boggs, about Mark's query. Roth and the senators received a reply from the Army and all of them forwarded a copy to Mark.

"I am currently stationed in Saigon, where I will remain, on temporary duty, until November 19, when I return to my home base in Hawaii.... I was trained in the Army to work in communications. I received a top-secret clearance and expected to go to work in a communications center. Instead, I was sent to Vietnam to work in a warehouse. I attempted to find out, through the proper channels and chain of command of the Army, whether I would ever work my primary military occupational specialty, but to no avail. I was always told that if I didn't like the way the Army was doing things, that I should write my representatives in government. So I did....

I sent out the letters around the 10th of September, and received prompt replies from both senators. I have not yet heard from my congressman....

As you can see, writing to Senator Williams was a complete waste of time. His answer would seem proper and logical if I hadn't received a reply from Senator Boggs. It is obvious that one senator is interested in the affairs of the people he represents, and is willing to put some time and effort into obtaining information. On the other hand, it seems that Senator Williams has little time to handle inquiries from a single soldier in Vietnam....

So, for all the men in service that read this who are thinking of writing their representatives in Congress because you can't get satisfaction through your chain of command, I would advise that a letter to Senator Williams would be useless and a waste of time. Senator Boggs, on the other hand, I believe will endeavor to help you and try to straighten the problem out."
Army Pfc. Mark L. Goodman, Sept. 30

Williams, a Republican from Millsboro, responded to Mark's letter on Sept. 16. His letter stated that "the Armed Services have the authority to determine where personnel is needed the most and where they can provide the most needed service." He went on to say that senators were not permitted to make recommendations about individual military assignments and that any senatorial inquiries about an assignment would be taken up by the serviceman's commanding officer.

"Since the Armed Services have full jurisdiction over assignments, the answer to your question would have to come down through channels which are open to you," Williams wrote.

Boggs, a Republican from Wilmington, replied to Mark's letter on Sept. 16 with a note indicating that the questions would be referred to the Department of the Army and that he'd write back after receiving a response. Mark updated his situation in November.

"Since I've written to you concerning our senators' help in finding out what my job is in the Army, a lot has happened. Right after the Congressional inquiry, my orders were revised and I have been extended here for six more months. I have been told that the inquiry was an influencing factor, which somehow seems wrong."
Army Pfc. Mark L. Goodman, Nov. 10 Mailbag

In his final letter of 1969, Mark appeared satisfied with his current job. His attitude about the war, however, remained unchanged.

"I am now working in the main communications center of Vietnam, located at Long Binh. I am working in the top-secret crypto section, so I cannot tell you exactly what I do. However, I do get a complete and firsthand look at all the aspects of the war from the messages received, and I am more convinced than ever that this war is not only killing people here, but also back in the states.

Although I cannot quote to you verbatim the messages that come through here, I can paraphrase, in my own words, what we receive. What I am concerned with is the casualty report sent through the Red Cross, which comes in daily. One tells of a soldier who has serious wounds in both legs, both arms and both eyes. Another tells of another soldier who was seriously wounded, and his mother, hearing the news, is on the verge of a nervous breakdown. It seems she has lost two sons already. I could go on but the stories are only more gruesome and would only make your skin crawl. The point is, look at the tremendous hardship and suffering this war is causing the American people, as well as the Vietnamese. It is senseless and wrong to feel that we are accomplishing anything constructive over here. I leave Vietnam in May and although I will have another year to serve in the Army, most likely in the states, I will participate in everything possible to make it known that being in Vietnam is wrong and that we should withdraw immediately. No one can say that I do not have a clear perspective as to what is going on, because I am here, I can see it, and I do not like it. I would like to get Agnew and all the rest of the pro-war people over here to see the war firsthand, have them talk to the soldiers to find out their opinions of what we are doing over here, and then see if he and the others can make the gross generalities they have stated recently.

The real truth is, this war stinks and should be ended immediately."
Army Pfc. Mark L. Goodman, Dec. 21

August 2
BOB: 104 DAYS TO GO
GENE: 123 DAYS TO GO

Eugene Barbato

...rote you I was at
...c. Now I'm down
... I was transferred
... May 15th. When I
...mpany's electronics section,
...ve it or not, I found another
Delawarean, Bob Geuting
from Green Acres and g...
from Sallies. You don't...
great it is to talk ...
who knows the sam...
pla... home th...
...aters out...
...conting...
...ve wi...
...r our wo...
...ve get one: We se...
...month ago, and we
...iting for it's arrival
...like the snapshot.
..."Dynamic Duo" in

Army Sgt. Larry Gray (top) served three tours in Vietnam and later worked for the FBI. High school rivals who called themselves "Delaware's Dynamic Duo," Army Sgt. Robert L. Geuting and Army Spc. Gene Barbato, sent joint letters to the Mailbag during their tour. Navy medic David Steinberg, attached to a unit of marines, comes up for air after the siege of Khe Sanh.

BATTLEFIELD FRIENDSHIPS GENERATED LETTERS AND PHOTOGRAPHS TO THE MAILBAG. "Many people that I've met in Long Binh have been very helpful to 'the new guy in town,' me, and I've even made a friend whom I consider one of the greatest to enter my life," one serviceman wrote. He continued:

"**He is a native Californian, and his beliefs are very much my own, which makes a friendship thrive continuously.** He'll be leaving in November, sorry to say, but hopefully I'll see him when I return. He is quite a musician and frequently writes his 'own thing.' He played with the Blues Project at one time so you know he has talent. His name is Sonny Carte."
Army Spc. George L. Allen, June 3

Meeting others from Delaware meant a lot to our servicemen, especially if months had gone by without seeing anyone from their home state. Delaware's small size provided common ground for conversation, whether or not the servicemen knew each other before they arrived in Vietnam.

"**It's just a little past 9 p.m. here now and I'm writing this by candle.** Our generator gave up about four days ago. Would you believe I got a buddy over here with me in the same gun section as I'm in? He is from Wilmington, Delaware, and his name is Tom Hudson! Have been over here almost 10 months now and [he] is the first buddy I've run into from Delaware! One more thing – this Feb. 22 is my Mom's birthday. Tell her Happy Birthday for me."
Army Cpl. Edsel Ford Norris at Fire Support Base Buell, Feb. 15

The Mailbag heard from Edsel's new buddy soon after.

"**When I entered this section, I was greeted by a guy from my home state.** He was very amazed because I was the first guy he had met from Delaware while in Vietnam. We got to be the best of friends and right away I began letting him know what was going on back in the world. His name is Edsel Norris….

Well, it's going to get boring real soon for me because Norris will be leaving to come home in April. I will hate very much to see him leave because we have been sharing our home newspaper and also the care packages that we receive from home.

Well, this is something that can't last forever because all the guys seem to be waiting for that time to come when our tour is up and we can catch the freedom bird back home. Edsel and I are looking forward to getting together when we both get home and just have a ball talking about our times while being in Vietnam. I never thought I'd meet such a great guy as Edsel."
Army Pfc. Thomas E. Hudson, April 14 Mailbag

The chance pairing of Wilmington high school rivals resulted in their shared nickname, "Delaware's Dynamic Duo." From the day they met at Tam Ky, their Mutt and Jeff correspondence provided us with witty commentary from the war zone.

"**Last time I wrote you, I was at Camp Eagle near Hue.** Now I'm down south at Tam Ky. I was transferred to B Company 801 MT BN on May 15. When I got into B Company's electronics section, believe it or not, I found another Delawarean, Bob Geuting. Bob is from Green Acres and graduated from Sallies. You don't know how great it is to talk with somebody who knows the same people and places back home that I do. We two First Staters outnumber any other state's contingent in our section, so we will fly a Delaware state flag over our work area when and if we get one. We sent for one about a month ago and we are patiently awaiting its arrival.

Hope you like the snapshot. That's 'Delaware's Dynamic Duo' in Tam Ky. That's Bob on the left (the sexy one with his shirt off) and that's me on the right (the handsome one with the shirt on). It is a good thing we are sitting because with both of us standing, we would look like 'Mutt and Jeff.' Bob is 6'4" and I'm 5'8".

Well, both Bob and I are getting SHORT. Only 3 months and days to go. We both have our R&R coming up, so that brightens things up a lot. Nothing like R&R for boosting morale. That's all from me. Now Bob will give you a few choice words."
Army Spc. Eugene Barbato at Tam Ky, Aug. 2

After noting he had 123 days left of his Vietnam tour, Gene then turned the pen over to Bob, who had 104 more days in country.

"**Gene is sitting right beside me.** Lately he's been coming down rather hard on me – reason – I've yet to write you. From the first few pages of the dual letter, you've learned that the impossible has happened, two First Staters in the same section of the same company.

Until I met Gene, I hadn't seen even one other person from Delaware. In fact, it could have happened that we might never have known the common denominator – it took almost a month after meeting up to resolve the common origin. It's great to be able to talk about the same stomping grounds (Pit, Rehoboth, etc.) and since Gene is out of Archmere and I am from Sallies we manage to swap a few cuts as well.

In fact, since Gene is only a year ahead of me in school (but still and all I outrank him – shows the quality Sallies product) quite a few names, friends etc., also find common ground.

Gene is still sitting over me. He says I'm using too much of his paper (says he has to fit it all in that tiny envelope). His feelings are understandable after that last sentence.

(Notice the lined paper – another Archmere necessity.)

Gene has told you of our move south. We're closer to the action – nightly flare and tracer displays, but as yet our perimeter has never even come close to seeing any Charlie.

B Company is a maintenance unit and has a fair brain trust that has brought the lifers around to the point of agreeing to do it our way, i.e., we're a lot better off than most people.

Both Gene and I are in the electronics section where things at least stay interesting once the sandbagging after a move is completed. The section has TO&E (Table of Organization & Equipment) to its two maintenance vans, which are the closest thing to home in Vietnam. They've got Formica-topped counters and two big fans which pull a constant stream of air across you if you sit close to the door. The best thing about them is the innumerable, two-pronged, straight from the world, 115-volt AC wall sockets. Love that power.

Gene's on me again. This time for writing too much. Actually, he's clawing me for the paper so he can write an Archmere P.S., which as a Salesianum gentleman I've got to let him do – that catch phrase can hang you sometimes."

Gene was the letter's closer. His P.S. ended with, "This is Gene again. I'll humor Bob and let him get away with those cuts at Archmere. I can't help it if he feels the need to deride Archmere because he wasn't lucky enough to go there."

We next heard from half of the duo when they were about to dismantle.

"As you can see from the myriad exclamation points above, below and around the sides of the word 'Short' (militarese for not much time left), things are getting close.

I've four times less time in country than Gene and he's down to 24 [days] or so. I promised few if any cuts but I've got to to mention the 29-zip Sallies-Archmere game. My brother sent me a sports page clipping which Gene didn't really appreciate. [Gene is an Archmere Academy alumnus]. He was quick to point out the Conrad and du Pont games but 29-zip is still 29-zip.

By the time this reaches you, I'll be on my way to Bien Hoa to process out. If we make the column, I'll have to read it in the world but Gene, having eons of time left, will still be in Vietnam with time to spare to read all that lurid prose."
Army Sgt. Robert L. Geuting in Tam Ky, Nov. 20 Mailbag

"I was reading in your column recently a letter from two Delawareans from the same section of the same Airborne Company at Camp Eagle near Hue.

Well, there are two Delawareans a little north of them at Landing Zone Nancy (yes, your namesake, Nancy, believe it or not), who are assigned to the same company and live in the same hooch.

My first week in Vietnam I was surprised when I met another GI from Wilmington at the 27th Engr Bn (Cbt) near Phu Bai, where I was assigned during January. But when I got up to LZ Nancy here at the 14th Engrs, and met someone else from Wilmington, that certainly made it seem like a small world, to say the least.

As for our jobs here, [Spc.] John [Lloyd of Newport] is the armorer for the company and I'm the mail clerk. John sends along a message: SHORT – 32 days before he goes home to his wife and son in Newport. He's already told me he's going to send me a postcard when he gets there. That certainly is thoughtful of him.

As for me, I don't go home, which is Talleyville, until December 30, but at the top of my Christmas list I'm asking for a 'drop' which will get me home by Christmas Eve."
Army Spc. Thomas P. Baker at Landing Zone Nancy, Sept. 9

The following letter was sent to the Mailbag by this serviceman's family members. The soldier's exuberance in seeing someone from his hometown is quite evident.

"Guess what? Remember a guy from 6th and Lincoln streets by the name of Ronnie Annone? His grandparents own the little lemonade stand and grocery store across from the pool hall. I ran into him today. It turns out he's in the same company I am in. He came across my name in the USO when I put my name in one of the books marked Delaware and he happened to be looking through it.

The whole time I had been working in the next building from him! We spent about four hours talking and killing a few beers. He had a lot of pictures from a lot of the guys at 6th and Lincoln streets.

Pfc. John Carrow is coming home around the 7th. Before he goes, Annone and I are going on convoy to pick him up and bring him back to our base 'cause I haven't seen him in about two years."
Marine Pfc. Joseph J. Deptula Jr., Feb. 13

Still others wrote to tell about the new friends they were making halfway around the world.

"I met a guy from Newark. He is Wilbur McVey. He has been here about two months."
Army Sgt. William H. Chance, Jan. 19

"I've met only one other First Stater since I've been in this rotten hole. He's Joe Clark from New Castle. The next time we get together, which should be soon, we'll get a camera somewhere and take a flick for you."
Marine Lance Cpl. John M. Nock, May 26 Mailbag

"Just a quick [note] before I depart to go on the operation. Thank Bill Moffa, Bobby Green and Joe Deptula for mentioning my name along with theirs. I went in the [Marine] Corps with them. Really, they're all good guys."
Marine Lance Cpl. Stuart D. Swalheim, April 17 Mailbag

"This letter is coming to you from Fire Support Base Ca Ru that is on scenic Highway 9 in the northern I Corps. Roddie Brodie (from Seaford) and I decided to write and let you know the southern part of our state is well represented in Lima Company."
Marine Lance Cpl. Steve Stone at Fire Support Base Ca Ru, June 23 Mailbag

Army Spc. Thomas P. Baker and Army Spc. John Lloyd sent a letter and a picture to the column in September (opposite). Army Sgt. Bob Matusik (center) and buddies show off a captured enemy rifle in South Vietnam's Highlands area.

"I'm with the 5th Marines at An Hoa. I met a high school pal of mine over here, Bill Moffa from Lima Company. We get together when we come to the rear and we talk about home and what we think about Nam.

Bob Green is also in Lima but every time I go up there, Bob is out in the bush someplace. They are both doing fine and will be coming home sometime in the near future."
Marine Lance Cpl. Norman Townsend at An Hoa, June 25

"A good friend of mine stopped by this week on his way back to the world, Spc. Joe Tomlin from my hometown of Lewes. He's going to be stationed in California. Great, huh? I'm going to Bangkok next month. WOW! Can hardly wait."
Air Force Airman 1st Class R. Lance Hall, Nov. 23

Letters about hometown meetings were countered by tales of a lack of them. "Greetings from the Sandbag Capital of the World…." began Air Force Sgt. James F. Wachter Jr. in his January letter. "I still haven't come across anyone from good old Delaware as yet." Others also expressed hope of meeting fellow First Staters.

"I sure will be glad to get home…. As far as I know, I am the only one from Delaware in all of Cam Ranh Bay. If you know of anyone, let me know, okay?"
Army Pfc. Elmer "Sonny" Blansfield at Cam Ranh Bay, March 20

The Mailbag put Sonny in contact with others from Delaware, he told us in April. "I see that you put the letter in that I sent you," he wrote. "Since you published it I have received a few letters from other guys from Delaware who are over here. I'm glad I'm not the only one."

"I've been in Vietnam for 6 1/2 months now and pretty soon I'll be on that freedom bird back to America!
In your April 3 column, I read where SP/4 Bob Marciniszyn is over here and stationed with the 71st TRANS Unit. Well, Bob, if you look to your right about a half a block, you'll see S-4 TRP COMD. And if you'll find the time, I'll be glad to talk about good old Delaware any time! I hope we meet before I leave in September."
Army Spc. Donald B. Patton, April 12

"I noticed in your article that Pfc. Harry Felsberg, who is from Wilmington, is over here in Cu Chi Hospital. Well, I'm about 60 miles south of there and will be going there in a week. If I can, I will look him up and let him know he's still thought of. I'm now sitting in the E.M. Club drinking beer. The fellows said [to] say hello for them. I've been here 2 months and have 15 to go, so wish me luck."
Army Pfc. Odell V. "Dollar Bill" Howie Jr., April 16

"Our small camp is located at the south side of the village of Lang Co. It is about 10 miles southeast of Phu Loc. If any other fellows from Delaware are passing through, tell them to stop by the Seabee camp at Lang Co."
Navy Petty Officer 3rd Class Robert W. Conley at Lang Co, June 28

TREAT THIS MAN WITH UNDERSTANDING

Treat this man with understanding.
He's dealt in a land you cannot know
His nation's call found him standing;
When others cowered - he dared go.
He went to fight for things held dear.
Although the peril didn't seem near,
He went twelve thousand miles away
To fight to prevent that terrible day
They'd pound on your door with swords and gun
A horde not unlike Atilla's Huns.

He's been in battle with the 101st.
In regions where he was the first.
He's fought in wet and filth and mud.
He knows what it is to sit alone and cry.
And wonder why this man had to die.
He's wiped from his face his best friend's blood;
Turned with a shrug and pressed on through mud
He's discarded much of what he was before
And filled the gap with a grim, hard, core.

Now he returns from so much giving
To resume the awesome task of living.
He's fought to save you from a terrible fate;
Now it's your turn to reciprocate
With a little kindness and a helping hand
For this man who would return your land.
He's been to war and done his best
And on his return makes but one request—
Be patient if at first he seems rude,
If his manner is coarse, or even crude.
He's done without so much for so long
That he'll probably do a few things wrong.
He'll soon adjust, so don't be demanding
Just treat this man with understanding.

Army Spc. Daniel A. Tressler Jr. was killed in action Feb. 2. To honor his friend, Army Spc. Bob "Weasel" Arnold asked the Mailbag to print this poem written by Spc. Tressler's buddy.

1969 WAS A BUSY YEAR FOR THE MAILBAG. With more mail than ever, the column celebrated its first anniversary on May 19. In its first year, we had packed 312 letters from Vietnam into 97 columns.

I commended our servicemen for their public service to us, writing, "Throughout the year, you have generously contributed your time and talents to the column – for which the entire state is thankful. You have kept us aware of what it's really like in that tiny battle-worn country. We've welcomed hundreds of First State correspondents from all areas of South Vietnam. Some of you even find the time to stop by the office when you get home or when you're on leave. You bring your pictures, your honors and your thanks in. Although I disagree with the reasons you are in Vietnam, I am happy to be able to afford you the chance to express yourselves. Keep up the good work."

We changed the format of the column. Until the Feb. 3 Mailbag, the policy had been to not print full military addresses, to protect privacy and ward off unwanted mail. Our servicemen addressed that issue.

"**In the last paper, you asked what we thought of publishing our addresses.** I'm in favor of it…. And, who knows, we just might get some mail from some long-lost and forgotten friends."
Navy Petty Officer 3rd Class Ralph "River Rat" Kessler, Jan. 8

"**I realize that you do not include the complete address in order to protect those of us who serve in Vietnam from perverts who might be inclined to cause some grief.**

I think this sweet, however, please be advised:
1. There are specific channels through which bad news can be relayed to us. All of us are well aware of that fact.
2. Most of us are bemused, if not amused, by the thinking that emanates from the vast craniums of perverted and pathetic souls.
3. We pay little attention to fake or non-existent, return-addressed letters. If a person hasn't the intestinal fortitude to correctly identify himself and give his correct return address for our future 'reference,' then the letter in question is not worth any degree of consideration on our part.
4. Using the optimistic side of the question, it would permit a flow of constructive ideas from the public who have the right to take issue with the things we say."
Army Spc. Michael E. Brelick, Jan. 19

After we started including full addresses, Mike wrote in March, "Some encouraging letters and baked goods have turned up here as a result, especially attributed to the printing of my full address, I might add."

Many servicemen let us know how much the column meant to them. One was Navy Petty Officer 3rd Class Richard Panadero, who wrote shortly before his tour was up: "I want to express my appreciation and thanks to the News-Journal for their generosity and thoughtfulness towards Delaware's fighting men in Vietnam. I have thoroughly enjoyed my free subscription to *The Morning News*."

The Mailbag gained additional media awareness in 1969 with a second television appearance. Army Spc. Robert W. Ketchum Jr. and Nancy E. Lynch were guests on Otto Dekom's "On Camera" show on WFIL-TV, Channel 6 in Philadelphia. Bob enlightened viewers from a serviceman's perspective on the bombing halt and the Paris peace talks. He was home on leave before returning to Vietnam to serve an additional six months at Tan Son Nhut near Saigon. Waiting for a sweep team from the 2nd Battalion, 34th Armor to check the road for mines, a tank driver (below) relaxes. Many tanks were named for that special girl back home and often included names of their crews.

After a mail run from the USS *Enterprise* to the USS *Dewey*, the choppy sea prevented the transport helicopter from landing safely, so the sailor was lowered to the deck. The Wolfpack (opposite, from left): Army Pfc. Frank Szczerba of Wilmington, Del., Army Pfc. Lenny 'Scratch' Scrantz of New Orleans, Army Spc. Thomas 'The Lover' Menacher of Oshkosh, Wis. and Army Pfc. Richard 'The Head' Kennett of Menomonee Falls, Wis.

As I mentioned before, it is very lonely here on the O.P. One of the reasons for this is because there is a shortage of mail. With your help and the cooperation of your readers back in the world, we could remedy this situation. I am enclosing a photo of our group along with our address in hopes that there is someone back there who would like to write (particularly young, unmarried women)."
Army Pfc. Frank Szczerba, Feb. 6 Mailbag

"Today myself and my buddy, Jim Myers, were talking about life here in Vietnam and he came out with 'why can't people write us more often than they do?'

Being so far away from the things that a person loves and learned to accept as a part of life is rough. It's very easy for a person to feel that he has been abandoned and no longer a part of the life he knew at home. It's really funny what effect a few words from home can have on a man over here. After a long time without hearing from people back home, a man ceases to care and that is not exaggeration!

Why is it so hard for people back there to write? I don't mean just the guy's parents but his friends, his girl, and friends of the family. The argument that 'well I would, but I don't have his address or haven't had time' doesn't work.

I get the feeling from some people that I write to that they won't write to me unless I write first. For one thing, I'm sure you know that a normal working day here is twelve to fourteen hours long. Another is, you are quite tired at the end of the day and just want to go to sleep when you get back from work. Those guys out in the field, I don't know where they get the time to write, for they're always on the move. There is not an abundance of things to write about – you have to be careful of the things you say to keep from worrying the people who are going to read these letters.

Also, in some areas, letters are destroyed after they are read, so that the questions that you asked will be forgotten by the time your son writes back. The attitude I mentioned before – not writing unless written to is wrong….

I'm writing this for the many GIs that are over here. Maybe someone, after reading this, might start to think when they wrote to somebody over here last. Believe me, letters can make a man feel ten feet tall."
Navy Seaman Michael S. Solomon in Da Nang, July 31

"MAIL OVER HERE IS THE NEXT BEST THING TO BEING HOME," WROTE ARMY PFC. JIMMY "RAT" GROSS IN JULY.
"If anyone wishes to write us, we'll be more than glad to answer any questions if we can." Mail was always welcome, as few things could lift a soldier's spirits like a letter from home. Mail was so important to servicemen that when few letters were received, the Mailbag heard about it.

"I am a member of the Wolfpack. The primary task of the Wolfpack is to man the bunkers around Brigade Headquarters just outside of Chu Lai Air Base.

Myself along with four others do something a bit different than the rest of the Wolfpack. We occupy an outpost just outside of the bunker line. Our job is to spot anything out of the ordinary, and then take the proper measures to ensure the safety of Headquarters and Chu Lai.

It's good duty because we don't have to put up with any of the harassment from the 'lifers' in base camp, but it's also very lonely.

Everyone up here on the O.P. reads your column. In fact, there is only one thing we read and enjoy more, but we don't expect you to compete with Playboy Magazine.

"Why is it so hard for people back there to write? I don't mean just the guy's parents but his friends, his girl, and friends of the family. The argument that 'well I would, but I don't have his address or haven't had time' doesn't work." Navy Seaman Michael S. Solomon

Most soldiers complained about a lack of mail, not an abundance. "In the last two weeks, I have been getting letters from girls in the Wilmington area," one soldier began. His correspondence, honestly sent as a distress call, begged an answer and topped our list of all-time funniest letters.

"They all say that they saw my name in the 'Dear Nancy' column. I don't ever recall writing to your paper and having anything put in it. I am interested in finding out just who it is that is putting my personal letters in the paper for the entire world to read. I would like to know [from] whom and from where did this letter come. I am not holding your paper responsible, however, I would like to know why you failed to contact me and ask my permission to run the article!

It might turn out that the letter was run by someone I know, if so, I want to know.

I am sorry for bothering you like this, because I know you must be very busy, but the fact that my personal life is being published doesn't appeal to me."
Army Spc. John E. Rubincan, Oct. 8

My response followed in the Oct. 23 Mailbag.

In answer and defense, John, let me say that you're making an assumption that I, as a reporter, used or may use the vehicle of the press as a forum for exposing your personal life "for the entire world to read."

First, my column is not one of lonely hearts, gossip, or character assassination. It is a medium for the exchange of ideas, thoughts, gripes, and humor between Delaware servicemen in Vietnam and me.

All letters that are published in the column come either directly from First Staters themselves or from their families. There is an unwritten understanding that letters, or parts of letters, will be published in the Mailbag.

Since February of this year, complete addresses of servicemen have been published in this column. Mail is a precious commodity in the combat zone, as you know, and we felt there were many, many persons in the state who would correspond with our servicemen if they had their addresses.

From time to time, I run names, addresses and a little background material on servicemen who are newly arrived in Vietnam and who have requested a complimentary subscription to The Morning News themselves or through their families.

Your name has appeared only once in the column, on Sept. 22, under the "Welcome To" section, as yours was a new name and we were in hopes you would want to contribute to the column, either by letters or pictures or both.

I am sending you a copy of the column. I am sure you will find nothing objectionable in the two short paragraphs about you. As you said, you have already heard from Wilmington girls who saw your name in the column and wanted to write to you.

And, John, it was not I who blew the whistle on your whereabouts. It was your mother.

John responded, as any gentleman would.

"What can I say? I received a copy of your column yesterday and read the answer to my question. You see, one of the girls who wrote said that 'part of your letter was in the paper.' This, of course, is what upset me. I had no idea it was my mother who sent in the information. I see by the article that there was nothing objectionable about it. I hope that you will accept my apology and not get the wrong idea of what I meant in that letter. I really am grateful for your running my name because I, like all the others GIs in Nam, know just how important mail is. And because of you I have received lots of it. Thanks again and I wish you the best of luck with your column."
Army Spc. John E. Rubincan, Oct. 29

John's letters actually sparked a special correspondence between him and the Mailbag. His continuing observations and insights throughout his tour added much to the column.

HUMOR CONTINUED TO PLAY AN IMPORTANT ROLE IN KEEPING A SENSE OF NORMALCY DURING TRYING TIMES.
Marine Earl E. Hopkins waxed poetic in February with "Dedicated to the Green Beret." He sent the six-verse poem to the Mailbag to humor Marine Lance Cpls. R.W. "Bobby" Green, W.R. "Bill" Moffa and T.R. Christopher, whom he tagged the "Devil Dogs."

We're the men, U.S. Marines
Dirty, rough and fighting mean,
From the states we came this way
Couldn't care less about the Green Beret.

We stalked the paddies both night and day
Don't need no chutes or a Green Beret,
We have no wings upon our chest
Fighting Marines, our country's best.

With steel pots upon our heads
Fighting Cong to make men free
100 men overrun today
We saved them all, Green Beret.

I saw Marines who gave their lives
So Green Berets could return to their wives
If I die in this far land
I hope it will be for a better man.

While they jump and sing their songs
We search the fields and kill the Cong
We're the men who fight each day
Since '65 it's been that way.

Back at home a young wife waits
Her brave Marine has met his fate
He has died so others could live
For his land that's what he'll give.

A soldier described his job and kept news from Vietnam light.

"**Well, hello once again from Mr. Impossible.** Would you believe a war is going on, someone ran off with my clean clothes and the ones I have on stand up in the morning without me. It's very hot and dusty and the shower went dry. I asked the 1st sergeant for a pass and he gave me KP today, guard tomorrow and CQ the following day. Oh well, this wouldn't be too bad but as I ate chow today, two ants walked off with my tray – and you asked me if I'm going to extend. Well, this is a big question mark right now. I guess if those two ants bring my chow back again, I might just do it.

Well enough for the joke. We have just moved my squad up to Lou's Castle. It is the main fire support base for the 11th Cavalry's operations. My main job now is sweeping a road three miles long every morning for mines. They moved us up here after one of the tanks blew up. All I can say is the Vietcong must know that Mr. I. and the Impossibles are here now, because the road is clear.

We are now in the Tet season and our area is fairly quiet. At the end of our sweep each day, there are thirty to forty little kids waiting for us. We always give them candy and soap and they are so happy. I believe if a mine was ever planted, one of the kids would let us know before we hit it. You'll be surprised what a candy bar can do."
Army Sgt. William H. Chance, March 6 Mailbag

An American-built swing set at an orphanage near Chu Lai provided hours of play-time for this youngster likely wearing a dress donated by Americans. In October, Army Sgt. James M. Carney sent an open letter (opposite) to the Mailbag.

C

HEADQUARTERS
MILITARY ASSISTANCE
COMMAND VIETNAM

BE IT KNOWN AMONG MEN, WOMEN, CHILDREN AND ANIMALS OF A CIVILIZED
OR UNCIVILIZED NATURE, THAT ON OR ABOUT THE 13TH DAY OF
OCTOBER IN THE YEAR OF OUR LORD 1969, THERE WILL BE
RELEASED BACK INTO CIVILIZATION A SUNBAKED, MUDCAKED, WATERLOGGED
AND SLIGHTLY UNSTABLE INDIVIDUAL KNOWN AMONG HIS FRIENDS, ALLIES,
LOVED ONES AND ENEMIES AS JAMES M. CARNEY ALIAS, ME

THIS POOR UNFORTUNATE SOUL WHO NOT LONG AGO WAS A NORMAL,
HEALTHY, AND OUTSTANDING MEMBER OF SOCIETY IS ABOUT TO BID FAREWELL
TO THE PLEASANT, SERENE LITTLE STRAW HOUSES, OPEN SEWER DITCHES AND
SIDEWALK COMMODES OF VIETNAM.
THE KNOWLEDGE THAT HE MUST LEAVE THE "BEAUTY" HAS CAUSED MUCH
MENTAL ANGUISH.
HE IS KNOWN TO HAVE CONSUMED VAST AMOUNTS OF ALCOHOLIC BEVERAGES
WHEREAS, HE WILL REMAIN IN A STATE OF DRUNKEN STUPOR FOR AN INDEFINITE
PERIOD OF TIME. THIS INDICATES THAT HE HAS ADJUSTED TO THE PATTERN OF
LIFE WHICH CONTROLS THIS PARIDISE OF SOUTHEAST ASIA.
TAKE SPECIAL CARE IN READING THE FOLLOWING ADVICE AND HEED THESE
WARNINGS. " YOU HAVE BEEN WARNED."
A. PLACE YOUR WOMEN, CHILDREN, ALL DOMESTIC AND IF POSSIBLE
NON-DOMESTIC ANIMALS IN A SECLUDED STORM OR BOMB SHELTER.
B. HIDE ALL ALCOHOLIC BEVERAGES AND/OR LIQUORS, THIS INCLUDES;
    1. MOUTHWASHES
    2. AFTER SHAVE LOTIONS
    3. RUBBING ALCOHOLS (DENATURED OR OTHERWISE)
    4. ANTISEPTICS
    5. ANYTHING WITH THE FAINTEST TRACE OF ALCOHOL

AFTER A REASONABLE PERIOD OF TIME (AT LEAST SIX MONTHS) HE
CAN SLOWLY BE EXPOSED TO THE ABOVE MENTIONED ITEMS, BUT ONLY
UNDER STRICT SUPERVISION AND CONTROL.

C. HE HAS SURVIVED THE WORST THE WORLD HAS TO OFFER: RAIN,
HEAT, SAND, RAIN, INSECTS, MUD, HEAT, MORTAR ATTACKS, RAIN, RATS, WIND,
FILTH, RAINY MUD, RAINY RAIN, MUDDY HOT RAIN, BUT WORST OF ALL, THIS
POOR SOUL HAS SURVIVED THE VIETNAMESE PEOPLE AND THEIR DRIVING HABITS.

D. PAY NO ATTENTION WHEN HE STIRS SOY SAUCE IN HIS SOUP AND
POTATOES, OR MIXES RAW SNAILS WITH HIS RICE (HE HAS BEEN CONDITIONED
TO DO THIS IN HOPES OF IMPROVING THE TASTE). DO NOT BE TOO HARSH
WHEN HE PREFERS HIS CHOPSTICKS AND FINGERS TO KNIVES AND FORKS, OR
SLOPS FOOD ALL OVER THE TABLE AND FLOOR.
ALSO UNDERSTAND THAT HE STILL DOESN'T KNOW THAT A WASTE BASKET HAS
BEEN INVENTED.

E. DO NOT BE EMBARASSED OR RUN AWAY IF HE DECIDES TO URINATE
ON THE STREET WHILE DOWNTOWN OR SPENDS AN HOUR ARGUEING PRICES WITH
THE MERCHANTS, HOPING TO SAVE A PENNY OR TWO. HE WILL GET OVER
THIS IN TWENTY YEARS OR SO.

THROUGHOUT THE YEAR, SOLDIERS FORWARDED THEIR GRIPES. One, about food conditions, seemed, finally, to resolve itself. Army Spc. Michael E. Brelick previously dished on food quality. "They say that 'the way to a man's heart is through his stomach.' Nothing could be more valid when it applies to a soldier, especially this one in his current situation." He went on to say the food was practically inedible and the water was often full of dirt. In his follow-up letter, Mike wrote the chow had improved.

"**Reference my last letter to you that appeared in your column in the 26 Dec. [1968] edition of** *The Morning News.* Relief from agonizing stomach aches, distressing heartburn and, yes, even hunger has arrived ... in the form of a new mess sergeant.

The caliber of 'inspiration' that he has instilled in his crew of cooks is the sort of 'blessing' many of us have been anticipating for some length of time. It was an impossible feat for the food to become worse. At any rate, with the recently improved food conditions, it appears the long-awaited days of hefty artillery men are here again."
Army Spc. Michael E. Brelick, Jan. 19

One soldier who had previously vented about draft dodgers and the Paris peace talks added more annoyances in this letter. His gripes mainly addressed ongoing issues at home.

"**Being that I'm stationed here in Saigon, I don't have too many gripes except for the traffic situation.** I work at Long Lines Det. New MACV. I've really got it made as far as working conditions go.

As far as for my gripes about what's happening back in the states, I've got a ... few.

Poverty – Over here, people live in cardboard houses or just sleep on the streets. They don't demonstrate and make fools out of themselves.

Police Brutality – People always say that police are too rough in putting down riots. But, according to certain individuals, it's just fine if someone throws bricks, rocks, etc. at police. I think that the police are doing what they do in self-defense when they strike a person. They've got a job to do and they do it."
Army Spc. Paul J. Walker III, Feb. 24

Others gripes ran the gamut.

"**Our only complaint is that we get a little tired of hearing about how hard our 'Office Pogue' statesmen [marine office clerks] have it in the rear.** If they wanted to see the real Vietnam, and the real reasons for being here, all they'd have to do is spend thirteen months living from a pack in the hills and paddies of this torn country. We're not complaining because we do live in the bush, we just wanted to put a word in for the 'grunts' in Vietnam. Grunts are the real Marine Corps and grunts are the real Vietnam!"
Marine Lance Cpls. R.W. "Bobby" Green, W.R. "Bill" Moffa and T.R. Christopher, Feb. 24 Mailbag

"**I'm stationed outside of Can Tho and can't wait to get out of this overgrown swamp.** This place must have a monopoly on mud."
Army Spc. Robert Mahan near Can Tho, Oct. 9

"**We are now into the monsoon season and I just can't believe the amount of rain that can fall over here at one time.** We have had rain for over two weeks now (and I do mean rain) with only occasional let-ups."
Army Spc. Mark D. Castelow, Oct. 12

A soldier at the 578th Light Maintenance Company in Phu Bai listed a slew of gripes when he wrote the Mailbag. He vetted a disturbing sequence of events in his letter.

"**I'm writing now because I am bitter.** However, my feelings do not affect the facts which I will relate….

My name is Eric Budin. I don't use a military title, that is their idea, not mine. I'm in the 578th Light Maintenance Company located in Phu Bai. The company area has never taken a mortar round and the whole base has been hit about three times since I've been here. I've been here since December. The rockets landed about three miles away and if somebody had not awakened me, I would have slept through every attack. What I'd like to do is give you a glimpse of the war that I see. Try humming the theme song from 'The Green Beret' while you read. I had been in the company about three days when I witnessed the first event, which was the beginning of a consistent pattern. I was standing outside of my hooch at about eleven o'clock in the evening talking to a few guys, when I witnessed the company commander, obviously intoxicated, relieving himself right behind the mess hall. In fact, he was standing next to a storage bin in which vegetables are stored. He has been seen twice doing this. As I was a security guard at the compound gate for six weeks, I can honestly say that he is intoxicated at least half of the evenings as I witnessed his return almost every night from a not too distant club.

I've seen times when my first sergeant couldn't walk a straight line. He has been medevaced three times in five months for alcohol poisoning. The sergeant that took his place in his absence has been told to stop drinking by the doctors as his liver is almost gone. I've seen other NCOs so drunk during an alert that they had to be carried back to the hooch afterwards. These are my leaders. They are responsible for the welfare of one hundred and fifty men in this company. This is nothing unusual. There are thousands of career men in the service who are here because they couldn't hold a responsible job outside of the service. We have been awakened at eleven-thirty for shakedown inspection. For awhile, we had to put up with a ten-thirty bed check with all the rest of the harassment. That was too much.

We staged an organized protest exactly at bed-check time and put an end to that. Fortunately, no one was prosecuted. They tried and convicted several GIs in San Francisco for doing the exact same thing. These things might seem small to the observer, but their effect on morale is magnified many times when they take place in a country where death is a constant reality and the people that it is all for have a concealed (but not always) contempt for GIs.

Last night someone in this company threw a tear gas grenade into the NCO's hooch, the thoughtlessness of this action is not debatable, however, what followed was equally thoughtless. We were called to a full uniform formation at two o'clock in the morning. We spent a full fifteen minutes dressing and covering to perfection in semi-darkness. We were then addressed by our CO, who took the situation well into hand. He ordered us to return to our hooches and clean every bit of our ammunition for immediate turn in, to be followed by an inspection…. I'm really not as bitter as I seem. Actually, I'm learning much about myself and people over here. I hope to learn much more. But I can't thank anyone for the opportunity."
Eric M. Budin in Phu Bai, June 6

Navy Hospital Corpsman Larry D. Gum shared his ration card and immunization certificate, his dress insignia and an enemy soldier's necklace with Buddha pendant.

E82 – 2314

E91 3"

155-07

Another serviceman vented in letters written two weeks apart but sent them to the Mailbag in the same envelope.

"My division officer was something else too as was my chief petty officer. My division officer recommended me for NESEP (college officer training program). This man was just too much. A slob would credit him too well. He wanted his men shined and brassed up at all times while he slouched around. I couldn't stomach some of his policies and my fat mouth caused my recommendation to be pulled…. The same was true of our chief petty officer. There were cases of literal assault by him against some of our men. This was needless and straight to his face I told him this was unnecessary and not a very good way to handle men. From my first evaluation to the second one was unbelievable change in words….

This chief took official business trips (15-20 days) to the Philippines. On one of these official business trips, he married one of the local girls (of doubtable character) in the Philippines. At the time of my discharge from the armory, I was called a disgrace to the Navy but surely a better chief could be found than this one who is supposed to be a credit to the Navy….

On one night of a rocket attack, we had a boat not more than 300 yards from the enemy rocket launch site. Swish, the rockets get launched. Our patrol calls in and gets clearance from the Marines in the general vicinity to open fire on the rocket launch site. Now dig:

Our officer calls the boat and tells them not to fire. They can't believe their ears. Don't fire! So they don't fire. Then four days later, this same officer issues a written order on the order of this: In the future if rocket launch sites are sighted notify this command and open fire!...

This division could go out of business. A sentry with any type of throwing arm could handle our job of dropping an occasional grenade. Our boats have twin .50-caliber machine guns. What do these guns do? Sit and rust. We now test fire them once a week (good morale booster). Since the rocket attack, I've changed. I now anxiously wait August – CONUS [continental United States] – Discharge – OUT! Still, whenever I do something I do it with pride as this is how I was brought up.

Navy Petty Officer 3rd Class Robert C. Jennings acquired these patches (opposite) during his tour on the USS *Dewey* (above), a Farragut-class guided missile destroyer.

The news in *Time* [magazine] really depressed me for awhile. The Pueblo incident. The U.S. was wary of going in after the Pueblo because of the incident it might cause, possibly a national crisis, another conflict (war)! What in God's good name could cause a national crisis than some nation coming onto the high seas and taking over a U.S. vessel? What more aggression, causing a national incident, could the U.S. ask for? Talk about getting walked all over! And talk about reasons for resuming the bombing, the rocket and mortar attacks we caught here in the Da Nang area should be reason enough….

As you can see I am a very fired up young man. I stand up for what I like and I say what bothers me and what I don't like.

The news from the U.S. is so depressing you'd be surprised at the number of men looking for out-of-country employment. I guess they feel Australia, nationalist China, Japan or the Philippines offer more. I am coming home because I love my country and I love my fiancée and I want to help. I am going out to Arizona to school and into the police department there….

One day our armory officer noticed we were filling sand bags too full so he wanted us to take one (1) shovelful out of the already filled and tied sandbags, not pour it out, but shovel it out, shovelful by shovelful – I swear!..."
Navy Petty Officer 2nd Class Terry Reiswig, April 9

"I wrote the enclosed document [the April 9 letter] almost two weeks ago and since then a few more things have happened. Last night another rocket attack at 7:45 p.m. Seven days ago was the last one around midnight. The war and PEACE TALKS go on!

The chief I wrote about has finally been brought up on charges, ranging from theft to assault. I guess in time everybody gets his due. Somebody got fed up with his system and finally got enough on him to give him the ax. It'll take an act of Congress to demote him but he sure does deserve it and I'd like to see him leave here in whites (a reduced rate) for all the crap he pulled and thought he'd get away with.

Well, only about 110 more days in the Navy! I'll try to drop by your office if I can."
Navy Petty Officer 2nd Class Terry Reiswig, April 21

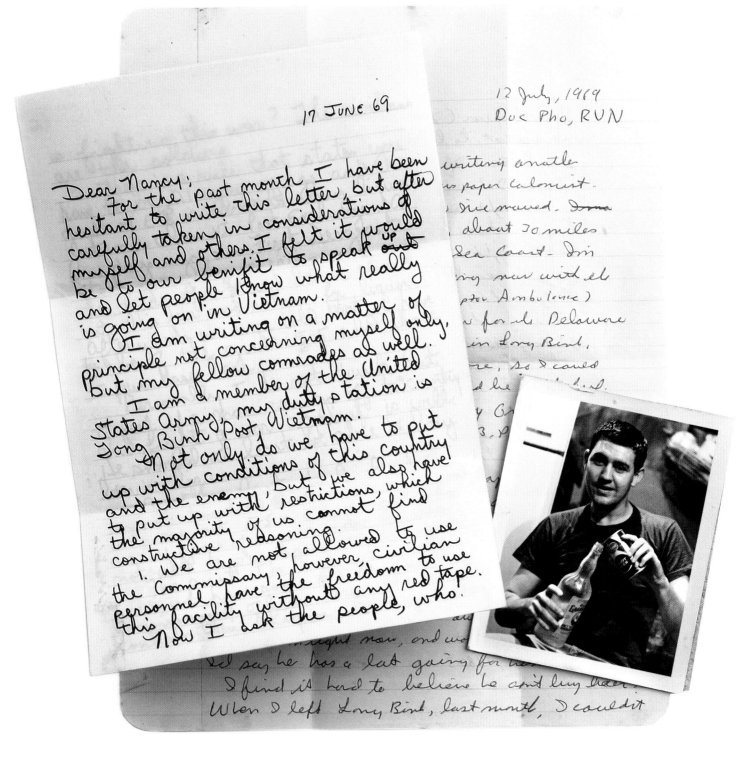

17 JUNE 69

Dear Nancy;
For the past month I have been hesitant to write this letter, but after carefully taken in considerations of myself and others. I felt it would be to our benifit to speak up out and let people know what really is going on in Vietnam.

I am writing on a matter of principle not concerning myself only, but my fellow comrades as well.

I am a member of the United States Army, my duty station is Long Binh Post, Vietnam.

Not only do we have to put up with conditions of this country and the enemy, but we also have to put up with restrictions, which the majority of us cannot find constructive reasoning.

1. We are not allowed to use the Commissary, however, civilian personnel have the freedom to use this facility without any red tape.

Now I ask the people, who.

12 July, 1969
Duc Pho, RVN

writing another
newspaper columist.
rice moved. Doma
about 30 miles
Sea Coast. I'm
ing now with el
ptor Ambulance)
for de Delaware
in Long Binh,
re, so I caued
d he
y Gr
3. P

sight now, and wo
I'd say he has a lot going for me
I find it hard to believe he ain't buy them.
When I left Long Binh, last month, I couldn't

A buddy of Army Spc. Donald B. Patton makes his point about liquor restrictions in the combat zone.

OCCASIONALLY, THE MAILBAG RECEIVED ONGOING CORRESPONDENCE FROM SOLDIERS TAKING ISSUE WITH EACH OTHER. Such was the case with two Wilmington servicemen, one stationed in Long Binh, the other in Chu Lai. The men sparred in several columns.

"**For the past month, I have been hesitant to write this letter but after carefully taking into consideration myself and others, I felt it would be to our benefit to speak up and let people know what really is going on in Vietnam.**

I am writing on a matter of principle not concerning myself only but my fellow comrades as well. I am a member of the United States Army, my duty station is Long Binh post, Vietnam.

Not only do we have to put up with conditions of this country and the enemy, but we also have to put up with restrictions that the majority of us cannot find constructive reasoning.

We are not allowed to use the commissary. However, civilian personnel have the freedom to use this facility without any red tape. Now I ask the people, who is fighting this war? The civilians or the soldiers.

There is a rule that states you have to be 21 years of age and a grade of E-5 or above to buy liquor at our Class VI post exchange. A few days ago, our first sergeant took every man's ration card, in the grade of E-4 and below, crossed out his beer and rations for liquor. Afterwards we were told that we have to be of the grade E-5 and above to purchase beer. Personally, I do not drink but I feel if a man can go off to a country and fight a war against his will, he should at least be able to buy beer or liquor.

Another fact to look at is several hundred soldiers (men) who are not E-5 or E-6, etc. but who are 21 years of age or over, are also not able to purchase beer or liquor. The point I'm trying to make here is we have some NCOs and commissioned officers here who cannot control their liquor, but yet they are permitted the privilege because of their rank.

I'll say this, take the E-4s and below and let the lifers fight the war and then they would understand how we feel about the restrictions we face everyday….

There is a lot of dirt being done in Vietnam that is not being published in the *Army Times* or any place else."
Army Spc. Donald B. Patton at Long Binh, June 17

Donald was countered a few weeks later in the Mailbag.

"**Long Binh post has an approximate population of 70,000.** The conditions of Vietnam are offset at Long Binh by air conditioning, bars and clubs, running water, flush toilets, and the large PXs, almost always full.

Compared to the fellows in the field (like I am right now, and was at Lai Khe), I'd say he has a lot going for him. I find it hard to believe he can't buy beer.

When I left Long Binh last month, I couldn't buy liquor. I'm a specialist fifth class, but it was no sweat to buy beer. Even a private can buy beer.

If what Spc. 4 Patton says is true, I'd suggest he write to Mendel Rivers [chairman of the House Armed Services Committee].

I might add that this rule about liquor does have some justification. But I might also add, just because he can't buy it, doesn't mean he can't drink it.

One of my former officers lent me his ration card, or else he'd buy a drink for me. Also the numerous EM [Enlisted Men] clubs offer mixed drinks. I don't think Spc. 4 Patton was representing the full picture. But I agree with his basic premise: things aren't fair.

But it's a hardship tour (especially for the guys in Long Binh taking it easy) and if you can't take it for a lousy year, then you aren't made of much on the inside.

I've been here 20 months, and only 176 days until I'm out. I've flown all four corps areas of Vietnam and have found that for every rule, there is a way around it."
Army Spc. Larry R. Kipp in Chu Lai, July 1

Donald volleyed back a few weeks later:

"**First, I'd just like to say I've checked into the approximate population of Long Binh post and found it not to be the 70,000 Spc. 5 Kipp referred to, but a lesser amount of 35,000….**

The information printed in your column written by Spc. 5 Kipp is undoubtedly false when pertaining to the unit I'm presently assigned to.

Spc. 5 Kipp stated Long Binh post was offset by the following conditions: bars, clubs, running water, flush toilets , air conditioning, and large PXs, almost always full….

For instance, we don't have running water (I shave in a basin each morning, not a sink); we don't have flush toilets, and if you think PXs are large, maybe you've been over here too long.

Every PX I've been in outside of Long Binh is double the size of our biggest one, such as PXs in Saigon, Bien Hoa Air Base and the Cholon area. But none of these areas is supposed to be as big as Long Binh….

I don't know what kind of inside track you have with officers, but our officers don't buy liquor for enlisted men. And as for your former officer who lent you his ration card, call yourself lucky because a specialist fifth class doesn't usually walk into a PX and purchase liquor with an officer's ration card and spec. 5 stripes and get away with it.

I readily suggest you spend some more time at Long Binh, but the next time how about opening your eyes and looking before you try to criticize facts presented by someone who knows.

As for the guys in Long Binh taking it easy, I can only say you're the type of specialists we need no more of in this Army.

It's people like Mr. Kipp that make people like me get out of the Army as quick as possible. I don't need Brownie points and I will always call the shots the way I see them.

I'm down to 52 days and things are still as before. I only hope they stay that way: Quiet."
Army Spc. Donald B. Patton, August 25 Mailbag

CRITICISM OF "LIFERS," CAREER MILITARY PERSONNEL, DOMINATED MUCH OF OUR CORRESPONDENCE. Writing to the Mailbag gave GIs an opportunity to vent. "As for this base camp, we have to pull guard for the lifers and the 1st Sgt. has a guard for himself, believe it or not," wrote one. "We have guard mount at seven o'clock. They tell us we are not allowed to drink anything." He continued:

"**We are not allowed to smoke and we cannot have any radios or tape recorders and, last but not least, we cannot sit down.** You might think I'm crazy but this is right inside of the base camp....

I guess you can see why we hate the Army. We have too many bosses. Ask any GI who has been in a unit like mine. Last night we had a shakedown inspection, but we don't mind it so much now because all of us are under 15 days.

The new guys who are just coming into this unit have a real big surprise in store for them, if you know what I mean."
Army Spc. Bob "Weasel" Arnold, May 18

"Short timers" and "lifers" often traded barbs in the Mailbag, as was the case between Army Spc. Ronnie Wright, who worked in the mortuary at Tan Son Nhut Air Base, and Army Sgt. Maj. Charles W. Ballard.

"**As for the social aspect of my tour here, it's been pretty nice.** I don't get any harassment from the lifers, for I've somewhat acquired the art of putting them right in their place.

I don't know where the lifers ever got the idea that a couple extra stripes put them way up on a pedestal somewhere above fellow GIs and myself.

One dedicated military-minded man had the nerve to jump in my face boldly and ask me if I had a problem because I talk about the military and the lifers so coldly. Bluntly, I told the lifer that 'as long as he stayed over here and as long as I stayed over here, that he was my problem while he's living and he also could become my problem if he should die over here.' Just that little statement shocked him so much he just turned and walked away.

Since I've been in the Army, I've found that some of these high-ranking military men have all the physical features of a man but the mental features of a child; these are the ones I consider lifers.

In this Army, I don't feel you really have got to be qualified for most of the jobs. What you have got to do is stay in for 20 or 30 years and rank and medals will naturally come to you....

I strike a hard blow at this Army system and the lifers in general, for I want out of this Army, and in 37 days this should come about for I'll be getting out of Vietnam and out of the Army.

I'd also like to close by saying I'm not all for the draft evaders but I feel I came into the Army unwillingly to be led by the unqualified, to do the necessary, for the ungrateful (the lifers)."
Army Spc. Ronnie Wright at Tan Son Nhut Air Base, July 25

Army Spc. Ronnie Wright (on left) relaxes with Army Spc. Renee Mendez at Tan Son Nhut Air Base where Ronn worked in the mortuary. In his letter (opposite) to the Mailbag, he encouraged families of fallen troops to "dig deeper into the actual cause of some of these deaths." He hinted some men may have lost their lives "through some freakish accident caused by [their] country's misjudged military tactics."

"**One of the men showed me your column in the 7 August 1969 edition of** *The Morning News* **and I was concerned that some mention was not made for the other side of the coin.**
Every walk of life, be it the military service, civilian industry, PTAs or even the United Nations, will have people that may not be, or to 'experts' seem unqualified to be in that position. It is true that in the service today stripes/commissions are easier to come by and has resulted in personnel 'not fully qualified' being promoted. However, this is true in fast-growing civilian industry as well.

The writer sounds typical of the smug, self-centered unadjustables that are above reproach, experts in everything, never err and yet are quick to criticize all others. A good long look in a mirror may prove this to be in error.

Many of the young/old men over here have learned the hard way and no teacher is greater than experience. A military-minded man I may be, but one who has served for 24 years, raised a family and traveled the world so that the youth of today can say and do what this writer has done, which is to betray to the public his immaturity and unreasonable blindness.

We the 'unqualified' are fighting and dying here so we may never have to fight within our own shores. The esprit de corps of the men here in Vietnam is only a small part of the pride that this 'lifer' has when I put the uniform on. I am proud to have had the opportunity to serve my country. Yes, even your writer who found us 'unqualified and ungrateful.'"
Army Sgt. Maj. Charles W. Ballard, Aug. 20

"I strike a hard blow at this Army system and the lifers in general, for I want out of this Army, and in 37 days this should come about for I'll be getting out of Vietnam and out of the Army." Army Spc. Ronnie Wright

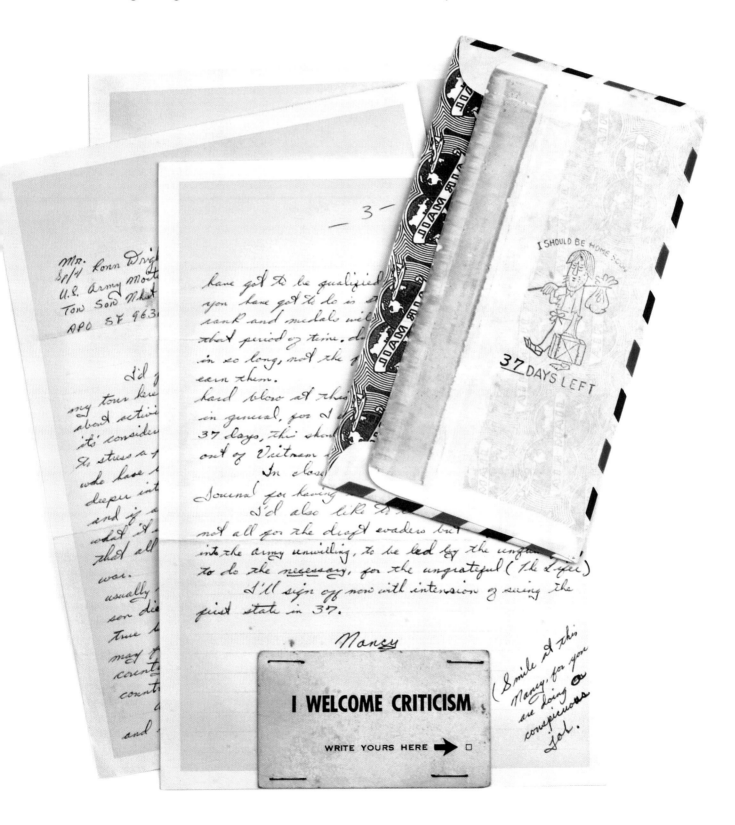

"MY BEST WISHES TO ALL DELAWAREANS STILL SERVING IN VIETNAM. 10 DAYS LEFT," ARMY CAPT. BOB RALSTON WROTE IN HIS LAST LETTER TO THE MAILBAG IN MAY. With the Nixon administration's ongoing troop withdrawals, the Mailbag regularly received lots of "last" letters from Vietnam. "I've just come in out of the field for out-processing," wrote Army Spc. Mike Rowan from Chu Lai in November. "See you people soon." Air Force Airman 1st Class Edward J. VanSant responded to that a month later when he was getting short. "I was glad to hear that my buddy Mike Rowan made it home for Thanksgiving. I was hoping to make it for the coming holidays but I should be home in 26 days and that's not too long."

Whether they were getting "short" or just leaving Vietnam, many servicemen still took time to write the column.

"As for my ship, we are headed home. We left the gun line at six o'clock Tuesday morning and arrived in Subic Bay, Philippines, Wednesday morning to offload ammo. Now we are en route to Yokosuka, Japan, for a few days, then home.

They say the [USS] *New Jersey* is doing a lot for the war effort, but I am sure looking forward to going home for awhile."
Navy Petty Officer 3rd Class Edward F. Blest aboard the USS New Jersey,
April 3

Army Spc. Mike Rowan, based at Landing Zone Bayonet near Chu Lai, was exuberant when his tour ended. "I've just come in out of the field for out- processing," he wrote the Mailbag on Nov. 17. "See you people soon."

"This will be the last time I'll be writing to you from the Nam. I only have about 3 weeks to go over here and in the Army. It sure will be good to get back to Wilmington again. I hope I don't get lost. With the new Interstate 95 almost finished, I won't know where I am…. It's been a real interesting and worthwhile tour over here for me. The only thing I didn't like was that since Sept. 1967 I never met another GI from Delaware."
Army Spc. Richard Glazier, June 8

Others let us know their departure dates were fast approaching and weren't too sad when they had to cancel their subscription to *The Morning News.*

"Upon receiving this letter, would you please cancel my subscription to *The Morning News.* I have been in country 19 months and I am going home May 20."
Navy Petty Officer 3rd Class Jim Bourbonnais, May 16

"My tour over here is about to come to an end. Therefore, would you please stop my subscription upon receipt of this letter. Our mailroom is right over my office and they are constantly flooded with newspapers for people who have already left. Since the papers can't be forwarded, they are left with the job of disposing of them. I hope to spare them the task of burning my papers."
Army Spc. Thomas H. Hutt, May 31

One marine who was "short" sent news of other Delawareans.

"I guess most of the guys over here would call me a short timer. I have 18 days left. Really it is pretty short but not as short as I would like. I'll be home the beginning of July if everything goes well.

Cpl. Moffa is here at An Hoa still and is doing fine. Cpl. Christopher is doing fine also. He is now at Camp S.D. Butler in Okinawa. I got a letter from him yesterday. Also, my two good friends, also First Staters, should be home right after me, Cpl. Alpaugh and Lcpl. Brainard. Cpl. Moffa and I ran into Pfc. Deptula about a week ago, so he is doing real well. I also ran into Pfc. Loughrey the end of April in Da Nang on my way to Sydney R&R. I got a letter from him and he is also doing fine.

As you can well see, Nancy, there are a lot of First Staters over here. You may not believe it, but all the men I mentioned, we ran around together before we came in. Can't wait till all of us are home again.

I'll see good 'ol Delaware in a few weeks."
Marine Lance Cpl. R.W. "Bobby" Green, June 15

One serviceman who was extending his tour took time to send news of his friends that were headed home.

"It's with sadness that I say Mr. Impossible and the Impossibles are breaking up. As I write this letter, two of the Impossibles are boarding a Boeing 707 and heading home after serving a real fine tour over here. In twenty-one days, we lose another one.

Myself, I may go into a new job. I may become the 919th Engineers' reconnaissance sergeant. This is up in the air right now. If I do take this job, I will do it upon my return from the states. I plan on taking a thirty-day leave and then returning for another tour of duty here."
Army Sgt. William H. Chance, May 15 Mailbag

Most servicemen counted days, hours, even minutes, until their DEROS (Date of Estimated Return Overseas). "Life is not too bad here but, of course, it can't compare to life in the world. I count every single day until I'll be able to go home," wrote Army Spc. Eugene Barbato on May 3. Although we received a lot of "last" letters, some wrote to say they were not coming home – yet.

"Just a few lines to say hello to all the Delawareans. Am looking forward to returning within the next 170 days. I've been in Vietnam some 43 months and I can really say at this time that I miss Delaware. By the way, if anyone cares to shorten my time over here mentally, ask them to drop me a letter."
Army Staff Sgt. Richard Williams Jr., March 12

"I get to come home in September. I have been over here for six full months now. I have five more months and days left."
Army Spc. Richard W. Hudson in Phan Thiet to friend Walton Johnson, April 10 Mailbag

"I've had quite a few things happen to me since I wrote you last. The most important is that I'll be coming home pretty soon for a 30-day leave. I received this leave for re-enlisting for another year."
Army Pfc. Larry Smith, July 8

THE SHORT TIMER

In honored old age, dignified manhood, and innocent boyhood, we find a delightful creature know to all of us as a Short Timer.

Short Timers come in all sizes and weights, in jeeps and three-quarters, all are dedicated, enslaved, and bondaged to the same urge: To enjoy every minute of every hour of every day and night in the nearest club, dayroom, or bunk, and to protest if there is any unwanted interference from the CO, First Sergeant, or MP's.

Short Timers can be found everywhere, on top of, under, climbing, sitting on, standing by, preparing to, shivering in, dripping with, hiding from, breathing down, two steps ahead of, getting ready for, running after, bragging about, and mostly smelling like who knows what. Mothers love them, Mama-Sans watch out for them, and the MP's prey upon them.

A Short Timer is a composite: He has the appetite of a ditch digger, the digestion of a pot bellied stove, the curiosity of a vacationer, the imagination of a PIO reporter, the irresponsibility of a recruit, and all the glamor of faded and torn fatigues.

No others can be so late to rise, so ignorant of formations, so early to meals, or so able to skip details. No body gets so much fun out of marking calendars, counting days, gaping at replacements, razzing the mess sergeant, or hollering the most popular word within the Republic...SHORT!! Nobody else can cram into one pocket two beer can openers, a dog-eared Vietnamese-English dictionary, an outdated roll of film, a rusty and corroded P-38, 20¢ in MPC, 500 piasters, a picture of his girl, one bent dog tag, a full size shorttimers calendar with days marked out, and his most prized and valued possession, a copy of his DEROS or better yet, ETS orders.

A Short Timer is a magical creature. You can restrict him to the company area but his mind and heart are dancing on that big silver dustoff. He may be court-martialled, given several Article 13's, placed on extra duty, fined, and verbally reprimanded, but to no avail. He is still the only one who brightens the thoughts of his loved ones when he gets to San Francisco, places a collect Long Distance call, and shouts, "Hey, guess who's home".

Those with minimal time remaining were called "short timers." Although he didn't say how much time he had left, Army Spc. Chris "Wandering Gypsy" Walton (on right) humored us with a treatise on the subject which appeared in the April 7 Mailbag.

SERVICEMEN ON TOUR IN VIETNAM FREQUENTLY USED THE MAILBAG TO CORRESPOND WITH LOVED ONES. Family matters and friendships were frequently in their thoughts. One serviceman had this request:

"I've read your letters in *The Morning News* and thought maybe you could tell my girlfriend that I'm fine and in good shape. And it will help my family to know also. I'd sure appreciate it. My girlfriend's name is Barbara and she'll know it's me because there's not many fellows from Delaware in the Seabees of the U.S. Navy over here."
Navy Petty Officer 3rd Class Robert W. Conley, March 14

After we published his letter, he sent a follow-up three weeks later.

"I just received a letter from my girlfriend and she was really happy that I wrote to you and told you everyone was fine. I want to thank you…. I'm leaving Da Nang soon to join the rest of Fox Company up at Vinh Dia near the DMZ…. Well, I don't want to say too much, I know other fellows have some news for home also. But if you could put it in the paper, tell everyone I'm fine and be sure and tell Barb I'm fine and getting a nice tan over here."
Navy Petty Officer 3rd Class Robert W. Conley, April 5

The Mailbag published announcements of other kinds as well. Whether it was a birth announcement or birthday, engagement or anniversary, many special occasions were highlighted in the column.

On this front, the Mailbag in 1969 welcomed five babies born stateside to proud papas serving in the combat zone. Elissa Seiple, wife of Marine Sgt. Stewart L. Seiple of Wilmington, sent a note asking that he be congratulated on two counts: his Jan. 9 birthday and the Dec. 30, 1968 birth of their first child, Kristin Michelle. Elissa said her husband had already served 13 months in Vietnam and was on a Caribbean cruise (military, of course) and was due home in about two months. Elissa also alluded to a full plate at home with her serviceman absent. "They always say," she wrote, "if the Marine Corps had wanted the men to have wives, they would have issued them."

Army Pfc. Peter J. McCorkle in Tien Phoc was so succinct with his child's birth announcement, he forgot to mention whether he had fathered a daughter or son, the date of birth and his newborn's name. He wrote in May, "I wish you could pass on through your column also how proud I am of my newly-born child."

Also in May, Army Spc. Darwin R. Wall, a military policeman, became a father, four days after his 23rd birthday. He told us his son Stephen Scott weighed 9 pounds, 1 ounce, and was a firstborn child.

To his baby son Francis P. Cahill Jr., nicknamed "Little Pat," whom he had not yet seen, this proud father penned a touching letter his wife Sherry shared with the Mailbag.

"Dear Son, while I sit over here you're probably saying, 'Mother, who's my daddy?' Well, don't worry son, I am over here in Vietnam fighting in a war because this country is too small to defend itself so your Uncle Sam sent me here.

I am sorry, son, but soon I'll be home with you and never will leave you or your mother again as long as I live. You tell your mother how much I love her and that these tears in my eyes aren't because I'm happy. I'd give my life just to see you and your mother just for five minutes.

This is an ugly place I'm at now and now that I am here I know I'll never let you see war or death as long as I live. Son, you tell your mother I said to take good care of you and tell her I said that she better take a piece of paper and pencil and write whatever you want to say to me. Love always, Daddy"
Pfc. Francis P. Cahill, Oct. 20 Mailbag

One serviceman waited for a special occasion to sing praises to his wife and new mother.

"I am writing to you concerning my wife Lynn. She gave birth to our first child on May 8, a beautiful little girl named Sharlyn. Needless to say, I was here in Vietnam at the time.

The Morning News and News-Journal gave fine recognition to the event and I am very thankful. But I would like to ask you a big favor: If at all possible, do you suppose you could write a little something about my wife in your column?

She's the greatest woman alive. I know it and I want everyone to know it. I will be home just in time for our daughter's first birthday, so until then, my wife will be both mother and father to her. She understands why I have to be here and she waits patiently for the day we will be together again.

Her birthday is tomorrow [July 29], so if at all possible, please wish her a very happy birthday for me and tell her I am very proud of her and send her all my love."
Pfc. Gregory W. Drummond, July 28 Mailbag

Marine Cpl. John M. Nock summed up what familial support meant to him in his June letter. He wrote, "One of the bad things about this place is the thought that everyone [at] home has forgotten where you are and what you are doing. I am very fortunate myself because I have a wonderful family that never forgot."

Air Force Staff Sgt. Robert E. May (on right) displays his Delaware flag which was flown on more than 20 missions over North Vietnam.

SERVICEMEN APPRECIATED ALL OF THEIR HOMESTATE FREEBIES. Delawareans continued to give thanks for their monthly bennie boxes from the nonprofit organization SOS Vietnam, their complimentary subscriptions to *The Morning News* and their free state flags and bumper stickers.

According to its August newsletter, SOS Vietnam, the nonprofit Interdenominational Center at Red Lion Methodist Church in Bear, had sent 6,156 5-pound boxes to Delaware servicemen in Vietnam since its first mailing in February 1968. Most letters the Mailbag received included thanks to SOS, such as when Army Spc. Terry W. Arnold wrote in February. "The one thing I forgot to mention is please print a few appreciating words to inform the public what an outstanding job the people of SOS Vietnam have done." Others wrote their appreciation for the organization as well.

"**I would like to thank the SOS Vietnam organization.** Those people can't get enough thanks for the tremendous job they [do]. I wish more people cared about the men over here like they do."
Army Spc. Richard Glazier, June 8

"**I wish to publicly thank the people involved in SOS Vietnam.** The work they're doing to help encourage Delaware servicemen in Vietnam. Their work is appreciated."
Army Pfc. Phillip R. Sheppard, June 26

"**Would you believe that the wonderful people of SOS Vietnam not only sent me a Christmas package which included a canned ham and fruit cake?** Those beautiful people wrapped each individual article in Christmas paper. Wow! Thank you all so much.

There are some other pretty wonderful and special people in Delaware. I'm speaking of Mrs. Fran Mangum and all the members of the Diamond State German Shepherd Dog Club. I have already thanked them in a recent letter but I'd like to thank them again through your column. They are really wonderful, thoughtful people."
Army Sgt. Robert S. Biss, Dec. 1

SOS Vietnam received national attention in 1969 when its founder, the Rev. Irwin R. Pusey, was tapped for a Valley Forge Freedom Foundation award. Pusey's all-volunteer organization earned a Pepsi Cola "People Are Great" salute and received a certificate of appreciation from the city of Da Nang in Vietnam that year.

When Army Spc. Robert Mahan wrote to the Mailbag in October, he had this to say about the organization. "Since I've been in Vietnam, I have received a monthly 'care package' from the Red Lion Methodist Church in Bear, Delaware. Their SOS Vietnam program 'saves' nearly 400 First Staters each month with food and other assorted surprises." He added, "I was very glad that they are finally getting the recognition they deserve from the Valley Forge Freedom Foundation and the Pepsi Cola 'People Are Great' salutes."

Servicemen also expressed appreciation for their complimentary subscriptions to *The Morning News*. "I have enjoyed receiving the Wilmington *Morning News* as I can keep up with events in Delaware," Air Force 1st Lt. Sam Jorgensen wrote in August. He added, "I delivered *The Morning News* when I was a boy in Bellefonte."

In one case, it was the column that brought two pen pals together. "Your article has brought me a new friend and correspondent which I am grateful for," wrote Navy Hospital Corpsman Larry D. Gum. "It really helps morale when a girl you don't even know read your name in the paper and cares enough to write. (Thank you, Linda)." Larry again thanked the newspaper in another letter.

"I now have five months before I return to Delaware and am thankful for *The Morning News* for the months already passed and am looking forward to the remaining months. Thank you for letting us express ourselves to thousands with one letter."
Navy Hospital Corpsman Larry D. Gum in Da Nang, April 21

Others sent praise and thanks.

"I've been receiving *The Morning News* for six months and it has really helped to know exactly what's going on in your own hometown…. It really helps the morale when you can look at the paper and tell the standings of your local teams, such as the Blue Bombers and W.H.S.!"
Army Spc. Donald B. Patton, April 12

"The only reason for this letter is to thank *The Morning News* for the paper I have received for the past year. Now that I have only 26 days left in 'Nam it gives me pleasure to cancel my subscription. I will be getting out of the Navy as soon as I get back to the states. I would like to thank all the people of The *Morning News* and SOS Vietnam for the OUTSTANDING job they are doing for the boys over here."
Navy Petty Officer 2nd Class Robert J. Manelski, July 7

Army Spc. Eugene "Gene" Barbato last wrote the column when he was short and had this to say: "All I can think of is going home soon. I've really enjoyed your columns in *The Morning News*. Thanks." His friend, who co-wrote the letter, added his thoughts.

"I've received *The Morning News* regularly since December and read your column diligently but never got up enough spirit to send off a thank you to you and to the News-Journal Company for the welcomed brown paper roll. So now I write and express my thanks and add a special one for your column.

It's really cool to read the paper and know that at least one four-inch column is aimed at me and the rest of the over-there First Staters. The paper loses all the impersonal edges and becomes a letter – your reply to ours – since I'm now in the club."
Army Sgt. Robert L. Geuting at Tam Ky, Nov. 20 Mailbag

For years, the Delaware State Development Office sent the official, full-color, silk-screened, 3-by-5-foot flag to all Delaware servicemen in Vietnam free of charge. Once the word was out on the popular perk, everyone wanted one.

"I'm from Wilmington and I also take a lot of ribbing about 'poor little Delaware.' The guys say that if you close your eyes upon entering Delaware, you'll be out of the state before you can open them. I wonder if you might be able to help me in obtaining a Delaware state flag…. I might be from a small state but everyone is sure going to know it."
Army Pfc. Phillip R. Sheppard at Camp Eagle near Hue, April 30

Army 1st Lt. James L. Deese had almost given up hope of receiving his state flag before it arrived. When it finally came, his excitement was obvious. "Today Christmas came a little late with my Delaware state flag," he wrote in January. "It's now hanging in my office over my desk adding cheer!"

Delaware servicemen were eager to proudly display their home-state flags – although on some occasions, that was easier said than done.

"I have a Delaware flag that my family sent to me but have no place to put it yet. I get a lot of ribbing about being from such a small place, but I'm mighty proud of it."
Navy Seaman Michael S. Solomon, May 24

"It is a little wet here with monsoon season in full bloom but something else has dampened my spirit more than the weather. On one of our not so often sunny days at this time of year, I proceeded to fly the U.S. flag with my Delaware state flag below it. I was told within an hour by my B.C. (battery commander) to take down my state flag because personnel of the 101st Airborne Division are not permitted to fly their state flag.

Now I appeal this question to the people of Delaware. Should I be able to fly the flag of Delaware or not?

I feel as an American citizen and as a citizen of the state of Delaware, who is proud of his country and of his state, I should have this right. Is it too much to ask for after coming halfway across the world to fight this war and not be allowed the simple patriotic privilege to fly your state flag? I also wish to thank you for sending this flag. It has been a big morale booster not only for me, but also the guys in my battery. Maybe someone ought to send a letter to the Department of the Army and ask for this privilege for the men in Vietnam as a Christmas present."
Army Spc. Peter J. McCorkle at Fire Base Roy, Dec. 23

In 1969, the Mailbag requested "Discover Delaware, the state that started a nation" bumper stickers as another freebie for our troops. In no time, the stickers were also a must-have item in Vietnam, as Army Spc. Larry Kipp related.

Writing in July, Larry had recently relocated from Long Binh to Chu Lai and had this request for the Mailbag. "I want to thank you for the Delaware stickers but, alas, they're all in Long Binh. If you could send some more so I could decorate Chu Lai, I would be grateful."

In the best tradition of sharing at Thanksgiving, Army Sgt. Robert S. Biss rallied support for a turkey-less dinner with all the trimmings for his detachment. A sampan provided transportation for many South Vietnamese on the country's abundant rivers and deltas.

December 1, 1969
Monday night.

Dear Nancy,

Thought I'd send some pic[tures]
the detachment's feast on Thanks[giving]
all started about a month ago
decided it would be a little [more]
[home] we made our own
[turk]ey. Certain guys [made]
[some]thing. For the salad we [made]
[pint]s of dressing ~~in four~~. Three
[we]re Italian ~~so~~ an antipasto
[a]ctually about enough for 50
[we were about] 16. Of course before
[we had] to have cocktail, so we had
[the m]ix sent. On our own even
[a] case of steak (120), about
[c]hicken, and four pounds

DESPITE THE WAR'S DAILY DRAIN EMOTIONALLY, VIETNAM IN 1969 AFFORDED SOME "GOOD MOMENTS," AS ARMY SPC. DAVID G. DALLER OF CLAYMONT CALLED THEM. Writing from Tay Ninh on March 9, David concluded, "And you and I know that we can use all the good moments we get."

Although we received many gripes about Vietnam over the year, soldiers could still appreciate the beautiful scenery Vietnam had to offer. Army Cpl. Bohdan R. "Bo" Tanchuk praised the scenery in June, "I thought I should mention this: the Vietnamese beaches are really beautiful. I saw Cam Ranh Bay and snuck out to the beach for a dip – water temp 85°, air temp 110° hot! The sand is beautiful, the water very clear."

Army Capt. William J. Taylor III also wrote from Cam Ranh Bay in June, "This place is like a huge beach. It's also rather pretty. Sunday after inspection I will put in a little time at the very attractive Navy beach. They make nice pink frozen daiquiris there." One month later, he indulged Mailbag readers with tales from his recent R&R.

"My trip to Long Binh and Saigon turned out to be all that I could have hoped for. I was even treated to my first nocturnal rocket attack while at Long Binh…. I took a ride on one of these little motor-powered jobs with the seat in front. The fellow I was with and myself were laughing frantically all the way as we blazed ahead through potholes and weaved around, narrowly missing trucks and the like….We just had a change of command here at the 97th M.P. Battalion…. As adjutant, I read the appropriate orders in the same sort of voice I would use to umpire a tennis match at the Delaware Girls' Grass Court [Championships]."
Army Capt. William J. Taylor III, July 17

Others wrote about their R&Rs as well.

"Once again I find myself splashing ink about; this time in pursuit of a 'dream' that occurred from 13 May to 20 May in Sydney, Australia. I was there on R&R soaking up fall sweater-weather temperatures, attempting to remain calm when negotiating turns while riding on the wrong side of the road; and, of course, getting my eyes full with all the miniskirts blowing about.

True, wool is a good buy in Sydney and I hastened to take advantage of the sweater sales that were currently taking place, purchasing two. I discovered one to be quite adequate for strolling through Hyde Park, cruising on the Hawkesbury River, or photographing the city from the observation deck of my hotel, the Koala Park Regis. However, when I went touring on the Roll Royce Owners' Club rally on Saturday, in a '21 Rolls Royce open touring car and on the Veterans' Car Club rally the following day in a '26 30/98 Vauxhall open touring car, I found myself wearing both sweaters.

The two cars were truly phenomenal machines. The '21 Rolls Royce, Ghost series, was judged the 'best Rolls Royce in Australia' for three years in a row. The only fault that I could find with it … was its brakes. It had two mounted on the rear wheels. We had an occasion, incidentally, to lock up all two of them, when some clown came barreling through a stop sign at one of the intersections along our route. The brakes stopped the wheels without any difficulty, but persuading the tires to stop the car was something else.

The '26 30/98 Vauxhall, of which 310 were built, had a racy looking all-aluminum body making it the most 'dashing' of the two cars….

After the two rallies, I was practically convinced that the wrong side of the road was not so bad after all. Yet my first experience riding in the cabs caused me to wonder. My cab drivers impressed me with their incredible talent for two-wheeling around corners, cutting off double-decked buses and 'blitzing' through red lights….

No matter where I went, it became clearly apparent that the miniskirt was not the phenomenon that it has been in the states, but a way of dress for the female populace of Australia, age 35 or less; the average hemline height being at least mid-thigh. This is not as amazing as it might seem because girls down there do not marry until around 30 as a rule. Consequently, they can afford to do a little more advertising….

Sixty days remain."
Army Spc. Michael E. Brelick, June 18

"My R&R in Sydney was just great. I have never seen so many beautiful girls in short miniskirts anywhere in my life. As I said, it was really great. Too bad my stay there was only six days long."
Army Spc. Eugene "Gene" Barbato in Tam Ky, Nov. 20 Mailbag

Another Army friend, once so active with the sentry dogs, wrote about an unforgettable holiday. To celebrate Thanksgiving in 1969, he organized a gala feast. In his letter, he told how all the guys pitched in to make the meal memorable.

"Thought I'd send some pictures of the detachment's feast on Thanksgiving. It all started about a month ago when we decided it would be a little more like home if we made our own dinner on Thanksgiving. Certain guys sent home for different things. For the salad we had 12 bottles of dressing. Three of the men are Italian so an antipasto was made – actually about enough for 50 people – we have about 16. Of course, before dinner we had to have cocktails, so we had whiskey sour mix sent. On our own over here we got a case of steaks (120), about six pounds of chicken, and four pounds of pork chops. No, we didn't have any turkey. We also bought liquor, champagne and beer (20 cases). We got tables, lettuce, tomatoes, and cucumbers from one of the mess halls. We had 50 loaves of French bread and 50 sandwich loaves baked for us downtown. And for table cloths, we used our sheets.

What a meal! Unfortunately, everyone was so anxious to eat that no one thought to get a picture of everyone seated during the blessing. About 2 p.m. we all sat down and Vinny Imgoglia said the blessing. Then we all dug in. What a wonderful day it was. And about 5 p.m. we opened our detachment to everyone who knew us and made a party out of what was left.

We truly had a lot to be thankful for that day. It was a good time."
Army Sgt. Robert S. Biss, Dec. 1

Bits and pieces of more mundane news in Delawareans' letters reassured us throughout the year there was some normalcy in Vietnam.

"**The last time I wrote I was up at Lai Khe, NNW of Saigon, but have since moved to Long Binh, the world's largest paperwork factory.** When Charlie attacked Long Binh a few weeks ago, he should have used flaming arrows instead of bullets, then we would have been in a mess, what with all those duplicates and 'true copies' and files and files of files!

They have been doing a lot of building around here and soon (next month?) a complete underground water system will be finished; hot and cold running water, flush toilets, tile showers, etc. I heard the grand opening begins when some general from USARV comes down and flushes the 1st toilet!

I think it should be noted that the 1st Infantry Division is soon to be awarded the Vietnamese Cross of Gallantry for some real fine action last summer and fall. Although our platoon (IVth Plt, Lai Khe Dust-Opp) isn't in the 1st, we feel real close to them and were proud to have served with them, especially the guys in the First of the Second (1/2) and 'Doctor Delta.'"
Army Spc. Larry R. Kipp in Long Binh, March 11

Always busy, the Information Office of the 23rd Infantry Division's headquarters in Chu Lai covered all news from the division and published *Under the Southern Cross,* a weekly newspaper. The withdrawal of National Guard troops (opposite) from Wilmington, Del., in January made headlines around the world.

"**Can't say that I've been up to much 'cause my bird has been in check now for over two weeks and we're still working on it.** I got to fly about two days ago, just put in enough time to rate my flight pay for the month. Even flew left-seat for about 10 minutes.

Handling that aircraft was really something. WOW, I was all over the sky. But it was a great feeling and I'm hoping that I'll get another chance sometime."
Marine Lance Cpl. John J. Jones, May 1 Mailbag

One gambling airman told us about a raffle his base was involved in that was trying to raise funds for a Vietnamese Children's youth center. He bought a ticket on my behalf and explained:

"**Thought I'd buy you a chance on the 'Tall Man Project' drawing in December.** If you win the car, you can take me for a ride in 164 days. 'The Tall Man' is the new base commander's idea. Only one problem – everyone at Tan Son Nhut is selling the worthless things – who do we sell them to???

On the eighth of November the New Christy Minstrels and Miss Kim Weston are giving a concert. It is being sponsored by Reader's Digest and the U.S.O. shows. It should be real good. On the ninth, USARV is presenting 'You're a Good Man, Charlie Brown' – another night of fine entertainment.

As long as they keep booking groups like this, I don't care how long I stay here. Just think, we even get Bob Hope this year – maybe.

Guess I'd better run now. Good luck on the drawing."
Air Force Airman R. Lance Hall at Tan Son Nhut Air Base, Nov. 6 Mailbag

STATE AND NATIONAL ISSUES CONTINUED TO MAKE HEADLINES AROUND THE WORLD. In Delaware, the exit of National Guard from Wilmington in January 1969 was a newsworthy action that was reported on in Vietnam, prompting Air Force Sgt. James F. Wachter Jr. to write,"I'd like to inform you that Wilmington, Delaware, was a top story on the news today over here. It was about the governor pulling out the National Guard troops in Wilmington. I was glad to hear that."

Other national events, like Neil Armstrong's July 20 moonwalk and U.S. Sen. Edward M. Kennedy's lack of judgment at Chappaquiddick, garnered scant attention from Delawareans in Vietnam.

"**As you might well know, things have been rather peaceful in Vietnam for the past few weeks.** I pray it stays this way. Maybe a bit of the incredible achievement of the Apollo 11 mission to the moon rubbed off on the NVA and NLF and they decided to reassess their goals about this war."
Army Cpl. Bohdan R. "Bo" Tanchuk, Aug. 4

Kennedy, whose passenger, 28-year old secretary Mary Jo Kopechne, was killed after he drove his car off a bridge on Chappaquiddick Island near Martha's Vineyard on July 18, failed to report the accident in a timely manner. A 1966 Henry C. Conrad High School grad shared his opinion when he wrote to the column.

"**As for the Edward Kennedy mess, he is just as human as anybody else.** If it is suspected that a crime was committed, then it should be investigated fast and thoroughly mainly because of his high position on our government. It's probably too late to hold an autopsy. Everything has been stalled too much and put off."
Marine Sgt. Jim Harris of Wilmington, Oct. 15

A Delaware issue, which required a state constitutional amendment, was a proposal to establish legalized gambling in the state. Paul C. Hassler of Wilmington Manor, a regional manager for the Fruehauf Corp., pitched a $150 million gambling-convention-entertainment casino for New Castle County and suggested such a complex could produce almost $20 million annually for the state in tax revenue. One frequent Mailbag writer tendered his comments.

"**I have received word concerning the $150 million amusement complex as proposed by Mr. Paul C. Hassler and think this is just an outstanding idea that could do nothing but help our home state.**
From a strictly financial point of view, while stationed in California I made a couple of trips to Las Vegas and had the opportunity to see how it could help the local economy and at the same time stimulate the tourist business. A town of such a small native population has had to increase many fold just to accommodate all the tourists. This expansion means only one thing – money.
The way I see it, the operation and construction of such a project would open up countless new jobs and opportunities for Delawareans...."

One other thing I've noticed about servicemen is that generally they like to gamble and have a good time when possible. When you consider all of the GIs returning home from here in Delaware and all the neighboring states, this can mean quite a bit of money.
I am really anxious to see how this all turns out – with hopes that it is approved because I feel it can do nothing but help the economy and residents of the state of Delaware."
Navy Petty Officer 3rd Class Stephen A. Nash, June 24

Other Delawareans added their two cents.

"**First of all, why not?** We already have legalized gambling in the form of Delaware Park, Dover Downs, etc. do we not? Agreed on a much smaller scale than that which Mr. Hassler has proposed, but gambling just the same. I do not feel that to legalize gambling and to build a casino would bring in or encourage organized crime more than it probably already has.
So, as you can guess, I say yes, legalize gambling. Besides bringing more tax money to the state, it will put the underground gambling out of business."
Air Force Staff Sgt. Robert E. May, Aug. 20

"**As for a gambling casino for Delaware, I am a fervent believer in the art of the cards and dice.** I think it would be a good thing financially. It would bring more people to the state which means more money also for businesses as long as it is handled properly and controlled."
Marine Sgt. Jim Harris, Oct. 15

Delaware's General Assembly did not legalize slot machines until 1995 when it passed the Horse Racing Preservation Act, permitting gaming at racetracks in Stanton, Dover and Harrington. Within two years, slots revenues tallied $300 million and temporarily revived the ailing horse-racing industry.

FEW THINGS UPSET OUR SERVICEMEN MORE THAN PACI-FIST PROTESTERS. News of antiwar demonstrators and draft dodgers at home generally raised the collective blood pressure of troops in Vietnam. Delawareans were no exception. One soldier dissed the demonstrators at Nixon's January 20 inauguration.

"**Today as I listened to my radio, I heard of the antiwar demonstrators.** This not only upset me but my whole squad. For twenty months over here fighting for what I feel is right and to have these young, good-for-nothings run around and yell victory for the Vietcong. You don't know how it makes my blood boil. For those who say these things, a word from me and my squad: stay home, we don't want you over here. I hope the day never comes when people like you have to go out and fight for your freedom.

I'm proud of my country and the people in it. There is an old saying, you have a rotten apple in every barrel, and on Jan. 20 we found 5,000 rotten ones. I hope the day never comes when I come face to face with one of these kind. I don't believe we have a name for their kind."
Army Sgt. William H. Chance, Jan. 21

"**Draft dodgers – WOW – No sweat they don't have to come in the Army.** Give them 2 choices. Send them to a communist country or send them over here and send them out on a night patrol wearing white sheets without weapons and, of course, in VC-infested territory. The U.S. has taken care of me, now it's my turn to help take care of it, even if it is in a small way. The U.S. is the GREATEST country in the world and everyone should want to keep it that way."
Army Spc. Paul J. Walker III in Saigon, Feb. 24

"**I really don't have any big opinion about the 'WAR' but I will say this for all of the dissenters who are over here, if you went 'over the hill' the only person you would hurt would be you for your attitude.** Your outfit would be better off without you.

For dissenters here in southeast Asia, or at home, if you think we have it so bad, go live in North Vietnam for awhile.

No one at home will miss you. Besides with your mentality you could probably help end this war a lot sooner by helping Hanoi. The confusion you would create would be so great they would have to stop fighting to get their senses back. No one likes war, gentlemen, but for some reason man insists on it, yesterday, today and probably always. So it is up to someone to try to stop it, peacefully, if possible. However, we can't always do that, so some of us end up fighting for peace.

So all you draft dodgers, SDS [Students for a Democratic Society] people, etc., I say please go hide in your holes, caves or what have you, wherever it was you came from and pull them in after you. Believe me, NO ONE will miss you one bit....

Just remember there are a lot of good men dying over here. Men who ASKED to come over because they believe in what they are doing and in what OUR COUNTRY is doing. They don't deserve to be given a back seat to the collection of 'KOOKS' and 'DING-A-LINGS' who do the demonstrating."
Air Force Staff Sgt. Robert E. May, May 8

"**At present, I am in Vietnam trying to defend the draft dodgers and hippies.** Of course, there are the few who really appreciate what we are doing over here and they show it by the care packages they send."
Marine Lance Cpl. Robert J. Rogers, July 9

As 1969 wound down, Nixon tried to defuse anti-war sentiment at home. On Sept. 26, at his first radio-television news conference in more than three months, he told Americans he planned to withdraw at least 60,000 troops by Dec. 15. He also announced cancellation of the November and December draft calls that would have affected 50,000 men and trumpeted a one-third drop in battlefield casualties since 1968.

Some servicemen supported Vietnam Moratorium Day on Oct. 15 when millions across the country demonstrated against the war in their cities and suburbs. For the march on the nation's capital a month later, more than a quarter-million people massed to show their opposition to the war.

"**It has come to the attention of the men in my group that many people think that the soldier is 1) in favor of the war and 2) against the moratorium.** Speaking for the men in my unit, and relating to you my conversations with many men over here, the typical soldier is most definitely against this 'hit and run' war over here and is in favor of anything done in the United States to get us out of Vietnam as soon as possible. I feel that the reason people think that the soldier is against the moratorium is because of statements made by so-called influential people reinforcing this belief. I refer specifically to the speech given by Army Chief of Staff William C. Westmoreland at the dedication of the Douglas MacArthur Academy of Freedom at Howard Payne College in Brownwood, Texas. In this speech, Westmoreland says, 'My guess is that the vast majority of U.S. soldiers in Vietnam are rather disappointed to see this development,' and 'the fighting man in Vietnam is disillusioned and disappointed by the Moratorium Day demonstrations.' He told a news conference there had been no reaction surveys, 'but the impression I have received from Vietnam is that they are somewhat disillusioned by the demonstrations. They don't understand what it is all about.'

We know what it is all about. There as many peace signs over here as in any demonstration back home. Black armbands were worn October 15 as they will be worn on November 15.

Perhaps the best way I can explain how we feel over here is to quote Arthur Goldberg when he spoke on October 15 at Lafayette Square across from the White House. He said that since the President has committed us to a withdraw[al] of forces, he will never get a better bargaining position than he has now. The Vietcong have the staying power so there is really nothing to be gained from staying here. That is how we feel. If all the hecklers are so against the moratorium, they must be in favor of the war. Instead of heckling and ripping apart doves from in front of the [U.S.] Custom[s] House, enlist in the Army, come over to Vietnam, and take my place. Then maybe you'll see how senseless this war is, how these people do not care who governs them as long as they have food in their bellies, and that the majority of soldiers are not disillusioned by the moratorium but are in favor of it, if it will help to get them out of Vietnam."
Army Pfc. Mark L. Goodman, Nov. 10 Mailbag

Mark's views won the endorsement of other servicemen. Here's one example:

"**Just a few words to comment on the letter written by Pfc. Mark L. Goodman....** My compliments go out to him for writing such a fine letter. I agree with him. The Vietcong are Vietnamese so they can't go home. To the Vietnamese people there is but one country, not two as the Eisenhower, Kennedy, Johnson and Nixon administrations have decided.

Anybody who has read the Geneva Accord of 1954 recalls that the division was temporary not permanent. When President Diem failed to implement the general elections for all of Vietnam in 1956, he violated the Geneva agreements. The door then opened for the civil war which ensued. Eisenhower, Kennedy and then Johnson sent American soldiers to aid a man who broke the agreements. The result was an unnecessary slaughterhouse for Americans, most of whom could not cast a vote to determine their own destiny.

The Vietnam Moratorium people realize that the U.S. has indeed made a very grave error. They call for complete withdrawal to end the senseless killing of both GIs and Vietnamese. They do not wish to kill GIs as some people say, only to bring all GIs home. Most Americans are unfortunately opposed to the moratorium. They see everything in terms of honor and pride. They apparently do not realize the amount of human suffering their pride and honor are costing.

Pfc. Goodman scoffed at the hecklers of the moratorium people and extended an invitation to those people to come here to take out their hostilities against the enemy over here. I wish to second that invitation.

We soldiers who wish peace over here must realize however that these people are misguided. They spent their time listening to Gen. Westmoreland and to 'lifers.' Any GI can tell them however that 'lifers' are the first ones to become 'cheerleaders for war' and the last ones to fight it.

Ironically, it is yesterday's peace protester who is out front in the infantry today while the warmonger lifer is making it with a girl and a bottle of whiskey.

My concern goes out mainly to the 'silent Americans.' It is these people who don't concern themselves with Vietnam until it is their father, their son, their brother, their husband, or their boyfriend who is over here. These are the people who get up in the morning, go to work, return home with their families and don't concern themselves with the rest of the world. It's too bad these people assume an 'I don't give a damn attitude.' These people don't realize how lucky they are. They spend their entire lives attending to their own selfish desires.

They live like leeches off the lives of the brave young Americans who have died here. It is to these people who I would like to send a personal invitation to come over to Vietnam and see what the world and life is all about. The unfortunate thing is that most of them would return home and once again live their selfish lives."
Army Pfc. Harry Darr, Dec. 1 Mailbag

On Nov. 30, Mark L. Goodman wrote again to thank all those who supported his thinking. "I would like to thank all who wrote me in response to my article in your column concerning the soldier's opinion of the demonstrations protesting the war. Over here, I attempted to wear a black armband to show my support for the moratorium but I was only laughed at and then given a direct order to remove it 'because it was un-American.'"

Peace Day Let Down GIs: Westy

BROWNWOOD, Tex. (AP) — Army Chief of Staff William C. Westmoreland said Saturday that the fighting man in Vietnam is disillusioned and disappointed by the Moratorium Day demonstrations.

He said national leaders also are vitally concerned about reaction in Hanoi to the cries for immediate U.S. withdrawal from Vietnam.

"My guess is that the vast majority (of U.S. soldiers in Vietnam) are rather disappointed to see this development," Westmoreland told a news conference.

Westmoreland spoke Saturday at the dedication of Douglas MacArthur Academy of Freedom at Howard Payne College.

The general, former commander of U.S. forces in Vietnam, told the news conference there had been no reaction surveys made in combat units "but the impression I have received from Vietnam is that they are somewhat disillusioned by the demonstrations. They don't understand what it is all about."

STARS AND STRIPES
PACIFIC
APO San Francisco 96503
Published daily: $2.50 per month. Second-class postage paid at San Francisco. Calif.

Army Pfc. Mark L. Goodman wrote in support of the moratorium to end the war and enclosed this *Pacific Stars and Stripes* article.

Everyone makes mistakes and even a country can make a mistake.

The United States is the most powerful country in the world, so let's be strong and admit we have made a mistake.

I have fought with ARVN troops and, as strange as it may seem, they don't really take this war seriously. For instance, I have set up ambushes in the jungle and they make one hell of a racket all night which the NVA or VC could easily hear and know our exact location – if they were anywhere in the area.

I've also fought and talked with Cho Hoys [participants in a program to get North Vietnamese or Vietcong soldiers to switch sides and fight for the South Vietnamese government forces] who only fight on our side because we pay them more money and they have better food to eat.

They even informed me that if the U.S. pulls out of Vietnam, they would go and join up with the NVA forces again. To me, this is total confusion. If the people aren't taking this war seriously, they can't really care if their country is run by democracy or communism....

I believe it's time for peace now."
Army Spc. Robert S. Baker, Nov. 24 Mailbag

"**I would like to give my congratulations on the Vietnam Moratorium, a protest which was very carefully planned and very well organized.** I just wish that I could be there to protest along with all of you. (Keep up the good work, just remember peace is the only way and it's we the people who can make it.)

I would like to give a few more of my viewpoints on Vietnam and the military establishment and I figure no one is more qualified than the men fighting this war in Vietnam. As you have already deducted, I am against the war in Vietnam, primarily because I feel the Vietnamese could care less about what kind of government they have ruling their lives. As a majority, the people are not actively involved in the political arena, nor do they know that much about such ideologies as socialism, communism and democracy.

I do believe that if the U.S. pulls out of the Republic of South Vietnam, they could easily go under communism. However, I don't believe the people really care. It's true the people are all farmers and will always be farmers no matter what.

It is true the U.S. is pulling troops out of Vietnam but not at a fast enough rate as far as I am concerned. Every day that goes by means that many more Americans are killed for nothing but land that we will not even be concerned with in the future.

To me, being over here seems just to be another way for a grotesque population control.

I realize the United States is looking for an honorable way to pull out of Vietnam without getting a bad reputation but I can't see all the lives being lost while they're looking for such a program.

His November letter wasn't the first time he wrote of his desire to see the war end and to have an era of peace begin. An earlier letter, titled "What We Go Through," gave Mailbag readers pause.

"**The infantry GI in Vietnam [goes] on a mission which usually lasts between seven to 14 days.** We fight our way through the jungles trying to locate the enemy. All the time we are in the jungle, we have to go without washing for we have to conserve our water for drinking purposes only. We are always wet from head to toe and just covered from filth from the swamps and canals we have to cross. We are very susceptible to diseases such as impetigo, ringworm, malaria, hepatitis, typhoid and many others.

We go night after night with very little sleep with the thought on our mind, are they going to find us or are we going to find them? When we do make contact with the VC or NVA troops after a killing spree is over, we have to try to find humor in what we have done. We can't think that these people had families to go back to and people who loved them as we are loved or we would probably go insane. Instead, we have to think of these people as animals and we are hunters.

After our missions are over with, we are just filthy and usually covered with leeches and our feet are so swollen from being wet we can hardly walk. We live in a very barbarous way and we don't act like rational human beings. We, the majority, say we've had enough, we want to come home, and it's not too late for peace. Please help us."
Army Spc. Robert S. Baker, Sept. 18 Mailbag

1969 – YEAR IN REVIEW

FEBRUARY 16
Allied forces observe a 24-hour ceasefire during Tet, the Vietnamese New Year. VC and NVA truce violations result in U.S. deaths.

MARCH 2
Throughout South Vietnam, village and hamlet elections are held. The enemy does not attempt to disrupt the high voter turnout.

MARCH 16
The battleship USS *New Jersey* pulls off the coast of South Vietnam after providing American and ARVN forces with impressive fire support.

MARCH
The Air Force begins 14 months of secret bombings of Cambodia.

APRIL 3
The commander of the U.S. Military Assistance Command Vietnam (MACV) confirms more Americans have been killed in Vietnam than during the Korean War.

MAY 8
The North Vietnamese issue a 10-point proposal contingent on complete U.S. troop withdrawal as a condition for peace.

JUNE 8
President Richard M. Nixon announces 25,000 U.S. troops will be withdrawn by the end of August.

SEPTEMBER 3
Ho Chi Minh, president of North Vietnam, dies.

SEPTEMBER
Army Lt. William L. Calley Jr. is charged with the murders of civilians at My Lai.

SEPTEMBER 16
Nixon announces another troop withdrawal, bringing the total to 40,500.

NOVEMBER 12
Journalist Seymour Hersh breaks the story of the My Lai massacre.

DECEMBER 15
Nixon announces a third round of troop withdrawals will be completed by April 15, 1970.

AFVN Newscaster Face

S&S Vietnam Bureau

SAIGON — An American Forces Vietnam Network (AFVN) newscaster who last week charged AFVN with censoring the news said Thursday that he will face a court-martial for an earlier dispute with AFVN superiors.

Spec. 5 Robert Lawrence stated he was informed he could accept an Article 15, a nonjudicial punishment administered by the commanding officer — in this case, Lt. Col. James Adams, officer in charge of AFVN. Under terms of the Article 15, Lawrence could have been fined, restricted, or reduced one grade in rank. Lawrence said he chose trial by summary court-martial, although its penalties can be much more severe than an Article 15's.

According to Lawrence the incident took place Dec. 29, when he was preparing his evening newscast, Sgt. Robert Mac-

Stars & Stripes Jan. 10, 1970

Richard Panadero YN3
MCB 74, Co. II
FPO New York 09501

FREE

VIA AIR MAIL
CORREO AEREO
PAR AVION

WILMINGTON MORNING PAPERS
c/o DEAR NANCY COLUMN
ORANGE STREET
WILMINGTON, DELAWARE 19801

rt-Martial

The inspector general for the
U.S. military command is investigating the censorship
charge. Lawrence and others
concerned with the case have
been ordered not to discuss the
with reporters until the in-
ation is completed. The
ght against Law-
are not con-
censorship

AIR MAIL
CORREO AEREO
PAR AVION

ARMY POSTAL SERVICE
22 FEB 1969

The Treasure Hotel
Vacancy

MAILBAG (NANCY)
EVERY EVENING NEWSPAPER
NGE
ON, DELA

s Repe
Alerted
Assaila.

"FOR THE TROOPS"

THE ROUNDUP

No. 12   18th Military Police Brigade, Vietnam   December 1969

The VC sappers crept
the diversion they knew w
RPG round landed insi
confusion.

They proceeded to carry
failed because of the one el
sentry dog.

The alert dog and
quick-thinking handler te
to spoil the early r
attack. One sapp
penetrated was ki
penmeter was
ensuing skirmish,
fled before
accomplish the

When cha
Rush N. Mor
handler at
Company (Sentry
MP Battalion, was t.
another handler, Spec
M. Walker, that his dog
alerted several times durin
night to noises and
the north

1970

ON APRIL 20, PRESIDENT NIXON ANNOUNCED THE PHASED WITHDRAWAL OF 150,000 U.S. TROOPS FROM SOUTH VIETNAM, REKINDLING THE HOPES OF MILLIONS OF AMERICANS FOR AN END TO THE WAR, NOW ENTERING ITS NINTH YEAR. THE TROOP REDUCTION, SCHEDULED FOR COMPLETION BY MAY 1971, "MEANS THAT WE FINALLY HAVE IN SIGHT THE JUST PEACE WE ARE SEEKING," HE SAID.

Within days of Nixon's announcement, and even as troops withdrew, the war seeped into Cambodia, South Vietnam's neighbor to the west and once a part of French-ruled Indochina, following a political coup there. Nixon called the April campaign an "incursion" and within three months it ended, but the maneuver further roiled antiwar demonstrators in America.

Hours after the U.S. invasion of Cambodia, students at Kent State University in Ohio on May 4 protested the involvement of their country in the widening war. Empowered to restore order, the state's National Guard shot and killed four students and wounded 11 others before the violence ended.

A national outrage over the Kent State shootings erupted May 5 and students coast to coast staged a strike supported by a majority of campuses in the country. The undeclared war in Vietnam continued to polarize Americans.

Another war of longstanding duration, and nearly as unpopular with some, also drew swords. The battle of the sexes segued into a general strike on August 26, a day to remember for liberated women who were encouraged to march, demonstrate and sit in, to stop typing, vacuuming, buying, and making love, all for the sake of equality. Specifically, women were striking for free 24-hour child-care centers, free abortions on demand and equality with men in education and employment.

Almost everyone in 1970, it seemed, had a dog in one fight or another. And there were more of us than ever before: the total U.S. population topped 200 million.

In Delaware, former Gov. Charles L. Terry Jr. died unexpectedly in Dover on February 6 at the age of 69. The April 18-25 Week of Concern, an ambitious letter-writing campaign addressed to North Vietnam on behalf of Delaware's five prisoners of war and the country's 1,400 POWs and others missing in action, had far less local impact than its sponsor, People of Wilmington Care, had hoped.

In June, Selective Service offices throughout the state were ransacked. Col. Clifford E. Hall, the state director of Selective Service, proudly reported that in the four weeks following the incidents his offices had issued all orders for the July call-ups on schedule. National headquarters, he added, sent help immediately to right the files. Since much of the information was stored on microfilm, very few records were actually lost.

In off-year elections, U.S. Rep. William V. Roth was elected to the Senate seat vacated by fellow Republican John J. Williams, the "Conscience of the Senate," who, due to his age, 66, felt obliged to retire to his State Street home in Millsboro. A promising newcomer, Pierre S. "Pete" du Pont IV, a Republican from Delaware's best-known family, convincingly won his first term in the U.S. House.

But the war weighed on everyone's minds. According to data from the National Archives and Records Administration, war casualties in 1970 totaled 6,081, the fewest since 1966. Delaware bore 19 losses, a figure also significantly less than in prior years. Despite the lower death toll and increased troop withdrawals, the war still conflicted Americans at home and in the combat zone.

Delawareans serving in Vietnam continued to see the conflict in the starkest black and white. Shades of gray seldom entered their opinions.

"It's a futile war and what are we going to be able to claim as a winning factor? It sure won't be the [47,000] young men who have put down their lives on something which their country has only declared as a police action," Army Spc. John P. "Pat" Little of Greenville wrote to the January 22 Vietnam Mailbag.

Army Sgt. Kenneth D. Keogh viewed the situation very differently when he sent his letter, dated March 3, from Quang Tri. "I know I can't, but can you blame these people for the way they feel? They don't want to fight or kill but they must. The people from the north intruded [into] their homes and these people decided to make a stand. As you know, they asked for our help."

Nicknamed "Teach," Army Spc. William W. Hutchison Jr. finally landed a rear job as a reporter and photographer for the 23rd Infantry Division's Information Office in Chu Lai. A wooden peace symbol (opposite), carved and sold by South Vietnamese street vendors, was common in country from 1970 on.

IN AN UNPRECEDENTED NEW YEAR'S VISIT, VICE PRESIDENT SPIRO T. AGNEW TOUCHED DOWN IN VIETNAM AS PART OF AN 11-NATION ASIAN TOUR. He told troops at two firebases that the American public was proud of them and they should not be misled by the news media. Agnew expressed the opinion the war could be ended during 1970, "so we all can go back to being civilians again."

Unaware of the vice president's pending trip, a frequent writer and war skeptic in fact had encouraged Agnew and "all the rest of the pro-war people" to see Vietnam firsthand in his December 21, 1969 letter to the Mailbag. He commented on Agnew's in-country comments in this letter, his first in 1970.

"**I never heard Agnew say that the war could be ended within this year.** I did not see Agnew either because the Army is very careful who talks to influential dignitaries over here on supposed 'fact-finding' visits. Anyone who might give a 'false impression' of the opinions of the servicemen, in other words, anyone against the current policy, is carefully kept away. The Army has many ingenious ways of making things appear as they are not."
Army Spc. Mark L. Goodman, Jan. 20

Within hours of his arrival in Vietnam, Agnew waved goodbye and left U.S. troops to deal with Tet, the Vietnamese lunar new year in early February when the Vietcong and North Vietnamese army traditionally increased hostile activities, and the April invasion of Cambodia.

Servicemen of all stripes offered their takes on these events as well as the extraordinary charges in January of news censorship by the U.S. Command and the continuing fallout from the 1968 My Lai massacre of Vietnamese civilians. Air Force Airman 1st Class R. Lance Hall had plenty to say about the censorship issue.

A regular writer to the Mailbag and man of many opinions, he weighed in on the January 1970 censorship case involving Armed Forces Vietnam Network (AFVN) newscaster Army Spc. Robert E. Lawrence of Atlanta. Lance supported Lawrence, who, on the air, accused the U.S. Military Assistance Command Vietnam (MACV) of censoring news broadcasts.

Lawrence, an AFVN newscaster since May 27, 1969, told American troops during a live telecast Jan. 3 from Saigon they were receiving censored news reports. In a 90-second statement he read live at the close of his regular 11 p.m. broadcast, Lawrence charged that, "In the military in Vietnam, I've found that a newscaster at AFVN is not free to tell the truth and, in essence, to 'tell it like it is.'"

An AFVN sportscaster, Marine Cpl. Thomas M. Sinkovitz of Harrisburg, Pennsylvania, followed Lawrence with a sports report which he prefaced with his on-air comment, "Thank you, Bob, in more ways than one." He later said his remark was meant as a "complete endorsement" of Lawrence's charge.

Lawrence, Sinkovitz and four other enlisted men at AFVN, who also alleged censorship, were immediately suspended from their duties pending an investigation by the inspector general of the U.S. Command.

Throughout January, Air Force Airman 1st Class R. Lance Hall (opposite) sent the Mailbag many newspaper articles from *Pacific Stars and Stripes* about the AFVN censorship case.

Lance fired off his first letter on the case soon after Lawrence's broadcast.

"**Enclosed is an article from *Pacific Stars and Stripes.*** I sincerely hope that you can find room in your column for a copy. I was watching the night [Army Spc. Robert E.] Lawrence made his statement. After saying 'I'm probably in trouble for telling you the truth tonight,' he added, 'GOODBYE and good night.' I haven't heard any more or even watched to see if he is still on. I've wanted to but have not been near a TV since. I'll bet the brass dropped their Flash Gordons that night.
He asked that we do all we can to help. I can't help but would like everyone to know that the censorship on AFVN is unbelievable."
Air Force Airman 1st Class R. Lance Hall, Jan. 5

The inspector general's investigation, completed January 20, 1970, fully exonerated the AFVN of charges of censorship. Lawrence, Sinkovitz, and the four others who worked at AFVN were reassigned. A brief announcement by MACV on January 21 said the investigation of Lawrence's allegations found his "views" to be "incompatible" with the policy of Armed Forces Radio-Television Service.
Lawrence's new job: a chaplain's assistant at Kontum, 270 miles northeast of Saigon. Sinkovitz was assigned to the 1st Marine Air-Naval Gunfire Liaison Company. U.S. Rep. John E. Moss, a Democrat from California, chairman of the House Foreign Operations and Government Information Subcommittee, ordered a congressional investigation into the matter.

Another soldier provided some inside information on the censorship case.

"**I am serving in the 1st Air Cavalry Division known as the 'First Team.'** ... Just returned from Saigon, working as a Cav news and feature liaison with the Armed Forces Vietnam Network Television Station (AFVN-TV).
While there, I worked in TV production and continuity, writing information-type announcements and commercials and also doing announcing work, in addition to putting together Cav feature film clips.
This year the Bob Hope Christmas Show was shown live from Long Binh to about 150,000 troops in the III Corps area. I worked on audio from the station end.
The censorship charges were also made while I was there. Although I'll have to reserve final comment until the current [U.S. House] investigation has been resolved, I might add that every newsman who was in the department at the time of the charges has been removed, from the officer in charge down to the lowly, so-called 'young, inexperienced newscasters.'"
Army Spc. Clay Rutter, March 9 Mailbag

No Policy of Radio Censorship, Broger Insists

The others pertain to informa-tion which would affect the safe-ty of U.S. forces or which... he said.

"We balance it where neces-sary," he added.

Broger said military newscas-ters are briefed in advance about the policies and problems... news in a foreign... final analy...

Broger said, however, that such a story "if played succes-sively and repeatedly" could be an "irritation" to the Saigon government. In that case, the Army command in Saigon might feel that the station was unnecessarily offending... Vietnamese government... Forces...

IG Probe Ends

AFVN Policy Right: MACV

SAIGON (UPI)—The U.S. Command said Tuesday the American Forces Vietnam Network (AFVN) had not violated Defense Department policies despite charges it has censored news beamed to servicemen in the Vietnam war zone.

Military investigators made the conclusion in a re-port to Washington after a two-week investigation of charges made by a GI newscaster in live television in South Vietnam Jan. 3.

The newscaster, Spec. 5 Robert F. Lawrence, 27, of Atlanta, Ga., said in a news program broadcast to Ameri-can servicemen that military newsmen had been suppressed. He called on his audience to "help stop censorship at AFVN and any station under military rule."

Lawrence was removed from the staff of the military broadcasting network and as-signed as a chaplain's as... ant in Saigon. He was ordered martialed for refusing... of a superior in an... ned before he... charge...

Fear New Red Laos Offensive

WASHINGTON (AP) — State Department spokesmen ex-pressed concern Tuesday that the inc... fighting in Laos may be... of a dry sea-son off... Vietnam-ese fo... lo-cal... troo...

They're 'Pedalling' Security

... more than 70 bicyclists start the ... mile race in Dalat Tuesday. The ... run from Nha Trang to the Mekong Delta city of Long Xuyen, is aimed at showing the security along the roads. The race is run only in daylight hours. (AP Radiophoto)

For Censorsh...

Hous...
GI N...

mittee... caster's... to cer...

AFVN New...

...GON (AP) — Two mili... ...smen who accused... ...ntured Friday... ...American Forces Viet... ...(N) to other... ...command in...

chaplain's... Thomas M... abbre to d... val Gladice... The spo... they will... duties... terminated... and... a number of

...smen (UPI) — Police ...smen said Saturday 193 persons were killed and 11,346 were injured in 10,095 traffic ac-cidents in Saigon last year.

free?

AFTER 5 DAYS RETURN TO
AIC R. Lance Hall
CMR I-5476
APO S/F
96201
ZIP CODE

Nancy Lynch
News-Journal Co
Wilmington, Delaware

GIs Avenge Loss Of Copter, Kill 27

S&S Vietnam Bureau

SAIGON — U.S. armored cav-alrymen killed at least 27 Com-munists Tuesday afternoon in a sharp battle only two miles from the Cambodian border and 78 miles north of Saigon, a U.S. spokesman said.

Troops of the 11th Armored Cav. Regt. moved into the area three hours after enemy gunfire brought down a U.S. Army light observation helicopter shortly after noon Tuesday.

The GIs, riding armored per-sonnel carriers and tanks, ...ded heavy machine-gun and ...le fire with the enemy and ...re supported by helicopter ...ships, artillery and U.S. Air ...ce fighter strikes.

...ere were no American loss-... the ground action. One of ... downed helicopter's crew-... was killed and one ...ed.

Meanwhile, a beefed-up Com-munist platoon, holed up in stur-dy bunkers, dueled U.S. 4th Div. infantrymen for five hours in the central highlands Monday and killed five Americans and wounded five, a U.S. military spokesman said.

Enemy losses in the clash, 16 miles north of An Khe in Binh Dinh Province, are unknown.

...aped in ...horities also reported 166 terrorist incidents in the week ending Jan. 14 in which 92 civil-ians were killed, 264 wounded and 105 kidnaped.

Of those killed, 45 were in IV Corps, south and southwest of Saigon.

As the fighting dragged on, in-fantry reinforcements rushed to the scene. U.S. artillery worked over the Reds until the enemy pulled back late Monday after-noon.

To the south, Communist gun-fire brought down a U.S. Army AH1 Cobra gunship late Monday morning near Song Be, 69 miles north-northeast of Saigon in Phuoc Long Province. Two men aboard the gunship were wounded.

In other actions:

— First Air Cav. Div. helicop-ter gunships killed 12 enemy sol-diers 75 miles northeast of Sai-gon.

— Six U.S. troopers of the 11th Armored Cav. Regt. were wounded when attacked by Com-munists firing rocket-propelled grenades 55 miles north-north-west of Saigon. Communist loss-es were unknown.

— First Inf. Div. troops unearthed a two-ton enemy arms cache 25 miles north of Saigon.

U.S. Artillery Colonel Killed

SAIGON (AP) — The U.S. command announced Tuesday that the deputy American artil-lery commander for South Viet-nam's two northernmost prov-inces was killed in action three days ago.

An announcement said that Col. John M. Jennings, 42, of the XXIV Corps tactical zone artil-lery, was killed by Communist small arms fire which hit an ob-servation helicopter in which he was riding.

The helicopter was on a recon-naissance mission in Quang Tri province south of the Demilita-rized Zone. It crashed but was not destroyed, the command said.

He had been serving in Viet-nam since May 5.

NCO's Murder Charge Confuses Judge

NHA TRANG, Vietnam (AP) — The trial of a U.S. Army ser-geant accused in the fatal shoot-ing of a Vietnamese civilian was postponed Tuesday because of confusion over the actual charge against him.

"I can't ask for a plea," said the military judge, Lt. Col. Ken-neth A. Howard. "Like the ac-cused, I'm not sure of what the accused is accused of."

He postponed until early March the trial of Sgt. Bruce A. Knerr, 20, a 173rd Airborne Bri-gade trooper charged with fatal-ly shooting a Vietnamese man last Sept. 12 in Binh Dinh Prov-ince.

At issue was whether the Army erred in changing the charge against Knerr from un-premeditated murder, and whether the case had been adequately in-vestigated before coming to trial.

It was the second post-ponement in two days in the trial of a 173rd Airborne Brigade

soldier charged with the murder of a Vietnamese man. The cases are not directly related to each other.

Monday, Howard postponed until March 2 the trial of 1st Lt. Frank B. Bonvillian II, 24, so that Bonvillian's father could fly here from Texas to testify in his son's behalf.

Bonvillian, a former platoon leader, is charged with pre-meditated murder in the fatal shooting Aug. 7 of what Army spokesmen have said was a wounded Viet Cong prisoner.

Knerr's defense counsel, Capt.

Elliott H. Vernon, 27, said the sergeant's company commander originally preferred charges last Sept. 19 of unpremeditated mur-der.

Subsequently, he said, the words "with premeditation" had been placed on the formal charge sheet presented at the trial.

Howard ordered the trial post-poned until the first week in March so the prosecution could determine which charge should be preferred against Knerr and whether the case had been prop-erly investigated.

6 Pacific Stars & Stripes
Thursday, Jan. 22, 1970

AFVN ↑

This one is a real...

A Killer at 15— Courtesy of V.C.

TAY NINH, Vietnam (Special) — He is 15 years old but looks 11. He is four feet, three inches tall and weighs 60 pounds fully dressed. He has a quick smile and can shoot a pistol from either hand while dodging and driving a motor cycle through city traffic.

His name is Tran Hoang Minh and in May, 1969, he shot and wounded a Saigon official. Tran was trained by the VC to be an assassin.

How he came to be doing these things began one day in December, 1967. Tran came home from school, where he was in the sixth grade finishing his primary education, and played around the house until his father, a fisherman, came home in the evening for supper.

It was nearly dark when supper was finished; the candles were lit. His mother and older sister were cleaning off the table and putting the cooking pots away while he, his two older brothers and younger brother, talked to their father at the table. Two Viet Cong recruiters knocked on the wooden frame of the open doorway and entered. Before the night was over they had persuaded Tran to join them. At the age of 13 he began to train, intensively, for warfare.

After training for six weeks in the jungle, Tran was assigned to a Viet Cong provisional mortar company operating throughout the Tay Ninh Province, part of the 25th Inf. Div.'s area of operations. After 14 months with the mortar company he was considered capable enough to handle some more training and a more complex job. He was picked for sapper school, and received extensive training in deception and subversion tactics.

After four months of training he was a qualified assassin, sapper and intelligence agent, ready for a job. The job he got was a tough one.

He was to become a double agent; a false rallier. The first step was to Chieu Hoi (Rally), which he did, near Go Dau Ha, on Nov. 7, 1969. He had worked hard at developing a good story; he was confident, he had an infectious smile, and after all he was only 15. And as a clincher, Tran disclosed the whereabouts of two NVA cadre and some crossing sites on the Vam Co Dong River.

The cadre were arrested and Tran later accompanied Navy men on the river, pointing out the NVA crossing sites.

At the same time he was doing another job. He was gathering intelligence about the naval installation at Go Dau Ha, to make an overlay of the positions there for the planned NVA January, 1970, offensive.

He was also reconnoitering the Go Dau Ha bridge for placement of demolitions.

His more than casual interest in the city's defenses eventually aroused suspicions, and he was brought into Tay Ninh City for questioning, where he admitted to being a false rallier.

Since that time he has identified four other teen-age Viet Cong, three of them double agents like himself. The fourth was an "inner group" leader in the Tay Ninh Military (VC) Intelligence Section, living in town legally, but under cover.

Because Americans tend to trust children, the VC deliberately recruit them, Tran explained to the 25th Div.'s 1st Brigade Intelligence Team, train them and teach them to kill, gather information, lie with a smile and destroy.

Tran Hoang Minh was a friendly youngster . . . a friend maybe, until you turned your back. He carried a K-54 pistol and orders to assassinate any officer or official he could safely kill.

Tran Hoang Minh shows his ability with a pistol while riding a motor scooter (top photo). Above and right, he field-strips a rifle. (USA)

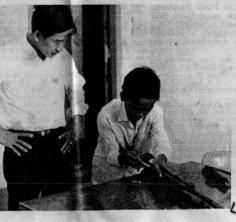

194

Army Spc. Richard S. Lovekin sent the Feb. 6 *Pacific Stars and Stripes* article (opposite) that same month with a note, "My Lai incident murder – I doubt it!!!"

THE MY LAI MASSACRE WAS FIRST REPORTED IN NOVEM-BER 1969, MORE THAN A YEAR AND A HALF AFTER THE MURDERS OF SCORES OF UNARMED CIVILIANS IN THE SOUTH VIETNAMESE VILLAGE. Army Lt. William L. Calley Jr. was charged with the responsibility for the atrocity. Some servicemen came to his defense.

The first soldier to share his thoughts in the Mailbag felt so strongly he wrote letters just weeks apart.

"**Lt. Calley is no more guilty of shooting and killing civilians than you are.** He was sent over here to do a job; why in the hell should he be punished for doing his job?

The people over here are scared to death of the Vietcong because he is everywhere and can be anyone. It's no problem for a Commie to come down from the north and obtain the needed papers to be a South Vietnamese national. He can be a friendly *papason* [older man] by day and at night slip through the wire and set satchel charges [bags containing small explosives] to blow some unsuspecting GIs away. You never know who is friendly or who are Vietcong until they kill or maim. So in my opinion, Lt. Calley is only guilty of doing his duty to his country."
Army Spc. Richard S. Lovekin, Jan. 3

"**I just read that ex-governor [George C.] Wallace [of Alabama] had a meeting with Lt. Calley.** In the meeting, Wallace said that he is proud of Calley for defending his country and so am I. That was his job and that is exactly what he did.

In my last letter, I sent an article about a 15-year old boy who was a sapper [a Vietnamese civilian carrying a satchel charge] and willing to kill the GIs he befriended and that is too evident and too well known for anyone to really press any kind of charges against Calley.... One of my buddy's hooch maids set a satchel charge at the bottom of his locker. Luckily, it was found before anything could happen.... This is going on constantly all over this damn country. You can't trust anyone."
Army Spc. Richard S. Lovekin, Feb. 24

Others voiced their opinions.

"**I won't say much about the alleged massacre.** They were told what to do and they did it. There are a lot of women and children that would just as soon kill you as look at you. They're VC too. Have you heard anything about punishment to the VN [Vietnamese] officer that shot the two MPs in the Ivory Tower in Saigon? No – and you won't."
Air Force Airman 1st Class R. Lance Hall, Jan. 27

A hot topic for Army Pfc. Mark D. Castelow (left) was the My Lai massacre. He defended Army Lt. William L. Calley Jr., pointing out the Vietnamese, including children, often befriended American troops during the day and tried to kill them at night. Like covered wagons in the Wild West, tanks (opposite) circle in a night defensive position, leaving rice paddies in ruins from their ponderous weight. Failure to put up a defensive screen of heavy chicken wire left one tank vulnerable to enemy RPGs and cost the crew their lives.

> **"How do you think Lt. Calley would have felt if he just passed by the village and that night watched one of his fellow 'fighting' men die alongside of him from a round of ammunition fired by one of these very same villagers, possibly a little, very innocent (looking) kid?"**
>
> Army Pfc. Mark D. Castelow

A military jury convicted Calley of murder in 1971 and sentenced him to life in prison. After repeated appeals and sentence reductions, he was released in November 1974.

Another case of atrocity was equally troubling to a soldier who sounded off on the 1970 conviction of Marine Pvt. Michael A. Schwarz, sentenced to life imprisonment at hard labor for killing 12 Vietnamese civilians during a February 19, 1969 patrol. This letter was the 500th received by the Mailbag.

"Well, I have gotten so tired of reading stories about mass murders and killings in Vietnam villages that I just felt that I had to write this letter. If I were in Lt. Calley's place I would lose what little faith I had, if any, in the entire U.S. government. How can they accuse one man of killing some estimated numbers (not even quotable) of Vietnamese when that was what he was sent over here for?

Out there in the field you could walk past a little, very innocent kid and that same night he could be assaulting your night defensive position. We had an incident where one dead Vietnamese discovered was identified as a man who was one of our barbers during the day and a VC sympathizer at night.

As far as My Lai is concerned, I would feel that it was just one less village to really have to worry about.

If the choice had been mine, I believe it would have been the same. How do you think Lt. Calley would have felt if he just passed by the village and that night watched one of his fellow 'fighting' men die alongside of him from a round of ammunition fired by one of these very same villagers, possibly a little, very innocent (looking) kid?

I'm sorry if I sound radical, but I have very little compassion for the people trying to live a double life in these villages. They are trying to walk the middle of the road, which is a very shaky road to start with.

I hope some of the people who read this letter will tend to disagree with my viewpoints. As of yet, I haven't been shown anything, either from the government or the people, to convince me that my attitude and that of Lt. Calley is or could be wrong. Think about it!"

Army Pfc. Mark D. Castelow, Feb. 21

"Just recently a Marine named Pvt. [Michael A.] Schwarz was convicted of murdering 16 innocent civilians in South Vietnam in 1969. He was sentenced by military court-martial to life imprisonment for this supposed war atrocity.

In passing judgment upon him, one has used superior intelligence and probably knows more than me.

First off, the action took place at night while on patrol. This is a major step in discovering the truth about the Vietnam war. The truth is that the Army doesn't know how to fight this war because we can't tell apart the VC from the South Vietnamese people and for that reason no one can determine reasonable judgment within human limits unless they are God. As [U.S. Sen. George S.] McGovern said, 'This war seems like an impossible task.'

So the Marine Corps has now played the role of God in passing judgment that cannot be determined by human limits. I call out in sympathy for a boy who became a man sent to no man's land in [a] hell of fire.

I motion that if Pvt. Schwarz is not pardoned from these incredible accusations that some of the 18 million men who have served in Vietnam organize a nonviolent march to the Capitol and demand a presidential pardon....

Secondly, I think that Pvt. Schwarz is not really guilty for this reason. In Vietnam, it is so dark at night that you can't see 2 feet in front of you. Those innocent civilians should have been in BED by then unless they were helping the VC set booby traps."

Army Spc. Charles Leach, July 1

TET

A New Year for

VIETNAM

WILLIAM F. BUCKLEY JR.

How Will Reds Celebrate '70 Tet?

The sun has entered Aquarius, and the Chinese New Year, better known in Southeast Asia as Tet, is at hand.

What will the enemy do? For symbolic reasons, there is great call on them to do something. The great Tet offensive of 1968 had profound political consequences in America. It is (I believe) inconceivable that Eugene McCarthy would have done so well in the New Hampshire presidential primary but for the general despair about Vietnam generated by that kamikaze assault on American installations and South Vietnamese cities. We know now that it was a military disaster for the enemy, but it looked for a great while as though it would be worth it to them in political tender, which is the tender they have mostly dealt in throughout the course of the bloody war.

The Mekong Delta is the likeliest area because it was there that the war, in fact, began, in part because the enemy coveted the great rice bowl of the region. It is useful to remember that 85 per cent of Vietnam is in friendly hands, and that 85 per cent of the area that isn't in friendly hands lies within the Mekong Delta—to which, however, the enemy has had for the first time to send North Vietnamese regulars because their efforts there can no longer be sustained by indigenous revolutionaries. This causes a special problem because of a historical antipathy by southerners to the Prussians from above the 17th parallel. Still, it remains the likeliest place for the assault.

It may be that the North Vietnamese haven't the military energy to do something spectacular this time around; or it may be that they will decide to await a more propitious season, perhaps in the spring or early summer. On the other hand, one must prepare oneself, and it is surely important to consider now what possibly the enemy could achieve, say in the Mekong Delta where it continues to be stronger than in the northern regions.

The answer, of course, is that over a short but melodramatic period a very few people can achieve a great deal, almost anywhere. The analogy is strained but useful, that if the Black Students Union can occupy Cornell University, the Viet Cong can probably take a village, town, or even a small city, if it chooses: a) to concentrate its power in a particular area, and b) to assign soldiers to a suicidal mission.

As ever, the enemy would have in mind a political rather than a military objective. The goal wouldn't be to hold down for a few days or a week a few towns and villages, but to suggest to the world that Vietnamization is a hallucination and that the military reserves of the enemy are infinite.

It would appear obvious to me that one should anticipate flash successes by the enemy in the next weeks or months. The military effect of them should be calibrated, and will be. Their political success should be studied much more intensely. Germany never seemed so strong as during the winter offensive it waged in

December of 1944, and the great Battle of the Bulge is said to have prompted even General Patton to muse at a dramatic meeting of Allied generals that the Germans might yet win the war. Ninety days later, Hitler had committed suicide.

General Giap is not likely to commit suicide, although it is not inconceivable that he will be shot, even as some of his predecessors were executed for miscalculations. The general believes that he knows America, and he has every reason to excuse the military casualties he suffered two years ago at Tet on the grounds that he came close to paralyzing the American will. Mr. Nixon, confident that the stamina was there, gradually roused it, and today it carries us forward, towards Vietnamization, towards an objective which can truly be called national.

Can we be unbalanced again by anything that it is within the power of the North Vietnamese to do? It is a subject of much political speculation.

The opponents of the Vietnam war and, derivatively, of the policy of Vietnamization, are strangely quiet these days, as if the concertmaster had taken a leave of absence. They gorge on bad news from Vietnam (nothing brightens their day so much as, say, news of high American casualty figures). But like the Viet Cong, they are still capable of spasmodic efforts which, even like a dying battery, can make a great light, even if it is a terminal effort.

Washington Star Syndicate

TET, THE VIETNAMESE NEW YEAR, ALWAYS SPELLED TROUBLE FOR U.S. GROUND TROOPS. Servicemen had plenty to say about the enemy efforts in February.

"**Tet is two weeks away and everyone is running around in circles getting ready.** I just hope I don't have guard from the 5th to the 9th of February because I won't get any sleep. Activity around the camp here has stepped up considerably. It's really funny, the NVA and VC have had four months of miserable weather to attack and now they step up the activity just when the weather is about to turn back to the good old hot and dusty."
Army 1st Lt. Henry A. "Alex" Wise, Jan. 19

He added a wry comment two weeks later.

"**The action has really picked up now but things here at Eagle are relatively quiet.** I'm glad I'm not at Evans or Sally. They receive sniper fire all the time. Not so here. All the brass is too worried about their own skins so they provide us with all kinds of support for defense of our perimeter."
Army 1st Lt. Henry A. "Alex" Wise, Feb. 3

Another wary soldier made plans to get out of Vietnam during Tet.

"**I plan to get away from all of this because on February 7 I am taking my R&R to Sydney, Australia.** I hope to have a really great time and I will let you and the readers know all about it in a future letter. I planned my R&R to fall right at the beginning of Tet, the Vietnamese New Year, which is a bad time to be in Vietnam.
Army Spc. Mark L. Goodman, Jan. 20

Tet was Vietnam's biggest celebration and always presaged increased firepower from the enemy. Servicemen shared their thoughts on the Vietnamese new year and one sent conservative columnist William F. Buckley Jr.'s take on the action.

Most American servicemen supported
Nixon's incursion into Cambodia, an April
campaign that ended in three months.

INVADING CAMBODIA IN APRIL PROVED A HUGE MORALE BOOSTER FOR MOST U.S. TROOPS. "As for the raids into Cambodia, I think anything that has a chance of stopping a VC or an NVA from getting to South Vietnam and killing an American soldier is justified," Army Sgt. Horace G. Cole wrote on May 7. Other correspondents echoed his view.

"**You want some comments about Cambodia?** Outstanding! Should have been done a long time ago! You stay-at-home-and-criticize-the-war types couldn't begin to appreciate how popular President Nixon is in this outfit. From field grades down to SP/4s, all I've heard is praise.

The main concern is our honorable Congress, particularly the Senate, is going to sell out. This drive to cut off funds is pathetic and stinks with politicking and partisan motives. Fulbright and Kennedy are perhaps the most disgusting examples of this with the exception of [New York City Mayor John V.] Lindsay.

His statement to the effect that 'the real heroes of the war are the draft evaders' is disgraceful, irresponsible, and a complete repudiation of the sacrifices made by the forty thousand KIAs and three hundred thousand WIAs over here serving America when called....

This is my view of the situation. Let Nixon do what he thinks is right. Shake things up in the Cambodian sanctuary, knock the VC and NVA off balance for a while. Not only will our casualties very likely be lessened in the long run, but the time gained from the blow will allow the Vietnamese army that much more time to strengthen itself for that time when it will bear the whole brunt of the fighting."
Army 1st Lt. James D.E. Weisbrod, May 11

"**We did not go into Cambodia but we came very close.** We were all hoping we would go. We back President Nixon one hundred percent. His actions in Cambodia will save many lives in the future. I just wish people would realize how important the Cambodian crossover is to the Cambodian government, not to mention the South Vietnamese government. I guess there are people who never get tired of telling the president how to run the nation."
Army Spc. Richard W. Refner Jr., May 24

"**For the president to throw a new war on the radical left now was somewhat of a curveball and more like a knuckleball.** [Atlanta Braves pitcher] Phil Niekro couldn't throw a better one and the batter, we hope, is a communist out.

In criticizing the war effort in Vietnam and now Cambodia, the radical left has shown me one thing, 'they are throwing a way of life down my throat,' and saying, 'like it or lump it.' For them, life is one big party of dreams but dreams, my friend, are fought for and worked for. We are fighting in Vietnam for the freedom to dream and work upon dreams....

Remember one thing. Your president has money tied up from here to the moon. He has the responsibility for keeping the first nation first in his 4 years of office. He must maintain a position of strength, not weakness. Let's not have another president look like President Johnson did when he left office in 1968."
Army Spc. Charles Leach, May 28 Mailbag

"**First off, I would like to let all the people back home know that we, of the 31st Engr. BN, are behind President Nixon all the way in his decision to clean up Cambodia.** I think the people should know how we feel, for we are the ones to see life over here and have to do the fighting. All those protesting college students are yelling for the president to get us out of Cambodia and save lives.

Well, I've lost 2 of my friends since we have moved in here. I would like to see us finish the job that we were sent in here to do, not only for ourselves, but for the men who lost their lives trying to do their job.

I would like to thank all the patriotic Delawareans who are behind us and want our wonderful country protected against what is happening over here. I was married and I hate the thought of my daughter having to hide and beg for food all her life....

Our headquarters is in Quan Loi and right now we are the only combat engineers in Cambodia. We have been in the field since the beginning of March. We will be going back in to Quan Loi tomorrow for a rest."
Army Spc. Roger L. Grubb in Quan Loi, June 22 Mailbag

"**For those who think the president's move into Cambodia was a bad deal, I'm here to argue.** There are too many politicians trying to fight this war from their chairs in Washington, D.C.

I am here in Saigon and the decrease in terrorist activity against military berthing areas, restaurants [and], local bars, and [the decline in] seriously injuring a lot of innocent people is very noticeable! The first real sharp drop was noted in the first week of the Cambodian offense.

The effect of this is very heartening to the Vietnamese people and they are hoping the war will not last much more than a year. The Cambodian strikes really hurt the NVA and VC supply systems. It is really noticeable now and is improving."
Navy Petty Officer 3rd Class James R. MacSorley III in Saigon, Aug. 8

"**I feel President Nixon's campaign into Cambodia was a major victory for the free world.** Possibly, this can be attributed to the personal safety I now have, but enemy action has been greatly reduced and the South Vietnamese soldiers are taking on a leading role in ground activities. I believe within a year's time they will be able to defend their own country with a minimum of outside support.

Myself, like most Americans over here, want to return home to their families and loved ones. There is much bitterness and resentment, both here and in the states, but our government has taken a stand and, right or wrong, we must abide by its decision. That's what makes America the great nation it is. People may be individualistic in their actions, but we must have unity in support of our government or the flames of Rome are going to seem like the flickering light of a candle."
Air Force Tech. Sgt. Robert B. Darrow, Dec. 2 Mailbag

The first Delawarean believed to have been injured in the Cambodian invasion was Pfc. Richard J. Roan of Newark. He sustained his injuries on May 9, the 100th day of his Vietnam tour. We learned of his misfortune when he was in recovery in Valley Forge General Hospital in Phoenixville, Pennsylvania. Mailbag readers were encouraged to send cards and letters to him in the June 29 column.

Army Sgt. Johnnie C. "Little Sparky" Duricek Sr., assigned to the American Division's 196th Infantry Brigade, was the first serviceman to write about the war spilling into Laos. His letter included a hand-drawn battle diagram. Although Americans did not learn of incursions into Cambodia and Laos by U.S. troops until 1970, the Delaware Reconnaissance Team, the Army's special operations group, had been gathering intelligence in those countries since late 1967. These ominous patches were worn by team members. A collapsible canteen (opposite) was part of a GI's load-carrying equipment.

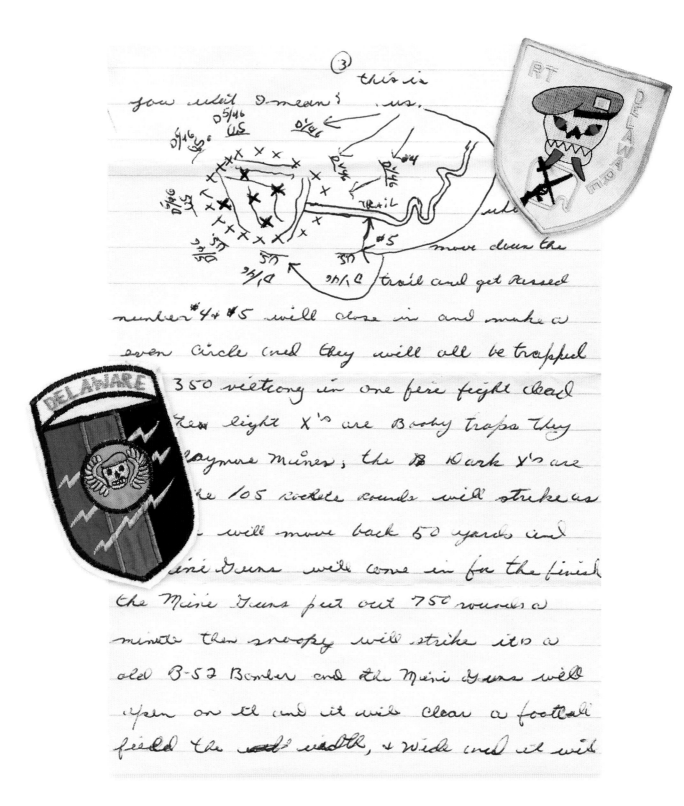

VIPs junketing to Cambodia and the outlandish preparations undertaken for their visit made me so angry I strafed the June 11 Mailbag with one of my infrequent editorial comments:

Saw via a newscast Monday night a film report of a recent visit by Gov. Raymond P. Shafer of Pennsylvania, assorted senators and others to Shakey's Hill, Cambodia, which could be classified as disgusting at best.

The VIPs were on a tour of inspection of Shakey's Hill, 107 miles north of Saigon and four miles inside the Cambodian border. Vast underground storerooms of enemy war materials had been recovered and captured by American troops.

Monsoon rains made Shakey's Hill no less than a quagmire. Soldiers were exhausted from combat. They received orders, however, to pretty the area for the advent of the VIPs.

Special tables were flown in, white linen tablecloths secured, haircuts all around, new hats, clean clothes. The area was made to look like a stateside super base waiting for inspection.

Soldiers were briefed on what they could or couldn't say to the dignitaries and even the captured weapons were replaced in their original caches to simulate recent discovery.

Ridiculous.

And the VIPs came away from Shakey's Hill convinced "our boys" are getting everything they need and want and war conditions in Cambodia are just peachy.

The soldiers themselves said they were living like animals and the whole visit was practically a sham. Ditto. Why take precious free time from these weary men to ensure that dignitaries would tarnish neither their minds nor their boots with the realities of war?

It would appear Vietnam and now Cambodia have become geographical showcases where political mileage is to be gained from apparent Utopian guerrilla conditions.

The same column featured a letter from a sailor who offered his opinion on how to deal with the war in general.

"Me and my buddy are sitting in the bunker and discussing the general situation here and back home.

We just brought up the thought that if England, France, Canada and all our little buddy-buddy 'allies' want us to do their fighting and protect the interest of the free world then it should be up to our discretion to carry it out the best way we could. We think President Nixon should go before the United Nations and submit an ultimatum to all countries, that if North Vietnam does not remove its troops from South Vietnam, Thailand, Cambodia and Laos that we will have no other choice but to make the country of North Vietnam incapable of carrying on these wars.

Not to wipe the whole populace out, just to make it incapable of being Russia's or China's springboard for liberation wars."
Navy Petty Officer 3rd Class Ron Weatherlow, June 11 Mailbag

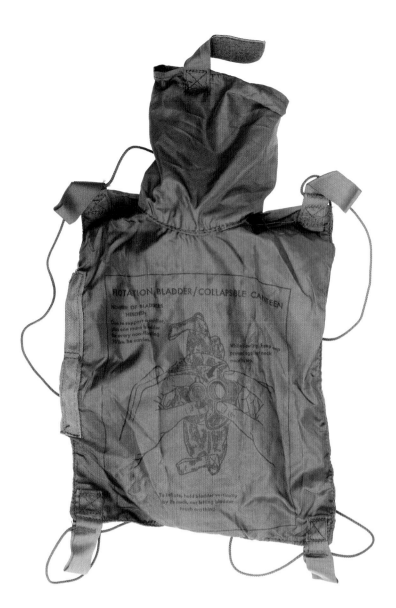

The Mailbag's first letter reporting combat in Laos, north of Cambodia and west of Vietnam, arrived late in 1970. The writer sent a chilling combat plan.

"We are fighting as a blocking point at Laos. We are on alert right now as there are three regiments of 350 Vietcong headed our way and they are carrying rockets, AK44 & 47 mortars and are moving and headed in this direction. We are supposed to attack them as they cross the rice paddies and dikes.

We are close to the trail that they are following.... When they move down the trail ... [we] will close in and make an even circle and they will all be trapped and 350 Vietcong in one fierce fight dead. The eight Xs are booby traps, claymore mines, the dark Xs are where the 105 rocket rounds will strike. Then we will move back 50 yards and the mini guns will come in for the finish.

The mini guns put out 750 rounds a minute. Then Snoopy will strike. It's an old B-52 bomber and the mini guns will open and [they] will clear a football field, everything down to the pulp."
Army Sgt. Johnnie C. "Little Sparky" Duricek Sr., Nov. 12

COMMENTARY ON TROOP WITHDRAWALS AND THE CAMBODIAN CAMPAIGN FILTERED IN. For many, the war finally was winding down. Navy Petty Officer 3rd Class Ron Weatherlow supported Nixon's decision but still had his doubts. He wrote, "Am behind the president's troop withdrawals but I do not believe we will ever be able to totally withdraw all combat troops until North Vietnam is made incapable of carrying out its wars of liberation." We continued to receive letters of support for the president's actions.

"Before I went to that beautiful but somewhat primitive country, I thought that we should be there militarily. However, I felt that Nixon's plan for withdrawal after the establishment of a 'Vietnamization' program was just another 'sell-out' to the Communists and I was therefore against it. Now that I have been there and have seen the war from my own vantage point, observed the people, the country and the ARVN's (Army of the Republic of Vietnam) accomplishments, I am positive that President Nixon's formula for our honorable withdrawal is the only one and is achieving a tremendous success.

I have spoken with many of the officers and men who are stationed around Saigon and who were under direct influence of the Cambodian sanctuaries. My own conclusion after considering everything is that it was the smartest and most rewarding move that the United States has made since the Inchon Landing in Korea by General Douglas MacArthur. The increased morale of the ARVN troops has been boosted tremendously because of their impeccable performance there and the pressure around Saigon has been reduced to almost nothing.

I have read the wild comments by the stateside liberal senators, congressmen and newspapers as they screamed that we were enlarging the war and that the ARVNs had no right to 'invade' Cambodia. I have also noticed that these same liberal sources neglect to point out that the ARVNs crossed the border to fight North Vietnamese Army soldiers armed with Russian-made weapons and who had 'invaded' Cambodia years before. We have pulled out completely and the ARVNs say that they will leave immediately, if the NVA will do likewise. Of course, they (NVA) won't do that.

For sure, a person must go to Vietnam in order to get a true idea of the situation and thus intelligently reach a conclusion on our commitment there."
Army Capt. James D. Rawlins Jr., Dec. 28

Conversely, one Army officer took issue with President Nixon on a couple of fronts, offering irrefutable evidence in his letter.

"I am stationed in a literally unheard of place called Quang Tri. President Nixon stated in a speech back in May that there were no troops north of Da Nang except the marines. I must rebut this by saying I am approximately 150 kilometers north of Da Nang and 13 miles south of the DMZ and I really haven't seen more than a dozen marines in the four months I've been here.

Nixon also mentioned the McNamara electronic eyes (radar) along the DMZ that keep the NVA on the other side. The personnel in my company maintain these sets and there are definitely troops on these sites operating them. He insinuated that these were self-sustaining, which they are definitely not.

Just to set the record straight, we are here and we are definitely doing a job for both the Vietnamese and the U.S. government."
Army Capt. Joseph E. Parker Jr. in Quang Tri, Aug. 29

A year and a half later, Quang Tri Province would make headlines when the North Vietnamese launched a major offensive south across the DMZ. Within days, the United States retaliated with bombing sorties deep inside North Vietnam, the first since 1967.

In May 1972, Nixon ordered the mining of major North Vietnamese ports, including Haiphong, and air strikes targeting railroads, causing serious economic disruption. Quang Tri City was liberated from the Communists by South Vietnamese forces four months later on September 15.

As this tank maneuvered into position for a night bivouac, its massive weight sank into mud. Tanks destroyed thousands of rice paddies throughout Vietnam.

Army Sgt. Kenneth D. Keogh saw plenty of action in Quang Tri,
about 25 miles south of the Demilitarized Zone that separated
North Vietnam from South Vietnam. In his letter (opposite),
Army Pfc. Buddy Wyatt praised the South Vietnamese people.

IN 1970, SUPPORT FOR THE WAR REMAINED MIXED. Our correspondents tended towards more philosophical outlooks on the conflict. They wrote more frequently about an honorable end to the war and the South Vietnamese as an oppressed people. First, commentary from those who believed the United States belonged in Vietnam.

"**Many of the men feel this is a political war.** But if Nixon pulls out, what were all the American lives for? What did they die for? And [what will] the men who will never be normal again gain? So don't pull out, let's fight and win.

Now I'm in Long Binh. I have seen little action but I'm going to Tay Ninh to be a door gunner under my own free will.… If I get killed I want it to mean something, not just so some politician can get votes.… I'm asking Nixon not to pull out. We've lost too many lives and it'll be for nothing. I'm for peace but under our terms!"
Army Pfc. J.W. Bowden in Long Binh, Feb. 19

"**Yes, it would be nice to bring us all home … but imagine the price we would pay just standing on the side watching this country's freedom fall apart.**

Well, here we are and here we'll stay. I guess until we can leave in a really honorable way. For those of you who disagree with what I've said, I would like for you to read something that I've heard: "For those who must fight for it, freedom has … a meaning which the protected will never know." But I'm fighting for freedom and if I die, that's the way it must be.

I only have, as of today, 134 days left in the Army. I'll be home for good in mid-July and I can say that I've served my time in hell!"
Army Sgt. Kenneth D. Keogh in Quang Tri, March 3

"**I have quite a while to go.** More than 300 days.… But from what I've seen, I definitely do believe that we should be here. These people are just as good as us and most certainly do work harder. One thing I am not too clear on, though, why are they paying me $65 a month extra for hazardous fire pay when the Vietnamese women, who work like dogs doing everything from filling sand bags to riding on a wet garbage truck, only get about $1 a day? I do not believe that is too awful fair, even with a low economy over here."
Army Pfc. Buddy Wyatt, April 6 Mailbag

"**I don't totally agree with this war.** I do feel, however, that since the United States has sent so many men, invested so much money and lost so many soldiers that anything less than an honorable peace, either military or political, would be most undesirable.

I'd like to think that by myself and all my fellow soldiers over here laying our lives on the line every day would lead to a just peace and not just troop withdrawals that would leave the country open for the Communists. I think that those who died here and those now fighting deserve better than that.

I've been here 10 months and I'm looking forward to getting home, but I'd rather stay here and fight another year than to see the United States suffer a political defeat by pulling out all U.S. troops and leaving the country to the VC or NVA."
Army Sgt. Horace G. Cole, May 7

"**What do I have to say about Vietnam?** It's a place you can see movies and pictures of and hear stories about, but never really believe until you're here. The country is much more developed now than when we first arrived yet the masses still live under conditions worse than those of our poorest people in the states.

It's a place where most of the people can't remember a time when there wasn't war. If the Vietnamization of the war works (and it appears to be in our area) maybe things will change for the people. I guess the best thing this place does for the American soldier is make him appreciate what he has back home."
Army 1st Lt. Bob Bowers near Long Binh, Aug. 20

"**We are very proud to be doing our part over here.** I'm with the 4th Infantry Division here at An Khe and have been in Vietnam since Aug. 15."
Army Pfc. Hall A. "Andy" Macklin III at An Khe, Sept. 21

"**I'm very glad that I came in the Army and even more so that I came over here.** I never really appreciated being an American until I came over here. I'm very proud to be serving my country and I also feel that if we pull out, all our men would have died in vain. Because if we pull out, the North Vietnamese will take over."
Army Pfc. Anthony J. Colicchio at Landing Zone Cindy, Oct. 7

American troops often helped the South Vietnamese fortify their military bases by stringing concertina wire around the perimeter. Ly-Tin was near Chu Lai.

LY-TIN

Another soldier believed the war was a mistake.

"**You cannot have peace by continually killing people.** It has to be a mutual agreement between two bodies, even if one … has to bend over backwards. For who are we to say which form of government is best for a people we know so little about?

War is gross and hideous and our elders have the gall to say, 'What has happened to the younger generation?' when it is only the younger generation that is over here trying to make up for one of the biggest mistakes in history.

I pray that at some time soon we may all be able to live in peace."
Army Spc. John P. "Pat" Little, Jan. 22 Mailbag

Others were more practical in their opposition.

"**My beliefs on Vietnam, I feel, are quite similar to those of a lot of GIs.** We shouldn't be here, at least the way the war is being conducted. This war is one BIG waste of money which could be used for more important things in the U.S.A. I believe the people here should have a chance to decide what type of government they want to live under.

I have no logical way of accomplishing this, but I feel President Nixon's move to Cambodia was a stepping stone to the solution. There has been considerably less action here in the past three or four months as a result of that decision to go into Cambodia."
Army Spc. John R. "Rob" MacNab near Cam Ranh Bay, Sept. 9

"**Many men have voiced their opinions on the 'war' here in Vietnam and their reasons.** I feel we are doing the country a grave injustice by our presence here which has inflated their economy out of all sane proportions. The black market is rampant and little or nothing is being done to check it....

With God's will this farce here and this terrible waste of U.S. money will soon be over."
Army Spc. Philip C. Winkler in Vung Tau, Nov. 11

Those who objected to the course of the war were just as fervent. One, a crew chief on a Cobra helicopter, was a frequent Mailbag writer who always signed his letters, "Your Man in Nam." He wrote to the Mailbag in January with a strong message, critical of U.S. strategy. Months later, his feelings remained the same.

"**I believe we are making a terrible mistake over here.** No matter how long we stay, there will always be Commies in this country. As soon as we withdraw all of our troops, the Commies will take it all over. This war is not run by soldiers but it is run by politics. The military leaders should cut the ropes that bind them and fight a real war. The only way to really make this country an independent nation is to ensure that the Commies will stay out and one of those ways is to destroy the North Vietnamese."
Army Spc. Richard S. Lovekin, Jan. 3

"**We have lost too many good men over here, not even worrying about all the billions of dollars spent over here, to pull out and let the Commies take over.** It's not too late to do what we should have done in the very beginning. Now the NVA is going into Laos and Thailand. The only way we can ever hope to even slow down the Communist aggressors in this part of the world is to go into North Vietnam and destroy its power.

'War is hell,' as the phrase goes, but this war could be less hellish if it was fought right. If this war doesn't start being fought right, we may as well chalk [up] all the lost lives and money spent here as a complete loss."
Army Spc. Richard S. Lovekin, March 11

TROOPS WHO HAD DAILY CONTACT WITH THE SOUTH VIETNAMESE ACKNOWLEDGED THEIR FORTITUDE. The deputy senior advisor to a Regional Force Battalion south of Da Nang came in contact with them often, teaching them English while learning their language. He sent two letters, four months apart.

"**My greatest impression so far has been the unbelievable ambition of these people.** Compared with the average American, their ambition far surpasses ours. They can make beautiful objects or arms of war with the simplest materials, using no modern tools. It shocked me at first, for something like this was never mentioned before I arrived here. They have an incredible desire to learn. They want to know everything about our civilization, Europe and the whole world in general. They believe that, like Americans, someday they will discover resources, so far unknown, and build their country into a peaceful and prosperous one.

I have read and heard time and time again that these people do not really want to win this war. I do not think that this is true. Imagine, if you can, that instead of drafting for two years, as we do in our country, that we have a thirty-year commitment. Yes, the soldiers here are in service for the duration of the war. In some cases, that has been a lifetime. Is it any wonder that at times they despair? I have known Americans to despair at a lot less.

I am sure that some of what I have said here will be scoffed at. Nevertheless, I look at it this way. The United States has agreed to help these people get on their feet. I don't think that anyone has plans for an out-and-out military victory. After all, whose victory would it be, ours or theirs?

We are here, maybe for not much longer, but let's make the most of it and help these people gain their independence. Weren't we helped to get ours at one time? Perhaps some of our younger citizens tend to overlook this at times. I am here for one year, and I will do everything I can to help someone, less fortunate than myself, attain something he wants so badly, but has never really had the chance to enjoy."
Army 1st Lt. Domenic M. Grillo, Feb. 10

"**With what these people have to work with, they are merely an example of strong initiative, ingenuity and the desire to succeed.** It makes me nauseous to hear over and over the falsehood about the people here taking all that they can from us. I don't find any of them that way.

Aren't we supposed to be here to help them? Unfortunately, we have all of the materials that they need. Presently, they have some and are getting more, but it is still very difficult. Right here I am involved with teaching them how to use their supply channels and to forget 'scrounging.'

Things have been going quite well over here. The Battalion staff is doing very well and improving constantly. My Vietnamese has also improved slightly and I have made a vow to not falter. It really is difficult though.

I'm still doing all I can to help these people all get that freedom they want."
Army 1st Lt. Domenic M. Grillo, June 3

Others also viewed the situation from a humanitarian standpoint.

"**I have been engaged in pacification programs during my tour here in Vietnam and in this area we have made good progress in helping the people to a better way of life.**

We have helped bring security to areas where before there was only terror – and not only through U.S. presence but through increased Vietnamese confidence and ability to uphold law and order by their own police force.

Once security is in fact in an area, roads so essential to development are being built, agriculture is once again reaching toward potential, fishing industries are growing and local government, self-elected, is coming into being.

Dispensaries, schools and other necessary public services are being reinstituted. And, again, this is not solely a U.S. effort. The South Vietnamese, with U.S. advisory assistance, are carrying these programs forward.

I could go on with the many humanitarian things our country is doing here. I fear from reading the many U.S. papers we see over here that this aspect of our effort is being overlooked. The Vietnamese people are benefiting from this effort and the Americans at home should be proud of their contribution, along with the contributions of other free world forces to this effort."
Army Lt. Col. Pat Morris, Feb. 21

"**It's hard to understand why we're here.** It's taken me over eleven months of being around the Vietnamese people to finally come to the conclusion that what we're doing here is worthwhile."
Army Spc. Bob Sheppard, March 2

"**Most guys over here are down on the country and refer to the Vietnamese as worthless gooks.** In most instances, they use this as an excuse to be on their worst behavior.

What we fail to realize is the South Vietnamese are an oppressed people. They deserve a chance for a democratic government that we take so much for granted.

Just for the record, I don't believe we should be over here. Until someone comes up with a better idea or the Vietnamese are capable of conducting the war themselves, it appears to be the only solution.

Perhaps if I were out in the rice paddies, jungles, or boonies, I'd have a different attitude. But since I'm not, this is the way I feel about the situation."
Air Force Airman 1st Class Richard L. Holding Jr., Aug. 11

"**It's not a bad life here.** My compound lies just outside Da Nang and is right on the beach (South China Sea). I have a team of Bru (Montagnards) and I take them to the field along with one or two Americans. They're more or less my bodyguards. They're nice to have around and they are for the most part crack shots. They're pretty Americanized, and I can generally communicate without my interpreter, although the conversations are a jargon of pidgin English, Vietnamese, Bru and some French words."
Army 1st Lt. James D.E. Weisbrod near Da Nang, April 18

MANY LETTERS CONTAINED COMMENTS ABOUT EXPERI-ENCES IN THE WAR ZONE AS WELL AS THE FIGHT AGAINST COMMUNISM. "I have learned a lot in my past year and [being] here is something I'll never forget," Army Spc. Jim Gross wrote in his January 5 letter.

"I am over here in Vietnam for twelve months' service to my country. Out of my twelve months, I have ten and one-half months left. I feel that my being here is helping to ensure that my children and their children will not have to go through the same ordeal as I am."
Marine Sgt. William F. May in Quang Nan Province, Feb. 22

"I'll tell you the truth. I was sort of disappointed in the U.S. as first impression has a habit of doing to some people. You could never believe the degree of wasted materials over here, it was honestly a heartbreaker to know where our taxes have gone.

I've got a long ways to go on my tour, if it wasn't for the bugs and weather, it wouldn't be so bad. The country itself is beautiful, but the people have got a long ways to go.

As when in the states reading papers and watching TV news, I thought the country had improved a lot but I am afraid I can't see much in improvement, only in military status. But now with Laos and Cambodia on the verge of war with VC infiltrates, Vietnam is no longer the big issue. But we are still here.

Another thing we have got 450,000 (approx.) men over here now. But I think maybe 1/2 or less could do the same amount of work. A lot of coffee is drunk over here, probably more than in the states. Although I've been in the Army 15 months, I prefer the VN country for Army duty rather than stateside. In the states, it's a big Boy Scout camp. You are treated like kids instead of men. But over here, you are a man, you've got to be or you'll be going home in a plastic bag. Not saying the ones that do are not men."
Army Spc. Howard E. Brown, April 27

"Four years ago, I knew nothing about Vietnam. Now I know enough to appreciate the complexities of the problems over here. I have 215 Vietnamese working for me and I have learned a great deal about their country and their customs.

They are a wonderful, kind people, industrious in their own curious way. They are intelligent and shrewd and can even be treacherous when the situation requires them to be.

Unfortunately, American intervention has destroyed the local economy, bringing unimaginable inflation and black market dealings. Many Vietnamese foresee the departure of American troops and consequently are trying to reap the benefits of our presence right now.

The war has brought hardship and untold suffering to many of my workers and listening to their stories is a troubling experience.

Like most Americans here, I shall be happy to leave 'the Nam' to return to my own life. The sad part is that even as I leave, others will be coming here to replace me. Eventually, somehow, the fighting will cease though I have seen little progress in my months here."
1st Lt. John E. Flaherty, June 23

One wrote of his concerns, just weeks apart.

"Some of the things I read worry me. What is happening to the United States? It seems that the Communists are succeeding in destroying our country and we are helping them."
Army Spc. James R. Turner Jr., June 26 Mailbag

"I feel this way about Communism.... It will always exist and the only way to control it is to have a meeting with the various countries. By changing leaders and laws, in time I hope the status of the world will change. I believe we are doing just what the Communists want: to get our country into such an uproar and confusion that we will destroy ourselves."
Army Spc. James R. Turner Jr., July 10 Mailbag

On many occasions, parents of servicemen forwarded letters to the Mailbag. This letter was written by an 18-year-old who had been in Vietnam about three months. He wrote from Camp Radner near Da Nang:

"**I want to tell you a story about a great man.** If at first you don't think him great, read on and you will understand.

We've been about five miles haven't we, Stan? My feet are dead. No, kid, just two instead.

Then a booby trap that the point man didn't see, a grenade with a tripwire tied to a tree. The 18-year-old trustingly walked forward, looking all around. Then a sudden explosion and three hit the ground.

The radio man is up on the frequency, calling a medic. The 18-year-old tells the corpsman, 'Doc, I don't think I'll make it back. I don't think I'll ever see my homeland.'

'You know, Doc, my father always called me a boy, he never called me a man.' The corpsman was working diligently doing his very best. Then the 18-year-old said, 'Doc, go look after the rest.' Then the 18-year-old felt a sudden cringing pain and the corpsman knew he had been working in vain.

Americas' hardest-fighting men stand there in a daze. Each with a tear in his eye and a prayer beneath his breath. You ask me who he is, but I'll tell you no name. He's your son, or the boy next door. He's the great man who never gained fame. He's the boy who can't drink with his Pop or vote in his own country.

And the man who died to keep everyone home free. Well, Mom and Pop, I love you both so dearly. I am going into a hot, hot area tomorrow but don't worry, I'll write as soon as I get back."
Marine Lance Cpl. Stanley F. Pienkos Jr., Jan. 26 Mailbag

Stanley did get back and he did write to his parents.

One proud mother, Mrs. J.T. Jump, sent correspondence from her son which was printed as an open letter.

"**The place – the Republic of Vietnam.** The time – December 1970. We are approaching a time of year in Vietnam which could be very dangerous, as I know from past experience. There are several things that can happen:

1. The NVA launch an offensive of tremendous proportion late in the monsoon season or immediately after.
2. Very little combat, as it is right now.
3. The war can end with the U.S. as victors.

Let us talk about the last possibility. To do this the soldier and diplomat must do his job and do it well if our country expects a decisive victory over the NVA and VC, but most of all over Communism. That is all it would take. The biggest reason why this war has gone on so long is that we do not have the support we need. The youth of America scream 'Get out of Vietnam – Peace Now.'

Do you think we, the soldiers, want to see our buddies killed day in and day out or lose a leg, arm or worse? Do you think a soldier loves war any more than you the civilian? Do you think the soldier likes to leave his wife, children and parents? If you do, you are very much mistaken. I do not. I have a wonderful wife and a fine son I

Marine Lance Cpl. Stanley F. Pienkos Jr., a member of 1st Force Reconnaissance Company, the Marines' special operations group, described himself as "lean and mean." A pride of Chinooks (opposite), part of the 23rd Infantry Division's Aviation Battalion, awaits orders at the army base in Chu Lai.

left behind. No, I don't prefer killing the enemy to being a good husband and father. I want my family free and happy. This is why a soldier goes to war without balking.

You say to kill is wrong. We know that too. We have to see the guy's face when a bullet slams into his body. Believe me, it is a sight you never forget. Some of you never see these sights and you don't see our guys suffer. So how do you know what is right or wrong?

We want the war to end, preferably in victory for the U.S.A. Friends, the only way that we'll be able to do that is for all good citizens back in our great country to give us soldiers and our government all the support you can and for all of us to put faith in God and pray to Him for help. Let us hope and pray for an end to war and a U.S. victory so that those who have died have not died in vain.

We need 100% support of all Americans. Without that, the Communists will keep on fighting both the diplomats in Paris and the soldier on the line.

Please help us that we may have peace and stop the Communist malignancy at the same time."
Army Spc. David T. Jump, Dec. 23

SERVICEMEN BROUGHT READERS CLOSER TO THE WAR WHEN THEY SHARED STORIES OF GROUND ACTION, RANGING FROM CLOSE CALLS TO BEING DIRECTLY IN THE LINE OF FIRE. "Right now, I am taking time off from my watch on Liberty Road. We have to man O.P. [outpost] sites all along the road from An Hoa to Da Nang. Right now, our company has the stretch between Liberty Bridge and An Hoa," one marine wrote. He continued:

"**So far, our platoon has been pretty lucky.** We haven't lost anyone for over two and a half months (knock on wood). The VC and NVA aren't that many around here. But they do make their presence felt very often. Just the other day they blew up three ARVN trucks with box mines. In the past week, five trucks have hit mines.

Just the other day, a patrol out in the many rice paddies around here was hit by a .50-caliber machine gun. Luckily, no one was hurt. So it's easy to see that they do make living very uncomfortable."
Marine Lance Cpl. Richard J. Pierce, July 22

"**[At night] you can hear the M-155s going off.** They usually fire about ten miles out. Every once in a while they'll fire two and three miles out.

Just last night the mortars were firing aerial flares on the other side of Dragon Mountain, which is only 200 yards outside our perimeter. There were also 7 helicopters flying around the hill. I don't think they spotted anything because we didn't hear them shooting the mini-gun.

These are some of the things people at home never hear about. All they ever hear at home is if someone gets killed or if the B52s make an air strike. They never really know how well we are protected if there ever was a report of enemy action in our area. The helicopters could be in the air within a matter of minutes and the mortar rounds would be on their way as soon as somebody called in to give them the area.

Things aren't as bad over here as the people hear in some of the papers. At least not in the area where I'm stationed."
Army Spc. Clifford W. Hudson at Camp Enari, Feb. 9

Members of the Da Nang Dust Off motor pool of the Army's 571st Medical Detachment find a few minutes to relax. The McDonnell Douglas F-4 Phantom II (opposite) served as the principal aerial fighter for the Navy and Air Force.

"**You hear almost every day of satchel charges or terrorist actions in Saigon.** So far, I've witnessed only one explosion and that really jarred me because I was only a block away. There are a lot of people with disabilities, like one arm, no fingers on their hands, blind, and things like that. It almost makes you sick sometimes when you look at them.

Well, I guess I've said enough and will hope you believe that I'm just trying to be honest. I might add that I was mighty lucky to get stationed here. Sometimes, it just doesn't seem right that there are guys fighting and dying not more than 20 miles from here and I'm sitting here relatively safe."
Army Spc. Fred Carlisle in Saigon, Sept. 16

"**The action has picked up out in the hills with many of the fire-bases being mortared, even during the day.** This district is about the most pacified around here but there is a rumor in the air that our headquarters is going to be hit within the next two months. This doesn't please me in a great way.

Last night we had a false alarm when a guard started firing his rifle around midnight. Within five minutes I was ready to hold off the NVA Army with an M-60 machine gun, my pistol and rifle and my helmet and flak jacket. I'm getting too short to fool around. I've been shot at before and I don't want it to happen again."
Army 1st Lt. Henry A. "Alex" Wise III, April 28

"**We were patrolling in the Marble Mountain area about 15 miles outside the city of Da Nang and ran into some VC trying to get into the I Corps area to blow up the I Corps bridge.** We took two prisoners and killed six. During the fight, a bullet hit me in the right rib area. As I was falling, I managed to get off a few rounds. Lucky I had my flak jacket on. Other than having the wind knocked out of me, no Americans wounded or killed. I'll always wear my flak jacket from now on. You can bet on that."
Marine Cpl. Art Davis near Marble Mountain, Aug. 30

One soldier wrote about a disturbing incident of firepower at his base camp. This letter stood apart from the rest as the danger did not stem from the enemy.

"**Last night was some night.** About 3:55 in the morning some M-16 shots woke me up. I drive a gun jeep for the bunker line so I had to go check it out. When I got to the bunker, one of the guards was lying on the ground with his chest blown apart and the other guard was standing to the side with his weapon in his hand. I asked him what happened and he said, 'I shot him.' He was real calm. You know why?

He had been smoking grass! Lucky he didn't shoot me. I don't know if the man died yet but I imagine he will. Maybe his death will make a couple of youths take heed and not smoke any weed.

I'm at work now. I hope everything stays quiet."
Army Spc. James R. Turner Jr., July 22 Mailbag

"I am glad to serve my country, by having to serve a tour of duty in Vietnam. As I see it, I am doing my share to stop oppression, terror and turmoil and to keep the stain of blood off American soil. What's one small year to give for such a big cause?"

Army Sgt. Kenneth D. Keogh

U. S. Rep. William V. Roth of Delaware received many letters from constituents in Vietnam who had complaints, hurt feelings, job problems, or who just wanted to put their opinions down on paper. Even so, members of Congress made a concerted effort to let servicemen know their efforts were appreciated. The House of Representatives passed a resolution directing that each lawmaker commend those serving in Vietnam for their individual sacrifices. Roth wrote letters to all Delawareans serving in Vietnam, and included a copy of the resolution with it.

One soldier responded to Roth with a letter of thanks. Roth shared the letter with the column and it was published in the Mailbag.

"Since I have a few minutes to myself, I thought I would write and thank you for your consideration for the Vietnam veterans.

I received your letter a few days ago and was surprised to hear that I, from the State of Delaware, was the only one in my unit to receive a letter from his state representative.

I guess that goes to prove one of the many reasons behind our state's nickname: The First State.

I would also like to say that I am glad to serve my country, by having to serve a tour of duty in Vietnam. As I see it, I am doing my share to stop oppression, terror and turmoil and to keep the stain of blood off American soil.

What's one small year to give for such a big cause?

Liberty and freedom mean a lot to me. I only wish a lot of other people felt the same way – but take it for granted.

A little more than seven months and I'll be home for good. I'll be glad I have served my one year and that I have served it proudly."
Army Sgt. Kenneth D. Keogh, Feb. 2 Mailbag

NOT EVERY DAY DID A COMPANY COMMANDER TAKE TIME OUT TO WRITE A COMMENDATION AND SEND IT TO A HOMETOWN NEWSPAPER. But the commander of the Army's 169th Engineering Battalion did just that on behalf of Spc. William E. Havens. His letter appeared in the February 5 Mailbag.

"**I am writing this letter for a man in my company.** He lives in New Castle, Delaware, and is serving very proudly in the United States Army.

He has been presented with three of the Army's highest awards. He was presented the Purple Heart for being hit in the line of duty. In another case, he was awarded the Bronze Star. While serving in my company, he was awarded the Army Commendation Award. This man who I am speaking of is Spec. 4 William E. Havens.

Spec. Havens is working TDY [temporary duty] with the 169th Engr. Bn. from the 101st Airborne. Havens is a proud member of the Army and if you could, it would do him honor to run an article in your paper. Havens will be leaving on June 3, 1970."
Army Capt. Robert E. Darn, Feb. 5 Mailbag

Army Spc. William W. "Hutch" Hutchison Jr. (above, right) with a fellow reporter from the 23rd Infantry Division's Information Office in Chu Lai before they take off on assignment. The Army's Long Range Patrol (opposite) rescues a wounded Vietcong for interrogation.

EVEN THOUGH THE WAR WAS WINDING DOWN, OUR TROOPS IN VIETNAM WANTED MAILBAG READERS TO KNOW ABOUT THEIR JOBS, VARIED AS THEY WERE. Army Pfc. Charles E. Comegys kept his job description short in his April 28 letter, saying only, "My job is cooking for the Army. We have about 150 people in all." More often, additional information was forthcoming.

"**The Army sent me to school to be a mechanic and/or crew chief on the UH-1 (Huey) [helicopter].** I learned all that I could learn in that too short (and in my opinion) inadequate course. They spent a lot of money to send me to that school. Then when I came over here last March 24 [1969], they put me OJT [on-the-job training] on the Cobra, the Army's first purely attack helicopter. I was surprised how fast I learned to work on it. I'm now a crew chief on a Cobra. The grunts (infantrymen) call it 'Blue Max' because it brings the maximum on Charlie."
Army Spc. Richard S. Lovekin, Jan. 3

"**I am presently assigned as the Deputy Senior Advisor to a Regional Force Battalion just south of Da Nang.** In this type of assignment, contact with the Vietnamese is constant; we literally eat, sleep and co-exist with them. At times, there can be a language barrier. However, we do have an interpreter assigned to the battalion and nightly I give classes in English to the staff officers while learning Vietnamese at the same time. I must say their command of our language is much better than mine of theirs."
Army 1st Lt. Domenic M. Grillo near Da Nang, Feb. 10

"**Boarding a Vietnam-bound plane is not easy, nor is service here.** The lights go on at 5:30 a.m. and the day runs till 5:30 p.m., 7 days a week. That is, if you're in a maintenance outfit like myself. The people who really have it rough are the 'ground pounders' and the 'gun bunnies.' These men are usually at it 24 hours a day. They do the most and complain the least."
Army Spc. Bob Sheppard, March 2

"**I got here December 12, 1969.** I have 251 more days left in the Army. That is active duty. I took basic training at Fort Bragg, N.C., then without a leave, I went to Fort Lee, Va., for 10 weeks of 76W20, that's my MOS. POL, gas, diesel and all kinds of petroleum products. Then I had a 19-day leave. Then I came over here for 14 months, until Feb. 5, 1971.

When I first got here they were in need of 11Bs, that's infantry, so I went through a week of combat training…. I went through a booby-trapped trail, went through a combat attack assault. We had a Vietcong sapper [an infiltrator carrying a small bag of explosives] to make it like a real assault. Then we had a class on Vietcong mines of all kinds and how to set them off when one is found. Then we went to a rifle range for night firing and to zero our M-16 rifles in and we also had to fire the M-50 and M-60 machine guns and then the M-71 hand-grenade launcher. So after my week of combat training, I went in the jungle to do my thing, which I did.

I was in the jungle for about four months. When they had enough 11Bs, they took me out and I started my job where I was supposed to at first. So here I am in the 199th C.T. INF BDE at Class III POL.

I sleep at the section. There are three of us that stay here, (myself), another Spec. 4 and a staff sergeant. I drive a tanker deuce and half. We just got two brand new trucks. I got one, I guess I was lucky. I haul mojos [grenade launchers] to forward firebases. We have four firebases to haul to. One of them is named after you, Firebase Nancy, Mace, Libby, Xon Loc. That's pronounced 'swan lock.'

Well, it's about 4:30 hours and I have guard tonight. I get it once a week. I pull four hours. I guess it's not too bad. "
Army Spc. Kenny Wyatt, May 28

"**The PSYOPs stands for Psychological Warfare.** We print propaganda to get Charlie (VC) to *chieu hoi* (join our side). The leaflets we print are dropped by planes and then the VC read it.

Da Nang is a pretty city. The French really build nice hotels here. By the time you receive this letter, I'll be in Tokyo, Japan. I'm going to school to learn offset press mechanics.

The school is about three weeks long. It is just like R&R. When I come back from Japan I'll have about 175 days left in Vietnam, getting short, but not short enough."
Army Spc. Ron Suppi in Da Nang, April 25

"**I am a District Liaison Officer in Phu Tu District, Thuan Thieu Province.** In actuality, the job entails no work whatsoever….

Tomorrow I officially become a 60-day loss to the Army and unofficially I'm hoping for a five-day drop. That would be nice.

I did see [Army Spc.] Jeff Fishwick about two months ago but not since then. His job is about as time-consuming as mine.

Since I've been out here in the District, I have become more familiar with the Vietnamese but I must say that I still wonder why we're still here. The MACV team who are supposed to be advisors and coordinators don't do anything, or should I say very little.

There is also a mobile training team who train the PF platoons for three hours everyday. Then there are the rest of us from the 101st whose sole job is to monitor two radios 24 hours a day – quite a waste of manpower since there's never any traffic."
Army 1st Lt. Henry A. "Alex" Wise III, April 28

"**I'm flying UH-1 helicopters ('Hueys').** I'm getting to see a lot of the country from the air."
Army 1st Lt. John "By" Bishop in Duc Pho, June 1

"**Well, the rains have started here.** It rains every day and makes life here worse than ever. I drive a gun jeep for the bunkers on Long Binh Post and I'm usually soaked before the night's over. This base is supposed to be the safest in Nam but we have a lot of vital supplies here that the VC would like to get their hands on. Since the Cambodian mess, our forces have destroyed many of the supplies that the NVA have brought from the north. Therefore, they will have to steal, using sapper techniques."
Army Spc. James R. Turner Jr., July 10 Mailbag

During the war, the United States dropped propaganda leaflets from the air to entice the enemy to join American forces. The mock playing card, aimed at Vietcong sympathizers, urged them to remain loyal to the South Vietnamese government. "Avoid your fate of lonely death by turning yourself in," it read in part. The North Vietnamese had similar items, like the small card which read, in part: "Friends, there is no safe haven for you ... come over to our righteous Republican side and turn yourself in to preserve your life."

"I am a security policeman in the 3rd Security Police Squadron. I work the day shift on security. I miss most of the excitement such as rocket and mortar attacks and hijackings of C-141s (by Army personnel) but I do get a nice tan.

As far as I can determine, this is a political war. Political wars should be fought in Congress or over a peace table. We Americans are over here only to show our force to all of the world but not being allowed to show our strengths. We in the military have our hands tied behind our back and this should not be so.

The only thing North Vietnam is after is publicity. And since they have not been getting a lot lately, there has been quite a noticeable lack of enemy activity."
Air Force Airman 1st Class Bruce D. Shur at Bien Hoa Air Base, Aug. 23

"Actually, there isn't much I can say about this place that you probably don't already know. I don't get out in the boonies like some guys because I work on planes. At least I know that we try to help those guys out there the best we can."
Marine Cpl. Ted Short in Da Nang, Sept. 17

"I am attached to the Military Sealift Command at the Binh Thuy Navy Base. Our unit is involved with bringing supplies and other needs into the Delta by means of LST ships. Also, we control tugboats moving barges of rock to build roads in the Delta."
Navy Seaman Harry G. Porter in Can Tho, Sept. 19

"My life in Vietnam has not been at all difficult so far. I work long hours and there's not much diversion, but that's what I planned on so it's been quite painless. As for my ability to offer insights on 'the war' to the people at home … I've had little contact with either the Vietnamese people or the actual fighting of the war."
Army Lt. William J. Wheeler in Phu Thai, Oct. 4

"I am a medic with the 566 Med Co in Qui Nhon. I don't see so much of the combat but I always see the results."
Army Spc. Gerald A. Roy Jr., Oct. 15

"I'm an air traffic controller at the airfield here. One of my friends is a pilot from Wilmington. The next time I can get him over here, we'll send a group shot."
Army Sgt. Joseph LaFollette at Fire Support Base Buttons, Oct. 24

"I'm an Air Force-type cop and do about the same job as most civilian policemen do. I can't say that I enjoy being in the Air Force, but since I am I wouldn't have any other job. Every night is different and exciting."
Air Force Sgt. James A. Clark in Cam Ranh Bay, Nov. 4

"As far as my work goes, I work on a SP-2E airplane, which is the largest and most complex plane that the Army has. It is an old Navy plane and it really takes a lot of work to keep them up in the air. We have six of these planes and every Sunday one of them goes to the Philippines to get washed and it usually stays three or four days. We have a company roster to determine who is going each weekend. We also have a beach party every Sunday afternoon. So I really don't mind it too [much] over here but I would much rather be back in the good old First State."
Army Spc. James R. Wright, Nov. 10

"Serving here in Vung Tau, myself and one other lab technician operate a Mobile Petroleum Laboratory. [The lab] is responsible for testing and certifying the quality of the vast quantity of fuel which is stored here. We supply fuel for helicopters and air planes to the Army and the Australian forces here in Vung Tau. The Navy and Air Force also need our fuel for their boats (ships?) and planes. All land vehicles receive fuel from us also.

While my chosen field is medical technology, I worked in DuPont's Petroleum Laboratory in Deepwater [N.J.] for 2 1/2 years and attended the Army's school at Fort Lee, Va. Although I worked as a medical lab tech at Fort Wood, the Army decided I would be more useful in Nam operating a petroleum lab in Vung Tau.

My wife, residing in Missouri, is an LPN and the both of us are looking forward to advancing our careers in medicine in Delaware when I leave the Army."
Army Spc. Philip C. Winkler in Vung Tau, Nov. 11

"My assignment, presently, as assistant civil engineer, is varied in scope and includes travel in parts of South Vietnam. This contributes to rapid passing of time as I have yet to be bored with the tasks or sights to be seen."
Army Lt. Rodney A. Brice, Nov. 19

"Since I've last written you, I've acquired a new job. I'm a door gunner on a UH-1H helicopter commonly called a 'Slick.' I'm still in the same company and we are called the Warlords. We are aero scouts. That means we go out and look for trouble. I've seen quite a lot since I started flying in October and I hope I don't ever have to experience the sights again.

I only hope that what we are accomplishing over here is not in vain. But when you see things like dispensaries hit and medevacs shot down, you really wonder what kind of people are these people we're fighting. I don't think we will pull out of Vietnam for 3 more years at least."
Army Pfc. John R. Elliott, Dec. 16

Troops make time for the necessary cleaning of the barrel of a 105-mm howitzer at San Juan Hill, a mountaintop fire support base about 10 miles west of Duc Pho.

"My MOS is 11C20 which is a mortar specialist. I am also the gunner of my squad.... At the present, I'm out in the middle of some farmland sitting on a foxhole. So, while sitting here waiting for the day to pass, I decided to write and thank you for your Christmas card."

Army Spc. Thomas B. Montaque, Dec. 25

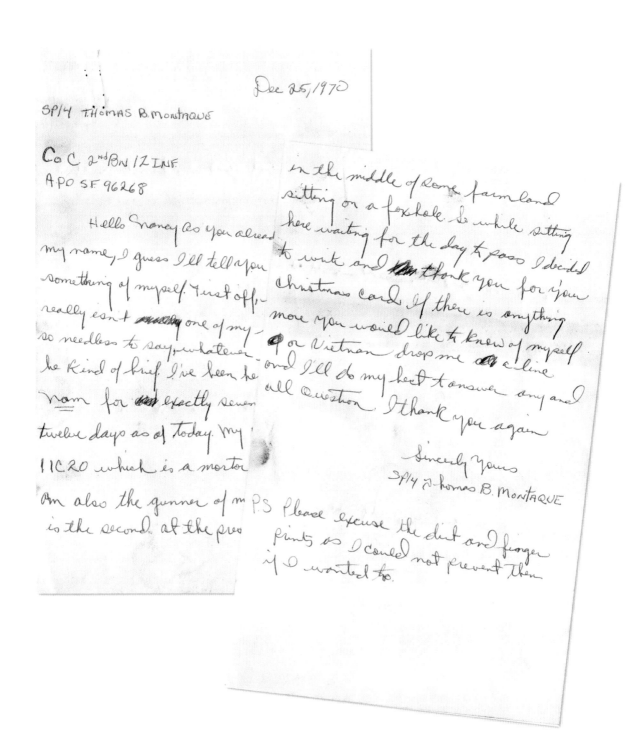

The mobile bridge was one of the Army's most utilitarian pieces of equipment, allowing troops, vehicles and and supplies to ford small rivers.

"**I'm stationed about 7 miles south of the DMZ in a small village called Dong Ha....** I drive a 5-ton truck hauling 8-inch and 175-mm ammo. I don't meet very many of the First Staters. Walter Lacey was near here until he moved farther south."
Army Spc. J.L. Absher, Dec. 28 Mailbag

The August 17 Mailbag deviated from standard protocol and printed an offbeat description of an MOS, a military occupational specialty. It came to the Mailbag from Bob Wiesner, who served with the Air Force in Vietnam. The letter itself, titled "To Be Of (In) Service," was written by an unidentified sergeant from Maine, stationed in Bien Hoa.

In a confused state of mind, I left college to venture forth into the better prospects of life. I blindly set out to conquer my inner conflicts, engage in something constructive, and enjoy and be educated by the variety life has to offer.

Within three months after I left school, the Selective Service politely informed me I would be drafted shortly. To avoid the possibility of being forced to commit any belligerent acts, I wisely chose to fulfill my military obligation in the United States Air Force. I met the qualifications and was assured by the recruiter I would be trained in an interesting career. This selection was made hastily, but proved to be an excellent choice.

I refer to this chapter in my life as a four-year detour from academic to practical learning. It resembles a scholarship program with a 'learn as you earn' curriculum.

In the Air Force I was lucky enough to discover a distinct profession of which I am proud. It has enabled me to learn and use a number of technical skills envied by the less fortunate.

The work is very interesting and richly rewarding, commanding the respect and compliments of everyone.

When the time arrives, if I should elect to be discharged from the Air Force, I'll have no need to worry about continuing this profession as a civilian. Jobs in this field are plentiful, offering excellent salaries and, of course, overwhelming prestige.

I realize at this point your curiosity has developed to its peak, and you long for me to reveal my occupation. But first allow me to briefly explain my value in Vietnam.

During the course of each day, I am required to carry out as many as 23 sensitive assignments, which, if not successfully completed, could cause serious damage to the Air Force mission. In turn, this could easily sway the American position in Vietnam to sheer disaster. My performance must be precise and persistent to ensure the utmost quality for such a distinctive position in our country's defense.

Above all, my mental faculties must be constantly working, providing top security and always improvising new tactics in my field to keep our war methods superior to the enemy's.

Although my job will leave a small mark, a mere milestone in the course of history, I can feel your yearning and desire that I disclose my profession.

I have the exclusive mission as the sound and distinctive pilot of an Air Force garbage truck.

Moving into a night defensive position, a convoy bogs down
in mud. When the first armored personnel carrier got stuck,
the one directly behind tried to free it but also got mired.
The tank pulled both carriers to high ground.

GRIPES, TOO, SERVED A PURPOSE IN THE WAR ZONE, IF FOR NO OTHER REASON THAN TO OFFER AN OPPORTUNITY TO VENT. One regular correspondent started his new year by letting off some steam in an early morning letter, striking back at a reader who had complained about the bountiful Thanksgiving feast he organized in 1969.

"**Happy New Year…. I do have one small gripe.** I learned from a friend at home that there was at least one person who reads your column who didn't think our Thanksgiving dinner was too great. It seems that she can't understand how we could obtain a case of steaks for our greedy party when so many (she says) of our men over here are starving.

I would like to say a few things. First, in our defense, we invited anyone who walked past that day to come in and help themselves. We were only too glad to share what we had with others. Next, I have never seen or heard of any American, Korean, Thai, Filipino, Australian or any other free world soldier, including the Vietnamese, starving in this war. Our men are the best-fed soldiers in the entire world. We have the best equipment, the best living conditions, and the best food ever. Even the C-rations, which I have eaten my share of, aren't bad.

It seems to me that this pseudo-nutrition expert has been slightly misinformed and, as far as I'm concerned, she is an ignorant 'establishment pig' who should get her facts straight before speaking or not speak at all. However, if she is really convinced that we are starving, I suggest she send her next paycheck to the wonderful people at SOS Vietnam. Now they don't supply us with three hot meals each day but their packages contain so many useful and original items that our minds are taken away from the pain in our stomachs."
Army Sgt. Robert S. Biss, Jan. 2

Another frequent writer griped about a common bumper sticker that was seen back in the States.

"**There is only one thing that Delaware does that brings me down, that being the bumper stickers that say, 'Back Our Boys in Vietnam.'** Number one, there is not one GI over here who likes to have people call him a boy. In my estimation, none of us are boys.
Anyone who goes through what we are going through now, and does such a good job, can't be called a boy. So the next time you write about us in Vietnam, please try to remember to say, 'the men in Vietnam.' Because we are."
Army Spc. John E. Rubincan, Feb. 21

One soldier was up in arms over a controversial action that would curtail the supply of refreshments. He stressed the importance of items such as sodas and ice cream to soldiers who spent most of their time in sweltering heat.

"**I received a circular in the mail which stated that the radical left has started a movement to boycott Coke.** Here in Vietnam the sun can burn you to a crisp in 45 minutes. Some have nearly died from sunburn…. At one time here [at] Cam Ranh [Bay], the heat reached 138°. The coldest it ever got was 58°…. We need Cokes here. Coke sells us an entire canned case for $2.40 here. Can you say the same for you?…
Think of that 19- and 20-year-old boy who is forced into manhood here. Some soldiers in the field never get Cokes or ice cream. They carry 30 pounds of field gear in this heat. These men in Vietnam are showing moral fiber and self-sacrifice. Some have a wife but children they've never seen…. Now you begrudge us a Coke."
Army Spc. Charles Leach in Cam Ranh Bay, June 4 Mailbag

Another griped about limited supplies in letters three months apart.

"**I am a machine gunner and the resupply system here is terrible.** To prove this point, we were in the Arizona and the man carrying our gun wrench and cleaning gear was medevaced. (The Arizona is one of the roughest areas around here. There are many booby traps and VC/NVA in there.)
Well, we were in the Arizona for twenty-eight days before we got a cleaning rod for the gun. It took us another two weeks just to get a wrench to fit the gun's gas system. And one of the gunners in the other gun team stole a wrench from motor T. We had to use our own tee-shirts to keep the guns clean and then when clean tee-shirts came into the platoon you couldn't get one unless you had an old tee-shirt.
Shirts and pants? The only time we get clean shirts and pants is on special days (that's the way it seems anyway)….
And another thing that upsets us is when the company comes into the rear. They give us two hot sodas and expect that to make us happy while other companies that go to the rear have big cookouts with steaks, hamburgers, cold beer and sodas. Then, at night, the office boys give the line watch to the guys who came into the rear for a rest."
Marine Lance Cpl. Richard J. Pierce, July 22

Army Spc. William W. Hutchison Jr., with the Information Office of the 23rd Infantry Division, also known as the Americal Division, shot this aerial of a Vietnamese village near Chu Lai. Even when lighting up (opposite), servicemen could signal their take on the war.

"**Well, I have to complain about Marine Corps supply again – that's if we have one.** It seems like whenever you need something is when supply doesn't have it. Like bore cleaner. I haven't seen a can of that since I stole a can from supply in the rear. That was about a month and a half ago. I still haven't gotten a gun wrench or an M-60 cleaning rod. And M-16 cleaning patches are as rare as hen's teeth. But I can put in one plus for supply – they did get us rain suits. Even if they were fourteen days too late."
Marine Lance Cpl. Richard J. Pierce in An Hoa, Oct. 19 Mailbag

Other letters were full of general discontent with the war.

"**I'm at Bien Hoa and I guess it's about like any other base in Vietnam.** You'd rather be home but we're here so what can I say? I DEROS 19 June '71. Why I'm here I can't say because, to me, this war is useless. The superiors (meaning [those] over enlisted men} say because of the Monroe Doctrine pertaining to the spread of communism that the U.S. would go to [Vietnam's] aid. Well, that was drawn up years ago and what the hell does it have to do with today?"
Air Force Sgt. Stanley Connie Walker in Bien Hoa, Oct. 8

"**Well, the monsoons are upon us and it has cooled off considerably.** I am flying down to Saigon tomorrow. Will see my nephew Bob and also contact a few people I know there and try and finagle a transfer out of this 'hell hole'.... All I can say, Nancy, is that in all of my years of service I have never been assigned to a unit such as this one. The place smells to high heaven."
Army Master Sgt. James T. Joyce in Phu Hiep, Oct. 23

"**Since I've been in Vietnam I've seen enough of the war to say that the war is still alive and going – but at a slower pace (fortunately).**
   Unfortunately for those of us presently here – and more so for those arriving in the next few months, the 'game' of war seems to be taking precedence over the seriousness of war. Current austerity programs, and increasing paperwork, and stateside type training all have made it to Vietnam at last. (To my chagrin) not necessarily agreeing with it all – I do see its usefulness to a small degree – and as an officer I intend to do the best job I can – not to win a game – or an inspection – but to remind my men the war is still a war, until the 'freedom bird' lands at Travis Air Force Base."
Army 1st Lt. Robert A. Nowaczyk, Dec. 29

LIFERS, CAREER MILITARY MEN, TOOK IT ON THE CHIN AGAIN IN 1970. "Having less than 50 days left in the Army, I've been reflecting on my time in involuntary servitude," one soldier wrote. "In general, I have concluded that the armed services are made up of NCOs and senior officers whose minds have been molded to the standards of the 1950s crew-cut chauvinist group." He continued:

"**They have failed to recognize the social changes in the past decade.** Therefore, [they] will be unable to cope with the growing discontent within their own ranks as well as the contempt of American youth in general.
   I think it's time our armed forces re-evaluate their standards before they contribute any further to the deterioration of the quality of our men in service."
Army Spc. Richard W. Hudson, Jan. 9

"**All I want to do right now is to get out of here and away from all these lifers.** That is the only war that I am fighting right now (the lifers). I have got a girl in Newark that I want to marry as soon as I get out of here and that is all. This damn war doesn't even make any sense at all."
Army Pfc. Richard A. "Smitty" Smith, Feb. 2

"**It seems like the lifers are always picking on us for something. Four or five days ago, our company made a beer run to Da Nang.** We were the only squad with some money so we bought five cases. We would get one case a day and would not be permitted to drink any beer after five o'clock. Around six o'clock we were talking about the lifers in our company and one of them was outside peeking in on us.
   He didn't like what we said so he took the rest of the beer and gave us our money back. He said we couldn't handle the beer. How far can a case of beer go with an eight-man squad?"
Marine Lance Cpl. Richard J. Pierce, July 22

28C SUNDAY NEWS, SEPTEMBER 20, 1970

Still ring-mastered by Bob Hope (▲) who has dropped in on more wars than any non-combatant in history, showfolk who volunteer for the boondocks find that the GI is basically the same as his old man in World War II. He wants to see girls—particularly Raquel Welch (←) and Joey Heatherton (→), today's pinup queens—and hear Hope harass the brass with gags that haven't changed basically since Gettysburg.

The GIs Haven't Changed

By JEROME CAHILL

A report that the boys in Vietnam don't groove with the old-style entertainment brings a retort that they still demand a GG rating—girls and gags—for shows

IN THE FILES of the USO, the voluntary civilian organization that has been boosting GI morale at home and overseas for almost three decades, is a letter from a Long Island girl that tells it like it is.

"My boy friend has been killed in Vietnam," the girl wrote.

"I just received his last letter and it is all about the Bob Hope Christmas show put on by the USO. It was the first real entertainment he'd seen in a long time, and it was the last nice thing he saw . . ."

Officials cite the letter as a small but compelling piece of evidence that whatever may be said of the entertainment tastes of today's GI, the ski-snooted comedian and other veterans of USO's celebrity circuit still pack plenty of box office clout with overseas military audiences.

USO headquarters dug out the letter as it joined with the Pentagon in an angry rebuttal of a news story out of Columbus, Ohio, the other day that such big name entertainers as Hope, George Jessel and Art Linkletter were "unacceptable" to most U.S. troops overseas.

Kenneth D. Smith, entertainment coordinator for the U.S. Army in Europe, reportedly had this to say in the controversial story:

"The kind of entertainment popular 20 years ago, when Americans were serving in Korea, fails to bring laughs and applause from soldiers turned on to pot smoking and rock music."

At the Pentagon, where Hope ranks up there with the flag, apple pie and motherhood, the reaction was instantaneous. One of the brass called Smith at his home in Columbus, where he was vacationing. The hapless Smith said he was misquoted, and promptly dropped from sight.

In a press release trying to set the record straight, the Pentagon made no secret of where its sympathies lie.

"Defense officials are convinced that Mr. Hope and the other entertainers mentioned in the story continue to enjoy enthusiastic acceptance with a great majority of our troops overseas, as evidenced by the standing room only attendance whenever they perform," the release said.

"These entertainers perform an invaluable morale service for American servicemen overseas."

Edward M. Kirby, director of public relations for the USO, put it more bluntly: "This man Smith has no connection with USO and does not know what he is talking about.

"I have seen Bob Hope operate in three wars and if there is anyone in show business who is very 'persona grata,' it is Bob Hope, the nearest thing to an American court jester of class and distinction," Kirby went on.

"If you have seen him walk onto an improvised stage in a cow pasture or a boondock before 1,000 or 15,000 smiling GIs, you see and hear immediately that he is welcome—that his very presence makes the GIs feel important and remembered by the people back home who sent them there."

Bringing beauty to the boondocks was really all Raquel Welch had to do on recent Vietnam visit with Bob Hope.

THE USO spokesman, refuting the implication that the celebrity circuit shows are fobbing off outdated entertainment on GI audiences, said reactions to performances are carefully monitored so as to give the boys what they appreciate.

"When it became apparent to us that GIs wanted more rock and roll, they got it," Kirby said. "When black GIs made it known they wanted more black entertainers, they got them. In fact, some 25% of our sponsored shows feature black entertainment from soul singing groups like James Brown to Miss Black America, ranking alongside the Miss America show in popularity."

Keystones of the celebrity shows today as in World War II, when dad was a dogface, are pretty girls and jokes ribbing the brass. Such winsome lasses as Joey Heatherton and Raquel Welch are now attracting wolf whistles that once went to Frances Langford and Dorothy Lamour.

Hope still makes a specialty of needling the military hierarchy. As Kirby pointed out, "In military circles, jokes kidding the socks off the brass have been socko with soldiers from the days of Grant down to Eisenhower, who always enjoyed a Bob Hope belly laugh at his own expense."

The Pentagon, and the USO, frankly concede that they draw the line on acts in which entertainers inject antiwar political comment. "We're interested in entertainment, not politics," a Pentagon spokesman said.

Added Kirby: "Once or twice we've had an entertainer try to put in political overtones, but the GIs resented it, and let them know it with their boos. When those shows came back, they were not scheduled again."

Peace groups opposed to the American involvement in Vietnam have raised questions, if not pressure, on the USO to stop supporting that involvement with its clubs and shows. To which the USO replies: "It's not the war but American soldiers we are supporting."

"We are there because our guys are there," is the way Kirby put it. "When peaceniks tell us we ought to get out, I ask them, 'Would you take an Army nurse or doctor out of Vietnam?' We are in the same position. We're there because we're needed."

USO entertainers performed before a total military audience of 8,732,556 last year without rating a single GI complaint, and Kirby sees no reason to change. The Pentagon agrees.

OCCASIONALLY, EVEN ENTERTAINERS CAME UNDER FIRE. Show-business icon and morale-booster-in-chief Bob Hope, an annual fixture in Vietnam with his USO-sponsored Christmas shows, was center stage in a flap in 1970 over his relevance to U.S. troops. Kenneth D. Smith, entertainment coordinator for the Army in Europe, actually caused the stink while vacationing at home in Columbus, Ohio, where he was quoted as saying such big-name entertainers as Hope, George Jessel and Art Linkletter were "unacceptable" to most troops overseas.

According to a news account sent to the Mailbag, Smith said, "The kind of entertainment popular 20 years ago, when Americans were serving in Korea, fails to bring laughs and applause from soldiers turned on to pot smoking and rock music."

Both the Pentagon and USO fired off rebuttals.

A release from the Pentagon stated, "Defense officials are convinced Mr. Hope and the other entertainers mentioned in the story continue to enjoy enthusiastic acceptance with a great majority of our troops overseas, as evidenced by the standing-room-only attendance whenever they perform."

Entertainer for all seasons, Bob Hope was a tireless showman in Vietnam. American servicemen eagerly awaited his in-country visits. Injured troops (opposite) in this 1960s photo, enjoyed preferential seating close to the stage.

The USO's director of public relations, Edward M. Kirby, added, "This man Smith has no connection with USO and does not know what he is talking about. I have seen Bob Hope operate in three wars and if there is anyone in show business who is very *persona grata* it is Bob Hope, the nearest thing to an American court jester of class and distinction."

Smith said he had been misquoted and dropped off the radar screen. The Mailbag asked for comments and our servicemen wasted no time rallying in support of Hope.

"In reference to your question about Bob Hope and George Jessel being wanted over here as entertainers, from experience I can say that both are top-notch people and the GIs really enjoy them. When I was here in '68-'69, I sent most all of the men from my battery to see the Hope show. Of course, the girls added a lot to it but the boys talked of Bob. Anyone (like Smith) who would say that he isn't wanted is crazy. I can see why he dropped out of sight. He should – and leave the entertainment to us."

Army 1st Sgt. James T. Joyce, Oct. 6

"I was reading one of your columns and you asked what we in Vietnam thought about Bob Hope. Well, I've talked to a lot of guys here on firebase LZ Cindy and they all feel the same way I do. We would be glad to see anybody just as long as they're from the world."

Army Pfc. Anthony J. Colicchio at Landing Zone Cindy, Oct. 7

"I think that Bob Hope will also be a very popular show. I, for one, would sure like to be in Da Nang to see his Christmas show live instead of watching it on TV.... Some of the guys I know would all like to see his show too. Of all the people I asked, they said they think Bob Hope will still be around when others are long gone. So keep on coming, Bob. You're always welcome at Hotel Company 2/5."

Marine Lance Cpl. Richard J. Pierce in An Hoa, Oct. 19 Mailbag

"The field troops may enjoy Bob Hope, but George Jessel isn't too popular with anybody over here. He never showed up for a USO show at our compound about 7 months ago."

Army Spc. Robert P. Stout Jr., Nov. 15

III MAF
BOB HOPE SHOW
DANANG RVN
RESERVED SEAT
ADMIT ONE

Downtown Da Nang was filled with street vendors and open-air markets where staples as well as black-market items sold briskly.

THE DIFFICULTY OF KNOWING THE REAL ENEMY WAS A CONCERN TO THOSE SERVING IN VIETNAM. "I read your column about the two-faced people here. It happens every day," one serviceman began in his letter. He continued:

"**Our shop is peaceful during the day.** At night, while we work in the dark, we get shot at from the same people. It seems like the people here don't know which side they really want to take.

The trash trucks have a Vietnamese woman who speaks English and sometimes she asks us what we make in the shop and what it is for. If the Vietcong knew what [my shop] was for, they would try to blow the place sky high. I feel these kind of people should be kept out of our bases and where we work."
Marine Lance Cpl. James W. Miller in Da Nang, March 22

Other servicemen corresponded about the hustlers and Saigon in general.

"**You wrote that Delawareans 'tell it like it is.'** Well, I'm stationed a mile from Saigon and to actually tell it like it is would give a lot of people the impression that there is no war going on over here. But, being honest like I am, I'll give you my best description of Saigon and its people.

My best description of the people here would be friendly. A lot of times too friendly. Like any GI tour in the world, the people try to make an extra buck from some GI. I'm not holding that against the Vietnamese in particular because it's the same anywhere. To really get along here, you have to know how to bargain and I mean bargain! A shop owner will start at maybe 1,000 piasters (about $8.25) for some object and you start at 500. The guy will give you a weird look like you are out of your mind. After about 10 to 15 minutes of haggling, you finally agree on a price. Of course, there are a lot of bars in Saigon. To describe the different kinds of bars would fill a book and some of the things that happen in them I won't elaborate on unless you really wish me to."
Army Spc. Fred Carlisle near Saigon, Sept. 16

"**Saigon is building up very fast.** There are more and more people coming to Saigon every day. The people try and make as much off the GI as they can. What they can't make, they try and steal. There are a lot of cowboys here. You can't travel alone….

There are a lot of people selling things on the street. Almost everyone in Saigon is selling something. You can buy anything on the street….There are a lot of hustlers here. They all say they have #1 girls. They are the ones everyone stays away from."
Army Pfc. Laurence Joseph Cervelli in Saigon, Oct. 19

Another wrote of corrupt politicians and their role in the growing black market.

"The [Phu Tu] district chief, a Vietnamese, is just another profiteer on the black market within his own district. He sells ammo boxes to the civilians, as well as the other items we provide him with. It's really sad since this is a relatively poor district and the people really appreciate what you bring them for their projects. Altogether, there are about five officers and eight enlisted U.S. types who just sit here idle all day and a corrupt District Chief, which actually is nothing unusual."
Army 1st Lt. Henry A. "Alex" Wise III, April 28

Other soldiers provided readers at home alarming insights on the underground economy as well.

"Concerning Koreans and the PXs in Saigon where both Korean and Thailand troops use the PX facilities, the situation is ridiculous. The same Koreans and Thais are at the PX every day buying up anything and everything they can possibly sell on the black market. Talking with some of these soldiers, I found out that their commanders, with the understanding that the soldiers will give them a percentage of the profits, issue them new ration cards as often as every day to purchase tape recorders, radios, refrigerators and other hard-to-get items, which command a tremendously high price on the black market.

As a result, by the time the American soldiers can get to the PX, there is absolutely nothing left. If an American should happen to be there when a new shipment comes in, he better be prepared for the stampede of foreign troops. I was almost trampled to death by some Thai soldiers pushing and shoving to buy some speakers that had just come in. It is a poor situation."
Army Spc. Mark L. Goodman, Jan. 20

"I'll have to agree with all that S/4 John Rubincan [wrote in December 1969] about the Korean troops, black market and PXs. Now I would like to add yet another group of people to the list – the Filipino troops. My office is in the same building as the Tan Son Nhut PX and I've seen it all (plus). On mornings that they have, for instance, refrigerators for sale, the Flips used to line up fifty strong to wait until the ten o'clock opening. They always knew when the 'good stuff' was going to be sold due to the too many Flips employed on the PX staffs. Our own GIs haven't a chance in hell. When a Flip fills his ration card, he merely returns to his HQ and is issued another. I've known several that did this weekly.

They are not engaged in combat but civic action that allows them to be in or near a PX constantly. A standing joke at TSN [Tan Son Nhut] is that the only Purple Heart received was from injuries obtained at a PX.

One good thing to be said for our side – the TSN PX is now off limits to Koreans and Flips. Now all we have are Vietnamese officers and I've heard that they too will soon lose their privileges. (I hope.) This is as it should be. American PXs should be for American military personnel only! I can't even enter the Cholon area commissary. If we can't use them – close them. Civilians can purchase there now, but many are soon to lose this privilege. This is really a hemorrhoidal subject in Saigon.

The black market itself seems to be underwritten by the [Ambassador Ellsworth] Bunker regime. One day, I was sitting in a Tudo Street bar and a buzzer sounded. It meant nothing to me but all the prostitutes ran to the back and threw on their waitress uniforms (knee-length white coats), thus an immediate transformation from prostitutes to waitresses (the illegal to the legal). In walked two American MPs, several white mice and a fat little man with a big button that read 'Customs Inspector.' We all about died laughing at that one. While the MPs drank their 'Bud,' the others began to carry out cases of American beer and whiskey procured through various illegal outlets (PXs, etc.). When they finished, they left and went on to the next bar where the same routine was followed. The next day – business as usual."
Air Force Airman 1st Class R. Lance Hall, Jan. 27

John, the soldier Lance referred to, who did write extensively on the black market in 1969, added a postscript. He wrote on February 14, "You might be interested to know that all of the Koreans are now not allowed to enter any of the PXs in Vietnam."

"[When] the time comes for us to fight in our own land, let's see if their protest signs will stop a platoon of Commies. It's not that I'm hoping this will happen to our country because I want to come home, knowing our country is safe for me. And that it'll stay safe for me and my kids and they can enjoy the freedom I've had."

Marine Lance Cpl. Michael Di Pasquantonio

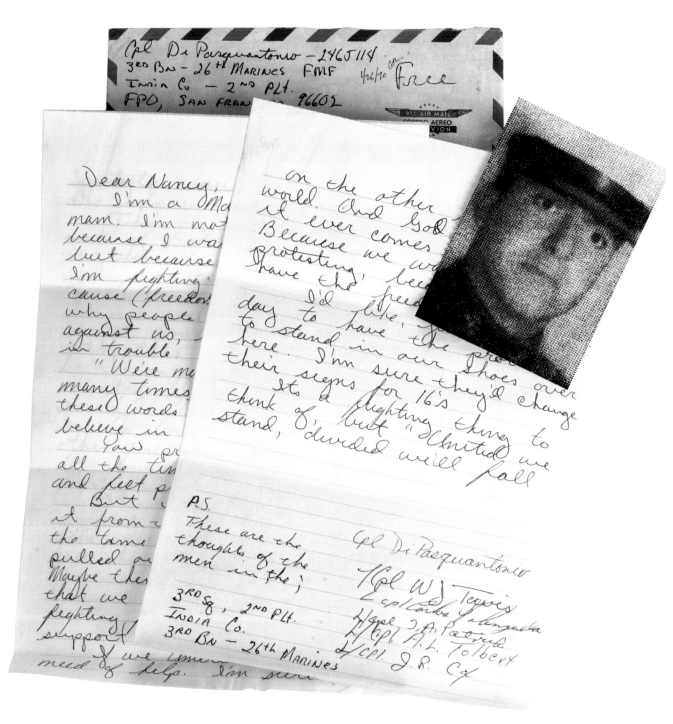

Marine Lance Cpl. Michael Di Pasquantonio's letter was endorsed and signed by five of his buddies in India Company, 3rd Squadron, 2nd Platoon.

A SERVICEMAN CHALLENGED PROTESTERS TO "STAND IN OUR SHOES" FOR JUST ONE DAY. He had served in Vietnam since October 1969 and, along with others in his outfit, took issue with what he perceived as a lack of support from home.

"**I'm a marine in Vietnam.** I'm not here just because I was sent here but because I feel that I'm fighting for a worthy cause (freedom). I can't see why people want to protest against us helping a country in trouble.

'We're not going to.' How many times have you heard these words. Or, 'don't believe in it.'

You probably couldn't count all the times on your hands and feet put together.

But what if you heard it from the servicemen when the time comes for us to be pulled out of Vietnam!? Maybe then the people would see that we believe in what we're fighting for and put some support towards our cause.

If we Americans were in need of help, I'm sure the protesters would appreciate all the help we could get.

Then the protesters say 'Pull out of Vietnam' and mind our own business. If we did, and just stood by and let Communism take over, we'd be in real trouble.

It would bring bad relations with other countries and we'd be the only non-Communist country left (and how long would it last?).

As long as America helps other countries, we'll never be alone in the never-ending fight for peace and freedom.

It seems to me the only support we have in Vietnam are the men fighting over here and the Vietnamese people. And it's pretty bad when support comes from a foreign country.

I'm not getting down on all the people of the U.S. because I know there are people who believe in the war (most are probably veterans).

I don't see how people can be against something they know nothing about!

If the protesters would take some time to look at what they're doing, they'd realize it's wrong.

Every time they hold a moratorium, they build up propaganda for Hanoi to use against us over here.

But it's not just the protesters, it's the news media also. They can talk for hours about riots and protests against the war but how much time do they take for the group called 'Tell it to Hanoi?'

Really, I don't think the president wants to pull out. By this I mean his feelings as a man, not as the president of the United States speaking for the people.

All it is is the Commies working in the states and all our higher educated college students are eating it up. They say they're being individualists, standing up for what they think is right! But is it their thoughts?

And when the time comes for us to fight in our own land, let's see if their protest signs will stop a platoon of Commies. It's not that I'm hoping this will happen to our country because I want to come home, knowing our country is safe for me. And that it'll stay safe for me and my kids and they can enjoy the freedom I've had.

We're not just fighting for the Vietnamese people, but for the U.S. as well. The only thing is, we're on the other side of the world. And God help us if it ever comes to our side because we won't win by protesting, because we won't have the freedom to protest. I'd like,

just for one day, to have the protesters stand in our shoes over here. I'm sure they'd change their signs for [M-16s].

It's a frightening thing to think of but, united we stand, divided we'll fall."
Marine Lance Cpl. Michael Di Pasquantonio, Jan. 8

Lance Cpl. Di Pasquantonio's letter was published in the January 26 Mailbag, 10 days before he stepped on an enemy mine in Quang Nam and was killed. The 135th Delawarean to die in Vietnam, he was due home in August 1970. Lance Cpl. Di Pasquantonio was 20 years old.

Others voiced their dismay.

"**We wish we had more support back home.** It really hurts when you read about the people back home fighting and killing. It seems like there is more hate back there than there is here."
Marine Cpl. Gene Emmell, Feb. 22

"**It seems the people doing the most complaining are the protesters back in the states.** They're all experts on the war, yet none have ever been here. I hope the people back home realize this and don't pay them any attention."
Army Spc. Bob Sheppard, March 2

"**We're a long way from home.** We just want to be heard above or at least at the same level as the hippies or Peaceniks in Rodney Square [in Wilmington] who have never been here, never seen the people. They care so much for their ideas, but what about these people?"
Navy Petty Officer 3rd Class Ron Weatherlow in Gia Le, May 14 Mailbag

The killings at Kent State University further fueled their sentiments. My good friend from Kennett Square, Pennsylvania, sounded off a week after the shootings.

"**As for [New York City Mayor John V.] Lindsay's lowering the flag to half staff in honor of the students killed at Kent State, what honor should be given to rioters?** The feeling around here is that it was overdue and fully deserved. Their deaths engendered no sympathy whatsoever; conversely, most people were pleased about it.

We get tired of reading and hearing about the students who seemingly need only the flimsiest of excuses to go on a rampage of burning and destroying. And if they're going to assault soldiers with loaded weapons, then let them pay the price and good riddance! How many of you have seen what an RPG [rocket-propelled grenade] does to a man or even what an AK-47 round will do as it rips away pieces of flesh and shatters a bone? Don't let 300,000 casualties go for nothing. Sure, it's easy to say, 'Stop it now, stop the blood and the killing.' But I hate to think of lying in a hospital with a crippling wound only to find out it was for nothing."
Army 1st Lt. James D.E. Weisbrod, May 11

Unfortunately, Jim did end up lying in Valley Forge General Hospital in Phoenixville, Pennsylvania, until he recovered from an injury sustained eight months after his tour in Vietnam began.

Another serviceman in Vietnam expressed his disgust with campus disorder and demonstrators at home. "Your Man in Nam" lashed out in letters 10 days apart.

"**I am just one American soldier out of the many thousands here in Vietnam.** I know that most of us share the same views and hopes for our homeland. From what I hear in the news and read in the papers … I'm not sure I want to return home and have to put up with all of these ignorant hippies and people (all a bunch of Commies). I have learned many things over here and one of them is endurance. But I can still only put up with some things for so long, then I explode inside and stand up for what I believe is right. I'll always stand up for what I believe is right. It's the American way – my way. I'll protect my wife and my family and loved ones with my whole life.

All this campus disorder and unnecessary trouble and turmoil doesn't make much sense to me at all. There are lots of ways to get the things you want and I feel that these people are going about it the wrong way….

I didn't especially want to come into the Army, but I didn't go out and burn my draft card or take off to Canada or take any of the other ways I could have thought to get out of it. I didn't really want to come to Vietnam either, but here I am. It would take a long time to write down all the reasons why I came here without making a big fuss, so I'll just mention the most important ones to me.

1. Above all, I did it for my wife and family. I did it to try and prolong their freedom and keep them out of harm's reach and away from these Communist terrorists who have no respect for life, freedom or the properties and welfare of others….

2. I am over here because I love my country and respect its laws. I am prepared to die for it and everything it stands for. Many people can't imagine how good they really have it back there. If they could only see this country and live here among all of the filth and death which is constantly around me, they (well, most of them anyway) would surely thank God and appreciate what they have.

3. I am over here doing a job. I am doing my job (a crew chief on the Army's only true gunship – the Cobra helicopter) the best I can for all of Americans who have died in this blood-soaked country fighting to preserve all Americans' freedom."
Army Spc. Richard S. Lovekin, Feb. 14

The Army's Cobra gunship, a fearsome fighting machine, was flown by the 147th Helicopter Company, based in Bien Hoa and Vung Tau.

"The situation at home is almost as bad as it is over here…. There are countless lunatics running around with guns and knives just killing at random. I'm here now and put my trust in the police to take care of my wife and family, but when I come home (REAL SOON) I'll become their Number 1 defense against all this damn violence that's going on.

Hell, the damn college students aren't even students anymore. They are troublemakers and damn drug addicts. They are enrolled at school to learn all they can because they will be the next leaders of the country. So why in God's name can't they realize this before it's too late? Maybe they'll see the light before it's too late. I sure do hope so. I wouldn't have any of these idiots running the country if I can help it.

I'll close for now and go send my ship back up (a Cobra gunship). I'll leave you with this one last statement: Don't halt the bombing. Move into North Vietnam and show them we mean business. That's the only way we can ever stop the Commies here. As soon as we pull all of our troops out, they'll come down and take over anyway, no matter what they say or promise to do!!!"
Army Spc. Richard S. Lovekin, Feb. 24

Other soldiers had strong words for protesters in their letters.

"I'm getting 'short' and I am almost afraid to return to the world because of all the foolish violence going on in most of our major cities. It is bad enough fighting these people without having to return home and possibly having to fight my fellow Americans. My fellow 'grunts' and myself agree that after fighting in this God-forsaken place that when we do return home we shall not have such persons as antiwar demonstrators and the like deprive us of the freedoms that we have fought for…. I want to be able to walk down any street, in any town, in any state, in peace without having to lower my head in shame at such sights as draft dodgers, flag burners and rioters.

I wish that everyone could have an opportunity to see our nation from the outside, especially the protesters, so that they too may see that they are shaking the foundations which made our country great."
Army Spc. Frank J. Hensley, May 27

"My wife and son live in Wilmington and how I wish I was with them but I've got a job to do and there isn't anything I can do. I'm serving my country and I'm proud of it. That's the reason I'm writing this letter.

It just makes me sick to read about protesters who desecrate our flag or carry Vietcong flags. It just isn't right. Too many people have died over here.

Everyone wants peace, that's only natural. But don't condemn us who are fighting and dying for our country by calling us murderers and killers. We're not.

This is a war and people have to die. You protesters are contradicting what you're preaching by using violent means. If you say this is the only way, then you're wrong.

There's too much violence in the world now. I'm sick of it as all of us are over here. We want to come back to a peaceful United States. How about giving it to us?

A buddy of mine is going home with a leg missing. Show him he lost it for something. Show us that you care about us. Believe me, we need it.

Next time you see someone supporting Charlie (the Vietcong) by desecrating our flag or carrying a VC flag, think about my buddy or the other guys who have died over here."
Pfc. Joe Farenski, May 28 Mailbag

"The American scene is really bad, with everyone killing each other or putting one another in the hospital. After reading all of this and listening to it on the radio, I decided to write a short essay on it….

In writing this, I hope someone can get an understanding of what it's like to be depressed and to fear for your life or [that of] some friend of yours.

Many of us here in Vietnam have been following the stories about unrest on the nation's campuses with subdued anger. It is demoralizing to read about our underprivileged counterparts vandalizing campus buildings, manhandling the institutions' leaders, and generally making 'asses' of themselves.

It is painful to the thousands of less pampered 'students' here who take their lessons from instructors dressed in black pajamas and sandals, where classrooms are sandbagged, hot, sweaty, jungle clearings, where the Saturday night date is a cold beer and a letter from home; and where the grades are not 'As,' 'Bs,' or 'Cs,' but sudden death, crippling wounds or maybe victory.

But we don't expect you people back in the world to be concerned, you did your share in [1944], or was it [1952] and now you're too tired to do more than mutter: 'What's this world coming to?'

Well, don't worry, people, because someday soon this war is going to end, and a half-million angry men are going to be descending on the 50 states with dreams of home and families and education and jobs. And when these men hit the campuses, I sincerely hope that someone tries to stop an ex-Marine from going to class or that some sorry, smelly, flaky social reject tries to plant a Vietcong flag next to the artificial leg of a Seabee, or spits in the burned face of an Army medic.

I guarantee it will only happen once."
Marine Cpl. Brandt E. Tue, June 30

"We all wonder how our country has changed in the year we've been gone. All these riots and demonstrations kinda make a guy think. I am wondering which country needs the most help. I can sum up my feelings about dissenters in a few words. If you don't like the way our country is run, a boat leaves every day."
Army Spc. Gerald A. Roy Jr. in Qui Nhon, Oct. 15

"You know, if everyone in the U.S. would have to come over here for 1 year I think they would appreciate what they have in the good old U.S.A…. They would not be so inclined to fight or march on trivial things as they are…. I just get hung up every once in a while and wish everyone would stop burning, looting and rioting."
Army Pfc. John R. Elliott, Dec. 16

Striking feminists in New York City join women nationwide on Aug. 26 in their crusade for equality with men. Although they could not fight on the front lines, women held jobs in the combat zones as nurses and American Red Cross and USO volunteers. Nancy Sobolewski (opposite, right) of Wilmington, Del., and Christina A. Reichel of Silver Spring, Md., were among about 100 women serving one-year tours in Vietnam in 1969 with the Red Cross Supplemental Recreational Activities Overseas (SRAO) program. Carter Taylor of WIlmington, Del. also served with the SRAO program.

A FEMINIST REVOLUTION FOREVER CHANGED WOMEN'S CIVIL RIGHTS IN THE LATE 1960S AND EARLY 1970S. The women's movement in general and its August strike in particular engendered several responses. In October, Army Spc. Gerald A. Roy Jr. sent a letter from Qui Nhon. "I find the Women's Liberation movement very funny. Maybe they should be sent to Nam and be able to fight alongside of us." An Army nurse took issue with her fellow feminists.

"**I read about the Women's Liberation movement and somehow I have not been very sympathetic with them.** I suppose I prefer to be feminine and do not want to be treated as an equal to men. I have no complaints about our present role in society. Everyone knows we are the stronger sex, so why take over completely? I prefer to let men be the dominating force in our society."
Army Nurse Corps Capt. Helen Polauf, Aug. 21

A soldier continued the discussion.

"**I just received the Stars and Stripes newspaper and on the front page was an amazing story about the Women's Liberation movement.**
I feel that if any woman wants the same treatment as men, then let's see them come here where men are dying, backs are breaking, and our minds are being subjected to constant mental strain.

I am married and I consider my wife as an equal. Where I may be strong physically, she is strong morally. The things that I may not be able to do my wife can, such as giving birth to a child. My wife may be soft and cute, but she is my idea of a real woman.

A real woman doesn't want to be treated kindly like a man, but to be treated kindly by a man."
Army Sgt. Frank J. Hensley, Aug. 30

Another soldier had no problem with the feminist movement, as long as equal rights corresponded with equal work.

"**I have read about Women's Liberation and heard on the radio of the strikes for Women's Rights.** I think if women want to be on an equal basis with men, fine, if this is what they want. But I think they should have the same obligations also. I have seen what the women of Vietnam have to go through to make enough money to support their families since their husbands are in the service. The women here dig ditches, wash clothes for 7 to 10 men, clean trash from the roadsides, etc., all to make $30 to $60 a month. The women in the United States complain about doing laundry for 2 or 3 people with all the conveniences, like automatic washers and dryers. As I said before, if they want Equal Rights, fine, but the obligations go hand-in-hand so then women could be drafted."
Army Spc. John R. "Rob" MacNab near Cam Ranh Bay, Sept. 9

AMERICAN WOMEN IN VIETNAM WERE SCARCE. Visitors from home, especially young, attractive females, always brightened tours in Vietnam. Such eye candy prompted these men to comment.

"**Now I'll tell you about the excitement that went on here today. Miss America and her party were here in BMT [Ban Me Thuot] today.** They were at the special forces camp adjacent to our compound. They were only here for around an hour, but it was a monumental task getting them here. Our colonel went to great lengths. It was really quite a thrill though."
Army Pfc. George Wojciechowski in Ban Me Thuot, Aug. 21

"**I forgot to mention Miss America visited the USO at Freedom Hill last Friday (August 28)....** The show was really decent!"
Marine Cpl. Art Davis near Da Nang, Aug. 30

Nancy "Sobo" Sobolewski was one "Doughnut Dolly" who told me first-hand of a woman's place in Vietnam. "You've heard of 'Queen for a Day?' In Vietnam, it's like you're queen for a day, 365 days a year. The work is fantastic but, of course, you'll have ups and downs," she said of the 40 hours weekly she spent as a staffer. My friend from our undergraduate days at the University of Delaware had spent a year with the American Red Cross in Vietnam as a recreation specialist. In 12 months, she had traveled extensively throughout Vietnam visiting major bases, firebases and landing zones. She sat up nights cutting out Valentines, pinning the little hearts on fatigues as men dragged out to battle. She attended rice wine parties with our Special Forces and caught the Bob Hope show in Long Binh. She even saw entertainer Martha Raye in the field – drinking the Special Forces under the table to boot. So it was understandable when Sobo decided stateside life was just too dull to stay home.

Following her first tour, she returned to Vietnam in September 1970. This time, Nancy worked in Special Services, a branch of the Army, to staff a recreation center in a base camp. Her job description was the same: to maintain high morale through diversified and competitive recreation such as dances, parties, tournaments and crafts.

Nancy visited the News-Journal office between tours to share some of her experiences. Although she had faced military alerts many times and was fired upon only once by the enemy, she recalled her scariest moment occurred when she first landed at Tan Son Nhut Air Base to begin her duties.

"You have to remember to always keep low and if you hear incoming (shells or rockets), hit the dirt," she told me with more than a little authority.

Hardships were many for a female during a year's tour but especially "landing at a firebase with no john. You learn not to drink Cokes during the day. You have to be really camelesque about the whole thing." But the men out on the firebases were so glad to see the "round eyes," as they called the Red Cross girls, they would construct makeshift toilets from old ammo boxes and designate the area with half moons.

At the centers, there were facilities for table tennis, pool, shuffleboard, cards, and other games. When the round eyes were on site, servicemen acted differently. "Lots don't talk. They will just come in for a game of pool and walk out. Others come in and tell you off about something." But, Nancy said, the more universal greeting was, "God, it's girls! Hey, fellas, some round eyes are here."

She crossed paths with few Delawareans on her travels but she said she would always remember Army Chaplain (Capt.) Francis J. Duncan, a Catholic priest from Elsmere, and his kindness.

THOSE SERVING IN ANCILLARY COMBAT CAPACITIES ALSO ENLIGHTENED US ABOUT ASPECTS OF THE WAR WE OTHERWISE WOULD NOT HAVE KNOWN. We learned much from chaplains and nurses. An Army chaplain who wrote that his job was "varied and quite rewarding" added this information:

"**I travel all over the 1st Cav Div area of operations and visit many fire support bases.** I usually conduct 10-16 services per week and the men turn out in large numbers. I haven't found but two men from Delaware and they are on their way home now."
Army Chaplain (Maj.) Tom Carter in Phuoc Vinh, Feb. 24

Another man of the cloth shared his insight on the war.

"**Now that it is almost time to leave I get around to writing.** This is just about par for me. Being a priest, I like to talk but hate to write. I don't know if this is a trait of the profession or just me.

I am assigned to the U.S. Army Support Command, which is a logistical depot for II Corps area in RVN. From here, everything from tanks to toothpicks is sent by convoy or plane to logistical support areas for distribution to the units in the field. This place can be compared to an oversized Gaylord's or Wilmington Dry [Goods].

I am assigned to the post chapel and since I am one of two Catholic priests this means a lot of area coverage. I visit units throughout II Corps area besides ride the convoys when time permits. The duty hours are long and the workload is heavy but it makes the time go by rapidly. The job of these rear line troops is greatly underrated. The convoy runs are over poor roads and the trucks provide Charley with a moving target for practice. My notion about support troops has changed considerably during this assignment.

Civic action also provides an outlet and a change. There are 3 orphanages and 3 refugee camps in the area. All of the work is coordinated through the Civil Affairs Officer for the American and VN military.

I took leave in January to Hong Kong and this week I am leaving for R&R in Japan. Perhaps the shocker is that I have extended my tour of duty in RVN for another six months. I will be home for leave in September and then return to RVN. My next assignment will be with the 25th Infantry Division. This will provide me with a different type of trooper and also a new mission and territory.

My thanks … to the people of SOS Vietnam in Bear, Delaware. They are doing a great job and even this Catholic likes to receive a package stamped from the Methodists."
Army Chaplain (Capt.) Francis J. Duncan in Cam Ranh Bay, Aug. 12 Mailbag

Army Chaplain (Maj.) Tom Carter (opposite) conducted many services at fire support bases. Church in the combat zone was anywhere two or more gathered together.

"Things at the 93rd are very busy, but that's to be expected. We work 12 hours a day, 6 days a week, but love every second. These guys of ours are fantastic and the best patients ever...."

Army Nurse Corps 1st Lt. Valerie D. Sloboda

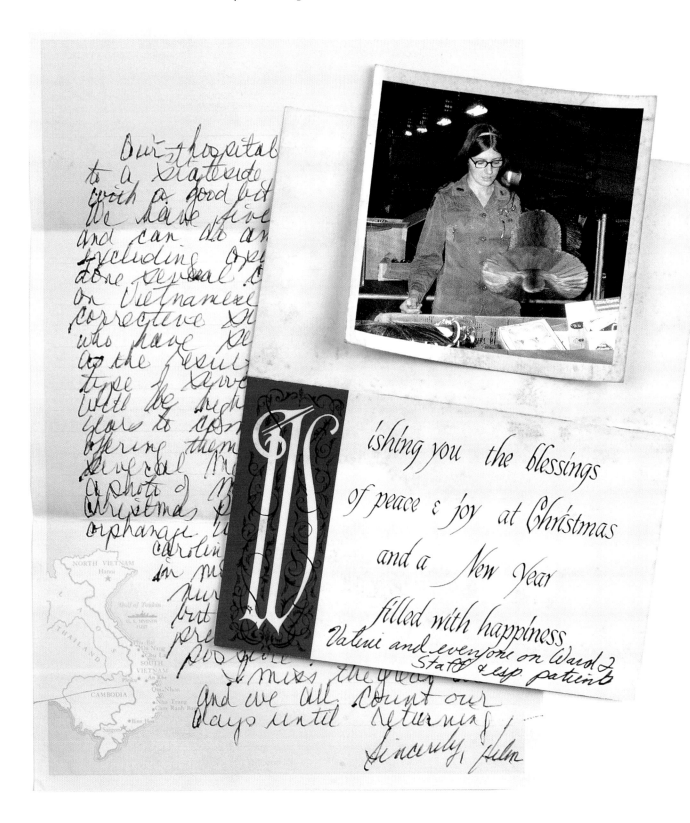

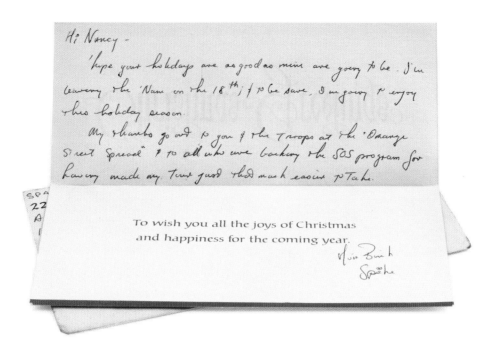

Nursing was another vital facet of the war. One nurse mentioned the long hours she and the other medical staff clocked at the 67th Evacuation Hospital in Qui Nhon, where she had been stationed for eight months.

"**We work six days a week, twelve-hour shifts.** We keep pretty busy but do have slow periods as well as high peaks, such as the past spring offensive.

It is really rough for us all to see our young men suffer the results of war. We also do elective surgery on GIs and Vietnamese. We care for wounded Vietnamese civilians, Army and Vietcong.

Our hospital is very similar to a stateside general hospital with a good bit of improvising. We have five operating rooms and can do any type surgery, including open heart.

We have done several closed-heart procedures on Vietnamese. We do a lot of corrective surgery for children who have severe contractures as the result of polio.

I feel this type of service for the Vietnamese will be highly appreciated in the years to come."
Army Nurse Corps 1st Lt. Helen Polauf in Qui Nhon, May 21

Another, Army Nurse Corps Lt. Col. Helen J. Mackey, had family ties to several wars. Helen spent 13 months in Bien Hoa before reassignment, first to Korea, then to Fort Leavenworth, Kansas, where she was chief nurse at the base hospital. Helen served two tours in Korea, the first during the conflict in a MASH unit.

Helen, one of six children, and three siblings served in the armed forces. Two sisters served in World War II, one in the WACS and one in the WAVES, and her brother was in the Air Force during the Korean War.

Army Nurse Corps 1st Lt. Valerie Sloboda (opposite) sent a Christmas card and thank you letter on behalf of the patients in Ward 2 at the 93rd Evacuation Hospital in Long Binh. The Mailbag also heard from Army Nurse Corps 1st Lt. Helen Polauf.

Another nurse had familial ties to the war as well. Army Nurse Corps 1st Lt. Valerie D. Sloboda was the second in her family to serve in Vietnam. Her brother was in the Air Force for a year's tour in 1966. We first heard from Valerie shortly after her promotion to first lieutenant in October 1970. She put in a year's stint at the 93rd Evacuation Hospital in Long Binh before being reassigned to duty in Colorado.

"**Things at the 93rd are very busy, but that's to be expected.** We work 12 hours a day, 6 days a week, but love every second. These guys of ours are fantastic and the best patients ever.…

I do have a request to make and hopefully you can help me. Christmas is coming and It's really lonely here at that time, especially for the wounded. If possible, could you get Woolworth's [or] one of our large stores to send some decorations and hard candy and cookies? These things are rare and it would really make the patients on Ward 2 happy and brighten up their Christmas."
Army Nurse Corps 1st Lt. Valerie D. Sloboda in Long Binh, Nov. 2

Thanks to many volunteers who contributed time and money, the Mailbag rounded up provisions enough for 75 men and decorations for Val's entire ward. She received eight boxes from Delaware to brighten the holidays for all her patients.

We last heard from Val in early 1971, when she sent her thanks.

"I arrived home in late December, just in time for Christmas," she wrote, "but before I had left Vietnam, the entire ward was decorated – we used everything. The tree was in the center of the ward, we kept it lit. Streamers from ceiling to floor. And every patient received a gift. It was wonderful and everyone enjoyed it." She continued the thanks in her last letter, adding, "[Christmas] was beautiful, a well-remembered time. I'm doing fine now, working intensive care here at Ft. Carson. I hope the pictures help you and thank you for everything. It was appreciated by all beyond words."

DESPITE ALL THE CARPING, OUR MEN IN VIETNAM EXPRESSED THEIR THANKS OFTEN. Thanks for their free subscriptions to *The Morning News*, for their bonuses from the Veterans Military Pay Commission, but mostly thanks for people back home who cared.

"As you might recall, I wrote you last month concerning the feelings of myself and my friends over here. Since then, we have received some 100 letters and numerous packages. You people have shown us your support, and we'd like to thank you."
Army Sgt. Michael J. Freebery, Jan. 7

"I receive your newspaper here regularly, for which I want to thank you. It is really great to be able to read all the hometown news so relatively soon after it happens."
Army Spc. Craig M. Lindell, Jan. 19 Mailbag

"I had no idea that the people of Delaware were so concerned about servicemen in Vietnam. It makes me very proud to be a First Stater and I'd like to say thanks and keep up the good work."
Army Pfc. Tom Yeatman, Feb. 16

"What I am writing this letter for is to thank all the wonderful people back there in the wonderful state of Delaware. It's people like you who really keep a marine's morale from totally falling apart.... Thank you all very much and I'll be back home in January of 1971."
Marine Sgt. William F. May, Feb. 22

"I'd like you to know it means a great deal to all of us over here to know the people back home are thinking of us. It's a pleasure to be a resident of the First State."
Air Force Tech. Sgt. Francis Sontowski, Feb. 17

"The reason why I'm writing is to thank you for sending me *The Morning News*. To me, it's worth its weight in gold because it is the only way I have to find out what is happening back in the First State. And, believe me, after I get done reading it, it doesn't get thrown away until a day or two later because while I'm reading it, there are usually two or three guys flipping a coin or cutting a deck of cards to see who is going to get your paper after I'm done with it. Since I've been here, you have become almost as popular as Dear Abby in the *Stars and Stripes*."
Army Spc. James R. Wright, Nov. 10

Army Pfc. William W. Hutchison Jr. enjoys the *The Morning News* and his state flag (opposite). Navy Petty Officer 3rd Class James R. MacSorley III told us he was grateful for his bonus from Delaware. He added, "The Navy is liberal on haircuts, sideburns and beards now. It makes for a lot of hippies and the Army hates us for it."

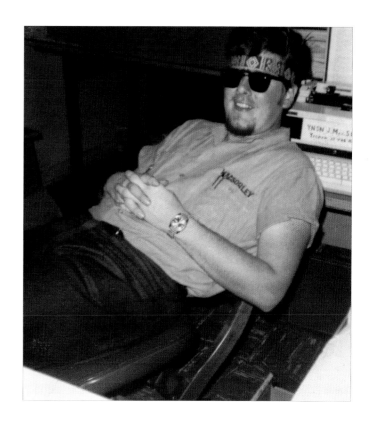

All Delawareans with proof of service in Vietnam were eligible for a bonus, up to a maximum of $300. Army Spc. Darrel O. Neidigh inquired about the bonus in November, saying, "I understand that Delaware gives a bonus to Vietnam veterans. I would like to know how one goes about claiming this bonus. The extra money will come in handy for I plan to marry upon returning home." Others were grateful.

"I received my check for $300 from the [Delaware Veterans Pay Commission]. That's a nice bundle to add to my Australia R&R fund due to be spent in early February [1971]."
Navy Petty Officer 3rd Class James R. MacSorley III in Nha Be, Nov. 2

One wrote of his appreciation in letters less than two weeks apart.

"Other men from different parts of the USA don't believe what is happening in Delaware. The people are sending packages and the state is giving bonus checks to Delaware servicemen. They all say that Delaware must be a fine place to live in if the people care that much."
Army Pfc. Tony V. Eoppolo in Quang Tri, Nov. 26

"I don't believe all the packages and letters I have received since I came to the Nam from the good people of Delaware. It gives me a warm feeling to see everyone give 100% to make us happier and enjoy these holidays in good spirit. Being thousands of miles from our loved ones, [receiving] a package or letter from a new friend really picks me up."
Army Pfc. Tony V. Eoppolo in Quang Tri, Dec. 6

"Morale is a big factor here or anywhere and I'm sure being able to read about the local news and events will be a big lift to me," wrote Air Force Sgt. Doug Williams on December 6. Others also stressed the importance of mail as a morale booster.

"This is about the biggest mess that I have ever seen but the only thing that keeps a good man going is the mail he receives from the world (which is the United States). Whether it is a package or just a few lines on a piece of paper, it is appreciated…. Don't let us be forgotten. It may be the last time you may hear or see him."
Navy Seaman William S. Crum in Nha Be, Sept. 27

"The soldier and his high morale, no matter what the situation, are as evident now as ever in our nation's past. There are many contributing factors and among them one of the greatest is the people at home who give a damn.

The friends and important ones who write about home, the people who find a man's name in a paper and write just to say hi, and all the great groups and organizations who take the time to put together care packages addressing them "To an American Soldier." Thank these people, Nancy, for they do a bigger and more important job than they can imagine."
Army Lt. James W. Roy in Cu Chi, Oct. 10

"Our company's mail is intermittent; some days it comes and some it doesn't. When it doesn't, the mail clerk is put up on a very bad spot. Everything has been discussed, from hanging to tar and feathers. That just shows how much mail is appreciated over here. It's one of the contacts to the outside world."
Army Spc. Dayne R. Smith, Oct. 25

SOS Vietnam, the Interdenominational Center at Red Lion Methodist Church in Bear, always received plaudits from our troops who were the beneficiaries of the non-profit's monthly 5-pound bennie boxes filled with cookies, candy, canned goods, and personal items.

Dedicated to "Serving Our Servicemen," SOS Vietnam was founded by the Rev. Irvin R. Pusey, Red Lion pastor, as an all-volunteer organization in December 1967. By the end of May 1970, SOS had mailed 9,972 gift boxes – nearly 25 tons of food and personal items – at a cost of $15,955.20. SOS packed more than 400 boxes for the December holidays.

Also in 1970, SOS reached out by advertising its mission on six billboards throughout New Castle County.

"I would also like to thank all the wonderful and unselfish people involved in the successful operation of SOS Vietnam. All of you have certainly helped immensely in my tour of duty over here. All of you deserve all the recognition you can get."
Army Pfc. Mark D. Castelow, April 3

"I would like to thank all the people at SOS Vietnam for the wonderful gifts from 'home.' I should hope to see you all soon. May God bless you all."
Army Sgt. Frank J. Hensley, Aug. 22

"I never received my state flag. Maybe the VC have it."

Army Spc. James R. Turner Jr., Dec. 23 Mailbag

For many, displaying the Delaware flag was a photo opportunity. In October, Army Spc. Roger L. Grubb (opposite, left) proudly displayed his free state flag with fellow First Stater Maurice Alonzo Smith. These soldiers stationed in An Khe posed with their flag: Army Pfc. Tony V. Eoppolo, Sgt. Richard W. Refner Jr., and Pfc. Hall A. "Andy" Macklin III, who sent the photo to the Mailbag.

"Thank you to the people who made it possible for me to receive *The Morning News* **and [to] the SOS Vietnam people.** In my 19 months here, they have helped my morale and [that of] all my buddies who shared the packages and papers."
Navy Petty Officer 3rd Class Michael S. Solomon, Oct. 6

"I would like to say thanks to the great people involved in the SOS Vietnam program in Delaware for the fine job they are doing in boosting the morale of the Delaware servicemen in Vietnam. It is always a thrill to get a gift from home and they always put something in the package that is on your mind but not obtainable in Vietnam. It's just great!"
Navy Petty Officer 3rd Class James R. MacSorley III in Nha Be, Nov. 2

Other programs received praise as well.

"I don't know if you know of a group called Project GI but I would like to tell you about them. They are a group of high school kids who got together and sent Christmas cards to us. It was really great and it makes one feel good knowing that even high school kids care."
Marine Lance Cpl. Timothy R. Akers, Dec. 6

"Christmas has just passed and the various troop units have constructed their own unique seasonal decorations for mess halls, barracks, and day rooms. Many stateside organizations sent Christmas trees and decorations to add a little more cheer. The USO shows, Special Services and Red Cross programs are just a few more of the many activities going on throughout Vietnam to make the Christmas season as cheerful as possible for the troops. The Bob Hope show was here on Christmas day and was watched by 22,000 men. It was an excellent program which we all enjoyed.
I would like to take this opportunity to tell you about one of our best morale programs in Vietnam throughout the year. This is the Military Affiliate Radio System, or MARS, that passes telephone calls from our men throughout Vietnam to their families and friends at home. The Army has 50 stations here serving nearly all troop locations. Calls are placed from Vietnam to MARS or amateur radio stations in the states who patch the call to the families over the regular telephone system. Calls must be initiated by the serviceman in Vietnam. The only charge is from where the call

enters the states to the called party. As you can imagine, now is a peak time for MARS calls. Approximately 40 to 42 thousand calls are completed each month. This does not count the 'busy's' and 'no answers.'"
Army Lt. Col. Richard C. Everts in Phu Rang, Dec. 28

Servicemen also wrote the Mailbag asking for assistance. Many requested the popular state flag.

"In my company, I'm the only Delawarean and also the squad radioman. Since half the guys are from the West Coast and don't know where Delaware is located, I would like to know how I could obtain a state flag so I could hook it on my radio and show it off."
Marine Pfc. Michael "Ski" Sadlowski, March 10

"Would it be possible to come by a state flag? (At a nominal fee of course.) I want to prove to local troops Delaware wasn't something in ole Greek mythology. Well, got to go fight the local war, which consists of some VC fly drinking from my now-hot beer."
Army Spc. Richard A. Flood in Tuy Hoa, Oct. 9

"The reason I'm writing is to see if there's any way I can get a state flag. We are making our barracks into a psychedelic shack, so to speak, and I want it to hang over my area. "
Army Pfc. Bob Campbell, Nov. 16 Mailbag

"I did receive the state flag and it pretty well covers one wall in my hooch.... The guys over here are a great bunch of people and we have a good time and make the most of the facilities we have to enjoy ourselves. "
Army Sgt. James "Don" Winchell, Nov. 11

"I'VE MET A FEW GUYS FROM DELAWARE BUT WE'RE FAR AND FEW BETWEEN," WROTE AIR FORCE AIRMAN 1ST CLASS RICHARD L. HOLDING JR. IN AUGUST. Meeting others from Delaware in Vietnam was random at best and many servicemen turned to the Mailbag, which published complete military addresses, to try to locate First Staters in the war zone. "By reading *The Morning News,* I've met another marine from Delaware, Lance Cpl. N.W. Diehl Jr. from Odessa, also Spc. Larry Lavender from Blackbird," Marine Cpl. Art Davis wrote in his August 30 letter from Da Nang. Many in 1970 connected with each other.

"I just learned that Jeff Fishwick just moved in up the road at the 101st Military Intelligence unit so I'll have to steal a vehicle (mine was salvaged a month ago) and go up and see him. He'll probably be shocked to see me."
Army 1st Lt. Henry A. "Alex" Wise III, Jan. 19

"There's something I'd like you to say to the Class of '67 from Newark High School. There's three of us guys from that class that hung around together in school that are stationed near each other, myself, Cpl. Ivan Trustler and Cpl. Robert Park.
We're all in Da Nang. The other two are in the Marines. I see Ivan every day. I'd also like to wish everybody in the No. 1 state a wonderful, safe and beautiful 1970, plus a special hi to my family, grandmother and my close friends."
Army Spc. Ron Suppi, Jan. 15

"On my flight over, there was another Delawarean aboard. His name is Sgt. John Hendrix, an amateur heavyweight boxer from Elsmere. I could hardly believe it, but one week after I started work here at CICV another Delawarean joined our branch. He is Pfc. Tom Gentile from Middletown. He is working in IV Corps Tactical Zone while I work in II CTZ."
Army Pfc. Robert P. Stout Jr. in Saigon, Feb. 21

"Since I've been in Vietnam, I have met about 10 other First Staters. I fact, one is a guy I used to go to school with. This is the last place I expected to meet one of my friends."
Marine Cpl. Gene Emmell, Feb. 22

"I did get in touch with two Wilmingtonians here. One of whom, Pfc. Larry Feldman, 1st Recon, is a cousin of mine. I haven't seen him in almost 2 years. Also, Pfc. Fred Ingersol, whom I went to school with. It was great to see someone you know!"
Navy Petty Officer 3rd Class Michael S. Solomon, May 23

By fall, he had met two more First Staters.

"I met a Delawarean a few weeks ago and it's funny because we grew up together and didn't recognize each other at first. His name is Kenny Shore (Wilmington) and last week we met another guy that we grew together with – Joey Glazar. It was nice to see old faces again."
Navy Petty Officer 3rd Class Michael S. Solomon, Oct. 6

A chaplain with the Army's 101st Airborne Division sent this group picture of four Delawareans in April. From left are Chaplain (Capt.) Robert J. Martin Jr., James E. Shetzler, Robert E. Ewing Jr. and John K. Livingston. Army Pfc. Bob Campbell (on left) sent a photo in November with best friend Christopher Esham. "This picture is of my next-door neighbor from the world. I met him in Bong Song one day. It seemed impossible to actually run into a friend as close as he was to me. He even used to date my sister."

The encounters rolled on throughout the year.

"You might be interested to know that I ran into a First Stater here by the name of Airman 1st Class Bob Christiansen. This is the second time Bob and I have been stationed together. The first time was October of 1968 at tech school at Chanute Air Force Base in Illinois."
Air Force Airman 1st Class James D. Buckland, July 15 Mailbag

"I had the very happy pleasure of meeting a fellow Delawarean here in my battery newly arrived just two months ago. Since his rank is a little higher, I don't know his first name. He is Staff Sgt. Messick."
Army Pfc. Jim Lacey, July 17

"Most of the First Staters I've met have already left for the land of the big PX. One First Stater who was in my unit was Joseph Filliben of Wilmington."
Army Sgt. Frank J. Hensley, Aug. 22

"Here with me in my platoon [1st Platoon, Company G, 2nd Battalion, 1st Marines] is a close friend and fellow Delawarean, Cpl. [Michael "Ski"] Sadlowski of Heritage Park. I've been in Vietnam for over 9 months and have been wounded twice and awarded the Vietnamese Cross of Gallantry in addition to two Purple Hearts. The time is drawing near when both Ski and I will return home to Delaware and we both would like to thank you and all the others from our state who have never forgotten us over here."
Marine Sgt. George W. Kearney, Nov. 3

"Here in my unit, the 371st RR Company, there are 3 First Staters, which is a fair amount for a unit that has a total strength of so few men. The three of us are Spc. Steven Price from Dover, Spc. Wayne Etzweiller from Elsmere and myself."
Army Spc. Scott D. Norris, Nov. 9 Mailbag

"Had another Delawarean join the unit recently. [Staff Sgt.] Bill Brown, who is on his second tour like myself. He lives out around 6th and Broom [streets, in Wilmington]."
Army Staff Sgt. Joe Miller in Phu Bai, Dec. 6

A Virginia Military Institute graduate regaled us with a rare sighting, a group picture of several Delawareans.

"Can you believe it? Four First Staters all in one unit in the Republic of Vietnam! After chapel services (yes, we all attended!) we had our picture taken together and have enclosed it in this letter.

Here are a few details of who we are: John K. Livingston from Wilmington. John graduated from Wilmington High in 1967. His wife and child live in New Castle while his mother and father live in Wilmington.

Robert E. Ewing Jr. from Newark. Bob graduated from Newark High in 1966. His mother, father, grandmother and lots of kin live in Newark.

James E. Shetzler, who brags on Newark as his home where his wife and child live while Jim is in RVN. Jim's parents live in New Castle. Jim claims to have graduated from William Penn High School and also attended a couple of years at the University of Delaware (and since he has become a chaplain's assistant – we have to believe him). Jim also says to let everyone back home know he is the 'shortest' (he'll be home before the rest of us).

And finally, yours truly, Capt. Robert J. Martin Jr., Chaplain, US Army (now maybe you see why we all got to church that day!). My wife and 3 children live in Newark while my parents reside in North Star. I realize that since none of the schools I graduated from (Lansdowne High School – outside of Philadelphia, Virginia Military Institute, Union Theology Seminary [in] – Richmond, Virginia) are in the state of Delaware, my claims to have graduated from them will be more than suspect."
Army Chaplain (Capt.) Robert J. Martin Jr., April 27 Mailbag

A co-authored letter from two Army lieutenants was loaded with job and background information about them and four other Delawareans.

"**Two Delawareans from the Saigon area send their greetings from themselves and from all six of the Delawareans in their battalion....** Bob and Jay met over here in Saigon and live across the hall from each other in their downtown Saigon BOQ.

Bob is from Newark and graduated from Newark High in 1964 and the University of Delaware in January 1969 in Engineering Administration. He is Officer in Charge of the MACV [Military Assistance Command, Vietnam] Dial Telephone Exchange which provides communications to the Saigon area and to General Creighton Abrams. At home, Bob's wife, the former Carol Tyler, is patiently waiting. After his tour in Nam, Bob will return to the First State in Newark, where he will go into management or technical sales.

Jay is S-2 Security and Intelligence Officer for the agency and is in charge of the training of ARVN Signal Corps troops who are schooled and who work on the agency's facilities. He also plays middle linebacker for Telephone Operations Company in Saigon which is now 21-0 and leading the Saigon area standings. Jay graduated from Brandywine High in 1964 and Oklahoma State

University in 1969 in radio-TV. When Jay leaves the Army and Vietnam next July [1971], he will become an Easy Rider and probably follow the south wind to Puerto Rico.

Here is a picture of Bob (the tall one with the hat) and Jay (the short one who lost his hat) in front of the Telephone Operations Company. We're keeping real busy over here but can't wait to get back home. We both read the comment a Delawarean put in your column a couple of weeks ago saying that we in Saigon should think of the guys out in the boondocks once in a while. We always are thinking of those guys and are doing everything that we can, in our way, to help them. We both realize that they are doing the biggest job in this country and always are very thankful that we got such a good assignment.

Other Delawareans here sending their greetings home are: 1st Lt. Bill Roemer, Staff Sgt. Bob Layton, Sgt. Larry Cervelli and Spc. Don Toomey.

So from sunny Saigon in scenic Southeast Asia, Lts. Bob Gibson and Jay Goodley signing off and saying we miss you back there in the First State. And although we do feel extremely fortunate with our nice Saigon assignments, Saigon will look best to us from the window of the big, beautiful FREEDOM BIRD.
Your Friendly Saigon Signalmen, Bob & Jay"
Army 1st Lts. Robert Gibson and Jay Goodley, Dec. 11 Mailbag

Army Capt. James D. Rawlins (opposite) went on patrol the final day of in-country training near Camp Evans soon after his December 1969 arrival in Vietnam. Army 1st Lts. Robert Gibson (left) and Jay Goodley sent a joint letter to the column detailing their duties with the MACV Dial Telephone Exchange.

FAMILY WAS FRONT AND CENTER TO SERVICEMEN 12,000 MILES FROM HOME. An Army officer who was a dentist with the 101st Airborne Division sent a moving letter to his daughter that he shared with Mailbag readers.

"At present, I am writing you with a request that you print the following: An Open Letter To My 7 1/2-Year-Old Daughter.

Dear Monica,

Granny wrote and told me that you asked her why your daddy went to Vietnam. I am sorry, sweetheart, that I did not tell you before I left the United States to come here.

The reason I did not tell you, I suppose, was because I thought you might be too young to understand. But now I realize that you are a very bright little girl who will try to understand her daddy.

First of all, Monica, I want you to know that the Army did not make me come here. I asked to come here for one year. I asked because I am a patriot and I felt it was my duty. A patriot is someone who loves his country and helps his country's leaders protect it from danger.

There are good people and there are bad people in this world. The good people work very hard to feed and clothe their families and themselves. The bad people make the good ones give them their hard-earned money and if they don't, the good people are put in jail or killed.

Our country, the United States of America, is ruled by good people. We are a very strong country but some of our friends are little countries and not very strong.

South Vietnam is a very small country ruled by good people. North Vietnam is also a small country but it is ruled by bad people. These bad people wanted to take over South Vietnam and make them give up their money and food. North Vietnam sent their soldiers into South Vietnam to force the people to give up. But the good rulers of South Vietnam asked our country, the United States, to please help them because they are our friends.

Therefore, our country sent many American soldiers to help protect our friends in South Vietnam. Our soldiers have never tried to take over North Vietnam. They have only stayed in South Vietnam to fight off the invading enemy soldiers from the North.

Every day some more American soldiers are killed trying to protect our friends in South Vietnam. Our rulers think that we should continue to help our friends until they have been trained and supplied well enough to take care of themselves.

If we do not help our friends when they ask for it, they will be destroyed by the enemy. That would only make the enemy want to take over another country and then another and another until finally we would have no more friends. Then the enemy would try to take over our country and we would have to fight them in our streets.

If this ever happened, Monica, your life, your sister's and your mother's would all be in danger.

When I was a little boy growing up, I never had to be afraid for my life because our soldiers were keeping the bad people away. They did this because they loved our country and little ones like me who lived in it.

Now, I am old enough to take my turn and help protect you and the others because I love you and our wonderful country. So, whenever anybody asks why your daddy went to Vietnam, you just hold your head up high.

Love, Daddy"

Army Capt. James D. Rawlins Jr., April 4

The Mailbag gladly – and regularly – announced special events such as births and anniversaries. Engagements, especially those made through the column, also received attention. In 1970, we celebrated one birth, three anniversaries and our second Mailbag match.

The Mailbag congratulated Army Lt. Michael J. LaGarde on the birth of his son in the June 24 column. Sean Michael, born June 6, weighed eight pounds, 12 1/2 ounces and measured 22 1/2 inches from head to toe.

In the same column, the Mailbag heard from Linda Sue Buchanan, who confided she and Army Spc. Billie R. Buchanan celebrated their second anniversary 12,000 miles apart on June 22. They had toasted their first on July 4, 1969, when Billie returned from basic training. The Mailbag wished them a better third.

Marine Lance Cpl. Paul Maxwell couldn't forget his first anniversary on March 5. His wife sent this greeting to the Mailbag: "Happy Anniversary to my husband whom I miss very much. With all my love forever, Dee."

Army Pfc. Jim Lacey took the initiative in his round-about message to his wife which he wrote on July 17. "I was wondering, well, you know how girls are, different dates mean things – special occasions, etc. I was wondering if you could print this for me. Just a few words but they would mean a lot to someone very, very special in my life. Vanessa: On our 8th. Love always, Jim."

Our man with the sentry dogs, Army Sgt. Robert S. "Bob" Biss, was the second Delaware serviceman to credit the Mailbag for his engagement. Navy Petty Officer 3rd Class Terry Reiswig had given readers his good news in his April 9, 1969 letter to the column.

Bob, a military policeman, was a frequent correspondent and sent many pictures of the sentry dogs, including his beloved King, during his 26 months in Vietnam. He returned to Delaware in April 1970 and stopped by the News-Journal office in September with fiancee Sharon Keirn. They said they got to know each other through four months of letter writing while Bob finished his second tour in Vietnam.

Sharon explained she started writing to Bob after seeing his name in the Mailbag one day during her lunch hour. He was a random selection but they corresponded regularly.

When he came home, Bob and Sharon learned they had more in common than stationery. Coincidentally, they lived not far from each other and even graduated from Mount Pleasant High School three years apart.

After dating, they became engaged on August 8 and planned to marry in the summer of 1971. When they stopped by the office, Bob had started his junior year in college, and, because of his love for dogs, planned to continue his studies at veterinary school after graduation.

The Mailbag received many letters from men who missed home.

"**It's really a pleasure to be able to read your hometown paper when you're 12,000 miles from home.** You know, you really don't miss home until you're far enough away from it and you know it's going to be quite a while before you get back to it again."
Air Force Airman 1st Class James D. Buckland, July 15 Mailbag

"**I thought it was about time that I should write you. I [have] under six (6) months in the Nam.** The 'war' isn't so bad, but being 12,000 miles from family and friends, especially 'That Special Girl,' is agonizing."
Air Force Airman 1st Class Bruce D. Shur at Bien Hoa Air Base, Aug. 23

"**Well, a lot of guys over here think this place is pretty bad.** All you have got over here are your buddies and your mail.… Tell my family and friends and especially my son I will be home soon."
Army Spc. David R. Moore, Sept. 6

"**I won't be home for Christmas again.** I will be home for my 22nd birthday. I spent my 21st here. Say hi to my friends for me. Send my love to my Mom and Dad and my sister."
Army Sgt. Laurence Joseph Cervelli in Saigon, Oct. 19

"**I enjoy my work over here very much.** But I do long for home a lot. It is always good to know that people back home do not forget what we are doing over here. I am waiting for the day when I will be coming home. I left too many important things at home, including one girl who I think about every day."
Navy Seaman Harry G. Porter in Can Tho, Sept. 19

Harry reached us in more ways than one with his next letter.

"**I would like to wish everybody at home a very Merry Christmas and a Happy New Year.** Today is Thanksgiving. I sat down and thought about what I have to be thankful about. I am thankful that I am fortunate to live in a country like the United States. I know there are people back home who are not thankful of this. In my opinion, these people would be more thankful if they would spend some time in a foreign country, such as Vietnam, and see how fortunate we really are. Being over here has helped me to mature and see the light. I just wish more people could see how lucky they are instead of complaining about the things that are wrong with our country.

I am also thankful for the great family and friends that I have. Also, people like you that show someone cares at home. You deserve some kind of medal for your service to servicemen from Delaware in Vietnam."
Navy Seaman Harry G. Porter in Can Tho, Nov. 26

DAYS COULDN'T GO BY FAST ENOUGH FOR SHORT-TIMERS. Everything else besides going home paled in comparison. "I have only 21 days left over here and in the Army and then home for good sometime around the 13th or 14th of July," wrote Army Sgt. Kenneth D. Keogh in June. The joy between the lines was evident in these letters.

"**My time is getting short over here.** I only have about 73 days left. My ETS should be about 17 April."
Army Sgt. Robert S. Biss, Feb. 4

"**I come home in 40 days.** I'll come in and see you when I hit Delaware. "
Army Spc. John E. Rubincan in Saigon, Feb. 14

"**I'll start making plans for leaving Vietnam on May 1.** I'll start cleaning on May 7, leave the company to go to Cam Ranh Bay on May 12 and leave Cam Ranh Bay on May 15 to be coming back to the 'world' or the states for permanent!!!"
Army Spc. Zachary D. McGriff in Phu Bai, March 6

Army Spc. Arthur J. Anderson III (right) chats with another serviceman from the 1st battaliion, 509th Infantry. Family man Army Spc. Roger L. Grubb (opposite) named his jeep for his wife.

"**All I can say about this tour is it has been an experience.** I have been in many outfits in 23 years but never like this one. Oh well, 16 more days isn't hard to take."
Army Sgt. 1st Class Jim Danby, Aug. 26

"**This may come as a surprise to you as it did to me.** I am leaving Vietnam. Our unit, Construction Battalion Maintenance Unit 301, is decommissioning after we go back to the states in a few days. Before, it was just a rumor. Now it is a fact."
Navy Petty Officer 3rd Class Richard J. Steele in Chu Lai, Sept. 23

"**I'm getting short.** I leave here Feb. 5, 1971, 113 more days E.T.S. in other words. When I get back to the states I'll be out of active duty. My two years will be up.… I sure can't wait until I get home. It will be great to be in the good old United States."
Army Spc. Kenny Wyatt with the 25th Infantry Division, Oct. 14

"**These fellas over here kept asking me if Delaware was a suburb of Philly [Philadelphia] or Brooklyn, then when I started getting the paper, they read it more than I did.** I should be getting home around the end of January [1971] and I'm counting every hour until DEROS. Not only am I coming home, but I'm getting married to a little girl from Delaware.

Well, that's about it. If you know of any other guys from home that are stationed near my APO, I would appreciate their addresses. It's good to talk about the Blue Hens or Rehoboth Beach."
Army Sgt. Charles L. "Chuck" Gebhart, Oct. 19 Mailbag

"**Sorry, I have only had a chance to write one letter before but you know how busy an infantryman is.** I wanted to write this letter to tell you I'll be back in the world in just two weeks.… I want to thank all the great people of Delaware who really back us up and give us their support, especially my wife, Ann."
Army Sgt. Richard W. Refner Jr., Oct. 21

"**Just a short note to say thank you for all of the moral support during my tour here in the 'sun and fun capital of the world.'** Fortunately, it has been a very quiet but lonely tour and naturally I sure will be glad to get home – especially for Christmas."
Army Spc. William R. Stevens Jr., Nov. 24

"**My tour is just about finished and I will soon be home.** The paper has kept me well informed on what has been going on back home. It will make my job of adjusting after a year's absence a whole lot easier."
Army Spc. Gary L. Pinder, Nov. 27

"**It won't be too much longer and I'll be home drinking beer with all my friends and that really sounds good to say.** The monsoons are up here now and it certainly is miserable. I don't believe I've seen the sun in the past couple of weeks and, boy, is it cold. Don't forget to put my address in your column so all those young lassies can drop me a line."
Army Spc. Robert E. Ewing, Nov. 30 Mailbag

"**It has been a real experience being over here in so many ways and I know I have been very fortunate and lucky.** Got to get that hold baggage packed."
Army intelligence officer James H. Ellett Jr., Dec. 31

Soldiers perform a never-ending job, repairing razor wire around the perimeter of Firebase San Juan Hill west of Duc Pho. During his R&R to Sydney, Australia, Army Spc. Mark L. Goodman makes some new friends (opposite). The famous Sydney Opera House was still a work in progress.

"We are located about 25 miles south of Da Nang [at] a place called Hoi An. While on guard if I've got tower watch, I can stand up and see LZ Baldy, Oun Son Mountains and can just barely make [out] Da Nang." **Marine Cpl. Art Davis**

"I arrived back in Vietnam on the 8th of September after a year's tour of duty at Fort Riley, Kansas. I was with the 13th Artillery, 24th Infantry Division until it was deactivated on 15 April and redesignated the 1st Infantry Division, whose colors were returned from Vietnam.

You may remember reading or hearing of this event. My unit was redesignated as the 5th Artillery, which is the oldest active unit still on military duty, having been started in June of 1775 by Alexander Hamilton during the Revolutionary War. It is known as Alexander Hamilton's Own.

My life as a professional soldier has been done with pride, intelligence and a whole bunch of guts. I love the life of a soldier very much and think it is wholesome for all youngsters today."
Army 1st Sgt. James T. Joyce, Sept. 23

OUR SERVICEMEN OFTEN SHARED SNIPPETS OF INFORMATION TOTALLY UNRELATED TO THE WAR. "As I'm safely back in the 'world' again, please cancel my subscription to *The Morning News*," requested Marine Maj. F. Alvin Huey in February. He added, "Next duty station is Hawaii." Others added commentary about their experiences in Vietnam.

"I was down in Saigon just before I went on R&R. It sure is funny to see how the other half of this war is fought. I couldn't believe the conveniences they have which we in the north look upon as luxuries: indoor bathrooms, hot water, beds, sheets, air conditioners and paved roads.

The most surprising thing was the nightlife and activity on the streets at night. Oh yes, another is telephones. I thought Vietnam was a hardship tour for everyone. Not so. The PX near Camp Alpha has more items in it than any PX in the states I have been in. The grass really is greener on the other side of the fence sometimes. Jealousy."
Army 1st Lt. Henry A. "Alex" Wise III, Jan. 19

One soldier wrote of his excitement about receiving his free subscription to *The Morning News* so he could keep tabs on his favorite sports team.

"I can't wait until the first paper arrives. It'll be about the closest thing to being home. It's be easier to follow the Phillies then. I've been thinking about the [Philadelphia] Eagles since last season. They should be in training now. Their preseason games should begin in about two months. I have a feeling they should really make some noise in the NFL this season. I sure hope so.
Army Pvt. Robert G. Hatfield, June 29

"**I went on R&R about three weeks ago.** I went down to Sydney. Boy, it's a beautiful place. I sure had a great time. The people are so friendly and the town is clean. The girls are something else. It sure is a change from the slant-eyed girls you see over here all the time. While I was down there, I saw a great show by Engelbert Humperdinck. He was really good. If I am still here in Nam in January, I will try and go back down to Sydney."
Marine Lance Cpl. Richard J. Pierce, Oct. 19 Mailbag

"**On June 16 I went to Da Nang for an in-country R&R.** I got a chance to go because I was named Soldier of the Month for May. The beach was something else. I've never seen anything close to it back in the world. I am working night shift now and time continues to pass rapidly. I've applied for an R&R to Sydney, Australia, for November. Can't wait."
Army Spc. Robert P. Stout Jr., Aug. 4

SERVICEMEN ALSO SHARED THEIR R&R EXPERIENCES WITH READERS. Two soldiers traveled to Sydney, Australia, while another's good duty earned him an in-country R&R in Da Nang.

"**Sydney is definitely an oasis in the desert that is this part of the world.** I found it to be more like an American city than Honolulu – where I was stationed for two months. Sydney has the shortest skirts and the cheapest liquor of anywhere in the world. The city is spotless and the people are super-friendly. As one Australian girl said to me, 'it's too bad all the people in the world aren't like the Australians, and then there would be nothing but friendship.'

The entertainment in Sydney rivals that of New York. While in Sydney I saw Jose Feliciano who put on a fantastic show and I also saw the Australian production of 'Hair,' which was an unbelievable experience.

I ate at some typically English restaurants and visited the zoo, which was different, to say the least.

But all good things had to come to an end and I left the beauty of Sydney to return to the ugliness of Saigon. There is, however, a ray of hope. This month I am taking a seven-day leave – now the taxpayers know where all their money is going – and going to Tokyo and Osaka to see Expo '70.

As you can see, I am implementing to the utmost the trite phrase someone thought up 'Join the Army and See the World.'

Well, I must get back to doing my small part for this useless war so I'll close now. If you can possibly do it, I would advise everyone to try and see both Sydney and Australia. It will be a trip I guarantee you won't forget, as I know I won't."
Army Spc. Mark L. Goodman, March 6

"It just feels like Christmas in the air – and Christmas is truly becoming a contagious feeling, a feeling, simply, of joy and happiness. What more could we ask?"   Army 1st Lt. Rodney A. Brice

THE MAILBAG WAS ON A ROLL IN 1970. The column received national attention twice, in the June 8 *Straus Editor's Report*, a Washington, D.C., weekly trade newsletter for editors and publishers, and in the June 27 *Editor & Publisher*, a New York-based publication featuring spot news items.

With all the varied and plentiful material the Mailbag received in 1970, the column expanded to three times a week less than a month after celebrating its second anniversary in May. In July, the Mailbag received its 500th letter, from Army Spc. Charles Leach, and proudly displayed pictures of First Staters in uniform at the Delaware State Fair in Harrington.

The Ilikai East Service Club in Cu Chi, home of the 25th Infantry Division, requested – and received – a complimentary subscription to *The Morning News*. The Saigon USO Club requested the Sunday paper but the News-Journal did not publish a Sunday edition until September 1975 so we had to turn them down.

The Mailbag inaugurated a Valentine's column and added a Top Drawer section to recognize the many awards, decorations, medals and promotions First Staters earned and a DEROS section to salute the increasing number of Delawareans coming home.

The Mailbag also reported the closing in July of the USO in Dover, Delaware's capital, after 29 years.

The column promoted the News-Journal's Vietnam Conflict Map, at 50 cents apiece, and Christmas cards depicting daughters of an American prisoner of war sold locally by People of Wilmington Care for $2 a box.

THE HOLIDAY SEASON WAS A TIME FOR REFLECTION AND HOPE. We couldn't help but marvel at the optimism of this soldier whose holiday cheer was not marred by being in Vietnam. He ended 1970 on a positive note, and decorated his correspondence to reflect the season.

"**It seems strange at first to think of Christmas in the perpetual summer of Vietnam.** But artificial Christmas trees are popping up all over, typical colored light displays are being rigged and there are carols being played on the radio. And what better time to celebrate Christmas than during the Vietnam springtime with all its flowers and birds. And no commercialization to mar the image.

While virtually all of us wish that we could be back in the states for Christmas, every indication is that we'll have a good one here. It just feels like Christmas in the air – and Christmas is truly becoming a contagious feeling, a feeling, simply, of joy and happiness. What more could we ask?"
Army 1st Lt. Rodney A. Brice in Long Binh, Dec. 25

Even though he wrote long before the holidays, Army Pfc. John R. Elliott ended his October letter with a thought for all of us to ponder every day of the year. "This world would truly be a better place … if people started caring about other people and not entirely about themselves only."

The News-Journal Co. brought the war closer to home by selling Vietnam maps at its statewide offices. People of Wilmington Care sold holiday cards that demonstrated the plight of American prisoners of war. As the year came to a close, many servicemen sent colorful holiday greetings to the Mailbag.

1970 – YEAR IN REVIEW

JANUARY 18
The North Vietnamese contend allowing American POWs to send a postcard home once a month and to receive packages from home every other month constitutes prisoner accountability.

FEBRUARY 17
President Richard M. Nixon announces Vietnamization, the increasing participation of ARVN troops in the war, is on track.

APRIL 30
Nixon announces an incursion of American troops into Cambodia.

JUNE 22
The Navy presents 273 combat boats to the Republic of Vietnam Navy in Saigon, bringing to 525 the total watercraft transferred since June 1968.

JULY 6
A Congressional fact-finding mission to South Vietnam reports optimism about ending the war but cautions the country's economic reliance on rice cultivation cannot support the war.

AUGUST 20
A Department of Defense study concludes three out of every 10 servicemen interviewed used illicit drugs during their tours in Vietnam.

AUGUST 30
In country-wide elections of 30 South Vietnamese senators, voting is marred by fraud charges and Vietcong sappers killing 42 civilians.

OCTOBER 8
MACV announces redeployment of 40,000 troops stateside, leaving 344,000 servicemen in Vietnam.

OCTOBER 15
Marines vacate their base at An Hoa and turn it over to ARVN forces.

NOVEMBER 19
U.S. Special Forces fail to liberate American prisoners in a helicopter raid of the Son Toy POW camp 20 miles west of Hanoi. The NVA had emptied the camp after being tipped off about the raid.

DECEMBER 10
Nixon warns the North Vietnamese if they ramp up fighting in South Vietnam as American troops withdraw, U.S. troops will resume bombing North Vietnamese targets.

DECEMBER 31
American war casualties in 1970 total 6,081, lowest since 1966.

1971

AS THE WAR CONTINUED, WITH NO END IN SIGHT AND MINIMAL PROGRESS IN THE PARIS PEACE TALKS, OUTRAGE AT HOME OVER THE CONFLICT ESCALATED TO UNPRECEDENTED LEVELS. ON APRIL 30, LEGIONS OF ANGRY VIETNAM VETERANS VENTED THEIR OPPOSITION TO THE WAR AS THEY DESCENDED ON WASHINGTON, D.C., WITH MANY OF THEM SO INFURIATED THEY HURLED THEIR COMBAT MEDALS ON THE CAPITOL STEPS.

The massive show of displeasure by these vets, who had organized as Vietnam Veterans Against the War, stoked the fires of the omnipresent antiwar demonstrators who, three days later, staged their own protest in the nation's capital. Police arrested thousands for civil disobedience but a court ruling later held the arrests were unconstitutional.

While Vietnam dominated the news in 1971, the war and its fallout at home did not have a monopoly on front-page headlines. In March, the 92nd Congress proposed the 26th Amendment, which gave 18-year-olds the right to vote. The amendment was ratified by the legislatures of 39 of 50 states, the required three-quarters of the states needed, and became valid on July 7.

Convinced victory in Vietnam was unattainable, Daniel Ellsberg, a Harvard University-educated analyst for the Rand Corporation who had served in the Pentagon and the State Department as a civilian in Vietnam, deliberately leaked the Pentagon Papers, the Defense Department's classified – and damning – documents on the conduct of the war, to *The New York Times*. On June 13, the *Times* published the first installment of the 7,000-page document. Nixon's attorney general, John Mitchell, then obtained a court order that prevented the newspaper from publishing additional installments for 15 days, until the Supreme Court overturned the order, enabling publication to resume.

Ellsberg knew he would not remain the anonymous source of the leak for long. After going underground for more than two weeks, he turned himself in to the U.S. Attorney's office in Boston on June 28 and was charged with theft, conspiracy and espionage. He believed he would spend the rest of his life in jail but the Nixon administration's clumsy attempts to discredit him prompted all charges to be dropped.

On September 13, 29 inmates and 10 hostages were killed at the Attica (N.Y.) Correctional Facility as state police and guards, acting on orders from New York Gov. Nelson A. Rockefeller, stormed the prison four days after about 1,000 inmates had seized control and taken 42 guards and civilians hostage. The prisoners demanded better living conditions at the facility that housed 2,225 inmates but was designed to hold 1,200. Rockefeller ordered the assault after the breakdown of talks between inmates and a team of high-profile negotiators. The New York State Special Commission on Attica would later write, "With the exception of Indian massacres in the late 19th century, the state police assault which ended the 4-day prison uprising was the bloodiest one-day encounter between Americans since the Civil War." The state settled a wrongful death lawsuit with slain inmates' families 27 years after the riot and, in 2004, awarded $12 million to the families of the prison employees killed at Attica.

In Delaware, business and government leaders cringed at the release of *The Company State*, consumer advocate Ralph Nader's scorching treatise on the influence of the venerable DuPont Company on the state and its government. Ironically, on June 28, Gov. Russell W. Peterson, a former DuPont chemist, signed into law the Coastal Zone Act, landmark environmental legislation which banned further industrial development along Delaware's entire coastline. But Peterson had no time to bask in the success of his signature political accomplishment. Within hours of the bill signing he would announce that the state would end its fiscal year two days later not with the surplus he had pledged but with a $5 million budget deficit. Peterson's political slide gathered momentum, bottoming out when he lost his bid for re-election in 1972.

Delawareans still refer to June 28, 1971, as Black Monday. On the war front, the South Vietnamese assumed a greater role in combat in their own country, and in Cambodia and Laos as well. The Paris peace talks languished as South Vietnam's president, Nguyen Van Thieu, amid claims of election rigging, won another four-year term. Despite an apparent military buildup by North Vietnam, the withdrawal of American troops from the war zone continued.

U.S. war casualties tumbled downward in 1971, with the 2,357 deaths recorded by the National Archives and Records Administration the lowest figure since 1965. According to data from the Vietnam Veterans Memorial, Delaware lost eight servicemen. By contrast, the South Vietnamese sustained more than 21,000 casualties while enemy deaths totaled about 97,000.

Marine Pfc. G. Hunter Metzner (opposite), based in Hoi An, wrote that he helped train ARVN forces to fight the Vietcong "so we can go home." Every serviceman wore identifying dogtags and most carried sunblock and a whistle with their gear.

FEWER AMERICAN DEATHS DID NOT, HOWEVER, TRANS-LATE INTO LESSER FEELINGS ABOUT LOSSES THAT DID OCCUR. Air Force Sgt. Daniel P. Stokes, assigned to the 366th Security Police Squadron at Da Nang Air Base, didn't try to conceal his anguish in his August 10 letter, the 750th received by the Vietnam Mailbag. He wrote, "On July 5, I lost five friends. Da Nang was rocketed and a barracks took a direct hit, killing 5 and wounding 32 others. This was my first contact with war in regards to the loss of human lives since I came in country in April.

"When they died, I also died. Something died within me. I have not as yet determined what is gone, but I know the feeling [I have is] that the only thing we're accomplishing over here is denting the population."

And the still-undeclared war, in its eleventh year, clearly weighed heavily on this soldier whose jarring letter also was printed in a summer column.

"**Here in Vietnam it is like a hellhole and, baby, let me tell you, that's not my bag.** I'll be glad when it's over. There'll be no more incoming rockets to splatter you around like you were paint. No more snipers. No more jungles or silent dead. No more clattering choppers and no more friends moaning, 'Help me, I'm hit.'

There's talk about moving out of Vietnam. Sure there's talk, but I'll be damned if I see any guys leaving. Sure, last year half a million GIs left Vietnam. But this year 200,000 of them came back.

The lucky ones come back to the world with two arms and two legs, but how about the ones that get crippled for life or even the ones who don't make it back? That's why Vietnam is a HELLHOLE.

Nancy, now when a man goes back to the world, he still finds himself caught in a war. A different war. This is a war of war and peace. He can't find a job. He doesn't know what to do or where to start. Maybe a GI wants to go back to school, but he still needs a job to pay dues and buy books. Remember he can't find a job yet. Sure when an employer hears you have been to Vietnam they say that they will help, but none did.

What's a man to do when he has lost all potential for making new plans and having new dreams?"
Army Spc. Joseph C. Dawson, July 16 Mailbag

As often occurred with the Mailbag, the column became a forum for debate, with Joe's views drawing a sharp response from another soldier.

"**There are some funny things involved in this letter.** No. I is that this person is assigned to a [brigade] level [Headquarters and Headquarters Company] which is never out in the field. The closest they ever get to the field is pulling berm guard. That is the funny part. No. II is where does he get the right if he hasn't been to the field to write this kind of letter? I will agree that most of what he says is true but not all of it. He says that when a GI goes home he can't go to school because he can't get a job. Most GIs when they come home don't want to work. They just want to collect unemployment.

About school, has this guy ever heard of the GI Bill? That's what it is for.

Navy Seaman Harry G. Porter (opposite) clearly expressed his opinion about troop withdrawals and the war. Enemy propaganda included "bounty cards" offering rewards for U.S. troops.

No. III is about people coming home. I am stationed where I can see freedom birds come and go. A guy I met on the way coming over is stationed at 90th Replacement Battalion. He has told me that there have been some weeks that maybe 200 or 300 people come into this country. And about leaving this country he says sometimes there are as many as 3,000 leaving. I think this guy should get his facts straight."
Army Sgt. Ralph J. "Butch" Anderson, July 30

Other servicemen expressed their frustrations with the war's pace and tactics and the fuzzy numbers of troop withdrawals.

"**This war is lazy!** I think these people are lazy. They just don't seem to be doing enough to help themselves. The U.S. has the power, men and capability to stop this war without atomic weapons but they don't! Why? With our capabilities we don't have any business letting Americans and especially Delawareans get killed. I could say a lot more but my morale is low enough, so I'll try to forget my gripes."
Air Force Tech. Sgt. Gerald W. "Jake" Jackson, Feb. 11

"**The battery I'm with moved from Bu Dop to Fire Support Base St. Barbara where I'm commanding three howitzers.** My commander and the rest of our battery are a little north of here with three howitzers at Katum.

Tay Ninh Province is the nicest area of Vietnam I've seen since I arrived here in November [1970]. Nui Ba Den or Black Virgin Mountain is an ancient hideout and sanctuary which provides us with not only scenery but artillery targets. We're only 7 kilometers north of it and our 155-mms pepper it daily. But it's been hit by everything the Army and Air Force have and the VC are still on it and in it."
Army 1st Lt. Robert A. Nowaczyk, Feb. 15

"I really don't know what's happening in this troop withdrawal. In my opinion, I think that the troops that do withdraw are being relocated in places like Cambodia and Laos. It seems to me that the war is expanding."

Navy Seaman Harry G. Porter in Can Tho, Feb. 11

Worn combat boots were among the items that returning servicemen were allowed to ship stateside. Uniform patches (above) were another form of expression. Army Spc. Robert P. Stout Jr. (opposite, right) stood by two Korean soldiers in a Saigon alley.

"It's too bad we didn't bomb Hanoi like we should have. It is my belief that if we would have shown North Vietnam we weren't fooling around, this thing would have ended long ago. Sure the troops are being withdrawn little by little but there will never be a total withdrawal. We'll have troops here just as in Korea. I think when the NVA find our strength becoming weak here in the south, they will just strike back stronger than ever."
Army Pfc. Richard H. Volk, March 17 Mailbag

"In one of your recent articles you mentioned that the number of [newspapers being sent] to Delawareans is increasing and wondered why since we are all supposed to be leaving. Well, the way it is written, combat troops are being pulled out, and only advisors will remain. An interesting point is the fact that my unit was "transferred" to the Naval Advisory Group! I am now an advisor and am allowed to remain in Vietnam? There are a lot of ways the government fools the people. The reports of "400 less men in Nam this week" get to me! They send 2,000 men home and bring in 1,600 new advisors, therefore 400 less men. However, there are still new troops arriving in Vietnam every day! It looks good on paper to see 400 less men, but actually 2,000 went home. The people are given a false picture of the situation and feel the war is ending sooner. The public doesn't see the 1,600 new men sent here (or hear about them) for a year or more. I think Congress has its head up its butt! Maybe in 10 more years the U.S. will be out of Vietnam."
Navy Petty Officer 3rd Class James R. MacSorley III, Nov. 3

Whatever the numbers, servicemen were coming home, and so were some of the units – and aircraft – that played major roles in the war. We noted in the September 20 edition of the Mailbag:

Air Force Sgt. Keith M. Williams of Smyrna helped close the final chapter in the combat history of the workhorse of the Air Force tactical air units in Vietnam.

The 1970 graduate of John Bassett Moore High School served as an aircraft maintenance specialist with the 35th Tactical Fighter Wing that flew the F-100 Super Sabre on its last mission in Southeast Asia.

Phan Rang-based aircrews flew four fighter bombers on the final strike in 1971 and dropped 750-pound bombs on an enemy bunker complex. That sortie was the last of more than 157,000 logged by the 35th since its arrival in the combat zone in 1966. The wing was deactivated as the eighth increment of U.S. troop redeployments from Vietnam. The F-100s also returned stateside.

The Super Sabre, introduced to the Air Force inventory in 1954, was the first fighter aircraft to attain supersonic speeds in level flight.

With troops withdrawing from Vietnam, reams of paperwork and mountains of packing preoccupied many. One sent travel tips from *The Southern Cross*, voice of the 23rd Infantry Division (Americal). Although specific to his unit, the tips were timely reads in a July column.

"For the men of the 23rd Infantry Division, [going home] can be something of a headache as nine copies of DEROS orders and at least four copies of an inventory of goods being shipped are required.

There are lots of things that may not be shipped home as 'hold baggage' from Vietnam. This list includes: narcotics, tobacco products, medicines, goods with federal stock numbers, pornography, camouflaged uniforms, food products, firearms, ammunition, alcoholic beverages, flammable goods and batteries.

Authorized war trophies may be shipped home as long as they have been registered with a Military Intelligence Company in the area.

One set of jungle fatigues, as long as they have been worn, and two pairs of worn jungle boots may also be shipped home with the hold baggage.

It's never too early to think about getting your things together either. Best time to ship your belongings home is when you get your orders. Allow 30 to 45 days for your shipment to reach its stateside destination."
Army Spc. William W. "Hutch" Hutchison Jr. in Chu Lai, July 30 Mailbag

"**Very few of Vietnamese actually appreciate what we are doing. All they want is the American dollar. The only reason I have stayed here so long is to get out of the Army as soon as possible.**"

Army Spc. Robert P. Stout Jr.

The war's complexity proved frustrating for many servicemen. Here's one example of the conflicting feelings felt by so many:

"**Vietnam is, or was, to me a very beautiful, raw and weird place.** Sometimes you can be in a place where there is not conflict, just the plain, serene everyday-type living. Then again you can be at a place where war is second nature and to live depends on who you serve. This I'm sure is natural in any war or conflict, whichever terminology you wish to use, but it's new to me and the feeling is puzzling.

You can't believe the beauty and fertility of the land, but war exists and it's left to fallow. This land could be prosperous but isn't because of the present state of the country. Slowly but surely, our efforts in helping the people are beginning to take effect. But why has it taken so long? I, for one, can only say that the answer lies at the feet of the politicians and the people of this land. If they would set a standard goal as to what they wanted, then their problems would be over.

But when a man is threatened by both sides and fears for only his family, then the man will never be neutral. He'll be an enemy one minute and a friendly the next. These people have very strong family ties and until you can prove to them that you have the right solution, you might as well forget about their support.

Our time of fighting in this war should have ended long ago. Enough time has been spent on training in the Army of the Republic of Vietnam. I find it hard to believe that in 11 years these people can't learn to defend themselves through our training.

Don't get me wrong, I don't knock our government for being here, I just say this war has been a war of politics, there's not way of getting around that. If we were asked to just help when we got here, then why are we still here?

It didn't take Korea this long to stop Communist aggression. Does the [government of Vietnam] really know what it wants? I don't think so! If they did, then the U.S. would be out by now. At this late stage all we should be doing is partially supplying them with materials, but not with personnel. The training and advisory days should be over.

A good example is my year here. I do absolutely nothing but play the part of an advisor, but without the ability to advise, because my counterpart knows more of what is going on than I do. He's had the opportunity to work with many advisors before me and if he doesn't know his job by now, then *xin loi* ("that's too bad."). Everybody's tired of this war. It's killed a lot of men and when you actually think of it, what has it gained? A decree of friendship signed on the dotted line or maybe thanks? Are we really needed anymore? I don't know, I'll leave this up to the politicians."
Army Spc. Darrell E. Bauguess, July 15

Fighting a war demanded round-the-clock vigilance. Servicemen wrote whenever they found the time. This soldier took pen in hand to sound off at 1:30 a.m.

"**Saigon was off limits today because of a big parade, sort of like the Moscow May Day parade – a big show of strength.** They must have shown all our tanks, APCs, choppers, rifles, etc. I just cannot agree with the war as it has been run by our leaders.

How do you feel about what *The New York Times* published recently concerning our involvement here in Southeast Asia? I won't comment.

I want out of the Army. Like Paul Newman said in the movie *Cool Hand Luke*, 'What we have here is a failure to communicate.' It makes me sick to see all the money and lives just wasted.

That's how I feel because I do not see anything gained from ten years of fighting. To put it lightly, the war, excuse me, police action, has destroyed the American economy.

Very few of Vietnamese actually appreciate what we are doing. All they want is the American dollar. The only reason I have stayed here so long is to get out of the Army as soon as possible."
Army Spc. Robert P. Stout Jr., June 20

**OUR CORRESPONDENTS OFTEN COM-
MENTED ON THE INCREASED LEVEL
OF SOUTH VIETNAMESE INVOLVEMENT.**
President Nixon's "Vietnamization" strategy
was conceived to give forces greater respon-
sibility for protecting their own territory.
One serviceman touched on those topics in
two notes.

"**I've been here 6 months along with another
Marine (Bill MacInerny).** I am from Milford
and Pfc. MacInerny is from Wilmington.…
We are infantrymen in a program to teach the
Vietnamese soldiers and [to help] show them
the way to break down the Vietcong's infra-
structure. We go on all patrols, ambushes and
operations with the Vietnamese soldiers, showing and helping them fight the Vietcong in the
proper way."
Marine Pfc. G. Hunter Metzner in Hoi An, Jan. 28

"**CAG, the unit I am in, is scheduled to pull
out May 13, 1971.** We have spent our time
training ARVNs to take over our area of operation so we can go home. The casualty rate for
our unit is really low. We only make contact
maybe two or three times a week."
*Marine Pfc. G. Hunter Metzner in Hoi An,
April 2 Mailbag*

Others wrote:

"**I'm a company commander of Alpha Co.
3/1 Americal Division.** The war has slowed
down quite a bit since my last tour and I
think Vietnam finally has a chance to make
it as a free and independent country. After
spending two tours over here it's rather
important that these people have a chance."
Army Capt. William E. Ferguson, Jan. 21

"**I've been in Vietnam since last June [1970]
but it seems like it's been a lifetime.** My
company is in the process of deactivating and
I hope I'll go back home instead of having to
go to another unit in Vietnam. It is also good
to see the ARVNs going into the field instead
of us."
Army Spc. John B. Minker III, Jan. 26

A soldier from Company A, 34th Armor, fires an M-60
machine gun near the Boi Loi Woods.

Most ground troops carried their gear in a rucksack or backpack that could weigh 75 pounds or more and included water, food, ammunition and a first-aid kit. Army Pfc. Paul E. Vaughn said of his rucksack: "My home is on my back."

6545-01-094-6136
INSERT, FIRST AID
KIT CASE

8510-162-5658
SUNBURN
PREVENTIVE PREPARATION
(CREAM PASTE)
Contents:

SOME SERVICEMEN DESCRIBED THEIR DAILY RIG-ORS IN GRAPHIC DETAIL. And they didn't hesitate to express their feelings about the war.

"I'm a 'GRUNT.' That's short for combat infantry soldier. My job is to take an area and find the VC or NVA. My home is on my back, we carry everything we need.

I carry a 75-pound rucksack backpack. It is made up of 10 quarts of water, three days of food, my M-16 ammo, two hundred rounds of M-60 ammo, machete (knife), a shovel, poncho, poncho liner, three smoke grenades, four hand grenades and the M-16.

Our main area of operation is around the A Shau Valley. It is raining quite regularly now and we are hardly ever dry.

My own view of the war is we should get out now! Mainly because if the ARVNs aren't ready now, they never will be ready."
Army Pfc. Paul E. Vaughn, June 11 Mailbag

"I can say the same about the life of a grunt. He is the MAN among MEN. He fights the battles with the last ounce of strength. He is the one that doesn't shave or shower for 9 days or more. He is the man that you don't hear about back in the "world." I've been in the field for 5 months and just got out of the field almost 2 months ago…. As I said before, the GRUNT is the one that does the JOB over here. The WORST JOB!

My own personal view of the war is to get out NOW. Why is because the ARVNs are not doing the job we want them to do. And as soon as we do get out, the VC and NVA will be right back in the same place they were before…. So I say we should get out."
Army Spc. Richard J. White in Cam Ranh Bay, June 16

Other servicemen gave Mailbag readers accounts of action near them as well as their insights.

"The blow-up of the ammo dump at Quang Tri on the 22nd of June was an enormous blast and was felt for a distance of a couple of miles. It causes me to shudder a little to think the North Vietnamese have an alley through a bunker line and easy access once through the line.

I think an instance such as the above would cause the United States Army Vietnam to take a close look at their regulation that the soldier, unless in actual combat, has to keep his weapon locked in the 'ARMS ROOM.'"
Army Chief Warrant Officer Herbert V. Melson at Da Nang Relay Station, July 1

"I am attached to an attack support squadron and am one of three corpsmen. I get to know all my men in the squadron and if someone is hurt I am the one they see. I always check their records for the place of birth and where they live.

Being in Vietnam I am always on the go but if I meet someone from Delaware I always make it a point to stop and talk to him."
Navy Hospital Corpsman Joseph H. Opdenaker Jr. aboard the USS Enterprise, Oct. 20

Sgt. Ronnie Morrow (third from left on tank) sent the Mailbag a picture of the "Fighting Five" near Khe Sanh. He wrote in June, "We are proud of our battery for we have very many kills to our credit. I for one think every NVA dead is one less that can kill an American."

"Well, everything has been calm, cool and quiet, Charlie-wise, here of late. We knocked out about fifteen rocket launch sites that he had set up in the mountains to the north of us and thank goodness that we got them before they got us. That old 122-mm rocket can do a lot of damage."
Air Force Master Sgt. James T. Joyce at Phan Rang Air Base, Feb. 25

"I'm new to 'THE NAM' but [I] get a little used to it as times passes. There's not much to say about it really. I get to see a lot of it but if you've seen one tree or one hill you've seen them all…. I don't get to see any cities or villages. I'm in an infantry unit whose motto is 'NO SLACK' so, as you can see, it's not all fun and games."
Army Pfc. Kenneth J. Norris, Nov. 18

"Well, here I am in vacation land. Beautiful southeast Asia Vietnam. The sandbag capital of the world….

I am a radar operator on a Q-4 radar…. Unfortunately, I am in Nam now. I am stationed about 6 miles from a big base camp by the name of Chu Lai. I am on a firebase by the name of Fat City…. If you've ever seen the trash dump at Ellendale, you've seen this place….

I know I live in the state that started a nation, but I think I am the only dude from Delaware in Vietnam now.

I guess I can say a few words about our so-called war. I work seven days a week. Most of the time I can't even tell anyone what day of the week it is or the date. The day I look forward to each month is payday. I get lots of mail when they decide it's time to send it to us.

The United States government spends millions of dollars over here each year on equipment. The problem is, it seems we don't get it. But the South Vietnamese has better equipment than us. But it's our government that gives them what they have now. Without the U.S., they probably wouldn't even have a shirt to wear."
Army Spc. William E. Justice, Sept. 19

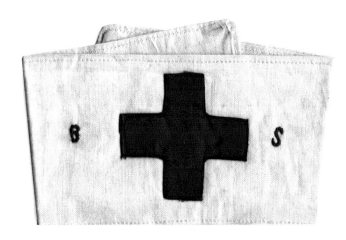

"As we were zooming along at about 100 knots we somehow or another topped a tree. The helicopter immediately shuddered and shook but our pilot brought it under control. We landed shortly thereafter and as I got out I saw about five feet of tail boom laying on the ground."

Air Force Master Sgt. James T. Joyce

"**On the 30th of June I was going to fly by chopper to Tan Linh but unfortunately we had what could have developed into a serious accident along the way.** After leaving Phan Rang we had to fly low, under the pattern of the planes incoming and outgoing from the air base.

As we were zooming along at about 100 knots we somehow or another topped a tree. The helicopter immediately shuddered and shook but our pilot brought it under control. We landed shortly thereafter and as I got out I saw about five feet of tail boom laying on the ground. So, after thanking God for a safe delivery, we got on another chopper and came back home. Scared? Hell, yes."
Air Force Master Sgt. James T. Joyce at Phan Rang Air Base, July 18

My friend and Wilmington Friends School graduate Army Capt. John B. "By" Bishop made some headlines as well as some television newscasts when he told reporters about his arduous trek to safety. We had his story in the March 10 Mailbag.

By, a helicopter pilot from Kennett Square, Pennsylvania, who had been in Vietnam since May 1970, was shot down over Laos on March 3. Afraid his mother might receive a telegram from the Pentagon declaring him missing in action, By attempted to get to a phone as fast as he could. South Vietnamese soldiers brought By and his crew, minus their gunner, safely back to South Vietnam within a few days.

After getting past network newsmen and their questions, By headed for the phone and called home – collect. Due to DEROS in May 1971, By's next travail involved contacting malaria. The April 5 Mailbag reported him stateside and recovering at home.

The Vietnam veteran would receive a Silver Star in 1972 for his gallantry in Laos. The old adage, "Like father, like son," aptly applied to By. His father, Robert B. Bishop, had received the Silver Star in World War II while serving with the Marines.

The citation for By's Silver Star read in part:

Capt. Bishop distinguished himself while serving as a rotary wing aviator with the 174th Aviation Company. On 3 March 1971, nine helicopters were transporting South Vietnamese army troops to Landing Zone Zulu when the lead craft was hit with intense hostile anti-aircraft fire. Unable to keep the craft in the air, Capt. Bishop skillfully maneuvered through the exploding enemy rounds and managed to execute a safe landing.

Upon trying to evacuate his helicopter, he found the left door was jammed and that the craft was burning. With great calm and presence of mind, he helped his crew and the South Vietnamese army troops out through the single door and prevented a delayed exit from the craft which could have been fatal.... He quickly and efficiently organized the men … and finally found the South Vietnamese landing zone they were seeking and shortly afterward they were all evacuated from the area.

Not all accidents in Vietnam were combat-related. Air Force
Master Sgt. James T. Joyce wrote of a near-disaster after
taking off from Phan Rang Air Base. In the field, both sides
cared for their wounded. A U.S. first-aid kit (opposite) is
shown with an enemy medic armband.

SERVICE IN VIETNAM WASN'T ALWAYS NERVE-WRACKING. Some troops were either temporarily out of the war zone or saw little combat in country.

"**At the present, we're tied up off Hong Kong.** There are so many bargains you tend to blow some coin without even knowing. I guess we're as bad as a bunch of women at a big sale. We'll be here two more days and back out on Yankee Station (Gulf of Tonkin) for about thirty days.

Believe me, that's a long time and who cares where you pull in, just let me off for a while. The United States looks better every time I think about it, which is most of the time."
Navy Petty Officer 3rd Class Clifford T. "Tom" Hitch aboard the USS Hancock, March 5

"**I have been in Vietnam almost two months now and nothing much is happening where I'm at, I mean no action.** And I thank God for that.… I am a heavy equipment mechanic. My unit is building a road."
Army Pfc. Richard W. McGinness in Phan Thiet, May 31

"**We're not too busy, fortunately and unfortunately.** Fortunately because that means not too many troops are out in the field getting hurt; unfortunately because that means we have nothing to do most of the time. Flying is what we'd like to do, so if we don't get to do that, anything else seems like nothing. We maintain field sites at Quang Tri and Phu Bai where things aren't very much more busy than here. Our primary mission is to pick up ARVNs since most U.S. are out of the field and the 101st [Airborne Division] has their own Dust Off [helicopter ambulance]."
Army 1st Lt. Kenneth D. Warner in Da Nang, Aug. 23

"**I don't think it too surprising that you may be receiving less and less mail….** As the war winds down, the attitude pervades many 'why keep working?'

Of course, many of our guys are getting their asses kicked but many news articles reveal troops are more and more reluctant to go into the field.

Also in the news are the men involved at Khe Sanh, where I have a couple of friends helping to provide fuel support to the many choppers, planes and trucks there. I hear from them what a hell of a job it is.

Perhaps you are not aware that the Australians and Koreans and Thais are still active around Long Binh, Bear Cat and Vung Tau and actually fighting V.C. Just 20 miles northwest of Vung Tau sits Nu Dot, the main Australian base in Vietnam.

Flying a helicopter ambulance for the 571st Medical Detachment, Dust Off, made Army 1st Lt. Kenneth D. Warner's day. His detachment, based in Da Nang, maintained field sites at Quang Tri and at Phu Bai (opposite).

During a recent liaison visit to inspect POL [petroleum, oil and lubricant] facilities there, I ate lunch with the Aussies and while I found them high spirited (an understatement!) and cheerful, they voiced the same sentiments as we GIs, i.e., it all seems so pointless.

Vung Tau has been reopened, unofficially, as an R&R Center again and the 25th Infantry Division has erected tents and facilities on our beach and support troops from Long Binh send 30 to 60 guys here a week for 3-day passes.

Being one of the few towns in Nam that is 'on-limits' and obviously caters to the Americans with its bars, beaches and bordellos, it offers an excellent place to 'rest and recuperate.'

Those of us here in Vung Tau help in every way we can to keep it all going."
Army Spc. Philip C. Winkler in Vung Tau, March 19

Even my Rehoboth Beach friend wrote of calm conditions soon after he arrived at Da Nang Air Base. His first letter to the Mailbag was dated four months before his friends were killed in a rocket attack.

"**Things here are relatively quiet, although the outskirts of the base get hit fairly often.** There's not too much to do besides write letters and drink beer. The base is really large and the facilities are really good. Of course the town is off-limits with the Laos thing and everything. What do you expect?"
Air Force Sgt. Daniel P. Stokes, April 12

SANDBAGS AND BARBED WIRE COULD BE A SOLDIER'S BEST FRIENDS. Readers of the June 9 Mailbag found out all the details about life on Firebase Katum, thanks to an article and photos prepared by the Information Office, Headquarters, U.S. Army Vietnam. The item featured Army 1st Lt. Robert A. Nowaczyk of Claymont, the executive officer of Battery C. We reprint the piece here.

This is home for the men of Battery C, 2nd Battalion, 12th Artillery. It is desolate country out here, just three and a half miles from the Cambodian border. It is dusty and hot during the dry season. It is muddy, wet and hot during the rainy season.

Battery C consists of 160,000 sandbags, scores of rolls of barbed wire to protect the perimeter and numerous 155-mm howitzer artillery pieces. Most important, there are about 100 men in the battery who call this firebase home for now. The battery moves at frequent intervals.

1st Lt. Nowaczyk's job is supervising the men of the battery in their operation of the guns. It is a job with a lot of responsibility. If a gun fires short or long, it could injure friendly troops so there is no room for mistakes. If a gun is slow in firing, it can cost men in the field their lives.

Battery C has been credited with saving the lives of many soldiers of the Army of the Republic of Vietnam stationed nearby whenever they have come under heavy enemy attack. The quick and accurate firepower of Battery C has been a major factor in repelling such attacks. The men are proud of this and they realize how valuable their support has been.

Hours are long and hard. Artillery is heavy work. Most of the battery's fire missions are at night, but there are always sandbags to fill, barbed wire to string, bunkers to build – with periodic moves, construction is never finished.

There are no post exchanges, clubs or snack bars out here. 1st Lt. Nowaczyk and the rest of the men of the battery improve their own environment as much as possible. They built a basketball court and strung a volleyball net. Many men in the battery keep pets, including numerous dogs, two monkeys, a python and a fawn.

Life is pretty much the same each day. During the day, the men work on fortifications and maintenance of the guns. Each man pulls guard duty at least every third night now, although this varies from one location to another.

The battery sometimes separates into two gun elements. One will go on what is called a "hip shoot." The purpose of the shoot is to increase the range of artillery. By moving the element to another forward operating area, the battery's field of fire is increased and they can fire on enemy locations which were out of range before.

Sometimes, a "hip shoot" lasts only a day with minor fortifications for the guns. At other times, it may last longer with more elaborate fortifications.

Occasionally a helicopter loaded with PX goods will land here and the men will mob around it, buying the things they have trouble getting, such as film for their cameras.

Life goes on for the men of Battery C, but for 1st Lt. Nowaczyk, his favorite topic of conversation starts out something like this: "When I get home…"

A Chinook helicopter from the 269th Aviation Battalion carries this 50-foot watch tower from the Ba Bep Bridge to Fire Support Base Crockett to support the 2nd Battalion, 34th Armor. Soldiers eagerly lined up to make purchases (opposite, top) when the PX chopper made its weekly landing in the field. In their moments of relaxation, soldiers took time to feed the native fauna. Army 1st Lt. Robert A. Nowaczyk surveys his surroundings.

FOR SERVICEMEN IN 1971, THE MOST COMPELLING
NATIONAL EVENT WAS THE 10-MONTH TRIAL OF ARMY LT.
WILLIAM L. CALLEY JR. Calley, charged with ordering the murders of scores of unarmed South Vietnamese civilians in the village
of My Lai, was convicted of premeditated murder on March 29 and
was sentenced two days later to life in prison. On April 1, President
Nixon ordered Calley released from jail pending his appeal. On
August 20, his sentence was reduced to 20 years. He eventually
served just months in a military prison at Fort Leavenworth, Kansas
before he was transferred to Fort Benning, Georgia, where he was
placed under house arrest. Through appeals and clemency petitions,
Calley's sentence was repeatedly reduced and he was eventually
released from custody in September 1974, five years after the original charges were filed, and went into the insurance business. Of 26
servicemen charged in the massacre, only Calley was convicted.

We first heard reaction about Calley from a Marine Corps military policeman who worked with sentry dogs.

"**When I first got to Vietnam I thought that we were trying to win
this war but with the restrictions that are put on the men over here,
it doesn't seem that way.** We have to get fired upon before we are
allowed to return fire and that is only on the command of an officer.
The only place where we are allowed to open fire is in the 'bush.'

Now since the conviction of Lt. Calley, it seems as though the U.S.
government and the 'high brass' are against the men over here. This
is my own opinion but I know quite a few men over here that share
this opinion with me."
Marine Cpl. Larry T. Larson, April 1

Others added their thoughts.

"**On the subject of Calley, I'm afraid you've hit a soft spot.** The
majority of the guys including myself disagree with the verdict
(STRONGLY). But then, what can we do? Here we've been sent to
Nam to protect our national resources and our buddies. But if it
takes killing someone, then it's a no-no?

If you knew the number of GIs killed by children and old men and
women, you'd probably go into a state of shock. Just the other day here
at Da Nang, 2 children were killed and another injured when the two
cluster bombs and B-40 [Chinese Communist] weapons they were
carrying blew up on them. They were 5 to 10 years old. I say better
them than us. What were they going to do with them? They were
about 1/4-mile from base and 200 yards from our off-base bomb
dump.

You don't know who your friends are. Therefore, in the best
interest of his troops, I think Calley was justified at My Lai. Granted,
morally it was wrong. What would you have done in his place?"
Air Force Sgt. Daniel P. Stokes at Da Nang Air Base, April 20

"I disagree with [the verdict] wholeheartedly. I can't see the Army
convicting a man for what they themselves have trained him to do.

At the time of their deaths, maybe they [civilians] were defenseless
but how about the night before when they were probably setting
booby traps? People say, how can you kill a little baby six or seven
months old? I'll tell you how I would do it. Just as I would kill the
20-year old Vietcong. I'd just consider myself doing a public service
to the GI who that baby might walk up to in 5 years and drop a
grenade at his feet."
Army Spc. George Wojciechowski, May 1

A lightning rod of controversy, Army Lt. William L. Calley Jr. was sentenced to life in prison on March 31, 1971, for the murders of unarmed men, women and children at My Lai three years earlier. In the combat zone, servicemen (opposite) overwhelmingly defended Calley, who was released in 1974.

"9 out of 10 guys that are over here feel that [Calley] is innocent of murder.

Some of us even wrote our Congressmen to see if anything was being done to get him set free. Of course, they told us they were watching what was going on, but they have been doing that since 1963 with the war.

Sometimes we think it is better to stay over here than come back to the states. Who wants to fight a war and come home and see riots and demonstrations? Tonight on the news we see there were 7,000 demonstrators in Washington. What happens to them? Nothing.

P.S. Here is our motto: The Only Thing I Feel When I Kill is The Recoil of My M-16."
Army Sgt. Ralph J. "Butch" Anderson, May 9

"I feel that Lt. Calley should be cleared of all charges brought against him or everyone above in his chain of command should be tried for the same charges.

While going through basic training every GI is taught exactly the same thing, to kill.

They are also taught to obey orders from their higher-ups. Lt. Calley was told to take no prisoners and he obeyed that order. He was also in a free-fire zone, where you shoot anything that moves in order to stay alive.

The people who were killed had no business in that area. The people in Vietnam all look the same so you really can't tell who the enemy is and who isn't. Lt. Calley was over here doing his job and trying to stay alive as thousands of other American soldiers are doing who have no right to be here in the first place.

I only wish I was home right now so I could be in Washington, D.C., with the rest of the Vietnam veterans trying to end this useless war."
Army Pfc. Kenneth P. Baker, May 28 Mailbag

"I have noticed that the majority of the individuals who have written to you have given their full support to 'Scape Goat Calley.' They have, as a majority, defended his actions and his motives as they believe them to exist.

To a certain extent there is validity to the concept of the Military Machine using this man to pay the brunt of a brutal mistake. However, the entire Vietnam War has turned into a brutal miscarriage of human justice.

In the beginning, the cause and meaning of Vietnam was good, but now, more than 10 years later, exaggeration and frustration have given this conflict a tinge of economics and politics. War, death, and destruction are wrong and they always will be wrong but then this is only my opinion and perhaps the politicians do not share my views.

My own personal opinion is that the mere presence of this country in Vietnam is wrong and if judgment must be made, it must come to the heart of the problem. If the United States government and military wishes to prosecute Lt. Calley on the charge of murder, then it also must prosecute itself for creating a monster that converts men into monstrous killers.

I would like to conclude only by saying that while sentiments are running high toward ending this fiasco; I do believe Mr. Nixon has put into effect the only feasible plan of withdrawal. I am, of course, referring to Vietnamization."
Air Force Sgt. Douglas B. Williams, June 16 Mailbag

And there was more on Calley and his superior, Capt. Ernest L. Medina, whom Calley said had ordered him to kill everyone in My Lai.

"Now, a little about Calley. After reading the 'Secrets' [Pentagon Papers] the *[New York] Times* printed, I'm really convinced that Lt. Calley was and is the scapegoat. I just hope they don't convict Capt. Medina too. After all, only one scapegoat is needed. Right?"
Air Force Tech. Sgt. Gerald W. "Jake" Jackson at Bien Hoa Air Base, June 27

"I have 37 days left in this country (Thank God).... You have been asking about the Capt. Medina court martial. Well, this is one guy who hopes to hell he gets off, because one scapegoat is enough and that one is Calley."
Army Spc. Scott D. Norris, July 30

Mellow Yellow, a helicopter ambulance from the Army's
571st Medical Detachment, ferries injured soldiers to the
95th Evacuation Hospital in Da Nang.

TWO WAR-RELATED TOPICS OF GREAT INTEREST ON THE HOME FRONT CAUSED LESS OF A STIR IN THE COMBAT ZONE. The Mailbag received only one letter on President Nixon's proposal for an all-volunteer military service and one about the publication of the leaked Pentagon Papers, the Department of Defense's classified study of the Vietnam War.

"**I would like to comment on Nixon's proposed volunteer army.** I intentionally do not include any discussions of Vietnam, for the ethics of our involvement is another subject.

There seems to be a new era of thought that is becoming dominant today. Whereas, it was once considered only reasonable to expect one to serve his country, the idea seems to have become repulsive, if not comical. It has certainly become the jest of many conversations.

Strong criticism is made of the military draft. Now the 'in idea' is to have a highly paid volunteer, professional army.

Also, many feel that an increase in taxes to cover the expenses would well be a substantial contribution on the citizens' part. Others believe that the military will ruin a young man's career plans and chances to obtain his goal. All of these statements sound appealing, but let's examine them further.

To accept the idea of a professional army is to almost equate it with accepting a mercenary army. However, many will claim that this is not so, but then what incentives for this army are being suggested; higher pay, benefits, etc. In other words, MONEY. Money seems to be the motivating factor. All sights seem to have been lost on some basic motives: service to country, freedom and to mankind.

Still supporting the volunteer army are those who feel the citizens should pay more taxes to cover the expenses. This seems to erase any further obligation on the citizens' part. However, it takes more than monthly payments to preserve our country. Even a car owner does more than just make payments. He washes and waxes it and services the engine to ensure continuous operation. Why shouldn't we take our turn to ensure continuous operation of our country?

Perhaps one of the biggest arguments against the draft is that it ruins the young man's career and chances for success. But then again, what made that education and success possible? It would be fair to say this country; after all it was America that made schools, scholarships and freedom of choice possible. Why then shouldn't we take our turn in preserving what so many before us have preserved so that others may also benefit.

What our country has gained has taken much time and effort, but to lose it would take but little. All of us who share the good of our country must share what we consider the bad, for those who take all without giving, are probably the most unfortunate of all."
Army Staff Sgt. Roy C. Thornton, Jan. 4

"I was glad to see the Pentagon Papers printed. [Daniel] Ellsberg has done this country a great service. Now the American public can judge for themselves whether this war is worth it. I got so tired of hearing people say 'Well, the government must be doing the right thing!' or 'There must be a good reason for the war that we don't know about!' Now, there are no reasons we don't know about; people can't escape a decision now.

The public holds the government up on a pedestal; it considers the government invincible. Remember the government is made up of people, and people make mistakes, no matter what their occupations.

Now the thing to do is admit to our mistakes. As far as I'm concerned, the U.S. is the greatest place in the world to live, work and play, but it is not perfect. The world doesn't expect perfection, why should we try to fool ourselves?

Why try to hide errors? Let's show the world we're great enough to learn from our mistakes. Admit we were wrong and get out of Vietnam."
Army Spc. John W. Hopper, July 17

Nancy Sobolewski, one of our few female correspondents, sent an update in May. "Here I am in a new post. I am now club director at the 90th Replacement Battalion in Long Binh. The job is challenging and the move sudden. Will fill you in on news and views and travel adventures." Army Spc. William W. Hutchison Jr. (opposite, far right) and members of the 23rd Infantry Division's Information Office receive plaques in Chu Lai for winning the Americal Division's volleyball championship.

SOME SERVICEMEN, WHILE UNDERSTANDING THE MILITARY'S MISSION, HAD TROUBLE FIGURING OUT WHAT U.S. TROOPS WERE SUPPOSED TO BE DOING IN VIETNAM. This officer sounded bored when he wrote.

"**I am being transferred in country again.** This will be my third unit since my arrival in February. I have been in an 'EXCESS' slot during 5 of my 9 months in country and the Army complains about too many personnel here. I am not griping to you, just telling it as it is. There are so many personnel sitting around just waiting to go home."
Army Chief Warrant Officer Herbert V. Melson, Nov. 25

"**I've changed jobs since my previous unit stood down (212th Combat Aviation Battalion).** I'm now Special Services Officer for the 11th Combat Aviation Group. This place, as is most of Vietnam, is terribly over-strengthened. There are assistants to assistants to assistants here. Many just don't have a job at all. This is especially true for officers.

Since 'my thing' is theatre, I'm going to try and do some here – maybe 'Zoo Story' or something….

P.S. Saw Bob Hope yesterday. A tremendous American and a great show as usual. Will be on TV Jan. 17. Planning on catching it?"
Army 1st Lt. Steven S. Neilson at Marble Mountain Army Airfield near Da Nang, Dec. 22

Many servicemen took the time to write about their jobs. Some letters were quick and to the point; others offered plenty of detail.

"**I have been in Vietnam five months now and I DEROS June 1971.…** I work in a motor pool as a clerk and mechanic…. I am not much of a letter writer but I hope you understand. There isn't much call for writing over here."
Army Pfc. Charles A. Sparpaglione in Qui Nhon, Jan. 8 Mailbag

"**I work at a direct support base at Phu Loi.** I work very hard and I'm always busy. I really don't mind because it makes time pass quickly. My main job is armament but I also work in hydraulics and the machine shop. These people [the South Vietnamese] are very nice and great to talk to, although they are sometimes hard to understand. They call me 'Woolie.'"
Army Spc. William D. Taylor in Phu Loi, Jan. 16

"**After receiving my orders, I was sent to Force Logistics Command where I am currently serving my last five months as an administrative clerk for FLC's Truck Company.** I am also a shotgun for convoys and single runs going to Hill 37, Fire Base Ross, Hill 55, LZ Baldy, Phu Bai and a few other places. As you can see, I really get to see a lot of the country.
Marine Lance Cpl. Kenneth H. Moye in Da Nang, Feb. 6

"**I am an aircraft mechanic and work on 0-2A type airplanes.** It is a two-engine Cessna used to carry smoke rockets and flares. The 0-2 flies FAC (Forward Air Controller) missions which consist of spotting the target, marking it with smoke rockets and giving the fighters the exact position so they can play wipeout. At night, the flares are used to illuminate the area so as to keep 'Charlie' (Vietcong) from mounting massive attacks by being able to spot him beforehand in most cases.

When they come back from a mission, that's when my work begins. Getting them ready for their next flight. They are used in the air over Vietnam 24 hours a day performing the important tasks of 'watchdog.'

It is an interesting job and I am proud to know I am helping my country in this war. I have five more months to serve here. I hope all GIs are out of Vietnam soon! I sure miss home, good ole Delaware."
Air Force Airman 1st Class Jehu J. Justice at Bien Hoa Air Base, March 5

"**Presently, I'm stationed in the 1st MAW (Marine Aircraft Wing) at Marble Mountain Air Facility which is located just north of Da Nang.** I am a squad leader in Zulu Company which is in charge of security. We have to push back attacks on our lines and area surrounding our base.

I have just finished flying with the air wing and occasionally fly medevac missions. Recently, I've been flying medevac missions in Laos and things get pretty sticky there at times."
Marine Lance Cpl. J.H. "Josh" Marvil, March 8

"**Well, our home base is Port Hueneme, Calif., and now the main camp here in Vietnam is South Camp Hoskins in Da Nang.** MCB [Mobile Construction Battalion] has been here since November 1970 and we are leaving the end of April. I'm the only Seabee in MCB3 that is from Delaware that I know of. I'm on a well-drilling detachment over here – Det. Hydra – we drill water wells for different camps all over Vietnam. Our team just got back from down south. We drilled six wells down there."
Navy Petty Officer 3rd Class Richard A. Mazol, March 17

"**Sorry this will be so short but I'm on my dinner break now.** We've really been working – now 12 hours a day and no days off. A lot of ARVNs left here this month so we're training six new crews now. The major wants me to have them all certified before the end of the month so we don't have any free time."
Sgt. Robert V. "Vance" Wilson in Phu Cat, April 7 Mailbag

"**As for my work here in Vietnam, I'm in a small engineers' detachment which is located at Lifer Gulch (Long Binh).** We don't spend very much time at the Gulch though. We're usually off working in other places such as the 90th Replacement Battalion, Song Be, Bien Hoa, Tan Son Nhut, Saigon, Vung Tau, etc., etc…. All I can say is that I sure am thankful that I'm lucky enough to live in the United States and will be real happy to get back."
Army Spc. John W. Huston, April 19

"**I am assigned to the Postal Squadron here in Saigon.** I work with the mail going back to the states and I go along as an armed guard on mail runs going to different parts of Nam. My return to the states is in December, so I am hoping to be home for Christmas."
Sgt. Glenn Barrentine Jr., May 15

"**I am Senior Chaplain's assistant with the 2nd Brigade.** Basically, I am an administrator. We coordinate the chapel activities for the men of the 2nd Brigade as well as the local support units.

Our four chaplains are constantly on the move, often in the 'bush.' Services are held whenever we have men, whether in the rear, on firebases, on landing zones or in the middle of nowhere.

As senior man of 5 assistants, I am responsible for transportation for the chaplains, for maintenance of our 3 chapels in the rear and for the rear administrative duties. I also play organ for 4 services each Sunday plus memorial services. I am very happy to report that we have fewer and fewer of the latter each month."
Army Spc. Carlton W. "Buddy" King III, July 12

"**I am with HHC, 52nd Aviation Battalion, working in the signal office.** We're stationed at Camp Holloway, Pleiku. My main job is pushing a pen and a lot of paperwork. It's an interesting job, though, which helps."
Army Spc. Jeff Miller, Aug. 9 Mailbag

"**Since coming to Vietnam in November 1970, I have been assigned to the 169th Engineer Battalion (construction).** The mission of the battalion is to reconstruct 8.7 kilometers of QL-20.

For the last six months I have been the equipment platoon leader in a construction support company, the 544th Engineer Company. Our mission is to produce crushed rock and asphalt for the 169th."
Army Lt. Joseph L. Ignatowski, Aug. 30

10 Nov

Dear Nancy,

As a recipient of The
Taiwan with frequent TDY's
your column and the news fr
Tactical Airlift Wing which
and Cam Ranh Bay for 16 day
one not familiar with 13th
country the 374th falls un
Air Division which schedul
most versatile aircraft fl
and passenger flights. It
makes it possible to servi
South Vietnam. Places suc
Tay Ninh are flown into on
fields of Danang, Chu Lai
always preface their landi
U.S. mail. Its a case of
when there is some aboard.
a different impression of
tedious life of the troops
and news from other friend
welcome.

The fact that I only spent 16 days a month in
allows me to fully appreciate the hospitality and
Taiwan. Taiwan serves as an excellent home away
The chinese and taiwanese cultures offer the sig
and bargain   er an endless source of adventur
a mo   to fly back to CCK (Ching Chu
               try. The USAF is a guest of
             re the base the Nationalist
             a combined effort by both A
             ce since January 1966.

           nk you and the people at
           and possibly see if a
           uld sure look good poste
           ly in country. Someone from hom

Thanks again,

1/LT Charlie Sparkman

MR 1144   CCK TAIWAN
50 TAS
APO San Francisco 96319

"I work for the 374th Tactical Airlift wing which flies the C-130 out of Tan Son Nhut and Cam Ranh Bay for 16-day shuttles…. The C-130, being a most versatile aircraft, flies combat support, air rescue, cargo and passenger flights. Its capability to land on short fields makes it possible to service the remote bases and outposts in South Vietnam.

Places such as Loc Ninh, Firebase Pace and Tay Ninh are flown into on a daily basis along with the larger fields of Da Nang, Chu Lai and Phu Cat. The American controllers always preface their landing instructions with a query about U.S. mail. It's a case of preferential treatment on the days when there is some aboard.

South Vietnam from the air gives one a different impression of the war as well as an escape from the tedious life of the troops on the ground. The mail, packages and news from other friends stationed in South Vietnam are always welcome.

The fact that I only spend 16 days a month in Vietnam allows me to fully appreciate the hospitality and beauty of Taiwan.
Air Force 1st Lt. Charlie Sparkman, Nov. 10

"Just a few lines to let you all know I'm fine and so are all the other First Staters I've met which have been very few and I hope will soon be a lot less…. I'm stationed at Long Binh, the largest enclosed Army base in the world. I'm part of the great 1st Signal Team…. I'm one of the luckier guys over here. I have an air-conditioned office, like my job and work with some of the greatest guys."
Army Spc. Lawrence B. Buchert, Dec. 6 Mailbag

Army Spc. Thomas A. Ashley gave us a ghost story for the June 7 Mailbag.

Tom was a "Blue Ghost," a member of Troop F, 8th Cavalry, 23rd Infantry Division, based near Quang Tri. The troop provided vital support for Vietnam's spring incursion into Laos to cut enemy supply lines.

Tom's job as a helicopter mechanic in the troop was an interesting one. Operating out of I Corps in the northernmost part of Vietnam, Blue Ghost helicopter teams of Cobra gunships, light observation copters and troop-carrying helicopters provided convoy escort and armed aerial reconnaissance for the Vietnamese ground troops.

Much of Troop F's mission was to screen areas not covered by infantry units and to survey landing zones. As in all aviation units, keeping the aircraft ready to fly 24 hours a day hinged on critical maintenance.

For his work, Tom, a 1969 graduate of Rising Sun (Md.) High School, was awarded the Air Medal for valor as well as the Army Commendation medal.

The C-130, which was a versatile aircraft, capable of takeoffs and landings from unprepared runways. It was also used for combat support, air rescue, cargo and passenger flights, Air Force 1st Lt. Charlie Sparkman wrote. Military payment certificates were the only legal tender for American servicemen stationed in Vietnam. U.S. dollars, also called "greenbacks," were not accepted. As a cashier, Army Spc. Douglas C. Vas Dias handled payment certificates worth millions each month. We also heard from helicpter mechanic, Army Spc. Thomas A. Ashley.

While others were making their move homeward, Army Spc. Douglas C. Vas Dias of Cinnaminson, New Jersey, was hard at work counting money in Vietnam. We explained his job in the June 21 Mailbag.

Those soldiers in Vietnam, like Doug, who fight with typewriters and adding machines against insurmountable paperwork, see to it that the troops get their paychecks, in spite of deadlines and confusion in the disbursing office.

Doug is a cashier with the disbursing division of the Army Finance Center and Accounting Office near Long Binh. Working in the third-largest Army finance center in the world, Doug sees approximately $115 million sorted and distributed throughout the Republic of Vietnam each month. Most of it is pure paperwork, but more than $9 million in cash goes through his hands every payday.

An important function of the disbursing division is converting U.S. dollars into piasters, Vietnam's unit of currency. About $160,000 is converted each week at the exchange rate of 276 piasters to the dollar.

Doug, whose wife lives in Salem, N.J., is a 1968 grad of Holy Cross High School in Delran and attended Santa Fe (N.M.) College before joining the Army.

Army Spc. William W. "Hutch" Hutchison Jr. had a job that kept us informed on what others were up to. "Being in the [23rd Infantry] Division Information Office has its advantages and one of these is seeing what is going on throughout the division," he wrote. For the August 6 Mailbag, he supplied us with news of another Delawarean, Army Capt. Blaine P. Turner of Wilmington of the 196th Infantry Brigade. Hutch sent us a story from *The Southern Cross*, his division's newspaper, on Blaine, a monk and a mountain.

DA NANG (196th Inf. Bde. IO) – They're not "pills," but they do give them out; they're not avid climbers, yet they will walk to the top of a mountain to insure a person's health. They could be called "Mountain Healers."

In a recent exhausting expedition a psychological operations (S-5) team from the 196th Infantry Brigade scaled Marble Mountain just outside Da Nang to deliver aid to a monk and his 15 neophytes.

"We got a lot of satisfaction out of it," commented Captain Blaine P. Turner, Wilmington, Del., S-5 for 1st Squadron, 1st Calvary, and leader of the excursion. "It's the other side of the war, the good side, as opposed to the killing."…

The delight on the monk's face turned out to be only part of the reward the men received for their arduous climb. They were escorted by a young amputee, a ward of the religious order, into caves to view massive Buddhas carved into the side of the mountain.

All too soon it was time to go. Ceremoniously, the monk bowed to them showing profuse thanks on his face. Any occidental-oriental gap that existed before had now been bridged.

The journey downward proved to be quite a bit easier than the one up. In a final backward look, the men knew that they would return, drawn by a need to aid the mountain dwellers and the mysticism of Marble Mountain.

"AFTER A DOG HAS SAVED YOUR LIFE, YOU CAN'T HELP BUT BECOME ATTACHED TO HIM," MARINE CPL. LARRY T. LARSON WROTE IN THE APRIL 23 MAILBAG. During the war, lives of countless other American troops were spared by dogs trained to range off-leash ahead of patrols to detect enemy ambushes or concealed land mines.

The role of war dogs in Vietnam was not a new topic for the column. In 1968 and 1969, Army Pfc. Robert S. Biss wrote frequently about his favorite subject and always signed his letters, "Bob and King," to include his special canine pal.

A marine, unaware of our previous coverage, wrote that he felt the dogs and their significance in the conflict had been slighted.

"**You read about the fabulous jobs the men in Vietnam are doing, but you only read about selected groups such as MACV, Infantry, Flight, Advisors and Special Forces but you never, I haven't anyway, heard of the great job the Sentry Dog section of the Military Police is doing.**

Your military police are here for security but the Sentry Dog team is your backbone for security at night while everyone is asleep. Between the hours of 6 p.m. and 6 a.m. if you look very close just inside the perimeter fence of some ammo dumps, POL [petroleum, oil and lubricant] yards, heliports, and food and part storage areas, you just might catch a glimpse of an M.P. handler and his dog walking, watching and waiting for any signs of VC or NVA 'sappers' trying to invade your post. If they do get in it is your job, and your dog's, to see that they don't do the job they were sent to do. If it wasn't for these men and their dogs, a lot more damage to these areas mentioned above and the deaths of many people might very well take place."
Marine Pfc. Fred W. Gibson, April 16

Sentry dogs had served effectively in Southeast Asia since 1965, but as the withdrawal of servicemen from Vietnam accelerated in 1971, the dogs began coming home too. In August, there were about 5,500 working dogs worldwide and about 1,400 in Vietnam.

By the end of the summer, the first group of about 50 Army scout and tracker dogs had returned stateside for cross-training or retraining and redistribution. Other military working dogs no longer needed in Vietnam were reassigned to fill requirements elsewhere in the Pacific theater.

Marine Cpl. Larry T. Larson relaxes with his best four-footed friend, Shep. "I've grown quite close to him for I've been with him since I got in Vietnam," he wrote. Not all canine warriors made it home. Their remains were buried at the War Dog Cemetery on a hill outside Da Nang. Sentry dogs and their handlers (opposite) train in Vinh Long. On alert, Army Pfc. Don Kunstrom and his dog walk his post on the perimeter of a helicopter support base in the Mekong Delta.

"Your military police are here for security but the Sentry Dog team is your backbone for security at night while everyone is asleep."

Marine Pfc. Fred W. Gibson

viewing vietnam

The ferocious guardian Of men's lives

TAN SON NHUT AB (7AF) – In an age when "man's best friend" maintains his status primarily as a pet, the U.S. Air Force dog in the Republic of Vietnam earns his praise as a worker, guarding men's lives and multi-million dollar aircraft and equipment during the blackness of night.

While man negotiates salary increases, shorter working hours, greater promotion opportunities and additional benefits, the Air Force military working dog walks a lonely damp, dark post on an air base perimeter for the price of his handler's praise, a daily ration and a clean kennel.

With his acute senses reaching into the darkness beyond his handler's perception, the dog must warn of any intrusion on their post. If the trespasser proves difficult to apprehend or attempts to harm the security policeman, the dog must respond with a ferocious attack.

Such has been the life of the U.S. Air Force sentry dog here since July 1965, when 40 canine teams were sent to the Republic of Vietnam from the United States to prove their ability in the Southeast Asia climate.

But the Air Force Military Working Dog Program in Vietnam encompasses more than just sentry dogs.

In 1966, four Air Force sentry teams received patrol dog training in We[...] 1968, 30 Strategic Air Command dog teams received advanced tr[...] The patrol dogs are now well-represented among the 275 [...]

A graduate of advanced obedience and detect[...] enforcement as well as for perimeter defe[...] patrol, building search, and tracki[...] worked off-leash and amo[...] attack and any pers[...]

Additional[...] canine[...]

...EETING -- A1C Robert Poe and Ralph greet [...]der to their post on the perimeter of Bien [...] with anything but open arms. While on [...]e sentry and patrol dogs not only increase [...]rity policeman's ability to detect and [...] intruders, but because of their known [...]d speed, act as a deterrent to potential [...] USAF Photo By MSgt. Sam Sears)

NOSING AROUND -- Cinder, a marijuana-sniffing German Shepherd, and A1C Elbert L. Woods, her handler, walk their "beat" through the military passenger terminal at Da Nang Airfield. In addition to being able to detect the drug in any hiding spot, a dog acts as a deterrent to people attempting to smuggle. (USAF Photo By TSgt. Carl D. Tomlin Jr.)

UP AND OVER -- Prin[...] the training course at Phan Rang A[...] ...dler, A1C Stephen W. Pelsor. The dog[...] ...ly to reinforce their confidence in themselve[...] (USAF Photo By Sgt. Rodney Eagan)

ONE VERY SERIOUS MATTER WE ASKED SERICEMEN TO COMMENT ON WAS THE USE OF DRUGS IN THE COMBAT ZONE. Letters arrived from all over Vietnam. Army Capt. Paul D. Lovett III of Centreville, a 1968 graduate of the U.S. Military Academy at West Point who was awarded two Bronze Stars and two battle medals for his command of A Battery, 5th Battalion, 42nd Artillery during his tour, had much to say from Firebase Nancy in the September 3 Mailbag.

Capt. Paul D. Lovett

Army Capt. Paul D. Lovett III considered drugs a bigger problem than the enemy for his unit.

"I've commanded A Battery for nearly eleven months so I've become very well acquainted with the drug problem. Although I've spent all of my tour in the field, my biggest problem has not been the enemy, it has been drugs. I know many estimates have been made about the number of users in Vietnam. I can say that on average, 14% of my unit (approximately 130 people, average unit strength) used heroin.

It is very easy to identify a 'freak.' He is generally inefficient, he eats very little, drinks much liquid but never alcohol, usually appears tired and associates only with other 'freaks.' They seldom participate in unit activities.

Heroin is as easy to buy as a straw hat from the Vietnamese. It's called 'coke' and is 96% pure. The pushers range from ARVN soldiers to 10-year-old kids. It is a white powdery substance usually sold in a cylindrical plastic vial in .1 gram portions.

Users smoke it and snort it in A Battery, but no one shoots it up (injects it by syringe). Once a person is stringing heroin, he will take every chance necessary to obtain the substance. His need for it overpowers his sense of reason. Although six persons have been successfully convicted of possession of drugs in A Battery, four more have been 'busted' and are awaiting trial.

The amnesty program is totally ineffective. Of approximately seventeen individuals who have gone on the program from A Battery, no one has 'come down.' The recent tests for personnel returning to the states are good for temporarily eliminating the user from his heroin, but I am not convinced that these people will never have the problem again.

To solve the problem, heroin must be eliminated at its source. Otherwise, the enemy will promote it and the Vietnamese will make money from it. This will have to be left to the higher authorities.

In my own unit, I feel I have done best by taking a hard line on the users. The straight people realize that their privileges are limited by the 'freak' because he abuses them. They also realize they are doing the work he will not do.

So often, the officers and senior NCOs of A Battery are tipped off and given probable cause for search. This usually leads to a court martial if it is properly carried out. I only wish that I had learned these procedures earlier and I hope others will take the time to figure them out.

The drug situation in A Battery has been reduced greatly since three members have been out in the stockade.

This has been a long dissertation but I think it covers the situation pretty well. Print what you would like. I'll sure be glad to get home on the 10th of September."

In short order, Army Spc. Carlton W. "Buddy" King III of Seaford, who worked in the HHC, 2nd Brigade Chapel of the 101st Airborne Division, shared his unique experience on drugs from Phu Bai when he wrote to the Mailbag on September 17.

"I'd like to add a few comments on the drug situation. Capt. Lovett had some very good comments in the Sept. 3 paper.

Unfortunately, the court martial route has proven to be the only effective method to control drug abuse. We in the chapel program work closely with the drug amnesty program.

An addict is able to turn himself in with no fear of punishment in order to get medical help during withdrawal. The addict is given every break in order to make his rehabilitation as easy as possible.

Despite all this, the program has proven largely ineffective. The number one reason is that the men don't turn themselves in until it's too late. If his mind has been away from reality for long enough, he'll have trouble recognizing reality when he comes down.

Once in the program, the addict must sincerely want to get off drugs. If he doesn't, then all the medical help and counseling we can give will mean nothing. This is even more important after the man has been declared 'clean' as a shockingly large percentage go right back on the stuff.

When a man comes to us to request amnesty, our first objective is to establish a mutual confidence. He's generally not sure whether he's doing the right thing, fearing pressures from this chain of command.

Some are afraid of talking with an officer (our head chaplain is a major) so we encourage him to rap with us on a first-name basis. We play games with him in order to help him relax. We've had a couple of Frisbees and even a pinball machine donated by a toy store in Seaford.

Once this rapport has been established, we do our darndest to keep his mind occupied while he's experiencing withdrawal. He is kept in a medical facility with 24-hour-a-day care. We visit him regularly there, offering whatever help we can.

Then the hard part begins. It's only natural that he'll get the urge to go back on drugs since that has been his way of life. We encourage him to call us, to come over and rap at any time. I sleep in the chapel next to two emergency phones and the chaplain is readily available as well.

We're happy to rap with the man if it'll help convince him that dope is a 'bummer.' We all know we're playing for fairly small percentages but even one successful case is better than none.

Amnesty is a good program on paper. For those who genuinely take advantage of it, it works beautifully. However, the majority seems not to have the willpower to make it stick; the court martial is about the only method for such guys.

Drugs are still very easy to get. The Vietnamese will find a way to make money from [them] as long as we're here. There's a simple and obvious way to solve that problem. The only people who really want GIs here are those with economic interests in drugs and the black market. The majority of Vietnamese resent America's presence and would like us all to leave. I'm perfectly willing to oblige, but the politicians have different opinions."

Despite an anti-drug crackdown, drug use continued among American soldiers. During his tour, Staff Sgt. Albert T. "Chris" Lewis saw both sides of the drug problem as he worked with abusers and addicts at Pioneer House. This picture of Chris receiving a medal appeared in the Sept. 13 Mailbag.

Drugs were such a serious problem in the combat zone, the U.S. Command took action in September, ending all rest and recuperation (R&R) flights for American servicemen from South Vietnam to Hong Kong. Any GI booked for a Hong Kong R&R after September 30 instead went to Taipei. Halting the Hong Kong circuit came as a result of five fatal drug overdoses of American servicemen in Hong Kong that year. Others wrote on the hot topic throughout the year:

"**Our squadron doesn't have much of a problem.** I think we've had two cases since I've been here but there are other squadrons on base that get two or three cases a month. Overall, here at Phu Cat, the percentage is relatively low."
Army Sgt. Robert V. "Vance" Wilson, June 30

"**I also believe the Army is being blamed for an awful lot of drug usage that is not necessarily its fault.** Drug usage is entirely the fault of the individual. The younger generation should find something worthwhile and accomplishing to occupy their minds and not be so free to blame emptiness on the Army. What happened to INITIATIVE?? Sorry I got carried away, Nancy, but it really hurts to see so many young people throw away their lives aimlessly."
Army Chief Warrant Officer Herbert V. Melson at Da Nang Relay Station, July 1

"**All services have got something going over here now.** To get out of country you have to submit to a urinalysis test that can tell if you have any narcotics in your system. If you do, they hold you here and get you off the habit and then send you home. If you don't have any in your system, to the Freedom Bird you go."
Army Spc. Scott D. Norris, July 30

"**I am in a section of eleven men.** There's one big problem over here. That is dope. I know of some guys on dope for the simple reason that it is so easy to get. But dope isn't my bag."
Army Spc. William E. Justice, Sept. 19

"**As far as I know, it isn't too bad.** We only have about seven guys [in my company] that are hooked on heroin but some of the newbies coming in are starting to use it. They just don't listen to someone that has seen what it can do to a person. All they ever say is it can't happen to me. But it does.

Some think it's a big thing. One guy came up to me and said that I have moved up the drug ladder to smack. They just don't know what it does to you. I have seen guys go home hooked and say I can't quit 'cause I'm hooked. But now that they have the drug test they are starting to get help. This is the best thing these guys that get hooked have going for them at the moment."
Army Spc. Joseph L. Conway, Sept. 21

Drug abuse was rampant in the combat zone and received lots of media attention. Marijuana and heroin were readily available and inexpensive.

"**We have a problem but since all the officers here fly, and about half the EM [enlisted men], as crew chief or medic, our problem is cut down right there.** Everyone is smart enough to realize that drugs and flying is like playing Russian roulette. Two of our drug users just kicked the habit themselves by having buddies watch them and keep them away from the drug. They went cold turkey right here in our company area and deserve a lot of credit. I hope they can stay off it, the temptation is always there and close by. This just points out, though, that if the individual finally wakes up and decides to quit, he can do it. The centers the Army runs are great helps, but the willpower has to be there first."
Army 1st Lt. Kenneth D. Warner in Da Nang, Oct. 11

One helicopter pilot provided insight on the issue when comparing his exposure to drug use in his two tours in Vietnam.

"**As an E.M. with the 1st Cavalry in I Corps, we didn't come in contact with the civilian population for months at a time.** I only saw two villages the whole year I was with the Cavalry. Therefore, drugs were scarce.

Maybe one or two guys smoke marijuana but no one was on drugs. Time also passed more quickly so we didn't need anything to make it go any faster,

Here with the 162nd Assault Helicopter Company at Can Tho in IV Corps we have an entirely different situation. I am probably closer to the enlisted men, having been one myself for 2 1/2 years, than any of the other officers and many of the NCOs.

Here we have a large drug problem. Recently two men from my platoon took overdoses of heroin. There are ten EMs right now taking the amnesty program at the base dispensary from this company.

We are located near one of the largest populated cities south of Saigon. Skag, heroin and marijuana are easily accessible to the men on this base. Also, the men get free time to do little or nothing. So to 'escape' or speed up idle moments, they go to town or just to their rooms and 'shoot up' and get 'strung out.'

I hope that gives you an idea as to the types of units that have bigger drug problems than others."
Army Lt. Barry G. Pollock in Can Tho, Oct. 23

"In this company, I think it's no problem. We have only a few smackers but no [opium] as long as I've been here. I really hate to see a guy hooked on smack 'cause that can really rip a body apart and also make that GI broke most of the time.

The biggest problem I think here in Nam is drinking.

A person gets drunk and can't control himself [and] goes walking down the company area saying, 'Hey, I'm going to kick everybody's ass.' I hope he feels big when we end up cleaning up after him when he falls and makes a mess. A guy who smokes goes somewhere and listens to music and doesn't bother anybody.
Army Spc. Ray Huffman near Da Nang, Nov. 26 Mailbag

MP's helping

drug battle

DA NANG (XXIV CORPS)--In an effort to curb the ever-increasing use of drugs, the MPs of Camp Horn, assigned to the 504th Military Police Battalion, Company B, 2nd Platoon are using an experimental program of assistance to unit commanders.

An incident file is kept showing the location of drug offenses and bits of evidence such as empty vials. When a buildup of evidence is noted in one particular unit, the company commander is notified.

"We explain that there is reason to suspect drug abuse in his unit. We also tell him the proper legal method to conduct a search or shakedown," says

First Lieutenant Frank Travis, the founder of the three-month-old program.

When the company commander decides to conduct a shakedown, the MPs are also there to assist. If something is found, they know what action to take.

"Statistics on this kind of thing are hard to find, but we have noted a marked decline in the number of incidents after the commander has been notified and action taken. The users are becoming smarter, however, and know the limits of the law, what we can and cannot do. This, of course, makes our job harder." Travis added.

FIRST IN VIETNAM

the OBSERVER

Vol. 10, No. 26   Saigon, Vietnam   October 29, 1971

Moving from Quang Tri to Mai Loc, a convoy of tank trucks from the 528th Quartermaster Company hauls high octane JP 4 to the ever thirsty gun ships operating out of the bag farm at Mai Loc during Operation Lam Son 810. Line at the left of the photo is the whip antenna on the convoy's lead jeep. (USA Photo)

Move is

Team effort

CAMP EAGLE (101ST ABN DIV) – As the Vietnamization program progresses and the Vietnamese Army takes over more and more of the combat duties here, the role of the American Army turns toward support of the Vietnamese Forces.

A recent operation near Khe Sanh during Operation Lam Son 810, clearly demonstrated the efficiency and team work of the two nation's armies.

The 159th Aviation Battalion, used 14 of its CH-47 Chinooks, to extract three 105mm howitzer batteries, the 258th Vietnamese Marine Battalion, the 54th Regiment, Army of the Republic of Vietnam and the 1st ARVN Ranger Group. The extraction by the 159th, which is the only Chinook Battalion in the world, was being made from firebases Hope, Gate, and Sarge, and took only five hours to remove more than 3,200 personnel, their equipment, as well as 18 105mm howitzers and their ammunition.

The 159th's Major Earl H. Webb, the S-3 officer, explained that the huge success of the mission was due to the extensive planning of the Vietnamese and U.S. forces.

"Planning for the actual extraction of all these troops took seven days, and we had a direct liaison with each ground unit before the operation. A great deal of timing and well performed air control was needed to keep the operation on schedule and to prevent any mid-air crashes," Webb noted. "At times there were more than 100 helicopters flying in that area. Besides our Chinooks, there were 'Slicks', Cobras, and command and control birds supervising from the air".

"With that many birds in the air simultaneously it was quite a job keeping everything scheduled properly. It went like clock work though, and a large part of the credit for handling all the aircraft belongs to the tower operators at Mai Loc, and the Pathfinders, who directed the birds at the pick-up points and landing zones. Everyone did their jobs superbly."

Webb concluded, "This is one of those few missions that just goes so perfectly. We relocated approximately 284 tons of equipment and personnel in 184 sorties. It's one of the largest operations of its type this division has undertaken."

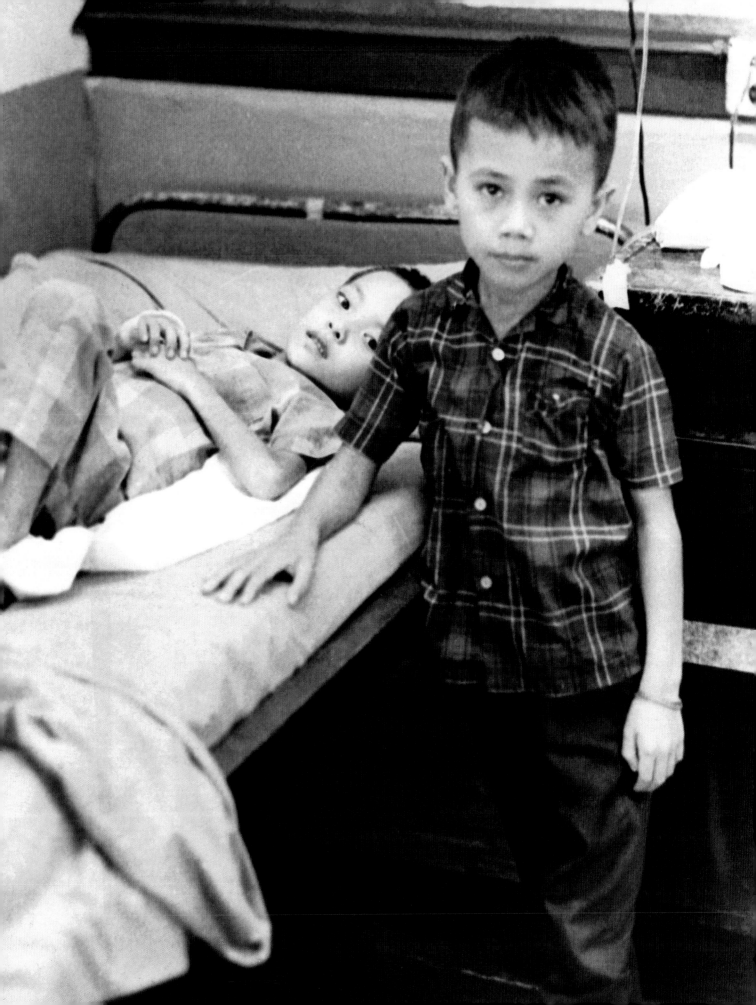

PERHAPS THE ONLY THING TOUGHER THAN SERVING AS A SOLDIER IN THE COMBAT ZONE WAS GROWING UP SURROUNDED BY WAR. Servicemen were especially sensitive to the plight of Vietnamese children, particularly those orphaned by the war. One soldier, an information specialist based in Chu Lai, sent Mailbag readers his treatise on "the tragedies and atrocities experienced in the Vietnam War." He called it "Our Enemies?"

"**Could you point your rifle at these two boys and pull the trigger?** Could you wantonly murder their mothers and sisters? I hope not. I certainly couldn't.

Yet it has happened. Every soldier who has fought, especially those who have had friends blown away by booby-traps, never to see the actual enemy, know the frustration involved – the need to retaliate. Fortunately, most have held back. But one man did not!

To the pictured small eleven-year old boys, the Vietnam war is already enough of a nightmare of screaming bombs, hidden booby-traps and shadowy figures in the night.

Never knowing when another loved one will be gone. Finally to become victims themselves. So young to have spent long, painful months in a hospital, never sure if they will ever get a chance to run and play again as every young child should.

They do not need to have the added fear of being massacred in open ditches by GIs who need revenge for fallen comrades. To condone such actions, whether a soldier is ordered or not, is a crime almost as appalling as the one committed by the man who pulled the trigger. Taking a life would never have helped any of my dead buddies.

Unfortunately, the other side commits enough atrocities without American soldiers blowing their cool and adding to the horror of an already unbelievably horrible war."
Army Spc. William W. "Hutch" Hutchison Jr., June 1

At Henry C. Conrad High School near Wilmington, fellow members of the Class of 1968 knew Navy Seaman Harry G. Porter as "Spider." In Vietnam, the sailor was a storekeeper who got very involved with an orphanage.

"**I visited the orphanage today for the first time.** I was really, really impressed at the job that the Catholic sisters are attempting to do here. At the present time, there are a total of 182 children ranging anywhere in age from 2 days to 15 years. The only problem is that it exists on contributions from people but no support from the government. If anyone would like to contribute to the orphanage, anything would be appreciated. Things like clothing, toys and canned goods are needed. Just about anything would be of use to them. If anyone would like to contribute, the contributions can be sent in care of me."
Navy Seaman Harry G. Porter near Can Tho, Feb. 7

Nguyen Van Hong, wounded in a movie theater after the Vietcong detonated a bomb, was successfully treated for a leg injury by American doctors at the 91st Evacuation Hospital in Chu Lai. Army Spc. William W. Hutchison Jr. described Nguyen and his friend as two of the "many innocent victims of this savage war."

"**There is one favor I would like to ask of the people of Wilmington.** A friend of mine and myself are starting a course in art at a local orphanage. But we are in dire need of art supplies such as brushes, crayons, paper, rulers and watercolor paints. If any organization or any function or any people would like to contribute, it would be deeply appreciated."
Navy Seaman Harry G. Porter near Can Tho, Feb. 11

After reading those letters, Wilmington-area Girl Scout troops rallied support. Harry responded with specific requests in his next letter to the column.

"**I am glad to hear that there are some people interested in the idea of providing items for the orphanage.**

The item most badly needed is clothing for newborns to about 6 or 7 years old. The reason for this being is that most of the older children have a regular uniform that they wear for classes. In the way of toys, probably the simple toys would be the best. There is also a lack of personal items such as toothbrushes, hairbrushes, combs, soap, etc.

Also, a friend of mine, YNSN Jim Sorensen, and I are going to start an art class at the orphanage but as of this time, we are without supplies to do so. So supplies such as crayons, tempera paints, brushes, clay and paper would be greatly appreciated.
Navy Seaman Harry G. Porter near Can Tho, April 14 Mailbag

In the June 11 Mailbag, Girl Scout Troop 478, which met at Alfred I. du Pont Elementary School, let readers know they had shipped Harry a box full of baby shoes, diapers, coverlets, soap, shampoo and hand towels, and planned to do more when they reconvened in the fall.

U.S. troops continued to show empathy for the young victims of the war and helped the children when they could. In the January 20 column, Mailbag readers learned about a 4-year-old boy with a potentially fatal heart condition and the servicemen who helped save his life.

Le Van Hoa's only hope was to undergo open-heart surgery. A physician at the hospital, where Le's mother worked, learned of the child's plight in October 1970, and brought it to the attention of a chaplain with the battalion. The chaplain notified 2nd Lt. William F. Wiggins, who served on the Saigon Support Command's civil affairs staff. Officers at the 93rd Evacuation Hospital in Long Binh and those of the 79th Maintenance Battalion worked with Bill for months to provide the necessary medical attention for the young boy. This life-saving surgery was to take place in Los Angeles and paperwork was the biggest obstacle in getting the child to this country. Bill worked closely with Vietnam's Ministry of the Interior to obtain a visa and passport for Le. He also got permission from Le's mother to make the trip and consent from the village and province chiefs where Le lived. Bill then accompanied the youngster for his stateside surgery at no expense to the boy's family.

Also, the doctor who first brought Le's condition to the attention of the chaplain left Vietnam for his home in Los Angeles, where he performed the surgery and served as Le's guardian for the child's month-long recuperation.

offer some positive solutions. They could accept the answer they have already received, but why should they have to do this, when I feel certain that with the amount of U.S. dollars and U.S. servicemen in Vietnam, coupled with the present corruption in the Vietnamese government, the U.S. must have some contacts in the Vietnamese government who could settle this question favorably. My problem is to find these contacts! ...

I hope that you will print my letter because it is so important not only to the girls, but also to myself and many others at the USAICCV-LDSC. The chance for them to improve themselves and eventually to help their country might just depend on you."

Army Spc. Michael M. Maloney in Long Binh, March 19

Army Spc. Michael M. Maloney of Wilmington, stationed in Long Binh, also requested assistance from those at home to help Vietnamese students who were having problems obtaining exit visas. He had quite a story to tell and a picture to go with it.

"**The topic I have written about is of great importance to me and many others at the U.S. Army Inventory Control Center Vietnam....** This is my first chance to help someone on a personal basis, thus, it is very important to me.

The girls I have described are everything I have said and more. They are outstanding computer programmers but have reached the highest level of education available here in the computer-oriented studies and yet still have the zeal for learning that so often is lacking in the Vietnamese population.

Their basic problem is that they are not able to obtain an exit visa for student travel since they attended a Chinese high school and the requirement is to have attended a Vietnamese high school. They have reached the point where they simply do not know where else to seek help.... They have been told by sources in their government that if they make a $1,200 payoff to the 'right people' they would be able to obtain the visa.

Since the structure of the government of South Vietnam is so much different from that of the United States, I personally do not know whom to contact for assistance. I have contacted Sen. Boggs, Rep. du Pont and Gov. Peterson about this problem. They have contacted officials in the State Department and also advised me to contact the American Embassy in Saigon. The State Department is still working on the matter and the U.S. Embassy would not help at all.

The treatment I received from the Vice Consul in the Visa Section was unbelievable. He had no courtesy whatsoever, which completely shocked me for someone in his position, and said that he did not want to get involved.... I hope to find some loophole ... or learn the name of a person, office, or organization that might be able to

After offering his take on the war, one serviceman provided a look at the hardscrabble existence of the South Vietnamese.

"**I really have no definite views on the U.S. policy in Vietnam.** One view our government takes on our actions in Southeast Asia is the renowned Domino Theory. They say if we fight in Vietnam and stop Communism before it spreads we will never have to fight Communism in the U.S.

If there is a slim chance that our being here will keep us from fighting in the states, then I am for staying here. Nobody from back home can really comprehend the filth ... and the oppression in which these people live.

I was on a truck which was making a run to the dump. When we stopped the truck we were swarmed by a bunch of people who wanted our worthless garbage and scrap. It was not garbage to them, it was a precious commodity. I see little boys 13 years old in uniform, ready to fight the VC. This is the same age as my younger brother Greg.

But, on the other hand, it is disgusting to see Americans killed for a war the U.S. is really not doing its best to win."

Army Spc. Tim Davis in Nha Trang, Jan. 8 Mailbag

This Army captain, lauded by Army Spc. Francis M. Jornlin II as a commander, formed a different opinion of the populace from his more southern location in Vietnam:

"**Since I have come in country, I have commanded A Battery, 5th BN, 42nd Artillery.** We've moved several times but right now I do have two fire support bases, Michelle and Nancy, in Long Thanh Province. The province is about twenty miles east of Saigon and is the most productive in South Vietnam. It's most active in the banana, timber and rubber industries. The people of the province have a great deal of pride and that has done much to ward off the VC."

Army Capt. Paul D. Lovett III, March 22

MAILBAG READERS LEARNED MUCH ABOUT THE VIET-NAMESE CULTURE AND LANGUAGE THROUGH SERVICE-MEN'S LETTERS. First, on March 12, the column was called to task by Army Spc. John R. "Rob" MacNab over genies we had written about when covering Tet, the Vietnamese new year, in February.

The traditional Vietnamese calendar runs in cycles of 12 years and a genie, in the form of an animal, represents each year. The hog or boar was the genie for 1971.

The February 3 Mailbag listed the cycle in the order of appearance of the genies as well as their Vietnamese names: Ty (mouse), Suu (buffalo), Dan (tiger), Mao (cat), Thin (dragon), Ty (snake), Ngo (horse), Mui (goat), Than (monkey), Dau (cock), Tuat (dog) and Hoi (hog). That section of the column ended with Happy Hoi.

Rob wrote on February 18 and his letter was in the March 12 Mailbag. "I am sending some information on Tet. In one of your articles you said this was the year of the hog. Not so, it's the year of the pig." My response:

Not to be flip, but I got it on good authority, namely the "Viet-Nam Bulletin," a weekly publication of the Embassy of Vietnam, that the Year of the Pig is analogous to the Year of the Hog and the Year of the Boar. To the Vietnamese, they are all the same.

For your information, the pig is much respected in Vietnam and is a source of food for most people. Nearly every farmer owns a sow or two with broods of piglets in times of prosperity.

That written, the March 24 Mailbag quoted more on the pig from a later embassy bulletin:

Any special occasion is marked by the roasting of a pig, the traditional meal for those who come to pay their last respects to the dead in post-funeral ceremonies.

At wedding ceremonies, the bridegroom's family must prepare a roasted pig festooned with paper flowers in its ears and a bright red sash down its back to present to the bride's family. This marriage pig is carried before the wedding cortege by an attendant in special attire.

A pig, either whole or just its head and tail, is frequently offered to one's ancestors as a sign of respect and memory. The head is presented to the most important person, for example, to a village chief, while the tail goes to the second most important person.

A traditional feast may have as many as 11 different recipes for pig: boiled, roasted, hammed, pasted, and seasoned with rare and perfumed vegetables. Even tripe and coagulated pig's blood are used in exotically prepared recipes.

Pork is considered nourishing. Mothers eat pigs' feet with lotus grains and rice to improve baby milk and wives will fry hog testicles with vegetables or rice to stimulate their husbands.

Working men enjoy blood coagulated with salt and served with heavily seasoned vegetables, believing it refreshes human blood and regulates digestion."

Learning the language in South Vietnam was difficult but this soldier sent Mailbag readers a primer on basic lingo.

"**About Vietnam – I hate it.** You can't understand these people over here and the weather is much too hot for me.

In case you'd like to know a few Vietnamese words, here are a couple and their meanings:

BAN means friend
GO means girl
BOO KOO DEP means very beautiful
UN KOON AP means I love you very much
TEE TEE means very short or small
LA DAY means come here
DEE DEE NOW means to get lost

There are many other words I could put down but I don't want to write a dictionary.

Formal letters aren't my bag either, that's why I'm not going to write anything formal. I have lived in Milford all my life and wouldn't trade the state of Delaware for any other, even though I have just about been in every state in the good old U.S.A."
Army Pfc. John H. Collison, Jan. 17

Marine Lance Cpl. Timothy R. Akers shares a light moment with Ruben Ochoa, his company's runner, and Gai, a Vietnamese boy they "adopted." Army Spc. Michael M. Maloney (opposite) sent a plea to help Vietnamese students.

WAR MIGHT BE HELL, BUT THE VOLUNTEERS AT SOS VIET-NAM, SPONSORED BY THE INTERDENOMINATIONAL CENTER AT RED LION METHODIST CHURCH, MADE SERVICE-MEN FEEL LIKE THEY WERE IN HEAVEN. Servicemen couldn't get over the goodwill of SOS Vietnam and the 5-pound bennie boxes the nonprofit mailed monthly to every Delaware serviceman in Vietnam. One lieutenant sent praise twice.

"A few days ago I received my fourth package from SOS Vietnam, a program sustained by the Interdenominational Center in Bear, Delaware, to send cookies and other foodstuffs to Delaware servicemen. And this package was no exception. So impressed am I with what these people collect, wrap and mail that I'd like to share with your readers the contents of this last well-received package.

In a box measuring about 6" x 8" x 12" came: Swiss Miss chocolate mix packet, dry milk packet, Instant Breakfast, iced tea mix, tomato juice, mixed fruit, raisins, soap, Slim Jim, gum, Lifesavers, foot powder, insole cushions, fresh cookies (about 2 dozen), stationery and envelopes, and the publication, *Our Daily Bread*, and words of cheer from Isabel Church, newsletter correspondent.

These foodstuffs are a welcome addition to the regular mess routine and provide excellent snack material. Each month the contents are different – one package even had crackers and a non-refrigerated type cheese spread! Tremendous.

My sincere thanks to this group of dedicated volunteers who reportedly send out well over 400 such packages each month. This group is making the tours of us Delaware servicemen more agreeable in a very real way."
Army 1st Lt. Rodney A. Brice, March 9

"Receipt of each box was often followed by an unusually large number of 'visitors' who 'happened by.' While it was said that the large box on my desk hadn't even entered their minds, they never refused the offer of some fresh cookies and, like me, were impressed with the large contents of the box. My sincere thanks to this wonderful organization."
Army 1st Lt. Rodney A. Brice, Oct. 1 Mailbag

Others added their own salutes:

"I'm not too good at writing letters, but I had to write so I could thank you for your wonderful package. I really loved the yo-yo and it's a Duncan! You should have seen the guys here trying to play with it – we really get a kick out of it.

It makes you happy that someone home is thinking of you. If you have anyone who wants to drop a line to me, I'll gladly answer. It's good to know what's going on back home."
Army Spc. Robert D. Coxe, June 14 Mailbag

"I'd like to take time to thank everyone at SOS Vietnam for the packages. It's great to know that there is one state that has so many people who care about their fellow statesmen. Delaware is, as far as I know, the only state that does so much for their men who are so far away from home. Thank you."
Sgt. Robert V. "Vance" Wilson in Phu Cat, June 30

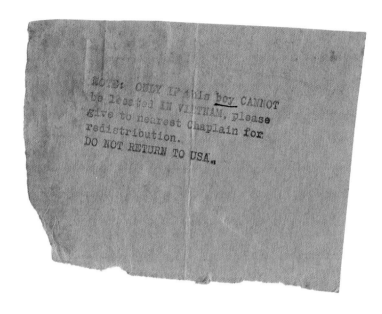

Servicemen never complained about their monthly bennie boxes from SOS Vietnam, but Army Spc. John R. "Rob" MacNab had a big problem with the organization's mailing label and its reference to the recipient as a "boy." Sgt. John Autenriet (opposite) of Valparaiso, Ind., reads mail from home delivered by the resupply chopper.

"Thanks for everything you're doing and thanks especially to Gov. [Russell W.] Peterson for his Christmas letter. It got here today (just a bit early) and to those folks at SOS [Vietnam]. Every month when I get my box someone remarks how they wish their state had something like that."
Army 1st Lt. Kenneth D. Warner, Nov. 8

One serviceman did take issue with SOS Vietnam, not over the contents of the bennie boxes but on the wording of their packaging.

"Please pass on to SOS, the note on their care packages should be changed. [SOS tagged every box with: Note: Only if this boy cannot be located in Vietnam, please give to nearest chaplain for redistribution. Do not return to USA.]

I haven't found too many boys in Vietnam. I would really like to thank SOS, they make it seem that someone does care. Just try to change that boy stuff."
Army Spc. John R. "Rob" MacNab, Feb. 18

After Rob's letter, we talked with Merle Fausnaught, SOS president, and he said a word change was in the offing as this complaint is not a new one to SOS. Fausnaught explained the stamp bearing the note was a relic dating back about three years and no one has bothered to get the wording changed to 'man,' 'serviceman,' 'Delawarean,' or 'First Stater,' none of which, we assumed, would be offensive.

DUE TO THE 12,000 MILES SEPARATING DELAWARE AND VIETNAM, PLANNING STARTED EARLY FOR FILLING AND SENDING HOLIDAY AND CHRISTMAS PACKAGES TO THE WAR ZONE. The October 18 Mailbag published the USO's sixth annual holiday gift survey of military personnel in the Vietnam-Pacific area. There was a distinct shift in requests, viewed as good news:

This year's survey, for the first time, no longer includes past combat zone staples: heavy-duty work socks, foam insoles for combat boots, shoeshine equipment or insect repellent.

Things may be looking up.

Although the American role in Southeast Asia is indeed changing through the process of Vietnamization and troop withdrawals, approximately 160,000 men of the American armed forces are expected to remain in Vietnam throughout the holiday season. USO strongly advises against any diminution of gift promotion activities.

USO is issuing its updated 1971 holiday gift suggestion list early this year, to give time for clubs, groups and individuals to complete their projects.

USO has found the following gifts top Santa's list: cassette tapes, small transistor radios, instant breakfast drinks, canned foods, meats and fruits, camera film, dry soap, holiday decorations, Christmas trees, small mirrors, candles, small flashlights and batteries.

By no means are we forgetting the distaff side. Women in the service have again listed their standard annual choices, including shampoo, rollers, hair setting lotion, cologne, fashion magazines, dry shampoo, lipstick and nail polish.

Holidays in Vietnam were especially hard on servicemen and during those times, they wrote, little things meant the most. They often told us that any comfort from home boosted morale. The Mailbag for the second year sent a card designed by News-Journal editorial cartoonist Jack Jurden, prompting responses:

"**There are 2 weeks until Christmas officially happens, but for me, Christmas has been happening right along.** Every day I get a copy of *The Morning News* or another local paper I receive from Dover, it is a bit of home wrapped in brown paper. In this day when money is so tight, it is gratifying to see these newspapers come as a free gift.... I did receive your Christmas card which caused me to write this letter. These are the things that Christmas should be about. People caring about people and extending greetings. Too bad we can't have peace and it seems war is becoming more popular than peace.... It will be good to get back to Delaware where the people really care."
Army 1st Lt. David Neylan, Dec. 11

Servicemen wrote about how they spent their holidays.

"**Happy New Year to you and all First Staters.** On this end of the world it should be a good year, only four months to go and that's almost short!

Like many have written, adjustment to the past holiday season in Vietnam was not without certain unique aspects. It was a fairly good time because everyone tried.

It was a time when a six-inch surprise Christmas tree from home, already overburdened with four-inch candy canes, took half an hour to balance on the contents of SOS's thoughtful monthly care packages and our blow-up Santa deflated under the weight of our American Red Cross care bags hung around his neck, when my men's greatest fear (otherwise known as First Sergeant) turned up at 3:30 Christmas morning to give them cookies and let them hear a tape of his children singing *Jingle Bells*; when Santa's sleigh was a hovering helicopter playing carols and Santa was the great American, Bob Hope.

Thank you, Nancy, The News-Journal Co., SOS, American Red Cross and all the people of Delaware for making this soldier's Christmas away from home a much better one.

New Year's for this lucky individual was that week of this year known as R&R. For me, that meant my wife and Hawaii (I have no idea where they get those 2 Rs). That event required adjustment too.

After almost eight months here, I'd nearly forgotten some of the luxuries of the world. It was almost surprising to order a rare steak and have something that was not only rare but a steak too. Another amazing thing was not having to take a 2x4 to the shower with you to beat the rust out of the pipes or 55-gallon water drum or having to wait until 4 p.m. for the sun to heat the water in that 55-gallon drum for a 'hot' shower. This event, of course, is no hardship, as showers are only every third odd day in the wet season and the Army provides 2x4s and it's good exercise too.

It's the little things, like the technology behind turning a knob and having all these things happen at once that makes me appreciate our military-industrial complex at home.

The only difficult adjustment in Hawaii, however, was its legalized fireworks. Thank goodness for a wife that holds on tightly or a lot more stores and restaurants would have been entered in the diving position and a lot more small palms, bushes and flower gardens would have been crushed.

Much like Delaware, the First, Hawaii, the 50th state, goes out of its way to make its visitors feel welcome and enjoy themselves."
Army Lt. James W. Roy, Jan. 8

"**Here's a real interest story.** A former member of our unit, now living in Fullerton, California, together with 4 other vets of Vietnam, have acquired 1,500 Christmas trees with all the decorations. They will be sent here about the second week of December. Our unit has the honor of distributing them throughout Vietnam. Our project is known as Operation Christmas. I understand that another group is sending another 1,000 trees."
Capt. Francis Simeone, Nov. 5

"**We plan several parties for local children as well as for GIs.** We have no trouble getting volunteers to help; it seems the GIs would rather help give a party for the Vietnamese children than for themselves, which is most gratifying. Plans for the next three Sundays include special music from our own choir, the local Vietnamese Protestant Church choir and the 101st Division Soldiers Chorus.

Our division, the last in Vietnam, is starting to go home. It probably won't affect me since I'm due to leave in February [1972] anyway. I'm hoping for a drop that would send me home sometime in January. Right now, I don't know whether I'll be reassigned or getting out.

All I know for sure is that I'll be out by midsummer and will begin grad school next fall. It sure will be good to get back to the real world where a man is respected for what he is and what he can do, not the rank he wears.

I'll come by to see you when I get back, hopefully in mid-January."
Army Spc. Carlton "Buddy" King III, Nov. 29

> ## "Thanks ever so much for the Christmas card. It was filled with much meaning.... I also wish to thank all of the people who have been writing. May God bless them always.
>
> **Army Spc. William D. Taylor in Phu Loi, Jan. 16**

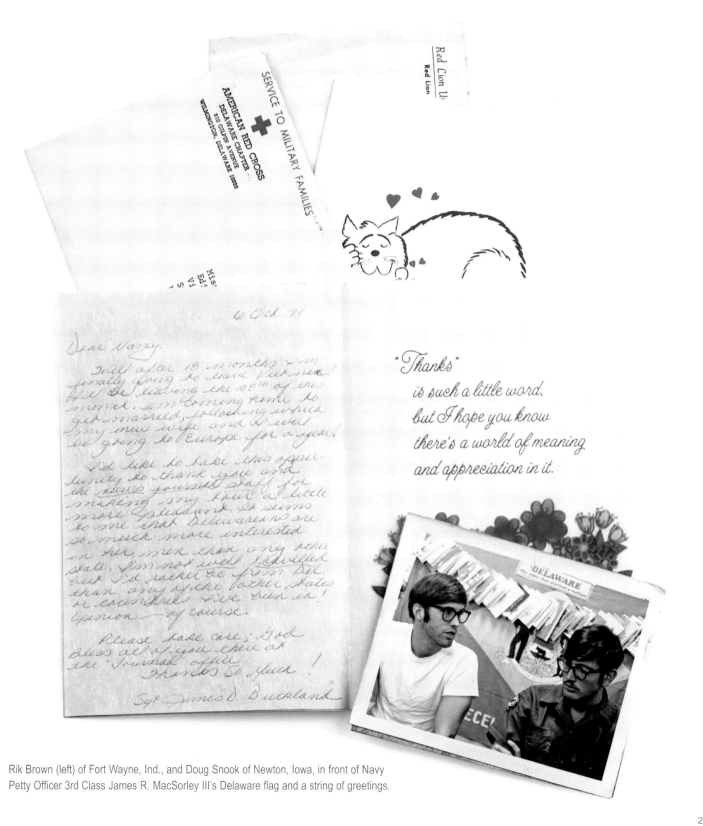

"Thanks"
is such a little word,
but I hope you know
there's a world of meaning
and appreciation in it.

Rik Brown (left) of Fort Wayne, Ind., and Doug Snook of Newton, Iowa, in front of Navy Petty Officer 3rd Class James R. MacSorley III's Delaware flag and a string of greetings.

WAR OR NO WAR, SERVICEMEN ATTAINED SIGNIFICANT PERSONAL MILESTONES AND SHARED THEIR THOUGHTS ABOUT THEM WITH THE MAILBAG. In a time of war, however, even the happiest moments were soiled with sorrow.

Memorial Day, our country's legal holiday in memory of fallen members of the armed forces of all wars, was a day of especially horrific memories for former marine Michael Lee Rose of New Castle, who, on that holiday in 1969, lost six buddies in battle in the A Shau Valley.

And because he could never forget, Mike dedicated his May 29, 1971 wedding to their memory. That's the way Mike wanted it. His thoughtfulness moved many readers of the May 31 Mailbag, reprinted here and based on information Mike told me.

A special memorial prayer for the six who died was incorporated into the marriage ceremony at Holy Spirit Catholic Church in New Castle.

"We were all coming home the same time," Mike, 21, recalled. But the 3rd Battalion, 9th Marines encountered hostile action in the vicinity of Quang Tri, near Landing Zone Stud.

Mike explained that all seven of them were due to leave South Vietnam the same day, and had only 10 days left in country when the combat began for their outfit.

"A lot of my company was wiped out," Mike, a former squad leader, said. When it was all over, Mike realized six of his friends had been killed. "They were my brothers."

U.S. control of the A Shau Valley began early in 1969. There was a lengthy fight, ending in victory [in] the valley, one of the key communist infiltration routes into the northern provinces of South Vietnam.

The sweep was called "Dewey Canyon" and when it was all over, Marines killed at least 1,405 North Vietnamese regulars in the drive, destroyed 66 trucks, six big 122-mm artillery pieces, 61 anti-aircraft guns and uncovered almost 400 tons on munitions – the largest weapons cache ever seized by the allies in Vietnam.

The operation cost the Marines at least 117 dead and 662 wounded.

And so, to his buddies, because they were brothers, Mike dedicated his wedding. The six who were killed in battle were all corporals. Mike says he doesn't know their [full] names because that was never important. What they went through together at A Shau is their bond. Mike will never forget that day.

The dead are:

Wilson from Arkansas
Meyers from California
Oliver from California
Hawk from Seattle
Mike from Tennessee
Tervenino from Brooklyn.

Mike was engaged a year and a half. His fiancee always wanted a June wedding. But she was very happy to be married last Saturday, the day closest to Memorial Day, so the memory of those close to Mike could be dedicated.

Mike enlisted in the Marines when he was 18 because he felt an obligation to serve his country. After basic training at Parris Island, S.C., Mike left for Vietnam in 1968. During his 13-month tour, he was wounded three times.

Mike's been back in town for some time. He works here and plans to settle his new family here. He doesn't talk much about May 30, 1969 – it's too hard. Nor will he discuss the awards he received for gallantry and bravery. It's just Mike's way.

We would like to dedicate today's column to those six men, as well as to the memory of all Delawareans who fought so bravely and died for what they believed was right in South Vietnam.

And to Mike for having served his country without demonstration, without reservation, without hesitation.

Other servicemen wrote the Mailbag with relationship news and family matters.

"I arrived here in Vietnam on January of '70. I went home on an extension leave from the fifth of December that year to the fifth of January '71. It was really nice to be home again. One never seems to appreciate a city like Wilmington until they have to leave it.

I had one daring adventure while I was home! I got engaged to a girl by the name of Miss Ellen B. Magee. We had dated for four years and felt that this Christmas being special to us was the right time….

The wedding is now waiting for the both of us to finish our schooling.

I stopped over at the 531st Engineers to see that fellow from Lynnfield [Army Spc. John W. Huston] about a month ago. I too am stationed at Long Binh. Unfortunately, he and the rest of his company moved to Vung Tau the day before I stopped over there.

The best news of all is that I'm short. I'll be back in the states and out of the Army on the ninth of August."
Army Spc. David Burns in Long Binh, June 24

Marine Cpl. I. Haass dedicated his poem, "The Battle," to fellow marine Larry T. Larson after both had received "Dear John" letters. Army Spc. David Burns (opposite), a flight engineer with the 273rd Aviation Company, worked on the giant CH-54A Sky Crane helicopters. During his tour, he received the Air Medal and Army Commendation Medal.

"**I really enjoy reading [my newspapers] about what's going on and which of my buddies is getting hitched.** I got married to my high school sweetheart, the former Donna Lloyd. We married and lived in California where I was stationed. We had many a wonderful time and [I'm] looking forward to settling down with her again.

I'm building up to the point that very recently, January 4th at 6:59 p.m., I became the proud daddy of a very good looking son, all 7 lbs. 9 oz. of him. He's 12 pounds now, named him Jeffrey Thomas. I have dozens of pictures of him and my beautiful wife.

But there won't be any moment hardly that's going to top our reunion in Alameda, Calif. When the ship pulls in, they'll be at the pier waiting. I've come back before and no one was waiting [for me but] I was so happy for guys that did [have someone waiting]."
Navy Petty Officer 3rd Class Clifford T. "Tom" Hitch aboard the USS Hancock, March 5

Affairs of the heart sometimes ended with bad breaks. Troops dreaded the "Dear John" letter from a significant other ending the relationship. We learned indirectly of such a missive to Marine Cpl. Larry T. Larson from Marine Cpl. I. Haass at the American Consulate, who dedicated his poem, "The Battle," to Larry. "Larry and I have been together since he got to Vietnam," he wrote, adding he too had received a "Dear John." The poem appeared in the February 26 Mailbag.

On one occasion, a misunderstanding during a soldier's hour of grief prompted a letter to the Mailbag. In a letter unusual for its negative content, the Delaware Chapter, American Red Cross absorbed the writer's wrath.

"**What I have to say really makes me disturbed about the Red Cross.** Here is what I can piece together from what my Mother's letter told me.

My grandfather died the night of 22nd of July '71. My parents called the Red Cross to try and see if they could get me home for the funeral because I'm named after him.

They said that they couldn't because he wasn't of my immediate family. But [they said] that my unit commander was notified. I didn't receive any word from the Red Cross at all. When I got the letter today, I went to the Company commander and he said that he would check my job and its importance and most likely grant the emergency leave.

What I'm mad about is that the Red Cross is supposed to be there for emergencies like this, for a soldier [who] is serving his country many miles from home. I'm deeply depressed about the whole thing.

Mail is the most important thing in my life (besides going home) over here. And when I get a letter like this it can really hurt because the Red Cross is supposed to help us, not make our tour worse."
Army Spc. Joseph L. Conway in Phu Tai, July 28

THE BATTLE

MANY TIMES DID I GET WOUNDED
MANY TIMES DID I GET PAIN
I HAVE FOUGHT, FOUGHT MANY BATTLES
BATTLES ON THAT ROAD TOWARDS HOME.

BUT EACH BATTLE WAS A VICTORY
FOR WOUNDS DID HEAL AND PAIN DID CEASE
AND ONCE AGAIN I COULD DREAM OF
                              PEACE.
ONE MORE BEND ON THIS LONG ROAD
ONE MORE BEND AND I'LL BE HOME
NO MORE BATTLES, NO MORE WOUNDS
NO MORE PAIN FOR I'LL BE HOME.

BUT IN THIS BEND THERE LURKS AN
                              AMBUSH
UNEXPECTED AND UNKNOWN TO ME
NOT PREPARED FOR ANOTHER BATTLE
I GO DOWN AND FEEL THE PAIN.

I AM WOUNDED I AM DYING
OF A DIFFERENT WOUND AND PAIN
FOR MY LOVE HAS FOUND ANOTHER
OH! OH! THE PAIN.

After a little sleuthing, we found Emily L. Markwood, casework supervisor for the Delaware Chapter's Service to Military Families Department, and, apparently, got to the bottom of Joe's problem. Her letter was printed in the September 13 Mailbag.

Replying to the letter of Spec. 4 Joseph L. Conway, Wilmington, please be advised that the Service to Military Families of the Delaware Chapter has no record of the parent of Serviceman Conway making a request to the Red Cross in Wilmington for an emergency leave to attend the funeral of his grandfather.

We have checked the records and consulted with Red Cross duty workers who are on duty 24 hours a day every day in the year, to assist men and women in the armed forces and their families and there is no record of any request from the family of Joseph L. Conway for an emergency leave.

Markwood enumerated Red Cross procedures in emergency cases and underscored the granting or denying of an emergency leave was made by the serviceman's commanding officer or the designated military leave authority, not the Red Cross.

WITH TROOP WITHDRAWALS AND VIETNAMIZATION ONGOING IN 1971, THE MAILBAG RECEIVED MANY STORIES ABOUT THE "SOFTER SIDE" OF THE WAR. Some were humorous, some were moving but all made good reading.

Edward J. Rucinski III was one of the first Delawareans to take advantage of the two-week stateside leaves the military had approved in December 1970. Ed was home for Christmas and New Year's and told us in the January 11 Mailbag he thought it was a good idea to allow servicemen to return home, especially for the holidays.

Ed, a gunner on a helicopter, said it wasn't that tough on him emotionally to head back to combat after relaxing with family and friends. "Besides," he said, "I'm used to leaving." His physical return to Vietnam proved difficult, though. After being refused stand-by on at least two flights out of Philadelphia, he was in jeopardy of not reaching Oakland, California, in time to take off for Saigon. But he made it.

Two months before Ed returned home for good in April, he was awarded the Air Medal with "V" device for valorous actions as crew chief of a command and control aircraft during an intense firefight with the enemy.

Army Spc. William W. "Hutch" Hutchison Jr., with the 23rd Infantry Division's Information Office, and his IO volleyball team were subjects of a September 17 Mailbag sports special on the Americal volleyball title:

TMF [Target Mission Force] had been unbeaten in the 32-team field until its first match with IO, which it lost, 15-4, 15-7.

IO drew from an office staff of 13 enlisted men and three officers to defeat the much larger TMF team 15-11, 15-1, for the title. And Hutch, our very own First Stater, was a first-string IO team member. Rah, rah, Hutch.

The victorious team was recognized with plaques and TMF received second-place trophies at ceremonies at division headquarters.

IO then went on to the Military Region I [I Corps] volleyball championship to take second place. They bested Da Nang Support command, 15-3, 15-3, and then went down in defeat by the 101st Airborne Division (Airmobile), 15-13, 6-15, 2-15.

Miss America always caused a stir in Vietnam and 1971 was no exception. Army Pfc. Anthony Francisco was on the scene, along with 6,500 other "Screaming Eagles" of the 101st Airborne Division at Camp Eagle near Hue. The August 30 Mailbag had the scoop:

The revue was held in the Eagle entertainment bowl and featured songs, dancing and several audience participation numbers. The Eagles, never at a loss for a scream or two, showed their appreciation by outbursts of applause throughout the performance.

The Eagles were transplanted from firebases and field locations in Vietnam's dense tropical jungles that permeate the division's area of operation.

Miss America 1971, Phyllis George of Denton, Texas, headlined the entourage of seven that included [six state pageant winners]. The Miss America show, now in its fifth annual eye-full, is sponsored by the USO and the Department of Defense for the entertainment of all servicemen abroad. During their 22-day stay, Miss America and her troupe are scheduled to entertain troops throughout the Republic of Vietnam.

One soldier shared big plans with Mailbag readers in his letter from Camp Eagle near Hue.

"I always read your articles and I can't see why everyone wants to leave Viet Nam. Personally I find this country fascinating. As a matter of fact, I've been talking to a real estate agent in Phu Bai and am buying a small two-room grass house outside of Phu Long village. The house is on a small plot of land with three rice paddies already built. He is giving me two water buffalo and six chickens as a bonus. Tomorrow I'm going to ask my C.O. for a few days off a week so I can start planting my rice."
Army Spc. Kevin M. Lyons at Camp Eagle, Aug. 11

Lest there be any question Kevin was spoofing us, his dad, Wilmington attorney Edmund D. Lyons, pointed out that fact in a letter three days after Kevin's letter was printed. He said his son had written him beforehand that his real estate venture was a "test of your publication."

While a student at Wheaton College in Illinois, Army Spc. Paul Joseph Kuhwald wrote several poems. Vantage Press published his collection, which he titled "Alive And Free," in hardback in December 1971. Months before the book was released, on July 11, Paul, a helicopter medic stationed in Long Binh, wrote a poem especially for the Mailbag, titled "To You At Home," which we printed in the August 13 column.

Spined and clawed at break of day –
Skewered by the tear-stained eyes
of these quiet people
as calloused hearts beat
war rhythms into greenbacked ears.

We, the blinded instruments
of one nation's injustice to life,
crawl and cry
for outstretched arms
for love, for home –
and our brothers from jungle and sickle lairs
struck by the womb's fear of death
they seek the open veins
of your strangered babes.
Both sides torture any hope of youth,
the Caesars and saviours pawn
our maturing souls
in hope of a few paddies, in hope of peace.

Should your sons die so far from home,
will tears and empty promises
add one moment to our lives?
Reach for us now,
We may not see tomorrow!

Competition was keen among 32 teams for bragging rights at the Military Region I Volleyball Championship. Army Spc. William W. Hutchison Jr. (opposite, right) led the 23rd Infantry Division's Information Office (IO) team to the finals, losing to the 101st Airborne Division (Airmobile) in the late summer tourney.

The Morning News, Wilmington, Del. • Monday, January 4, 1971 11

Nancy's Vietnam Mailbag

By NANCY E. LYNCH

Hi there—

Bonanza of bonanzas was delivered to us last week by Capt. JAMES D. RAWLINS JR. of Seaford, who just got home. Jim brought snaps of as many as five First Staters together.

Jim shares with us some of his observations after a year's tour in Vietnam and some belated holiday messages from our First Staters:

"Before I went to that beautiful but somewhat primitive country, I thought that we should be there militarily. However, I felt that Nixon's plan for withdrawal after the establishment of a 'Vietnamization' program was just another sell-out to the Communists and, therefore, I was against it.

"Now that I have been there and have seen the war from my own vantage point, observed the people, the country and the ARVN's accomplishments, I am positive that President Nixon's formula for our honorable withdrawal is the only one and is achieving a tremendous success.

"I have spoken with many of the officers and men who are stationed around Saigon and who were under direct influence of the Cambodian sanctuaries. My own conclusion after considering everything is that it was the smartest and most rewarding move the United States has made since the Inchon landing in Korea by Gen. Douglas MacArthur.

"The increased morale of the ARVN troops has been boosted tremendously because of their impeccable performance there and the pressure around Saigon has been reduced to almost nothing.

"I have read the wild comments by the stateside liberal senators, congressmen and newspapers as they screamed that we are enlarging the war and that the ARVNs had no right to 'invade' Cambodia.

"I have also noticed that these same liberal sources neglect to point out that the ARVN crossed the border to fight North Vietnamese army soldiers armed with Russian-made weapons who had 'invaded' Cambodia years before. We have pulled out completely and the ARVNs say they will leave immediately if the NVA will do likewise. Of course, they (NVA) won't do that.

"For sure, a person must go to Vietnam to get a true idea of the situation and thus intelligently reach a conclusion on our commitment there.

"By saving some clippings from your column, I was able to locate other First Staters in my area, Phu Bai so just before I left for home, I arranged a meeting of six of us and took pictures.

"The group includes:

Charlie and Leonard and Bob and Larry and Jim
. . . together

"Pfc. LEONARD D. SHATLEY (222-36-0086, CO E 3-506 INF (RADAR), APO SF 96383) from Coventry, who sends a 'Merry Christmas and Happy New Year' to his family;

"Spec. 4 LARRY E. HARMON (221-34-5460, C CO, 159th ASHB, APO SF 96383) from Newark, who sends his message: 'Merry Christmas to everyone and give my love to Mary.'

"Spec. 4 ROBERT A. COEN (221-36-3541, 101st ABN DIV AG POSTAL, APO SF 96383) from Afton, who is a postal clerk in the 2d Bridgade APO and a real credit to his unit. He sent 'Happy holiday to everyone and I hope to be home soon.'

"Spec. 4 JAMES M. WILSON (222-34-8284, HHC 8th RRFS, BOX 641, APO SF 96308) from Wilmington, who said, 'Merry Christmas, Happy New Year and I hope to be home real soon. Keep those cards and letters coming.'

"Spec. 4 CHARLES R. SARRIO (213-56-2186, HHC 8th RRFS, BOX 647, APO SF 96308) from Rockville, Md. Although he is from our neighboring state, he feels he qualifies as a Delawarean by proxy because he reads every Wilmington Morning News paper he can get his hands on and spends his time with James Wilson and Curtis Wayne. His evaluation of the Morning News was, 'It's No. 1 in my book.'

"Two other men unable to make the group photo were Spec. 5 CURTIS WAYNE (HHC 8th RRFS, APO SF 96308) from Gordy Estates, who had to report for night perimeter guard duty, and Pfc. GEORGE S. WOOTTEN (HHC 2d BDE 265th RRU, APO SF 96383) from Landenberg, Pa., who was tied up with some security work.

"I want to thank you and all those persons who sent me the Morning News and the Delaware State flag, thereby making me feel missed by my fellow citizens. After a 30-day leave in Seaford, I shall go to Ft. Carson, Colo., for a two-year assignment.

"Best of everything to you and your fellow workers."

★ ★ ★

Gov. Russell W. Peterson was recently made honorary chairman of the USO in Delaware and awarded a certificate by United Service Organizations, Inc.

Presenting the certificate to Peterson were William M. Gourlay, USO regional executive, and Robert G. Hackett, state USO chairman.

Delaware's single USO Club, in Dover, closed in July after 29 years of being a home away from home for thousands of servicemen. The Dover club closed because there weren't enough persons attending to make it worthwhile.

★ ★ ★

Until Wednesday. . .

Nancy

Army Capt. James D. Rawlins Jr. struck it rich with his rare shot of five First Staters together. From left, Army Spc. Charles Sarrio, Army Pfc. Leonard D. Shatley, Army Spc. Robert A. Coen, Army Spc. Larry E. Harmon and Jim. Army Spc. James L. McCormick (opposite, on left) sent this photo with Army Lt. Walter C. Hopkins, the only other Delawarean in his company.

IF NEWS OF FIRST STATERS FINDING ONE ANOTHER IN VIETNAM GAVE US A LIFT AT HOME, THE OFTEN-RANDOM MEETINGS OCCASIONED MUCH HIGH-FIVING IN THE COMBAT ZONE. It was especially good to hear from two or more in one letter, as the Mailbag did early in 1971. About a week after Army Capt. James D. Rawlins Jr. sent a group photo of several Delawareans, two soldiers co-authored a letter to the Mailbag.

"**My co-writer and I would like to introduce ourselves.** I am Sp/4 James Michael Wilson and here with me is Sp/4 Curtis Simmons Wayne. We are both from Wilmington.

Curtie and I are both graduates of Henry C. Conrad High School, Class of '68.

My name being Wilson and his Wayne, we were in the same home-room class all through high school. You can imagine my surprise when I found him living in the room next to mine upon his arrival last July.

Me being in this strange foreign country and running into an old high school buddy, well, it was like old times!

Curt and I are stationed at 8th RRFS (Radio Research Field Station), in Phu Bai. We are both Communications Center specialists.

Since we have to be here, the fact that we're old pals has helped to make our tour a lot easier to take.

Your column has really provided us with a lot of entertainment, as well as helping Curt and I see just who else is in Nam that we might know. I don't get [*The Morning News*] on a regular basis, but when I do get it, all the guys in my room want to read it.

Keep the papers coming, but you can stop it for me on the first of June. I'll be home! Curtie will be back in the world July 22. So until then, God Bless and continued success with your column."

Army Spcs. James Michael Wilson and Curtis Simmons Wayne, Jan. 5

The meetings, chance or otherwise, happened throughout the year. Sometimes, the Mailbag sparked unintended but welcome communications.

"**Have heard from several of my old friends who have seen my name in the paper and have really enjoyed hearing from them.** You have a wonderful lost-and-found column. Capt. Hill at MACV Team 44 received a letter from his grandmother in Wilmington. She enclosed my last contribution [to the Mailbag] mentioning the fact that he was here. He was tickled with it."

Air Force Master Sgt. James T. Joyce at Phan Rang Air Base, Feb. 25

"**Just a line to tell you that we will be having an officer coming to my unit from Wilmington later on this month.** His name is Lt. j.g. Foresman. I was really surprised when I heard this because our unit only consists of a total of six men."

Navy Seaman Harry G. Porter in Can Tho, Feb. 7

"**This place is okay because, first, the town is on limits and, second, because there is a beach that we can use that is really great.** From my old unit another guy from Delaware came up here with me. His name is Steve Price.... From what I hear, there are others from Delaware here at the 330th too, but as yet I haven't met any.... Say hi to my family for me and also to my niece Lee."

Army Spc. Scott D. Norris at Nha Trang, March 29

"**Although I am not exactly thrilled with Vietnam, I feel I can put up with my tour here.** I am currently stationed at LZ English with the 173rd Airborne Brigade. It is not one of the garden spots in the world, but, again, I expected I would have it a lot worse off than I do.

A few weeks ago we had some guys come into our detachment who had spent a few months in Nha Trang. One of them is named Ken Robinson and he lives in Newark. We had some good times talking about Delaware. He has 6 months left in country and I have 8. That is 250 days and you can believe I am counting them down."

Army Spc. Tim Davis, April 28 Mailbag

"I've been in the Army a year and seven months and have met only one person from Delaware and then I come to Vietnam and find our fire-base commander is from Wilmington – what a coincidence!

He gave me his flag, which is hanging high over my hooch, and his subscription to my hometown paper. Capt. Paul Lovett left about two weeks ago, so he's back in the world by now and I'm sure my parents have looked him up by now.

Captain Lovett did an outstanding job as battery commander and I only wish I could be under him for the remainder of my time here. He cleaned up the heroin problem, which was quite an accomplishment. And treated the men fairly, which, by the way, is not the way it is now."
Army Spc. Francis M. Jornlin II, Sept. 15

"I got a paper today and saw a friend's name in it, Pfc. Tony Eoppolo. I knew he was in Nam but didn't know where. I graduated from high school with him. So thanks a lot for having the column."
Army Pfc. Anthony J. Colicchio, Oct. 19

"**You people make me feel like a real king.** I got letters from all sorts of people and friends. Some people wrote and said, 'Good luck, Joe, and return soon.' Some person who sent a box of homemade cookies didn't send their name. But the cookies were just great.

You said you wanted some names of people serving over here from good ole Delaware. Here are some: Thomas Poore, Claymont, Joseph Beam, Newark, and Robert Lewis of Brookside. These are just a few. Delaware has its share of men over here."
Navy Hospital Corpsman Joseph H. Opdenaker Jr. aboard the USS Enterprise, Nov. 17

"**I'm sure Joe Opdenaker will be glad to know there is another Delawarean nearby....** I receive the same response when I tell my shipmates where I'm from. I'm going to try and fly our state flag from our mast, if I can obtain permission. So tell Joe to keep an eye open."
Navy Petty Officer 3rd Class Alan Marc Solomon aboard the USS Constellation, Nov. 25

"**I finished a tour in Germany and only met one Delawarean there in 18 months.** Since I've been here, I've met four. As a matter of fact, there are two plus myself in the same battalion at Marble Mountain Army Airfield in Da Nang. Capt. Bill Kenderman went to the U. of D. and is the commanding officer of the 62nd CAC, which is about 100 feet from my front door."
Army 1st Lt. Steven S. Neilson in Da Nang, Nov. 30

"**I've only met one other First Stater on the base.** His name is Pat Dolan and he is a staff sergeant from Elsmere…. However, his family moved to San Antonio, Texas, some time ago.

I'd appreciate it if you could locate a Delaware state flag for me. I would like to hang it in my room so everyone will know where I'm from…. P.S. Tell everyone to look for me on the 'Bob Hope Christmas Special.' I'll be the only one with a sign that says 'Delaware!'"
Air Force Airman William E. Hudson at Cam Ranh Bay Air Base, Dec. 18

And, sometimes, not meeting another First Stater was the story.

"**I keep a close watch on your Vietnam Mailbag too because I'm still trying to meet another Delawarean before I get out of the Army.** I came in the Army in Oct. of '69 through my Media, Pa., draft board and so far I've met guys from everywhere imaginable except Delaware."
Army Spc. John W. Huston in Long Binh, April 19

But help was on the way.

"**Good to see you continue to be the eyes and ears for the public from the GI in Vietnam.** Please accept my second tour greetings and assurances that I'll look up Spc. John Huston.

I'm the XO of the 240th Aviation Company (Assault Helicopter), the Greyhounds. 'Go Greyhound and leave the flying to us.' So much for the commercial."
Army Capt. Jon M. Peterson, May 8

Air Force Airman 1st Class Jehu J. Justice (above) received lots of mail after his name and address appeared in the Mailbag. Others used the column to send messages to loved ones, especially around the holidays. Soldiers and a nurse (opposite) relax at the Officers Club on Red Beach in Da Nang.

MAIL AS A MORALE BOOSTER WAS AS IMPORTANT IN 1971 AS IN EVERY OTHER YEAR OF THE CONFLICT. This airman said it all when he wrote from Bien Hoa Air Base.

"**I received your letter and was very glad to hear from you.** I'm always glad to hear from anyone from good ole Delaware. Since my name was in your column, I have also received letters from different people who saw it. I would like to thank everyone for their nice letters! Here in Vietnam, mail is really an important morale factor. In my opinion, I would say the most important of all."
Air Force Airman 1st Class Jehu J. Justice, March 5

Jehu correctly put mail on a pedestal, next to news from and about family. Some found the column an appropriate forum for messages to loved ones and updates on their families' activities.

"**I would like to ask that you publish at least the following for me in your column:** A very special thanks to my loving wife for all her thoughts during my second tour in Vietnam."
Army Chief Warrant Officer Herbert V. Melson in Quang Tri, April 28

"**Just a short note to keep up with my cousin Frank [Jornlin] who wrote you several weeks ago from outside Saigon.** My job

is a flight deck troubleshooter working 'on the roof' of the Connie. We have now joined the Tonkin Gulf Yacht Club, otherwise known as Yankee Station.

The XO of our squadron is a Wilmingtonian, Cmdr. Jack Miller, as is AT1 Monty Horowitz. Three Delawareans out of 200 or so isn't too bad at all. Would also like to rattle off a hello to Frank at Firebase Nancy and see if I can beat him back to Wilmington."
Navy Petty Officer 3rd Class Philip E. Jornlin aboard the USS Constellation, Nov. 2

"**I am the supply officer on the Army's only helicopter repair ship.** My wife is living in Delaware and is expecting our first child. Keep writing. It sure gets lonely out here."
Army Capt. Jerold S. Gold aboard the USS Corpus Christi Bay, Nov. 5

"**To my fiancee Carol, I would like to wish you all the happiness in the world during this holiday.** I miss you a lot and hope you are taking good care of yourself. I would like to thank you for all you've been doing for me while so far away from you and home during my tour in Vietnam.

Honey, I want to wish you a Merry Christmas and Happy New Year despite us being so far apart from each other."
Army Pfc. Alfred Donald Thompson at Fire Support Base Gibraltar, Nov. 30

SOMETIMES THE TABLES WERE TURNED AND THE MAIL-BAG RECEIVED CORRESPONDENCE FROM FAMILIES AT HOME ABOUT THEIR LOVED ONES IN VIETNAM. Daphne A. Crum, mother of Navy Seaman William S. Crum, who called himself the "Spirit of Peace for Everyone," expressed this post-Mother's Day thought in the May 19 Mailbag:

You have head from "Peace" and I'd like to send my thanks and appreciation from a "Mother of Peace" who is very proud of my son who would like to make this a little better world without violence. He realizes each of us owes a little to this once-great country and has a respect for those in authority. I wait impatiently for Bill's return in June.

Another proud mom from Wilmington shared with the May 26 Mailbag a verse penned by her son, Charles E. Crick Jr., who joined the Navy in June 1970, and was serving aboard the USS *Enterprise.* He called it "What is War?"

What actually is war?
It can be described in many ways
Such as fear, hate and hell.
But why do we have to go and die?
Is it really worth it?
Well, just look at a little girl
Playing jump rope or with dolls;
Or look at a little boy with a bat, ball and glove
It is called freedom, yes, just a word
But look at the millions of people
Who have died who have tried to keep that wonderful word strong
Yes, many of my friends have given up their lives for our great country,
I would gladly be proud to do the same
Just walk around your block
And look at all of the little children playing
Or go to your school in time for a football game
Would you do the same as I?
Join the service and try to show
That you do care for this great land.

Another woman wrote the lead letter in the Nov. 22 Mailbag.

The wife of a Delaware serviceman in Vietnam waits for her husband to return home. He won't be there for Thanksgiving dinner Thursday or for Christmas or even for next Fourth of July.

As a waiting wife, this young woman perhaps shares many of the same thoughts as you, another waiting wife. She asked that she not be identified, but her name really isn't important.

What she says is.

Think of her when you sit down to turkey and pumpkin pie and how she must feel. If you can't imagine how she feels, she'll tell you. This is her point of view:

It is a sad and lonely time – these days of war – a time when men are torn between their hearts and their minds – leaving their loved ones behind because duty calls. Their country needs them.

I am proud of my husband for what he is doing even though it is very hard living apart – not knowing what destiny has in mind for him. It is even harder when I see people ridicule soldiers, protest, burn draft cards, turn to drugs. These people are hurting my husband, my country, and, in Vietnam, are endangering lives around them.

I feel just as everyone else does about the situation in Vietnam. I want more than anything else for my husband to come home. But it is his duty and if it means he is doing something for the good of our country and our future, I can only pray that he is able to do it well and that others will do their best in helping us help our country.

I am happy to say that I am an American and when asked what my husband does, I stand proud and hold my head high and answer, 'He's in the U.S. Army serving in Vietnam.'

I pity those who cannot be proud of their servicemen because they are the backbone of this country, they are fighting for our right to be free.

I look in disgust at the younger generation (and I am only 21) who won't or can't salute our flag or stand to the national anthem. I can't let myself think Vietnam is for nothing because that would mean my husband's life may be put on the line for nothing – then my life would mean very little.

This is the second time my husband has been to Vietnam. The first time as an enlisted infantryman, the second as a helicopter pilot.…

But this is my first time as a waiting wife. I hope it will be my last. But if duty calls, he'll have to go and I know it's for us and for the generations to come.

Addison wrote: "The grand essentials in this life are something to do, something to love and something to hope for…" My husband, just as the rest of our men, is trying to keep this country the kind of place to always be able to have these things.

The Waiting Wife's letter prompted an enthusiastic response from this sailor aboard the USS *Enterprise.*

"**The article in your Vietnam Mailbag sure did me a lot of good, the article about the wife of a Delaware serviceman.** Well, Nancy, I agree with her 100%. As I sat here reading it today I wonder what my wife and family are doing now that the holidays are near. So I believe this woman deserves a Well Done, not only as a lonely wife but as a great Delawarean."
Navy Hospital Corpsman Joseph H. Opdenaker Jr., Dec. 7

There. Two colors. In addition:
The colors of the Coat of Arms and other elements of the State Flag shall be the following: Husbandman, trousers of gray brown, shirt of red, hat and hilling hoe of brown; Rifleman, suit of green, binding, bag and leggings of buff, hat of brown, powder flask and feather of gray; Shield, frame of shaded yellow, top panel of orange, center panel of blue, lower panel of white; Ox of red brown, grass and corn of green, wheat and branches underfoot of yellow, heraldic wreath to be blue and silver (twisted); Ship under full sail to have a dark hull and white sails.
That should settle any disputes for the time being.

Soldiers were always happy they had their state flags to show off.

"Special thanks to the people of Delaware for the flag (a bit big for the bush) and their terrific support. Let's hope the Delaware General Assembly passes the law forbidding Delaware men from serving in undeclared wars. Remember, when the power of love overcomes the love of power, peace will reign."
Army Pfc. William W. "Hutch" Hutchison Jr., May 3

"I am currently serving with the 35th Security Police Squadron at Phan Rang Air Base. Most of the guys have their state flags on display in their rooms. I would appreciate it if you could possibly send me one."
Air Force Airman 1st Class Mike McGraw, July 10

Army Spc. Neil A. Fairchild, a sports fan and former Christiana High School Viking, cheered on his old football team for its Thanksgiving game from his post at Quang Tri. He also mentioned in the November 26 Mailbag he had seen John Holley of Newark.

University of Delaware fans mentioned support for their favorite football team.

"I've got clippings taped on the wall of my hooch about [the University of] Delaware's successful year on the gridiron – really wish I was there to see the games and the Boardwalk Bowl."
Army 1st Lt. Steven S. Neilson at Marble Mountain Army Airfield near Da Nang, Nov. 30

"I especially enjoy reading the sports section and seeing where the Hens have romped again. It really helps when I hear that too-often received slight, 'Delaware, is that in Ohio?' It's, 'Go Hens' and keep sending that *Morning News*."
Army 1st Lt. David Neylan, Dec. 11

THOUGHTS OF HOME PROVIDED A DIVERSION FROM THE EVER-PRESENT THREAT OF ENEMY FIRE. This letter, from a soldier based in Saigon, led to some interesting research.
"I read an article of yours the other day where the Delaware flag is supposed to be the most expensive because of its 17 colors, etc. Well, it's the prettiest flag around here, but you'll have to count those colors again. Maybe I have the wrong flag hanging here by my desk. It certainly doesn't have 17 colors."
Army Spc. Robert P. Stout Jr., May 3 Mailbag

We did some research only to conclude that no one really knew how many colors grace the state flag so we turned to the Delaware Code, the state's final legal authority. We reprint the Mailbag here:

This whole thing started way back last summer when we discovered Delaware's was the most expensive flag of the 50 states, namely because it has so many more colors than any other, each of which requires a separate silk-screening.
Rechecking our statistics, we find Gov. Russell W. Peterson's office in Wilmington, after a color by color count, places the total at 12 but really only 11 if you don't count the fringe.
The [Delaware Public] Archives in Dover says the total is 16, according to the Delaware Code, Title 29, Sec. 506.
The Department of Community Affairs within the Division of Economic Development says there "are possibly" 12 colors.
Bob Stout said we were wrong at 17; he feels there are far fewer than that.
We've read the Delaware law and by our newest calculations, we count 14 colors. To avoid further dispute, we abstract from the law which calls for a flag with a background of Colonial Blue surrounding a diamond of buff in which is placed the Coat of Arms of Delaware.

C-RATIONS OR ROAST BEEF? Mess hall menus provided plenty of food for thought. Lighter fare included this officer's comments on victuals in Vietnam.

"In the Dec. 30 [1970] issue of *The Morning News,* there was an article on page 23 entitled 'I'll Never Cook Again After This,' and it took some shots at 'lifers.' I passed it around the company and everyone got a big laugh out of it. The part that said enlisted men never complain about the chow has got to be the biggest put-on since the Trojan Horse…. A poor meal in our mess hall incurs my wrath because my men deserve the best and not because I personally don't like it. The lifers complain because they have been out in the field eating cold C-rations with the troops and expect a little more for their people than greasy eggs and cold sausage.

I had better close for now and head for the mess hall. We are on a fire support base for 4 days and the chow at our mess is good. But I'll complain until it is perfect because my troops deserve steaks and lobsters, because the American GI is the greatest in the world and I'm proud of my company and each man."
Capt. William E. Ferguson, Jan. 21

A Navy cook, a frequent writer to the Mailbag in 1969, stirred the pot on the food issue from Pearl Harbor.

"We got back from Vietnam this past September so maybe I shouldn't be writing to you, but I saw an article in the Feb. 3 column that I don't understand. You asked any cooks to write their feelings about military cooking, so here goes.

I'm a cook aboard the USS *Joseph Strauss* (DDG-16), home-ported in Pearl Harbor, Hawaii. A lot of the guys complain about the food, roast beef all the time not enough, etc. Well as a cook, all I can do is cook it. They don't realize that we only have $1.52 to feed each man on per day. Also, we cooks don't have the say over how much food is broken out to be cooked.

So in other words, if the men want steak and lobster every day, they better get busy and write somebody high up and stop bugging the cooks. After all, we have our problems also."
Navy Petty Officer 3rd Class Edward F. Blest, Feb. 17

One serviceman, who took such delight in the yo-yo he received in one of his bennie boxes, offered the best recipe for a repast when he wrote.

"Our Thanksgiving was somewhat okay. We had a halfway good meal, but I still [would] rather have been home with my wife and family."
Army Spc. Robert D. Coxe, Nov. 25

Servicemen enjoy a few beers in their former mess hall, which had been destoyed by one of the many monsoons that ripped through Vietnam in 1971.

"WE'RE STILL GETTING OUR BUILDING REPAIRED FOLLOWING TYPHOON HESTER," ARMY SPC. CARLTON "BUDDY" KING III WROTE ON NOVEMBER 29.
Typhoon Hester moved through the South China Sea and struck central Vietnam on October 23, with winds reaching a peak of 100 mph. The category 2 cyclone caused heavy damage to both Vietnamese and Americans, killing 85 Vietnamese and three Americans. Each typhoon brought war to a virtual standstill as the hard wind and rain felled trees, unroofed scores of buildings, cut power, flooded areas, and in a few cases, created powerful mudslides resulting in fatalaties.

In 1971, 34 tropical storms formed in the western Pacific and 24 reached typhoon intensity, of which six reached super typhoon strength. The final and strongest typhoon of the season, Irma, reached a peak intensity of 180 mph on November 11. Fortunately, the Category 5 storm remained at sea, affecting only shipping and causing minor damage to the islands of the West Pacific. At the time, the typhoon held the record for the fastest intensification in a 24-hour period.

Complaints about the monsoon season were common but we were informed that getting acclimated to what seemed to be a perpetual summer could be a challenge as well. "As everyone says, it's hot over here," wrote Sgt. Robert V. "Vance" Wilson from Phu Cat. "I thought it was hot when I was stationed in America but this place definitely takes first prize."

Typhoons wreaked havoc throughout Vietnam, ripping apart scores of buildings (above). Earthen berms fabricate a patchwork of terraced rice paddies near Chu Lai.

Others added more information.

"We are now going into the hot season and it is starting to climb into the 90s every day. At night if there is a breeze blowing, it isn't too bad. But without the breeze and no air conditioning you sort of swelter. But I hope to rectify the air conditioning problem before too long. Then get a good night's rest."
Air Force Master Sgt. James T. Joyce at Phan Rang Air Base, Feb. 25

"It's starting to get pretty hot over here now so water will be a big problem. We really look forward to resupply day. They bring out hot chow, sodas and beer along with our C-rations and ammo. I'll say one thing about Vietnam, it will really make you appreciate America and the things you have a lot more."
Army Pfc. Richard H. Volk, March 17 Mailbag

"Well, the temp has been in the near 90s to 95 the past two and a half weeks. In March here it's like June, July and August in the states (hot). But it won't be long now before I'll leave here. Only 37 more days."
Marine Cpl. Art Davis, April 5 Mailbag

"As soon as I get another camera, I'll send you a picture of my famous red, white and blue hooch, the flag over it and the only Delawarean on Firebase Nancy. If possible, could you send me a new flag due to the fact that mine is faded white since Capt. Paul Lovett had it before I did. That hot sun is murder."
Army Spc. Francis M. Jornlin II, Dec. 10

Taking his leave, Army Sgt. Crouse accepts his farewell gift from the 571st Medical Detachment in Da Nang. Army Spc. Frank Bohrmann (opposite), a crew chief with the 571st, relaxes at the airfield.

THOSE CAREER MILITARY MEN KNOWN AS "LIFERS" OFTEN TOOK A HIT FROM THE YOUNGER ENLISTED MEN AND DRAFTEES. These servicemen were pretty fired up when they wrote.

"**Well, it's been a long time since I've written to you.** I wouldn't have written now, but I feel that it is necessary. I've been in country for almost 8 months and it's getting worse every day. I don't mean the enemy and I don't mean Vietnam itself, what I'm talking about is the lifers who are in charge of us.

As you know, this is supposed to be a combat zone but if you ever came over here, you would think you were still in the states. I'll give you a few examples of what I mean.

We recently, here at Landing Zone Cindy, took a couple of mortars that were launched by NVA, who aren't very good at hitting their targets, lucky for us. Well, that same morning, our colonel had us out in our perimeter policing up cigarette butts. How would you like to go out there and do that knowing that there could be a NVA sniper out there waiting for you? This is just one of the small things that they do.

I would like to tell you of the biggest one they have ever pulled off yet. We have bunkers on our perimeter; now in these bunkers, you have a 79 grenade launcher [the M-79, a single-shot, shoulder-fired weapon that fires 40-mm grenades, nicknamed 'Thumper' for its distinctive discharge sound], a machine gun and your M-16 rifle, plus all the ammunition for these weapons. Well, today the colonel said that we have to turn in all our 79 ammunition that we have in our bunkers to our central place on the LZ. In other words, if we get hit, we don't have any 79 ammo. We would have to run all over the LZ to get ammo while mortars are coming in.

I feel that they're really trying to get rid of us. What would you think if you were over here? I hope a lot of people read this and if you care about any of us over here, write and tell your congressman or anyone else that you think would do some good. Remember someone you know may come over here sometime!

P.S. I hope you will print this as soon as possible. If there is a way, can you put something on the front page so everyone will get to read this? I'll leave it up to you. Oh, and can you put the congressman's name and address in the paper?"
Army Pfc. Anthony J. Colicchio, Feb. 28

"**I haven't had anything to say really, but here I am in Vietnam and I have been scheduled to march in a parade.** To me, this is very silly and idiotic. Why of all places do we have to march in a parade? I'm here supporting a mission and that doesn't involve marching in a parade.

Better yet, we are marching on the flight line. When we get hit that is one of the main targets. Why should we have to take a ridiculous chance just because our base commander is leaving and he wants a parade?

There are quite a few other people over here who are asking the same question. I really don't mind marching but why in a combat zone? To me, this is out and out stupidity. It's like asking Charlie, or rather daring him, to hit us."
Air Force Airman 1st Class Thomas F. Scott, May 19 Mailbag

This sergeant played devil's advocate in his letter.

"**I enjoy receiving your newspaper and especially enjoy reading your column, and so I suppose I'll take a crack at 'sounding off.'**

Freedom and equality for all! Surely this statement summarizes the desires of many during this century. And rightly so for everyone wishes to acquire the two.

But in this quest for true freedom and equality for all, some groups are being forgotten. One is the military.

Upon reading a newspaper, one discovers that certain individuals of the military are the center of jokes, cartoons and editorials. Even their personal lives are attacked. For them there is no freedom of privacy. ROTC students are being ridiculed by fellow classmates and now ROTC has been eliminated by many colleges. Students who desire ROTC are no longer free to make a choice concerning attendance.

The military in its entirety is receiving discrimination. Today our military is attempting to compete with industry for manpower. However, certain individuals and groups attempt to thwart recruiting efforts on campus by the military. No one seems to mind General Motors or Coca-Cola.

In this time of our quest, let not others lose so we may gain. If we are sincere in this desire, then let it be for everyone. But then, is it sincerely for everyone that we seek these gains?"
Army Staff Sgt. Roy C. Thornton, March 26

THE MAILBAG RECEIVED NEWS ON A VARIETY OF SUBJECTS.
Some servicemen wrote in with a few words about the column.

"**I only wish I could do more than just say THANK YOU for the paper.** A person back in the states just doesn't know how much your paper helps a man over here in Vietnam."
Army Spc. James R. Wright, Feb. 14

"**I wrote to ask if it would be possible to send the Monday, Wednesday and Friday editions of the paper to me regularly.** I'm not sure how the system works, but the Tuesday, Thursday and Saturday editions do not seem to carry your column.

The column of yours carries interest here to even Californians who read [The Morning] News after I'm finished. I like it because some familiar names have popped up in it. I've got many classmates here in Vietnam who attended [the University of] Delaware with me. I guess I'm wondering if they are located near me in Tay Ninh Province."
Army 1st Lt. Robert A. Nowaczyk, Feb. 15

"**Please put my name back on your mailing list.** I had really enjoyed getting *The Morning News* on my two previous trips to Vietnam. Now, after a wonderful 30-day leave, I'm on my way back to the same duty station in Ben Luc, this time for six months. I expect to be stateside again in November. Thank you for the newspaper and I also thank all those concerned for the wonderful SOS packages I've been receiving. It's nice to know people at home care."
Navy Petty Officer 3rd Class Lawrence S. Kazimir, May 14 Mailbag

One serviceman notified us that he extended his tour in Vietnam.

"**Well, I thought I should be getting another letter off 'cause a lot has been happening here.** I was going to be home in April but I have extended my tour over here another 7 months…. Being no fool, the only reason I extended was to get an early out of the Navy. I should be able to get 9 months knocked off my 4 years. I will trade 7 months here for 16 months somewhere else anytime."
Navy Petty Officer 3rd Class James R. MacSorley III, April 2

Another wrote about his R&R and a music festival.

"**I was home from Dec. 17-Jan. 19.** Sorry I didn't get a chance to stop in. Leave was OK but coming back here was a drag. The curfew here in Saigon has been raised from 10 p.m. to 1 a.m. effective April 1. R&R to Hawaii for June. My first R&R was to Sydney. I loved Sydney, especially the friendly people. No views on the Laotian operations, etc. since I'm in a sensitive spot here at CICV…. *Hoa Binh* (PEACE)."
Army Spc. Robert P. Stout Jr. in Saigon, March 30

"**I went to an International Pop Festival held here in Saigon on May 29.** Great bands entertained the large crowd. The bands were from the U.S., Philippines, Korea, Vietnam, Australia, etc. It was sort of like a small-scale Vietnamese 'Woodstock.' I am enclosing a card advertising the festival. Another souvenir for your collection."
Army Spc. Robert P. Stout Jr. in Saigon, June 20

Entertainment and down-time were high notes for servicemen in the war zone (opposite). Bands frequently played at the Officers Club in Da Nang. Army Spc. Robert P. Stout Jr. sent this card promoting an International Pop Festival in Saigon.

March 30, 1971

Dear Nancy,
It's been ... since I've written ... real busy ... flying.

I wa... Jan 19. ... a chan... was O... here ...

Count those colors again. Maybe I have ... flag hangin ... desk. It ... have 17 col ... R+R ... June. My 1st ... I loved Sy... friendly pe...

has boxes from SOS-Vietnam ... to Da... they only send them ... e tour (12 months)? ... for me, I... please ...
It's a...
peop...
an...
pe...
vie...
sin...
he...
...on.

LẦN ĐẦU TIÊN TẠI Á-CHÂU
THE FIRST TIME IN ASIA
Ngày Nhạc Trẻ Quốc-T...
International Pop Festi...
• Cuộc đua tài giữa những ban nhạc...
  Đại Hàn, THQG, Việt Nam...
  A Musical competion between well-know...
• Cuộc trình diễn thời trang đánh c...
  theo kiểu y phục đẹp, lạ, độc đáo ...
  và những Phần thưởng giá trị kh...
  All the spectators can participate in the...
  medals, etc....
• Nơi trình diễn được dựng lầu...
  ảnh hưởng.
  Arrangements will be made to preve...

29-5-1971
TẠI SÂN VẬN ĐỘNG HOA LƯ
Từ 9 giờ đến 18 giờ

Đại lộ Thống Nhứt
Đường Hồng Thập Tự
Đường Đinh Tiên Hoàng
Phan Đình Phùng

Đường Đinh Tiên Hoàng
SÂN HOA LƯ

HOALU Stadium 2 Đinh Tiên Hoàng St, Saigon

'NH
EACE)

THE MAILBAG TOOK PRIDE IN HELPING SERVICEMEN FIND ANSWERS TO THEIR QUESTIONS. Occasionally in the column, we showcased matters of interest both to our troops and to our readers at home. On January 25, we printed the daunting POW experiences of Air Force Col. Norris M. Overly, neither a Delawarean nor in service in Vietnam when the Mailbag was published. After we listened to his compelling remarks to relatives of POWs in Philadelphia, we felt they warranted repeating.

Imprisoned in the "Hanoi Hilton," the old French POW camp in North Vietnam's capital, he discussed his five-month ordeal that began after he was shot down during a night reconnaissance mission, his eleventh flight over North Vietnam, on September 11, 1967, near Dong Hoi.

When he arrived at the POW camp, he was stripped of his uniform, shaved and issued black pajamas. He spent the next 24 hours being interrogated. He said he and the other prisoners were treated like criminals. The North Vietnamese, he added, did not abide by the Geneva Convention concerning humane treatment of captives because the conflict was not a declared war.

Placed in stocks for 29 days and not allowed to move, Overly, then a major, said had he not been in such good physical condition, he would not have survived the physical abuse. His only sustenance was watery soup and bread. His weight plummeted from 155 to 115 pounds, then stabilized at 135.

More alarming than his physical decline was his mental decline. Overly said he felt forgotten while he vegetated in prison and described his captivity as a Pavlov dog-like existence. He said he was a "very bitter man" during his first two weeks of capture. "It was hell and I was making it a worse hell for myself." After praying, Overly said he found new strength. "I knew at that point, I could make it, that I could get through it."

When he was shot down, Overly, then a major, said he was a "very bitter man" for his first two weeks of capture. "It was hell, and I was making it a worse hell for myself." Overly said he got down on his knees and prayed. Excerpt from the Jan. 25 Mailbag

At the time of his talk, the highly decorated career airman was a student at the National War College at Fort McNair in Washington, D.C. He spoke about his POW experiences on his own time. "This is a peoples' war," he told this audience. "Everyone is involved. Men. Women. Children."

The Mailbag strived to be informative and helpful. "I have just begun receiving *The Morning News* and happened to run across your column. You mentioned some benefits Del. GI's receive if they are aware of them. I was wondering if you could fill me in on this information?" Army Spc. John W. Hopper asked in his May 16 letter.

In late September, we printed a timetable for veteran benefits that had recently been released from Aberdeen Proving Gound's information office in Maryland. As the young men returned stateside and began to look for jobs, continue their education or cope with mental and physical service-connected illnesses, they inquired about veterans benefits. Educational benefits, job training, compensation and medical care were offered in the program. GIs had up to one year to convert their group life insurance without exam (if totally disabled), file for dental care, and receive employment compensation. Eight years were allotted for use of all GI education and training entitlements. There was no time limit to obtain a GI home loan, compensation for injury or disease, obtain VA hospital care or employment assistance and job training.

In October, 1st Lt. Douglas A. Smarte responded to the article. "Your Sept. 24 column which included information about VA benefits was particularly educating." He continued, "The article answered many questions and I'm sure many First Staters will be able to take advantage of their benefits quicker and with less confusion after having read the article."

After their interrogations, enemy prisoners in this South Vietnamese holding cell in Phan Thiet await relocation. Army Spc. Richard Glazier, an intelligence analyst with Advisory Team 37, interrogated more than 100 captives.

LEAVING VIETNAM COULDN'T HAPPEN SOON ENOUGH FOR MOST SERVICEMEN. Mailbag readers enjoyed the jubilation they expressed over homecomings. Catch the spirit in this officer's brief message, with its nod to Motown.

"STOP! In the Name of Love!

STATE OF MIND: Elated

REASON STATED: ETS 3 June or, in other words, Baby, I'm comin' home!

Have really appreciated a state that gives a damn about its people and the paper, the goodie boxes from Red Lion Church and the flag. So, without further ado, this is Jay Goodley in Saigon digging you."
Army 1st Lt. Jay Goodley, May 14

Others, perhaps not quite as enthusiastic as Jay, also wrote their glad tidings.

"Just a note to let you know that I have an early out from Vietnam and will be returning on the 8th of May. My new assignment will be at the U.S. Navy Autodin Switching Center, Hancock Air Force Base, Syracuse, N.Y. A recent arrival to our office at HQ USARV is Staff Sgt. Ronald K. Salisbury, who is from Dover."
Army Lt. Col. Richard C. Everts, May 7

"I am writing to let you know that I am finally getting short. I didn't think the time would ever come but at last it is getting close."
Army Spc. Charles Sparpaglione, June 7 Mailbag

"Should arrive back in Seaford (my home) the last week of June. It's been an interesting year here at Pleiku, but I'm glad it's over."
Air Force Sgt. Winfield H. Gray, June 23 Mailbag

"Now that I have reached the happiest part of my military career, the part of getting short, you can cancel my *Morning News* subscription. I am scheduled to depart from Vietnam June 27th and ETS shortly after that.

By the way, while canceling my subscription, could you possibly start one up for Spc. Jerome Lynch from Wilmington? Just send it to my old address. He was always glad to see me get a paper because he knew he would be reading it soon.

Also, if I may, I would like to thank all of the people in Delaware who are showing they care [and] the SOS Vietnam group from Bear for their support…. See you soon."
Army Spc. John J. Dempsey, June 19

"On July 1st, after 8 months in the field with Battery C, I was lucky to be chosen for a new job with Headquarters and Headquarters Battery in Phu Loi. I was the executive officer for 'Charlie' and now I have a similar position in HHB but with a little different mission…. Also, I expect to be home in late August or early September."
Army 1st Lt. Robert A. Nowaczyk, July 4

"I would like to thank you and all Delawareans very much for contributing time and money to send me packages and holiday greetings and make my stay in Nam a little happier. I'd also like to say that I'm proud to do my part in serving this great nation of ours. P.S.: Short!"
Army Spc. Tony V. Eoppolo in Quang Tri, July 31

"I will be home on Sept. 3rd and I can put my eighteen-month tour in one sentence: We have done all we can for these people and only they themselves can end the war now."
Army Spc. T.E. "Ted" Elisee in Saigon, Aug. 7

"Due to a change in my military obligation, I will be departing sunny and wet Vietnam on 26 September. Please do not mention my early return in your column until late October. My mother is not expecting me until early November and I want to surprise her."
Army Lt. Joseph L. Ignatowski, Aug. 30

"My next assignment is Fort Lee, Virginia. During my interim 30-day leave, I expect to sightsee from California to Georgia. Am sure I now have a much better appreciation for the good ole U.S. of A."
Army Capt. Rodney A. Brice, Sept. 19

"Well, after 18 months, I'm finally going to leave Vietnam! I'll be leaving the 28th of this month. I'm coming home to get married, following which my new wife and I will be going to Europe for a year!"
Air Force Sgt. James D. Buckland, Oct. 6

"Just a few lines to tell you, the paper, and SOS Vietnam that I'm on my way home. To say I'm glad to be leaving would be an understatement and after I'm almost finished my second tour I hope to never come back…. To all of you who have stood behind us … and who have been so wonderful I send my deepest appreciation and thanks."
Army Sgt. 1st Class Eugene F. Nittinger, Oct. 17

"Well, this should be my last letter from Vietnam. I will be leaving here on the 15th of November for Long Beach, California, to get processed out of the Navy. It will be great to be a civilian again."
Navy Petty Officer 3rd Class James R. MacSorley III, Nov. 3

"I'm getting ready to pack my bags and leave here for good. I just wish everyone else could do the same. I plan on being home around the 9th of February…. Everything here is fine, the number of troops here are less than they were three months ago, which I am very glad to see."
Navy Petty Officer 3rd Class Harry G. Porter, Nov. 23

"Hope your holidays are as good as mine are going to be. I'm leaving the 'Nam' on the 18th and, to be sure, I am going to enjoy the holiday season. My thanks go out to you and the troops at the 'Orange Street spread' [News-Journal Co.] and to all who were backing the SOS program for having made my tour just that much easier to take."
Army Spc. John J. Monaghan Jr., Dec. 13 Mailbag

Another of our regular correspondents took a few minutes to write the Mailbag after he no longer had a military prefix.

"**I ETS'd five days ago – Nov. 3rd – at Oakland Army Base.** It feels good to be out of the "Green Machine" and back to the states, even Delaware. The weather is a bit too cold but I'll try to fight it.

Let's hope President Nixon has everyone else out of S.E. Asia soon. Many will come home for Christmas but they'll return after their leave. However, Bob Hope will be there again to cheer everyone up. I'll really hate to miss him!"
Robert P. Stout Jr., Nov. 8

And one serviceman wrote with more than a touch of envy.

Actively against the war before he joined the Air Force, Sgt. Daniel P. Stokes offered candid commentary from Vietnam.

"**It seems as if everyone else in the column was 'short.'** I am, and will be for a while, a 'new boy' in country. My DEROS doesn't roll around 'til the 2nd of April 1972."
Army Spc. John W. Hopper, May 16

The Mailbag's best news of 1971 was that our troops were coming home. The New-Journal's annual June audit counted 250 free subscriptions winging to Delaware servicemen in Vietnam, down from a high of 773 in March 1968. By mid-September, subscriptions had dropped to 173.

Numbers also were down for SOS Vietnam, the volunteer organization that provided a monthly bennie box to every Delaware serviceman in the combat zone. Their May count was 312, a new low for the year and, by August, the number plummeted to 180.

The Mailbag celebrated its third anniversary in May and applauded First Staters in uniform who by then had penned 725 letters expressing their views, humor and gripes. But we, too, were downsizing. In July, due to the decreasing volume of mail from Delawareans serving in Vietnam, the Mailbag dropped from three to two columns a week.

Gov. Russell W. Peterson on April 9, Good Friday, asked all Delaware residents to observe a minute of silence at 3:15 p.m. as a tribute to prisoners of war and those missing in action. He also designated May 1 SOS Vietnam Day and on November 16 signed into law a bill authorizing $500,000 to continue payments of bonuses to Vietnam veterans.

Despite the encouraging news of troop withdrawals and the progress of Vietnamization, my friend, Air Force Sgt. Daniel P. Stokes, wrote a provocative letter from Da Nang Air Base.

"**The President has said that he will end the war.** He or anyone else will not end this war. He may end the United States' involvement here, but this is an internal conflict where the only feasible remedy is within the [Vietnamese] people.

The majority of the Vietnamese would be happy if we would just leave them alone. Before our involvement, they were happy eating their fish and growing their rice.

We, the Americans, had no right appointing ourselves the watchdogs of the World. In my estimation, we are nothing more than a bunch of money-hungry parasites exploiting the underdeveloped nations of the World [taking] from them anything we can.

In the case of Vietnam, we have taken their freedom. After all, it was our bombs, our Calleys and our superior attitudes towards these people that have driven many of them to turn toward [North Vietnam]. Perhaps not physically but mentally. How they have put up with the harassment by GIs and some of their own people is beyond me.

There was a time not so long ago when I would get goose bumps and have a feeling of elation when I heard the National Anthem. It's gone now.

If I knew before I came here what I know now…. As somebody once said, "War is a symptom of man's failure as a thinking animal."
Air Force Sgt. Daniel P. Stokes, Sept. 9 Mailbag

1971 – YEAR IN REVIEW

JANUARY 6
Secretary of Defense Melvin R. Laird announces Vietnamization is well ahead of schedule and U.S. combat missions in Vietnam will end the following summer.

MARCH 24
The Defense Department says the North Vietnamese have started to move artillery supplied by the Soviets to the western end of the DMZ.

MARCH 29
Army Lt. William L. Calley, Jr. convicted of murder for the My Lai massacre.

APRIL 7
President Richard M. Nixon announces more troop cutbacks and says Americans will leave Vietnam by June 30.

MAY 12
The last major Marine offensive, Operation Imperial Lake, ends with 305 enemy killed and the loss of 24 marines.

JUNE 13
Pentagon Papers published in *The New York Times*.

JUNE 21
U.S. military strength in Vietnam stands at 244,900.

JULY 12
With continued withdrawals, U.S. military strength drops to 236,000.

OCTOBER 3
Amid protests and violence, Thieu is re-elected to another four-year term as South Vietnam's president.

NOVEMBER 26
Nixon, frustrated by the stalled Paris peace talks, orders the Air Force and Navy to resume bombing North Vietnam.

NOVEMBER 29
North Vietnam signs an agreement with the Soviets for economic and military assistance.

DECEMBER 31
U.S. troops in Vietnam number 156,800. More than 50,000 Americans have been killed in the undeclared war.

MENT OF THE ARMY
TH COMBAT AVIATION BATTALION
O San Francisco 96266
"FIRST IN VIETNAM"

MENT OF THE ARMY
INFORMATION OFFICE
8TH ENGINEER BATTALION (C)(A)
RANCISCO 96353

WILMINGTON
WILMINGTON
.S.A.

WARHAWK

BATTLE
E EFFICIENCY

QUADRON 97
E OFFICE
601

PEACE HELL
BOMB HANOI

COMBAT ZONE
Free

COMBAT ZONE

Yours Truly,
Frank J. Ransley

Nancy Lynch
The News Journal Co
ington, Delaware
19899

VIA AIR MAIL
CORREO AEREO
PAR AVION

FREE

Sorley III USN
rity, Saigon
rsonnel
6621

y's Vietnam
urnal Co
nge St
Delaware 19899

ficer, presented
to CPT Gibson.
in the Flag Detail were
aptain James R. Bowies,
Command Sergeant Major
William E. Ford, Sergeant First
Class David Emory, Sergeant

coordinating fire for 14 105s, six
155s and one 175. The
combined artillery expended
32,471 rounds and took 1,838
enemy lives in support of the
(Continued On Page 6)

Despite increased U.S. troop withdrawals, the war raged on throughout Vietnam, much of it from fortified mountaintops, like this one near Phu Bai. The Army used its nimble light observation helicopter to sniff out an often-nimbler enemy. Many LOHs, including this one (opposite), were named by their crews.

1972

THE TIDE FINALLY WAS TURNING. AFTER 11 WRENCHING YEARS, PEACE SEEMED WITHIN GRASP IN 1972 AS MORE AND MORE U.S. UNITS STOOD DOWN AND TROOPS RETURNED FROM VIETNAM AT UNPRECEDENTED LEVELS. AMERICA'S LONGEST WAR, ITS FIRST UNDECLARED WAR, WAS ABOUT TO BECOME HISTORY. BY MIDYEAR, 48,000 U.S. TROOPS WERE BASED IN VIETNAM, THE LOWEST NUMBER SINCE APRIL 1965, AND THOUSANDS MORE WERE EXITING EVERY MONTH. ON AUGUST 11, THE ARMY'S U.S. COMMAND ANNOUNCED THE PULLOUT FROM FIELD DUTY OF THE 3RD BATTALION, 21ST INFANTRY, THE LAST OF 112 BATTALIONS IN SOUTH VIETNAM.

Earlier in the year, Secretary of Defense Melvin R. Laird said that no more than 50,000 men would be drafted in 1972, half as many as in 1971 and the lowest figure since before the Korean War. President Nixon trumped that news in August by announcing the draft would end altogether on July 1, 1973.

Achieving this longtime goal, Nixon's advisers believed, compensated for his failure to end the conflict while bolstering his image with 25 million young people eligible to vote in their first presidential election.

Nixon also ordered troop strength in Vietnam reduced to 39,000 by September 1, a figure that contrasted starkly with the more than 540,000 servicemen in the combat zone in January 1969, when he took office. On October 26, Henry Kissinger, Nixon's assistant for national security affairs, announced "peace is at hand." By late November, 31,000 U.S. troops remained in Vietnam, the lowest number in more than seven years.

Delaware servicemen were coming home too. By June, The News-Journal was sending fewer than 100 free daily papers to Delaware servicemen in the combat zone, down from a high of 773 in 1968. By December, fewer than 50 Delawareans were receiving the newspaper.

Delaware had four losses, but only two were confirmed at the time: Air Force Tech. Sgt. Donald R. Hoskins of Dover on April 26 and Air Force Maj. Gerald Francis Ayres of New Castle on June 18. Marine Capt. Larry F. Potts of Smyrna was shot down April 7, declared an MIA and later died in a POW camp. Although his remains were never recovered, he was officially classified as a KIA several years later. Air Force Col. Paul O. Meder of Dover was shot down in Laos on December 21. Initially listed as an MIA, his partial remains were recovered in 1985 and he was laid to rest in Arlington National Cemetery.

Troop withdrawals and talk of peace eclipsed the nation's other news, which included Nixon's trailblazing trip to China in February, a failed assassination attempt on Alabama Gov. George C. Wallace in Laurel, Maryland, in May, the bungled burglary of the Democratic National Committee's Watergate headquarters by Nixon campaign operatives in June and re-election of the Nixon-Spiro Agnew ticket in November with 61 percent of the popular vote.

In Delaware, Republican Russell W. Peterson became a one-term governor, narrowly defeated by Democrat Sherman W. Tribbitt, while an outspoken, 29-year-old Wilmington Democrat, Joseph R. Biden Jr., upset august Republican J. Caleb Boggs for a seat in the U.S. Senate.

Delawareans, like all Americans, were buoyed by the tentative wave of hope for war's end. Despite their philosophical differences concerning the conflict, everyone was tired of the discord that had polarized them for more than a decade.

VIETNAM, A COUNTRY NO LARGER THAN THE STATE OF WASHINGTON, HAD MONOPOLIZED A GENERATION OF YOUNG AMERICANS, DEFERRING THEIR DREAMS AND DASHING THEIR FUTURES. Hundreds of thousands of WIAs and KIAs later, a perennially elusive exit now seemed possible. Our servicemen's enthusiasm for leaving the combat zone was palpable.

"I'm finally on my way home. And is it ever a great feeling," wrote Army Spc. Lawrence B. Buchert on February 29. "It's somewhat like a dream come true. I've only spent eleven months here, but that's far too many. I received a 30-day drop and, hopefully, if I ever finish cleaning today, I'll be going to the replacement station tomorrow. Gosh, it seems like everyone's going home and everywhere I go there's a line to wait in. But being I'm coming home, I really don't mind."

Another soldier shared his enthusiasm:

"April 3 I'll be homeward bound for the states. Boy, I sure can't wait!
After I ETS out of Oakland, Calif., I'll be coming home to Delaware. It's really going to be great to be home with my wife, family and friends."
Army Spc. Robert D. Coxe Jr., March 8

And one sailor was so excited about his homecoming he wrote the Mailbag at 2:30 a.m.

"Everyone aboard the *Enterprise* is especially happy. Reason being, tomorrow at 1300 hours, we pull into San Francisco – HOME.
It's been a long and tiresome nine months. There have been a few joys and a few heartbreaks. But I want to express my gratitude to all the wonderful people who have taken their time to send us those boxes of goodies. Also, for the state flag and sticker.
I'm proud to be a First Stater, even though there are only four or five of us aboard this floating city."
Navy Petty Officer 3rd Class Charles E. Crick Jr. aboard the USS Enterprise, Feb. 11

For all the euphoria expressed by those leaving Vietnam, though, one serviceman reminded us the war was not over.

"We are keeping busy because of all the units standing down. The way everything is looking, Long Binh depot will be the last one in Vietnam…. Without people like you I think we'd be forgotten. People have to realize there's still a war going on over here. People are still fighting and dying over here."
Army Spc. Charles J. Backus in Long Binh, Feb. 23

Rustic hooches outside Da Nang dramatized the hardscrabble existence of most South Vietnamese.

Runway 17 at Marble Mountain Army Airfield (opposite) near Da Nang was one of the busiest during the war. Marines had pulled out of Da Nang by 1972 and left the facility to the Army. South Vietnamese ARVN soldiers carried two-sided identification cards like the one shown here. The ever-popular state flag got a hand or two from Army Spc. Francis M. Jornlin II at Firebase Nancy while Navy Petty Officer 3rd Class Alan Marc Solomon flew his from the mast of the USS *Constellation*.

Others filed differing takes on the conflict.

"**Things are pretty much the same.** We're working very hard to keep from becoming too bored. Christmas sort of passed right along with the rest of the month. If it weren't for all the great folks who sent me cards, and again for SOS Vietnam, I wouldn't have realized Christmas was even around."
Army 1st Lt. Kenneth D. Warner, Jan. 2

"**I'm stationed at a base called Anson.** It's about seven miles from the town of Qui Nhon, which in the past several days has made the headlines due to terrorist attacks. However, we are not bothered much here at the base.

There is also a Korean infantry division here that we are supporting. From what I hear and read in the papers, Americans seem to be getting scarce over here and I hope it won't be long before there won't be any."
Army Spc. Michael Przybylek near Qui Nhon, Jan. 19

"**I am presently flying for an assault helicopter company supporting the ARVNs and Koreans in II Corps.** The weather is in the process of changing from the monsoon season to the dry season. The combination of the improving weather and the Tet season is causing an increase in flying, even with the phasing out of American troops."
Army Lt. William John Downes, Feb. 7

"**I wanted to send you a list of units still in Vietnam but my commanding officer says it's still confidential information.** He may be wrong. I'll check and let you know later.

I'm assigned to the 196th Brigade in the 1st Military Region [I Corps]. We have started to turn in equipment so we should be home around April, I hope.… We recently captured some NVA who were following our patrol. They admitted that they have orders to avoid contact unless they have been fired on. They still manage to lob rockets in every once in a while but then again we still bomb North Vietnam."
Army Spc. Woodrow Wilson Cahall III, Feb. 18 Mailbag

"**Just dropping a line from the Gulf of Tonkin, where lately we've been real busy.** We were pulled out of Hong Kong early in order to make Charlie's New Year's celebration, otherwise known as Tet.

We were still able to contribute greatly to Hong Kong's economy in the five days we did stay and most, but not all, are returning with some booty to show for their expenditures.

The flight deck of the *Constellation* has been a hectic place the last few months. Our planes are flying around 100 sorties a day and our workday runs 14-16 hours. Don't know what I'd do with a normal 8-hour day anymore, but I expect I'd make good use of the time….

Currently we will be involved over here in Nam until the 23rd or 24th of March and then we'll start on our voyage back to stateside with arrival in San Diego scheduled for April 17."
Navy Petty Officer 3rd Class Philip E. Jornlin aboard the USS Constellation, March 24 Mailbag

"Just an unsolicited first-hand report on this offensive. I'd like to say that the real shame is … the poor peasant who has moved from Quang Tri and farther to Da Nang. I don't suspect the news let people know that lots of civilians were killed by the NVA as they tried to flee. It's a real shame to see the road jammed with people going to they don't know where just because the government can't agree on anything. And anyone who says it's our fault just doesn't know what he's talking about."

Army 1st Lt. Kenneth D. Warner near Da Nang, May 19

SOME SERVICEMEN TOOK THE TIME TO REFLECT ON OTHER MATTERS IN THEIR LETTERS. An Air Force sergeant offered his perspective.

"**I want it over as much or more than anyone else but I do not want to leave any POW here when we leave.** I don't think very much of pulling our ground forces out away from our perimeters, leaving the VC and their rockets and mortars 10 miles from base.

I do not think anything in Paris is going to end things here unless we use more force on Hanoi and Haiphong to prove we mean it. I think people are tired of us getting involved in places around the world in every situation and then leaving them and trying to ignore the fact that they are getting killed and wounded daily.

I know that First State servicemen and vets get treated better back home than any others. I think nationwide the serviceman and vet is getting the shaft. To the GI here, the deserter to Canada or Sweden gets more feeling and sympathy and understanding than the returnee with an arm or leg blown off. This, however, is a nation-wide picture and not a Delaware picture…. So, here I am with the 366th TFW [Tactical Fighter Wing] 'Gunfighters' in Rocket City as a quality control inspector working on Phantom fighters, liking the job immensely.

Well, anyhow, the next time you pass Brandywine Park, Delaware Memorial Bridge or Frederica or eat a Penny Hill donut, fight the store crowd at [Wilmington] Dry Goods, think of the ole sarge because he wishes like hell all this was over and he could be doing those things again."

Air Force Technical Sgt. Sam Jenkins in Da Nang, March 8

"**I don't have much to say about politics or the war except I don't like it here.** I think this war is useless and I want to come home. Also, I'm confused about what is happening at home. I've heard that they told everyone there are no ground combat troops over here. I guess since you work with the newspaper you would know. I'm a grunt now because my artillery unit stood down and we went to the bush. If they're lying to the public, I think they should know. Also, a lot of times they twist the words around so it sounds like something else. If so, I'd appreciate it if you told the people exactly what is going on."

Army Spc. Gary Ford, July 15

A minister, who had served with the Army Chaplain's Corps since 1966, wrote about spending time on the road.

"**I too have felt the impact of the drawdown.** I am now 1st Signal Brigade Staff Chaplain. 1st Signal Brigade has communication responsibility for all of Vietnam and Thailand. Although I live here at Long Binh, I will be traveling all over Vietnam and Thailand visiting the chaplains and men of this brigade."

Army Chaplain Charles D. Burge at Long Binh, May 5

Intrigued by the presence of U.S. troops in their country, South Vietnamese young-sters (opposite) gathered in their rural village during a medical civic action program, known as a MEDCAP operation. Many servicemen carried an ammo pouch or wallet which ensured they had an extra two rounds of .357 or .38 bullets.

One of my Army friends, who was awarded the Bronze Star as a rifleman assigned to the 1st Cavalry Division (Airmobile) near Bien Hoa, brought Mailbag readers up to date.

"**The first five months over here I spent in the bush about 35 miles northeast of Saigon**. I was then one of those folks who attempted to keep the enemy from overwhelming Saigon, Bien Hoa and Long Binh. And whether people there realize it or not, there are still people out pounding the bushes.

At present, I'm an armorer for Bravo Company, 2nd Battalion, 5th Cavalry, 1st Air Cavalry Division, one of our last combat units. I ensure that machine guns, rifles, etc. are in working order for those who must still go into the jungles.

I'm in Bien Hoa right now and am living rather comfortably compared to when I dwelt in a hammock and poncho a few months ago. Well, thought I'd inform you that the war at present is somewhat different from what some people think."
Army Sgt. Matthew D. Mason III in Bien Hoa, Feb. 19

We heard from this marine only once, when he was stationed on the fringes of Vietnam.

"**Sorry I haven't written up to now.** I finally found time to write and let the people know a little bit about what's going on. I'm not in Vietnam for one thing, nor am I in the Army.

I'm in the Marine Corps and I'm now stationed in Nam Phong, Thailand. That rings a bell, doesn't it? I thought it would. The Marines landed here on May 21, 1972.

There was a total of about 405 U.S. Marines here at one time. We were all here by June 19. It cost the U.S. government approximately $7 million to get us all to Nam Phong.

Some marines came here by plane while some, including myself, came to Nam Phong by ship (USS *Mobile*). We landed at the port city of Ban Sattahip and from there we took buses to Nam Phong for a total of about seven days by ship and one day by bus.

I was recently stationed in Okinawa. At the present time (since we've been here), we're living in tents and sleeping on cots with rubber air mattresses. Our showers are outside and we have outhouses for our bathrooms. We're in the middle of nowhere while the Army and Air Force are living in barracks and their bases are near cities.

They have liberty every night while we have to wait from eight to 12 days in between for ours. We also have a group of the Navy (Seabees) here with us. They have been doing an outstanding job of making this place a little more comfortable for us.

Our main mission is to support our own Marine Air Wing that goes on bombing missions in Vietnam. We are approximately 350-400 miles from Bangkok and 80 miles from Laos.

P.S. I forgot to tell you that the government of Thailand does not like the idea of Marines being in Thailand."
Marine Pfc. Garry J. Morengo in Nam Phong, Thailand, Sept. 1 Mailbag

ALTHOUGH THE MAILBAG PRIMARILY FEATURED CORRE-SPONDENCE FROM OUR TROOPS, THE COLUMN OCCASION-ALLY SUPPLEMENTED INFORMATION PROVIDED BY THE SERVICEMEN. Our series on Tet, the Vietnamese new year and a period of heightened danger for Americans in country, appeared in the January 24, 28 and 31 columns and was based on a fact sheet provided by the Military Assistance Command Vietnam (MACV).

Tet, celebrated Feb. 15-17 in 1972, is Vietnam's biggest celebration of the year. Chinese in origin, the 3-day event signifies the beginning of the Oriental or lunar new year as well as the advent of spring.

For the Vietnamese, it is a time of solemnity, gaiety and hope, a time to pay homage to ancestors, visit family and friends, observe traditions and to celebrate. Tet is also the time to correct faults, forget past mistakes, pardon others for their offenses and pay debts. To owe money during Tet is considered bad luck. Truly a comprehensive holiday, all Vietnamese give it full observance.

Taboos associated with Tet include:
•Never clean a house during Tet
•Don't borrow fire from a neighbor
•Don't insult others
•Don't show grief
•Don't break any dishes

Months before Tet, businessmen prepare for a stellar selling season. Items in greatest demand are food – not only to eat but also to place on ancestors' altars – clothing, gifts, candies and flowers. Everyone dresses up for the holidays. According to tradition, those who go out on the first day of Tet wearing old clothes admit to the basest form of poverty. Consequently, it is very difficult to get tailoring done just before Tet.

Downtown streets are covered with flowers. Stores, including sidewalk stalls, are decorated. Professional scribes sell scrolls with messages for the Tet season. Art dealers sell symbolic drawings inscribed with words of wisdom and formulas for chasing away evil spirits.

All preparatory events for Tet come to an abrupt halt at noon the day before the start of the holiday. Everyone hurries home to celebrate. Most employees get time off with pay. Many receive bonuses. Streets are quiet on the lunar new year eve as families remain at home to participate in ceremonies. At midnight, firecrackers herald the new year.

A midnight ceremony is held for the good spirits and family ancestors at a candle-lit altar in the open air near the house. After this, the family may go to the pagoda and burn incense and pray for a prosperous new year. They take home a bud from a plant or tree as a symbol of happiness. On Tet morning, special foods are placed on the family altar for the returned ancestors. These meals are repeated twice a day until Tet is over. Then children receive gifts and the family exchanges new year's wishes.

For a visitor, Tet is a fine time to make real friends among the Vietnamese people. A phrase like "Happy Tet" is meaningless. To a man, a proper greeting would be, "I wish you a happy and prosperous new year. Greet a married woman with, "I hope that next year you will have a (or another) boy."

For children up to 15 and all single Vietnamese, a small red envelope has a very special significance. To make a real impression, a visitor should write on it, "Chung chuc tan xuan," which means, "Many wishes for the new spring." Some gifts are taboo, such as medicines, vitamins, sharp objects or anything not new.

Visits are an important part of the Tet celebration and a foreigner should accept invitations to visit whenever possible. Male visitors are considered improperly dressed if they are not wearing a jacket and necktie. If gifts are offered while visiting, accept them. They will likely be rice cake or other delicacies and tea. It would be unpardonably rude to refuse them.

All American military personnel should use military bus transportation during Tet to allow the Vietnamese maximum use of public transportation. In Saigon and some other metropolitan areas, taxi, cycle and pedicab rates can be expected to double during the holiday period.

By observing rules of courtesy and consideration, visitors can enjoy Tet. To the Vietnamese, what a man does during Tet forecasts his actions for the rest of the year.

THE NOVEMBER 27 MAILBAG REPORTED FOUR "FREEDOM TREES" WERE PLANTED EIGHT DAYS EARLIER ON STATE GROUNDS NEAR LEGISLATIVE HALL AND THE HALL OF RECORDS IN DOVER. They were dedicated to Delaware's only POW, Navy Cmdr. Robert B. Doremus of Newark, and the state's three MIAs, Air Force Maj. John M. Martin of Dover, Marine Capt. Larry Fletcher Potts of Smyrna and Marine Gunnery Sgt. Edward Arle Willing of Wilmington.

Cmdr. Doremus eventually returned home safely. According to information compiled from government and private sources, he was the flight officer on an F4B Phantom jet off the USS *Midway* when it was struck by a surface-to-air missile (SAM) over North Vietnam on August 24, 1965. He and the commanding officer, Fred A. Franke, ejected and were captured as soon as they landed in a rice paddy. Soon after the incident, both men were listed as KIAs, but they actually spent the next seven and a half years in a Hanoi prison. They were released after the January 27, 1973 peace accord ended the war and were reclassified as returnees. Cmdr. Doremus retired from the Navy as a captain.

Delaware's three MIAs were later declared killed in action in Vietnam. Capt. Potts and Gunnery Sgt. Willing are named as Delaware dead on the Vietnam Veterans Memorial in Washington, D.C. and are honored with Maj. Martin and 163 others from the state who died in the war on the Vietnam Veterans of America, Delaware Chapter 83 memorial in Wilmington.

Mailbag reader and state worker Elaine di Benedetto of Wilmington contacted us soon after that column's publication to tell us Delaware might have a second POW. Navy Lt. James J. Connell Jr., listed as a POW from California, was born and raised in Wilmington.

The story she related unfolded in the December 4 Mailbag. Jimmy, she said, was her sister-in-law's brother as well as the nephew of Wilmington City Council President William J. McClafferty. Jimmy was the son of the late James J. Connell of Wilmington and Ann Connell, who was living with her daughter and son-in-law, Maj. A.P. di Benedetto, in Thailand.

Jimmy, a graduate of Salesianum School, was reportedly shot down in Vietnam in 1965. After he was declared a POW, his wife and children moved to California, according to Elaine. He too was later declared dead and is listed as a Delaware fatality both on the Wall in Washington, D.C. and on the memorial in Wilmington.

Earlier in the year, on May 29, the Mailbag paid respects to Delaware's KIAs on Memorial Day. We wrote:

It's a day for reflection, for remembering past wars and their terrible tolls, a day for honoring those men and women who participated, willingly or unwillingly, in this century's wars and died for their participation.

Memorial Day, as near as we can document, began with Gen. John A. Logan in 1868 when he was commander-in-chief of the Grand Army of the Republic. In that year, he issued an order designating May 30 as the day for decorating soldiers' graves.

We'd like to pay our respects to all the country's war dead, but most especially those First Staters who served us without comment in Vietnam and died for their efforts.

We know a little bit more about these men. Some corresponded with us; some we remember from high school or college – we all remember those men at some point before they put on a uniform.

So, to the families of Delaware's servicemen who have died in combat in Southeast Asia, from James H. Johnson Jr. of Milford, who died Oct. 3, 1963, to Donald S. Hoskins of Dover, who died April 26, 1972, our thoughts are with you today as we salute your – and our – fallen servicemen.

We also wrote about ways of building awareness of servicemen held captive or missing in action. This item appeared in the June 2 column:

POW bracelets are making waves these days.… Delaware state legislators have taken up the torch and at least 10 of them are sporting nickel or copper bracelets inscribed with the name of an American serviceman being held a prisoner of war or missing in action in Vietnam, his rank and a date.

The column explained how to purchase the bracelets from POW-MIA advocacy groups, and mentioned other POW-MIA items as well, including bumper stickers, license plate frames, calendars and recordings.

POW-MIA bracelets were frequently worn in support of servicemen taken prisoner or missing in action. Army Spc. William W. Hutchison Jr. wore this bracelet in honor of his friend, Marine 1st Lt. Larry F. Potts, initially an MIA. After Hutchison returned from Vietnam, he tracked down 1st Lt. Potts' commanding officer, who told him the marine suffered a broken leg after he was shot down on April 7, 1972, his 25th birthday, and later died in a POW camp. Although his remains were never recovered, he was posthumously promoted to captain and declared dead several years later. To ward off evil spirits and disease throughout the year, South Vietnamese perform the lion dance in Saigon (opposite) during Tet, the Vietnamese new year.

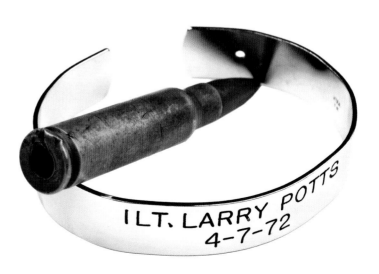

From top: Air Force 1st Lt. William Paul Curtis Jr. (on left) shares some down time with Air Force Sgt. Melvin Evans of Baltimore (center) and Air Force Lt. Col. Gerald P. Foss of Dover, Del., at Tan Son Nhut Air Base. Army Spc. Stewart Revel sent a picture to the Mailbag from his post in Cam Ranh Bay. Underway, Navy Petty Officer 3rd Class Alan Marc Solomon stands at the stern of the USS *Constellation*. The carrier, whose scheduled deployment was extended to combat the enemy's Easter Offensive on March 30, participated in 11 campaigns during the Vietnam conflict. A soldier (opposite) works on an engine in the 571st Medical Detachment's motor pool in Da Nang.

WITH THE TROOP WITHDRAWALS AND INCREASED VIETNAMIZATION, THE MAILBAG HEARD LESS THAN IN PREVIOUS YEARS ABOUT JOBS IN THE COMBAT ZONE. What we did hear, we eagerly printed.

"**In my last letter, I told you I was working in the television repair shop.** Since then, I have been transferred to my old division, the electrical division. My transfer was due to a shortage of electricians on board.

I am now working in the catapult and elevator shop which I was in before. My job is to maintain and repair the electrical circuits of our bomb and deck-edge elevators, escalators and conveyors, catapults and arresting gear, JP-5 fueling stations and pump rooms and our different cranes on board. In addition, I work in the television repair shop in my spare time and also stand switchboard watches on our ship's service generators that produce electricity for the ship. Needless to say, I'm kept quite busy."
Navy Petty Officer 3rd Class Alan Marc Solomon aboard the USS Constellation, Jan. 13

Alan included in his January 13 note some interesting stats about his ship, which was then the world's largest conventionally powered attack aircraft carrier. Commissioned October 27, 1961, and named for the U.S. frigate and national shrine afloat in Baltimore, the USS *Constellation* housed 3,000 officers and men plus 2,000 more in the air wing. The stats:

Length: 1,072 feet, 7 inches

Height (keel to flight deck): 97 feet

Horsepower: 250,030

Speed: more than 35 knots

Meals served daily: approximately 15,000

Daily food prep: 1,000 loaves of bread, 5,260 pounds of meat, 10,150 pounds of vegetables

Also aboard: an 86-bed hospital, dental clinic, post office, cobbler shop, laundry, weather bureau, tailor shop, soda fountains, a TV and radio station, air conditioning and fresh water.

But still no girls or trees.

"**I am working in customs here in Cam Ranh Bay.** I check my fellow GIs' hold baggage before it is sent to the states. I enjoy this job because I like seeing my fellow Delawareans go home. Also, I can't wait to get back to Delaware. I hope all of us First Staters get home soon."
Army Spc. Stewart Revel in Cam Ranh Bay, Feb. 24

"**My job is wire maintenance for the Joint Overseas Switchboard, which means I repair all equipment and the switchboard whenever trouble arises.** The hours are 7 p.m. to 7 a.m., which makes for a long night at best.

As for Vietnam, I would rather be some place in the world like Delaware. This place can get to you after awhile being that everything is so dirty around here. Saigon is one big mess and that's the best one can say about it."
Army Spc. Darrell T. Grubbs, Feb. 12

"**I'm serving my tour in Vietnam with the 3rd Aerospace Rescue and Recovery Group with my specific detachment located here at Tan Son Nhut Air Base.** We here at Detachment 14 work under a unique situation in that we work out of both Tan Son Nhut and Bien Hoa air bases, providing local base rescue support to both these installations.

Tan Son Nhut remains our home base, where our maintenance people work long hours keeping our aircraft on alert status.… All of us here work so that our motto, 'That Others May Live,' can be realized."
Air Force 1st Lt. William Paul Curtis Jr. at Tan Son Nhut Air Base, Aug. 15

The Mailbag's 800th letter from the combat zone came from a sailor serving off the coast of Vietnam.

"**I went to boot camp at Great Lakes, and then I was sent to school in Memphis to learn about jet engines.** After I completed school, I was sent to Okinawa for about a year where I learned a lot about planes from the squadron that I was attached to and that was VC5. I like it over there and I think the United States is wrong in giving it back. Right now I'm on the USS *Constellation* (CVA-64), which is operating off the coast of Vietnam. We are due to return to the United States in April of 1972.

I'm working in engine buildup aboard the ship and my rate is ADJAN and it is a hard rate but I like my work. There are a few guys from Delaware on the ship but I haven't met them. I work with a few guys from New York and New Jersey.

We don't have much problem with drugs on the ship and there are 5,000 guys on my ship."
Navy Aviation Machinist John Collins aboard the USS Constellation, Jan. 12

Sturdy Caribou Proves An Untiring Workhorse

A "Caribou" pilot barely clears the trees as he prepares for a full flap short landing at Tra Bong. The 1,000-foot runway must be approached precisely. At the exact moment, the pilot swings the transport over tree tops and comes to an immediate stop no less than 50 feet from the end of the steel-meshed runway.
(USAF Photo By TSgt. Ed Canivan)

The twin-engine Caribou (left and opposite), subject of an article in the *Pacific Stars and Stripes*, proved an invaluable asset during the war. The utility transport's short takeoff and landing capabilities made it an ideal aircraft for delivering troops, supplies and equipment to isolated outposts. Soldiers Jim Phillips (left) and Robert L. Settle boosted troop morale one note at a time as members of the 266th Army Band in Long Binh. They and other bandsmen also enhanced pacification efforts with their concerts. When they weren't performing, they built bunkers and served as perimeter guards.

I have mixed feelings about the Army band system. It's been an easy way to spend my time and I'd probably choose it again if I had to, but I wouldn't enlist.

It's very frustrating, though, to see how the Army can screw up something you care about. Quite often, there are people in a band who are more qualified and better musicians than the NCOs and warrant officers in charge. But seldom are they allowed to direct. The one thing about this is after awhile, a person stops caring so much if the music gets any better. No matter how much you care, you know that as long as the music is functional, the Army will be satisfied. This is bad, to be sure, but I really don't know of any solution as long as people are forced to give a couple years of their lives to the big green machine.

The Zero-Draft Program will definitely hurt the band system I feel since I see little reason for an accomplished musician to enlist in the Army band. I have gained virtually nothing musically from the band system, only from association with other musicians and exposure to a variety of music."
Army Spc. Robert L. Settle in Long Binh with the 266th Army Band, June 6

Early in 1972, the Mailbag heard from a Wilmington man who served in the Marines three years before our first letter was received.

"**My part in Vietnam was way back in 1965-1966 so I guess I'm one of the old-timers.** I was a photo-recon pilot based at Da Nang and on the Navy carriers *Hancock* and *Intrepid*. I flew 224 combat missions over both North and South Vietnam and was awarded the Distinguished Flying Cross and 13 Air Medals plus all the other assorted decorations that all the veterans come home with.

Just recently, I resigned my commission as a captain in the Reserve and I am presently employed as a pilot for Western Airlines out of Los Angeles and flying routes between California, Mexico, Hawaii and Alaska."
Gail William Sublett, Feb. 10

Sometimes the news we received wasn't good. The Mailbag frequently learned of war injuries, as was the case with Army 1st Lt. William L. Melson of Wilmington, grandson of Family Court Judge Elwood F. Melson Sr. In early 1972, Bill was recovering at Valley Forge General Hospital where he had been since October 1971 and would stay for at least three more months. We encouraged readers to send notes and cards to cheer Bill and printed this about him in the March 3 column:

Bill was wounded in action as a company commander and lost a leg last Sept. 25 after being in country four months. Bill's a grad of P.S. du Pont High School and Wake Forest College. He was a teacher in Virginia before joining the Army. After basic training at Fort Dix, N.J., and Fort Benning, Ga., he went to Vietnam to serve in the Americal Division's 11th Brigade. His wife is from Holliston, Mass.

When Air Force Sgt. Robert Lee Reed stopped by the office in February, he had finished his Vietnam tour and was on leave before reporting to Andrews Air Force Base near Washington, D.C.

Bob worked at Cam Ranh Bay as a crew chief on the Caribou, an Air Force cargo plane. He brought an article on the aircraft from the *Pacific Stars and Stripes*. In part, the article described the Caribou as having a loud engine, uncomfortable seats and vibrating like a mechanical weight-reducing belt. Advantages included getting into the air quickly and requiring a minimal landing strip.

Its mission was to get loads and vital supplies to camps, no matter how many trips or whatever the danger. The light transports carried 15 to 20 tons of men, mail, food, animals, munitions or weapons daily.

When we first heard from this soldier, we were intrigued with his assignment. Unusual in nature, it stood apart from standard combat jobs. We fired off a letter to him in Long Binh and requested more information and a picture. He sent both and Mailbag readers learned about another dimension of the war.

"**You asked for more information about myself and the Army band system so I'll try to oblige.** I graduated from Rising Sun High School, Md., in 1966 and from Campbell College, Buies Creek, N.C., in 1970 with a B.S. in music education. I enlisted in August 1970 to escape the draft. I thought I'd play it smart – enlist for the extra year, get in a band somewhere and be pretty sure of not getting sent to Nam. Little did I realize!

Anyway, from October 1970 until I came over here in March, I was stationed with the 324th Band at Aberdeen Proving Ground, Md. They played for a lot of parades, quite a few military ceremonies in Pennsylvania and Maryland and some concerts in local elementary schools.

The official function of an army band is to improve troop morale, provide music for military ceremonies and improve community-post relations. Over here that means play for stand-down ceremonies and change of command ceremonies. Occasionally we do play in the Vietnamese community. About four mornings a week we play a 15-minute pops concert on USARV hill, this is why the band cannot go home, even though we've received stand-down orders three times in the past year or so.

IN THE COMBAT ZONE, SERVING AT SEA CAME WITH ITS OWN SET OF LOGISTICS. Residing aboard a sailing city frequently on the move wasn't easy and required adaptation. There were fewer sailors than soldiers serving in Vietnam. In an attempt to balance our coverage, the Mailbag in July began saluting our sailors and their ships based on those receiving complimentary subscriptions to *The Morning News*. We located 17 First Staters aboard 11 ships. Nine of the 17 men were on three ships, the USS *Newport News* (with four), the USS *Saratoga* (with three) and the USS *Constellation* (with two). Or so we thought.

A few weeks later, we started getting corrections and additions. One of our first letters was from a seaman aboard the USS *Newport News* who gently corrected us, and rightly so:

"Hey, I read your column in the paper about everybody from Delaware on the USS *Newport News*. Everything you wrote about the ship was correct except for one thing: its length. I think the figure you mentioned was in meters, not feet. Anyhow, through some mathematical calculations (conversion of meters to feet) I found the length to be more like 700 feet, give or take a few feet.

At this writing, we are scheduled for an in-port visit to Subic Bay, Philippines. It will be from August 3rd to 10th. A break in the action. The captain announced today we will most likely visit Hong Kong in mid-September.

Oh yeah, another thing, there's this guy who's a cook on board the ship from Delaware. His name is CS3 R. L. Jones. Anyhow, he told me to let you know he's here. His address is the same as mine but he's in S-2 Division."
Navy Seaman Glenn Alan "Ace" Loveless, July 26

Then we learned of six more sailors, including four on the USS *America*, from families whose sons were not receiving the free newspaper. We also heard from a sailor from nearby New Jersey.

"I received the July 15 copy of the News-Journal today and I saw my name listed as a mystery person. I thought I'd drop you a line and let you know I am alive and well in the South China Sea. The *Saratoga* is presently off the coast of North Vietnam on Yankee Station. We just left Hong Kong where we had an in-port period from July 20 to July 27. Our line period was extended ten days because the carrier *America* can't quite carry her load so we are helping out.

As it stands right now, we are supposed to pull into the yards at Portsmouth, Va., on 29 November, but our schedule only goes up to 30 September. Everybody on the ship is still hoping we leave for home around October 5, but nobody knows for sure….

Right now, I'm 20 years old and will turn 21 on Sept. 15, when we'll still be at sea. I graduated from West Deptford High School in Woodbury, N.J., in May of 1969. I spent the summer racing cars at the drag strip and just more or less bumming around. I left for basic training in September and went to Great Lakes.

After basic, I was assigned ABH 'A' school in Lakehurst, N.J. While there, I received orders to N.A.S. Bermuda and went to work in the crash crew there. I spent two years in Bermuda, March 1970-March 1972. I reported aboard the *Saratoga* in June of this year.

I now work in V-3 Division, which is the hangar deck. My job on the ship is an airplane director. The work isn't that hard, but the hours are kind of long: 12 to 18 a day.

The captain of the ship just came on the ship's public address system and told us that there has been quite a bit of MIG activity over ships here in the past few days, so we had to shut off all our exterior lights because we might be prime targets for the MIGs. He also said that they are building up for an attack, so I guess only time will tell. I am hoping for a three-month cut once we get to the yards, which would put me out in June 1973, the sooner the better."
Navy Petty Officer 3rd Class Robert Davidson aboard the USS Saratoga, Aug. 18 Mailbag

This sailor clarified information on his ship's length.

"When you said the ship was 213 feet long and we would be home in October some time I figured it was time the public found out the truth. For one, the ship is 717 feet long and weighs 21,000 tons. Two, we do not know when we will be home. We suspect sometime in November or December but have no definite date."
Navy Seaman Thomas W. White aboard the USS Newport News, Aug. 11 Mailbag

A family member told us this sailor was 18 and had enlisted in the Navy for four years. Then the sailor shared some of his views with Mailbag readers and gave us news about two of his shipmates.

"Here we sit off Vietnam and waiting out another refueling and a bomb shipment. They don't call the *America* the 'forever sail' for nothing. I've been here for awhile. Came on as an electronics man and switched over to boatswain's mate. I just needed a feeling of accomplishment in what I did, I guess.

Well, Brian [T.] Eide is safe now. No one can foul his life up anymore. It's out of the Navy's hands now. I salute him. He's gone through more hell than anyone can imagine, just like any boatswain's mate.

They don't realize we're the ship's eyes in all weather, we steer her, fuel her and take on the bombs by the hundreds. We die here but no one knows it. But that's war.

But this isn't even war. Someone better get some stuff straight someplace. Either we're fighting or we're not. This isn't a chess game. Even though it might seem like it at times. We on *America* don't even know when we'll see home again.

Now, don't get me wrong, I like the Navy. I'll be going up for my third-class test soon. As a boatswain's mate. Wouldn't see it any other way. It's a good place to hide, get killed or just serve time.

The thing that bugs us is when will we get home? I've got a great family and a loving woman back there and I want to see them both, but here I sit, floating in the ocean.

But as someone once said: 'Ours is not to reason why, ours is just to do or die.'

And life goes on. So with that, I'll end. Seaman John Brezinski, myself and the fabulous, fun-loving, fearless, frolicsome, fantastic Fourth Division wish Brian Eide the best of luck and the world a hearty 'SHIP-OVER!'"
Navy Seaman Gerald H. Olszewski abard the USS America, Sept. 4 Mailbag

Another sailor brought Mailbag readers current on his activities.

"I am a Third Class Commissary Man in the Navy. My friend Glenn Loveless showed me your column of Aug. 14, 1972 and I thought I would help you get your record complete. You mentioned you would like to hear from me, so briefly, here's a profile of myself. I am a 1967 graduate of Salesianum School and I attended St. Edward's University, Austin, Texas, and the University of Delaware for awhile before I entered the Navy in March of 1969.

After completing boot camp, I was sent to commissaryman 'A' School in Newport, R.I. From there, I was transferred to the commissary store, Submarine Base, Groton, Conn.

There I met my wife Nancy and maintained a residence at New London, Conn., while keeping my permanent residence at the home of mother and stepfather, Mr. and Mrs. Robert S. Donahue [in] Wilmington.... From what I understand I too now live in Delaware as my family has recently moved into Woodland Apartments in Wilmington.

I reported to the USS *Newport News* on November 1, 1971 and have been with her continuously since I have no definite idea when the ship will be home, but I do know when I'll be back for certain. If all else fails, then I'll be home in 180 days."
Navy Petty Officer 3rd Class Robert L. Jones aboard the USS Newport News, Aug. 29

Readers learned of a reunion at sea from this sailor:

"I'm writing this to inform you of another First Stater I met here on board. His name is ADJ2 Paul McCafferty. His squadron is HS-7. He's a jet mechanic on helicopters. He lives in Westview, the same community I'm from. I can't remember his address exactly. We've known each other quite a few years now. I can remember playing ball together when we were grade-school age.

I sure enjoy the papers and the boxes from SOS Vietnam. It sure makes you feel good, knowing that you're remembered back home when you're so far away. My mother used to help with the packing at SOS as I had a brother over here in the Marines last year and also several other relatives over here then."
Navy Petty Officer 3rd Class Gilbert Arterbridge Jr. aboard the USS Saratoga, Aug. 12

The USS *Anchorage* (LSD-36), a Navy dock landing ship launched in 1968, served as a launch platform for large landing crafts. After the war ended, the *Anchorage* carried marines back to the United States.

The WAVES (Women Appointed for Voluntary Emergency Service), the women's branch of the Navy, made a splash in the August 14 Mailbag.

According to the latest Z-Gram from [Navy] Adm. Elmo R. Zumwalt Jr., once the amendment to the U.S. Constitution granting women equal rights is ratified, there is no reason why women sailors couldn't serve at sea, become aviators or attend the [U.S.] Naval Academy in Annapolis.

Zumwalt, chief of naval operations, said he felt after the ratification of the amendment, now being considered by the states, it will be legal to assign women to combat jobs.

The admiral's orders opening Navy billets to women goes a step further than the Army's recent decision to double the size of the Women's Army Corps and opening all but combat jobs to them.

In his recent four-page message to all ships and stations, Zumwalt called the assignment of women aboard warships "the ultimate goal" that will be timed to coincide with implementation of the new legislation.

The amendment, regarding equal rights for women and men, was proposed by the second session of the 92nd Congress on March 22, 1972, when it passed the Senate. The House previously passed it on October 12, 1971. The seven-year deadline for ratification of the proposed amendment was extended to June 30, 1982, by the second session of the 95th Congress, but the amendment failed to be ratified by three-fourths of the states by that date.

EVEN IN 1972, PACIFICATION, OR CIVIL ACTION WORK, WAS ONGOING. Mailbag readers, over the Year, had received – and honored – many requests from Delaware servicemen for clothing, toys, canned goods and health articles for South Vietnamese orphanages. An officer told us about his work and what he hoped to accomplish on behalf of war orphans.

"**I have been in the Army since June 1969 with intermediate stops in Georgia, Boston and Hawaii before coming to Vietnam.** Currently I am assigned to the 509th Radio Research Group Headquarters in Saigon. I know your reaction is 'oh, another Saigon warrior.' While this is my home base as plane and manpower officer, I must travel frequently all over the Republic.

It has been an interesting tour but believe I'll be happy to return to the United States. I am undecided as to future plans because I am waiting for approval of my law school applications. If they are favorable, I should be separated in August which coincides with the end of my term here. If the applications are not favorable, I will probably accept a position with the Army Security Agency in Augsburg, Germany. Not a bad consolation prize.

One of my primary reasons for writing to you is to solicit your support for what I consider a worthwhile program. Our group headquarters, in conjunction with the Junior Officers Council (I am the current president), has been sponsoring outings and other diversions for a local orphanage in Saigon. The Santa Maria orphanage has over 500 children that are sons and daughters of refugees who have been killed by the VC/NVA and, of course, our own bombs.

Unfortunately, bullets don't differentiate sentiments and loyalties.

Anyway, each of us at the headquarters donates $2 to $5 from their monthly pay for support of the kids. Many of us spend one or two days and evenings a week at the orphanage repairing equipment and providing much-needed services the orphanage cannot afford.

However, the crying need most of the children have is for decent clothing. I know many of your readers give to UNICEF, United Way and other worthy charities, but it seems to me that direct donations of wearable, small, lightweight clothing for kids directly involved with one of your own neighbors (albeit a technical resident) is eminently preferable to giving to a faceless relief organization.

Many of these children will grow up to be responsible adults if given the care and opportunities we so often take for granted in the states.

Any small measure of contributions would be greatly appreciated."
Army Capt. James W. Foster in Saigon, March 27 Mailbag

South Vietnamese children (opposite) were intrigued by American servicemen and eagerly posed for pictures. These war orphans were playing near Chu Lai.

OFFBEAT NEWS ARTICLES ABOUT VIETNAM FREQUENTLY FOUND THEIR WAY INTO THE MAILBAG. This item, a bit of premature postwar economic elbowing noted in the January 14 column, was a good example:

There's another war, of sorts, in the offing off the South Vietnamese coast. It concerns oil and five countries are in the process of applying to South Vietnam's National Petroleum Board for drilling rights.

Of the 22 firms that have applied, 15 are American. The others are French, British, Japanese and Israeli. All apparently want to begin drilling under the Viet-Khmer continental shelf.

Vietnamese geophysical studies indicate that a large layer of sedimentary rock, which often covers oil pockets, extends from Phan Thiet on the center coastline to Ca Mau on the southern tip of Vietnam, and runs from Tay Ninh near the Cambodian border along the Mekong Delta and under the Pacific Ocean to Malaysia.

Or this tidbit, in the March 20 Mailbag:

Any takers for the South Vietnamese deep sea fishing project? With a coastline of approximately 1,000 miles as well as a rather sophisticated river and canal system. South Vietnam is looking to the fishing industry to play an important part in the country's national economic development.

According to the "Vietnam Bulletin," the semi-monthly publication of the Embassy of Vietnam in Washington, there are only 10 fishing trawlers currently plying the coast with the majority of fishermen using their own boats.

The South Vietnamese government is encouraging the development of the fishing industry, given the natural advantages and promises some form of assistance to investors.

Fresh fish is the common food for the Vietnamese. Dried fish, canned fish, fish sauce, fish meal and fertilizer are apparently in great demand.

Or this, in the May 19 Mailbag:

Good news for First Staters: the Saigon Chamber of Commerce is planning to promote the export of mineral water.

According to a report published in a recent issue of the "Vietnam Bulletin," a semi-monthly publication of the Embassy of Vietnam, many springs are known to provide "mineral water of high therapeutic value, the most famous being the Vinh Hoa Springs in Phan Thiet Province.

"Vinh Hoa mineral water was first commercialized in 1928 with a production, at times, reaching 100,000 liters a year. Interrupted by the first Indochina war in 1945, production was resumed on a fairly large scale in 1956 by the government-owned Vinh Hoa Mineral Water Co."

Any entrepreneurs in the group?

Or this, from the June 12 Mailbag:

Good news for shrimp fanciers.

Word has it that an unidentified Saigon financier plans to begin shipping frozen Vietnamese shrimp to the United States by the end of the year.

The businessman is apparently building three freezing plants in Kien Hoa Province at the mouth of the Mekong River, 50 miles south of Saigon.

The shrimp, which usually cost 77 cents a pound in Ben Tre, South Vietnam, will be sold for up to $3 a pound in America.

And then there was this item, in the August 4 Mailbag:

Electric cattle prods are out…

We couldn't help but chuckle at the recent United Press International release out of Saigon about the U.S. Command ordering medical evacuation teams flying in the An Loc campaign to turn in the prods they had been issued to knock unwanted passengers off their helicopters.

Everyone found this November 7 Mailbag item humorous:

After four years and $375,000, the Navy has decided the flight characteristics of Frisbees cannot be adapted for warfare.

In an extensive scientific study conducted from Hurricane Mesa in Utah and the Navy ammunition depot at Crane, Ind., the Navy has decided Whamo Manufacturing Co.'s plastic toy, referred to in the report as an "air-launched gyroscopically-stabilized disc," is not what they're looking for.

According to Lt. Cmdr. Hugo A. Hardt, who took over the testing program two years ago, the naval air systems command was looking for a new way of delivering flares.

Navy ordnance experts at Crane used the data from Frisbee flights conducted at Hurricane Mesa to develop a disc-shaped flare that could be launched at night from airplanes to light up battlefields as the disc spun through the air.

Flares now used by the military burn for three to five minutes as they float to earth by parachute. Hardt said the Navy was hoping the Frisbee-type flare would do the same job at less cost than the $50 parachute flares.

Navy scientists found, however, that their burning characteristics caused them to "develop thrust and takeoff straight up like a rocket" instead of spinning off in horizontal flight.

Although it was felt this problem could be solved, Hardt said the flares required a "monstrous and expensive launcher" which would have made the idea impractical.

Well, back to the drawing boards, fellas….

It is suggested that remarks not be made about the neatness of the uniforms of the Marines, Navy or Air Force but have a word of praise for his Class As [service dress uniform]. Never ask him why the Joneses' son held a higher rank than he did and, above all, never mention the term 'extend.'

If you are out to one of your favorite nightclubs and after a few hours of drinking he suddenly calls the waitress 'numah one girl' or uses his hat for an ashtray, he is still rational. He will probably keep listening for 'Homeward Bound' to sound over AFVN. If he does, comfort him, for he is still reminiscing.

Be especially watchful when he is in the presence of women, beautiful women. His intentions may be dishonorable, but strictly sincere. Above all, keep in mind that beneath that tanned and rugged exterior there is a heart of gold (the only thing of value he has left). Treat him with kindness and tolerance and an occasional fifth of good liquor and you will be able to rehabilitate that which once was (and now is a hollow shell of) the happy-go-lucky guy you once knew and loved.

Last but not least, send no more mail to his APO, fill the ice box with beer, get the civvies out of mothballs, fill the car with gas, and get the women and children off the streets because the kid is coming home!"
Army Sgt. Frank J. Hensley, March 6 Mailbag

After all that, we added this about Frank in the April 17 Mailbag:

First Staters aren't usually last, but Sgt. Frank J. Hensley … has the rather dubious distinction of being one of the last remaining members of the 101st Airborne Division (Airmobile) to leave Vietnam for redeployment to Fort Campbell, Ky.

The division's colors were returned to its home base at the Kentucky fort after being in Vietnam since the early days of the buildup of American forces in Southeast Asia.

Frank is a squad leader with Company C, 2nd Battalion of the division's 501st Infantry.

Occasionally, the Mailbag offered items for reflection, as in the March 10 column:

A rather interesting development occurred in the Defense Department recently. Defense Secretary Melvin R. Laird has ordered the Pentagon to review its practice of stamping a special number on the records of servicemen discharged for using drugs, permanently identifying them to prospective employers as drug abusers.

Laird was quoted as saying this practice "may be inconsistent with our policy directive on invasion of privacy and could have an unjust and unfair impact on some discharged personnel."

U.S. Sen. Harold Hughes, D-Iowa, had earlier threatened legal action or legislation to stop the practice following its disclosure by a Pentagon official who said employers need to know whether or not a man has a drug problem.

Over the years, the column had been used by many servicemen to signal the coming their DEROS This letter for it typifies the feeling of getting ready to leave South Vietnam.

"In the very near future, the undersigned will once more be in your midst, dehydrated and demoralized, ready to take his place once again as a human being with the well-known forms of freedom and justice for all, engaged in life, liberty and the somewhat delayed pursuit of happiness.

In making your joyous preparations for welcoming him back into organized society, you must take certain steps to make allowances for the crude environment which has been his miserable lot for the past 12 months. In other words, he might be a little infected with Vietnamitis and overseasitis and should be handled with extreme care. A little time in the 'Land of the big PX' should cure this malady.

Therefore, show no alarm if he insists on carrying a weapon to the dinner table, looks around for his steel pot when offered a chair, or wakes up in the middle of the night for guard duty. Keep cool when he pours gravy on his dessert at dinner or mixes peaches with his Seagram's VO and insists on fingers and hands instead of silverware and prefers C-rations and hot sauce to steak.

Take it with a smile when he insists on digging up the garden to fill sandbags for the bunker he is building. Be tolerant when he takes his blanket and sheets off the bed and puts them on the floor to sleep on. When in his daily conversation he utters such things as *xin loi* and *choi oi,* just be a little patient, he will learn to speak his own language again sooner than you think.

Do not let it shake you up if, when on the phone, he says 'Roger, out' instead of goodbye or simply shouts 'working.' And leave quickly and quietly if by some chance he should utter *didi moi* with an irritated look on his face because it means no less than 'get the hell out of here.'

TIRELESS PERFORMER AND AMBASSADOR OF GOODWILL BOB HOPE WAS STILL ENTERTAINING AMERICAN TROOPS IN VIETNAM DURING THE HOLIDAYS IN 1971. Our Mailbag correspondents waited until the new year to file these reports:

"I did get to see the Bob Hope Show at the Eagle Bowl at Camp Eagle. It was really a good show and since I was in the fourth row from the stage, I had a good seat."
Army Pfc. Kenneth J. Norris, Jan. 3

"As for the Bob Hope Show, well, he didn't make it to Cam Ranh [Bay] because 'Charlie' was a little mad during the holidays. But he did make it to Bien Hoa and Long Binh. A few of the guys went to Long Binh to see him but I couldn't – we were on alert and I had to go out on patrol.

But we did give Bob a little gift from the Security Police Squadron. It was a sign that said '483rd S.P.S. ... Pigs for Peace' and the guy who kissed Miss World was from Cam Ranh too! At least that's what he says! He's from Texas and you know how they are!

One person described Texas [being] like Vietnam. He said, 'Texas is like Vietnam … full of sand and people who talk funny!' So we still have a sense of humor.

To answer your question, I'd say approximately 300 GIs from Cam Ranh saw Bob at Long Binh. Most of them drew straws and the lucky guys got to go."
Air Force Airman William E. Hudson in Cam Ranh Bay, Jan. 19

DELAWAREANS ALWAYS HAPPILY REPORTED MEETING OTHER DELAWAREANS IN VIETNAM. They often sent the Mailbag pictures to prove it.

"Happy New Year from all the guys from Delaware in my unit.... We're all married too (my wife told me to be sure and include that in there this time). I'm glad this part of the year is over. It's even lonelier here at this time of the year.

Congratulations to the University of Delaware for being No. 1 in small college football. Too bad they didn't beat Temple in that disputed game. At least they beat Villanova and their 'self-proclaimed All-American.' However, I wouldn't be surprised if they could have beaten Toledo but they didn't get the chance to play them. The Boardwalk Bowl must have been just that, a 'walk.' I'd hate to have been on C.W. Post's side that day."
1st Lt. Barry G. Pollock, Jan. 1

"The gruesome twosome in the picture is Spec. 5 Paul Fangman and me," wrote Army Capt. Jerold S. Gold of Newark (right) on Feb. 1. Paul was a fellow Delawarean from Claymont. They both served aboard the USNS *Corpus Christi Bay*. Although servicemen enjoyed some liberties in their downtime, such as pool games (opposite), cards and sports, nothing compared to the freedoms they knew awaited them when they returned to the world.

Delawareans often encountered one another by chance, as was the case with this soldier, who had inspired an avalanche of mail for servicemen in 1968 when he wrote to the syndicated Dear Abby column.

"This letter is going to be the shortest I have ever typed. One thing must be done. I have found someone from Delaware and his name is Spec. 5 C. James Moore. He is from Laurel and he is married. We were talking about my mail in 1968 and he wanted to hear all about it. He did not believe it and asked me where I was from and I told him Delaware and that was it. Could you see that his name is put on the paper list, also the SOS [Vietnam]?"
Army Spc. William D. "Dave" Rice, June 26 Mailbag

Others told of meetings.

"I've done some searching in the 69th Signal Battalion and I've found two other Delawareans here. One lives only 8 miles from my own home in Wilmington. It took me to travel 12,000 miles to meet Sgt. Mosley. Also, there is a fellow from downstate named Gustavson. I believe he's from Felton, but I'm not sure.

Anyway, that's all I've met here."
Army Spc. John F. Glenn Jr., June 30

"Before I close, I'd like to tell you a little about another First Stater on the 'Wacc.' He's Seaman Edward 'Seasick' Cycyk. He's a graduate of P.S. du Pont [High School], class of '71, and worked at John Wanamaker's before entering the Navy."
Navy Seaman Neal Kelley aboard the USS Waccamaw, Oct. 24

When Army Spc. Charles J. Backus (bottom) sent a picture from Long Binh he added, "A bunch of guys over here kid me 'cause Delaware is small. I tell them there's more to a state than size. I'm proud of being from Delaware." Air Force Airman William E. Hudson responded rapidly after receiving his sticker in January. "I want to thank you and the state Division of Economic Development for the New Year's gift," he wrote from Cam Ranh Bay. "I have enclosed a snap to show how proud I am of all the great Delawareans. After all, we're No. 1, right?"

EARLY IN 1972, THE MAILBAG SHARED THE EUPHORIA OF SERVICEMEN COMING HOME. For those not yet on their way, we mailed 175 "Discover Delaware, the state that started a nation" bumper stickers, a freebie provided by the Division of Economic Development. We promoted them in the January 10 column when we wrote:

We know First Staters are proud of their state and want to ward off smart-alecs who persistently ask, 'Delaware? What state is that in?' Maybe this will help.

Take heart, they're on their way – Delaware will be heard from. Hope you like them. We hope to bring you other 'goodies' during the year, just to let you know we care.

One serviceman sent proof his sticker was on the job.

"I would like to thank you first of all for the 'Discover Delaware' sticker. I was really glad to see that. I was going to stick it on the company jeep, but our captain probably wouldn't think too much of that so I just hung it on a wall."
Army Spc. Alfred Donald Thompson, Jan. 30

Another wrote of a quandary after he received his freebie.

"Now for a bit of distressing news. What am I to do with the bumper sticker, 'Discover Delaware,' that you sent me? I appreciate it, of course, but I don't even have a bicycle to put it on or even a radio wagon."
Army Spc. Jesse H. Walling, Feb. 1

The CH-47A Chinook helicopter, which entered service in Vietnam with the 1st Cavalry Division in late 1965, was the Army's principal transport for troops and artillery. With a top speed of 170 knots (196 mph), the tandem-rotor aircraft was faster than utility and attack helicopters.

For Delawareans still in Vietnam in 1972, displaying their state flag remained a foolproof way of meeting other First Staters. The official Delaware flags were free for the asking from the Division of Economic Development.

"I would really like [the state flag] very much…. I'm the only one on this big aircraft carrier from Delaware out of 4,500 guys so I would like to show them that Delaware is on the map."
Navy Steelworker Mark Bickling aboard the USS Coral Sea, March 7

"I would like a Delaware State flag as I am from Port Penn, Delaware. Lived there all my life. Now I am over here in Vietnam."
Army Spc. Donald L. Moore, May 12 Mailbag

Grateful troops continued to mention the flags in their letters.

"I finally received my flag and spent a nice Christmas in the rear. We were in the rear because my battalion stood down to go to Cam Ranh Bay. We're away from the cold, wet monsoon season of up north and enjoying the warm sun and dry weather down south here."
Army Pfc. Kenneth J. Norris, Jan. 3

"Oh, yes, the flag finally got through all the mail. It hangs proudly in the medical department letting all personnel know that men from Delaware are doing their part over here also."
Navy Hospital Corpsman Joseph H. Opdenaker Jr. aboard the USS Enterprise, Jan. 18

"My roommate has a Kentucky flag from his home state and I refuse to be outdone. We Eastern U.S. boys kind of hang together anyway and I'd be happy to see a Delaware flag waving beside his Kentucky. Delaware is all right. Peace would be nice."
Army Warrant Officer 1st Class Eric C. Darby, Feb. 11 Mailbag

"S.O.S. - VIETNAM"
INTER-DENOMINATIONAL CENTER,
BEAR, DELAWARE. 19701   JANUARY, 1972

Dear First Staters:

Here we are into a brand new year with brand new hopes for an end to all the ugliness in Vietnam. We hope you had as good a holiday as possible under adverse circumstances. Our hearts were with you through the season.

January as of this writing is almost ready to give way to the month of February and with the end of January, it also means the end of the football season, at least for awhile. The Super Bowl ended it on this past Sunday and millions of men are re-discovering their long-suffering wives, while others discovered that their's left them at the onset of the season. Comedian Totie Fields was able to get her husband's attention by devious means During the Super Bowl game she strolled past him wearing a nightgown made of Astro-turf! For pity's sakes...why didn't I think of that?

For the benefit of you men receiving a package for the first time, I'd like to explain briefly as possible about our organization. We began sending a-box-a-month to each Delaware man in Vietnam for whom we had a name and complete overseas mailing address. The names come to us via family, friends, the newspapers etc. Ours is strictly a non-political, non-profit, inter-denominational organization. We rely soley on donations from the public and by our various money-raising events. The cost runs high with packing and mailing supplies, food items and postage but we're happy to say, people have been very generous these past four years. We'll celebrate our 4th year in February so we've sent approximately 17,000 boxes to date. The whole purpose of the project is to let you over there, know that we over here care about you.

The little state of Delaware is about to establish a record in the annals of the Wilmington weather bureau. Wilmington has so far this winter of 1971-72 been entirely without snow! As a matter of fact we've had very little cold weather. It's been quite balmy so why go to Florida and spend all that bread? It's great weather for the golfers but a bad scene for the skiers around the area. Easter plants in some gardens are up about six inches or more... they think it's April so who can blame them? I think our car will be ready for the junk heap before our snow tires ever wear out. (They aren't even ON the car yet).

We hope you like Libby's selection this month. I was told to send on a recipe to you men. In the box you will find a can of date and nut bread, a can of pudding and a can of toasted cocoanut. You are supposed to concoct a super desert by putting a glob of pudding on a slice of bread and top it with the cocoanut crispies. Okay? perhaps it will satisfy the sweet tooth.

Just a reminder to send us your probable date of return to the world. There's nothing we'd like better than to remove your name from our list because you are coming home. God bless each and every one of you. Our thoughts and prayers are ever with you.

Sincerely,

Isabel R. Church.
(Isabel R. Church)

As reliable as the calendar, the all-volunteer SOS Vietnam mailed 5-pound bennie boxes to Delaware servicemen in Vietnam every month for about five years. The boxes contained canned food, homemade cookies, toiletries, games and a letter of support, like this one. Based at Red Lion Methodist Church in Bear, Del., SOS was founded in December 1967 by the Rev. Irvin R. Pusey to "Serve Our Servicemen" and sent tons of bennies to the combat zone.

THROUGHOUT THE YEAR SERVICEMEN, RETURNING OR OTHERWISE, REGISTERED ABUNDANT THANKS. Most often, it was for moral support from home.

"**First, I would like to extend my deepest thanks and appreciation to those who try and make our tour a little more pleasant by giving of themselves.** My special thanks go to SOS Vietnam and the Salvation Army. The packages I received were not only enjoyed by me but [my] shipmates as well. It is gratifying to know that someone really cares, especially the great people of our state."
Navy Petty Officer 3rd Class Alan Marc Solomon aboard the USS Constellation, Jan. 13

"**Well, once again I am writing a letter of great thanks and appreciation to the people in the great state.** I spent Christmas in a place that I would have thought people would have forgotten about. But the great people from Delaware came through once again. I received so many cards, care packages and stuff from everyone. You people are just heaven on earth for us guys."
Navy Hospital Corpsman Joseph H. Opdenaker Jr. aboard the USS Enterprise, Jan. 18

"**I have spent a tour here prior to this with the 1st Cavalry Division.** I came over with them and I shall hold the people of Delaware forever very near and dear to my heart. During that tour, I received many gifts and care packages from the folks at home. Those folks included the Chicago Bridge and Iron Company with whom I have never been associated, a sorority at the University of Delaware which solicited letters from the men in my unit so they, in turn, could write further, many others too numerous to mention [but] in particular, Mr. Stanley Hulse, proprietor of a beauty shop at 11th and Washington streets in Wilmington.

Mr. Hulse is a very special person. He took many coins from his own pocket to send goodies to Delawareans in Vietnam and corresponded frequently. God bless him.

[News-Journal columnist] Mr. Bill Frank, with photographer, also visited me during his trip here to see all the men from Delaware. I think he located some 300 of them.

So, Delaware, I salute you, I thank you, and I love you."
Army Spc. Jesse H. Walling, Feb. 1

"**Just a few words to thank all the people from the good ole U.S.A.** I mean the SOS [Vietnam] boxes and also the paper and most of all for the Delaware state flag sent to me. That is the prettiest thing over here."
Army Spc. Donald L. Moore near Da Nang, Aug. 28

Delawareans in Vietnam frequently wrote to SOS Vietnam to show appreciation for the bennie boxes filled with food, games and personal items sent monthly by the all-volunteer organization. SOS, in turn, shared these letters with the Mailbag. Here's an example:

"**I was really surprised to receive a package of goodies from you.** I didn't think you knew about me. I really appreciated it.

As for me, this war still wages on out here somewhere in the Tonkin Gulf.

We usually stay on the gun line for a month at a time and then go to the Philippines for about a week of rest. We're scheduled to leave the gun line soon. It really gets boring out here at sea for a month … no birds, no green grass … nothing.

I see the shore of Vietnam but it appears to be an isolated place four miles from shore. We fire our guns at the enemy but we never see them. It's really strange.

Sorry the letter is so short but I'm almost out of writing paper. The ship's store hasn't had any for about two weeks so I guess everyone is hard up."
Navy Seaman Glenn Alan "Ace" Loveless aboard the USS Newport News, Sept. 11 Mailbag

Readers first met Navy Seaman Neal Kelley of Wilmington in the July 31 Mailbag when we profiled Delaware's Navy men and their ships. A 1968 Corpus Christi High School alum, Neal, 21, attended the University of Delaware for a year and a half and worked at Laird, Bissell & Meeds in Wilmington for another year and a half before enlisting in the Naval Reserve.

After basic training at Great Lakes, Neal was sent to Norfolk, Virginia, where he was assigned to the USS *Waccamaw,* an oil ship. His interesting story was the 41 days it took to get to Vietnam. The *Waccamaw* shoved off from Norfolk with the USS *America* and other ships. Since the *America* was too large to go through the locks at the Panama Canal, the entourage had to sail around the southernmost tip of Africa to reach their Gulf of Tonkin destination.

Neal offered his appreciation for all things Delaware in his October 24 letter. "First, I'd like to thank you for your column, "Vietnam Mailbag," and the News-Journal Co. for the subscription to their paper. Also, I wish to thank the [Division of Economic] Development for sending me that Del. state flag. And last, but not least, my thanks goes to all the people connected with SOS Vietnam for all the goodies and thoughtfulness they've sent." He continued, "All of these bring a guy a little closer to home and don't think it goes unappreciated or unmentioned over here. Much talk among guys in the service centers around their state. And with these benefits, Delaware supplies a lot to brag about."

In 1972, SOS Vietnam entered its fifth full year of service. The January 21 Mailbag mentioned three Vietnam vets, Army Capt. Rodney Brice, Army Spc. Richard J. White and Army Pfc. Paul E. Vaughn, who helped SOS in December 1971 as its volunteers packed 140 5-pound bennie boxes for shipment to Vietnam. Rod made the trip more than once to Bear from Fort Lee, Virginia, where he was stationed. Overall, the nonprofit organization sent more than 16,000 boxes to Delawareans serving in Vietnam.

Army Pfc. Kenneth J. Norris, shown here, was among the servicemen who received Valentine's Day greetings from loved ones in the Feb. 14 Mailbag (opposite). For this day, hearts replaced stars as dividers between column items.

Although this serviceman didn't send a Valentine, he shared glad tidings with Mailbag readers.

"**I've gotten some good news since I wrote my last letter.** I've received a beautiful 6-month drop and should arrive back in the world by April 14, a little late to see our first baby being born, but in plenty of time to learn all there is to know about diapering."
Army Capt. Jerold S. Gold aboard the USS Corpus Christi Bay, Feb. 1

The March 13 Mailbag featured a postscript about Jerry and family:

Noah never made it and neither did the cookies.
Seems Jerry's wife, Maralyn, was in a family way when his letter and picture appeared in the March 3 column.
Jerry was hoping to get home in time for the birth of their first child. The Golds, using theories of two obstetricians, had planned on a son and decided to call him Noah. Noah never arrived.
Meanwhile, Maralyn and Jerry's mom were busily baking cookies last Wednesday in response to SOS Vietnam's plea for 150 pounds of cookies for the March bennie box to First Staters.
Nicole Lynn apparently couldn't wait for the cookies to come out of the oven and forced her mom to the hospital. All the cookies the Golds baked that day are still sitting at home but their intentions were certainly admirable.
Jerry's R&R to Hawaii was canceled and he is expected home about April 14. Congrats, Jerry – hurry home, you have a lot of cookies to eat.

FAMILY WAS ALWAYS TOP DRAWER TO SERVICEMEN SO FAR FROM HOME. For the second year, the Mailbag ran a Valentine's Day column which, in 1972, landed on February 14. We asked for greetings well in advance. Hearts and flowers poured in almost immediately.

"**In the spirit of St. Valentine's Day I would like to make an offering if I may.** Here it is: To my wonderful wife, Louise, the light of my love, the love of my life, forever. Happy Valentine. Guess who?"
Army Spc. Jesse H. Walling, Feb. 1

"**Something great happened to me while I've been in Nam. I** became a father. My wife, Bonnie, had a boy, 7 pounds, 11 ounces. I have just returned from leave and I got to say it was wonderful. My son is beautiful but mean. The only bad thing about it was it ended so fast.
 I saw your ad about Valentine lovers.… Would you please enter my wife and me? Tell her I love her very much and can't wait to return to my little family."
Army Pfc. Lannie K. Arnold in Da Nang, Feb.2

"**Carol, to the one I love a lot.** Honey, even though we are so far apart during this day, our hearts will always be together no matter what. I miss you a lot and hope you are taking good care of yourself. Please have a Happy Valentine's Day and remember there will be another one next year which we will celebrate together. Love always and forever, Donnie. XOXOXOXO"
Army Spc. Alfred Donald Thompson, Feb. 14 Mailbag

Until the mother of Air Force Sgt. C. David Webb contacted us, we had no idea he and his family shared such a rich multigenerational history of serving the country. In the October 16 Mailbag, we wrote about David's second tour overseas, one that took him to Taiwan with shuttles to Vietnam for two weeks at a time. There was more in the column:

David's mom has told us he is in his eighth year with the Air Force and has also been in Turkey and has seen quite a bit of the world from the air since he has been or is a crew chief on a C-130 most of his career.
David, who plans a career with the Air Force, has five uncles who also served their country as well as a host of cousins. For the record, John E. Adams Jr. died in 1945 in World War II; Calvin C. Adams served 12 years in the Navy and saw duty in both World War II and the Korean

War; Sgt. Roscoe B. Adams retired in 1970 after 20 years in the Army, including one tour in Vietnam; Chief Master Sgt. Clinton D. Adams retired in 1971 after 22 years in the Air Force, including one tour in Vietnam; Sgt. Robert D. Adams is currently stationed in South Carolina after three tours in Vietnam.

Before we're completely out of breath, we'd better add the cousins. Robert Hudson, Richard Hudson and Larry Callaway [who] have all served in Vietnam.

David's mom said at one time there were five in her family either in Vietnam or on hospital ships off the coast of Vietnam. She means it when she says her family is proud of its servicemen.

The Mailbag dedicated a Mother's Day column to all moms of Delawareans serving in Vietnam. We wrote on May 15, the day after the official celebration:

We have felt for a long time that the Moms of Delaware servicemen fight just as hard as their sons, only in a different way. We'd like to personally recognize their support in this column.

Army Spc. William D. "Dave" Rice, our notorious "Dear Abby" letter-writer, sent his mom a poem, closing with, "Thanks to Mom for being herself and I love you, Mom."

1st Lt. Thomas J. Ahern, an advisor to ARVN forces in Binh Duong Province, added his sentiments from Lam Son, some 20 miles north of Saigon:

My wife, Pattie, sent me the notice from your column about the Mother's Day greetings. Hope you will convey the best wishes of the day to my mother, Mrs. Rita M. Ahern of Woodside Manor. The same goes for my mother-in-law, Mrs. Mary B. Russell of Woodcrest.

From his post at Long Binh, Army Spc. Alexander Wilson III of Wilmington sent a special note to his mom:

To my dear Mom, Mrs. M. Pegram. Mother's Day is only once a year to mothers, but it is every day to their children because they can appreciate and give praise to her even when she thinks she has just had an ordinary day.

Mother, we feel the love you radiate and it is a very good feeling. As a matter of fact, it is the greatest feeling that mankind knows of … the feeling of love between mother and child.

Dear God, a thank you for my mother on this day and every day because without her where would we be?

This serviceman was in the field when he wrote his Mother's Day greeting. He discovered he had lost the address to the Mailbag and asked friends for an assist in delivering his note. He wrote:

"I'm a First Stater from New Castle who wishes to leave Nam soon but until then I would like to be in Nancy's column. It will be Mother's Day soon so I wish all the First Staters [would] have an ad in the paper about Dear Old Mom. Here's what I'd like to say to Mother:

Dear Mother, This is your son here in Da Nang and I would like to wish you Happy Mother's Day. I hope I'm home next Mother's Day to show you my feelings, like a present perhaps. But I ain't, so all I can do is wish you the happiest Mother's Day possible."

Army Spc. Lannie K. Arnold in Da Nang, April 30

vietnam mailbag

nancy lynch

Hi there—

Happy hearts, everyone, and assorted valentines to all First Staters in Vietnam. We have below, as promised, our annual valentine offering from Delaware to you. We're happy to note that two First Staters have sent valentines into the column.

We appreciate all the hearts and flowers from those who care. Delaware servicemen already know they represent the First State and this column, we hope, will show them we all care.

Greetings to all Delaware servicemen—a special valentine from us—and from your following below.

♥ ♥ ♥

To Pfc. JOHN R. SENIGO (221-32-6546, 557th MP Co, APO SF 96491) from Wilmington:

"Dear Russ: Hi, honey. Happy Valentine's Day. I miss you almost as much as I love you. I can't wait until you're home again. Everyone sends their best. Take care of yourself and when you're low just think of all the time we have to be together when you get back home again. Love always, Sharon."

♥ ♥ ♥

To SFC JESSE H. WALLING (221-20-2584, CoA 8th RRFS, Box 858, APO SF 96308) from New Castle:

"Happy Valentine's Day from Louise, Cathy, Judy, mom and dad, Trixie and the rest of the family."

♥ ♥ ♥

To Spec. 4 ALFRED DONALD THOMPSON (221-36-3576, Co B, 1st Bn 12th Cav. 1st Cav Div (AM), APL SF 96490) from Blackbird:

"Donnie, miles cannot diminish love, they only make it stronger. They just increase the hope we won't be apart much longer. I miss you, honey, but I know that as the new days come and go, we're never really far apart, for you are always in my heart. Love always and forever, Carol. XOX." (Carol, Donnie's fiancee, is in Hawaii now with Donnie who's on R&R.)

♥ ♥ ♥

To PFC. KENNETH J. NORRIS (222-36-5973, Co D, 2d Bn, 327th Inf, 3d Plt, 101st Abn Div (AM), APO SF 96312) from New Castle:

"On Valentine's Day and all other days too, just want to remind you that I love you. All my love. Lou Ann."

♥ ♥ ♥

To Lt. WILLIAM J. DOWNES (221-30-9977, HHT, 7-17 Air Cav, APO SF96226) from Newark:

"Happy Valentine's Day to the best husband ever. We'll celebrate it in 99 days. Love, Cindy."

♥ ♥ ♥

341

WITH STEPPED-UP TROOP WITHDRAWALS FROM VIETNAM, THE MAILBAG RECEIVED MUCH CORRESPONDENCE FROM SERVICEMEN LEAVING THE COMBAT ZONE. Some were from those ready to board their "freedom bird" and others were already home. There were also a couple of bittersweet notes from those reassigned or delayed in country.

"Great news for me is that on the 28th of February, 1972, I shall be separated from the U.S. Navy and leave Vietnam about the 20th of February headed for my home state. I just hope there are a couple of jobs left out there for us guys."
Navy Hospital Corpsman Joseph H. Opdenaker Jr. aboard the USS Enterprise, Jan. 18

"Just thought I would drop you a little note to tell you the great news that has happened to me.

My normal DEROS from Vietnam was in September, but now that the drops have come down, I'll be coming back home in April. It will probably be at the end of next month, but that is a lot better than waiting until September….

I have a lot of letters to write and tell everybody the good news."
Army Spc. Alfred Donald Thompson, March 30

"This is only my second letter to you and I'm writing mainly because I got shore duty orders stateside and I'm finally leaving. Can't say I've had it as bad as those guys on the mainland but being separated is rough. This is my third time over here on a carrier. This time it's the USS *Hancock*, celebrating its 28th birthday April 15th.

Our in-port periods have been rearranged over and over due to extensions on the line (combat zone on the Gulf of Tonkin) due to the big offensives right now. There are four carriers over here and I know we're flying our share, I have no trouble sleeping at night….

I deeply appreciated all the support I've gotten while over here from all my family and fellow Delawareans. I have a beautiful wife and 15-month-old son waiting for me in California, what a reunion….

A special thanks to my mother who has really kept those letters coming my way when I really needed them. Also, to my dad, grand-parents and my father and mother-in-law. The list is larger but now it's time for me to settle now to stateside living. I'll be heading for the states May 15th. I count every day and every day I thank God for the wonderful people back home."
Navy Petty Officer 2nd Class Clifford Hitch aboard the USS Hancock, April 9

"I am writing to tell everyone good news. I will be home in 17 days.… I hope that the people of Delaware keep up the good work because it means so much to us First Staters to know that people do care."
Army Spc. Stewart Revel, April 16

"Though I am in the Air Force, my entire tour here in Vietnam has been spent on assignment with the U.S. Army.… I hope to be on my way to Delaware by mid-September.… Also, in case they haven't received my letter, tell the 'Delaware Donut Dollies' who send out the SOS Vietnam goodie boxes that I'll be returning short-ly and my thanks to them also for their thoughtfulness."
Air Force Master Sgt. John T. Pacek at Camp Holloway near Pleiku, Aug. 7

Army Spc. Robert A. Coen was released early from his second tour and featured in the March 10 column. From the 120th Aviation Company, the "Deans," Army 1st Lt. Edward J. Mulderick (opposite) wrote he would be one of the last to leave Vietnam.

"Just a short note to let you know I'm coming home. My new DEROS date is Nov. 15. Our unit is standing down around the 13th so all 25 of us should be home by Thanksgiving. I think we're the oldest unit left here, if that is any distinction."
Army Spc. Robert L. Settle, Oct. 19

The Mailbag always welcomed Delawareans home with great enthusiasm. On March 10, we featured Army Spc. Robert A. Coen, home after 18 months as a postal clerk with the 101st Airborne Division:

We understand Bob is home early because he extended for an extra hitch overseas. We further understand Bob received not one but two Army Commendation medals.

Actually, Bob is not new to the column. He appeared in the Jan. 4, 1971 Mailbag in one of our largest "groupie" snapshots of First Staters in Vietnam provided by Army Capt. James D. Rawlins Jr. The picture showed five First Staters and two soldiers from Maryland.

Bob has a lot in store for him after he rests. His mom tipped us off that neighbors, friends and family will be celebrating a Christmas in March with all the trimmings for Bob since he missed two Christmases with his enlistment.

Servicemen continued to send thanks and news when they were both short and after they arrived back home.

"This is the last letter that will be written by me from Vietnam. First off, I would like to thank you and the News-Journal for the subscription that I received the 18 months that I have been here. I would also like to express my appreciation to the people of SOS Vietnam for all the goodies that made my stay here a little more comfortable."
Army Spc. Robert Kelly, June 12

"**I was really glad to get home.** And I just wanted to thank you for the newspaper and SOS [Vietnam] for the boxes every month. I really enjoyed them.

There is another man from Dog Patch – his name is Lannie Arnold and he is married and has a little boy. I would appreciate it if you would print this in your column and if he could get a copy to let him know that everybody here is waiting for him and so he'll know I wish him the very best of luck and tell him to hurry home."
Bill Moorehead, May 8 Mailbag

One told us that even though he was coming home, it would only be temporary.

"**By the time you receive this letter, I should be home.** I would have written a lot sooner but my drop came in with only a day's notice. I still have some time to do in the Army after my leave. My next assignment will be at Fort Campbell, Ky., with the 101st Administration Company."
Army Spc. Michael Przybylek, May 1

A few soldiers were not coming home right away and they told us why.

"**I figured it's about time I let you and everyone else know I'm here.** I've been here six months and I'll probably be here six months more. I'm in the 120th Aviation Company, the 'Deans,' which is the largest aviation company in Vietnam. The Deans were the first to come to Vietnam in 1961 and we'll be the last to leave.

My DEROS is in September, which should make me just about the last Delawarean to leave. Some honor, huh?

The Deans are based in Long Binh but we have small units in Saigon, Na Bhe and Phu Loi. I'm at Long Binh, which is the boredom center of Vietnam. I go on leave in 30 days, so that's my consolation.

Give my regards to Mr. Bruce Reynolds and his classes at William Penn and to my old friend, Sam Gish, if he's still in Delaware. And if he is, I hope my being here kept him there."
Army 1st Lt. Edward J. Mulderick in Long Binh, Feb. 20

"**Everyone is leaving here (RVN) and I'm starting to wonder if anyone is going to be left here to keep me company.** My July DEROS looks firm and it's a bit disheartening to see people who came in with or after you leave long before you do."
Army 1st Lt. Kenneth D. Warner at Marble Mountain near Da Nang, March 27

The April 28 Mailbag reported one serviceman's return to Vietnam.

Not everyone's coming home. We've recently heard from Mrs. Mary B. Sockriter from Lewes, whose brother, CMS Paul J. Glynn, whose family lives in Wilmington, left New Year's Eve and is in Da Nang.

Before going to Vietnam, Paul was a military aide to former President Lyndon B. Johnson. He served with Johnson in Washington when he was vice president and also when he became president.

Prior to that, Paul was on President John F. Kennedy's Air Force One as a flight steward. When Johnson left the White House, Paul left too and went to Texas with the former president and was stationed at Bergstrom Air Force Base there.

The sun sets on another day of war near Chu Lai. The A-4 Skyhawk (opposite) carried out some of the first air strikes by the United States during the war. A Skyhawk is also believed to have dropped the last U.S. bombs on Vietnam.

SINCE ITS 1968 DEBUT, THE MAILBAG HIT THE GROUND RUNNING AND NEVER LOOKED BACK. Our servicemen's overwhelming response grew the weekly column to twice a week in less than a month, then three times a week, a frequency it maintained for more than a year. We had tapped into something special. In the May 22 column, we recognized another milestone:

As promised, a celebration.

What better reason to celebrate than us – today we are four. On May 20, 1968, the first Vietnam Mailbag rolled off the presses.

It's been a success story all the way, bolstered by 833 letters from First Staters serving in the Republic of Vietnam – plus a few slipped to us from Cambodia, Laos and Thailand.

The column has sustained a consistent readership throughout. Again, thanks to you. You First Staters have provided us at home with much information about this "war," and its miseries and heartaches and loneliness.

And we've also shared your good times. Your special Thanksgiving and Christmas dinners in the combat zone, your often rewarding descriptions of pacification programs in Vietnam, and some rather humorous, if not ribald, accounts of the black market and Saigon bars. We've been informed as well as entertained by your correspondence.

And we've also traveled with you. From the bustle of Saigon to historical Hue, from jungles to firebases. Also to Da Nang, Phu Cat, Phu Lam, Bien Hoa, An Loc, An Khe, Vinh Long, Phan Rang, Ban Me Thuot, Quang Tri, Pleiku. These have all become household places the armchair traveler can identify with and visit through you.

We've been to all these places, through you. You've made us more aware than perhaps war correspondents of what it's like to really exist in Vietnam – and that's all some of you have done. Exist. Seldom totally prejudiced, most of you tell it like it is and that's what we've come to expect from you. You haven't let us down. Thanks.

You share your weather with us. Monsoons and all. Your seasons are so mixed up that when you get home not only do you have to readjust to civvie life again, you also have to get acquainted with Delaware weather, a breed unto itself.

And your pictures. These we enjoy just as much as your letters because it gives us a chance to see the face behind the words. And that's what we like. Sometimes you appear in the column individually, sometimes two First Staters together, occasionally three together, or, only once, five together in the largest "groupie" shot we've ever published. And it was great.

We've been the prime benefactor of souvenirs. During the monsoon season, many of your letters reach us with mud on them. Honest-to-goodness Vietnamese mud. But that's a fringe benefit.

Your uniform patches mean a great deal and we have a collection totaling about a dozen now. Each one different, too. And Vietnamese money. Both a note and a coin for 20 dong, the unit of currency in Vietnam. Some artwork, too.

Occasionally, you get very poetic and share your innermost thoughts and fears in verse. Several poets in the group. One of you, who has returned to the states, has published a book of his poetry that is already becoming a good seller on the market.

You keep us informed and that keeps the column going. As long as there is interest in the Vietnam Mailbag, we'll do the behind-the-scenes production work. After all, it is your show. And we intend to keep it that way until you're all home – whenever that is.

We've shared your enthusiasm over an early drop, that special letter from home, a hot meal, boots that fit, American beer and a day without rain. You've been through it all in the past four years and we're proud to say we've been right behind you.

During the Mailbag's five-year run, many, many servicemen called or visited us when they returned stateside. My good friend Air Force Sgt. Daniel P. Stokes stopped by the office on his way to Langley Air Force Base in Virginia. We wrote about his visit as well as the call from Army Spc. Francis M. Jornlin II in the March 13 column:

Danny got a two-month drop and is exceedingly glad to be stateside again. He's a bit pessimistic about troop withdrawals in Vietnam and believes most men are being reassigned rather than coming home. Danny, after his leave, expects to be at Langley about 20 months.

Speaking of drops, Army Spc. Francis M. Jornlin II boasts of a five-month early out. Frank was stationed on Firebase Nancy and says the Army has turned it over to the South Vietnamese.

Frank left Vietnam from Tan Son Nhut and says four or five planes – about 1,000 men – are leaving the combat zone daily. Frank experienced temperature extremes of 107 degrees when he left Vietnam all the way down to 30 below when he stopped in Anchorage, Alaska.

After his 30-day leave, Frank reports to Fort Hood, Texas, [where he] will finish his 11 months of duty.

As the Mailbag began, so it ended as a once-a-week column. On September 1, we announced, effective September 4, the Mailbag would appear only on Mondays. We were winding down too and viewed that as good news with more and more Delawareans returning home. Over five calendar years, we had a good run, a perfect bell-shaped curve, with columns published once, twice, then three times a week, then back to twice weekly, then once a week, based on a total of nearly 900 letters from Delawareans in Vietnam.

Our swansong column on December 11 was indeed bittersweet.

We'd been thinking about this column a long time, know-ing it had to come, but knowing, too, that when it did come, it would mean both happiness and sadness.

Happiness because perhaps this country's best Christmas present to itself (if you're a dove) is at hand. Happiness because finally we can say with certainty we're sending the complimentary subscription of The Morning News to fewer than 50 Delawareans stationed in or off the coast of South Vietnam. Happiness, because it looks like soon, and we're not sure when, those remaining men will ETS and head stateside on the freedom bird.

Sadness because there will be a void for us and for our ardent readers without the Vietnam Mailbag. Someone asked us once, "Surely it must be a chore to put together a column three times a week, or twice a week, or once a week?" as we have done for the past four years and eight months.

A chore? Unalterably no. Definitely no. Heavens no. Granted, some-times we ran late and our editor got a bit anxious, but we usually managed to get it together before deadline.

Sadness because we've enjoyed your frequent and abundant correspon-dence from the jungles, coastal areas, big cities and from off the coast.

You've made Vietnam gruesomely real to us and to your families and friends at home. In your nearly 900 letters since we've been in opera-tion, you've shared much with us. We've tried to share a little cheer.

We've been able to see your mood change from the terror and fear of the war that was never declared a war when we first began in 1968, to the somewhat more relaxed pace in 1969 with pacification programs to anxiety the next year over Tet, over new bombings, new raids, to your hopes last year for peace, to your boredom this year (for some of you) of doing nothing but marking time in a place where you neither asked to come nor were told when you were going to leave.

Throughout our time together, you've been happy, sad and most stops in between. You've shared … your feelings on the war, your humor, your gripes, your longings.

But, most of all, we've come to depend on you for your continued efforts to keep those of us back in the First State aware of what it is that's really going on in Vietnam.

Long ago, we adopted the belief, based on fact, that Delawareans "tell it like it is" and this added fuel to your literary fires. Perhaps we'll con-vert some of your reminiscences into a book some day…

There seems to be only one thing left to say: we'll miss you.

We deactivated the Vietnam Mailbag on December 18 with our fourth "Operation Christmas" column, featuring an annual exchange of messages to and from First Staters for the holidays. We closed the Mailbag, writing, "Again, our best wishes for the New Year … and PEACE."

Call it happenstance, but the Mailbag received two letters from a Navy seaman after the column ended. Here are excerpts from his previously unpublished letters.

"Hello, this is the first time I've written you. If this letter seems to be written badly, it is due to the fact that we are in the middle of a storm and the ship is rocking pretty good. I just want to thank you and Neal Kelley, a First Stater, for the article [in] the Vietnam Mailbag about me. Neal and I knew each other through his girl-friend. When she told me her boyfriend was in the Navy, I asked what ship. When she replied the USS *Waccamaw*, I just about fell through the floor! Here I am on the same ship thinking I was the only First Stater on board but I wasn't…. I have to stop here as we are going to refuel the USS *Midway* in about an hour and I want to eat dinner so, again, thank you very much."
Navy Seaman Edward Cycyk aboard the USS Waccamaw, Dec. 1

Ed voiced a generation's hope in his – and our – final letter, dated December 23, from the war zone. He lamented, "I know this is the season to be jolly but how can one be happy with all the hate and discontent in the world, especially over here? I'm just praying that everything will come out all right."

POSTSCRIPT

SOME AMERICANS RECOGNIZED VIETNAM AS AN UNWINNABLE QUAGMIRE AS EARLY AS 1968, YET THE WAR MARCHED ON FOR FIVE MORE YEARS AND SNUFFED OUT AN ADDITIONAL 21,031 U.S. TROOPS.

As a conflict of choice to contain communism, the war divided and frustrated Americans, inflicting angry wounds that fester to this day. Peace seemed improbable throughout most of the conflict's turbulent 11-year run.

On January 25, 1972, President Nixon publicly acknowledged numerous secret peace proposals his administration had extended to the North Vietnamese during the previous two and a half years. He also announced an eight-point peace plan that included a presidential election in South Vietnam.

The Vietcong responded by proposing a revision of the peace plan they had first put forward in July 1971. It called for South Vietnamese President Nguyen Van Thieu's immediate resignation, followed by negotiations with Saigon after it abandoned its policies of "waging war and repression." The North Vietnamese, through their delegation in Paris, also insisted on Thieu's leaving office and announced U.S. prisoners of war would be released only when the United States had withdrawn its support of Thieu and the war ended.

South Vietnamese forces in February 1972 made three incursions into Cambodia. On March 23, peace talks were halted. A week later, the North Vietnamese executed a major offensive into Quang Tri Province, south of the DMZ. U.S. forces retaliated early in April with the first deeply penetrating bombing of the north since 1967.

May was equally ominous. Nixon ordered the mining of Haiphong and Hanoi, major North Vietnamese ports, as well as air strikes on enemy railroads to destroy supply routes. The war dragged on through the summer. In September, Quang Tri City was liberated from the communists by the South Vietnamese.

Despite the continuing war, Henry Kissinger, Nixon's assistant for national security affairs, again met secretly in Paris with North Vietnamese delegate Le Duc Tho on October 8. Communist acceptance of a peace plan separating the military from the political settlement of the conflict constituted a monumental breakthrough. On October 26, Kissinger announced a nine-point peace plan, even though several issues had not been resolved. Thieu blasted the plan as a sellout.

Meetings between Kissinger and Tho resumed two months later but talks abruptly collapsed. Nixon again ordered massive bombings of Hanoi and Haiphong. A world shocked by the apparent re-escalation of hostilities watched with horror as the fierce aerial assaults razed North Vietnam's most strategic cities and resulted in the loss or capture of nearly 100 Air Force personnel and more than a dozen B-52 aircraft. On December 30, 1972, the United States halted bombings in North Vietnam.

Secret peace meetings resumed in January 1973 between Kissinger, who would win a Nobel Prize for his peace efforts, and Tho. On January 23, Nixon televised his announcement to the nation that an agreement for a formal cease-fire had been reached.

The accord, signed in Paris on January 27 by the United States, South Vietnam, North Vietnam and the Vietcong's Provisional Revolutionary Government of South Vietnam, was effective on January 28 and called for the withdrawal of all U.S. combat troops and allied forces within 60 days.

Factional fighting broke out almost immediately after U.S. troops left the country and escalated to major engagements throughout 1974. The North Vietnamese, aided by their southern allies, routed South Vietnam in December 1974 and major cities fell like dominoes to the communists. Soon after Saigon was captured with little resistance on April 30, 1975, the Republic of Vietnam surrendered unconditionally to the Provisional Revolutionary Government.

The undeclared war cost 58,193 American lives.

U.S. military involvement in Vietnam ended in 1973 with a paper-thin accord the North Vietnamese all but ignored. After months of ruthless offensives, the communists (opposite) overran South Vietnam, toppling Saigon on April 30, 1975.

1972 – YEAR IN REVIEW

JANUARY 25
Nixon discloses an eight-point peace plan which includes a new presidential election in South Vietnam.

MARCH 23
The Paris peace talks are suspended by the U.S. delegation.

MARCH 30
North Vietnam launches the Easter Offensive across the DMZ in Quang Tri Province.

APRIL 7
The U.S. retaliates by resuming bombardment of North Vietnam.

MAY 8
Nixon orders mining of North Vietnam's major ports such as Haiphong.

SEPTEMBER 15
ARVN troops recapture Quang Tri City.

OCTOBER 8
Henry Kissinger, assistant to the president for national security affairs, and North Vietnamese delegate Le Duc Tho, begin secret peace negotiations in Paris.

OCTOBER 26
Kissinger announces "peace is at hand" and discloses a nine-point peace plan, which Thieu promptly criticizes.

DECEMBER 8
Kissinger and Tho resume peace talks in Paris, which collapse Dec. 16.

DECEMBER 17
Nixon orders more bombings of Hanoi and Haiphong, resulting in the loss of 93 U.S. airmen and 15 B-52 aircraft.

DECEMBER 29
Nixon halts the bombing of North Vietnam.

DECEMBER 31
U.S. troops in South Vietnam number 24,200.

1973

JANUARY 23
After six days of discussions, Kissinger and Tho meet again. Nixon announces agreement for a formal cease-fire.

JANUARY 27
Delegations from the United States, South Vietnam, North Vietnam and the Provisional Revolutionary Government of Vietnam sign a peace accord to end the war. The cease-fire is effective January 28.

PART II

★ THE VETERANS TODAY ★
HOW THE WAR SHAPED THEIR LIVES

ROBERT S. BISS
ARMY 1968-1970

No one gains entry to Robert Samuel Biss's cherry-appointed home office and its woodsy vista without first passing by King, a perfectly confirmed German shepherd dog whose eyes monitor a visitor's every move from a large framed oil painting placed strategically in the room.

King remains Biss's gate-keeper today just as he was 40 years ago in Vietnam when the two served with the 212th Military Police Sentry Dog Company. First in Long Binh and later in Vinh Long, King was Biss's protector and pal, his life and lifeline in the combat zone for nearly a year.

Through his many letters, pictures and news clippings to the Vietnam Mailbag, Biss both educated and enlightened readers about the role of the sentry dog, offering an altogether different dimension of the war. We always looked forward to reading about his adventures with King. And we were moved that he signed his correspondence, "Bob and King." But we weren't prepared for his November 24, 1968 letter, written at 3:45 a.m.

"The saddest day of my Army career was November 13 [1968] when I took King back to Long Binh, and November 14 when I said goodbye to him," Biss wrote in an aching letter that touched dog-lovers everywhere. He had been promoted to corporal, a rank which prohibited him from handling a dog.

"I cried in the kennel," Biss recalls, glancing tenderly at King's portrait in his office. Man and his dog had had several good months and together had survived the ugly, controversial war. Biss knew the time had come for both to move on, he to military advancement in country and King back to Okinawa for retraining and assignment to another handler. At that moment, though, their diverging destinies made parting unbearable.

The sorrow that overcame him in Long Binh rekindled his childhood farewells, like losing his father, a welder and draftsman, to a heart attack. Biss, an only child whose mother was a registered nurse, floundered. "Dad died when I was 10. That sucked. I was a latchkey orphan because of the circumstances," he says. But the fair-haired boy made the best of his situation. He also made the track team in junior high school.

"In high school, I was more interested in science and exploding things than sports," he remembers. He first aspired to be a doctor but, given his fondness for animals, especially dogs, decided to become a veterinarian. "I always had a dog growing up. There was Chippie, a collie, then Blackie, a mutt, and Buff, a mixed collie."

After graduating from Mount Pleasant Senior High School in suburban Wilmington, Delaware, in 1964, Biss attended Louisburg Junior College in North Carolina and, after taking a semester off, received an associate's degree in arts and another associate's degree in science in 1967.

Army Pfc. Robert S. Biss and his beloved dog, King, served together for almost a year with the 212th Military Police Sentry Dog Company.

PFC. R.S. BISS
212th M.P.Co. (S.D.)
C/O 175th Avm. Co.
APO S.

FREE

26
AUG

February 4, 1970
Wednesday

January 2, 1970
Friday morning
2 a.

212th Military Po
Long Binh Post
APO San Franc
April 27, 1968

Dear Nancy,

Happy new year

I don't really
for you this time c
however, I'm send
from the brigade
the other sentry
981st M.P.Co. I

Dear Nancy,

I received your letter
I am quite pleased and surprise
idea. From what information you say
in your letter, I think the column would be
big hit with the readers. I believe you may
have some trouble getting us to write letters
to you - most of the information would probably
letters to our parents.
myself. I could

PFC. R.S. BISS
212th M.P.Co. (S.D.)
C/O 175 Avm. Co.
APO S.F. 96357

FREE

'20
JUL

VIA AIR MAIL
CORREO AEREO
PAR AVION

Miss Nancy Lynch
C/O The News Journal Co.
Wilmington, Delaware
19801

now, I close. King an
when are you going to a full page?

Bob + King

354

MAKING HIS CHOICE

"I wanted to continue on to one of the North Carolina schools but I didn't have the GPA [grade point average]." His choice after graduation was clear. "Either I would go to Canada or I would go into the service. I was too patriotic and too much of an American to go to Canada so I decided to volunteer for military service before they could draft me."

But which branch? "I pretty much settled on the Army through a process of elimination. One Sunday afternoon at college, I saw a picture of a marine on a hill in Vietnam, with a dog in *Look* magazine. Then I thought, 'Oh shit, does the Army have dogs?'" He asked the Army recruiter the next morning. "I was passionate over German shepherds. I loved Rin Tin Tin and Bullet [television cowboy Roy Rogers' German shepherd] as a kid. I thought they were the coolest dogs."

Then Biss had a revelation. "The thought that the Army would give me a German shepherd to hang out with while serving my country just blew me away." But it wasn't that easy. First he had to go through basic training, then military police school, then volunteer to be a dog handler. To be certain, he spent a day during spring break with a dog handler at Fort Story, Virginia. "I decided that was absolutely what I wanted," he recalls.

He enlisted in the Army in June 1967, and left for basic training at Fort Bragg, North Carolina, in August. After leave, he moved on to Fort Gordon, Georgia, for eight weeks of military police school. There, he told everyone he saw he wanted to be a dog handler. His persistence paid off but not before being rattled by a sergeant in the mess hall who told him all volunteer dog handler slots had been filled. "All the air deflated out of me."

Biss couldn't believe what he was hearing after all his hard work. "After a pregnant pause, the sergeant told me there was about a quarter-inch of space at the bottom of the registration form. 'I'll bet if you can get your sorry ass down to the orderly room, I can probably squeeze your name in.' I never ran faster."

Early in 1968, he got his orders to Okinawa for six weeks of training as a dog handler. "I walked off the plane and I couldn't believe it. I'm a beach person and, oh my God, there were palm trees everywhere. They put us on a truck to take us to the handling school where we would be assigned dogs."

All dogs entered the military program through the Sentry Dog School at Lackland Air Force Base in San Antonio, Texas, Biss wrote the Mailbag on August 24, 1968. Dogs, he explained, were donated or purchased for no more than $150 each. The German shepherd was the breed of choice for its "working ability, temperament, size and suitability for all types of climate and terrain," he wrote, noting the breed's senses of smell, hearing and vision surpassed those of a human by 40, 20 and 10 times, respectively.

At Okinawa, King was the first dog Biss saw and it was love at first sight. "Out of 40 or 50 dogs there, the law of attraction put us together. I couldn't believe it. And King loved me right back." From that random pairing, Biss and King, with "229M" tattooed inside his left ear, were inseparable. Schooling demanded much from both of them.

"The course is broken down as follows: first week is obedience, next two are for agitation, and the last three are for scouting problems, the last week of which is all-night training, which is the most realistic training that we received," Biss wrote in a letter.

"To graduate," he adds now, "we had to find one person hiding in a 500-acre sugar cane field. Because we knew how to 'work a dog,' we could find that person. We did it twice. King had it going on." Biss and King were ready for Vietnam.

They arrived in Long Binh in March 1968 as members of the first of two sentry dog companies in Vietnam, the 212th Military Police Sentry Dog Company. The 212th was reactivated in 1966 for duty in Vietnam and by July 1968 had about 240 men and dogs in six detachments.

For four months, Biss and King patrolled the ammunition dump. "Long Binh was horrible," he recounts, explaining it reminded him of a stateside base, but, next to King, "the sunrises and sunsets were the best part of Vietnam. I'd be on duty 6 p.m. to midnight or midnight to 6 a.m. That was unique to Long Binh."

OVERNIGHT PATROLS

During patrol one night, Biss and King took a break. "The sergeant checked on us and brought us C-rations. King and I sat down on a pallet. The dog of the other MP on patrol with us alerted. We heard a noise that sounded like 'fukoo' and thought the VC were messing with us," Biss remembers. "The MP set off a flare for illumination, called his sergeant, and put his dog to work searching various pallets. When we told the sergeant about the incident, he started laughing. 'You must have heard the fuck you lizard,' he said and left."

Biss wasn't sure he believed the story until he returned stateside. He read an article in *Playboy* magazine which specifically referred to the "fuck you lizard." "I said, 'son of a bitch, it really does exist.' It made a believer out of me."

Despite the distracting lizard, Biss and King kept busy. He had written the Mailbag on July 16, 1968: "About three weeks ago, I was in a demo with King, put on for a 3-star, the new Deputy Commanding General of United States Army Vietnam (USARV). The company spent almost the whole morning on police calls and clean-up details and he only stayed about 30 minutes. Everyone was so relieved when he left that we were off for the following two days.

"Words can't express the feeling of security I have when I have to walk down a completely dark air strip with just King. He is the compromising force between me and an intruder."

We put on many demonstrations for visiting dignitaries to the L.B. post. As a matter of fact, anyone of any importance who visits the post is automatically shown the dogs."

The pace accelerated when they transferred in July 1968 to Vinh Long, in southern Vietnam's Mekong Delta, where Biss and King helped protect the airfield from the Vietcong and guarded the helicopters. The base was frequently rocketed and mortared by the enemy. "That was the scariest part," recalls Biss. Indeed, he had shared his apprehensions decades earlier with the Mailbag: "Words can't express the feeling of security I have when I have to walk down a completely dark air strip with just King. He is the compromising force between me and an intruder."

After his promotion and after King returned to Okinawa, Biss instructed sentry dog handlers. And he did see King again in Vietnam with a new handler. Biss extended his tour twice, serving in 1968, 1969 and 1970. As he advanced in rank, he explains how he remained involved with the sentry dog program.

"As a corporal I was in charge of one of the two shifts each night at the detachment in Vinh Long [and was] referred to as NCOIC (noncommissioned officer-in-charge). A few months later I was promoted to sergeant and was then in charge of the whole Vinh Long Detachment, 212th Military Police Company/Vinh Long. Both positions required daily training for obedience and agitation. Often I played the role of the enemy and was the 'dummy' for the dogs to attack. Thank goodness for the thick 'attack suits.'"

After Biss was promoted, he could no longer work with King. But he remained involved with sentry dogs and their handlers, like Army Pfc. Don Kunstrom (left). Biss (opposite) in Long Binh.

LETTERS LEAD TO LOVE

During his service in Vietnam, Biss started corresponding with Sharon Keirn of Wilmington, who had seen his name while reading the Mailbag during her lunch hour at work and spontaneously wrote to him. They discovered they had attended the same high school but she was three grades below him. Through their long-distance letter writing, they also discovered they had much more in common.

After he returned stateside in April 1970, Biss and Sharon dated, got engaged and married in 1971. They have two children, Garret, a lieutenant in the Marine Corps stationed in Pensacola, Florida, and training to be a Marine Corps aviator, and Dawn Gilts of Orlando, Florida, who has a master's degree in social work and is a social worker at Florida Hospital/Orlando.

Although the couple divorced after 17 years of marriage, Biss says he and Sharon remain "best friends" and frequently see each other at family gatherings. "I really screwed up being a great husband, but I try really hard to be the best dad and father-in-law our two awesome children and their spouses could possibly have."

After graduating from the University of Delaware in 1971 with a degree in entomology, Biss ran the university's pest control division for housing and food services before operating his own pest control company in Newark. In 1978, he signed on with ICI Americas, now AstraZeneca, as a technical service representative. He transferred into executive sales and marketing two years later and retired in

1994. Since then, Biss has been self-employed as a free enterprise business consultant specializing in travel.

Long before his career, he had scrapped his dream of becoming a veterinarian. "I looked at the number of applicants and the number of acceptances and, statistically, the odds were not in my favor. I had a better chance of surviving a direct mortar hit in Vietnam than graduating from veterinary school."

Today, Biss, 63, who lives near Hockessin, Delaware, is not vocal on Vietnam and doesn't socialize with veterans. He has suffered marginally from post-traumatic stress disorder [PTSD] from his service in the war and says, at times, it affects his attitude and magnifies his perfectionism and need to control. "I feel I had a lot of dysfunctional behavior in my first 20 years. After Vietnam, I sought help to sort things out and dropped the baggage I was carrying."

He lauds Delaware as "the best state to have been from" as a serviceman in Vietnam. "They provided a free newspaper, the Vietnam Mailbag column, the state flag, a cash bonus and care packages from SOS Vietnam at Red Lion Methodist Church." His pride in his home state is evident. When he's asked where he's from, he responds, "I'm from the great First State of Delaware!"

Biss doesn't dwell on Vietnam today but one parallel he draws between Vietnam and Iraq is that "the serviceman today, as then, can be hanging out with the enemy and not know it" due to similarities in appearance of friend and foe.

Other than that, Biss says he's just glad he got through Vietnam alive. And he's forever grateful a dog named King was at his side.

RICHARD GLAZIER
ARMY 1967-1969

If Richard Glazier were a betting man, and he is, he'd wager the house that racetracks will always be in his future. After all, they've been in his past since he was a kid and they're in his present as Delaware Park's odds-on favorite public relations personality and winner-take-all television host.

Much of Richard Glazier's work in intelligence with the 1st Military Assistance Command Vietnam (MACV) involved secrecy. Today, the gregarious Glazier, in his office at Delaware Park, revels in his very public profile at the thoroughbred racetrack.

And, clearly, the lack of horseracing in Vietnam was a major issue for Glazier. As an Army intelligence analyst and interrogator based in Phan Thiet from 1967 to 1969, he made Vietnam Mailbag readers laugh when he griped in his first letter from the combat zone: "It's too hot here and there's no racetracks." During his R&R to Sydney, Australia, he spent "every day and night" trackside, only to face his own interrogation by military police before returning to Vietnam with the wad of legitimate winnings he pocketed.

But that was long ago and far away.

"I don't care what they call me here at Delaware Park, my bosses are the fans," fast-forwards the gregarious Glazier, 60, at ease in the TV Room, one of his three official offices at the Stanton, Delaware, thoroughbred track. Glazier's space inside the clubhouse mirrors a Circuit City showroom with 13 television sets covering an entire wall and six smaller screens, stacked three high, on his desk. All simultaneously broadcast horse races from around the globe.

The living color technology dominates the office, which also stables his mini-fridge, microwave oven, computer and microphone. A colorful Delaware Park wall poster backdrops Glazier's desk and his mascot, Bungi, a small, stuffed brown horse, hangs above it, tethered to the ceiling by a wire. "When I do my daily TV show, which is every live racing day, Bungi's trainer off-camera lowers him slowly. He comes down, like Groucho Marx's duck, and whispers in my ear the name of a sire – daddy – of horses that are bred to be good runners on the turf. He does OK, but nobody's perfect."

Glazier reaches for a box on a low shelf to his left. "Bungi has costumes, too. He dresses up for the 4th of July, Halloween, very hot days with a straw hat and lounge chair, rainy days with galoshes and umbrella and, depending on the secret name, an appropriate costume. When he whispered Brahms, Mozart or Bernstein, he held a musical instrument or a baton. For Galileo, he had a telescope. For Cat Thief, he wore a cat mask and so on. Whenever we can use a prop, we do. Sometimes it's clever, sometimes it's cheesy, but the fans like cheesy."

The phone rings. "Yeah, 1951 was the first Delaware Handicap, which was the New Castle Handicap before that." Glazier hangs up smiling. "Been here 21 years," he volunteers. "I love what I'm doing." The enthusiasm he exudes is more than contagious. He's a one-man entertainment system with more horse and track facts in his head than the *Daily Racing Form*.

Thoroughly in his element, his eyes steal to the mini-sets on his desk. "We're in the off-season now. Delaware Park runs from April to November as a summer track. So this is where I am all winter, in the TV Room," Glazier explains. "My other offices are in the press box and in the paddock when we're running."

He talks about what he does in the off-season. "We take the country's five biggest tracks running now: Aqueduct in New York, Gulfstream in Florida, Fairgrounds in New Orleans, Santa Anita in California, and Laurel in Maryland, and give results which are taped for Comcast 28 community television. The show airs at 11 p.m. nightly and 7:30 p.m. on Saturday, 364 nights of the year but I'm not on every night. I also give results every three races on the hotline which gets 5,000 calls a day."

Putting his workload in perspective, Glazier confides he's never seen the inside of the beach apartment that he and Amy, his high school sweetheart and wife of 36 years, have rented for a decade in Ventnor, New Jersey. "I'm always here," he shrugs, feigning dismay. "In the winter, I work five days a week and during the live racing season, I work six days a week but I love this place."

That love was an acquired taste. "I saw my first race as a young kid with my mother. Delaware Park would have a Ladies Day once in a while and my mom would take me. All I did was pick up losing tickets on the ground, cheer for a horse whose name I liked, and eat a hot dog. It was just a fun day for a kid."

The fun turned into curiosity a few years later, recalls Glazier. "When I was maybe 12 or so, my dad went to Brandywine Raceway, which was for trotters. As best as I recall, he maybe went once a year.

When he came home, he tossed me his program and I was very intrigued, to say the least, with all the past performance data."

As a student at Pierre S. du Pont High School in Wilmington, he remembers, "going to Brandywine was sort of a social place to go for the teenagers at P.S. du Pont. [The track] let you in free for the last few races, so we would go up there, watch and bet a few races and then head to the Charcoal Pit for a late-night snack. To most of my pals, it was just something to do."

But to Glazier, it was more than just something to do. "I really got into handicapping the races. Brandywine was at night, the time between races was less than the flats [thoroughbred tracks] and the program had all the info as opposed to Delaware Park where you had to buy a racing form in addition to the program, too much for a poor kid. Usually at Brandywine, you could pick up a discarded program when you got there late, where at Delaware Park, it was 25 cents for a program and 50 cents for a form. Today, it's $3 and $5.50, respectively."

Away from the tracks, Glazier, oldest of three sons of Amelia and Morris Glazier, a price clerk for Wilmington Plumbing Supply, excelled in basketball at P.S. du Pont. "In 1965, my senior year, we were co-champs of the Blue Hen Conference with Brandywine High School," he says proudly.

FAST TRACK TO INTELLIGENCE SCHOOL

In November 1966, he was drafted. "I took the test and qualified to be in intelligence so I enlisted in the Army for three years," he says. Basic training at Fort Jackson, South Carolina, was routine. "Intelligence school was January to March 1967 at Fort Holabird, in Baltimore. Baltimore, could I have asked for a better place? There was a bus, called the Pony Express, that took people to Pimlico [a thoroughbred track]. And you could take a taxi to the civic center in downtown Baltimore and catch a bus to Delaware Park. Both of which I did many times."

Glazier digresses and says his preference in tracks evolved over many years. "I started liking thoroughbred racing and losing interest in the trotters. By the time I joined the Army, I was really into the flats and the rest is history." He explains. "There are lots of reasons I like thoroughbred racing better: different distances, different surfaces: dirt and grass. I think the most significant reason I switched was I think flat racing is way, way more honest than harness racing."

And there's another reason. "One of my best friends growing up, Joey Glazar, no relation, but also a Vietnam vet, was the first one of my pals to get into the flats rather than the trotters and he used to drag me along with him to Delaware Park and Garden State Park and, pretty quickly, I changed allegiance."

In addition to easy access to racetracks, intelligence school afforded Glazier the opportunity to indulge his histrionic side. Of 35 men in his class, 33 received orders for Vietnam after their March 1967 graduation. Glazier and another soldier stayed at the school as interrogation instructors until they were deployed to Vietnam in September 1967. "There was a lot of role-playing [as an instructor]. I dressed up in different uniforms and played the role of a prisoner."

After landing at Bien Hoa, Glazier remembers he was "a little scared. I didn't know what to expect." He boarded an air-conditioned bus to Saigon to the 525th Military Intelligence Group. He was then flown to Pleiku, Ban Me Thuot and, finally, Phan Thiet, his final destination, 100 miles east of Saigon, where he replaced the intelligence analyst/interrogator for the army's Advisory Team 37. "It was a different world. My job changed every day and, as an advisor, I worked closely with the South Vietnamese."

Glazier speaks highly of the ARVN soldiers he worked with and has stayed in contact with one, Ngo Van Ngo, his interpreter in Vietnam, who now lives in Silver Spring, Maryland. "I call him Jack. I made good friends with the South Vietnamese," he says. "When we went out on operations together, there were usually two Americans and 12 to 15 South Vietnamese and it was complete trust."

Some were night missions. "It was so dark and quiet. There were a billion stars in the sky. It was so peaceful, it was hard to imagine a war was going on. I remember lying on a sand dune while the South Vietnamese platoon was on guard duty, taking good care of me. That was one of the best night's sleep I had over there."

Glazier also interrogated more than 100 enemy prisoners during his tour. "Most were *chieu hoi*, meaning they didn't want to be Vietcong, they wanted to join our side and were thrilled to have a meal and a bar of soap."

He questioned only one "tough guy," an NVA officer. "He had a head wound and the South Vietnamese had pounded on the wound with a rope. I was always the good guy with the soft touch. I asked

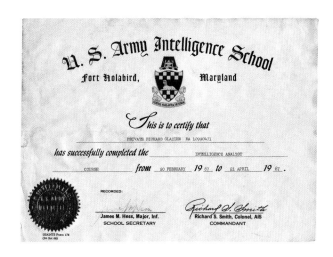

Despite the increased threat level around Tet, the Vietnamese new year, Glazier still took time to keep updated on his favorite sport – horseracing.

him about his family. For days, all he said was "f… you." I stayed at it and finally found his breaking point. I told him we'd take him to the hospital in Nha Trang where he'd have clean sheets and blonde-haired nurses. He had a lot of information and I got a good report out of him. He died a few days after he got to the hospital."

Glazier wrote daily INTSUMs in Phan Thiet until he left Vietnam in June 1969. "I'd gather reports from various intelligence units – Air Force, Navy, South Vietnamese and the 101st Airborne Division – on the previous day's happenings. The second section of my report [was intelligence on] enemy activity from agents. The next section was the next day's planned operations."

Glazier pauses. "I really liked my job," he says, adding a sad note. One of the soldiers from the South Vietnamese intelligence platoon was killed and Glazier paid his respects by visiting the man's home. "His family seemed quite touched that I came to see them and fussed over me," he recalls.

Despite the absence of racetracks in Vietnam, Glazier stayed in touch with the sport through his mother, who knew her son well. "She wrote me every single day I was in Nam so I would get mail every day, but the best thing dear old mom did was she went to the newsstand every Monday and bought and mailed me the *Morning Telegraph*, which is what the eastern edition of the *Daily Racing Form* was called in those days. The *Telegraph* would have all the race results of the big races run on Saturday. There was no Sunday racing then, so Saturday was *the* day," he recalls.

"This allowed me to keep up with all that was going on in horse racing and it also gave me the opportunity to make bets while I was overseas. I would have to make my bets a week in advance or sometimes by calling home on MARS [Military Affiliate Radio System]. I actually hit a few races and made some money. It was a great morale booster when I read that I cashed a bet."

Glazier even taught a few of his buddies how to read a racing form "and actually bumped into one of them at a track once. It was a million-to-one coincidence." He took his first R&R to Sydney where he was at trackside nonstop and "did pretty well. I took $200 with me and came back with $600. MPs interrogated me before I left. They thought I got the money on the black market."

"I made good friends with the South Vietnamese. When we went out on operations together, there were usually two Americans and 12 to 15 South Vietnamese and it was complete trust."

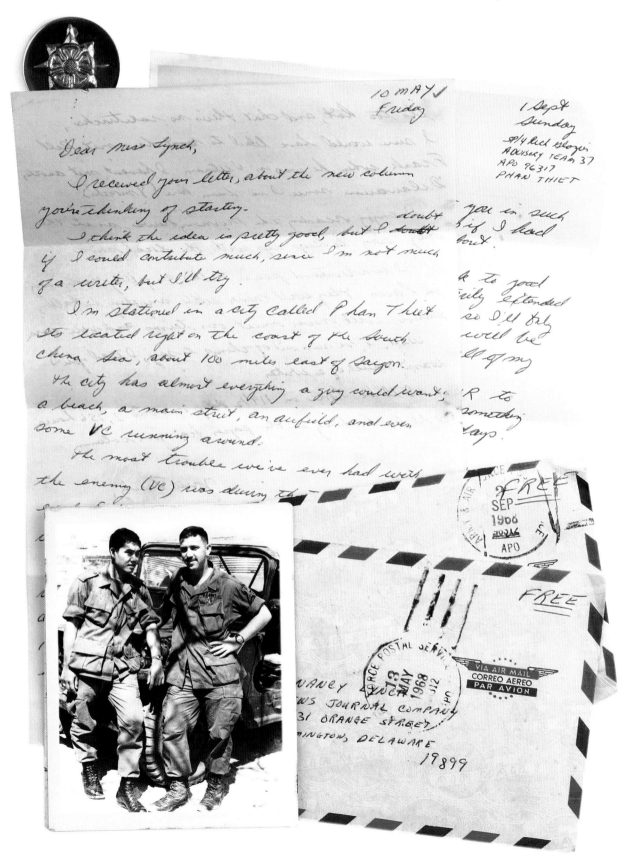

10 May
Friday

Dear Miss Lynch,

I received your letter, about the new column you're thinking of starting.

I think the idea is pretty good, but I doubt if I could contribute much, since I'm not much of a writer, but I'll try.

I'm stationed in a city called Phan Thiet. Its located right on the coast of the South China Sea, about 100 miles east of Saigon.

The city has almost everything a guy could want, a beach, a main street, an airfield, and even some VC running around.

The most trouble we've ever had with the enemy (VC) was during th

1 Sept
Sunday
SP/4 Rick George?
Advisory Team 37
APO 96317
PHAN THIET

you in such
if I had
bout.

to good
ily extended
so I'll only
will be
ll of my

R to
omethi
ays.

NANCY LYNCH
WS JOURNAL COMPANY
31 ORANGE STREET
MINGTON, DELAWARE
19899

JOIN THE ARMY, SEE THE WORLD

He liked his job in Vietnam so much he extended his tour. "Everybody from intelligence ended up at Fort Bragg. I didn't want to go to North Carolina and be a soldier again. My captain needed me and I wanted to be of service and if I stayed in Vietnam, I could get out of the Army five months early." And, for agreeing to stay in country, he was rewarded with a 30-day home leave. Almost as soon as he arrived, he hit the tracks, this time trotters in Harrington, Delaware. "I remember the Beatles' *Hey, Jude* was the number one hit then."

The best part of serving his country in Vietnam was seeing the world. In addition to visiting Sydney, he also took R&Rs to Bangkok and Singapore. In contrast, knowing what he knew as an intelligence analyst, the worst part was "seeing my buddies die. That goes without saying. As many dead VC as I saw, it didn't bother me, but the first time I saw a dead American, I couldn't get over that."

Glazier is especially moved each Memorial Day and takes a moment to recognize fallen troops from all wars on his television show which, by May, has moved from the TV Room to Delaware Park's paddock. "I go all out, I put the flag out and I tell people to sometime during the day remember those guys."

As an intelligence analyst, Glazier worked closely with ARVN troops and received the Medal of Honor from the South Vietnamese Army. To this day, he stays in touch with his interpreter, Ngo Van Ngo (opposite), whom he calls Jack.

THE LONGSHOT BEATS THE ODDS

He considers himself "one of the lucky ones" to have returned home intact. "Once in awhile, if I'm watching a movie about Vietnam, little things will come back to me but if I had it to do over, yes, I would do it again. I was hawkish then and I was behind what we were doing over there," he says. Negatives at home disturbed him. "When I came back, my buddies were doing pot and hash, the girls were loose – that part wasn't bad – and there was inflation."

Nonetheless, coming home in June 1969 had its advantages: hot showers, racetracks and separation from the Army. "When I came home from Nam I wanted to be a professional horse player. I've done it twice." He settled for Brandywine Raceway his first night home, then worked for 18 years as an accountant in West Chester, Pennsylvania. During this time, he also earned an associate's degree in business management from Goldey Beacom College in Wilmington. He and Amy wed in 1972 and have two sons, Michael and David.

In 1987, he lucked into his "dream" job at Delaware Park, one he wouldn't trade for his right arm. "My specialty is grass, turf racing. When Delaware Park is running, my routine is to check the turf on my show. I stomp around on it and say 'the turf is firm' or 'the turf isn't so good today.' Many fans seem to enjoy my antics."

He knows most of them head for bed when his show ends at 11:30 p.m. "I try to send them off with a smile by doing or saying something wacky, but usually I do a funny salute where I pretend to poke my eye or hit my head too hard or fall off my chair or get my hand stuck on my forehead, dumb stuff like that."

As a betting man, Glazier leans toward the number seven. "I was born on 11/7/47 at 7:11 a.m. and weighed seven pounds, seven ounces. Richard has seven letters, so does Glazier. There are two sevens in my phone number. My first girlfriend's first name had seven letters, I was on Advisory Team 37 in Vietnam, Michael has seven letters. Everything in my life has sevens and many times I've bet the number seven."

He shares an example. "Delaware Park was closed on 7/7/77 so I went to Belmont. Horse number seven scratched so I went to Meadowlands and bet on number seven in the seventh race. He came in seventh. I'm still trying to figure out how to win."

And nothing, Glazier readily concedes, beats winning. "When I did make my first bet," he says, "I probably won. I always tell newcomers that everyone at the track won their first bet and that's why they are all here. There's nothing more rewarding than studying those records, putting up your hard-earned money, watching your selection win and then getting money for being correct."

R. LANCE HALL

AIR FORCE 1969-1970

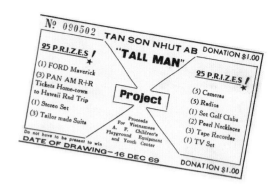

In his own words, Rupert Lance Hall "had it good" during his year-long tour with the Air Force in Vietnam. The opinionated former right-wing conservative from Delaware's oldest city, who today lives in Germany's oldest city, was stationed in Saigon at Tan Son Nhut Air Base where he worked in an air-conditioned office in the payroll division.

At home with Roman ruins in Trier, R. Lance Hall prefers living in Germany where he ended his 20-year military career. Hall was outspoken as an airman in Saigon during his one-year tour. He sent the Mailbag a "Tall Man" chance for a new car.

This was a year of discovery and adventure [for me] in Saigon and Asia," remembers Hall. "Saigon, the Paris of the Orient, was a very beautiful city even with the constant pollution from the tac-tacs killing the trees and foliage, the anti-bomb screens, the barbed wire and plain old garbage everywhere, not to mention the occasional rocket attacks." Tac-tacs, he explains, were vehicles with "motor bike fronts with a box on the back that would [hold] two Americans or 10 Vietnamese. They were noisy and smoky and used as taxis in Saigon."

Duty at the air base, a multi-purpose complex housing a finance office, base exchange, post office, chapel and movie theater, also afforded Hall the opportunity to travel, "up Highway One toward the north and to Hong Kong, Sydney and Bangkok." Duty at Tan Son Nhut also permitted Hall to write often to the Mailbag, speaking out forcefully on the My Lai massacre, news censorship at the Armed Forces Vietnam Network (AFVN) and Vietnam's black market.

With an older brother and sister, speaking out was an acquired trait for Hall, one learned early on and honed during his 20-year career with the Air Force. He explains, starting at the beginning. "I remember having a wonderful childhood and am amazed to this day that I and my friends lived through some of the things we did. Actually, we did nothing bad but dangerous, yes."

Like jumping off the railroad bridge over the Lewes-Rehoboth Canal in Lewes. "We were not allowed to jump off the easier and much lower dock at Angler's Restaurant. Also, playing on the sand dunes was very dangerous but a lot of fun. We also used to smoke in Mayor Otis Smith's very expensive barns, up in the hayloft of all places. And the most dangerous was playing in the ditch we called the 'falcon's nest' on DeVries Circle. We would go home at dusk and glow in the dark. It was polluted and really nasty as it was behind the old chicken plant. I now know it was another Love Canal."

Born three days before Independence Day, 1945, Hall was the youngest of three children of the late Rupert O. Hall, who retired from the Coast Guard, and the late Grace Johnson Hall, a dietitian with Beebe Medical Center. He grew up in Lewes, discovered by Henry Hudson in 1609 and established 22 years later by Dutch settlers as a whaling station on Delaware Bay. "I was fortunate enough to attend Lewes High School [now Cape Henlopen High School] for 12 years, graduating in 1963 with a great bunch of kids," he says. (In southern Delaware during Hall's youth, many towns had a single school building that housed all 12 grades.)

He attended Charlotte College in North Carolina for one semester, from February to June 1964, but "did not like it there as they spoke funny." Hall returned to Delaware and went to Thompson's Private Business School in Wilmington and later transferred to Goldey

considered his tour in Saigon "a year of adventure and discovery."

MAKING FRIENDS IN THE COMBAT ZONE

Upon his arrival in Vietnam in January 1969, as a member of the 377th Combat Support Group, he was welcomed by friends. "I was lucky enough to not feel that I was going to meet my Waterloo in Nam so the stress level was low for me," Hall says. Almost immediately, he was taken by the South Vietnamese people whom he described as "one of the nicest and friendliest folk going. I never met one to this day I did not feel comfortable around and like."

In fact, all the people Hall encountered in Vietnam left an indelible impression on him. Those relationships formed the most positive aspect of the war for him and included "the people I worked and lived with for that amazing year, not only the Vietnamese but folks from all participating nations, the people in the streets, markets and all over Asia that I was fortunate enough to have made contact with. I also met many wonderful and talented folks in the Saigon USO and also in a theater group I took part in."

Today, he wonders aloud about the loyal Vietnamese civilians who worked on base and what happened to them when the U.S. military left their country. "I'm sure they were rounded up and either shot or moved to the north for retraining and rice field slaves."

His worst memory of his service in Vietnam still sobers him. When he first reported to work, "I was instructed to go pick up plastic bags for the shredder. They took all newbies to the morgue and we were told to go in and tell the man at the desk we were to pick up plastic bags. It was just an initiation for new arrivals but it was pretty bad. I really don't want to go into detail but the bad was really bad as in the number of bodies stored there awaiting transport back to CONUS [continental U.S.]. It was a reality check for us all."

om Junior College there. He graduated in January 1967 with a ee in accounting and business administration.

hen was forced to (1) join the Air Force or (2) be drafted into Army. Well, as my mama didn't raise no fool, I opted for the Air e and never looked back," he recalls of his decision. Basic train- t Amarillo (Texas) Air Force Base where the running track was lly on storied Route 66, was "gawd awful." Hall next was ned to the Strategic Air Command Headquarters at Offutt Air e Base near Omaha, Nebraska "What a wonderful time in aha! Big city for me."

Throughout his tour, from January 1969 to February 1970, Hall says the days "flew by, other than the occasional rocket attacks and the constant death and destruction. The traveling I managed was a very enjoyable part of my year in Southeast Asia."

As a frequent correspondent to the Mailbag, he showed his playful side by sending me a chance on a car with a December 1969 drawing at Tan Son Nhut. "If you win, you can take me for a ride in 164 days." And when we didn't win, he sent a note of consolation the next month. "No new wheels for you or for me. What a bummer."

"I was damned proud to be serving my country in a war I felt was truly justified. I also felt at the time we were really helping the people of Vietnam."

9 Nov '69

arking and
something
been out
stop kissi
war. I
governme
are en
and to
poverti

me
direc
the
It's
sh
do
I
a

8 August '69

Dear Nancy,
          Here's another F.N.G. from
Nam, and I might add, a very
angry young (?) American!
          First of all, let me thank
W.M.D. for sending all of us
the paper and also for the assistance
in obtaining the state flags.
          This will be short. I don't
want to be hanged for bad-mouthing
the government. If we
mention w
have been
are losing
will lose
we are in
          To fully
situation.
should get
book — "Ou
the co-author
Mr. William
great book an
facts.

a real enjo
is the Charlie Brown

SERVING WITH PRIDE

Despite his considerable opinions, Hall says he was glad he fulfilled his military obligation. "I was damned proud to be serving my country in a war I felt was truly justified. I also felt at the time we were really helping the people of Vietnam. They all were very happy to have us there helping too. They never stopped thanking us while I was there. It sort of fell apart in the end but now I see it all in a different light."

Looking through that different lens, Hall adds that knowing what he knows now about Vietnam and absent the draft, he would not have served in Vietnam. "I have enjoyed my 20 years spent moving with the military but without the draft I would not have enlisted during the period I did. Sorry. I was never the military type." But, as the son of a career Coast Guardsman, Hall says he knew what to expect of his service and "that helped me remain sane."

He recalls his homecoming from the war was "very low key, family only and damned happy I made it home safe." But his quiet welcome paled to his childhood memory of a Korean War vet's homecoming parade. "It was a big event for Lewes. I remember thinking it was a huge affair for only one GI. Nothing like it for Vietnam vets as I can remember. For us, there's a wall in Washington with a *lot* of names on it."

After Vietnam, Hall was stationed from February 1970 to March 1972 at the Air Force Accounting and Finance Center in Denver. There, he learned the hard way how unpopular his uniform was off post. "We were 'advised' to either wear long civilian raincoats over our uniform going to work or wear civilian clothes and change after arriving. That pissed me off."

There was another repercussion: "I admit," he says, "I lost a lot of respect for my fellow civilian man while stationed in Denver and not being able to be proud to wear a uniform of the armed forces in any place to include my POV [privately-owned vehicle]. Americans went crazy then."

During his two years in Denver, Hall at one point was assigned to the MIA/KIA Special Actions Branch which provided funds to wives and widows from accounts of missing or dead servicemen for necessities like housing, cars and tuitions. "Very interesting and very political" is the extent of Hall's comments, although he wrote on June 27, 1970, his final letter to the Mailbag, "Now that I'm here in Denver, I wish I could have stayed in Saigon. We're working such stupid hours trying to get the system in operation to take over all the pay records etc. in Europe and Southeast Asia."

Hall wasted no time in volunteering for an extended tour in Europe to get out of the states. He was rewarded with orders for Zweibruken Air Base in Germany, where he served with the 26th Combat Support Group for nearly three years.

"Our job there was to open the base after the Canadians left to give us a convenient place to receive trainloads of equipment from our troops being thrown out of France at the time," he says. "That was when French and U.S. agreements ran out to have our troops stationed on French soil. They did not renew the agreements and we have never been allowed back in, officially anyway."

Hall in February 1975 received orders to return to the same job, even the same desk, in Denver. "During this tour we moved offices into a newly built finance center at Lowry Air Force Base which got us back on a real base once again. Had no problems with uniforms but the pollution now prevented us from seeing the mountains from Denver!"

NEW LIFE IN THE OLD WORLD

After two years in the Mile High City, Hall missed Germany so much he put in his paperwork to return. He received orders to report to Hessisch Oldendorf, a small base the United States was opening near Hanover. "This was a great five years after which I moved to Spangdahlem Air Base in the Eifel-Mosel River area." There, Hall would buy his first house and retire from the Air Force in 1987.

"I started my second career as a retail manager for the Army and Air Force Exchange Service (AAFES) with duty in Spangdahlem and Bitburg, Germany, and with facilities of responsibility in the Netherlands and Belgium."

After his second 20-year career, Hall retired again, on his 62nd birthday. "I'm now doing more of the things and hobbies I love, like studying medieval Cistercian architecture, traveling all over Europe to flea markets, buying antiques at auction and just plain old traveling. I especially enjoy the south of France along the Med [Mediterranean Sea] and northern Belgium at the beach in Knokke-Heist. The UK [United Kingdom] is a favorite too as now my dogs can travel there with me."

Hall is characteristically outspoken on Vietnam. "The war enlightened me to the horrors that a few power-hungry men have inflicted upon the many throughout the centuries," he begins. "Personally, I do not feel affected but a lot of men came back a different person, not on the surface, but underneath. I also realize pillar saints will continue to run our world and our country into bankruptcy trying to get their legacy. This has happened many times throughout history and man will never learn."

After an alert, Hall and other airmen gather at sand-filled barricades outside their hooch at Tan Son Nhut Air Base.

KNOWING THE SCORE

As a career airman, he says the war made him more aware of the need to make things happen. "I might not always have agreed with my supervisors, but I knew it was really a great game and what was important was the result or score. [Statistics] too, I suppose I'm trying to say, were important. During the war, the stats were shown as whatever Washington wanted. After all, they were running the thing."

And Hall knew the score. "I realized Washington was running things and ballsing it up bad. We (military members) gave it our all. Washington screwed it all up! What can I say? It has become my feeling that politicians and reporters should not have anything to do with a war. If we need a war fought, just sit back and let the military take care of it."

One issue embitters him. "We, military retirees, don't even get out teeth cared for and when Saddam [Hussein, late dictator of Iraq] came out of his hole, the first thing he got was medical and dental exams by our military doctors, on TV, doing their duty in Iraq. I would like to be able to see a dentist without having to go to a civilian one and paying through the ass for it. When I enlisted in 1967, I was promised lifelong medical and dental care. Our lawmakers keep gnawing away at our benefits to pay their overinflated salaries and to finance their silly wars and buy their pages gifts."

Hall, 63, segues to the parallels between Vietnam and Iraq, specifically, the visibility of the wars. He reiterates his belief that politicians and reporters should be banned from combat. "There are many things not really proper that happen in a war zone. They do not need to be splashed across the front page of newspapers and should not be shown on the six o'clock news. There are certain things that need to remain unseen."

He's pragmatic about the impact of war. "People have got to remember that we are still in Europe 60 years after the war here. We are still in Korea and we will still be in Iraq 60 years from now and we will be paying $18 a gallon for gas as no government has the balls to tell big business to make a car that runs on water."

And, naturally, Hall has opinions on other world events. "We do not need to build any new missile sites in eastern Europe as planned. And until there is a real war between the Jews and Palestinians and we have a clear winner, there will never be peace. Just like in Iraq," he says. "They need to duke it out between themselves. I think that's what we did in America, wasn't it?"

As to his former right-wing conservative positions, Hall concedes he is more liberal today "but I'm not a tree-hugger. In Germany they say *leben und leben lassen!* (Live and let live!). I agree."

Content in Germany where he lives in Trier, the country's oldest city, Hall, who has never married, has no plans to return to his homeland. He retains his U.S. citizenship with permission to reside in Germany. "Since I was a very small boy, I started saving for my 'Europe Fund.' Europe then was just someplace I wanted to travel to and when I got my first assignment to Germany, I just sort of stayed in the German pipeline," he says. "If I had been stationed in England all these years, I would have remained there. Home is where the hearth is."

And Hall has stoked fires afar too long. "Germany is now my home. I get homesick when I'm anywhere else. I've lived more than half my life here." And that life, he adds, "is just better, slower, and more enjoyable in spite of George Bush screwing the dollar-to-Euro rate. Like I said, breakfast in Luxembourg and dinner in Barcelona. I just travel when and where I want."

LARRY D. GUM
NAVY 1968-1969

A trim, jeans-clad Larry David Gum apologizes for running late. As fire chief of the Millsboro Fire Company, he's just returned home from responding to a single-car accident on a busy stretch of road near this burgeoning town on the Indian River about 15 miles from Delaware's oceanfront resorts. "Nothing serious," he reports. "The vehicle rolled over a couple of times and we had to use a hydraulic rescue tool to cut the driver free but he'll be OK."

Gum, a Navy hospital corpsman-third class in Vietnam from 1968 to 1969, is no stranger to serving others and takes his responsibilities with the local fire company very seriously. In 2007, he answered nearly every call. He's been a member for more than three decades and served from 1994 to 2000 as fire chief, a job, he says, his fellow firemen "coaxed me into taking back in 2008." The maroon polo shirt he wears with pride bears the gold insignia of the Sussex County Fire Chiefs Association.

His service with the 65-member fire company parallels his municipal involvement as mayor of Millsboro, a town of 2,500 whose residential building boom has slowed with the tepid economy. Gum expects the new housing again will attract out-of-state retirees who laud Delaware's low taxes and nearby beaches. "I was elected to the Town Council for three years in 1999, my first experience with politics," recalls the unassuming veteran. "Then I was re-elected to a second three-year term, then a third term."

In June 2008, Gum was re-elected for a fourth term. He's always run unopposed. Elected mayor by his council peers in June 2007, he still holds the title. "I look at it as serving your community. A great staff makes the job worth having."

Such selfless civic involvement has stood him in good stead throughout this life. An only child, Gum grew up five miles from Millsboro in Frankford where generations of Gums before him settled. As a youngster, the energetic redhead enjoyed helping out on his grandfather's farm. "Frankford was a small town with not much to do, but I rode bicycles with the other kids and played backyard basketball and side-yard football. The Gum family is a very small family," he adds. "My great-grandfather, Francis M. Gum, was a horse-and-buggy doctor in Frankford. Everyone called him 'Doc Gum.' My dad, Waples W. Gum, was a Navy veteran of World War II and served in the Pacific Theater."

Keepsakes from another era, Larry Gum's military effects include an enemy necklace with religious pendant and his Navy hospital corpsman patch. Today, Gum thrives on community service.

"All corpsmen were issued a .45-caliber pistol, just like the officers were. You never knew who the enemy was, like Iraq today, and medical personnel were prime targets. If a corpsman was injured or killed, who would treat the wounded?"

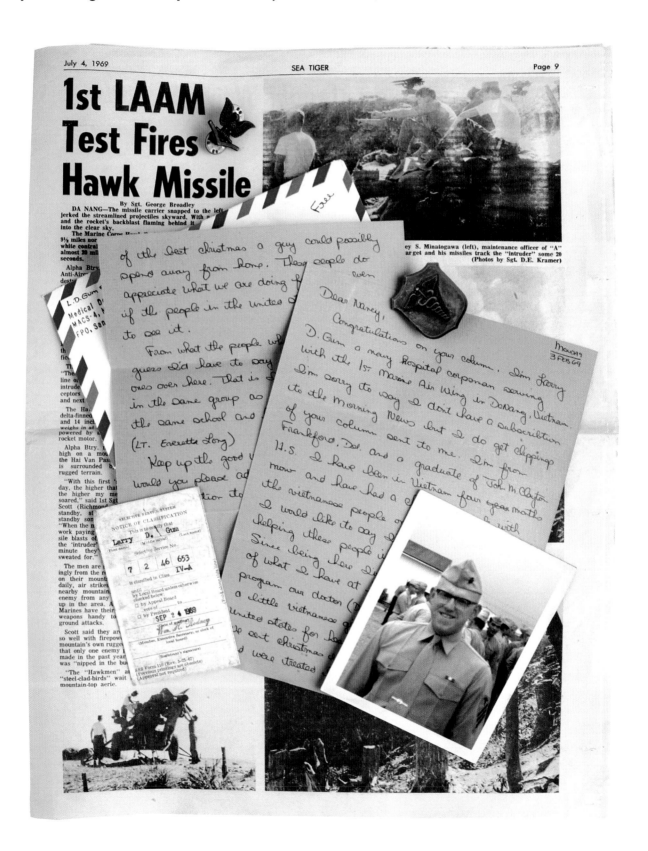

So it was not surprising that Gum chose to serve in the Navy like his father. He graduated in 1964 from John M. Clayton High School, housed in the building where he had attended school since first grade. He played football and basketball and ran track for the Clayton Bears. The summer following his graduation, he worked at Banks Hardware in Frankford. He was hired that September by the DuPont Company's nylon plant in Seaford for shift work. "I needed a worker's permit from the state because I was 17." Drafted in December 1965, he still has his Selective Service notice. "I joined the Navy instead. Two of my friends had enlisted, Robert Bentley from Dagsboro and my classmate Theodore Doukas from Frankford, who also became a corpsman. The recruiter said I could have a specialty if I qualified."

And it also was not surprising Gum chose and later earned the rank of hospital corpsman, HN, as his specialty after boot camp at the U.S. Naval Training Center in Great Lakes, Illinois. Just getting there was the first of many new adventures for the 18-year old. "In December 1965, I was leaving home for the first time. It was snowing like crazy at National Airport in Washington, D.C., and the propeller-driven plane vibrated terribly during takeoff. It was my first experience on a commercial airplane. We arrived at Great Lakes and were kept up all night scrubbing the floor with our toothbrushes."

Outside the barracks was no fun either. "There was cold weather and snow the whole winter I was there," he remembers. "The training was not an issue and after basic training I was awarded the position." That involved four more months of training in Great Lakes at the U.S. Naval Hospital Corps School. "I graduated in June 1966 and was given duty at the National Naval Medical Center in Bethesda, Maryland. What a place with all the naval brass and dignitaries from Washington. I even had the opportunity to meet and escort Supreme Court Justice Hugo Black to his annual physical. He was a very nice, polite man towards a new naval recruit."

Three months later, Gum reported to Indian Head Naval Ordnance School on the Potomac River outside Washington. "I was stationed with personnel from all services. Working off base on the live ordnance range at Stump Neck, where you learned how to dispose of unexploded ordnance safely, was an experience I enjoyed. One day I returned from the range to be told I had been transferred to the Fleet Marine Force (FMF) training facility at Camp Pendleton, California, for Field Medical Service training. For four weeks, 400 corpsmen were trained by a Marine drill instructor. He had experience in Vietnam and was trying to prepare us for what was to come. After graduation in May 1967, 380 corpsmen boarded buses to begin the journey to Vietnam. I was one of the 20 left behind."

After Pendleton, Gum went to Twentynine Palms, California, "to experience Marine Corps life. The interaction with the marines is something I will always cherish. One by one, my fellow corpsmen were assigned to Vietnam. Eventually I could stand it no longer and volunteered. I could not stand being left behind."

Gum graduated from the Fleet Marine Force's battlefield training school wearing a Marine Corps uniform with Navy stripes. Assigned to the 1st Light Anti-Aircraft Missile (LAAM) Battalion's aid station at Da Nang Air Base, he sent this article to the Vietnam Mailbag.

WELCOME TO THE JUNGLE

By September 1968, Gum was bound for the combat zone. "We all were given 30 days leave before being deployed to the Republic of Vietnam. Home for 30 days to let it all hang out and I did. Leaving home was terrible for my parents and I remember their sadness. Even my father, who doesn't show much emotion, was moved."

Gum left the United States from Travis Air Force Base in California. "It was a madhouse of military personnel coming and going. We landed at Camp Hanson in Okinawa where returning vets were crossing paths with their replacements. It was like boot camp with standing in line and checking to make sure everything was correct." His next stop was Vietnam.

"Flying into Da Nang Air Base, I remember the green of the jungle. It was beautiful and the land was dusty with reddish color dirt. I also remember the morgue at the end of the runway with silver caskets stacked up and I thought about my vulnerability. I can still see the caskets." After his plane landed, Gum noticed "troops coming and going in open wagons, large semi-trucks, like cattle wagons full of troops. The first night we learned what it was to be in a war zone when we were awakened by sirens and incoming rockets. Young kids were turned into vets!"

Gum landed in Da Nang with five friends. "We got split up and went to different units. All six of us came back. We were lucky," he says. A resident of his hometown, Army Private First Class William J. Bunting, was not as fortunate. He was killed in action on May 26, 1970, eight months after Gum returned to Frankford.

"ONE OF THE LUCKY ONES"

As a Navy hospital corpsman, he served with the 1st Marine Air Wing at Da Nang Air Base. He remembers his favorable assignment in Vietnam. "I was one of the lucky ones who had a hot meal and a dry bed every night. Others who served in remote areas were not as fortunate. I was assigned to the 1st Light Anti-Aircraft Missile (LAAM) Battalion that served as air defense where I worked at the battalion aid station. All corpsmen were issued a .45-caliber pistol, just like the officers were. You never knew who the enemy was, like Iraq today, and medical personnel were prime targets. If a corpsman was injured or killed, who would treat the wounded? We wore the Marine Corps uniform with Navy stripes. I was very proud to serve with the Marines. I was later transferred to MACS-4, the Marine Air Control Squadron located on Monkey Mountain."

For Gum, the best part of serving his tour in Vietnam was helping others. "Our job as corpsmen was sick call. We took care of the injured or sick marines." Responsibilities also included "doing all administrative work, sanitation and patrols," he wrote in his letter published in the May 8, 1969 Vietnam Mailbag. He lamented in-country accidents, such as friendly shootings or vehicle crashes. He also aided the South Vietnamese in Medical Civil Action Program (MEDCAP) activities throughout the Da Nang area. "I would like to say I'm proud to be over here helping these people in any way possible," Gum wrote in the February 13, 1969 Mailbag. "These people do appreciate what we are doing for them even if the people in the United States don't get to see it." Gum adds, "I have always wondered what happened to the friends I made there."

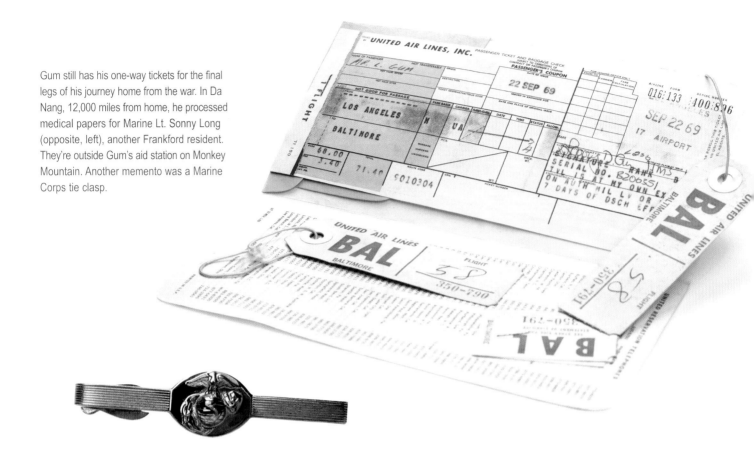

Gum still has his one-way tickets for the final legs of his journey home from the war. In Da Nang, 12,000 miles from home, he processed medical papers for Marine Lt. Sonny Long (opposite, left), another Frankford resident. They're outside Gum's aid station on Monkey Mountain. Another memento was a Marine Corps tie clasp.

In his February letter, he mentioned a young Vietnamese girl who traveled with her mother to California for heart surgery, arranged by the doctor in his MEDCAP unit. He told readers her family treated him and other American servicemen "like royalty" on Christmas Eve 1968. In his May letter, he had good news and noted his pleasure at attending the girl's homecoming party given in April by her grateful parents.

Working with the South Vietnamese in general and being in Vietnam in particular made Gum "more appreciative of what I have at home." He also shared with the column that, despite being from Sussex County, Delaware, which can get oppressively hot in the summer, he found Vietnam's heat and humidity "unbearable." He's grateful his one-year tour in the combat zone was "cut short by troop withdrawals. We called it short-timing and referred to those with less than 100 days [as] 'Short-Timers.'"

COMING HOME

Gum's circuitous route home included a transfer to a Navy fighter unit in Iwakuni, Japan, where he spent most of his savings on custom-made suits. He then was sent to Okinawa before returning to California. "After I got stateside," he remembers, "I was sent back to Okinawa with the 9th Marine Amphibious Brigade. I ran into an old friend there from Twentynine Palms, Chief Bickford. He saw I was within a 120-day window for my discharge date from the Navy. He asked if I wanted to be discharged early. I said, 'Yes.' I'd been

away from home for two-and-a-half years. He wrote the orders for me to be discharged. He made my day."

Prior to that red-letter day, Gum recalls he was required to take some "training to acclimate back to civilian life" in Long Beach, California. He also was regaining the weight he had lost. "In Vietnam, I contracted severe dysentery and came home weighing 120 pounds. I was 160 pounds when I went over." Gum's not sure how he got dysentery but clearly remembers his situation. "I just became very ill and couldn't do anything. I stayed in my hooch in Da Nang." With the proper dietary and sanitary conditions on the West Coast, he recovered his strength, gained weight and completed his readjustment training.

Unfortunately, returning to his normal weight meant he no longer fit into his Japanese-made suits, so he scuttled them. "Then I was given money to get home. I visited friends in California first and then flew home," he says. He still has the United Airlines ticket stub, dated September 22, 1969, for his one-way flight from Los Angeles to Baltimore. Cost: $68 plus $3.40 tax.

He also kept his Continental Trailways bus ticket which shows a one-way fare of $4.60 from Baltimore to Salisbury, Maryland. "I was trying to surprise my folks but when I got to Salisbury, I couldn't get a ride to Frankford so I called my parents to come pick me up. When I got to Frankford and saw my grandfather Gum on the farm, he asked why I wasn't in uniform. I told him people in uniform weren't treated very well, that in airports we were exposed, people would look at us and call us names."

LIFE AFTER THE WAR

Gum says he was treated fairly when he returned to Delaware. The DuPont Co. had held his job for him. "They said, 'Welcome back,' and considered my time with them as never having stopped. It was September 1969, and I had been drafted nearly four years earlier."

In spite of the chemical giant's magnanimity, Gum looked for work closer to home, in eastern Sussex County. After about a year of commuting to Seaford from Frankford, a 50-mile roundtrip, he took a job with Delmarva Power, working for 17 years at its Indian River Power Plant and then for another 20 years at the utility's district offices in Millsboro. Gum retired in 2007.

In 1971, soon after joining Delmarva Power, Gum married his high school classmate, Christy Hurley. "She had had a bad marriage and a young daughter," Gum says. He adopted her daughter, Amy, and the couple moved to Millsboro, where they built a house. "Her support and encouragement gave me the confidence to excel for the past 38 years," he says. Gum's sense of civic duty ramped up once he joined the town's fire company. No stranger to fire service, he also had been a member for several years of the Frankford Fire Company, like his father.

He's comfortable the second time around as Millsboro's fire chief. "I try to answer every call," he says. The company receives about 500 calls annually for fires, accidents and assists to other fire companies, and also makes about 1,800 ambulance runs a year. Every fireman's response is a volunteer effort. Only the six full-time and six part-time emergency medical technicians (EMTs) the company retains are paid personnel. Before they were hired, Gum rode the ambulance as an attendant "and used my experience as a corpsman."

Today, Gum is technically retired, but don't tell him that. "And don't tell my wife that. I'm anything but retired," he fires back. "I hear people say they're bored when they retire. I say they're not doing anything because I'm definitely not bored." With his dual duties as Millsboro's fire chief and mayor, he doesn't have time to be bored.

That said, Gum has always made family a priority. When Amy, her husband and their infant daughter, Courtney, faced financial difficulties, they moved in with Gum and Christy. After Amy divorced, she and Courtney continued to live with her parents. When Amy got back on her feet and moved out, Courtney wanted to stay and was raised by her grandparents, her legal guardians until her 18th birthday. She graduated from Sussex Technical High School in Georgetown in June 2008. Gum and Christy also dote on their grandson, Courtney's brother, Ben Simmons, a standout lacrosse player at nearby Sussex Central High School. "I try to get every home game in," Gum says. Ben also represented his school as an all-state saxophone player as a freshman in 2008.

Gum, 61, keeps a 35-foot motor home parked next to his house and has vacationed with his family in Florida each year since his retirement. "Christy and I have always enjoyed camping. Back in 1977, we went to California to see a military buddy. We drove in a pick-up truck and had never camped a day in our lives. I'll never forget her mom and dad stood in our driveway and cried when we left. I think they weren't sure we'd make it home."

The Gums bought their first motor home, a used 31-footer, in September 2006. They belong to the Funseekers Chapter of the Delaware Good Sam Camping Club. "We try to attend monthly campouts in different areas in New Jersey and the Eastern Shore of Maryland and local dinners when winter sets in. I enjoy the fellowship of the campers. It reminds me of the fellowship I experienced in the military and the fellowship I have in the fire service today," he says.

Gum's personal interests include photography, which he comes by naturally. "My grandfather, Harry Watson, who lived in Selbyville, was an amateur photographer. He developed his black-and-white pictures in trays in his kitchen. I was always amazed to watch pictures appear off white paper."

Classic cars are another interest. He stables a white 1962 Chevrolet Impala in its own garage next to his house and lovingly tends to it any chance he gets. "My dad gave it to me for Christmas a few years ago," he says proudly.

With his Vietnam experiences distant memories today, Gum occasionally taps into the luxury of hindsight to reflect on another undeclared war, the one America is waging in Iraq. "I think there are exact parallels with Vietnam," he says. "It's the same situation but there's no line, no DMZ, and you've got ethnic groups fighting, not north and south. I support our troops but I definitely have concerns. I'm very skeptical about what we can do in Iraq."

Gum does not hesitate when asked if he'd serve again in Vietnam. He points out he was the only family member in his generation to serve in the military. "Yes," he answers, "I'm too committed to this country. It's probably still one of the best systems around."

DONALD B. PATTON
ARMY 1968-1969

A study in multitasking, Donald Bernard Patton takes charge of the frenetic front office at the George V. Kirk Middle School. The no-nonsense principal talks on a phone, directs two secretaries, assists a third and soothes a sick student slouched on a couch. Another phone rings and he grabs the receiver while answering a question from a parent. The round-robin frenzy continues for several minutes as Patton channels chaos to calm. Then he points to a visitor. "OK, you're next," he says, exiting the office, his rich voice trailing him.

In the hallway, he confronts a gangly teen without a pass. "Just getting a drink of water, Mr. P.," he offers tentatively. "Water fountain's over there, son," Patton says, motioning to another hallway. "No, I like the water better over here," the student challenges. "You telling me I got bad water in this building?" Patton asks with incredulity. "No, sir," says the student, doing an about-face.

Patton rounds a corner and reaches his office, an oasis of quiet in the din of educating 925 seventh- and eighth-graders. He steps on a round rug woven with the colorful seal of the United States Army. Confident as a school principal, Patton acknowledges his demeanor wasn't always this assured. He says the rug symbolizes his service to his country and reminds him daily of his long journey from a fatherless kid reared in the public housing projects in Wilmington, Delaware, to an award-winning educator respected by his peers.

In July 2008, Patton left Kirk Middle School in Newark, Delaware, after six years as principal to head Bayard Middle School near his old neighborhood. "It's a school heavily populated with African-American and Hispanic students from low socioeconomic backgrounds. We're resegregating. The goal," he explains, "is to make sure there are high expectations and adequate resources for all students to be successful."

Patton, 60, who turned down jobs in Charleston, South Carolina, and Atlanta to take this post in inner-city Wilmington, which has borne its share of racial tension, is certain he is the right academic leader at the right time. "The tough part is getting everyone to see there is hope. Your personal situation should not define who or what you are or what you can be. I can pull this off because I am one of these students."

And he has embraced the challenge. "I am taking over a tough situation and will make it successful. I expect to see positive results in the first year." His tools for success include teamwork, solid professional relationships and leadership, all precepts he credits the Army with fostering within him.

Award-winning educator Donald B. Patton credits the Army for his success, both in Vietnam and in Delaware.

"There was no good part of Vietnam for me. I don't know of any positive experiences I gained except I came back. I was lucky."

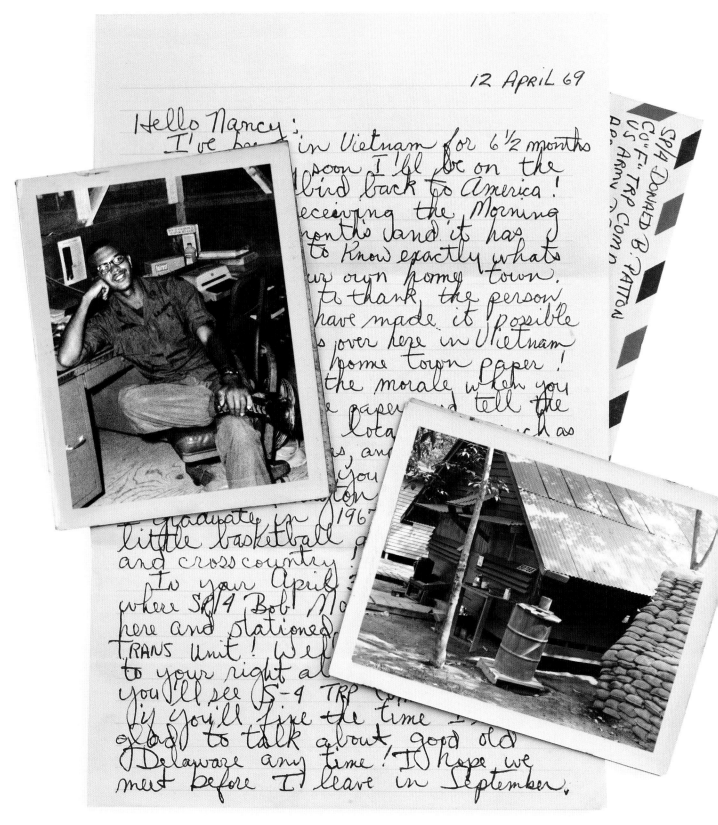

12 April 69

Hello Nancy:

I've been in Vietnam for 6½ months and soon I'll be on the bird back to America! receiving the Morning months and it has to know exactly whats us own home town. to thank the person have made it possible is over here in Vietnam home town paper! the morale when you the paper and tell the total as and you graduate in 1967 little basketball and cross country in your April where Sp/4 Bob M here and stationed TRANS Unit! Well to your right al you'll see S-4 TRP if you'll find the time glad to talk about good old Delaware any time! I hope we meet before I leave in September.

Sp/4 Donald B. Patton
Co"F" TRP Comm
US Army Comm

CONTRASTING LIVES

Military service both challenged and nurtured him and was in many ways a surrogate for the father who was absent from his life and the single mother who did the best she could for Patton, his identical twin, Ronald Burnett Patton, and his sisters, Barbara, Sherry, Bonnie and Karen. "We all kind of raised ourselves, cooked, cleaned and dressed on our own," he recalls. "My mother worked much of the time as a nurse's tech at Wilmington General Hospital and we saw her one or two days a week. My older sister was the caregiver and she was not home most of the time."

Two of his sisters, he adds, were raised by friends of his mother's. "We visited with each other as children, but did not live in the same house. As we became adults, we were able to connect like siblings who grew up living together. We loved each other and disregarded how we were raised separately."

An athletic but average student with untapped potential, Patton plodded through public schools. "I did not have support from home and did just enough in school to qualify to play sports, no more, no less," he says. He also joined a local Youth for Christ group which offered him an unexpected ticket out of the housing projects and an unforgettable life lesson.

"I got a full scholarship to Wilmington Friends School for tenth grade," he remembers. The Quaker-affiliated school in upscale Alapocas had previously enrolled mostly well-heeled students from upper-middle-class Wilmington neighborhoods and was anathema to anything Patton had experienced.

"I understood enough to know the world was made up of many people from a variety of races and it made sense to go to this school," Patton says, explaining that he accepted the stipend and reported to the Friends football camp in August 1964. "I played defensive end and they wanted me to play basketball too. It was a hard transition. I was the only black in a school of rich white kids. I had trouble adjusting."

Just getting to and from the private school posed its own problems. "I was picked up and dropped off by my white friend's parents. My neighborhood friends were all at Wilmington or P.S. du Pont high schools and they knew where I was every day. I was living a double life." By December, Patton called it quits at Friends. He rejoined his classmates at Wilmington High School, where he excelled in track and was a member of the Red Devils' undefeated cross-country team. Patton graduated from Wilmington High in 1967.

Patton went to work as an X-ray orderly at Memorial Hospital, where his older sister Barbara was the mailroom supervisor. He wasn't there long. "I was drafted in December 1967 and reported to Fort Bragg [North Carolina] in January 1968." He liked the Army's discipline and regimentation. "When I left basic I was a private. I took AIT [advanced infantry training] at Fort Lee [Virginia]. I was still a private. Then I went to Forest Park Army Depot in Atlanta. I advanced to corporal, then specialist fourth class. I was always looking to get to the next stop."

In October 1968, Patton's next stop was South Vietnam. "I was 18, scared, and didn't expect to return," he recalls, adding two of

In Vietnam, Patton quickly advanced to sergeant and was the battalion chief's driver. Patton's April letter (opposite) was the 300th letter the Mailbag received.

his neighbors had been killed in action. Army Pfc. Wilbert Rudolph Butler died February 7, 1966, and Marine Pfc. Paul Wayne Quick III died January 11, 1968. "They both lived right across the street from me."

'A FEAR OF BEING ALONE'

Although Vietnam's stifling heat did not ruffle him, he remembers many "dark, sad moments" after landing at Cam Ranh Bay. "It was the first time I had ever been that far away, I didn't know anybody, and I had a fear of being alone." After processing out of Tan Son Nhut, Patton traveled to the U.S. Army Depot Long Binh for duty with Company F Troop Command.

"Right after I got there, we were attacked. I remember being scared when I heard the alarm. It was the monsoon season and we fought a couple of days. I issued weapons. There was one soldier who was high on drugs and refused to follow orders. He would have gotten us all killed so we had to shoot him. That was my worst day." Overcome with the horrid memory, Patton's eyes well up.

At Long Binh, "I was where the jail was. It was hot, confined and in the war zone. It was the pits of hell." But he met three soldiers at Long Binh who befriended him. "I only remember Capt. Allen and Staff Sgt. Archie Fisher who lived in North Carolina. There was also another sergeant. They said, 'Don't be scared. You're going to be all right. We'll take care of you.' And they did. I was in Vietnam a couple of months and was made a sergeant. I was also made the jeep driver for the colonel who was the battalion chief. I replaced Fisher, who was an E-7. I was an E-5. I was a young sergeant."

In Vietnam, he says he was "blessed" he didn't use drugs, which were readily available and inexpensive. "I escaped by playing music and writing letters." He did see two Delawareans during his tour: Army Spc. Ronn Wright, who worked in the mortuary at Saigon Air Base, and Army Cpl. Dennis Taylor. Both were from Wilmington.

SPARRING BY AIRMAIL

He and Army Spec. Larry R. Kipp, whom he never met and who also was from Wilmington and served with the 54th Medical Detachment in Chu Lai, entertained Vietnam Mailbag readers by sparring several times in the column over buying beer and liquor at the Long Binh PX.

In his June 17, 1969 letter to the Mailbag, Patton groused about restrictions at Long Binh, specifically, not being able to use the commissary, and having to be 21 and a grade of E-5 or above to buy liquor at the post exchange. Patton didn't drink but felt the rules were too rigid for a combat zone. "If a man can go off to a country and fight a war against his will, he should at least be able to buy beer or liquor," he reasoned.

A few weeks later, Kipp, an E-5, countered Patton in his letter to the Mailbag by suggesting Long Binh was a plush place with air conditioning, flush toilets and running water. Further, he could buy beer but not liquor there. Kipp's solution: "One of my former officers lent me his ration card, or else he'd buy a drink for me. Also, the numerous EM [Enlisted Men] clubs offer mixed drinks."

Patton volleyed back in the August 25 Mailbag, telling Kipp he'd seen only the better parts of Long Binh, that he didn't have running water, and that his sergeant had crossed out beer and liquor on his ration card, meaning he couldn't purchase alcoholic beverages.

He concluded by chiding Kipp that his officers didn't buy liquor for enlisted men and that he should "call yourself lucky because a specialist fifth class doesn't usually walk into a PX and purchase liquor with an officer's ration card and Spc. 5 stripes and get away with it."

Today, Patton doesn't recall the exchange and says he wrote a lot of letters just to blow off steam. "I got through the year," he says, adding his only injury was shrapnel wound to his left hand. He returned stateside in October 1969. Ronald, his twin, was supposed to replace him in Vietnam.

"He went AWOL," Patton says sadly. "He stayed home and was found living with some young lady in the projects of Riverside [a neighborhood in northeast Wilmington]. He struggled with many challenges during his youth. Not having a father or positive role model was more difficult for him."

Ronald, according to Patton, drank heavily. "After things went bad in his marriage, job, and overall life, he lost his family. The result was more drinking to the point that was all he did. One day, he was so drunk he called his separated wife and said he was going to kill her. He stabbed her multiple times and attempted to commit suicide. The police stopped his car as he headed to the Delaware Memorial Bridge to jump off. He has been incarcerated ever since. But I'm not giving up on him," Patton says.

After Vietnam and a 30-day home leave, Patton reported to Fort Meade, Maryland, and was assigned to the 181st Ordnance Unit until his discharge in January 1971. "That was the catalyst that got me thinking about college and about my need to go to college."

To make that happen, he worked as a respiratory technician at the Delaware Division of the Wilmington Medical Center at night and commuted for years to Delaware State University in Dover, a two-hour roundtrip, during the day. "I took education courses because teachers and coaches had had the most impact on me. I knew I wanted to teach."

After graduating in 1976 with a degree in business education, Patton first taught business classes to seventh-, eighth- and ninth-grade students at Warner Junior High School in Wilmington. To broaden his professional opportunities and pay scale, he left academia to work for the DuPont Company and for seven years sold industrial finishes. When the chemical giant sold that division, "I was a part of the sale but decided I did not want to relocate with the new company so I went to work for Sherwin-Williams for two-and-a-half years before they asked me to relocate to New York. I left Sherwin-Williams and went to work for Pratt & Lambert for 10 years. They were sold to Sherwin-Williams."

LEARNING TO BE A LEADER

Concurrently, Patton coached high school basketball for 16 years. "Many schools offered me the opportunity to stop traveling and do what I enjoyed doing: teaching. I taught business education at Christiana High School for three years while coaching basketball at Newark High School." In 1999, Patton was named acting assistant principal at Christiana. He left the high school in 2000 to become assistant principal at Kirk Middle School and was named principal there in 2002.

He credits the Army for his rise to administrative positions. "I had many growth experiences in the Army and developed organizational and leadership skills. The Army gave me the tools I probably would not have otherwise had," Patton says. "In the end, those helped me become a better leader."

Until recently, Patton was a licensed practical nurse (LPN). "I took the state boards in the mid-1980s. I wanted to have options. I never worked as an LPN because there were many things going on in my life at that time. I renewed my LPN license until I became an assistant principal. At that point, I decided not to renew and stay in education." Another side to Patton is his love of tennis. He is on the court whenever time permits.

Of all his accomplishments, raising student achievement at Kirk outweighs nearly all else. "When I first came to Kirk, it was a school in disarray, at the bottom of the middle schools in our district and very low in the state, but I wanted the challenge," Patton remembers.

"We had to rethink the way we educated our students without lowering our expectations. It was a fight in the beginning because many teachers felt the way they were doing it was OK and they did not see a reason to change. We had to convince those teachers to leave and start from the beginning with high expectations, increased engagement levels, improved teaching

and learning practices and loads of professional development. We worked together to implement new strategies, best practices and new initiatives."

Under his leadership, Kirk was Delaware's only middle school in 2006-2007 to receive the Lieutenant Governor's Award of Excellence for showing double-digit growth in math and reading/writing DSTP [Delaware Student Testing Program] scores for three consecutive years. Last year, the school also was a Delaware State Chamber of Commerce Superstars in Education runner-up, based on the success of its Advancement Via Individual Determination (AVID) program, an international program that encourages schools to rethink how they teach and learn to increase student performance.

"You put a lot of yourself in it and form a lot of relationships," he says of the intensive process of turning a school around. Patton is quick to laud his capable and responsive staff of 75 at Kirk. "I told them, 'If you partner with me, we're going to do all right.' As an administrator, you're not a leader if no one is following. You're only in front."

The school's path to success, he says, also included "espousing interactive relationships with parents and the kids." Along the way, Patton was singled out for recognition. In 2006, he received Administrator of the Year awards from the Rho Chapter of Phi Delta Kappa, a national sorority of educators chartered in 1934 in Wilmington, and from the Newark Chapter of the NAACP. "The Phi Delta Kappa honor was especially appreciated because it was from educators," he says. He also is an administrative consultant

for AVID but shrugs off too much limelight. "I have had success and when people say, 'This guy is phenomenal,' I tell them I didn't invent it. I look at people and programs that do things well."

Ups and downs checker Patton's personal life. His first daughter, Donna Lynn, was born before he went into the service. He was 12,000 miles from home when his second daughter, Renee Joy, was born in June 1969. He and his wife, Shirley Washington, met in high school, married in 1968 and divorced in 1974. "We were very close when she died of breast cancer."

His second wife was Patricia Henderson, whom he married in 1977 and divorced in 1992. Patricia, also an educator, is a former principal of Bayard Elementary and currently principal at Elbert Palmer Elementary School in Wilmington. They had two children, Brian and Alexis. Patton now is in a committed relationship with Marqueia Davis and thoroughly enjoys his five grandchildren.

At the top of his professional game today, Patton seldom, if ever, discusses Vietnam with anyone. He belongs to no service-connected organizations and prefers to be "disconnected from the past." Occasionally, he sees Wright, who worked in the mortuary.

Patton, who describes himself today as honest, open and forthright, is introspective about his own changes from the conflict. "The baggage I brought back from Vietnam was isolation and an inability to be open and accessible mentally and physically. I've had to do a lot of reflective governance of me." He pauses. "There was no good part of Vietnam for me. I don't know of any positive experiences I gained except I came back. I was lucky."

"The Home of Quality Dentistry."

407-830-4401

JAMES D. RAWLINS JR.
ARMY 1969-1970

Guilt trumped curiosity to ultimately land Dr. James David Rawlins Jr. a year's tour in Vietnam. Though his route to the combat zone was circuitous, the gung-ho dentist from Seaford, Delaware, zealously embraced the opportunity to support his fellow servicemen when he received his orders in late 1969.

I felt guilty about having what seemed like a paid vacation while our military was facing hardships," Rawlins recalls of his Army posting – first to Aschaffenburg, Germany in 1966, then seven years later to Friedberg, Germany, where he was chief of the Friedberg Dental Clinic, previously immortalized as the third-floor living quarters of Army Pvt. Elvis Presley.

"The best part of Vietnam," adds Rawlins, 71, who retired as a full colonel in the Army Reserve in 1992 after 27 years, "was getting to see the culture and the beautiful country. I traveled all over by chopper. I really enjoyed my year there."

He served as the 2nd Brigade dental officer for the 101st Airborne Division in a clearing station unit in the combat zone. Located at Landing Zone Sally and later at Camp Hochmoth in Phu Bai, he did fillings, root canals and extractions for American servicemen and occasionally for the South Vietnamese. "I never fired a shot at anyone and I was only fired upon once, in Hue at the Imperial Palace when a bullet ricocheted off a bell about six feet away from me."

An intense, lithe man with a generous nature and a ready joke, Rawlins still practices dentistry at his multi-doctor office, Dental World, in Longwood, Florida, near Orlando. "When I first came here, there was Disney World, Sea World, Hubcap World and Liquor World. Now there's my place, Dental World."

He bought the 3,900-square-foot clinic in 1983. He and two associates offer comprehensive family dental care. In December 2006, he fulfilled his dream of treating his entire 19-member office staff and spouses or companions to an expense-free luxury Caribbean cruise. Rawlins even provided his "Chew Crew" with red polo shirts and baseball caps embroidered with the Dental World logo.

To know the happy-go-lucky Rawlins is to know his roots. In mid-sentence, he jumps up and leaves his kitchen, apparently on a mission. After a whirlwind reconnaissance, he flushes his 1955 high school yearbook from his high-tech home office in Altamonte Springs, a few miles from his dental office. He plunks the weathered volume down on the kitchen table, grinning boyishly. "Here it is," he says quickly, leafing through the pages.

He pauses, slowly fingering the "Aloha." "Here it is," he repeats enthusiastically, stopping at a fuzzy black-and-white photo of three gangly teens, co-captains of Seaford High School's football team. "That's me," he says, pointing a manicured index finger at the weathered image, "with Harlan White and Dave Messick. I was a fullback. Played three years of football, four of basketball and did three years of track. I lettered in all."

Dapper dentist James D. Rawlins Jr. outside his Dental World office near Longwood, Fla., half a world and half a lifetime from his clinic in Vietnam.

THE WHITE HOUSE

WASHINGTON

March 24, 1971

Dear Monica:

Your father recently sent me a copy of the patriotic
essay you wrote for class, and I can well understand his pride in your efforts.

It is easy to see that you have a keen awareness of
your responsibilities as a citizen. I hope you will
always be anxious to learn all you can about our
nation, and the men selected to lead our country.
Keep up the good work!

With my best wishes to you and your family for the
years ahead,

Sincerely,

Richard Nixon

Miss Monica L. Rawlins
Apartment 9
5300 Westbard Avenue
Bethesda, Maryland 20016

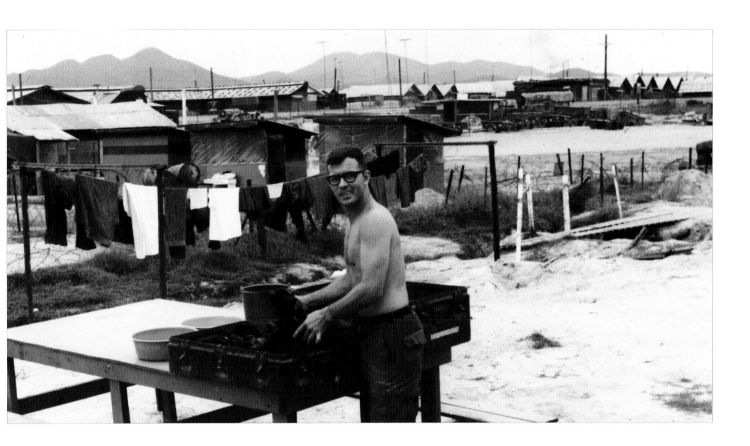

Rawlins' daughter Monica's prized possession is a personally signed letter from President Richard M. Nixon. Rawlins was based at Landing Zone Sally.

Rawlins, a young-at-heart grandfather on his second marriage, turns a few more pages. His peers tagged him "Life of Every Party" and "Biggest Flirt" in his yearbook. "I was kinda mischievous in school," he concedes this day, more than half a century later. But he knew he wanted to be a dentist. "I wanted to be my own boss. I saw my Uncle Jack in family practice." John C. "Jack" Rawlins spent decades of his career tending to the medical needs of the Seaford community as a family physician before his 1990 retirement.

Uncle Jack mentored his nephew, the only son of his older brother's four offspring, and took him to visit the University of Maryland Dental School in Baltimore. Rawlins chose Western Maryland College (now McDaniel College) in Westminster for his undergraduate work after Seaford High School but was turned down for his low grades. On his uncle's advice, he completed his freshman year at Salisbury State Teachers College, now Salisbury University, and transferred to Western Maryland in 1956.

"Just before the Christmas break, the first love of my life broke up with me and caused me to lose interest in everything academic, resulting in my flunking chemistry and ROTC, so I dropped out of school and worked for a year. I reapplied to Western Maryland but they said, 'No.' Jim Blackwell, a Seafordian and friend of my father's, said he would recommend me to Tusculum College, a small school in Greeneville, Tennessee," Rawlins recalls. He was accepted in 1958. "I studied well, majored in chemistry, minored in math, and graduated in 1961."

The same year, he married Ivonne Santa Cruz from Bolivia, who worked in Washington, D.C., as a secretary. "We met on the beach in Rehoboth [Beach, Delaware] on July 4," Rawlins says. After they wed, Ivonne quit her job.

Following graduation from the University of Maryland Dental School on June 6, 1966, he volunteered for the Army and served five years as a dental officer with the rank of captain. "I always wanted to go in the service, in the Army. Uncle Jack and his oldest brother, Victor, served in the Army and I liked the toys the Army had." He and Ivonne were based in Germany for three years. Their first daughter, Monica Lynn, who is married and lives in Lafayette, Louisiana, was born in 1962. A second daughter, Tanya Marie, today a major in the Army stationed at the U.S. embassy in La Paz, Bolivia, arrived four years later.

"I volunteered for Vietnam. I wanted to go," Rawlins says as enthusiastically as if he was again offering to go. He was given a month's leave before joining the dental unit of the 101st Airborne Division's 2nd Brigade in the war zone in December 1969. "There was one dentist for every 5,500 men. We had a day off every 13 days," he remembers.

From the day he arrived in Cam Ranh Bay, Rawlins was captivated. "Getting to be in the combat zone was definitely a unique experience. I had no fear. I was homesick for Germany but I found [Vietnam] so interesting. I thought we were definitely doing the right thing there."

In addition to caring for soldiers' teeth during his tour, Rawlins also treated the South Vietnamese. "I'll never forget, I was at an orphanage in Hue and the children were lined up. We were injecting them before doing extractions. There was not one whimper."

A MEMORABLE LETTER

Despite his compassion for the South Vietnamese, Rawlins, as a father, was torn by being so far from his family. Inspired, he says, by a letter from his mother who chided him for not telling his 7 1/2-year-old daughter Monica why he felt it was so important that he had volunteered for his combat assignment before he left, he penned her an explanation "in terms that I thought she would understand."

After he sent his letter to Monica, "I considered that many of my fellow soldiers had young children back home who might be able to relate to their missing fathers if they read (or had read to them) my letter." So he sent a copy to the Vietnam Mailbag, and asked whether it might be included in a future column. "When I saw it in print, it meant a lot to me and, hopefully, to others too."

Rawlins' letter, published April 20, 1970, touched many Mailbag readers for its simplistic yet honest message. His closing words ring true nearly four decades later:

"When I was a little boy growing up, I never had to be afraid for my life because our soldiers were keeping the bad people away. They did this because they loved our country and little ones like me who lived in it.

"Now I am old enough to take my turn and help protect you and the others because I love you and our wonderful country.

"So whenever anybody asks why your daddy went to Vietnam, you just hold your head up high and tell them, 'He went there because he loves me, my family, and our country.'"

"The only thoughts that I had and continue to have are those of so much pride in my father and for what our troops did then and continue to do for the sake of our country's freedom," Monica Rawlins Harlow says. "My father is really an amazing man and it is no wonder that he wrote that letter back then explaining the situation in the manner that he did. It still causes a little tear and a little lump in my throat. What a letter! I love it!"

Rawlins says he sent a copy of his letter and a patriotic essay Monica had written in school to President Richard M. Nixon "with the message that I was very much behind his actions in Vietnam and was enclosing [the essay] from my daughter that showed that even the very young were aware of what was going on." Nixon commended Monica in his personally signed March 24, 1971 letter to her.

HARSH WORDS FOR DISSENTERS

Aside from the death and destruction of the war, negatives of serving in Vietnam for Rawlins included "reading all of the antimilitary [rhetoric] and the lack of support from the people of our own country with the demonstrations and flag burnings." He has harsh words for dissenters, then and now: "Those ungrateful, selfish, ignorant, antiwar protesters who disgrace themselves by denigrating our military fighting men and women are undeserving parasites. Yet, our military men and women will sacrifice their lives for those same ungrateful slugs."

Internal strife in the war zone also nagged him. "There were two big problems in the military [in Vietnam]: the drug problem and the race problem, which was terrible. There were, on average, three murders a month because of these two problems in my brigade."

Strategically, Rawlins says he was "unhappy that we didn't seek military victory in Vietnam. LBJ [President Lyndon Baines Johnson] announced to the world that 'our mission was to discourage aggression' and we couldn't seek victory by playing defensive. But we never lost a single major battle."

After his tour ended in December 1970, Rawlins, who then was divorced, was assigned as the assistant chief of Dental Troop Clinic 2 at Fort Carson in Colorado Springs, Colorado, where he met and married his second wife, Nicole, who was born and reared in France. Rawlins says Nicole's 9-year-old daughter, Nathalie was a "bonus prize of that marriage."

Rawlins' open letter to his daughter Monica inspired her to write a school essay for which President Richard M. Nixon commended her. In this 1987 picture, the Rawlins army included daughters (left to right) Spc. Nathalie, Cpl. Tanya and ROTC Cpl. Monica with their father, who retired as a lieutenant colonel in the Army Reserve.

"Those ungrateful, selfish, ignorant, antiwar protesters who disgrace themselves by denigrating our military fighting men and women are undeserving parasites. Yet, our military men and women will sacrifice their lives for those same ungrateful slugs."

After a brief stint at Fort Sam Houston, Texas, Rawlins was transferred back to Germany for three and a half years. "As part of the downsizing of the military after we pulled out of Vietnam, I was riffed out of Germany and I signed out of the Army in February 1977 at Fort Dix, New Jersey In March, I signed up for the Army Reserve as a major and was promoted to lieutenant colonel several years later."

Soon after his separation from the Army, Rawlins visited his sisters in Delaware. Despite spending his entire childhood there, "I knew I wouldn't move back to Seaford," he remembers. He preferred Florida's year-round warm weather. "When Nicole and I traveled to Florida to visit my parents, who had moved to Merritt Island from Seaford while I was in Germany, I said, 'we're home.'" He got his license to practice dentistry in the Sunshine State and lived in Ocala for 14 months. "They needed a dentist at the women's prison in Lowell, so that's what I did."

He next practiced at a frenetic pace in Winter Park. There, he was the only dentist in a 23-chair denture clinic where he saw, on average, 120 new patients daily by 10 a.m. and would take impressions for one-day dentures and partial dentures. He saw an additional 65 patients who needed adjustments by 1 p.m. During the afternoon, he delivered dentures to the new patients he had seen that morning.

"Also, from 1 to 3:30 p.m., I would extract between 180 and 200 teeth from 20 to 30 of those 120 patients for immediate denture deliveries. I did this

five days a week for almost two years, from 1978 to 1980," Rawlins recalls. His office staff consisted of 15 lab technicians, more than a dozen dental assistants and four receptionists. "It was a real hustle job and I got burned out after two years."

He worked for another dentist for a year before taking over the four-office practice of Denture World in 1981 in Longwood. He immediately changed the name to Dental World, offered comprehensive family dental care, and bought the practice and the building in 1983.

His buoyant personality always has drawn patients to his thriving practice, including, for orthodontics, Brandy Johnson of Altamonte Springs, a national champion gymnast who competed at the 1988 Olympics in Seoul, South Korea.

"Over the course of my career, I've often had patients say to me, 'I hate dentists.' I just turn and look them right in the eye and say, 'I don't particularly care for you either.' This breaks the ice. Our two biggest enemies are fear and apprehension. I do my best to get rid of both." He sees his staff as family and treats them well. They reciprocate with long-term loyalty and describe the unflappable septuagenarian as "youthful, energetic, and charismatic."

Indeed, on his 67th birthday, Rawlins made local headlines by riding his unicycle to and from work, a 9-mile round trip, as well as in the homecoming parade at his college reunion. He and Nicole traveled to and from the Tusculum gathering, about a 1,300-mile roundtrip, on his BMW 1200 LT motorcycle, with its heated seats and GPS navigational system.

Rawlins, who deeply appreciated his tour in Vietnam, sees parallels with today's undeclared war in Iraq. "We cut and ran in Vietnam and there was a bloodbath. There are lessons we should have learned from Vietnam. I'm proud of George W. Bush for going over to Iraq and I don't want to see the resolve of the American people diminish."

Regardless of which war he discusses, Rawlins is adamant about one thing: "We all owe our comfortable lives and abundance of food, pleasures, luxury items and the freedom to enjoy them to those soldiers who sacrificed themselves to protect us and our country." As for Vietnam, he sums up his service without hesitation: "I'm happy I got to be there."

RICHARD S. LOVEKIN
ARMY 1969-1970

With a documented medical disability, Richard Stephen "Rick" Lovekin could have avoided service in Vietnam altogether. He chose instead to enlist in the Army and spent a year in combat as a door gunner on a Huey helicopter and later as crew chief on a Cobra chopper. Lovekin paid a high price for his decision. Within months of returning home in 1970, his marriage failed and he nearly died from alcohol abuse and depression.

Today, Lovekin, 59, is happily remarried and dotes on his four children, seven grandchildren and Bogart, his 170-pound Landseer Newfoundland, at his suburban Wilmington, Delaware, home. Although he takes medication for post-traumatic stress disorder (PTSD), he finds purpose in life and is proud to be a founding member of Delaware's Chapter 83 of Vietnam Veterans of America. He is fulfilled by the talks and slide shows on Vietnam he has presented, on his own time and at his own expense, to thousands of high school and college students for nearly 25 years.

As he runs a hand through a now-graying shock of hair, he starts his story.

"Everyone knew what was going to happen to them after high school – Vietnam. So I enlisted in the Army for two years to beat the draft," he recalls of his 1968 decision. "My main drive to enlist was that I saw everybody else in my neighborhood going into the service and I didn't want to be the only one who stayed home. I didn't have to enlist but I did."

A year earlier, Lovekin had suffered a punctured right kidney playing sandlot football near his home in Ogletown, about three miles east of the University of Delaware in Newark. "On the last day of school in 1967, I went to the boy's room and nothing but blood came out. I learned I had two small kidneys on my right side and one was removed. The doctor told me then I'd be exempt from service."

But in August of 1968, just two months after graduating from Christiana High School, the determined 19-year old reported to Fort Bragg, North Carolina, for eight weeks of basic training.

In high school, Lovekin had been best-known for his band, Rick and the Rockets, later The Quarrymen, but the war helped drive the musicians apart. "I played rhythm guitar and was backup singer," Lovekin explains. "Our lead singer punked out and joined the National Guard and the two other guys, brothers, went to Canada. We never heard from them again."

He felt uncomfortable at Fort Bragg. "It was infantry training and they were turning us into killers," he remembers. "That disturbed me. I suppose they had to do it but, to me, it was a game I tried not to take too seriously."

His education on base extended beyond military tactics. "It was the first time I had been in contact with people from all over the country. I'd had a lot of black friends growing up. My biggest problem was with the hillbillies."

From Fort Bragg, Lovekin was assigned to the Huey helicopter door gunner school at Fort Eustis, Virginia. Less than 24 hours after his December 20, 1968 graduation, he returned to Delaware to marry his high school sweetheart, Carol Bethard. He had orders to report to Fort Campbell, Kentucky, three days later.

"I was put in a holding company there and pulled maintenance," Lovekin says. "We set up a Vietnamese village and trained." He noticed war veterans on base didn't follow orders. "They didn't get up. 'Look, man,' they said, 'I just got back from Vietnam. You want me to do this chicken shit?' Those guys disappeared or were sent to the brig."

On March 20, 1969, Lovekin packed his duffle for Vietnam.

Soldier Lovekin on break during the Christmas holidays in 1969 at Vung Tau, a secure air base. Today, Lovekin honors Vietnam veterans through his stirring presentations on the war.

"I saw two helicopters collide, both were U.S., and I saw a helmet bounce down the runway with the pilot's head still in it. That sight and the smell of that crash is still with me today."

14 Feb 70

(2)

more peaceful and less destructive way.
I didn't especially want to come into the army, but I didn't go out and burn my draft card or take off to canada or take any of the other ways I could have thought to get out of it. I didn't really want to come to Viet Nam either, but here I am. It would take a long time to write down all the reasons why I ca[...]ithout making a big fuss, so I'll just [...] ones to me. ① Above all [...] and family. I did it [...] freedom and keep th[...] and away from the [...] who have no respec[...] the properties and [...] it seems that I can[...] away from my love[...] the US with their t[...] ② I am over here 'c[...] their laws. I am [...] everything she stan[...] imagine how go[...] [...] of the filth [...] and me, they (well [...] would surely thank God and [...] what they have. ③ I am over here [...] I am doing my job (As A CREW [...] ARMYS ONLY TRUE gunship - the [...]pter) the best I can for all of American[s who] have died in this blood-SOAKEN country fighting to preserve all americans freedom.

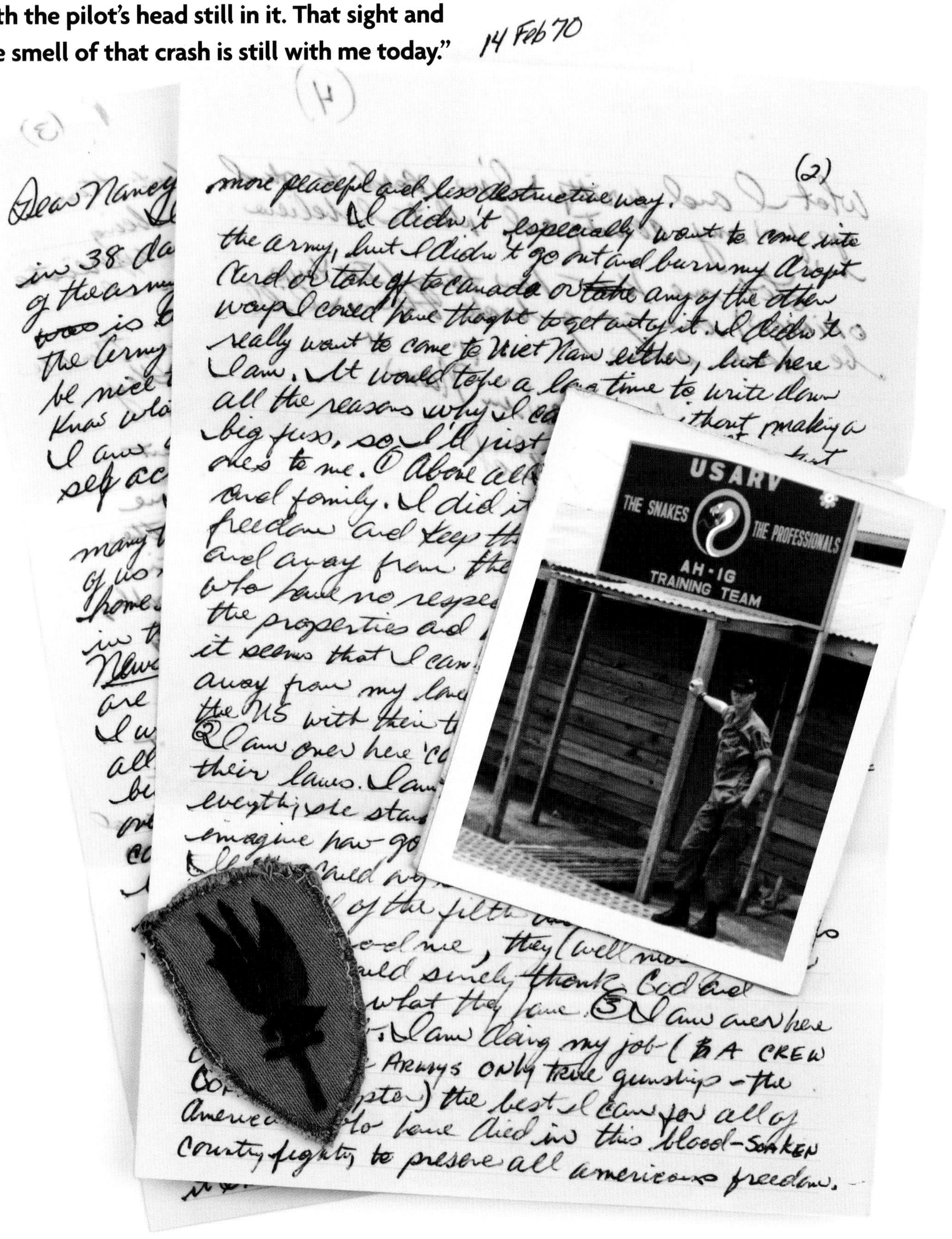

A DIFFERENT WORLD

After flying about 20 hours on a packed commercial jet from California to Alaska to Japan to Vietnam with more than 100 servicemen he didn't know, he recalls, "we did a corkscrew landing at Tan Son Nhut Air Base because there was a chance the base might be hit. It was a big shock getting off the plane, like landing on the moon."

Acclimating to Vietnam's withering heat and humidity proved difficult, but observing the abject poverty all around him during the bus ride to Long Binh overwhelmed him. "The people lived in thatched huts and makeshift housing. And the smells were terrible," he says.

In short order, Lovekin, the oldest of six children in a blended family, toughened up emotionally. "Growing up, I was disrespectful and did things to show off. I lost my real dad when I was 13 and I was angry. When I went to Vietnam, I put away my toys and picked up a rifle and became concerned about the people next to me. That may have been the best thing that happened to me."

Conversely, one scene he witnessed in Vietnam forever scarred him. "I saw two helicopters collide, both were U.S., and I saw a helmet bounce down the runway with the pilot's head still in it. That sight and the smell of that crash is still with me today."

To cope in Vietnam, Lovekin and his fellow soldiers developed their "don't mean nothing" mantra. "When something tragic happened, we'd automatically say this to get us through the situation, no matter how bad it was. It kept us from thinking about how bad things really were," he says. "And it usually worked."

Getting to know the 60 men in his unit, the 147th Helicopter Company based in Bien Hoa and Vung Tau, was a positive experience. "I was in aviation and that's where I wanted to be. I got into Cobras because they needed crew chiefs. I saw so many different people and learned how to deal with them – that has stayed with me to this day. I met some wonderful people."

'YOUR MAN IN NAM'

Lovekin was a frequent writer to the Vietnam Mailbag and always signed his letters, "Your man in Nam, Rick." In his January 3, 1970 correspondence, he defended Lt. William L. Calley Jr., charged in the My Lai massacre. "Lt. Calley is only guilty of doing his duty to his country." On February 24, he added, "It's not easy being over here. The pressures we go up against are immense and never-ending." In the same letter, he also decried the violence and protests in America. "The situation at home is almost as bad as it is over here though. There are countless lunatics running around with guns and knives just killing at random."

He shared a vignette of after-hours life in Vung Tau. "Half the people in town didn't care about you and half would try to take money from you. Most towns had what we called cowboys. One night, we got on the wrong side of town and a group of cowboys approached us. One of my buddies just clocked one of them and we started to walk away. They picked up stones and bottles and threw them at us. We ran for our lives. This was going on in a war zone."

Lovekin was attuned to the shift in the war's rhythm in his two years of service, especially during his 12 months in country. "It changed from when we thought we really could win to 'let's get our butts home alive.' With that change, Vietnam became not a 12-year war but 12 one-year wars. New guys coming in asked, 'Hey, man, where's the dope?' not 'Where are the guns?' or 'Where's the bunker? Have you been hit lately?'"

Days before he left Vietnam in March 1970, an appreciative Lovekin wrote, "It's really good to be able to voice my feelings and opinions and let people know how I feel…. This will probably be my last letter to you as I am coming home very soon…. I'm so short I can count my days to go on my two hands. Be home less than a week after this letter. WOW!!"

With more firepower than a tank, the Cobra helicopter was Lovekin's aircraft of choice. During a 1985 visit to the Vietnam Veterans Memorial (opposite), he reflected on those lost in the war. The total is now 58,260 names listed on the Memorial. Approximately 1,200 of these are listed as missing (MIAs, POWs, and others).

THE AFTEREFFECT

Within a few months of his shaky return to civilian life, he knew he and Carol were headed for divorce. "When I was at war, we were trained to kill and destroy. When I came home, my family wanted to treat me like I'd been away to summer camp. I know they didn't want to bring up bad memories but everything built up inside me," Lovekin remembers. "Anger was still a big problem for me. I used to snap over nothing. I know it affected the divorce."

From there, Lovekin spiraled downward. His PTSD symptoms, which he still deals with, included insomnia, nightmares, road rage and a need to be treated fairly. "I couldn't sleep. I drank too much. I hung around biker bars. I felt safe around them, they were outcasts and so was I. I didn't want to commit suicide but I didn't care what happened to me."

Then he met his future wife, Karen Tomlinson. "I was in Ohio. It sounds corny but I was a milkman and Karen was on my route. Her husband had been killed in a motorcycle accident and she was raising two young boys by herself. We like to say we saved each other." They married in August 1971.

Despite his happiness with Karen and their life together, his anger eventually strained his relationship with her, her sons and their children, especially Stephanie, their older daughter. "As a little girl," she recalls, "I was frightened of my dad. I didn't understand why he freaked out sometimes and why he never talked to me. It was always scolding that I heard from him. Of course, as a kid, I internalized it. I thought if there wasn't anything I could do to make my father smile or stop being mad, I must be a bad person."

"I know what I put everyone through and it bothers me to this day," Lovekin says. "I never hurt anybody but I'd punch walls and really scream and holler over little things. No one was allowed to run around the house because the noise reminded me of the war. Everybody in the house was walking on eggshells because of me."

Over time, Stephanie remembers, her interaction with her father improved. "He started coming to my high school softball games. Although he was physically there and said he was proud of me, I still never felt an emotional connection to him. It wasn't until one day, when I was about 25, he handed me a folder of newspaper clippings from every softball and volleyball game where my name was mentioned and pictures from my games and varsity letters I'd thought I'd lost that it finally clicked he truly cared and was proud of me."

THE RETURN STATESIDE

Throughout his tour in Vietnam, Lovekin says he was "never scared, just excited and nervous." His return home precipitated a lot of readjustment problems, starting with takeoff from Tan Son Nhut Air Base. "I left Vietnam at 7:30 a.m. on Friday and, because of the International Date Line, arrived in Oakland, California, at 7:30 a.m. Friday, the exact day and time I'd taken off." That was just the beginning.

After two days of debriefing at the Army base in Oakland, mostly standing in lines, Lovekin finally was ready to fly to Philadelphia, his final destination. Still in uniform, he arrived at San Francisco International Airport at 6 a.m. for his flight home. He couldn't help but notice "two guys dressed in black with microphones in their sleeves, like the CIA." They were, he learned, a security detail for Col. Harland David Sanders, founder of the Kentucky Fried Chicken restaurant franchise. Lovekin recalls Sanders, dressed in his trademark all-white suit, shook his hand and said, "'Son, thank you for serving. While you're here, my men will protect you.'"

Prior to leaving Vietnam, Lovekin says he had prepared himself for all manner of negative stateside reaction to his uniform and knew "to be aware of people looking to abuse veterans returning home."

What he had not prepared for was the reaction he received from World War II veterans. Soon after he arrived home, his stepfather, David Lovekin, who had served in the National Guard during the Korean War, took him to a veterans' gathering. He was taken aback after his stepdad proudly introduced him. "The room was quiet, like everyone was thinking 'so what?' Then their comments were, 'What are you doing home? The war's still going on,' and 'What kind of drugs are you doing, buddy?'"

THE HEALING PROCESS

Today, their relationship is even better, says Stephanie, 36, a married mother of two young sons who is a project manager at JPMorgan Chase & Co. in Wilmington. "I have come to learn that the Vietnam War changed my dad, that it was almost impossible for him to make a deep emotional connection to anyone after returning from the war. I know my dad really does love me and the connection has always been there, I just can't touch it. And that's OK because now I understand that it's how the Vietnam War shaped him. I want him to know that he didn't let any of his kids down in any way. He was always there for us, no matter what. And," she adds, "I want to make sure he knows how proud I am of him."

Lovekin, 59, is more spontaneous with his feelings today. "I love my family. Nothing else means as much." To spend more time with his family, he prefers a flexible schedule and works as a flooring salesman, the fifteenth job he's held since Vietnam. "I've never been fired, I've always walked away. It's still hard for me to put up with crap."

Since 1984, he has packaged his Vietnam experience in a compelling talk and slide show set to 1960s music for high school and college students in a multi-state area. He estimates he has given more than 1,300 presentations to more than 30,000 young people.

"It's a free program and lasts one to two hours," says Lovekin. "We tailor it for different age groups but we want people to remember what happened to Vietnam veterans and how we were treated when we came home.. There are people who confuse veterans with the war. We say, 'don't confuse the war with the warriors.'"

The highlight of his speaking engagements was an invitation from the U.S. Military Academy at West Point for him and nine others from the Delaware Chapter of the Vietnam Veterans of America to talk on campus. "We were treated like kings. They put us up for about a week. We had a wonderful time because of the camaraderie."

In addition to speaking to West Point cadets for two days, his group also shared their experiences with hundreds of area high school students, bused in by the academy.

Lovekin says he gives his presentations on behalf of all Vietnam veterans "because I want people to have a correct perception of who we are. This has channeled my anger. It's therapy. Do you know Vietnam vets are still considered a minority group? We were designated that in the 1970s with blacks and Hispanics," he says, referring to the Vietnam-Era Veterans Readjustment Assistance Act of 1974, which prohibits job discrimination.

When he's not speaking to groups about the war, Lovekin is active in Vietnam Veterans of America Chapter 83, which he helped found in 1983. The chapter is responsible for erecting in Wilmington a memorial, dedicated on Veterans Day, November 11, 1983, to Delaware servicemen killed in Vietnam. The chapter also promotes the memory of fallen veterans in its Delaware Hometown Heroes program and honors the state's Gold Star Families.

"We also give $1,000 U.S. Savings Bonds each year to one male and one female student at the Delaware Military Academy who exemplifies service to others," says Lovekin. "You don't read about us much but we have a lot of support from big companies. We're a real quiet little organization that does tons of stuff."

Lovekin, who was not wounded in Vietnam, lost a cousin, Army Sgt. Timothy Joseph Noden of Linwood, Pennsylvania, and Christiana High School schoolmates, Army Pfc. Alan G. Geissinger and Navy Constructionman Jon J. Hayden, both of Newark. He harbors no bitterness about the war today and says he would serve again if he had it to do over. "First, I'm an American and back then it was all about baseball and apple pie. You didn't question your government."

He does, however, lament the parallels of Vietnam with Iraq, another undeclared war nearly as far away. "We got into Vietnam in the beginning with the full support of the people, like Iraq. By the time LBJ [President Lyndon Baines Johnson] was in office, we had all these troops in Vietnam and could have ended the war but politics got in the way, like today."

America could have achieved victory in Vietnam, Lovekin believes. "We never lost a major battle. When we pulled our combat troops out of Vietnam, we had a treaty with North Vietnam. Two years later, they attacked and took over South Vietnam." He pauses. "We like to say we lost the peace, not the war."

Lovekin is proud to have served his country in Vietnam and shrugs off any plaudits. "I just did my job." And he eagerly shares that job through his programs for young audiences today." One of our ground rules is we don't discuss politics. We're not going to debate history. We feel that gets us away from what happened to us. My drive," he says, "is to make sure this generation of veterans is not treated like we were."

STANLEY F. PIENKOS JR.
MARINE CORPS 1969-1970

The uniform, Stanley Frank Pienkos Jr. says without hesitation, attracted him immediately, prompting him to enlist in the Marine Corps soon after a recruiter spoke at his high school. The dress blues' no-nonsense crisp lines and sharp contrasts appealed to the former track hurdler who would in Vietnam epitomize the highest ideals of the corps as a member of 1st Force Reconnaissance Company, one of the Marines' special operations groups.

"I just liked the uniform," Pienkos repeats from his well-appointed construction trailer in a New Castle, Delaware, industrial park. "One of the Marine recruiters came to school. As soon as I saw his dress blues, I thought he looked cool. I guess you'd say 'awesome' today." President since 1999 of Pienkos and Son General Contractors, a commercial and residential building business, he revels in life, liberty and loyalty to his country.

"[2007] was the first year in 37 that I attended my 1st Force Recon reunion and had a chance to see a few of my old team members. It was great," he effuses. For five days in May in Jacksonville, South Carolina, near Camp Lejeune where they went through advanced infantry training together, he and his buddies reunited. "We mostly brought each other up to date about our families and what we were doing today. We didn't talk that much about war stories."

But the men easily could have flashed back to Vietnam and their service as an elite band of brothers proud, as the Marine Corps put it, to "dare greatly" for both corps and country. Service that included putting on their camouflage faces, long-range missions, O.V. 10 Bronco prop planes, SPIE [Special Insertion and Extraction] rigs and patrol reports. But those memories are a world away from Pienkos' roots in Wilmington, Delaware.

The second of three children of Mary Lou and Stanley Pienkos, he was a happy towhead who grew up in Hedgeville, one of Wilmington's Polish neighborhoods, and attended a parochial grade school nearby. "I was an ornery Polish boy, always getting into trouble for boy stuff. I was an overachiever who was small and fast and ran track and hated school. I was a Boy Scout in a troop sponsored by the Pulaski Legion," he recalls. His late father was well-respected in northern Delaware's construction industry and was proud of his 55 years with New Castle Carpenters Local 626, a union membership that started with his father, Pienkos' grandfather. Pienkos himself joined the union in 1977.

Pienkos, his younger brother, Kenneth, and older sister, Dianne, attended Henry C. Conrad High School, where he was an average student. In 1968, his junior year, he married Paula Greenwell, a senior at the former Gunning Bedford High School. They had met four years earlier at the Merryland Roller Rink in Glasgow, about 15 miles south of Wilmington. He was 17 and she was 18.

Recently, the couple celebrated their 40th anniversary, a family occasion that included their children, Matthew, Sherri and Amanda, and grandchildren, Joseph E.P. Hawkins and Sarah Pienkos. "Paula and I've stayed together because we so incompatible," Pienkos teases. "Seriously, behind every good man, there is a strong and wonderful woman pulling the strings, but don't let anyone know."

Pienkos and his bride had scant time for married life before he enlisted in the Marines in December 1968. Basic training at Parris Island, South Carolina, was, for Pienkos, an experience that was "priceless, like the MasterCard commercial." He moved on to Camp Geiger within Camp Lejeune for advanced infantry training and later to Fort Benning, Georgia, for parachute school. "I wanted to be one of those guys with gold jump wings. It went very well." He was firmly on the fast track as a marine.

His next stop in June 1969 was Oceanside, California, where he joined the Marine Corps' 5th Force Reconnaissance Company for more training, specifically as a diver. "Every Friday, we'd have either a jump or a dive," he remembers. Four months later, his team flew to Okinawa, their last stop before Vietnam. They landed in Da Nang on October 24, 1969, two weeks before his 18th birthday. "Our first base was Hill 34," Pienkos remembers. "It was near the Navy's 1st Medical Battalion, between Da Nang and Marble Mountain. It was a resort compared to An Hoa [where 1st Force Recon was stationed before moving to Hill 34]. Instead of tents, we had hooches with tin roofs, screened sides and plywood floors."

A gung-ho Stanley F. Pienkos left high school to join the Marine Corps. He bought the WAR medallion in Vietnam and wore it the entire 259 days he was in country. Today, he captains his own construction company.

**"We were scouts, eyes and ears.
Our job was to not make contact with the enemy."**

THE SCOUTING REPORTS

Working together as a special operations team provided unmatched camaraderie, he says. "We were scouts, eyes and ears. Our job was to not make contact with the enemy." Pienkos leafs through several patrol reports from 1969 and 1970 marked "Confidential" and "Secret" which are now declassified. He selects one, dated February 12, 1970, for a patrol he went on from February 8 to February 12.

According to the report, written by Marine 1st Lt. Sands A. Robnick, the patrol leader, the team's mission was to "conduct an area reconnaissance to intercept and monitor routes of supply and infiltration. Be prepared to utilize fixed-wing aircraft on targets of opportunity. Be prepared to attempt a prisoner acquisition on order." After 68 1/2 hours of patrolling, Pienkos' team reported 11 sightings of a total of 33 enemy, three camouflaged huts and two concealed canoe-like boats called pirogues near the Buong River.

Enemy observations on February 10 included "… 1 VC/NVA working in a cultivated field. The enemy was wearing black PJs and he was picking the produce of the field and throwing it into a wicker basket off to the side of the cultivated area … 16 VC/NVA (including 3 females) moving west on a trail. All of the enemy were wearing black PJs and all but 1 were uncovered. The enemy that was covered was wearing a coolie hat. The enemy were carrying bundles of wood, wicker baskets and 1 was carrying a hoe. No weapons were observed."

The report also included information on terrain, "extremely steep with a thick single canopy approximately 20' in height. The undergrowth is approximately 10' high and consists of bamboo, vines, briars and scrubs. Movement is restricted at the rate of 100 meters per hour for a recon patrol and it is limited to ridgelines and trails."

Robnick concluded in his report that the "entire river valley … is a food-raising area. He also believes the enemy are exploiting the services of Montagnard tribesmen for the cultivation of these crops. He recommends that a prisoner acquisition be conducted in the vicinity." No contact was made with the enemy and the team was extracted by helicopter without incident.

Contact with the enemy during a war, however, was inevitable. "We lost a lot of good men but we never left anyone behind," says Pienkos. "We walked out together and we walked back together. We were all brothers."

As hellish as the war was for him and his fellow marines, Vietnam provided some upbeat moments. "I try to remember all the good times: the USO shows with the Dallas Cowboys Cheerleaders and Connie Stevens, the Bob Hope show, C-rations."

C-rations?

"I loved them, especially the green eggs and ham and the beans and franks."

He enjoys talking about lighter moments in Vietnam. "There were a lot of funny times," he says. "I remember we stopped during a night patrol and one of the guys was bored. He started throwing small stones at an orangutan in a tree. All of a sudden, there was screeching and the momma orangutan came down from that tree and knocked him out cold. How she knew who was throwing stones I'll never know but she clocked him."

Another night mission proved humorous. "Again, we had stopped but soon we were being pelted with small sticks and stones. We couldn't see and didn't know if it was the enemy playing with us. It was rock apes. They smelled us and started throwing anything they had at us. It should have been on *Candid Camera*. Another time, we heard this thundering noise and the ground was shaking and we thought, 'What the hell is that?' It was elephants. I was just a city boy. Nobody told me it was a jungle out there."

A TENDER POET

The tough marine, who has "1st Force Recon" tattooed on his right arm, also showed his tender side when the Vietnam Mailbag twice published letters he wrote to his family during his 12-month tour. Both touched readers, especially his second letter, dated March 7, 1970, which contained a poem. He prefaced it with, "Dear Mom and Pop, Hi, how is everything? I was here thinking and I wrote this. Boy, I should be a poet, huh?"

When you think no one cares
Look into the skies
Think back upon the day you left
And the tears in your mother's eyes.
When you think no one cares
That you're in a far-away land
Think back upon the day you left
And your father's shaky hand
When you think no one cares
Well, just listen, mister
Think back upon the day you left
And the break in the voice of your sister.
When you think no one cares
Consider all your friends
Then listen for many prayers
That are in the wind.
When you think no one cares
Just stop and look around
And think about the happiness
That just 19 years have found.

Pienkos, who wrote often to his wife and parents, signed this letter, "Your loving son, Stanley." He shrugs off any literary talent. "It was just something that came to me and I wrote it down. I've written hundreds of verses like that one. But I'm not a poet or a writer. Hell no, I can't even spell."

PATROLS IN THE JUNGLE

Throughout his tour, he went on countless patrols and says 17 missions were long-range, five days or longer. In Vietnam since 1965, 1st Force Recon was tasked with conducting "Key Hole" missions which involved silence and stealth and no contact with the enemy. This modus operandi allowed teams to carry out ground reconnaissance and forward observing. "I was in a very elite group, like the Navy SEALS or the Army Rangers or Special Forces. Today, it would be the Delta Force," Pienkos says.

For Pienkos and his team, putting on their faces was standard operating procedure before a patrol. "We used camouflage grease paint, black and green, and each of us had our own face, our war face. We always made ourselves up the same way each time. Mine covered my cheekbones and most of my face below my nose. We rubbed what was left over on our necks so our skin wouldn't shine. Basically, we covered everything not covered by our clothing. Then we'd put on our jungle hats and proceed to the chopper pad, ready for another patrol."

Patrols took him and his team to numerous locations, including Da Nang, A Shau Valley, Elephant Valley, Chu Lai, Spider Lakes and Nha Trang. Without the relative comforts of Hill 34, he remembers eating monkeys, snakes and rats on patrol. "When we were at Spider Lakes, we got socked in for 11 days. We had enough food for three days. We found a few rats and made soup which was especially good. It was red meat and we used ketchup and sauces left over from our C-rations in it."

Every scouting mission, he says, ended with a SALUTE, an acronym for a report on the enemy's Size, Activity, Location, Uniform, Time and Equipment. "You did your job. You took orders," says Pienkos, who was promoted to corporal in May 1970. Despite the prevalence of drugs and alcohol in Vietnam and the escape they provided, he had nothing to do with them. "Being in Special Forces, you had to stay in top shape. We were running seven or eight miles a day and we carried 120-pound packs. We were lean and mean."

Pienkos and six of his team members are pictured on the cover of *Force Recon Diary, 1970*, a 1992 book by Bruce H. "Doc" Norton, which chronicles Norton's second tour in Vietnam where he was assigned to 1st Force Reconnaissance Company as a Navy hospital corpsman. On the back cover, which shows an image of Pienkos' face, Norton wrote: "Whether patrolling the Thuong Duc Corridor west of Da Nang, training new teams, or taking a hill in the middle of NVA territory, this Force Recon company put its lethal skills to work to make sure its team could survive combat behind enemy lines – where one slip could mean body bags for everyone."

"Our motto was, 'Stop, look and beware because Force Recon is everywhere' and we were," Pienkos says. "Basically, that meant you'd better be scared to death of us." His memorabilia from the war includes what he calls a 'death card,' a colorful, playing-card-size calling card that 1st Force Recon left on enemy dead. Another memento is a small, tattered note pad he kept in his left uniform pocket at all times. Between its torn pages, he had carefully printed information: patrol name, patrol members' last names and first initials followed by a column of single letters. "Blood types," he explains. "We had to know everyone's, just in case." He turns to the back of the pad where a detailed, hand-drawn map covers two

Pienkos' worn note pad accompanied him on all patrols and included team members' names and blood types. He taped his dog tags together to silence them and received a special Marine Corps coin when he left Vietnam. Pienkos (opposite, front row, left) with members of 1st Force Reconnaissance Team.

pages. "I did this on my stomach during a mission. We didn't have photocopiers then so when I got back to my base this map was copied by hand. Kind of interesting, isn't it?"

By October 1970, Pienkos was headed home. "Our 30-man detachment was breaking up and 1st Force Recon was on its way to California. We flew from Da Nang to Okinawa to Guam to Hawaii to San Francisco to Philadelphia. I took a cab and got home about 3 a.m." He startled his wife, who was living with his parents during his absence. "I shouted, 'There's a man in the house.' I heard my father say to my mother, he called her Pat, 'Pat, get the gun. There's a man in the house.' I said, 'Pop, it's me.'"

Pienkos, 57, knew he could work with his father in construction but joined the Marine Corps Reserve after his active duty ended in 1972. He worked as a full-time recruiter from Wilmington for more than four years. Then, without warning, he suffered his first onset of post-traumatic stress disorder (PTSD). "I had to get rid of the uniform. I was whacked out and I let loose. There were fights. So I got out of the Reserve and started working as a union carpenter. I went to the VA [Veterans Administration] and I saw a shrink. I got my head straight and got back into the military."

In 1984, Pienkos enlisted in the Delaware Army National Guard and in 1987 was named the top National Guard recruiter in the country. Before his 1997 retirement as a first sergeant, he served part-time as a 'weekend warrior' for five years. "I enjoyed every minute of it," he says. In 1992, he started his own construction company. "I decided to call it Corps Construction for the Marine Corps. In 1999, we changed the name to Pienkos and Son General Contractors." The company works throughout Delaware, and does about 90 percent of its work for commercial clients, the rest residential.

Asked about this country's role in Vietnam, he is clear. "What did we learn? Nothing," he says. "We won battles but not the war. I think being over there was a good thing. I'd rather be fighting over there than here." He acknowledges PTSD was his personal toll. He had another episode in 1995. He's also worked through some depression with help from family members, especially Paula. "She was always there for me."

As for Iraq, Pienkos is equally clear. "We started something. We should finish it. If you're going to do it, do it or get the hell out of there. We started this war to find weapons of mass destruction. Now we have reservists serving three and four tours. Is Bush wrong? I think he did the wrong thing but this is no time to pull out our soldiers. The beer, beans and bullets days are gone. We lost one war and it wouldn't look too pretty if we walk away from this one."

Pienkos, who calls himself a patriot and says he would sign up for Vietnam if he had it to do again, puts his war experiences in perspective. "The first three months you're fighting because you're scared. The second three months you're fighting for Mom, apple pie and Chevrolet. The third three months you're fighting because you kind of enjoy it and the fourth three months you're fighting for your life. You're bobbing, ducking and weaving and want to go home in one piece. Vietnam gave me respect for life and people." Choosing his words carefully, he adds, "Vietnam made me a man."

WILLIAM W. HUTCHISON JR.
ARMY 1970-1971

Nearly 2,000 Americans would die in Vietnam in 1965, the year William Wilds "Hutch" Hutchison Jr. graduated from a rural public school. The undeclared war's alarming death toll, nine times the previous year's fatalities, ramped up anxiety at home. For the rail-thin teen from Clayton, Delaware, the Vietnam War was as remote and unreal as World War II and the John Wayne type of war heroes he watched on TV. The Green Berets, the Army's Special Forces, seemed larger than life and their role in the conflict reminded him of the make-believe world of his childhood.

"They were mythical creatures whose exploits resembled the playing 'war' of my youth when we fought and died gloriously, guns blazing," Hutchison recalls. "I especially enjoyed playing with Bob Comegys because he added authentic German military gear brought back by his doctor father from World War II. I was just as happy being the German even if the helmet was heavy enough to make my neck ache."

The second of four children of a work-at-home mom and a Delaware state trooper, Hutchison played war and cowboys for years with his pal in the quiet town of Clayton. In 1960, when he was in ninth grade, his family moved a few miles west of town to his paternal grandfather's farm.

A lean tower of graying hair and beard today, Hutchison easily summons the indelible images of the pastoral spread. "There was a huge elm tree, you could see it from Clayton, with a truck tire swing. And the farmhouse was old, built in the 1700s. I probably mentioned these things most in the letters I wrote home from Vietnam," he says. But he's ahead of his story.

"I grew up playing war and cowboys but I couldn't understand Vietnam," he recalls of America's ever-deepening involvement in a country 12,000 miles from his home. So, after his graduation from John Bassett Moore High School in Smyrna, he concentrated his considerable energies on staying in school and out of the draft. "I wanted to become a history teacher and I did. I carried 18 credits at Salisbury [Md.] State College [now Salisbury University] so that if I had to drop a course I would still be a full-time student at 15 credits and maintain my student deferment."

After earning his bachelor's degree in 1969, he moved back home and spent a long summer job-hunting, finally landing a position as a seventh-grade humanities teacher in the Dover-area Capital School District. "I thought I had it made until my mom called the school in November. She said I'd received a letter that started, 'Greetings…' I had been drafted."

Sailor for all seasons, retired teacher William W. "Hutch" Hutchison Jr. crews on Delaware's tall ship, the Kalmar Nyckel. In Vietnam, he was an infantryman and later a reporter/photographer with the 23rd Infantry Division.

THE DRAFT

Hutchison learned that his friend Roger Gourley of Frederica, a teacher in Milford, also had received the same letter. "We met in the Peanut Room in the basement of the Hi-D-Ho Restaurant in Dover to commiserate over some beers. I was so hung over [the next day] I missed my first day of school."

Even though he called in sick, Hutchison drove to his school district office and asked the personnel director to write to his draft board requesting a deferment, like the rest of the male teachers in his building had received. His induction was deferred, but only to the end of the school year. Two days after school dismissed in June 1970, he reported to Philadelphia for his Army physical.

"When we boarded the bus outside the Selective Service office in Dover, mine was the last name called, so I consider myself the last person to be drafted in Kent County under the old system. In January [1970] they started drafting by lottery and your number was based on your birthday," Hutchison recalls. "My number was in the low 200s, Roger's was 300-something."

Once Hutchison received his draft notice, "I became very interested in what was going on. I felt I couldn't go to war." He contacted the American Friends Service Committee, the Quaker social justice organization founded to support the interests of conscientious objectors, for information about relocating to Canada as a conscientious objector. "One of the things that stopped me was I wouldn't be able to teach in America and I couldn't teach in Canada until I became a Canadian citizen. Every alternative seemed so final: give up my family, go to jail. I think in the back of my very naïve mind I believed that I would never end up in combat in Vietnam."

During basic training at Fort Dix, New Jersey, Hutchison tried challenging his instructors, but to little avail. "I refused to raise my hand for the oath. I was hoping to create a stir but no one seemed to notice." He further tested them by refusing to pick up his M-16 rifle. "There were 100 of us. When they got done firing, they loaded up to go to dinner. I was told, 'you're going to stay here until you fire your weapon.' I saw no point in sitting at the firing range all night so I fired three bullets into a target and ended my first real protest."

At the conclusion of basic training, Hutchison and about 30 other soldiers, half of whom were college graduates, were shipped to Fort Polk, Louisiana, for advanced infantry training (AIT). It was the first time he had been in an airplane. "Our MOS was 11 Bravo (infantry). That's when I realized I was on the fast track to Vietnam."

After AIT, Hutchison had a 30-day leave before reporting to Fort Lewis, Washington, his last stop before Vietnam. Hutchison returned home. "My Dad suggested I could get a ride directly to Vietnam on a C-5 from Dover Air Force Base. I said no. I was not going to hurry the process in any way."

Captivated by a weather event, soldiers shoot an incoming typhoon on the South China Sea. A Vietnamese orphan in Chu Lai (opposite) holds her baby Ameri-Asian brother, almost her size.

ARRIVING IN VIETNAM

In November 1970, Hutchison was en route to the war zone with 15 soldiers from his company at Fort Dix. "When I stepped off the plane in Cam Ranh Bay, the first thing I felt was the humidity. It was even more humid than Delaware. Our bus had chicken wire over the windows. I joked to the driver, 'Is this to keep us from jumping out?' He said, 'No, it's to keep people from throwing things [like grenades] in.'"

The driver's words rocked the 23-year-old soldier. "For the first time I was scared. This is for real, I thought, and there's a chance I might die. I literally stayed scared the entire time I was in the bush but I believe being scared and being older than most of the guys I served with helped me survive in Vietnam."

Hutchison reported to the 23rd Infantry Division (Americal), 198th Light Infantry Brigade, 1st of the 6th Infantry Battalion, Alpha Company. "I took a training course in Chu Lai with all the other 'newbies' of the division before being sent into the field. Again my smart mouth pissed off one of the instructors and I was sent to burn shit."

Outhouses there, he well remembers, had eight to 10 seats. "I pulled half-barrels out of the shitters, which had a horrible, disgusting smell. I poured diesel fuel in them and set them on fire. The smell only got worse as you had to stir the stuff with a stick to keep it burning. I only did that once. I realized that you keep your smart remarks to yourself and use a long stick."

Hutchison then was flown from Fire Support Base Dottie to join Alpha Company in the field to secure pacification "villes" (villages) on the Batangan Peninsula south of Chu Lai. "I got my first chopper ride, on a Huey. Three of us with full rucksacks and our M-16s on our laps and we're sitting in the open door with our feet hanging out. The chopper banked and I was looking straight down at the ground. Since I was in the middle, I had nothing to grab hold of nor did I have a free hand to grab with. All I could do was stare at the ground wondering why I wasn't falling out and here I was not even in the field for an hour." As he exited the chopper, a body bag was loaded on, a grim reminder of the war's toll.

IN AND OUT OF TROUBLE

In the field, Hutchison realized he needed to learn lessons quickly from his fellow soldiers. "Most I learned by observing and asking questions. Some I had to learn the hard way. I got jock rot, a rash in my crotch, and went to the medic who told me to drop my pants. As I was doing so he exclaimed, 'Jesus Christ, you're wearing underwear.'" Hutchison would later tell his students, "I never met anyone who served in the bush who wore underwear. So if you want to know who has served in the bush, just ask them what color their underwear was."

His service in the bush started in the pacification villes but he spent most of his time patrolling at night in squads or smaller groups. "If we had been at full strength, we would have had 20 men split into two squads. Instead, we had six to eight guys operating at least a click [1,000 meters] apart to set up nightly ambushes with claymore mines in free-fire zones. That meant anyone moving around, especially at night, was considered the enemy and got shot at. We did have our claymores go off but with usually nothing to

show for it other than frayed nerves. One morning just before dawn our mechanical ambush blew away a water buffalo." The animal had made contact with the tripwire, sending a spray of 1,000 BBs across the trail where the mine had been set.

Hutchison recalls his first, harrowing night patrol. "We couldn't talk and [so we] communicated by touch. I was walking 'drag,' the last one in line. My job was to make sure that our rear was secure. Every hour or so, we would stop to catch our breath at which point I would face the way we came and keep watch. Suddenly I realized it was too quiet. The rest of my squad had moved and I didn't know it. It was pitch black and I was suddenly very alone and petrified. I moved a few yards, then realized I had no idea where anyone had gone. So I just hunkered down and waited." His squad doubled back for him. "I made darn sure after that I had physical contact with the guy next to me."

In all, he spent about seven months in the field. "I became the RTO, a radio telephone operator, and spent most of the rest of my time walking behind the lieutenant." It wasn't long before he was in trouble again.

While crossing a valley of rice paddies in daylight, his squad came under enemy fire which included heavy machine guns from high ground across the valley. Hutchison's lieutenant had him call in artillery and they "blasted the hell out of the hill." After the barrage ceased, the squad again tried to cross. Immediately they came under fire and again artillery was called in.

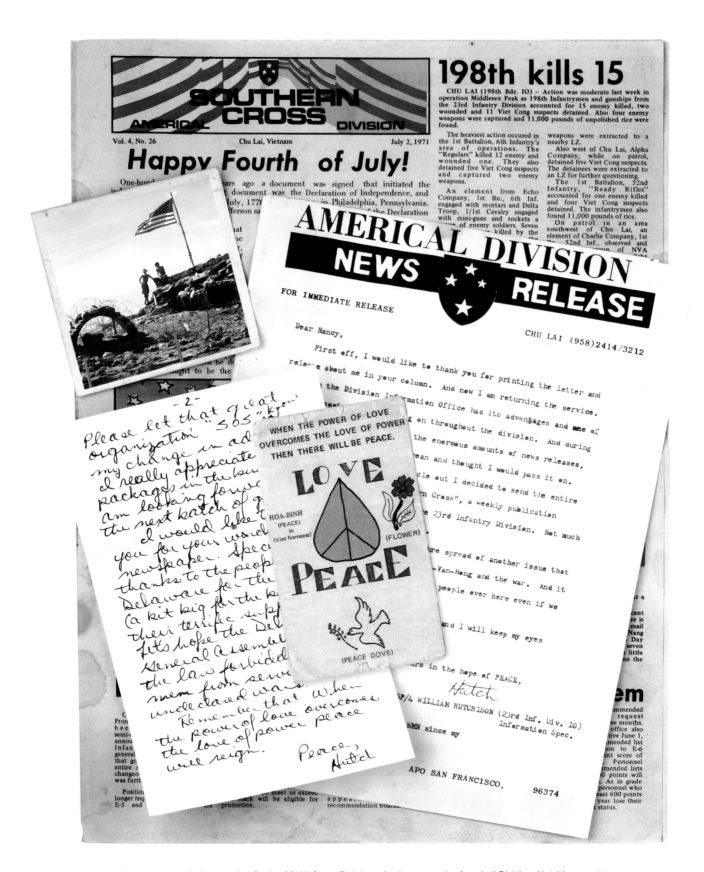

As a reporter and photographer for the 23rd Infantry Division, also known as the Americal Division, Hutchison wrote often for the *Southern Cross*, the division's newspaper. In this edition, he featured his nemesis, Maj. Gen. James L. Baldwin, who had earlier presented him with the Army Commendation Medal for valorous conduct as an infantryman.

As twilight and quiet settled on the area, the company commander radioed Hutchison to tell his lieutenant to take the squad across the valley and check out the enemy position. Hutchison tried to explain it was getting dark and hard to see. The captain repeated his order. "At that point, I began fiddling with my squelch button and said I had not heard the last message. I requested the message be repeated, which it was, but I said since I could not make out what was said, the unit would stay put until morning."

He told his lieutenant the radio battery died. "The company commander's helicopter was there at dawn. He thrust a new radio at me and snatched up my old one saying, 'Son, you had better hope this thing doesn't work.' In the night I had inserted an old battery and buried my good one. When we crossed the valley in company strength, we found a large, freshly abandoned tunnel and bunker complex."

"For the first time I was scared. This is for real, I thought, and there's a chance I might die. I literally stayed scared the entire time I was in the bush but I believe being scared and being older than most of the guys I served with helped me survive in Vietnam."

Hutchison continued. "Then we got a new platoon leader, a captain straight out of Ranger school. On our first patrol, with me carrying the radio behind him, he bent down and began to pick up something shiny. I dove to the ground and covered my head. With a shell casing in his hand, the captain turned around, spied me on the ground and said, 'I guess I shouldn't have done that.' 'Not if you want us to survive,' I replied."

After the patrol, the captain told Hutchison if he would stay with him until he learned the ropes, he would do everything he could to get him a rear job. "A week or so later, he was as good as his word," Hutchison remembers.

'V' FOR VALOR

Before the episode with his company commander, Hutchison, who was nicknamed "Teach" by his fellow grunts, had been nominated for a medal. He tells the story:

"While my unit was being moved by choppers to a new AO [area of operations], one of the chopper pilots spotted a VC with an AK-47 on the ground. After consulting with the lieutenant, it was decided that we would assault the village. The choppers dropped us off, hovering above the rice paddies that surrounded the little hamlet of thatched huts. As I leaped out of the chopper, with no idea where we were or what was going on since only our officer was able to talk to the chopper crew, I pitched forward into the knee-deep mud of the paddy, my overly-full rucksack helping bury my face in the mud and water. As I struggled to free myself, I thought I might drown. Once free, I struggled to try and get into a defensive position and clean the muck off my glasses. Of course, that was hard with almost everything wet and covered in mud.

"Once in position, our squad leader had us move forward into the ville in single file. I was directed to check out a well at the end of the ville. As I moved toward it, I felt my right foot give. I froze and told the sergeant who was behind me that I thought I had stepped on a booby trap. He dropped his gear and crawled to me, using his bayonet to probe around my foot. Sure enough, he uncovered a wire that led to a 155-mm artillery shell. After it was disarmed, I could finally move my foot.

Almost every grunt in the bush yearned for a rear job. Most were handed out based on seniority, those longest in the field got the job. But some rear jobs required special training. Hutchison's best friend from basic training and advanced infantry training lucked into one after being "medevaced from the field with boils on his ass." In the hospital in Chu Lai, he read that the Divisional Information Office needed an artist and he was a fine arts graduate of Syracuse University. He got the job and wrote to Hutchison. "I wrote him back and said that his first assignment was to get me back there with him."

His friend informed him there was a reporter/photographer job available. "So I wrote this long letter to the IO [information officer] telling them about my extensive background as a high school and college yearbook photographer and how I had written for my high school and college newspapers. I lied through my teeth."

The information officer replied, telling Hutchison the job was his – if he could get released from his unit. When he asked his lieutenant, who asked his company commander, Hutchison was flatly denied, with the commander "saying something about not letting me out as long as he was in charge."

"We dropped a concussion grenade down the well. Moments later, there was another explosion on the other side of the village. Half our guys had assaulted from the other side, supposedly to trap the enemy inside. Immediately, someone yelled for the medic. Then it was, 'Teach, Teach, Doc's been hit.' With only one medic for our platoon, I was designated to carry the medic bag for our squad as I had taken some first-aid training with the Frederica Volunteer Fire Company to become an ambulance driver.

"I immediately released my rucksack and took off running in the direction of the shouts. I ran across the ville to where a couple of guys were clustered around our medic, whose body was still smoking from having been hit by a 'bouncing betty,' one of the VC's ugliest mines, a grenade on a spring that when set off, bounced into the air and exploded. Doc, who had been bent over moving through a hedgerow, had taken most of the grenade in the face. I did the best I could for him. An LOH [light observation helicopter] came in and picked him up. We were told he died on the operating room table with shrapnel in his brain."

Hutchison's lieutenant recommended him for the Army Commendation Medal with "V" device for valor. "I told him I didn't want a medal. Doc was dead, I had failed. They kept saying it was an act of bravery. I said no, it was ignorance."

Hutchison had figured out what had happened. "Our lieutenant had taken us into a village that on the map was marked as a mine-field, what we called a booby-trapped ville. That VC had shown himself to draw us into his trap and we were dumb enough to go. Or should I say the chopper pilot and our lieutenant were dumb and we were totally ignorant of what was down there. We lost two guys that day and even though we did get one VC who was hiding in a tunnel off the well where I stepped on the mine, it was not worth the price we paid."

After the war, one of Hutchison's greatest disappointments was his inability to contact Doc's family and "tell them the truth about what happened." He couldn't remember Doc's real name and had lost his address book. "About 20 years later, I was able to cross-reference the names on the Vietnam Veterans Memorial with dates and was able to find him on the Wall: Stephen Warren. Through a Web site connected with the Wall, I made contact with his former girlfriend. But when she tried to contact his family, she couldn't find anyone."

When Hutchison found out he would get three days in the rear to receive the medal, he changed his mind about accepting it. Army Maj. Gen. James L. Baldwin, commander of the 23rd Infantry Division, pinned it on him. "I even got a new uniform out of the deal, the only one with my name on it while I was in the bush," he recalls.

Hutchison also was honored as the 198th's Soldier of the Month. "When the company commander, the major who I was in the dog-house with over the broken radio, saw that I was the one getting that award, he said, 'YOU!!' But he did go ahead and hand me my $25 savings bond and shake my hand. I just grinned."

A FEW CHOICE WORDS

He finally got his rear job as a reporter/photographer with the information office and his first assignment was a story and three pictures on a helicopter company. Hutchison didn't know the top from the bottom of a camera. "I asked who was the best photographer and begged him to help me." He shot an entire roll of black-and-white film. "They used one picture."

The rear was quite different from the bush and towards the end of Hutchison's tour, he extended "so I could go to Australia for two weeks and DEROS from the Army at the end of my extension. Unfortunately, my mouth got me in trouble again." One Sunday, his only day off, Hutchison returned to the information office from the beach "where several of us had consumed close to a case of beer each. I had a run-in with my commanding officer who I told to 'get fucked, sir.'"

The major threatened him with a court martial, citing dereliction of duty and disrespecting an officer. "I talked to some people at the Judge Advocate's office and they felt it would be hard to make the charges stick. I was technically not on duty and I was drunk." The major reconsidered. "Instead of court-martialing me, he said he was not going to protect me when the unit drew down and I would be going back to the bush. My reply was that I was definitely not going back to the bush."

Hutchison went to Gen. Baldwin's office, where he knew a captain from Philadelphia. When Hutchison told him he had already served 11 months and 14 days in country, the captain told him he could go home. A typhoon the next day disrupted his travel plans. "The following day, I walked into the major's office, snapped to attention in front of his desk, saluted and said, 'Sir, get fucked! And this time I mean it!'"

Hutchison dashed out of the major's office, leaped into a waiting Jeep and sped to the airport. "I climbed aboard a C-130 and had to sit straddle-legged on the flight deck, held down by a cargo strap. I was looking over my shoulder the whole time."

BACK TO THE BASICS

Despite orders to report to Fort Hood, Texas, Hutchison planned an end run. He had been accepted for graduate study at Salisbury State while he was in Vietnam. He learned that if he went to the Pentagon, he could get his Fort Hood assignment changed to the base closest to his home as he was getting an early out to go back to school.

"So my buddy and I drove to D.C., went to the Pentagon, found this office deep in the bowels of the world's largest office building and got our orders changed to Fort Dix." In January 1972, Hutchison was separated from the Army and attended Salisbury State for one semester on the GI Bill. He worked that summer for his father's fertilizer business, then spent nine months sailing the Caribbean. "In September 1973, I forced my school district to give me my old job back, citing the Soldiers and Sailors Act of 1947."

After his return to teaching, he became active in the teachers union as a local negotiator and president and was elected vice president of the Delaware State Education Association. He was active in protests, against the war, then the nuclear freeze movement, joining the Kent County Peace Fellowship and Pacem in Terris. Many years later, "I organized a protest outside the gates of Dover Air Force Base during the Persian Gulf War. I also refused to lead my students in the pledge [of allegiance], which got in the press. It was my little way of protesting." Hutchison taught for 25 years and moved into administration for seven years before retiring in 2003. He lives in Dover, Delaware's capital. His only child, Chela, is a registered nurse in Seattle.

Hutchison, 61, labels the war in Iraq "another Vietnam. The similarities are so scary. It's amazing how patriotism is used as armor to keep people from dissenting. There was no way we could have won in Vietnam, and there's no way we'll win in Iraq. I believe there are more terrorists in the world now than before we invaded Iraq."

Although Hutchison has dialed back his rhetoric over the years, he remains active in retirement, volunteering nearly 1,000 hours annually with the Kalmar Nyckel, Delaware's tall ship and goodwill ambassador, a replica of the Swedish vessel that sailed to America in 1638. Its 24 passengers established the first permanent European settlement in the Delaware Valley, the colony of New Sweden, which today is Wilmington, Delaware's largest city. "I spend most of my

Hutchison felt a kinship with the oppressed South Vietnamese whom he photographed frequently. He enjoyed his downtime on the beaches of Chu Lai (opposite).

time crewing, which keeps me active." In addition, Hutchison in April 2008 was named interim director of education, a paid position, for the Kalmar Nyckel Foundation.

Without reservation, Vietnam remains the seminal epoch in his life. "I remember more about every single day of Vietnam than I do any other period of my life, including last week," says Hutchison, who came home a much more committed activist and pacifist than when he left.

"War doesn't solve anything but it marked me, it changed me, it made me the person I am today but I could not, would not, go through it again." He looks away. "I went in the Army questioning authority. I came out knowing I would never again do something just because someone ordered me to if I thought it was wrong."

DANIEL P. STOKES
AIR FORCE 1971-1972

Within days of his April 1971 arrival at Da Nang Air Base, near Vietnam's pristine beach on the South China Sea, Air Force Airman 1st Class Daniel Pack Stokes experienced his first enemy assault, a brief but relentless barrage from Soviet-made Katyusha rockets. The former life-guard from Rehoboth Beach, Delaware's premier resort on the Atlantic Ocean, learned more about himself in those few minutes than he had in all his 20 years.

Daniel P. Stokes was a reluctant warrior in Vietnam, a "pacifist at heart who carried a gun." He has found his niche as a medical massage therapist.

The attack scared me shitless," Stokes remembers. And with the hindsight of 37 years, he refers to it as his "baptismal event," an episode that determined his actions for the rest of his tour.

Ironically, his original orders put the young airman nowhere near Da Nang, but in Bien Hoa, a relatively secure post about 350 miles south, near Saigon. "I considered myself lucky to have drawn such cake duty. My joy was short-lived however. Within a couple of hours of reporting to the Security Police Squadron at Bien Hoa, I was informed of new orders, an in-country transfer to the 366th Security Police Squadron at Da Nang. I was to leave the following day on a C-130."

Stokes, disheartened but not dismayed, recalls he spent his first night in Vietnam "to the sounds of Motown, GIs drinking beer and smoking pot and the occasional sound of a chopper or F-4 Phantom flying in the distance. When I fell asleep, I slept well." After breakfast the next morning, he headed for the flight line. Passengers included Vietnamese refugees and squawking chickens.

"Da Nang felt different," says Stokes, a trim man with a graying beard and earnest blue eyes. "The smells were the same as in Bien Hoa: AV [aviation] gas fumes, open cooking fires from the villagers just outside the fence, human excrement, body odor and dusty soil, but there was a palpable tension to the surroundings that confused

me and elevated my awareness. I didn't understand exactly what made it feel like that but I was pretty certain that I was going to find out soon enough."

Stokes soon felt different, too. "Oddly, I wanted something to happen. I wanted to see or hear action. The first few days at Da Nang were uneventful. I had been assigned to the swing shift 1430-2230 [2:30 to 10:30 p.m.] and was told to find a bunk in the hooch which my fellow swing-shift airmen were assigned to. I went to supply to get camo [camouflage] fatigues and was told they didn't have any. My hooch's *mamasan* [maid], hooked me up with two pair in one day, tailored to fit me, for $10 MPC [military payment certificate] and she never took a single measurement."

Choosing the hooch that was closest to the latrine and shower, Stokes noted the construction of his living quarters. The floor was a concrete slab, the walls were clapboard with screening at the top, and the corrugated metal roof was nailed down and secured with sand-bags tied together with rope. The hooch also had screened doors at each end. Free-standing metal lockers served as partitions.

"Generally, there were two guys to a cubicle with two double lockers. The beds were capable of being bunked but none were. Nobody wanted to be on the upper bunk, the logic being that the chance of getting hit by shrapnel during a rocket attack was greater the higher you were off the ground."

"He said, 'Hey, Stokes, why don't you grab a seat and play some cards? We got A-1 intel [intelligence] on getting hit tonight. You've been talking shit about wanting to see something happen. Tonight, you might just get your wish.'"

AN ATTACK IS IN THE CARDS

On his tenth day in the war zone, Stokes got something to eat after working his shift and settled into his hooch for the evening. "I still had not seen or heard anything remotely like action or combat. Random artillery shots came from east to west and you could hear them 'sucking air' as they went over us. The Katyusha rockets would run out of fuel and fall to earth. The only sound they made before impact was 'pushing' air. I later realized that if you heard one sputtering overhead there was little to worry about as it was still moving away from you. It was getting late. I was tired and wanted to go to sleep."

But Sgt. Willie I. Graves of Philadelphia, his hoochmate, hassled him. "He said, 'Hey, Stokes, why don't you grab a seat and play some cards? We got A-1 intel [intelligence] on getting hit tonight. You've been talking shit about wanting to see something happen. Tonight, you might just get your wish. You don't want to be sleeping and miss the show.'"

So he reluctantly joined Graves and three others. "Picture five guys sitting on a couple of folding chairs and empty ammo boxes playing poker on a makeshift table in a cubicle so small that if anybody but the guy at the entrance needed to leave, at least three of us had to make room. We weren't playing for money; we were playing to pass time."

Most of the men smoked and drank soda or beer. Hours passed. "We could hear our guns going off in the distance and I grew more and more tired. I started to leave to get some sleep. Willie grabbed me by the shirt. 'Sit your ass down, Stokes. There's plenty of dark left for Charlie to do his thing. We're getting hit tonight. Count on that.'"

They played another hand. A mix of songs by Smokey Robinson and the Miracles, Cream and Lynyrd Skynyrd wafted through their hooch. "Suddenly," Stokes remembers with the clarity of yesterday, "the table flipped, cards and chips flew and everybody rolled off their seats or just dove to the floor – except me. I had no idea what was going on. I hadn't heard or seen anything unusual. A moment later, the world came unglued."

An intense white light flashed outside the hooch, followed by an explosion so close and so powerful that dust rose several feet off the concrete floor from the concussion. "The noise was ear-splitting and was followed by several more explosions, but none as close as the first that I was aware of. It was a terrifying time. I always thought it was just a figure of speech when people talked about their life flashing before their eyes. But that is literally what happened to me. Images of my first or second birthday party, me and my little sister, Mimi, playing in Rehoboth Bay, my grandparents, younger brother, and other people and events of my life up to that very moment all actually flashed before my mind's eye in mere seconds."

The assault was over in minutes. "I found myself under Willie's bunk and partially under Willie as well. My ears rang for days after that night and I learned to cover them during subsequent attacks when possible," Stokes recalls. "I also had no trouble staying awake when we had A-1 intelligence of a pending attack."

Although there were minor injuries that night, he knew the 3:05 a.m. attack was a close call and wouldn't be the last. "It was a night of lessons. Outgoing rounds (artillery) suck air, incoming rounds (rockets) push air. Recognizing the subtle difference was all the heads-up Willie and the others needed. Man-oh-man, did I long to be home. It was a defining moment for sure … 254 days [left] and a wake-up…. I'm fucked."

Nonetheless, he says he observed "some horrific things" at Da Nang. Like the orange-robed monk who sat cross-legged and immolated himself outside the base's west gate to protest the war. And the airman burned over 75 percent of his body who carried his refrigerator to safety after an attack, not realizing he was injured. And the dazed soldier who came back to the compound covered with his buddy's blood after a rocket attack.

"There was a transformation in Vietnam. You observed and processed and you could bury yourself in alcohol or drugs, or you could protect yourself. I became increasingly vigilant and paid close attention to everything I heard, witnessed or sensed. I trusted my instincts. That was how I protected myself."

Stokes touched Vietnam Mailbag readers when he wrote on August 10, 1971, about the loss of five friends in a rocket attack on a barracks in Da Nang, his first encounter with losing buddies. As difficult as that was, he reflects on another kind of loss, the transformation he saw in the war zone.

"We all went into this conflict with varying degrees of innocence. The longer you were in country, the more you experienced the war's cruelty and unfairness. The more of that you were involved in, the quicker you lost your innocence. Soldiers who generally greeted one another with a smile and a wisecrack did so reluctantly after they had seen casualties up close and personal. Some handled their emotions well and recovered their sense of self after a short period of time. Others seemingly never got over it. They took their anger, fear and frustration to different levels to cope. Some became heroin addicts, some became ruthlessly cruel."

Assigned to the armory for part of his tour, Stokes says he was "in a position to see several hundred different men every day, one shift to deploy weapons and another shift to check in weapons. The friends I 'lost' were the guys who started their work shift joking with one another when they got their weapons and returned at the end of their shifts silent, exhausted and emotionally spent from recovering bodies and tending to the wounded. Watching the changes they went through was a great source of sadness … in retrospect, more so than any other singular event of my tour."

Stokes pauses to explain his own transformation. "During a year's tour in Vietnam, for the first three months you're trying to figure it out. From the fourth to seventh months you don't give a fuck, you do what you're told to do and adopt a 'whatever, don't mean shit' attitude. Then you get to the magic 100 days left and you realize you'll be going home soon and you do whatever you need to do so you can get there. That's when the superstition came in. When it was a full moon, I'd take a certain route to get to the latrine, staying in the shadows so I wouldn't be an easy target. When it was a new moon, I'd take the shortest path."

FRUSTRATION, FUN AND FRIENDSHIP

Despite the war's ugliness, he had reasons to give thanks. "I didn't really experience a lot of horrible things. I never killed anyone and I am very grateful for that. I was a pacifist at heart who carried a gun." At the armory, "I knew guys not by their names but by the butt numbers of their guns and where the guns went, the slot

DECIDING TO SERVE

Stokes used the lessons of his first attack to survive the Vietnam conflict, a conflict the pacifist struggled with long before he arrived in country. "The war was a real conundrum for me because I was actively against it. I took a bus to an antiwar rally in D.C. in 1967 when I was a sophomore in high school," he says.

"I really struggled. I had a cousin well beyond draft age in Toronto [Canada] who offered safe haven and I had another cousin who was a captain in the Marine Corps who had served three tours in Vietnam. I thought, 'geez, what am I going to do?'"

In 1969, Stokes was a member of Rehoboth High School's last graduating class before district consolidation. He mulled his future that summer on Indian Beach as a lifeguard with the Rehoboth Beach Patrol, a job he had held since 1968. "I knew I could do Toronto but I also knew I couldn't live with myself if I did. I could have gone to college too but I decided to join the Air Force for four years."

The agonizing decision made, he reported to Lackland Air Force Base in San Antonio, Texas, in October 1969. "When orders were handed out, I got security police. That freaked me out. It meant I was going to Vietnam." For his first few months in country, especially after experiencing his first enemy attack in Da Nang, Stokes says he "did a lot of observation to get a feel for what to expect. I recognized I needed to stay on the good side of anyone who could help me stay safe."

numbers. Sometimes a gun was still there but the man was not. It wasn't always bad news, though. A lot of guys rotated home."

Frustration was perhaps the worst part of his tour. Stokes recounts an example. "In 1971, troop withdrawals were ongoing and the MACV [Military Assistance Command Vietnam] rules of engagement for our base changed. What were once free-fire zones now required permission from MACV. A K-9 handler named Woods was on patrol with his sentry dog and got shot in the leg. We were not permitted to fire back. We had the perpetrator – the entire area was illuminated by pop flares, 18-inch aluminum tubes you'd set off by placing the top of the tube on the bottom and slamming the base with your helmet – and we were waiting for permission to light him up. It never came. The shooter, a man dressed in baggy black pants and shirt – carrying an AK-47 rifle at his side – casually walked back to the village and disappeared. He shot one of our own and there was no repercussion. Woods was medevaced to Japan. We never saw him again. Life went on. That was frustrating."

As a counterpoint, Stokes adds there were "some extraordinarily good times" in Vietnam. He tells this story: "As security police, we were in charge of guarding the air base. We were pissed off that chow was better for the officers. When the officers' food locker was replenished, we'd break in and steal steaks and lobster tails. We would then report the break-in. We never did catch the perps, but we sure ate well the following few days."

Stokes says he liked the South Vietnamese as a people. "Once you understood them, they were just like us and they were gracious when you treated them with respect." One, a barber named Hanh, befriended Stokes. "When I encountered him in downtown Da Nang City, he warned me not to continue down the street. 'You turn 'round. Go back that way,' he told me." Hanh steered him away from Da Nang's "cowboys," panhandlers and petty thieves who banded together and robbed and sometimes fragged [threw fragmentation grenades at] unsuspecting servicemen. "One of the hardest parts of Vietnam was maybe not doing more for people like Hanh. He was a good guy. I wonder what happened to him."

HOMEWARD BOUND

An unusual circumstance prompted Stokes's early out from Vietnam. "For years, I lived with my grandmother, Anna Pack, in Rehoboth Beach so she was considered next of kin. I got a Red Cross telegram saying she was exhibiting 'aberrant behavior' and her condition was being classified as a 'medical emergency.' It was February 1972 and her Christmas tree was still up and she said it wasn't coming down until Danny came home. People at home, especially her doctor, were worried about her declining mental state. Within 24 hours I was on a plane and gone, a month and a half early. What no one knew was she had bought one of the first artificial Christmas trees."

Stokes well recalls his arrival stateside. "We were *persona non grata*. The hardest part of coming home was the disdain with which we were looked upon. There was no thanks. My Mother said she hoped I was not bitter. I told her I was not bitter, just disappointed."

Although he wanted to go to college after completing his military obligation at Langley Air Force Base near Norfolk, Virginia, in August 1973, Stokes changed course. "I was not tolerant of the way people treated us so I became a certified arborist and did tree work for a living for many years in Wilmington [Delaware]. Outdoors, I didn't have to deal with college-aged, discontented know-it-alls whose most significant life experience may have been getting dumped by a girlfriend but who still thought they were authorities on the war."

A decade later, in 1983, Stokes married Diane Skomorucha. They divorced in 1997. Their daughter, Katie, 21, is working towards her nursing degree at the University of Delaware, and their son, Nicholas, 16, is a student at Delcastle Technical High School.

In the mid-1990s, he became a licensed massage therapist. There's a story behind that too. "When I was a little kid, I used to rub my grandparents' feet and they told me I did a wonderful job. I did it for the 50 cents they gave me to play pinball at the Flat Top in Dewey Beach." Stokes' grandparents, Anna and Harry Pack, owned and worked at the fabled Bottle & Cork, a rustic taproom in Dewey Beach, and were on their feet all day. "The truth is, I assumed their appreciation was out of duty rather than a compliment. Years later, at the urging of my parents, I looked into massage and found that I had a gift for it. It's a far greater gift than I imagined."

Today, Stokes, who lives in north Wilmington with his second wife, Susan Henderson, specializes in medical massage. He sees patients at his office as well as at Family Practice Associates in Wilmington, takes outcalls for geriatric and homebound patients, and does *pro bono* work. "The reason I do what I do is because it provides an opportunity for people to get well. I am incredibly grateful for the gift I have and being able to help is a great pay-off for my patients and me."

He considers himself one of the fortunate survivors of Vietnam. He suffers no residual side effects, mentally or physically, from the war, although he had one upsetting incident he dealt with a few years ago.

"The thing that caused me the most trouble was when we invaded Afghanistan in 2001, Operation Enduring Freedom. I was having heart palpitations and knew something was amiss. I went to the VA [Veterans Administration], described my symptoms, and they told me it was a textbook case of panic disorder. That's when they started calling up the reserve in preparation for going into Iraq. My nephew, Peter Martz, was the same age I was when I served in Vietnam and I'm positive that's when the trouble started. I was putting myself in the position of the young men and women and reservists being put in harm's way. That was the trigger for me. Had I not had children, I would have volunteered," Stokes says. "If there was a way to spare just one of them the trauma of that experience, I would have done it."

Would he serve in Vietnam again? "Actually, I enlisted in the Air Force in the hopes of avoiding Vietnam. Once I got my orders, the choice was made for me. In looking back, though, I learned so much from the experience of Vietnam that I feel it has had a profound influence on my life. The things I observed, the lessons I learned made it a very important and enlightening time for me. I came home with a better understanding of people." He adds that his war experience was, in many ways, responsible for who and what he is today.

As for lessons this country learned in Vietnam, Stokes, 58, is uncompromising. "We lost 58,000 men. What's ironic is we didn't learn anything and we're no smarter. And we haven't made the world any safer. Forcing your will on someone else never works. The only person you can change is yourself."

ROBERT A. COEN
ARMY 1970-1972

Robert Anthony Coen played out his field of dreams during the heady days of high school when he suited up as a starting pitcher for the Brandywine Bulldogs. For three years, he commanded the diamond and hurled his high school's varsity team to victory after victory. "I threw fastballs, then curveballs to keep the batter off guard. I did well," he downplays. In fact, he pitched so well that baseball scouts from the Cincinnati Reds and Pittsburgh Pirates flocked to the school in northern Delaware to observe the lanky, six-foot-three fireballer on the mound.

I knew they were there watching. I was a little nervous but it got me pumped up to the point where I wanted to do well. I wanted to make sure I gave them what they came to see," Coen says. "They were also scouting Garland Gills, our third baseman, who was a good hitter. We were both in our junior year so they couldn't talk to us until our senior year, it was a legal thing," recalls Coen. He had a stellar final season at Brandywine and pitched a second summer for the American Legion-sponsored Brooks Armored Car team.

At the peak of his game, he received a letter from legendary Pirates' manager Danny Murtaugh, a resident of nearby Chester, Pennsylvania, and friend of his mother's family. "The scouts had told him I was a pretty good ball player and he wanted me to try out for his major league team," Coen remembers proudly. He also received a letter from Selective Service.

"I got drafted on my eighteenth birthday in August. Come on down, you're the next contestant," Coen quips, parodying emcee Bob Barker's line on "The Price is Right" game show. But Coen knew Uncle Sam wasn't playing a game. "I may have given up a major league baseball career," he says, exhaling slowly.

Coen was drafted into the Marine Corps. "I thought I was already enough of a man. I decided I didn't need the Marines so I enlisted in the Army." During basic training at Fort Bragg, North Carolina, testing steered him towards work in the Army post office – and 12 weeks at post office school at Fort Benjamin Harrison in Indiana. "I saw my first Indy 500 race there. It was definitely not my sport," recalls Coen. He moved on to Fort Benning, Georgia, where he elected jump school. His rationale? "I earned $55 more a month."

From Fort Benning, he received orders in March 1970 for Vietnam. Coen was 19. "And it was off to the land of milk and honey. I expected it. The number one song then was Peter, Paul and Mary's *I'm Leaving on a Jet Plane*." Soon after his arrival in Phu Bai, a marauding band of South Vietnamese street thugs called "cowboys" boosted his wristwatch and fled on mopeds. "That was my welcome to Vietnam." That and a very forgettable first meal, C-rations of dehydrated eggs and ham.

THE PARACHUTING MAILMAN

During his tour, Coen was stationed in northern South Vietnam, in Phu Bai, not far from the old imperial city of Hue. He was assigned to the 101st Airborne Division's Administration Company. "I spent my year there as a postal clerk. I sold stamps and money orders and sent and distributed packages." Although his job required him to be indoors, he worked in a war zone and was issued an M-16 rifle. "I was not directly involved in combat, not like the infantry was."

His job, he explains, entailed delivering mail to servicemen. "I worked with about eight other guys in the administration building, which was a lot nicer than having to do anything outside. We were open from 8 a.m. to 5 p.m. six

The draft derailed star pitcher Robert A. Coen's dream career. The war changed his life forever. For good luck, he still carries the 101st Airborne Division's commemorative coin.

With the friendships came the inevitable losses. "That was the worst part. Guys you knew for all those months and then they were gone," Coen says, tears welling in his kind brown eyes.

Mailman Coen delivers his take on the war from Phu Bai. He enjoyed a special camaraderie with Lan (opposite).

days a week. If we got mail on Sunday, we'd work on Sunday too. We sorted the mail, put it in large canvas bags and sent it out by jeep or truck to different areas. The men got their mail through their barracks. They'd only come to the post office to buy stamps or send a package or money order."

He remembers an incident at the post office where he upbraided a high-ranking officer. "A full bird colonel wanted to cut in line. I told him, 'Sir, you can't do that.' He said, 'What? Who's your commanding officer?' I told him the name of my captain who later told the colonel I was only doing my job and that he had to wait in line, just like everyone else."

With his experience parachuting out of planes, Coen rotated jumps with another postal worker to nearby firebases to sell money orders. Heroic? "We didn't have a choice," he says. "These guys were getting paid every month and needed a way to send their money home. They needed a postal person but were on duty in the field and couldn't get back. Their pay was held by their commanding officers."

So Coen strapped on a money-order machine and an MACV machine to certify the transaction and jumped from a helicopter to the firebase. The equipment weighed 25 pounds. "I'd stay there three days, then take a helicopter back to Phu Bai. I made two jumps while getting shot at. You think sex is exciting, try dodging an incoming round."

In Phu Bai, Coen didn't always manage to dodge enemy fire. "There was always incoming. It was early evening and we heard it. We were running to get to a safe area. We were always told to get low because after it hit, it would throw up fragments and dirt. On the run out, something hit my left knee. I was the only one hurt. It could have been a lot worse." However, cellulitis, a complication, developed and Coen's knee swelled to three times its normal size. He had to keep his leg propped up and was out of commission for about 10 days.

Despite the hazards of the combat zone, he says there were some good times. His memories span a range of experiences but meeting servicemen from all across America and making new friends ranked highest.

"Whenever we could, we played pinochle and volleyball with the guys from Camp Evans near the DMZ. I'll never forget the songs popular then, *We Gotta Get Out of This Place* by the Animals and *Mama Told Me Not to Come* by Three Dog Night. There were so many different things, Fresca in cans, C-rations, the heat." And there was that drinking contest involving airmen and Lord Calvert whiskey. Coen won it but the victory grounded his routine for a few days.

With the friendships came the inevitable losses. "That was the worst part. Guys you knew for all those months and then they were gone," Coen says, tears welling in his kind brown eyes. There also was Lan. "She was my *mamasan,* a housekeeper." His picture of her shows a pretty young South Vietnamese woman who signed on the back, "I love you always. For ever I hope you don't forget me. I love you." Coen says they enjoyed a special relationship. "After I got home, I corresponded with her but never heard back. A sergeant over there said she'd moved."

A BITTERSWEET HOMECOMING

Before the end of his yearlong tour in Vietnam, Coen learned he would be reassigned to Germany for 18 months. "I told them that was too long to be away from home and they said if I re-upped for seven more months in Vietnam at my same job two things would happen. One, I'd get a 30-day home leave and, two, I'd get out of the Army nine months early." His decision was easy. "I figured with the war winding down, I'd be better off staying in Vietnam for seven more months and getting out than going to Germany for 18 months.")

Although he found it emotionally difficult to return to Vietnam after relaxing in Delaware for a month, Coen honored his obligation. "I'd already made the commitment." With the war waning and troop withdrawals well underway, the next seven months passed quickly at his new post in Da Nang and he was home for good in March 1972. Coen's mother, Sally, tipped off the Vietnam Mailbag that neighbors, friends and family planned a Christmas in March with all the trimmings for her only son as he had missed two holidays at home with his enlistment.

His homecoming was bittersweet. Coen was relieved to be stateside and appreciated the holiday cheer generated by his mother, his "faithful writer" while he was in Vietnam. "I was glad to be home, God bless America. If you live in this country, you should fight for it. My friends treated me well but with outsiders it was different." Coen says his experiences paralleled those of other returning servicemen. "There was no thanks, we never had any parades, there was not a lot of hoopla. We were called baby-killers and it was almost as if people didn't care if we came home or not. Just don't send their sons over to Vietnam."

Coen found room for books and photos in his cramped quarters in Phu Bai.

A SHOCKING DIAGNOSIS

Coen worked until July 2004, when he was diagnosed with Charcot's Foot, a neurological condition named for 19th-century French neurologist Jean Martin Charcot, which affected his left foot and his ability to walk.

He immediately underwent surgery to place pins in his left leg to support his ankle. "I was rehabbing well and walking with a cane. Then I developed an infection in October," Coen says. He was admitted to the Veterans Administration Hospital in Elsmere, Delaware, for treatment of the infection.

After extensive examinations, his physicians concluded that he had been exposed to Agent Orange, one of more than a dozen highly toxic herbicides used as defoliants in Vietnam to eradicate enemy cover. The U.S. military sprayed about 20 million gallons of herbicides in all four military zones in Vietnam during the conflict's duration. Although Agent Orange was the most prevalent, Agent White and Agent Blue also were applied in lesser quantities. These chemicals were identified by the color of the stripe on their storage drums

Coen's doctors said his exposure was neither related to his diabetes, diagnosed in 1985, nor natural causes. "I vaguely remember seeing Agent Orange during my second tour," he says. "Apparently, I was overexposed to the chemical but I was not aware, there was so much going on." The long bones in his left leg had nearly disintegrated and doctors told him his leg could fail at any time without warning, causing him to collapse. The shocking diagnosis came 32 years after he left Vietnam.

"They kept me in the hospital until December 23. I came home for Christmas." Coen did a lot of soul-searching over the holidays and came to a wrenching conclusion. "I figured the best thing to do was for them to take my leg. I went back to see my doctors on January 20. Five days later, they removed my leg below the knee. It was a tough decision but I didn't want to do any further damage."

A few months later, after making sure there was no infection in the stump, he was fitted for a prosthetic leg. "I healed pretty fast," Coen says.

No sooner than he had gotten used to walking with the artificial limb than the prosthesis was mistakenly thrown out at the VA Hospital. "Within a week, I got a new one and adjusted. I got good training. I learned fast because I wanted to walk again," he says.

At 58, Coen is retired and 40 percent disabled, a determination made by his doctors for the loss of one limb. "I get 100 percent medical coverage from the VA as the loss of my leg is service-oriented. Retirement isn't what it's cracked up to be, but I guess it would be better if I could get around easier," he says without complaint. He and his older sister, Lynda, now care for their mother who is 87 and suffers from dementia, in the house they grew up in. Their father, Francis Coen, a state constable, died in 1998.

His conversation turns briefly to Iraq, another undeclared war. "It's similar to Vietnam. It's a senseless war and we shouldn't be there. We should pack up and come home."

Coen doesn't dwell on opportunities lost or roads not traveled in his life. Shifting in his chair, he adjusts his prosthesis. "No, I'm not bitter," he says softly. "What's done is done. I'm still here to tell my story. I think of the guys who didn't make it back. They were so young."

In addition to the lack of appreciation for putting himself in harm's way, Coen initially found his readjustment to civilian life disconcerting. "Whenever a car backfired, you'd get down. It would freak you out, hearing that loud noise. And it was tough watching movies like *The Deer Hunter* and *Apocalypse Now* because they related so much to Vietnam and I wasn't ready to watch them so soon after getting out of the service."

His first post-Vietnam job was with construction giant Bechtel Corp. as a timekeeper and assistant office manager in Wilmington. Coen also reactivated his pitching arm and played two seasons of semi-pro baseball in the Delco League, based in Chester. "I used to hit pretty well too," he recalls, adding he later was the only non-parent coach of a baseball league for boys 13 to 15 in north Wilmington.

His Bechtel job dried up in 1974 after two years. "They wanted me to travel and I didn't want to live out of a suitcase, so I ended up being an insurance man like my dad for four years."

Coen had hoped to marry Mary Fleisher, his next-door neighbor in Linwood, Pennsylvania, where he had lived before moving to suburban Wilmington in 1964. "Her mother wanted me to marry her before I left for Vietnam but I didn't think that was a very good deal. She eventually married a friend of mine."

In 1976, he wed Debbie Ferguson, whom he had met at a Bechtel construction site. Their daughter, Melissa, was born the following year and today lives in Rochester, New York. Coen and his wife divorced in 1983.

He toiled at a succession of jobs after selling insurance, all within a block of each other in north Wilmington. He started as a cashier at a Pathmark supermarket. "They were training me for management when I ended up going to the Tally-Ho Motor Lodge as a desk clerk. When the owners bought the franchise for a motel and the Tally-Ho became a Day's Inn, I was the manager there."

26   The Morning News, Wilmington, Del. * * * Friday, March 10, 1972

vietnam mailbag

...ld appear to our wondering eyes but Spec. 4 ...COEN from Afton, who should have returned from Vietnam this week after a year and a half as a postal clerk in the 101st Airborne Division.

We understand Bob is home early because he extended for an extra hitch overseas. We further understand Bob received not one but two Army Commendation medals.

Actually, Bob is not new to the column — he appeared in the Jan. 4, 1971 Vietnam Mailbag in one of our largest "groupie" snapshots of First taters in Vietnam provided by Capt. JAME D. RAWLNS JR. from Seaford. The picture showed five First Staters and two soldiers from Maryland.

Spec. 4 Robert A. Coen

Bob has a lot in st... him after he rests. F... tipped us off that neighbors, friends and family... celebrating a Ch... in March with all the trim... R... ristmases with his enlist...

...it made, Bob. By the ...entary subscription to ...oth SOS Vietnam a ...lopment say you' ...well as the State ...for Delaware r...

★

...goes up ...Bulleti- ...Vietna ...aught ...nst ...er

...were due to pric... milk, edible oil, some vegetables and ...

Other categories on the upswing include ren... up 0.2 per cent for the middle class and 0.7 per cent... working class due to higher prices in kerosene.

Domestic help remained unchanged.

E97   3"   155-07

HEADQUARTERS
2D BDE 101ST ABN DIV AMBL
and
PHU BAI COMBAT BASE

419

KENNETH D. WARNER
ARMY 1971-1972

Kenneth David Warner pulls a stool up to the center island in the kitchen of his late 19th-century farmhouse, his engaging smile and sky blue eyes disarming. This, he knows, will be an interesting conversation, one he's not had since he left Vietnam in 1972 as a helicopter ambulance pilot with the Army's 571st Medical Detachment.

Before he begins reconstructing his mostly positive combat tour, he apologizes for the dishes in the sink and the bags of groceries on the counter. His morning got away from him, he fusses. But he admits to making, from scratch, the inviting plate of saucer-sized cookies nearby. "I'm a house husband," he confides matter-of-factly, leaning over the island. "I do the cooking, the baking and the wash in this house."

Warner, like his farmhouse in Middletown, Delaware, is a curious amalgam of modern and antique, of worldly and homey. The retired career military man who so skillfully flew UH-1 helicopters on hundreds of medical evacuations in and off the coast of Vietnam is equally comfortable today picking pie cherries from his backyard orchard and planning his family's dinner. He's rarely flown since Vietnam. "What I do not have today," he says, "is the excitement I had then and I really don't want to cheapen the memory." But he's way ahead of his story.

A story that starts in Newark, about 15 miles north of his farmhouse. A musically gifted youth who started playing trombone in junior high school, Warner graduated from Newark High School in June 1965. That fall, he entered the University of Delaware and would become a music education major. He tried out for and was accepted into UD's prestigious marching band as a trombone player and soon became friends with trumpeter Bill Meredith, "which is how I met my wife, Patsy, who is Bill's sister."

He also was a member of the university's ROTC [Reserve Officer Training Corps] program. "After I got my draft notice, I signed up for advanced ROTC, which allowed me to finish school and get my degree." He brushed aside admittedly bad advice from an education psychology professor on campus. "He recommended that I stick an ice pick in my ear to perforate my eardrum so I couldn't serve."

Warner remembers he "needed a couple of classes so I stayed an extra semester and graduated in January 1970." He and Patsy married the following month. He was also commissioned as a second lieutenant. "I went on active duty in March 1970 and went to officers' basic training at Fort Sam Houston, Texas."

Warner knew early on in his military career he wanted to continue flying, an interest he had developed before graduating from the university. He had taken lessons and earned his private VFR [visual flight rules] pilot's license at Cecil County Airpark near Elkton, Maryland. Then, after basic training, he was transferred to Fort Wolters, Texas, where he went to helicopter flight school and enhanced his VFR skills in a TH-55 basic trainer and learned to fly by instruments in a TH-13.

Army 1st Lt. Kenneth D. Warner, a helicopter ambulance pilot, waits between calls at the 13th Surgical Hospital at Quang Tri. Warner today trumpets music over medical missions and remains at ease as a househusband.

"I *loved* instrument flying. I always sought out ways to get more and, on some night missions and some bad weather days, both in and out of the combat zone, being able to fly on instruments got me out of lots of potential trouble."

But Warner truly enjoyed the challenge of flying helicopters, regardless of the weather. "Helos are inherently unstable," he says, adding that during his training, "one of my first attempts at hovering found us hurtling across the airfield towards the fuel truck in what seemed to be half a second after being given all the controls. In the TH-55 and the TH-13, we had to use both feet and both hands – controlling the throttle of the piston engine with the left hand – to keep the engine at a constant RPM. Every helo since then has had a turbine engine."

After his advanced training at Fort Wolters, Warner and Patsy relocated to Fort Rucker, Alabama, where he trained in the UH-1 helicopter. Their first child, Patrick, was born in December 1970. Before he received his orders for Vietnam in July 1971, he returned to Fort Sam Houston for a three-week basic medical emergency course.

"I wanted to go to Vietnam. I'd been indoctrinated by World War II movies, when the army was the good guy and the enemy was the bad guy," he recalls. Patsy and Patrick moved back to Delaware and Warner took off on a commercial flight to the West Coast. He arrived in Vietnam by way of Anchorage, Alaska. "I landed in Tan Son Nhut, then was assigned to Da Nang. I remember it was hot and sticky, messy, icky."

Once he settled in with the 571st Medical Detachment, known as Da Nang Dust Off, he was paired with a stick-buddy and a UH-1 Iroquois helicopter ambulance. "All army helicopters are named for Native American tribes. The H model was the one I flew all the time. It had a strong engine and lots of room. It was designed for medical evacuation and you could put three stretchers in each one." He remembers his first mission out of Da Nang clearly. "I sat and watched."

FLYING UNFETTERED

After observing a few more missions, Warner, now a first lieutenant, soon was flying often. "We always had a crew of four, two pilots, a crew chief and a medic. Their signature craft had "My Brother's Keeper" lettered in white paint across its nose, above the red cross centered on a field of white. Warner says the name was the medic's idea. "My work with Dust Off was unique because we went alone, unless guns were requested, without command and control oversight on our missions." Warner speculates the call sign 'Dust Off' may have originated years earlier with the first unit and, over time, grew to be distinctive and recognizable. The 571st Medical Detachment's motto was, "To Save A Life."

"In addition to medical evacuations, part of the flying I did was called 'ash and trash,' which meant delivering mail, payroll, parts, medical supplies, almost anything other than a patient or other passengers. The only way to travel over there was by helicopter."

Some of his transports were memorable for their drama. "I picked up two [male South Vietnamese] who got in a fight over which village somewhere between Phu Bai and the DMZ [Demilitarized Zone which divided North and South Vietnam] had ownership of a grave. Those guys were intense. And I know we picked up NVA. They were dressed differently than ARVNs. They spoke better English and were better organized." Warner explains why he knowingly would have given a ride to the enemy. "When a mission was called in, we went and completed the pickup. We picked up anyone who was at the coordinates. We sorted out our thoughts and reactions later."

One transport defied physics. "We were evacuating patients from somewhere north of Phu Bai after the U.S. had left the area, except for us, and on one mission we took off with 19 Vietnamese plus our crew plus all the gear we carried (medical supplies and a variety of small arms and ammo in case we were shot down) and a full load of fuel. Someone out there will say I am delusional, but we did it."

For this consummate pilot, the highlight of serving in Vietnam was flying missions. "The worse the conditions, the better. All I needed was the coordinates. I'd scarf missions off other pilots. I was pretty much unfettered by command, which meant I could really fly."

Warner elaborates. "I compare my flying in Dust Off with that of the pilots of World War I. The biplane pilots were making the parameters for the next generation of flying-by-hand pilots. They discovered the limit of the airframe and invented maneuvers used even today. For example, the Immelmann, named for the German pilot in World War I, is a turn that gets you behind the aircraft chasing you. We didn't do that, but we had the freedom to explore limits and to thereby expand the capabilities of our flying. And then, unintentionally, scare other pilots in the states after we got back."

Medics often had names painted on their flying ambulances. Warner liked the moniker for this craft, which he piloted often. O[n] standby, Da Nang Dust Off members (opposite, from left) Warra[nt] Officer Bobby Walker, Spc. Frank Bohrmann, Warner and Spc. Walter Tappy await another medevac.

He summed up his zeal for combat aviation for Vietnam Mailbag readers in his August 23, 1971 letter: "Flying is what we'd like to do, so if we don't get to do that, anything else seems like nothing."

To emphasize that point, Warner tells about a ride he took on the Air Force's CH-53, the helicopter used to rescue downed pilots, and after the flight comparing notes about day and night navigation practices. Air Force pilots, he says, "were either getting guidance from the ground signals, radar vectors from the command and control aircraft or both, plus homing in on the locator signal when they got close enough." Then they asked how Warner navigated.

"I told them I got a grid coordinate, usually six digits, eight if I was lucky, sometimes only four, and then I would plot a course to that spot, figure the distance, work out the time en route and go. When we got in radio contact with the person on the ground, we'd either ask for smoke or some other means of identifying the pickup site if it was not a firebase or some easily identifiable site. Sometimes, we'd get bad coordinates and then have to ask if the guy could hear us and guide us in, based upon whether we got louder or softer, then he'd see us and pop smoke. This was almost always a pickup from the jungle, not a firebase."

The Air Force pilots were intrigued. "One said he'd love to go on a mission like that to see how it actually happened. He never got to. Incidentally, this is another comparison to the World War I pilots. Navigation was essentially visual then, using roads and towns and other landmarks to figure position."

Warner frets his can-do attitude about flying came too late in the conflict. "I knew we were winding down militarily. I just wish I'd gotten there four years earlier, but I got a little taste of it." Especially at Firebase Fuller at the DMZ, where Warner says he experienced his closest call. "The enemy shot us down on a short final approach. We lost all control and the helicopter tipped. We were rocking and I remember an ARVN running out to help us and the chopper blade cut his head off."

Warner and his crew were not injured. "We got out and watched the aircraft burn with the ammunition in it going off and after a long time, or so it seemed, we were rescued by another aircraft, which I think was from Eagle Dust Off, the unit from the 101st Airborne Division. I did get the tail rotor chain and had a bracelet made of it for Patsy, which she still has somewhere. That was supposed to be the thing to do when you were shot down but I can't tell you how I know that."

KIAS AND RESCUES AT SEA

He recalls two medical emergencies at sea. One was called in by the destroyer USS *Joseph Strauss* off the DMZ. "There was simply no place to land on the ship so we had to hoist. The patient had hepatitis and was wearing a mask. We reeled him in and got him to the 95th Evacuation Hospital in Da Nang as quickly as we could.

"The only other ship mission I had was at night off Da Nang. The weather was lousy but I wanted the mission. A sailor had cut his finger off." While Warner hovered above the heaving stern deck in the darkness, shipmates strapped in the injured seaman with his severed digit. He too was flown to the 95th.

"Only rarely did we ever find out the final disposition of patients we evacuated, but I suspect they both got better," he says.

Pretty in pink, the commander's jeep at the 571st Medical Detachment was hard to miss after Warner and a buddy spent all night painting it "different." On one of only two at-sea medical emergencies, Warner hoists a patient with highly-contagious hepatitis off a Navy destroyer.

Sometimes, Warner remembers, he transported KIAs. "Our Dust Off pickups were, by doctrine, only for wounded or injured or sick. A KIA was a logistics item and Quartermaster aircraft were to pick them up. We called them 'log birds.' Log was for logistics. A few times we'd do pickups in the field for Long Range Recon Patrols (LRRPs), and when they had a KIA, if we didn't pick him up, they either had to stay in position – something they didn't want to do – or carry the body until a log bird could get him. I and a few other pilots had no qualms about picking up a KIA to relieve the unit of the stress, even though it was against doctrine. We made those decisions as there was no command and control directing us. Some pilots would not but, by and large, I think most would. I know I always had room for a KIA."

When he wasn't flying, Warner had a ground job working with drivers and mechanics in the motor pool at Da Nang. There, he observed firsthand the profound effects of drugs on American servicemen. In his October 11, 1971 letter to the column, he wrote, "We have a problem but since all the officers here fly, and about half the enlisted men as crew chief or medic, our problem is cut down right there. Everyone is smart enough to realize that drugs and flying is like playing Russian roulette."

His observations of some of the men in the motor pool still bother him. "A big percentage were on drugs, heroin and pot. Some were hardcore dopers. I saw a couple of soldiers who broke my heart. I'm sure they died after I left. Some didn't care, they didn't have anything at home."

Mail call, Warner recollects, was especially difficult for them, and for him too. "I used to experience physical agony when day after day some of the unit would show up, knowing their name would not be called but hoping anyway, only to be distressed once again.

"[Army Spc.] Ricky Langlois, a medic from Toledo, Ohio, and I would have a time counting letters to see who got more and, of course, I got bonuses for the SOS Vietnam bennie boxes from Red Lion Methodist Church. But always I would see the huge sadness and palpable disappointment in some of the men. I never knew how to comfort them and, to this day, wish I could have. They were good workers and solid producers in spite of their isolation and having resorted to drinking or drugs for solace."

To counter the emptiness of mail call for many in his unit, Warner interjects a humorous story about his commander's jeep. "Ricky [Langlois] and I painted it. We just wanted to make it different from any jeep on the airfield. We had enough white paint to mix with red to make pink. We stayed up all night painting Capt. Willie Boyd's jeep pink. The next morning, he took one look at it and said, 'By the end of the day that jeep better be back to green.' It was, but there was still a spot of pink paint on the tire. That incident is probably why I never got a medal."

Warner estimates he flew about 1,200 missions during his year in Vietnam. "A lot of that was just driving around town," he downplays, adding his base was Da Nang but he also flew to field sites at Quang Tri and Phu Bai and points in between. The worst part of his tour, he adds, was giving up that excitement of flying. "I just wanted to fly in the combat zone. At first, I wanted to fly gunships but I flew medevacs instead. Once I got into it, I realized what a plum job it was because of the freedom of lack of command."

23 Aug 71
Da Nang

Dear Nancy,

Greetings from DaNang! Here I am with the 57th Dust Off
unit - and here is our patch for you to add to your collection. We're
not too busy, fortunately + unfortunately. Fortunately because that
means not too ... are out in the field getting hurt,
... means we have ...
... like to do, ...
... no nothing ...
... where ...

11 Oct 71

almost everywhere ... first
... in my ...
... Bedford, Ohio.
... to say —

Ken Warner
(address on back)

A 'PARIAH' HEADS HOME

In July 1972, Warner's tour ended and he boarded the freedom bird to San Francisco. "I wore my uniform home but I felt like a pariah, like why am I even in this airplane? I felt like nobody wanted to sit next to me and, after we landed, not once did anyone ask to buy me a beer. I didn't tell anyone I was coming home from Vietnam because I didn't want to risk criticism. Many of the guys trashed their uniforms in the rest room but their short hair gave them away."

After a leave in Delaware, Warner and his family reported to Fort Lewis, Washington, his fifth post, where his second child, Meredith Ann, was born in 1973. His third child, Deanna, was born two years later at Fort Sill, Oklahoma. Despite the geographical hopscotching, Warner says he enjoyed his military career. "I really liked the Army. In 20 years, we moved 17 times. My longest tour was in Japan from 1975 to 1978 where I was a pilot. My next longest tour was Heidelberg, Germany, from 1988 to 1990."

It was also his last.

"I got out of the Army as a major and we came here in 1990. We bought this farmhouse from Patsy's mother – Patsy grew up here." How much longer they'll stay is now uncertain. The house is in the direct path of the projected widening of U.S. 301. "The state highway department plans to demolish this house."

Patsy, whom Warner credits with being "an absolutely fabulous army wife," is a former teacher and is now assistant principal at Brick Mill Elementary School in Middletown. Their roles are reversed and it's his turn to stay home while she works. Younger daughter Deanna lives in a small house on their 5-acre property. Meredith, an Air Force major and orthopedic surgeon, recently served tours in Iraq and Afghanistan and lives in San Antonio, Texas. She completes her four-year obligation to the Air Force in June 2009. Patrick, who owns a graphic arts business, lives in nearby Newark.

During the 2007-2008 school year, Warner and his wife hosted Denis Mosentsev from Rostov-Na-Donu, near the Azov Sea in Russia. He participated in the American Council of Education's Future Leaders Exchange Program and attended Middletown High School as a sophomore. "And I went back to being a high school parent again," Warner says with a sigh.

Although he's given up flying, he still has music in his life. He organized the Maximum Brass Quartet. "We play any place anywhere," he says. The quartet's paid gigs include playing at area churches and local weddings.

By choice, Warner, 61, belongs to no veterans' organizations and says the only stress he's had is "the way this country treated us when we came back from Vietnam. I liked what I did and I did a good job and I would do it again in a heartbeat." Many who know him well do not know he is a Vietnam veteran. "I ought to get over it after all these years, but I still don't tell people."

Warner does have serious reservations about America's role in Iraq, decades after that other undeclared war he knew so well. "I think President Bush had a no-win situation at the outset: go in and find no weapons or not go in and [late Iraqi dictator Saddam] Hussein unleashes a weapon. Either way he would be blamed. I said that at the time.

"I didn't tell anyone I was coming home from Vietnam because I didn't want to risk criticism. Many of the guys trashed their uniforms in the restroom but their short hair gave them away."

Warner and his wife, Patsy, met in Hawaii for his only R&R during his year-long Vietnam tour. With 17 moves in 20 years, the career officer refers to her as an "absolutely fabulous army wife."

"I don't disagree with going into Iraq," he adds, "but we should have gone in with a full army. I do think [Vice President Richard B.] Cheney and [former Secretary of Defense Donald H.] Rumsfeld pushed in too soon. Then Rumsfeld became arrogant, thinking, 'I'm smarter than the Pentagon.' I took issue with Rumsfeld for not following the advice of his general staff."

He says he "agrees completely" with prominent politicians that this country mismanaged the aftermath of our initial military victory and completely ignored history and the lessons of Vietnam.

As for his own history, Warner is comfortable knowing he contributed his best in Vietnam. "I did something I liked and was supportive of what I thought our government was trying to do over there at the time."

IN MEMORIAM

DELAWARE'S VIETNAM CASUALTIES

The Vietnam Veterans of America Chapter 83 memorial in Wilmington lists 166 Delawareans who lost their lives in the Vietnam War. The names of those casualties appear here, in chronological order by date of death. Information was taken primarily from the database of the Vietnam Veterans Memorial in Washington, D.C. For some of the servicemen listed, the Wall's database makes no reference to any Delaware connection. Also, in that database, there are two entries for James R. Adams and three for George E. Jones, but none contain information linking those servicemen to Delaware, so information about their service is not included here. There is no listing for a Charles G. Stoeckel in the Wall's database.

NAME	BRANCH	RANK	BORN	DIED	HOMETOWN
Johnson, James H. Jr.	Army	Capt.	April 11, 1932	Oct. 3, 1963	Milford
Holden, James E.	Army	Pfc.	May 10, 1942	Nov. 17, 1965	Millsboro
Cripps, George W., Jr.	Army	Specialist 4th Class	July 13, 1946	Jan. 13, 1966	Dover
Butler, Wilbert R.	Army	Pfc.	May 16, 1945	Feb. 7, 1966	Wilmington
Alley, Douglas D.	Army	Pfc.	June 24, 1945	Feb. 26, 1966	Newark
Smith, Frederick E.	Army	Pfc.	Oct. 27, 1944	Feb. 26, 1966	Wilmington
Sudler, Edmund L.	Army	Specialist 4th Class	Jan. 9, 1946	March 23, 1966	Wilmington
Donnelly, James V.	Army	Specialist 4th Class	Dec. 27, 1944	March 25, 1966	Wilmington
Hill, Richard K.	Marines	Pfc.	Feb. 6, 1947	March 26, 1966	Seaford
Morris, Arthur C. Jr.	Army	Sgt.	Oct. 19, 1929	April 3, 1966	Newark
Porter, Charles E.	Army	Sgt.	Jan. 6, 1930	April 8, 1966	Wilmington
Woodson, George W. Jr.	Army	Pfc.	Feb. 11, 1948	April 23, 1966	Philadelphia, Pa.
Tams, Robert N.	Army	Pfc.	May 18, 1945	May 10, 1966	Wilmington
Hess, Gene K.	Air Force	Staff Sgt.	Aug. 18, 1933	June 17, 1966	Townsend
Sornson, Edwin H.	Army	Pfc.	Sept. 18, 1946	June 20, 1966	Dover
Bowman, Robert M.	Army	Pfc.	Nov. 6, 1947	June 29, 1966	Wilmington
Connell, James J.	Navy	Lt. Cmdr.	May 6, 1939	July 15, 1966	Wilmington
McRobie, Norman W.	Air Force	Airman 1st Class	Oct. 6, 1940	Nov. 26, 1966	Delmar, Md.
Messick, James A.	Army	Staff Sgt.	Jan. 31, 1925	Jan. 8, 1967	Seaford
Lowman, William L.	Army	Pfc.	Nov. 8, 1944	Feb. 4, 1967	Smyrna
Bischof, Wolfram W.	Army	Sgt. 1st Class	March 11, 1937	Feb. 13, 1967	Wilmington
Thompson, Gerald R.	Army	Pfc.	July 12, 1940	March 5, 1967	Penns Grove, N.J.
LaSalle, Lawrence L.	Marines	Cpl.	Aug. 3, 1945	March 17, 1967	Newark
Leatherbury, Louis A.	Marines	Pvt.	Sept. 23, 1946	March 24, 1967	Wilmington
Brittingham, Elmore Jr.	Army	Staff Sgt.	Nov. 23, 1927	March 25, 1967	Wilmington
Press, Victor E.	Army	Specialist 4th Class	Dec. 27, 1941	April 1, 1967	Wilmington
Perry, George F. III	Army	Sgt.	Feb. 16, 1946	May 15, 1967	New Castle
Williams, George H.	Army	Specialist 4th Class	April 10, 1941	May 16, 1967	Wilmington
Alexander, Robert D.	Army	Pfc.	Jan. 11, 1942	May 20, 1967	Claymont
Glover, James Albert	Army	Specialist 4th Class	Jan. 3, 1948	May 31, 1967	Wilmington
Webb, Howard Lee	Army	Sgt.	July 21, 1942	June 8, 1967	Rehoboth Beach
Giacobello, Frank A. Jr.	Army	Specialist 4th Class	Sept. 11, 1947	June 14, 1967	Coatesville, Pa.
Crowder, Raymond D. Jr	Army	Specialist 4th Class	May 10, 1946	June 19, 1967	Chadds Ford, Pa.
Lowdon, Graham N. Jr.	Army	Capt.	July 7, 1938	June 28, 1967	Wilmington
Samans, Walter A. Jr.	Army	Specialist 4th Class	May 27, 1946	July 10, 1967	Richmond, Va.
Paoletti, Samuel	Marines	Cpl.	May 3, 1947	July 17, 1967	Stanton
Johnson, Robert E.	Army	Sgt.	June 10, 1946	July 21, 1967	Greenville
Pollard, William A.	Marines	Pfc.	Aug. 27, 1947	July 21, 1967	New Castle
Ludwig, Raymond J.	Marines	Pfc.	Nov. 28, 1947	July 27, 1967	Wilmington
Partin, George E.	Marines	Lance Cpl.	Feb. 12, 1947	Aug. 14, 1967	Georgetown
Hayden, Jon J.	Navy	Constructionman	Dec. 15, 1946	Aug. 16, 1967	Newark
Haddick, Harold W.	Air Force	Chief Master Sgt.	Oct. 3, 1922	Aug. 22, 1967	Dover
Amoroso, Francis B.	Army	Cpl.	Feb. 22, 1948	Sept. 3, 1967	Newark
Chason, Theodore J.	Army	Cpl.	July 23, 1947	Oct. 8, 1967	Wilmington
Morris, James T. Jr.	Army	Pvt.	July 31, 1948	Nov. 3, 1967	Wilmington
Palczewski, Edmund L.	Marines	Cpl.	Dec. 27, 1946	Nov. 3, 1967	Wilmington
Flaherty, Kevin G.	Army	2nd Lt.	Nov. 17, 1945	Nov. 4, 1967	Wilmington
Hezel, Karl D.	Air Force	Maj.	Dec. 8, 1933	Nov. 17, 1967	Cranford, N.J.
Martin, John M.	Air Force	Lt. Col.	June 17, 1931	Nov. 20, 1967	Dover
Jenkins, Lance N.	Marines	Lance Cpl.	May 14, 1949	Dec. 6, 1967	Vineland, N.J.
Branyan, Paul F. Jr.	Army	Cpl.	Jan. 3, 1947	Dec. 10, 1967	New Castle
Miller, James L.	Army	1st Lt.	June 25, 1943	Dec. 14, 1967	Seaford
Hamilton, Donald P.	Marines	Pfc.	Feb. 4, 1949	Dec. 19, 1967	Ellendale
Doyle, Robert W.	Marines	Lance Cpl.	April 9, 1949	Jan. 5, 1968	Wilmington
Berry, Paul L.	Army	Warrant Officer	July 9, 1946	Jan. 10, 1968	Melbourne, Fla.
Fones, Paul M.	Army	Cpl.	Dec. 14, 1942	Jan. 10, 1968	Bear

NAME	BRANCH	RANK	BORN	DIED	HOMETOWN
McFalls, Harry P.	Army	1st Lt.	Aug. 6, 1939	Jan. 10, 1968	Lewes
Quick, Paul W. III	Marines	Pfc.	Sept. 26, 1947	Jan. 11, 1968	Wilmington
Tracy, Robert L.	Navy	Hospital Corpsman 3rd Class	Jan. 1, 1947	Jan. 18, 1968	Greenville
White, Isaiah	Army	Specialist 4th Class	May 24, 1947	Jan. 27, 1968	Ellendale
Mereider, Robert J.	Marines	Pfc.	Jan. 16, 1948	Jan. 28, 1968	Milton
Thompson, Ralph L. Jr.	Marines	Pfc.	Nov. 3, 1948	Feb. 1, 1968	Wilmington
Anderson, Robert C.	Marines	Lance Cpl.	June 21, 1948	Feb. 3, 1968	Middletown
Dawson, Donald E. Jr.	Army	Sgt.	Aug. 26, 1947	Feb. 9, 1968	Wilmington
Paskins, Wayman E.	Army	Specialist 4th Class	April 25, 1947	Feb. 14, 1968	Greenwood
Faulkner, Richard J.	Army	Specialist 4th Class	July 22, 1947	Feb. 25, 1968	Wilmington
Brittingham, Linden W.	Marines	Lance Cpl.	March 6, 1948	March 1, 1968	Milton
Adams, Thomas B.	Army	1st Lt.	Dec. 6, 1946	March 4, 1968	Selbyville
Crowe, Douglas D.	Army	Capt.	Dec. 1, 1949	March 4, 1968	Newark
Kenton, Donald E.	Army	Warrant Officer	Jan. 5, 1947	March 6, 1968	Dover
Rolfe, Michael D.	Marines	Cpl.	Oct. 9, 1947	March 8, 1968	Rising Sun, Md.
Dobrzynski, Raymond P.	Army	Specialist 4th Class	Aug. 4, 1947	March 13, 1968	Wilmington
Mastromatteo, Frank	Marines	Lance Cpl.	Feb. 3, 1949	April 8, 1968	Upper Darby, Pa.
Jester, Wayne C.	Army	Pvt.	Nov. 19, 1948	April 10, 1968	Milford
Robinson, Lionel L.	Marines	Cpl.	Nov. 29, 1947	April 10, 1968	Wilmington
Ray, Nolan R.	Army	Specialist 4th Class	Aug. 18, 1944	April 12, 1968	Dover
Momcilovich, Michael Jr.	Army	Capt.	Sept. 13, 1943	May 5, 1968	Wilmington
Geronimo, Charles A.	Army	Staff Sgt.	Dec. 8, 1946	May 12, 1968	Wilmington
Coppage, George H. III	Army	Cpl.	Nov. 13, 1948	May 15, 1968	Camden-Wyoming
Cubbage, Clifton	Army	Pfc.	June 25, 1947	May 16, 1968	Bowers Beach
Kaminski, Joseph M. Jr.	Marines	Pfc.	Sept. 23, 1948	May 24, 1968	Wilmington
Grant, Gene T.	Marines	Lance Cpl.	June 25, 1948	May 29, 1968	Bridgeville
Weldin, Jacob Robinson	Army	Sgt.	Aug. 18, 1946	June 6, 1968	Wilmington
Cuff, Donald M.	Marines	Staff Sgt.	July 12, 1938	June 7, 1968	Wilmington
Collins, Toby E.	Army	Pfc.	Nov. 18, 1947	June 11, 1968	Dover
Faulkner, Elmer L. Jr.	Marines	Pfc.	Sept. 25, 1948	June 18, 1968	Greenwood
Chamberlain, Richard M.	Marines	Sgt.	April 29, 1947	June 21, 1968	Wilmington
Jones, Frank W.	Army	Warrant Officer	Oct. 7, 1946	June 30, 1968	Claymont
Bird, Leonard A.	Marines	1st Lt.	Sept. 14, 1943	July 13, 1968	Wilmington
Schulz, James W.	Marines	Cpl.	Dec. 11, 1944	July 14, 1968	Camden
Arnold, David M.	Army	Pfc.	Sept. 2, 1943	July 15, 1968	Hockessin
Gibson, Donald L.	Army	Specialist 4th Class	Feb. 28, 1945	July 19, 1968	Milford
Willing, Edward A.	Marines	Gunnery Sgt.	Aug. 28, 1949	July 21, 1968	Wilmington
Ross, Luther J. Jr.	Army	Pfc.	Nov. 6, 1947	July 22, 1968	Wilmington
Baker, William S.	Army	Staff Sgt.	Jan. 20, 1947	July 25, 1968	Middletown
Clough, Bruce E.	Marines	Pfc.	Feb. 12, 1949	Aug. 2, 1968	Magnolia
Mallard, Morris A. Jr.	Army	Sgt. 1st Class	July 23, 1933	Aug. 7, 1968	Wilmington
Henrickson, Jan V.	Army	Sgt.	March 11, 1948	Aug. 12, 1968	Hartly
Sinibaldi, Michael W.	Army	Cpl.	Oct. 1, 1949	Aug. 14, 1968	Kearny, N.J.
Dolbow, Bruce E.	Army	Pfc.	Sept. 10, 1948	Aug. 25, 1968	Felton
Glazar, Aaron Zane H.	Marines	Pfc.	June 4, 1947	Sept. 23, 1968	Wilmington
Williams, Robert E.	Marines	Cpl.	Dec. 23, 1948	Sept. 23, 1968	Newark
Reeder, Philip D.	Army	Pfc.	June 6, 1949	Sept. 27, 1968	Hockessin
Bleacher, Ronald T.	Marines	Cpl.	March 10, 1949	Sept. 29, 1968	Marshallton
Brown, Werner C. II	Army	1st Lt.	Jan. 5, 1945	Sept. 29, 1968	Greenville
Howard, Sylvester J.	Marines	Lance Cpl.	Dec. 30, 1948	Oct. 14, 1968	Wilmington
Dieffenbach Robert, Jr.	Army	Specialist 4th Class	Nov. 29, 1947	Oct. 18, 1968	Newark
Gott, John Joseph Jr.	Navy	Hospital Corpsman 3rd Class	Aug. 24, 1947	Dec. 18, 1968	Wilmington
Tressler, Daniel A. Jr.	Army	Sgt.	April 24, 1947	Feb. 2, 1969	Elsmere
Curry, Richard J.	Army	Maj.	Aug. 7, 1937	Feb. 23, 1969	Altoona, Pa.
Nelson, Frank W. Jr	Marines	Pfc.	Aug. 16, 1947	Feb. 23, 1969	Wilmington
Stevenson, Richard C.	Marines	Cpl.	Aug. 25, 1949	Feb. 23, 1969	Georgetown

NAME	BRANCH	RANK	BORN	DIED	HOMETOWN
Hill, Arthur S. Jr.	Marines	Sgt.	Sept. 2, 1941	March 4, 1969	Wilmington
Cassidy, Jeffrey T.	Army	Specialist 4th Class	Jan. 10, 1948	March 10, 1969	New Castle
Ripanti, James L.	Army	1st Lt.	July 11, 1947	March 14, 1969	Wilmington
Hitchens, Lawrence E.	Marines	Pfc.	March 15, 1950	May 17, 1969	Magnolia
Hall, Vaughn O.	Army	Cpl.	Jan. 25, 1948	May 23, 1969	Georgetown
Downs, Lloyd J.	Army	Sgt. 1st Class	Aug. 17, 1924	June 19, 1969	Claymont
Geissinger, Alan G.	Army	Pfc.	Sept. 16, 1947	July 11, 1969	Newark
Hayward, Arnold C.	Army	Lt. Col.	Nov. 4, 1932	July 11, 1969	Trenton, N.J.
Hastings, David L.	Air Force	Sgt.	April 17, 1948	July 18, 1969	Laurel
Donaway, Robert H.	Army	1st Lt.	May 14, 1944	Aug. 18, 1969	Felton
Burris, Reginald W.	Army	Specialist 4th Class	Jan. 18, 1949	Aug. 19, 1969	Ellendale
Acher, Robert P. Jr.	Air Force	Capt.	July 1, 1942	Sept. 2. 1969	Dover
Aikin, George Lee	Army	Capt.	July 31, 1947	Oct. 9, 1969	Wilmington
Moore, Abraham L.	Air Force	Staff Sgt.	Feb. 12, 1937	Oct. 11, 1969	Dover
Briggs, Frank H.	Air Force	Col.	April 17, 1928	Oct. 19, 1969	Wilmington
Rodowicz, Michael J.	Marines	Lance Cpl.	Dec. 17, 1950	Oct. 25, 1969	Claymont
Boxler, Charles E.	Army	Pvt.	Feb. 3, 1948	Oct. 28, 1969	Wilmington
Fuller, Robert J.	Army	Specialist 4th Class	Jan. 31, 1949	Nov. 10, 1969	Wilmington
Falkenau, Robert A.	Army	1st Lt.	Nov. 26, 1944	Dec. 6, 1969	Wilmington
Dempsey, Gary L.	Army	2nd Lt.	Nov. 15, 1948	Jan. 1, 1970	Yorklyn
Protack, Thomas John	Army	Sgt.	Dec. 15, 1948	Feb. 1, 1970	Wilmington
Stewart, James W.	Army	Specialist 4th Class	July 12, 1949	Feb. 2, 1970	Laurel
DiPasquantonio, Michael	Marines	Cpl.	July 10, 1949	Feb. 5, 1970	Wilmington
Murphy, William J.	Army	Sgt.	Sept. 16, 1950	Feb. 16, 1970	New Castle
Taylor, Eric W.	Army	Warrant Officer	June 30, 1948	Feb. 18, 1970	Wilmington
Hetzler, Raymond C.	Army	Specialist 4th Class	Oct. 12, 1950	Feb. 27, 1970	Wilmington
Miller, Glenn W.	Navy	Constructionman	Sept. 17, 1949	April 7, 1970	Wilmington
Gaworski, Francis X.	Army	Specialist 4th Class	Dec. 18, 1948	April 10, 1970	New Castle
Wilson, Rodney W.	Army	Cpl.	Jan. 30, 1950	May 25, 1970	Georgetown
Bunting, William J.	Army	Pfc.	April 4, 1950	May 26, 1970	Frankford
Webb, Earl R. Jr.	Army	Specialist 4th Class	Sept. 23, 1949	June 3, 1970	Newark
Bowman, Richard A.	Army	Cpl.	Jan. 12, 1950	June 9, 1970	Newark
Dadisman, Michael R.	Army	Specialist 4th Class	April 9, 1950	June 24, 1970	Newark
Jones, William E.	Army	Staff Sgt.	May 18, 1946	July 14, 1970	Millsboro
Moses, Jesse L.	Army	Specialist 4th Class	June 12, 1945	Aug. 4, 1970	Wilmington
Killmon, Frederick R.	Marines	Cpl.	June 2, 1950	Aug. 31, 1970	Delmar, Md.
Johnson, Robert B.	Air Force	Tech. Sgt.	May 29, 1936	Nov. 29, 1970	Monroe, Mich.
Rucker, John W.	Army	Sgt.	Nov. 27, 1947	Dec. 14, 1970	Roanoke, Va.
Tidwell, Joseph S.	Army	Pfc.	Dec. 10, 1948	Jan. 17, 1971	New Castle
Kerl, Michael J.	Army	Capt.	Nov. 8, 1946	Feb. 6, 1971	Drexel Hill, Pa.
Selak, John R.	Army	Pfc.	May 30, 1950	Feb. 21, 1971	Baltimore, Md.
Anderson, Charles R.	Army	1st Lt.	Aug. 2, 1946	March 3, 1971	Newark
Dennison, Richard S.	Army	Specialist 5th Class	May 16, 1950	March 5, 1971	Bethel
Bailey, Donald R.	Army	Cpl.	Dec. 14, 1950	March 31, 1971	Willow Grove
Schettig, Robert S.	Army	Chief Warrant Officer	Jan. 2, 1951	July 3, 1971	Spring Valley, N.Y.
Crosby, Rolin J.	Army	Chief Warrant Officer	Dec. 19, 1947	Nov. 6, 1971	Wilmington
Potts, Larry F.	Marines	Capt.	April 7, 1947	April 7, 1972	Smyrna
Hoskins, Donald R.	Air Force	Tech. Sgt.	Jan. 5, 1929	April 26, 1972	Madison, Ind.
Ayres, Gerald F.	Air Force	Maj.	Feb. 23, 1939	June 18, 1972	New Castle
Meder, Paul O.	Air Force	Col.	Dec. 29, 1931	Dec. 21, 1972	Jamaica, N.Y.
Nellans, William L.	Air Force	Maj.	Dec. 29, 1936	Nov. 2, 1973	Dover AFB
Adams, James R.					
Jones, George E.					
Stoeckel, Charles G.					

★ GLOSSARY ★

This glossary provides definitions for the military jargon most frequently used in letters written by servicemen to Nancy's Vietnam Mailbag and from the contemporary interviews of the veterans featured in this book.

AB – air base

AFB – Air Force base

AFVN – Armed Forces Vietnam Network, in-country radio and television broadcast outlets

AIT – advanced infantry training

AO – area of operation

APC – armored personnel carrier

APO – Army Post Office

ARVN – Army of the Republic of Vietnam

BC – battery commander

Bennie box – box of goodies from home

Booby trap – mines, concealed explosive devices placed by the enemy

BOQ – bachelor officers' quarters

Bouncing Betty – a jumping mine that shot out of the ground and exploded at groin height; a grenade on a spring, most often an M-16-A1 bounding antipersonnel mine

CA – combat assault

CEV – combat engineer vehicle

Charlie – nickname for the enemy, applied to both the Vietcong and the North Vietnamese Army

Chinook – CH-47 twin-rotor helicopter, used primarily for troop movement, artillery emplacement and battlefield resupply

CIB – Combat Infantry Badge for meritorious service in infantry combat

Click – (also klick or klik) a kilometer (1,000 meters)

CO – commanding officer

Cobra – AH-1 attack helicopter, shares a common engine, transmission and rotor system with the older UH-1 Iroquois (nicknamed "Huey"); sometimes referred to as the "Huey Cobra" or "Snake"

CONUS – continental United States

CRIP – combined reconnaissance intelligence patrol

Dear John – the dreaded letter from a serviceman's girl who has dumped him

DEROS – date estimated return from overseas

Diamond State – nickname for Delaware, described as a jewel for its strategic location on the Eastern Seaboard.

Diamond Stater – resident, or native of Delaware

Dink – slang reference to a native Vietnamese

DMZ – demilitarized zone, the invisible neutral line established by the 1954 Geneva Convention to separate communist North Vietnam from non-communist South Vietnam

Drop – time deducted from obligatory duty

DSU – direct support unit

Dust Off – medical evacuation helicopter (air ambulance)

EM – enlisted man or men

ETS – estimated time of separation from service

FAQ – forward artillery quadrant

First State – nickname for Delaware, first of the original 13 states to ratify the U.S. Constitution on December 7, 1787

First Stater – resident, or native of Delaware

FAC – forward air controller

FLC – force logistic command

FPO – Fleet Post Office

FSB – fire support base

Freedom bird – airplane transporting troops home

GI – low-ranking Army soldier, an acronym for Government Issue

Gook – slang for the enemy

Grunt – combat infantry soldier

Hooch – living quarters

Huey – UH-1 Iroquois, multipurpose utility helicopter, workhorse helicopter of the Army in Vietnam

In country – in South Vietnam

KIA – killed in action

KP – kitchen patrol (kitchen duty)

Land of the Big PX – United States

Leatherneck – nickname for a marine

Lifer – one serving a career in the military

LOH – light observation helicopter

LP – listen post, small night-time forward position set up outside perimeter of night position

LRP – long-range patrol; slang for freeze-dried rations (pronounced "lerp")

LZ – landing zone

MACV – Military Assistance Command Vietnam

MAW – Marine aircraft wing

MARS – Military Affiliate Radio System

Mechanical ambush – concealed explosive devices placed by U.S. forces

MEDCAP – medical civic action program

MIA – missing in action

Mojo – 105-mm or 155-mm artillery shells for cannons

MOS – military occupational specialty, the job assigned to military draftees

MP – military police

MPC – military payment certificate, a unit of military currency

Nam – shortened version of South Vietnam

NCO – noncommissioned officer

NLF – National Front for the Liberation of South Vietnam, a coalition of more than a dozen political and religious groups, many of them armed, opposed to the government of the Republic of Vietnam; commonly referred to by Americans as the Vietcong

NVA – North Vietnamese Army

OD – olive drab, the color of military fatigues

OP – outpost; observation post, daytime version of listen post (LP)

PBR – patrol boat river

PCS – permanent change of station, a military move from one assignment to another with orders

PFS – members of the South Vietnamese Popular Forces

POL – petroleum, oil and lubricants; or protective oil and lubricants

Pond, the – Pacific Ocean

Pop flare – illuminating device inside an aluminum tube discharged by hitting bottom of tube with the palm of the hand, a helmet or other hard object

POV – privately owned vehicle

POW – prisoner of war

PSP – perforated steel planking, used for helicopter landings

PTSD – post-traumatic stress disorder

PX – post exchange

R&R – rest and recuperation, time away from battle, either in or out of South Vietnam

RPG – rocket-propelled grenade

RTO – radio-telephone operator; radio transmitter operator

RVN – Republic of South Vietnam

SAM – surface-to-air missile

Sapper – North Vietnamese Army or Vietcong demolition commando, typically carried satchel charges when attempting to infiltrate areas controlled by the U.S. or South Vietnamese

SAR – search and rescue

Satchel charge – satchel full of explosives

SEAS – acronym for soldiers' derogatory comment, "Southeast Asia sucks"

SEATO – Southeast Asia Treaty Organization, a U.S.-sponsored organization of eight nations formed on September 8, 1954

Short, short-timer – not much time left in country before returning home, calculated by exact number of days, even hours and minutes remaining in country

SOG – special operations group

Sortie – single aerial mission, from takeoff to landing

Steel pot – helmet worn in battle, also known as a shell pot, often personalized by owner

TFW – tactical fighter wing

TMF – target mission force

TDY – temporary duty

USARV – U.S. Army Vietnam

USO – United Service Organizations

VAT – village assistance team, formed for civic action projects

VC – Vietcong

Vietcong – Military branch of the National Liberation Front, included both regular army units and guerrilla troops who operated in smaller geographical areas in South Vietnam

VOLAR – volunteer army

WAC – Women's Army Corps

WAVES – Women Appointed for Voluntary Emergency Service, the women's branch of the U.S. Navy

WIA – wounded in action

Wing stores – gun or rocket pods mounted on each side of a helicopter

World – home; back in the Good Old USA

XO – executive officer

Xin loi – Vietnamese phrase (pronounced sin loy) meaning "sorry about that," a sarcastic response used by soldiers

★ ACKNOWLEDGEMENTS ★

A book of this magnitude takes a team to produce. To these talented and tireless professionals, many of whom toiled for nearly two years, I owe gratitude beyond measure:

Larry Nagengast, the consummate editor, made the words better, chased the details and guided the team through the project. Art director Jaime L. Anderson marked each page of the book with her special gift for layout and design. Autumn B. Grinath's exceptional eye for coaxing the best out of a photograph shines in the book's hundreds of images. Award-winning lensman Kevin Fleming lent his artistry to the portraits of the dozen veterans we interviewed. Sara Tucker Garrison's corporate experience led us through the maze of marketing and media relations. Corey Groll gave us internet presence with his construction of our impressive and interactive Web site, www.VietnamMailbag.com. Donna DiFrancesco spent countless hours typing and indexing and always asked for more to do. Marianne Nagengast handily researched, organized, produced and checked numerous lists. Graphic designer Rob Waters and proofreader Kristie L. Moore enlisted late in the effort and contributed significantly in the battle to meet our deadlines.

Thanks also are due Jill Fredel, assistant managing editor of *The (Wilmington, Del.) News Journal,* who green-lighted our use of the servicemen's letters; *News Journal* librarians Anne Haslam and Cecilia James, who patiently unearthed scores of microfilm reels for our research; the friendly staff at the Brandywine Hundred Library in Wilmington, where most of the book was edited, and particularly staffer Anh Nguyen who translated Vietnamese; U.S. Sen. Tom Carper, who recounted his Vietnam experiences in the foreword; Russ McCabe of the Delaware Public Archives in Dover, whose early encouragement spurred us on, and, of course, gratitude to my former *News Journal* editors Fred Hartmann and Harry F. Themal for trusting me with a column of my own, Nancy's Vietnam Mailbag.

And thanks to the veterans themselves, who so selflessly loaned us their photographs, war memorabilia, uniforms, even their boots. Equally important, they shared their time and their memories: Richard S. Lovekin, William W. "Hutch" Hutchison Jr., Kenneth D. Warner, Stanley F. Pienkos, Robert S. Biss, James D. Rawlins Jr., Daniel P. Stokes, Richard Glazier, R. Lance Hall, Robert A. Coen, Donald B. Patton, Larry D. Gum and William D. "Dave" Rice. Special kudos go to former combat reporter/photographer Douglas R. Elliott for his many professional pictures. We also recognize all the unnamed veterans who endorsed our efforts from the outset. And, clearly, we could not have undertaken this project without the unconditional support of family and friends.

It's been a remarkable journey.

Thank you all.

AUTHOR'S NOTE

To safeguard wartime correspondence for future generations, I encourage all Vietnam veterans and their families to contribute their letters to the Legacy Project. This national, all-volunteer initiative, founded in 1998 by Andrew Carroll, editor of *War Letters*, honors those who have served our country in all wars by preserving their letters, and now their emails. To learn more about the Legacy Project, please visit their Web site: www.WarLetters.com or write to P.O. Box 53250, Washington, D.C. 20009.

ABOUT THE AUTHOR

Author-journalist Nancy E. Lynch started her writing career as a staff reporter for *The (Wilmington, Del.) News Journal*. For five years, her popular column, Nancy's Vietnam Mailbag, afforded our servicemen a unique opportunity to tell their stories from the combat zone, riveting readers at home.

The University of Delaware graduate has been a freelance writer for many years, contributing numerous articles to regional publications and teaming with photographer Kevin Fleming to produce six books on contemporary Delaware. With the publication of *Vietnam Mailbag, Voices From the War:1968-1972*, Ms. Lynch, who lives on Broad Creek in historic Bethel, Delaware, fulfills a decades-long desire to "properly salute my guys."

★ PHOTOGRAPHY CREDITS ★

Photos and illustrations not credited here were originally
published in Nancy's Vietnam Mailbag in 1968-1972.

Studio photographs of artifacts and letters by
Jaime L. Anderson and Autumn B. Grinath.

Arthur J. Anderson III
152, 249

Bruce Anderson
18-19, 271

Robert S. Biss
46, 47, 353, 354, 355, 357

Robert A. Coen
342, 414, 416, 417, 418

CORBIS
Bettmann 87, 95, 186, 187, 200, 272, 273, 283, 290, 324
JP Laffont 234
Jacques Pavlovsky 347
Harvey L. Silver 17

Douglas R. Elliott
3, 7, 20, 21, 24, 27, 28, 32, 35, 36, 41, 52, 53, 54-55, 60,
64, 74, 78, 96, 102, 103, 105, 106-107, 110, 111, 115,
120, 124, 132, 133, 142, 148, 150-151, 153, 161, 221,
237, 263, 270

Kevin Fleming
352, 359, 365, 371, 376, 382, 389, 395, 401, 408, 415, 421

Richard Glazier
48, 58, 94, 310, 358, 360, 362, 363

Douglas T. Grinath
251, 305, 317

Larry D. Gum
370, 372, 375

R. Lance Hall
364, 366, 367, 368, 369

William W. Hutchison Jr.
29, 39, 40, 56, 57, 59, 75, 76, 98-99, 112-113, 114, 126,
128-129, 130, 131, 134, 136, 137, 139, 140, 144, 145, 146,
164, 166, 182, 191, 197, 204, 208, 210, 214, 215, 218, 222-
223, 225, 227, 240, 250, 277, 297, 303, 304, 308, 316,
323, 332, 344, 400, 402, 403, 404, 405, 406, 407

Robert C. Jennings
162, 168, 169

Richard S. Lovekin
2, 34, 66, 93, 118, 156, 159, 195, 232, 388, 390, 392, 393, 428

The (Wilmington, Del.) News Journal
VI, 6, 8, 9, 10, 11, 12, 13, 14, 15, 23, 25, 183, 230

Donald B. Patton
170, 172, 377, 378, 379, 381

Stanley F. Pienkos
211, 394, 396, 397, 399

James D. Rawlins Jr.
247, 383, 384, 385, 387

William D. Rice
Title page, 81

Daniel P. Stokes
44, 313, 409, 410, 411, 412

U.S. Army, 25th Infantry Division
7

Kenneth D. Warner
V, 82, 84-85, 141, 212, 213, 228, 229, 268, 269, 274, 278,
280, 301, 306, 307, 309, 318, 321, 327, 329, 331, 334, 337,
345, 420, 422, 423, 424, 425, 426, 427

★ INDEX ★

The index for *Vietnam Mailbag* includes the names of men and women from in and near Delaware and, if known, their service branch, year(s) served in Vietnam and hometown. Page numbers locate their correspondence in the book. Index entries without page numbers are for individuals who were mentioned in the column but did not write or whose letters were not included in the book. For more index information, please visit our Web site, www.VietnamMailbag.com.

NAME	BRANCH	YEAR	HOMETOWN	PAGES
Brown, William	Army	1970-1971	Wilmington	
Brown, William H.	Navy	1971	New Castle	
Bruhn, Richard C.	Army	1971	Wilmington/New Castle	
Brumbaugh, William III	Air Force	1970	New Castle	
Brunner, James R.		1971	Newark	
Buchanan, Billie R.	Army	1970-1971	Bear	248
Buchanan, Keith	Navy	1970	Kennett Square, Pa.	
Buchert, Lawrence B.	Army	1971-1972	Seaford	279, 319
Buckingham, Warren	Army	1968	Middletown	
Buckland, James B.	Air Force	1970-1971	Wilmington	245, 248, 312
Buckley, Dennis D.	Army	1970-1971	Wilmington	
Buckman, Willard F.		1970	Wilmington	
Budd, David E.	Marines	1971	Smyrna	
Budin, Eric M.	Army	1969		167
Buker, Ken	Marines	1968		
Bullen, John R. Jr.	Army	1970-1971	New Castle	
Bunting, Thomas	Air Force	1972	Frankford	
Burge, Charles D.	Army	1972	Christiana	322
Burk, William A.		1972	Claymont	
Burke, Stephen F.	Army	1971	Wilmington	
Burkins, Lee C.	Army	1970	Wilmington	
Burns, David	Army	1970-1971	Wilmington	294-295
Buzin, Ronald M.	Army	1970	Wilmington	
Byrd, Nathaniel H.	Marines	1969	Wilmington	
Byrne, James A.	Army	1969-1970	Wilmington	
Cahall, Woodrow Wilson III	Army	1972	Wilmington	321
Cahill, Francis P. Jr.		1969	New Castle	176
Calio, James	Army	1969	Laurel	
Callahan, Thomas John	Army	1971-1972	Georgetown	
Callaway, Edgar W.		1970	Laurel	
Callaway, Larry				341
Calloway, Curt	Army	1968	Milford	75
Campbell, Robert	Army	1970-1971	Wilmington	243, 245
Campese, Francis J.		1971	Wilmington	
Cannon, John G.	Army	1971	Milford	
Capece, Daniel J.	Army	1971	Wilmington	
Caralivanos, E.H.	Navy	1968-1969	Newark	5
Carlisle, Fred	Army	1970	Milford	213, 228
Carlson, Ralph N.	Navy	1972		
Carney, James M.	Army	1969	Claymont	97, 103, 164
Carroll, Thomas H.	Air Force	1970-1971	Wilmington	
Carrow, John P.	Marines	1968-1969	Wilmington	24, 31-32, 65, 75, 158
Carter, Charles	Navy	1971-1972	Wilmington	
Carter, Tom	Army	1970	Wilmington	236-237
Casper, Peter		1971	Wilmington	
Castelow, Mark D.	Army	1969-1970	Wilmington	97, 167, 196, 241
Casula, James	Army	1968	New Castle	42
Casula, T.W.		1972	Wilmington	
Caughlin, Bob	Navy	1970	Philadelphia, Pa.	
Cavalier, Joseph A.		1971	Wilmington	
Cervelli, Laurence Joseph	Army	1970-1971	Wilmington	228, 246, 248
Chaivanik, Jack	Navy	1970	Connecticut	
Chall, Woodrow W. Jr.		1972	Wilmington	
Chance, William H.	Army	1968-1969	Wilmington	29, 108-109, 158 164, 175, 184
Charamella, Robert		1971	Wilmington	
Chastain, Gary D.	Marines	1968	Claymont	53
Chieff, James		1969	Wilmington	
Christiansen, Bob	Air Force	1970		245
Christopher, T.R.	Marines	1969	New Castle	164, 166, 175
Ciconte, Thomas A. Jr.	Army	1971	Wilmington	
Cierkowski, Edward J.		1969-1970	Wilmington	
Clapham, Reid		1969	Wilmington	
Clark, George W.	Army	1971	Dover	
Clark, James A.	Air Force	1970-1971	Newark	219
Clark, Joe		1969	New Castle	158
Clayville, Glenn A.	Army	1970-1971	Newark	
Cleary, Michael S.	Army	1970	New Castle	
Clemmons, Beauford V.		1971	New Castle	
Clendaniel, Gary V.		1971	Wyoming	
Clendaniel, Henry L. Jr.	Army	1971	Milford	
Clobes, Billy F.	Army	1971	Dagsboro	
Cloud, Jeffrey F.	Army	1971	Wilmington	
Cloud, Walter		1970	Wilmington	
Clough, Harold L.	Army	1970	Wilmington	

NAME	BRANCH	YEAR	HOMETOWN	PAGES
Coburn, Clarence	Army	1969	Wilmington	
Coen, Robert A.	Army	1971-1972	Wilmington	298, 342, 414-419
Coffin, Barry W.		1971	New Castle	
Coghill, Peter		1970	Wilmington	
Cohee, Phillip L.		1969	Felton	
Cole, Alexis	Air Force	1971	Wilmington	
Cole, Charles E.		1968		20
Cole, Horace G.	Army	1970	Wilmington	201, 207
Colicchio, Anthony J.	Army	1970-1971	Wilmington	207, 226, 299, 307
Collins, John C.	Navy	1972	Wilmington	327
Collins, Richard P.	Army	1970-1971	Lewes	
Collins, Robert		1968	Wilmington	
Collison, John H.	Army	1971	Milford	289
Collison, Terrance		1972	Hockessin	
Comegys, Charles E.	Army	1970	Wilmington	216
Conaway, Joseph H.		1970	Wilmington	
Conklin, Gary	Marines	1968	Wilmington	
Conley, E.L.		1972		
Conley, Robert W.	Navy	1969	St. Georges	159, 176
Connell, James J. Jr.	Navy	1972	Wilmington	325
Connell, John P. Jr.		1971	Wilmington	
Conner, Ray		1969	Odessa	
Connor, Michael F.	Army	1970-1971	New Castle	
Connors, John W.		1970	Wilmington	
Conway, Joseph L.	Army	1971	Wilmington	284, 295
Cook, David		1972	Wilmington	
Cool, Steven	Navy	1968	Wilmington	49
Cordeiro, Lawrence	Air Force	1971	New Castle	
Cormier, Paul L.	Army	1971	Wilmington	
Cornell, Craig		1972	Wilmington	
Corvette, Theodore E. Jr.		1969-1970	Wilmington	
Covelli, E.F.	Army	1971	New Castle	
Cox, Edmund S.	Army	1968	Wilmington	20
Cox, William L.	Air Force	1971	Smyrna	
Coxe, Robert D. Jr.	Army	1971-1972	Wilmington	291, 303, 319
Creasey, Kenneth H. Jr.		1972	Wilmington	
Cresson, Jim	Army	1968	Milford	33, 66
Crick, Charles E. Jr.	Navy	1972	Wilmington	301, 319
Crosby, Rolin J.		1972	Wilmington	
Cross, Clifford J.	Army	1970	New Castle	
Crothers, James A. II		1970	Rising Sun, Md.	
Crowe, Thurman		1968	Smyrna	
Crum, William S.	Navy	1970-1971	Wilmington	241, 301
Cuff, James J.	Army	1971	Centreville	
Culver, Melvin Jr.		1971	Newark	
Cummings, William L. Jr.	Army	1970-1971	Seaford	
Cunningham, Glenn	Marines	1969	Wilmington	
Curran, James		1972	Wilmington	
Curro, Robert W.	Army	1968	Chadds Ford, Pa.	79
Curtis, William P. Jr.	Air Force	1972	Wilmington	326-327
Cutsler, W. Barry		1970	Wilmington	
Cycyk, Edward	Navy	1972	Wilmington	335, 345
Czerwinski, Dominic G.	Army	1970	Wilmington	
Daisey, James C.	Army	1971	Wilmington	
Daller, David G.	Army	1969	Claymont	181
Daly, Daniel P.		1970-1971	Newark	
Dambach. Jeffrey K.	Army	1971	Wilmington	
Damiani, Olindo	Army	1968	Wilmington	33
Danby, James	Army	1970		249
Danner, Charles M.	Army	1968	Dover	79
Darby, Eric C.	Army	1972	New Castle	337
Darr, Harry I. III	Army	1969-1970	Wilmington	185
Darrow, Robert B.	Air Force	1970-1971	Wilmington	201
Dash, Tony	Air Force	1969	Wilmington	
Dauron, Gary M.		1970	Wilmington	
Davidson, Robert	Navy	1972		330
Davis, Art	Marines	1970-1971	Wilmington	213, 235, 244, 250, 305
Davis, George O. Jr.	Marines	1970	Smyrna	
Davis, Milton E.	Army	1971	Wilmington	
Davis, Tim	Army	1971	Claymont	288, 298
Davis, William F. III	Army	1970-1971	Marshallton	
Dawson, Jim	Army	1968	Wilmington	69
Dawson, Joseph C.	Army	1971-1972	Millsboro	258

NAME	BRANCH	YEAR	HOMETOWN	PAGES	NAME	BRANCH	YEAR	HOMETOWN	PAGES
Dawson, Joseph W. Jr.	Army	1968	New Castle	69	Ewing, Robert E. Jr.	Army	1970-1971	Newark	244, 245, 249
Day, John R.		1970	Wilmington		Fairchild, Michael A.	Army	1971	Newark	
Dayton, Herbert Spence III	Army	1970-1971	Newark		Fairchild, Neil A.	Army	1971-1972	Newark	302
Dean, Frank	Army	1969	Seaford		Falkowski, Mike	Army	1969	Wilmington	138
Dean, Lawrence	Army	1969	Blades		Fangman, Paul M.	Army	1972	Claymont	335
Deese, James L.	Army	1968-1969	Wilmington	37, 179	Farenski, Joe		1970	Wilmington	233
DeMoss, Bruce A.	Navy	1972	Newark		Faulkner, William	Army	1971	Wilmington	
Dempsey, John J.	Army	1971	Wilmington	312	Faw, Kenneth	Army	1968	Wilmington	
DeNight, Gordon		1968		63	Feist, Jim	Navy	1968		
Depew, Larry	Marines	1968	Greenwood	24	Feldman, Larry		1970		244
Deptula, Joseph J. Jr.	Marines	1969		158, 175	Felsberg, Harry			Wilmington	159
Derrickson, Milton L.		1971-1972	Frankford		Ferguson, Dale		1971	Newport	
DeShields, Raymond	Marines	1972	Concord		Ferguson, Frank		1969	Wilmington	
Destaffaney, John		1968	Wilmington		Ferguson, John W.	Army	1968	Wilmington	75, 79
Dexter, Louis	Army	1972	Bridgeville		Ferguson, Robert C.	Navy	1971	Claymont	
Di Biaso, Camilo Jr.	Army	1968	Newport		Ferguson, William E.	Army	1970-1971	Wilmington	262, 303
DiBendetto, Anthony P.		1968		29	Filliben, Joseph F.	Army	1970	Wilmington	245
Dickerson, John	Army	1968	Rehoboth		Finochi, Michael		1968	Wilmington	
Dickerson, Marshall G.	Army	1968			Fishwick, Jeffrey P.	Army	1970	Wilmington	216, 244
Diehl, Norman W. Jr.	Marines	1970-1971	Wilmington	244	Fitzgerald, James	Army	1968	Wilmington	5
DiEmedio, Joseph A.	Air Force	1971	Wilmington		Flaherty, Gerard C.	Marines	1968	Rehoboth	16-17
Dietz, George	Army	1971	Wilmington		Flaherty, John E.		1970	Wilmington	210
DiPasquantonio, Michael	Marines	1969-1970	Wilmington	230, 231	Fleetwood, Mike	Marines	1968	Seaford	24, 27
Divens, James Jr.	Army	1970	Swedesboro, N.J.		Fleetwood, William	Marines	1968	Wilmington	
Dolan, Pat		1971-1972	Elsmere	299	Fleischut, Skip	Army	1968	Wilmington	76
Donophan, Carl	Air Force	1972	Magnolia		Fleming, John		1971	Wilmington	
Donovan, William F.		1970	Wilmington		Flood, Richard A.	Army	1970-1971	Frankford	243
Doremus, Robert B.	Navy	1965-1973	Newark	325	Forbes, Robert G. Jr.		1971-1972	Wilmington	
Dorman, Gilbert		1968	Seaford		Ford, Gary	Army	1972	Wilmington	322
Doss, Jerry L.	Army	1971	Wilmington		Forrest, Joseph Jr.	Navy	1968	Wilmington	12
Dougherty, David	Army	1972	Wilmington		Fortner, John W.		1972	Wilmington	
Dougherty, Hugh R.	Army	1968-1969	Elsmere	5, 42-43, 59, 133	Foss, Gerald P.	Air Force	1972	Dover	326
Dougherty, Paul		1969	Wilmington		Foster, James W.	Army	1972	Wilmington	332
Doughty, Robert	Navy	1971-1972	Millsboro		Foulk, Robert		1968		
Douglass, James K.	Army	1970	Rehoboth Beach		Francisco, Anthony	Army	1971-1972	Wilmington	296
Dowd, James		1972	New Castle		Frase, Richard		1969	Felton	
Downes, William John	Army	1971-1972	Newark	321,341	Frederick, John II		1969	Newark	
Draper, Horace	Coast Guard	1972	Newark		Freebery, Michael J.	Army	1969-1970	Elsmere	100-101, 240
Drugash, Don	Army	1970	Seaford		Frey, Arthur	Air Force	1972		
Drummond, Gregory W.		1969	Wilmington	176	Friedal, C.M.	Army	1968	Wilmington	
Dukes, Harry H. III	Navy	1970-1971	Millville		Frost, Kenneth	Navy	1972	New Castle	
Dukes, William		1969			Fuller, Daniel L.	Navy	1972	Wilmington	
Duncan, Francis J.	Army	1969-1971	Elsmere	235, 236	Funk, Vance A. III	Army	1971	Wilmington	
Duncan, Lester P.		1972	Bear		Gaglia, Joseph	Army	1971	Newark	
Durante, Paul	Army	1972	Magnolia		Gaglione, Anthony	Air Force		Clayton	
Durham, Arthur J.	Marines	1971	Wilmington		Gainor, John W. III	Navy	1972	Wilmington	
Duricek, Johnnie C. Sr.	Army	1970	Wilmington	202, 203	Garver, Donald	Army	1971	Wilmington	
Dvorak, John		1969	Elkton, Md.		Gaynor, Joe	Navy	1968	Elsmere	15
Dzielak, Joe	Army	1969	New Castle		Gebhart, Bill	Army	1970	New Castle	
Eastridge, Steve F.	Navy	1968		73	Gebhart, Charles L.	Army	1970	New Castle	249
Eberly, Barry R.	Army	1971	Wyoming		Gebhart, Leonard M.	Army	1971	Hockessin	
Edwards, Joseph	Army	1971-1972	Wilmington		Gentile, Thomas	Army	1970-1971	Middletown	244
Eide, Brian T.	Navy	1972	Newark	330	George, David	Army	1968	Middletown	
Elisee, Theodore E.	Army	1971	New Castle	312	George, Eugene D.		1971	Claymont	
Ellett, James L. Jr.	Army	1970-1971	Seaford	249	George, Paul J.		1970-1971	Claymont	
Ellingsworth, Vernon R.	Marines	1970-1972	Wilmington		Georgia, Milan O. Jr.		1970-1971	New Castle	
Elliott, Douglas R.	Army	1969	Claymont	103, 124	Gerard, Kenneth	Army	1968	New Castle	63
Elliott, John H. Jr.	Navy	1971-1972	Newark		Geuting, Robert L.	Army	1969	Wilmington	156-158, 179
Elliott, John R.	Army	1970	Lewes	219, 233, 253	Giaccone, Robert W.	Army	1970-1971	Wilmington	
Elliott, Robert A.	Army	1968	Georgetown	31, 61, 66, 76	Gibson, Fred W.	Marines	1971	North East, Md.	280-281
Emery, Floyd C. Jr.	Army	1971	Wilmington		Gibson, Robert	Army	1970	Newark	246
Emmell, Gene	Marines	1970		231, 244	Gibson, William J.	Marines	1968	Newark	51
Eoppolo, Tony V.	Army	1970-1971	Wilmington	241, 243, 299, 312	Gilmer, Scott A.	Army	1971-1972	Wilmington	
					Glanzel, Kevin A.		1972	New Castle	
Esham, Christopher	Army	1970		245	Glazar, Aaron Zane H.	Marines	1968	Wilmington	24
Eskridge, Clifford	Army	1968			Glazar, Joseph C.		1970-1971	Wilmington	244
Essick, Bob	Navy	1969			Glazier, Richard	Army	1968-1969	Wilmington	31, 48-49, 75-76, 95, 108, 174,178, 358-363
Etzweiller, Wayne	Army	1970-1971	Elsmere	245					
Evans, Andrew R.	Navy	1970	Wilmington		Gleasner, Lee	Army	1970	Wilmington	
Evans, Cashar W. Jr.		1970-1971	Selbyville		Glenn, John F. Jr.	Army	1971-1972	Wilmington	335
Evans, Charles C.		1971	New Castle		Glogowski, Daniel M.	Army	1970	Somers, Conn	
Evans, Melvin	Air Force	1972	Baltimore, Md.		Glynn, Paul J.	Air Force	1972	Wilmington	343
Evans, Paul D.	Air Force	1970	New Castle		Godwin, Donald L.	Navy	1968	New Castle	49
Evers, Warren W. Jr.	Army	1968	Wilmington	66, 67	Gold, Jerold S.	Army	1971-1972	Newark	300, 335,340
Everts, Richard C.	Army	1970-1971	Wilmington	243, 312	Gooding, Robert H.		1971	Newark	
Evon, Earl Jr.	Navy	1968	Waterbury, Conn.	73					

NAME	BRANCH	YEAR	HOMETOWN	PAGES
Goodley, Jay	Army	1970-1971	Wilmington	246, 312
Goodman, Mark L.	Army	1969-1970	Wilmington	154-155, 184-185, 192, 199, 229, 250-251
Goodman, Robert A.	Air Force	1970		
Gooner, William R.	Air Force	1970-1971	Milton	
Gorman, J.F.		1970	Wilmington	
Gould, Allen E.		1971	Newark	
Govens, John H.	Army	1972	Wilmington	
Grady, Allen E.	Army	1971	New Castle	
Graham, Walter F.	Army	1970		
Grant, Ronald	Air Force	1971	Newark	
Grapperhaus, Ralph H.	Army	1972	Selbyville	
Graves, Richard T.	Marines	1971	Wilmington	
Gray, Gilbert	Navy	1969	Bladensburg, Md.	142
Gray, Winfield H.	Air Force	1971	Seaford	312
Green, Frank	Army	1968-1969		86
Green, James E.	Army	1971	Wilmington	
Green, Richard		1970	Wilmington	
Green, Robert W.	Marines	1969	Stanton	115, 158-159, 164, 166, 175
Green, Stephen M.	Army	1971	Wilmington	
Green, William H.	Air Force	1970-1971	Felton	
Greenwell, Alan	Marines	1968	Smyrna	5
Greer, Gary D.	Army	1970		
Greer, Riley		1969	Wilmington	
Gregg, Robert W.	Air Force	1970-1971	Newark	
Gregory, Wilbur T. Jr.	Army	1971	Wilmington	
Grier, Garrett		1972	Milford	
Grifantini, Paul M.	Army	1968	Wilmington	10, 76
Griffin, Charles W. Jr.		1970	Wilmington	
Grillo, Domenic M.	Army	1970	Wilmington	209, 216
Gross, Charles E. Jr.		1971	New Castle	
Gross, Jim	Army	1969-1970	Wilmington	162, 210
Grubb, Roger L.	Army	1970	Wilmington	201, 243
Grubbs, Darrell T.	Army	1972	Ogletown	327
Grygo, Raymond	Navy	1970		
Gum, Larry D.	Navy	1969	Frankford	115, 133, 179, 370-375
Gustavson, Walter	Army	1972	Felton	335
Haass, I	Marines	1971		295
Hackney, James M.		1970-1971	Newark	
Hahn, Daniel C.		1970		
Hall, R. Lance	Air Force	1969-1970	Lewes	96-97, 159, 182, 192, 195, 229, 364-369
Hallsted, Robert H. Jr.		1969-1970	Claymont	153
Hammond, William	Army	1972		
Hanby, Gary W.	Army	1970-1971	Wilmington	
Hanby, Wayne	Marines	1969	Wilmington	
Hanna, Gerald P.		1971	Wilmington	
Hannan, Thomas M.	Army	1971-1972	Wilmington	
Harcum, Weldon W.		1971	Houston	
Hardesty, Charles S.	Army	1970-1971	Seaford	
Harmon, Larry E.	Army	1971	Newark	298
Harrington, J. Saxton	Marines	1968-1969	Claymont	
Harris, Jim	Marines	1969	Wilmington	97, 148, 183
Harris, John C.	Army	1970	Wilmington	
Harris, Michael J.	Navy	1970	Newark	
Harrison, Jerry		1970	New Castle	
Hart, Bruce		1970-1971	Wilmington	
Hartsock, Glen		1968	Newark	
Harvey, Edward D. Jr.	Army	1971	Claymont	
Hatfield, Robert G.	Army	1970-1971	Newark	250
Hauser, Carl J.	Army	1970-1971	Hockessin	
Havens, William E.	Army	1970`	New Castle	214
Hawk, William F.		1972`	New Castle	
Hayden, Richard Jr.		1969	Wilmington	
Hayton, Paul S.	Marines	1971	Seaford	
Hayward, Pierre du Pont		1971-1972	Montchanin	
Hazzard, Terry L.	Army	1970-1971	Lewes	
Healey, Robert		1968	Wilmington	
Heath, Ricky		1970	Wilmington	
Hedgecoth, James E.	Army	1970	Wilmington	
Heeren, James	Army	1968	Delaware City	
Helwig, David R.	Army	1971-1972	Wilmington	
Henderson, Joe B.	Marines	1968	Wilmington	15
Hendrix, John E.		1970-1971	Elsmere	244
Henry, John C.	Army	1968		5
Henry, Robert W.	Army	1972	Bridgeville	
Hensing, Fred	Army	1968	Wilmington	72-73
Hensley, Frank J.	Army	1970-1972	New Castle	233-234, 241, 245, 334
Herlihy, Patrick E.	Marines	1970	Wilmington	
Herman, Donald L.	Army	1968		38
Hess, James D.	Navy	1970	Newark	
Heston, Earl A.	Marines	1968	Wilmington	12, 20, 33, 52, 77
Hetherton, John		1969	Wilmington	
Heuer, David	Army	1971	Wilmington	
Heuser, William Jr.		1972	Wilmington	
Heverin, Fred R.	Army	1971	Newark	
Higgins, Charles A.		1972	Wilmington	
Higgins, James E.	Army	1971-1972	Claymont	
Hijar, George E.	Marines	1968	Wilmington	63
Hill, John C.		1968	Dover	69
Hinderer, Robert		1969		
Hinkle, Lonnie		1970	Wilmington	
Hitch, Clifford T.	Navy	1971-1972	Wilmington	269, 295, 342
Hitchner, Vernon	Army	1972	Pennsville, N.J.	
Hobson, Thomas	Army	1969	New Castle	111
Hoddinott, Thomas F.	Navy	1969-1972	Wilmington	
Hoey, Robert A.	Army	1968	Wilmington	79
Hoffman, David A.	Army	1970	Wilmington	
Holding, Richard L. Jr.	Air Force	1970-1971	Townsend	209, 244
Holland, John		1969	Claymont	
Holley, John		1971	Newark	302
Hopkins, Earl E.	Marines	1969	Wilmington	164
Hopkins, Irving L.	Marines	1971	Odessa	
Hopkins, Walter C.	Army	1971	Lewes	298
Hopper, John W.	Army	1971-1972	Newark	275, 311, 313
Horowitz, Monty	Navy	1971		300
Horsey, Richard B.		1970	Wilmington	
Horstead, Terry L.	Air Force	1971	Newark	
Hoskins, Donald R.		1972	Dover	317, 325
Hosler, Jack	Marines	1968		
Howie, John		1969	New Castle	
Howie, Odell V. Jr.	Army	1969	Wilmington	159
Huber, Charles S.	Army	1970		
Huber, Clark S.	Army	1970	Kennett Square, Pa.	
Huber, Frank S.	Army	1972	Kennett Square, Pa.	
Hudson, Clifford W.	Army	1970-1971	Milton	212
Hudson, Larry		1970	Wilmington	
Hudson, Michael S.		1970	Dagsboro	
Hudson, Richard W.	Army	1969-1970		175, 225, 341
Hudson, Robert V.	Army	1968	Milton	12, 341
Hudson, Thomas E.	Army	1969	Wilmington	145, 157
Hudson, William E.	Air Force	1971-1972	New Castle	299, 335-336
Huey, F. Alvin	Marines	1969-1970	Seaford	250
Huey, Kenneth A.	Army	1970-1971	Greenwood	
Huffman, Ray	Army	1971-1972	Claymont	284
Huggler, Gary		1969	Newark	
Hughes, Larry	Army	1968	Wilmington	49
Hughes, Michael V.		1970	Harrington	
Hultberg, William J.	Navy	1970	Wilmington	
Hunter, Bruce	Army	1968	New Castle	5
Hunter, Michael		1969	Wilmington	
Huston, John W.	Army	1970-1971	Wilmington	277, 294, 299
Hutchison, William W. Jr.	Army	1970-1972	Clayton	191, 214, 240-241, 260, 276, 279, 287, 296-297, 302, 400-407
Hutt, Thomas H.	Army	1969		174
Hypes, Seth L.		1970	Newark	
Ignatowski, Joseph L.	Army	1971	Wilmington	277, 312
Ingersol, Fred		1970		244
Irelan, Art	Army	1968	Marshallton	51
Irwin, Donald		1969	Elsmere	
Irwin, Leo	Army	1968	Wilmington	
Ivie, Terry	Marines	1968		38
Jabluszewski, Thomas Jr.	Army	1970-1971	Wilmington	
Jackson, Charles		1971	Wilmington	
Jackson, Gerald W.	Air Force	1971	New Castle	258, 273

441

442

NAME	BRANCH	YEAR	HOMETOWN	PAGES
Nemeth, Stephen J.		1970	Newark	
Neylan, David	Army	1971-1972	Dover	292, 302
Nittinger, Eugene F.	Army	1968-69,1971	Wilmington	77, 312
Nock, John M.	Marines	1969		63, 115, 158, 176
Nock, Rick	Navy	1968	Wilmington	51, 63
Nogaj, John A.		1971	Wilmington	
Norris, Edsel Ford Jr.	Army	1968-1969	Glasgow	33, 51, 75-77, 157
Norris, Kenneth J.	Army	1971-1972	New Castle	265, 335, 337, 340-341
Norris, Scott D.	Army	1970-1971	Wilmington	245, 273, 284, 298
Nowaczyk, Robert A.	Army	1970-1971	Claymont/ Wilmington	225, 258, 270, 308, 312
Nufrio, Nicholas	Marines	1971	Newark	
Nylen, Bob	Army	1968	Wilmington	40-41
O'Connor, Paul William	Army	1971	Wilmington	
O'Dell, Bruce L.		1971	Wilmington	
Ohsol, Richard B.	Army	1969	Wilmington	139
O'Leary, Joseph		1972	Wilmington	
O'Leary, Michael		1972	Wilmington	
Olmstead, Gary	Navy	1968	Wilmington	63
Olszewski, Gerald H.	Navy	1972	New Castle	330
O'Neill, William E.		1970-1971	Wilmington	
Opdenaker, Joseph H. Jr.	Navy	1971-1972	Wilmington	265, 299, 301, 337, 339, 342
Osborne, William A.	Air Force	1971	Milford	
Ottinger, Terry W.		1970	Penns Grove, N.J.	
Owens, Archer A.	Army	1968	Wilmington	
Pace, Nolan S. Jr.	Army	1972	Seaford	
Pacek, John T.	Air Force	1972	Dover	342
Pacello, Eugene	Air Force	1972		
Pacello, Francis D.	Marines	1972	Wilmington	
Panadero, Richard	Navy	1969	Elsmere	137, 160
Pancoast, Ronald	Marines	1969	New Castle	
Park, Robert	Marines	1970	Newark	244
Parker, Joseph E. Jr.	Army	1970-1971	Wilmington	205
Parker, Paul		1969		
Patterson, Doug		1970	Dover	
Patterson, Ralph P.	Army	1971	Elsmere	
Patti, John R. Jr.	Navy	1972	Wilmington	
Patton, Anthony F.	Army	1970		
Patton, Donald B.	Army	1969	Wilmington	145, 159, 170-171, 179, 376-381
Peltz, Joseph		1971	Wilmington	
Perry, Charles	Air Force	1971	Dover	
Peterman, Jim	Army	1968	Milford	5
Peterson, D.T.		1971	Wilmington	
Peterson, Donald		1969	Frederica	
Peterson, Jon M.	Army	1968,1971-72	Wilmington	9, 21, 299
Pharis, Robert H.	Marines	1971	Stanton	
Phillips, Harold D. Jr.		1970	Laurel	
Phillips, Jim	Army	1972	Delmar	328
Pienkos, Stanley F. Jr.	Marines	1969-1970	Wilmington	211, 394-399
Pierce, Paul	Marines	1968	Wilmington	
Pierce, Richard J.	Marines	1970-1971	Wilmington	212, 224-226, 251
Pinder, Gary L.	Army	1970	New Castle	249
Pletsch, James	Coast Guard	1970	Smyrna	
Polauf, Helen	Army	1970	Dover	234, 239
Pollock, Barry G.	Army	1971-1972	Wilmington	284, 335
Polsky, Barry W.		1971	Elsmere	
Poore, Thomas		1971-1972	Claymont	299
Porter, George N.		1968	Lewes	38
Porter, Harry G.	Navy	1970-1972	Wilmington	219, 248, 258-259, 287, 298, 312
Porter, Philip W.	Navy	1972	Wilmington	
Porter, Richard C.		1971	Wilmington	
Potts, Larry F.	Marines	1972	Smyrna	317, 325
Preiss, Frederick J.		1971	Wilmington	
Price, Scott	Marines	1968	Wilmington	15
Price, Steven W.	Army	1970-1971	Dover	245, 298
Protokowicz, Edwin	Marines	1968	Wilmington	
Przybylek, Michael J.	Army	1971-1972	Wilmington	321, 343
Pugh, Robert J.	Air Force	1971	Wilmington	
Pyle, Burton F.	Army	1970	Newark	
Pyle, Donald A.	Army	1971	Wilmington	
Queen, Henry J. Jr.		1970-1971	Wilmington	
Quig, Michael G.	Navy	1970	Hockessin	
Quigley, Peter D.	Army	1971		
Quillen, Jimmy G.	Air Force	1970	Harrington	
Raczkowski, Philip J.		1971	Claymont	
Rago, Pete	Army	1968	Wilmington	12
Rainard, Walter L.	Army	1968-1969	Wilmington	4, 45, 122-123
Ralston, Robert G.	Army	1969	Wilmington	102, 135, 174
Ramey, Gordon	Army	1972	Blades	
Ramone, Francis M.	Navy	1970	New Castle	
Ramsey, George	Army	1970	Wilmington	
Ramsey, T.H.		1971	Newark	
Ranney, Vern H. Jr.	Marines	1969	Claymont	120
Rawlins, James D. Jr.	Army	1970-1972	Seaford	205, 247, 298, 342, 382-387
Reader, John R.	Army	1971	Wilmington	
Redmond, Edward C. Jr.	Air Force	1968	Lewes	49
Reed, Robert Lee	Air Force	1971-1972	Greenwood	329
Reeder, Douglas S.	Army	1971	Hockessin	
Refner, Richard W. Jr.	Army	1970	Wilmington	201, 243, 249
Reichel, Christina A.		1970	Silver Spring, Md.	234-235
Reichelt, Klaus	Army	1968	Wyoming	
Reiff, Gary E.	Army	1970-1971	Middletown	
Reiswig, Terry	Navy	1968-1970	Newark	68-69, 103, 140, 169, 248
Remmers, Louis C. Jr.	Navy	1968	Newark	49
Renzetti, John	Air Force	1972	Wilmington	
Revel, Stewart	Army	1972	Millsboro	326-327, 342
Revelle, Gary P.		1970-1971	Georgetown	
Reynolds, James W.		1970	Wilmington	
Reynolds, Norman L.	Navy	1971-1972	Claymont	
Rice, William David	Army	1968-1972	Elsmere	80-81, 335, 341
Rickards, John	Navy	1969	Selbyville	
Rideout, Franklyn		1969	Wilmington	
Riley, Harvey W.	Army	1971	Dover	
Riley, Robert C.	Navy	1968-1969	Wilmington	75, 100
Rineer, Joseph Jr.		1969	New Castle	
Rineer, Tim J.	Marines	1968	Claymont	12, 37
Rippe, Henry J.		1970	Kennett Square, Pa.	
Rivers, Rodger	Army	1968		
Roach, Walter Jr.	Marines	1969		
Roan, Richard J.		1970-1971	Newark	201
Roberts, Douglas L.	Army	1971	Wilmington	
Roberts, Michael A.		1970	Elsmere	
Robertson, Russell		1972	Wilmington	
Robinson, Hartford I.		1971	Smyrna	
Robinson, Ken	Army	1971	Newark	298
Robinson, Lee	Air Force	1972	Magnolia	
Robinson, Lester	Army	1972	Wilmington	
Rockwell, Lee C.		1971	Wilmington	
Roe, James	Army	1968	Seaford	
Roemer, William S.	Army	1970-1971	Wilmington	246
Rogers, Joseph D. III		1971	Hockessin	
Rogers, Mike	Army	1970	Wilmington	
Rogers, Patrick	Army	1972	New Castle	
Rogers, Robert J.	Marines	1969	Clayton	184
Rogers, Walter O. III		1971	Wilmington	
Romano, Frank	Marines	1969	Wilmington	
Romano, Pete	Army	1968	Bear	79
Rose, Michael Lee	Marines	1971	New Castle	294
Rostocki, Leon J		1970	New Castle	
Roth, David		1968	Wilmington	
Rousso, Samuel L.	Army	1971		
Rowan, Mike	Army	1969-1970	Wilmington	174
Rowe, James M.	Army	1968-1969	Seaford	49
Rowe, Richard J.		1971	Bethel	
Roy, Gerald A. Jr.	Army	1970-1971	Wilmington	219, 233-234
Roy, James W. Jr.	Army	1970-1971	Wilmington	241, 293
Rubincan, John E.	Army	1968-1970	Wilmington	120, 140, 163, 224, 229, 249
Rucinski, Edward J. III	Army	1970-1971	Wilmington	296
Ruffin, Patrick S.	Air Force	1971	New Castle	
Rupert, Ronald		1970		
Rusher, David	Navy	1968	Wilmington	59
Rust, Dale	Navy	1969	Millsboro	
Rutter, Clay	Army	1970		192
Rykiel, Robert R	Army	1970-1971	Wilmington	
Sadlowski, Michael J.	Marines	1970	Wilmington	243, 245

NAME	BRANCH	YEAR	HOMETOWN	PAGES
Sailer, Christopher		1971	Wilmington	
Salisbury, Ronald K.		1971	Dover	312
Santos, Emilio	Army	1968-1969	Wilmington	33, 51, 97
Sarrio, Charles R.	Army	1971	Rockville, Md.	298
Savage, C. Kenneth	Army	1969	Seaford	145
Savage, Leonard G.	Marines	1971	Newark	
Savage, William R.	Army	1972	Milton	
Saxton, David	Army	1968	Harrington	49
Saylor, Terrance E.	Army	1971	Newark	
Scarpitti, Richard N.		1972	Claymont	
Scheel, Phillip A.	Air Force	1971-1972	Wilmington	
Schirmer, Lawrence A.	Army	1971	Milton	
Schneider, Michael H.		1971	Wilmington	
Schnitzer, Alan	Army	1971	Wilmington	
Schollenberger, George	Army	1972	Laurel	
Schwartz, Barney		1970-1971	Wilmington	
Schwartz, Barry		1969	Wilmington	
Scott, George S. III	Army	1970	Wilmington	
Scott, Michael F.	Army	1970	Newport	
Scott, Robert	Army	1968	Seaford	79
Scott, Thomas F.	Air Force	1971	Wilmington	307
Seiple, Stewart L.	Marines	1969	Wilmington	176
Senigo, John Russell	Army	1971-1972	Wilmington	341
Settle, Robert L.	Army	1972	Wilmington	328-329, 342
Shaffer, Charles E. Jr.	Army	1972	Seaford	
Shaner, Sandy	Air Force	1968	Smyrna	31, 77
Shankles, Larry A.		1971	Newark	
Shannon, John W.	Army	1970	Wilmington	
Sharpe, Jim	Navy	1969		108
Shatley, Leonard D.	Army	1970-1971	New Castle	298
Shelton, John F.	Army	1970	Wilmington	
Shepherd, Donald L.	Army	1968	Newark	53, 79
Sheppard, Bob	Army	1970	Wilmington	209, 216, 231
Sheppard, Phillip R.	Army	1969	Wilmington	178-179
Sheridan, Gerald J.	Marines	1971	New Castle	
Shetzler, James E.	Army	1970	Newark	244-245
Shockley, Mike		1971	Wilmington	
Shore, Kenneth		1970-1971	Wilmington	244
Short, Theodore R.	Marines	1970-1971	Lewes	219
Short, Thomas	Army	1970	Georgetown	
Shroud, Robert H.		1971	Wilmington	
Shur, Bruce D.	Air Force	1970-1971	Wilmington	219, 248
Silinsky, Joseph C.	Army	1971	Pennsville, N.J.	
Simeone, Francis	Army	1971-1972	Wilmington	293
Simmons, Carlyle L.		1970-1971	Wilmington	
Simmons, T.L.		1971	Wilmington	
Skelly, Thomas D.	Army	1969	Wilmington	148
Skillern, Christopher L.	Air Force	1972	New Castle	
Skinner, William W. Jr.	Army	1970	Wilmington	
Skirvin, Denny	Army	1968	Wilmington	31
Slack, James M.	Army	1971-1972	Newark	
Slattery, Michael	Army	1972	New Castle	
Sloboda, Valerie D	Army	1970-1971	Wilmington	238-239
Small, David		1969	Wilmington	
Small, John A. Jr.	Army	1971-1972	Wilmington	
Smarte, Douglas A.		1971	Seaford	311
Smith, Alfred C.	Army	1968-1969	Wilmington	103
Smith, Dayne R.	Army	1970-1971	Wilmington	241
Smith, Gerald R.	Army	1968-1969	Newark	79, 142
Smith, H.U. Jr.	Air Force	1969	New Castle	
Smith, Henry L. Jr.	Marines	1968-1969	Wilmington	38
Smith, James		1968	Wilmington	
Smith, James M.	Navy	1971	Wilmington	
Smith, Lawrence	Army	1969-70,1972	Newark	105, 175
Smith, Maurice A.	Army	1970	Wilmington	242-243
Smith, Richard A.	Army	1970-1971	Lincoln	225
Smith, Thomas		1969	Wilmington	
Smith, Tim	Army	1968	Wilmington	12
Smith, Wayne	Air Force	1972	Newark	
Snodgrass, John J. Jr.		1970	Wilmington	
Snyder, John L.	Army	1970-1971	Elsmere	
Snyder, Kenneth M.	Army	1971-1972	Newark	
Snyder, Matthew H.		1971	Wilmington	
Sobolewski, Nancy	Army	1969-1971	Newark	234-235, 276
Solomon, Alan Marc	Navy	1971-1972	Wilmington	299, 320, 326, 327, 339
Solomon, Michael S.	Navy	1969-1979	Wilmington	133, 162, 179, 243-244
Sontowski, Francis	Air Force	1970	Wilmington	240
Sorensen, Jim		1971		287
Sparkman, Charles F.	Air Force	1971-1972	Wilmington	278
Sparpaglione, Charles A.	Army	1971	Wilmington (also Frankford)	
Speakman, Samuel Jr.	Army	1971	Fairfax	
Spence, Franklin M.	Army	1970-1971	Greenwood	
Spicer, Tracy L.	Army	1971	Newark	
Spiegel, Robert S.	Air Force	1971	Abington, Pa.	
Spry, Lawrence R.	Marines	1969	New Castle	90
Stallard, Earl		1968	Bear	
Stalnaker, George F.	Navy	1968	Wilmington	82
Stayton, Michael D.	Navy	1972	Harrington	
Stearrett, Francis B. Jr.	Army	1970-1971	Wilmington	
Stebner, Gary Lee		1971	Wilmington	
Steele, Richard J.	Navy	1970	Red Lion	249
Stephenson, Craig D.	Army	1970	Wilmington	
Stercho, A.G.	Army	1968		
Stevens, Joseph A. Jr.	Army	1970	Wilmington	
Stevens, William R. Jr.	Army	1970	Seaford	249
Stevenson, Tom		1968		
Stewart, Jim		1968-1969	Elkton, Md.	86
Stewart, Richard	Army	1968	Rehoboth Beach	
Stigler, Harry C.	Army	1970-1971	New Castle	
Stipo, John J.	Army	1971	Wilmington	
Stockwell, Stephen E.	Marines	1971	Wilmington	
Stoddard, Paul P.	Army	1968	Bear	52, 66, 82
Stokes, Daniel P.	Air Force	1971-1972		258, 269, 272, 313, 344, 408-413
Stone, Steve	Marines	1969	Laurel	158
Stonebraker, Thomas D.	Army	1971	Newark	
Stout, Robert P. Jr.	Army	1970-1971	Wilmington	226, 244, 251, 260-261, 302, 308, 313
Straughn, Charles R.	Marines	1968-1969	Newark	15, 33, 83
Straughn, Donald	Army	1968	Newark	
Strockbine, Robert	Army	1969	Millsboro	
Sublett, Gail William	Navy	1965-1966	Wilmington	329
Sullivan, Andrew L.		1971	Wilmington	
Sullivan, John K.		1972	Wilmington	
Summa, Samuel J.		1970	Ridley Park, Pa.	
Summerfield, Larry	Army	1968		
Suppi, Ronald W.	Army	1969-1971	Newark	216, 244
Swalheim, Stuart D.	Marines	1969	Hockessin	147, 158
Sweeney, Gerald P.		1971	Glasgow	
Sydnor, William		1969	Christiana	
Szczerba, Frank	Army	1968-1969	Wilmington	162
Tabo, Joseph S.		1970	Wilmington	
Talley, Wallace W. Jr.	Air Force	1970	Greenville	
Tanchuk, Bohdan R.	Army	1969	Bellefonte	90-91, 137, 181, 183
Tanner, Robert J. Jr.	Air Force	1971	Wilmington	
Taylor, Carter		1969-1970	Wilmington	234, 235
Taylor, Glenn E.	Army	1971	Salisbury, Md.	
Taylor, James	Army	1970	Oregon	
Taylor, Warren E.	Army	1969	Wilmington	147
Taylor, William D.	Army	1970-1971	Wilmington	276, 292
Taylor, William J. III	Army	1969-1970	Wilmington	105, 120, 181
Teagle, Henry C.	Army	1970	Seaford	
Teat, James E.	Army	1971	Middletown	
Temple, Al	Navy	1968	Wilmington	21
Temple, Bruce J.		1971	Wilmington	
Thomas, David R.	Army	1969-1970	Wilmington	
Thomas, Jesse L. Jr.		1971	Cochranville, Pa.	
Thomas, Marvin L.		1972	Wilmington	
Thomas, Norman		1969		
Thompson, Alfred Donald	Army	1971-1972	Blackbird	300, 337, 340-342
Thompson, Gerald W.	Army	1968	Dover	9, 37, 83
Thompson, Timothy W.	Marines	1970	Newark	
Thornton, Michael P.		1971	Wilmington	
Thornton, Roy C.	Army	1970-1971	Wilmington	275, 307
Thorstens, Gary H.	Army	1971	Claymont	
Tidwell, Joseph S.		1971	Wilmington	
Tilley, William	Marines	1968	Wilmington	5, 33, 65
Timko, Bob	Army	1968	New Castle	
Timmons, Ernest P.		1972	Millsboro	

NAME	BRANCH	YEAR	HOMETOWN	PAGES
Tindall, Stephen F.	Army	1971	Middletown	
Todd, H. B.	Marines	1968	Wilmington	15, 33
Tolbert, John	Army	1969		92- 93
Tomczyk, Edward J.		1971	Newark	
Tomlin, Joe			Lewes	159
Toomey, Don	Army	1970		246
Torres, Benjamin		1971	New Castle	
Townsend, Norman	Marines	1969		95, 159
Trager, John		1971	Wilmington	
Tressler, Daniel A. Jr.	Army	1969		160
Trumbull, Ghordis W.	Army	1970	Claymont	
Trustler, Ivan	Marines	1970	Newark	244
Tue, Brandt E.	Marines	1970	Dover	233
Tunstall, Donald W.	Army	1970-1971		
Turak, George J.		1969		115
Turner, Blaine P.	Army	1971	Wilmington	279
Turner, James R. Jr.	Army	1970	Wilmington	210, 213, 216, 242
Twilley, William B.	Army	1971	Wilmington	
Twitchell, Douglas G.		1971	Wilmington	
Tyler, James B. III	Army	1971	Wilmington	
Tyndall, Gary C.		1971	Seaford	
Tyndall, James D.	Army	1969-1970		
Undorf, Anthony	Army	1968	Wilmington	66
Uniatowski, Joseph	Army	1969	Wilmington	127, 142-143
Urmston, Randolph		1971	Wilmington	
Urquhart, Rudolph		1970	Wilmington	
Van Grofski, Thomas W.		1969	Wilmington	121
Vance, Mitchell D.		1970	Wilmington	
Van Gorder, Ronald L.	Army	1971-1972	Farmington	
Van Gorder, Terry		1968		
VanSant, Edward J.	Air Force	1969-1970	Wilmington	153, 174
Vas Dias, Douglas C.	Army	1971	Cinnaminson, N.J.	278-279
Vaughn, Paul E.	Army	1971-1972	Wilmington	264-265, 339
Vernon, Lawrence D.		1971	Hockessin	
Vestal, Daniel R.		1970	Wilmington	
Vickers, Ray L.	Navy	1972	Wilmington	
Vickers, Vincent H. II	Navy	1972	Wilmington	
Vines, William		1969		
Vinson, Gary L.	Army	1971	New Castle	
Vogelhaupt, H.R.		1970	Wilmington	
Voight, Gilbert A.		1971	Wilmington	
Volk, Richard H.	Army	1971	West Grove, Pa.	260, 305
Wachter, James F. Jr.	Air Force	1968-1969	Wilmington	33, 159, 183
Walker, George S.	Army	1968	Wilmington	10, 37
Walker, Lawrence R.		1970	Newark	
Walker, Paul J. III	Army	1969	Georgetown	119, 166, 184
Walker, Stanley C.	Air Force	1970-1971	Georgetown	225
Wall, Darwin R.	Army	1969	New Castle	176
Walling, Jesse H.	Army	1972	New Castle	337, 339-341
Walls, Harvey L.		1972	Georgetown	
Walls, Robert John	Marines	1971	Wilmington	
Walls, Winfield Scott	Army	1968	Millsboro	15, 63, 83
Walsh, Ralph	Army	1968	Wilmington	21
Walton, Chris	Army	1969		175
Walton, William B.	Army	1970	Wilmington	
Ward, Bruce C.	Army	1968	Wilmington	75
Ward, Charles R.		1971	Wilmington	
Wardell, Jimmie F.	Army	1968	Wilmington	70
Warner, Kenneth D.	Army	1971-1972	Middletown	269, 284, 291, 321-322, 343, 420-427
Warren, Kenneth D.	Navy	1972	Ellendale	
Warriner, W.C. Jr.	Army	1971	Greenville	
Warrington, Frederick III	Army	1971	Georgetown	
Warwick, Thomas P.	Army	1970-1971	Wilmington	
Watkins, Bill	Marines	1968	New Castle	21
Watkins, Charles A.	Army	1971	Wilmington	
Watson, Reginald E.	Army	1969-1970	Wilmington	
Watson, Richard E.	Navy	1971	Milford	
Watson, Thomas W.	Navy	1972	Wilmington	
Wayne, Curtis Simmons	Army	1971	Wilmington	298
Weatherby, Bob	Army	1968		76
Weatherlow, Ron	Navy	1968-1971	Wilmington	53, 203, 205, 231
Weathersby, Elijah	Army	1968	Lewes	63
Webb, C. David	Air Force	1972	Millsboro	340
Webb, Howard A.	Army	1970	Lincoln	
Wedmore, Jared C.		1971	Wilmington	
Weisbrod, James D.E.	Army	1970	Kennett Square, Pa.	201, 209, 231
Welch, David E.	Air Force	1971	Newark	
Welch, Sidney J.		1971	Wilmington	
Wetherhold, Richard R.		1971	Seaford	
Wethington, Ben C.	Army	1971	Milford	
Wetzel, Harry P. Jr.		1971	Newark	
Wheeler, William J.	Army	1970-1971	Wilmington	219
Whelchel, Gene		1969	Newark	
White, Charles		1971	Newport	
White, Don	Army	1968	Newark	20
White, Goster		1972	Belvedere	
White, Richard J.	Army	1970-1972	Wilmington	265, 339
White, Thomas W.	Navy	1972	Wilmington	330
Wickersham, Eugene P.		1972	Newark	
Wickersham, Larry	Army	1972	Wilmington	
Wicks, Sam C.		1971	Greenville	
Wieland, Robert N.		1971	Newark	
Wiesinger, Robert L. II	Army	1971	Wilmington	
Wiesner, Robert	Air Force	1968-1969	Wilmington	46, 221
Wiggins, William F.		1971	Wilmington	287
Wilczynski, Robert		1972	Wilmington	
Williams, Douglas B.	Air Force	1970-1971	Wilmington	241, 273
Williams, Evan T.		1971	Hockessin	
Williams, Fletcher	Army	1972	Newark	
Williams, Keith M.	Air Force	1971	Smyrna	260
Williams, Richard Jr.	Army	1969	Wilmington	93, 175
Williams, Stephen P.	Army	1970-1971	Wilmington	
Williamson, Bruce L.		1970	Bridgeville	
Willing, Edward Arle	Marines	1972	Wilmington	325
Willis, Stephen E.	Army	1970-1971	Seaford	
Wills, Barry	Marines	1972	Wilmington	
Wilson, Alexander III	Army	1971-1972	Wilmington	341
Wilson, James M.	Army	1970-1971	Wilmington	298
Wilson, Mike	Army	1971	Wilmington	
Wilson, Richard A.	Army	1970	Newark	
Wilson, Robert V.	Army	1971	Wilmington	277, 284, 291, 305
Wilson, Robert W.		1972	Wilmington	
Wimmer, Kenneth R.	Army	1970	Newark	
Winchell, James	Army	1970-1971	Claymont	243
Windon, Richard		1968	Wilmington	63
Wingate, Rockie L.	Navy	1971-1972	Wilmington	
Winkler, Philip C.	Army	1970-1971	Georgetown, Md.	208, 219, 269
Winterringer, Daniel	Army	1969-1971	Newark	
Wise, Henry A. III	Army	1969-1970	Wilmington	105, 199, 213, 216, 228, 244, 250
Woerner, Frank C. Jr.	Army	1968	Newark	5
Woerner, James Jr.	Navy	1969	New Castle	
Wojciechowski, George	Army	1970-1972	Wilmington	235, 272
Wood, Peter F.	Army	1971	Wilmington	
Woomer, Christopher W.	Army	1972	Smyrna	
Wooten, Edsell	Army	1972	Wilmington	
Wootten, Cardwell D.		1970	Wilmington	
Wootten, George S.	Army	1970-1971	Landenberg, Pa.	
Wright, Donald O.		1970	Bethel	
Wright, Frank Lloyd	Air Force	1968		69
Wright, James R.	Army	1970-1971	Newark	219, 240, 308
Wright, Ronnie	Army	1969	Wilmington	172-173
Wright, Stephen C.		1971	Rehoboth Beach	
Wright, Wayne H.	Army	1971	Wilmington	
Wright, William		1969-1970	Marshallton	
Wyatt, Buddy	Army	1970	Wilmington	206-207
Wyatt, George	Army	1970-1971	Harrington	
Wyatt, Kenneth A.	Army	1970	Lewes	216, 249
Wyatt, Lindley K.		1971	Wilmington	
Wyatt, Richard A.		1971	New Castle	
Wyks, Ed		1972		
Wyre, Eli M.	Marines	1971	Wilmington	
Yeatman, Thomas P.	Army	1970	Wilmington	240
Young, Barry Gene	Army	1970	Claymont	
Young, Philip S.	Marines	1968	Wilmington	61
Young, Rex O.		1971	Wilmington	
Zimmerman, Wayne R.	Navy	1968	Wilmington	31, 33, 53

VIETNAM
MAILBAG
VOICES FROM THE WAR: 1968-1972

POST OFFICE BOX 68 · BETHEL, DELAWARE 19931
WWW.VIETNAMMAILBAG.COM · 302.381.5993

★

PRINTED AND BOUND IN CHINA BY GLOBAL PSD

★

ISBN 978-0-615-24454-9 ·

THIỆN NGÔN
Sốc Ky
247
LTL 20
Military reservation
Xóm Rẫy
PHƯỚC AN
Tapang Prey
TL 13
Xóm Bà Điết
106°00'
82
11°30'
Ấp Trại Bí
88th NVA Regiment
Chà Ruốt
Tapang Sôm
TRAI BÍ
Bàu Tâm
Nàng Rà
Xóm Tra Vông
PHƯỚC HƯNG
THIÊN NGÔN
Xã Hao Duoc
23
Xóm Sóc Hóa
Ấp Mo Cang
PHƯỚC VINH
Phum Sralouvien
Trảng Công
Xóm Bàng Dung
Xóm Trà Cốt
Xóm Thôn Bần
Xóm Sóc Ốm